CATULLUS AND HIS RENAISSANCE READERS

CATULLUS
and his
Renaissance Readers

JULIA HAIG GAISSER

CLARENDON PRESS · OXFORD
1993

Oxford University Press, Walton Street, Oxford OX2 6DP
Oxford New York Toronto
Delhi Bombay Calcutta Madras Karachi
Kuala Lumpur Singapore Hong Kong Tokyo
Nairobi Dar es Salaam Cape Town
Melbourne Auckland Madrid
and associated companies in
Berlin Ibadan

Oxford is a trade mark of Oxford University Press

Published in the United States
by Oxford University Press Inc., New York

British Library Cataloguing in Publication Data
Data available
ISBN 0-19-814882-8

Library of Congress Cataloging in Publication Data
Gaisser, Julia Haig.
Catullus and his Renaissance readers/Julia Haig Gaisser.
Includes bibliographical references and index.
1. Catullus, Gaius Valerius—Criticism and interpretation—History. 2. Literature, Modern—15th and 16th centuries—Roman influences. 3. Love poetry, Latin—History and criticism—Theory, etc. 4. Epigrams, Latin—History and criticism—Theory, etc. 5. Authors and readers—Europe—History—16th century. 6. Rome in literature. 7. Renaissance. I. Title.
PA6276.G35 1992
874'.01—dc20
ISBN 0-19-814882-8

Typeset by Hope Services (Abingdon) Ltd.
Printed in Great Britain
on acid-free paper by
Biddles Ltd.
Guildford and King's Lynn

Dis Manibus Parentum,
Marito Filioque

PREFACE

SCHOLARS have not paid equal attention to the two great events in the Renaissance *fortuna* of Catullus. Generations of classicists and text critics have studied the rediscovery of Catullus around 1300 and his transmission and manuscripts in the fourteenth century. Few scholars of any field have taken an interest in the publication of the *editio princeps* in 1472, which allowed Catullus to be more widely read than at any time in his history. Although there are some important articles on aspects of the work of individual humanists, there is no general study that treats the reception of Catullus after the first edition or follows his fortunes through the Renaissance.

I first thought of writing this book as I was completing the article on Catullus for the *Catalogus Translationum et Commentariorum*. Searching out manuscript commentaries on Catullus, tracing the relations between them and the printed commentaries, and—above all—hunting for biographical information on the commentators, made me realize that Catullus' Renaissance readers (by which I mean those who annotated, edited, imitated, lectured, or commented on the text of Catullus) deserved both a more detailed and a more general treatment than that allowed by the *Catalogus*. The ideas and interpretations of the humanists, along with their text, influenced the ways in which future generations (sometimes even our own) would read Catullus; but they also provide windows into their own intellectual and historical worlds—which changed (often radically) from decade to decade and from city to city.

Since this book emphasizes the role of individual interpreters, I have let the humanists speak for themselves as much as possible, quoting liberally from their lectures, prefaces, poems, and commentaries. For the most part I have used the vernacular forms of their names (they were real people after all, not just denizens of an *apparatus criticus*), but I have not been perfectly consistent. Minor figures tend to keep their Latin names, as do the Portuguese scholar Achilles Statius (so well known under his Latin name that I could not bring myself to call him Estaço), and the Dutch humanists of Chapter 6.

The only untranslated Latin in the text is the poetry of Catullus. Poems imitating Catullus appear in the text both in Latin and in translation; other quotations appear only in English with the Latin text in the endnotes. All translations are my own, unless otherwise noted.

The jacket illustration is a detail from a wall painting at the Villa Oplontis, published with the kind permission of Dr. Baldassare Conticello, Archaeological Superintendent for Pompeii and Herculaneum.

This book has been written with the assistance of research grants from Bryn Mawr College, the American Philosophical Society, the American Council of Learned Societies, and the National Endowment for the Humanities. I am grateful to them all.

There can be no greater pleasure at the end of a long project like this than thanking the friends and colleagues who made it possible. I am especially grateful to Richard Hamilton, James O'Donnell, and Douglas Thomson, who read the manuscript (parts of it more than once) and offered valuable suggestions for its improvement, and to G. N. Knauer, who has been unfailingly generous with his learning and friendship. Many others have read parts of the manuscript, written letters of recommendation, sent me references, and provided much appreciated aid. They include Helen North, Michael Putnam, Phyllis Bober, Phyllis Gordan, Anthony Grafton, Joseph Farrell, Laura Abrahamsen-Lazos, Nancy Dersofi, John Salmon, Darby Scott, Anita Moskowitz, Paul Harvey, Catherine Lafarge, Silvie Davidson, Alain Gowing, Patricia Osmond, Craig Kallendorf, and Peter Godman. I have been helped by many librarians, but especially by Robert Babcock of the Beinecke Library and by Ann Denlinger, Mary Leahy, M. Winslow Lundy, John Dooley, James Tanis, Charles Burke, Florence Goff, and Andrew Patterson of the Canaday Library at Bryn Mawr College. I owe a special debt to my *Catalogus* editors, F. E. Cranz, who initiated me into the mysteries of bibliographical research, and Virginia Brown, who lured me into the world of the humanists in the first place.

J.H.G.

Bryn Mawr, Pennsylvania
August 1991

CONTENTS

ILLUSTRATIONS

ABBREVIATIONS

AJP	*American Journal of Philology*
BHR	*Bibliothèque d'humanisme et renaissance*
BICS	*Bulletin of the Institute of Classical Studies of the University of London*
BMC	*Catalogue of Books Printed in the XVth Century now in the British Museum* (London, 1908–49)
CP	*Classical Philology*
CQ	*Classical Quarterly*
CTC	*Catalogus Translationum et Commentariorum*, ed. P. O. Kristeller, F. E. Cranz, and V. Brown (Washington, DC, 1960–)
DBI	*Dizionario biografico degli italiani* (Rome, 1960–)
GRBS	*Greek, Roman, and Byzantine Studies*
GSLI	*Giornale storico della letteratura italiana*
IMU	*Italia medioevale e umanistica*
JRS	*Journal of Roman Studies*
JWCI	*Journal of the Warburg and Courtauld Institutes*
RhM	*Rheinisches Museum für Philologie*
RQ	*Renaissance Quarterly*
TAPA	*Transactions of the American Philological Association*

SELECTIVE CHRONOLOGY

FIFTEENTH- AND SIXTEENTH-CENTURY EDITIONS, COMMENTARIES, AND WORKS ON CATULLUS

(NB Dates are italicized when the work is unpublished or its date of completion is known to differ from the date of publication.)

1472 Catullus, Tibullus, Propertius, and Statius' *Silvae*. (Vindelinus de Spira, Venice). *BMC* v. 161–2.

1473 Catullus and Statius, ed. Francesco dal Pozzo (Puteolano). (Stephanus Corallus, Parma). *BMC* vii. 939.

12 August, 1473 Angelo Poliziano's subscription to his emendations of Catullus in Venice 1472. (Rome, Biblioteca Corsiniana, 50. F. 37, fol. 37).

1475 Catullus, Tibullus, Propertius, and Statius' *Silvae*. (Phillipus de Lavagnia, ?Milan). *BMC* vi. 702–3.

1475? Catullus. (?Ulrich Han, ?Rome). *BMC* iv. 26.

1481 Tibullus, Catullus, and Propertius. (Albertus de Mazalibus, Reggio d'Emilia). *BMC* vii. 1087.

1481 Catullus, Tibullus, Propertius, and Statius, ed. Giovanni Calfurnio. (Johannes Renensis and Dionysius Bertochus, Vicenza). *BMC* vii. 1041.

1485 Antonius Parthenius, *Antonii Parthenii Lacisii Veronensis in Catullum Commentationes*. (Boninus de Boninis, Brescia). *BMC* vii. 968.

1485 Angelo Poliziano's second subscription to his emendations of Catullus in Venice 1472. (Rome, Biblioteca Corsiniana, 50. F. 37, fol. 127 v.).

c.1487–93 Marcus Antonius Sabellicus, *Ex Catullo*, in *Annotationes in Plinium et alios auctores*. (Venice,? 1497). Goff S-6.

1489 Angelo Poliziano, *Miscellaneorum Prima Centuria*. (Antonio di Bartolommeo Miscomini, Florence). *BMC* vi. 638.

1493 Hieronymus Avantius, *Emendationes in Catullum*. (Johannes Tacuinus, Venice, 1495). *BMC* v. 530.

1496 Palladius Fuscus, *In Catullum Commentarii*. (Johannes Tacuinus, Venice). *BMC* v. 530.

1500 Hieronymus Avantius, *Emendationes in Catullum*, with texts of Catullus, Tibullus, and Propertius, edited by Avantius. (Johannes Tacuinus, Venice). *BMC* v. 535.

1502 Catullus, Tibullus, and Propertius, ed. Hieronymus Avantius. (Aldus Manutius, Venice).

1502 Franciscus Puccius' subscription to his emendations of Catullus (edition unknown).

1515 Catullus, Tibullus, and Propertius, ed. Hieronymus Avantius. (Aldus Manutius, Venice).

1521 Alexander Guarinus, *Alexandri Guarini Ferrariensis in C. V. Catullum Veronensem per Baptistam Patrem Emendatum Expositiones cum Indice*. (Georgius de Rusconibus, Venice).

1521–2 Pierius Valerianus, *Praelectiones in Catullum*. (Vat.lat. 5215).

*c.*1535 Catullus, ed. Hieronymus Avantius. (Trincavelli, Venice).

1548 Franciscus Robortellus, *Explicationes in Catulli Epithalamium*. (Laurentius Torrentinus, Florence).

1551 Bernardinus Realinus, *Bernardini Realini Carpensis in Nuptias Pelei et Thetidis Catullianas Commentarius*. (Anselmus Giaccarellus, Bologna).

1554 Marcus Antonius Muretus, *Catullus et in eum Commentarius*. (Paulus Manutius, Venice).

1558 Marcus Antonius Muretus, *Catullus et in eum Commentarius* (with the texts of Propertius and Tibullus edited by Muretus). (Paulus Manutius, Venice).

1566 Achilles Statius, *Catullus cum Commentario*. (Paulus Manutius, Venice).

1569 Catullus and Tibullus, edited by Victor Giselinus and Theodorus Pulmannus, with Propertius edited by Guglielmus Canterus. (Christopher Plantin, Antwerp).

1577 Joseph Scaliger, *Castigationes in Valerii Catulli Librum*. (Mamertus Patissonius, Paris).

1579 *Phaselus Catulli, et ad eam, quotquot extant, Parodiae*, ed. 'Sixtus Octavianus'. ('Ioannis Marcantius', 'York').

Introduction: *Fortuna Catulli*

Ad patriam venio longis a finibus exul
Benvenuto Campesani

IN 1915 William Butler Yeats published a poem entitled 'The Scholars':

Bald heads forgetful of their sins,
Old, learned, respectable bald heads
Edit and annotate the lines
That young men, tossing on their beds,
Rhymed out in love's despair
To flatter beauty's ignorant ear.

All shuffle there; all cough in ink;
All wear the carpet with their shoes;
All think what other people think;
All know the man their neighbour knows.
Lord, what would they say—
Did their Catullus walk that way?

Yeats' desperate, passionate Catullus is a child of early twentieth-century romanticism, conceived in reaction to the excesses of nineteenth-century philology. The picture prevailed—at least in the English-speaking world—until 1950 or so, when a new image began to emerge. The Catullus of our time is much closer to Yeats' bloodless scholars than to his amorous poet; for we tend to imagine not a desperate man in the thrall of passionate emotion, but a learned Alexandrian, a student of recherché Hellenistic poetry, a young man tossing on his sleepless bed not out of love's despair but because he is enamoured of the allusive poetics of Callimachus.

Our Catullus, like Yeats', is very different from the Catullus who lived and wrote in Rome in the first half of the first century BC. For whether we mean to or not, we impose on the ancient poet (or rather on the image of the ancient poet we have received from previous generations) our own ideas about history and poetry and our own experiences and expectations, so that willy-nilly we read him through the lens of our own time. And so did all our predecessors—from the nineteenth-century philologists to the Renaissance poets and humanists, medieval scribes, second-century scholars and rhetoricians, first-century epigrammatists, and even Catullus' immediate successors, the Augustans Vergil and Horace.

This book is about Catullus, but also about the changing perceptions and historical circumstances of his readers in the Renaissance and the ways in which they edited, interpreted, taught, criticized, imitated, and parodied his poetry from the appearance of the first edition (1472) to the end of the sixteenth century. We shall begin by tracing Catullus' fortunes from Antiquity to the eve of the first edition.

CATULLUS AND HIS POETRY

Gaius Valerius Catullus (*c.*82–*c.*52 BC) was Rome's first major lyric poet. He was born in Verona (so Jerome and the ancient testimonia), and his father was important enough to be on terms of hospitality with Julius Caesar, as we are told by the first-century biographer Suetonius in an anecdote illustrating the famous Caesarian *clementia*. Catullus, it seems, succeeded in damaging the great man's prestige irreparably with scurrilous poems on his protégé Mamurra, but Caesar magnanimously responded to his apology with a dinner invitation and continued on good terms with his father. The poet died in Rome at the age of 30; but our source (Jerome again) gives the date as 58 BC, which is contradicted by the internal evidence of the poems.[1]

Our information is scanty enough (and little more is known about the lives of most ancient authors), but Catullus himself seems to make up for the deficiency. No ancient poet except Sappho writes of emotions and personal experience with such intensity. The poems chart a complicated emotional landscape with two figures at the centre: the poet's brother, whose death has banished all his interest in both love and poetry (a loss recounted in poems about the separation and grief of lovers); and his mistress Lesbia, whom he loves and wants to respect—and who betrays him in every alley in Rome.[2] Catullus' brother is otherwise unknown, but Lesbia is generally identified with the notorious Clodia whose aristocratic pedigree and low morals Cicero satirized in the *Pro Caelio*.[3] There are also lesser loves—Ipsitilla, invited obscenely to a mid-day rendezvous (32), and the boy Iuventius, coy and unfaithful (24, 48, 81, 99). Names of friends and enemies abound, and many are historical personages—politicians (Caesar, Mamurra, Cicero, Memmius), poets (Calvus, Cinna, Cornificius), and the historian Cornelius Nepos, to whom the work is dedicated.[4] We can even glean a few dates from the poetry. Catullus mentions serving in Bithynia as a member of the *cohors* of Gaius Memmius, who governed the province in 57–56 BC (10), and he refers to Pompey's consulship of 55 BC (113) and to Caesar's invasion of Britain, probably the campaign of 54 BC (11, 29).

Catullus' vividness and detail invite the manufacture of biographies,[5] but poems have always been unreliable witnesses. 'We know how to tell many lies like the truth, and we know how to tell the truth when we please,' say Hesiod's Muses (*Theogony* 27–8). Catullus puts it differently:

> Pedicabo ego vos et irrumabo,
> Aureli pathice et cinaede Furi,
> qui me ex versiculis meis putastis,
> quod sunt molliculi, parum pudicum.
> nam castum esse decet pium poetam
> ipsum, versiculos nihil necesse est. (16. 1–6)

But it hardly matters if the poet hides behind his *persona* and mocks biographers.[6] It is less useful to the historian to arrange the Lesbia poems, for example, in a romantic chronology than to see the poetry as a work of the imagination that evokes, but does not chronicle, a portion of the world and society of late republican Rome. Catullus' portrait of his world has been well characterized in modern scholarship.[7] It is urban and urbane, violently partisan, morally lax, but with powerful undercurrents of the old Roman values of family, *amicitia*, and *pietas*.

It is also a world of poets and poetry—a certain kind of poetry. For Catullus and his friends (the likes of Cinna, Calvus and the rest) were part of a poetic revolution that ostentatiously rejected Roman models in favour of Callimachus and other Alexandrians, and they were as partisan in their poetics as in their politics. Some say the catalyst was the Greek poet Parthenius (brought home by Cinna as part of his booty from the Mithridatic war around 66–65 BC), but perhaps no catalyst was needed.[8] Romans had been travelling east and reading Greek poetry, even Alexandrian poetry, for generations. But whatever the source of their inspiration, the 'New Poets', or neoterics (a term used by Cicero in disgust and by modern critics in approbation), turned whole-heartedly and self-consciously to the principles of learning, craftsmanship, and attention to detail sponsored by Callimachus.[9] Like Callimachus, they eschewed epic in favour of smaller genres—particularly elegy, epigram, and epyllion (short erotic 'epic' on mythological subjects); they wrote love poems, satirized politicians (the more important the better), attacked bad poets, and praised the Alexandrians and one another. Their metres were various and for the most part familiar (hexameters, elegiac couplets, iambics), but their hallmark was the Phalaecean hendecasyllable, little used before in either Greek or Latin, as far as one can judge.[10]

The hendecasyllable is the Catullan metre *par excellence*, and the one for which later generations would remember him best. About two-thirds of his lyrics, the so-called polymetrics, are in hendecasyllables. The content is various (from the erotic to the scatological), but the metre is always light, graceful, intimate—perfectly suited to the cultivated ease and informality of the Catullan *persona*.[11] Their apparent simplicity should not deceive us, for the hendecasyllabics are as studied and carefully wrought—as Alexandrian, in fact—as anything in Catullus. Like the rest of the corpus they are both a product and an assertion of neoteric poetics. The programme is announced in the opening lines of the first poem, a dedication to Cornelius Nepos:

> Cui dono lepidum novum libellum
> arida modo pumice expolitum? (1. 1–2)

Lepidus and *novus* are catch-words in the neoteric vocabulary; *expolitum* puns on the polish given the papyrus roll and that applied to its contents by the artful poet; the diminutive *libellus* announces that Catullus plans a work on a small (i.e. Alexandrian) scale.

For both artistic and practical reasons, however, the programme poem cannot have been intended to introduce the Catullan corpus as it now stands. Catullus' characterization of his poems as *nugae* (1.4), though appropriate for the polymetrics, does not fit the longer and more ambitious epithalamia, elegies, and epyllion.[12] The length of the corpus also presents a problem. The text contains nearly 2,300 verses (2,289 in Thomson's edition), a sum that takes into account neither lost verses nor intervals between poems.[13] The facts of ancient book production make it virtually impossible that a poetic work of this size was ever accommodated on a single papyrus roll. Single books of poetry were written on separate rolls (e.g. a book of the *Aeneid*, a book of Horace's *Odes*, etc.), with a typical length of about 750 lines and an upper limit of around 1,100. There are some exceptions: the books of the *De Rerum Natura* range between 1,092 and 1,455 verses; Book 4 of Apollonius Rhodius contains 1,779.[14] Simply by adding more lengths of papyrus it would have been possible to manufacture a roll to contain a poem much longer than even Apollonius 4, but the result would have been almost impossibly cumbersome for a book of short (and shortish) poems. Moreover, the upper limit for the length of classical papyri is generally taken to be about 10.5 m.[15] A roll containing all of Catullus would have had to be substantially longer, at least if it were written in the manner of our two most ancient papyri of Latin poetry, PHerc 817 (*Carmen de bello Aegyptiaco*, 31 BC–AD 79) and the Gallus fragment from Qaṣr Ibrîm (*c*.50 BC–*c*.AD 25). If we base our calculations on PHerc 817, Catullus' *liber* would be 15.85 m. long; if it were written in the more modest fashion of the Gallus papyrus it would be a mere 11.62 m.[16] In either case, our hypothetical roll certainly could not have been described as a *libellus*.

It seems likely, therefore, that Catullus' poems appeared originally in several (probably at least three) *libelli*, which were joined together when the work was transferred from roll to codex, and that the dedication originally intended for a single *libellus* was used for the whole. The exact contents and arrangement of each *libellus* are unknown, but there are some probabilities. The work easily falls into three sections that might well have appeared in separate *libelli*. Poems 1–60 (848 lines in Thomson's edition) contain the polymetrics, 61–4 (795 lines) ambitious Alexandrian set-pieces (epithalamia, the Attis poem, the epyllion), and 65–116 (646 lines) elegies and epigrams. Whether these groups were arranged and published as books by Catullus or another is open to question. Catullus died young, and it is possible that the *libellus* announced in poem 1 (surely the polymetrics) was the only one published in his lifetime. The book shows signs of careful arrangement, but it may also include poems added by an editor after his death.[17] There are no dedications for the other groups of poems, which perhaps were posthumously arranged.[18] It is likely, for example, that the epyllion (64) originally occupied a roll by itself. There is an additional complication. The principles of arrangement discerned in the collection have been derived (naturally enough) from the extant poems, but there is a possibility, at least, that some of Catullus' poems did not survive. He has frequently been credited with *priapea*, and it is probable that a quatrain preserved by Terentianus Maurus and two one-line fragments found in Nonius and Porphyrion are genuine.[19] The place of such poems in the collection is problematic; perhaps they failed to survive simply because they were circulated separately.

Catullus and his friends had a profound influence on the next generation of poets. The Callimachean and Alexandrian literary ideas naturalized by the neoterics became the dominant poetics of the Augustans. The other New Poets played a role: their fragments, few as they are, have echoes in Augustan poetry.[20] The Greek Parthenius—perhaps their teacher, perhaps only a solitary late-blooming Alexandrian—had close ties with Cornelius Gallus and Vergil.[21] But the influence of Catullus himself is decisive. Whatever scenario one prefers for the origins of Roman elegy, some role must be allotted to Catullus; most would favour an amalgam of Catullan elegy and epigram, perhaps developed by Gallus in his *Amores*.[22] The basic situation of elegy (love-struck poet and faithless mistress) is certainly Catullan, as is the self-conscious preoccupation with writing poetry in the Alexandrian style. Horace, too, although he conspicuously fails to acknowledge it, owes many debts to Catullus.[23] Vergil uses Catullus' epyllion (64) in the *Aeneid* and in the *Fourth Eclogue*;[24] his most famous echo is Aeneas' moving protest to Dido in the underworld, which is modelled on a line from the frivolous *Lock of Berenice* (66): *invitus, regina, tuo de litore cessi* (*Aen.* 6. 460). (Cf. 66. 39: *invita, o regina, tuo de vertice cessi.*) Some scholars believe that Vergil is also the author of *Catalepton* 10, which parodies 4.[25]

CATULLUS IN THE SILVER AGE

Catullus' popularity continued through the Silver Age, but he was now popular in a different world and for different reasons. Alexandrianism, no longer avant-garde, had become a poetic cliché, its originality exhausted by the great poets of the Augustan age and their lesser successors. The hurly-burly of the late Republic, where great men could be assaulted in verse with impunity, had given way first to Augustan order and then to the dangers and sycophancy of the Empire. Caesar invited Catullus to dinner, Augustus exiled Ovid, Domitian's reign of terror silenced a generation. There were other differences. Catullus spoke as an equal to friends and enemies alike. Horace and Vergil lived on complicated and tactful terms with their great patron Maecenas, whose influence on their poetry is not easy to assess. Martial and Pliny were Catullus' greatest admirers in the Silver Age: the one shamelessly flattered Domitian and wrote to please the rich and famous; the other, rich himself, dabbled in poetry for amusement.[26]

For Martial Catullus is master and model: *uno sed tibi sim minor Catullo*, he says to his acquaintance Macer (Mart. 10. 78. 16). 'Second only to Catullus'. The wish is more modest than it seems, for Martial places Catullus in the second rank of poets. Epic poets come first. Thus in 5. 5, when Martial writes to Sextus, librarian of the emperor Domitian, he establishes a definite poetical (and social) hierarchy. Let my poems find a place, he says, next to those of Pedo, Marsus, and Catullus; Vergil's epic should be placed next to Domitian's.[27] When he sends his epigrams in homage to the epic poet Silius Italicus, a rich man, once governor of Asia, and the author of the *Punica* (the longest extant poem in classical Latin), he imagines that he is following in the footsteps of Catullus:

> nec torva lege fronte, sed remissa
> lascivis madidos iocis libellos.
> sic forsan tener ausus est Catullus
> magno mittere Passerem Maroni. (Mart. 4. 14. 11-14)[28]

(and read my little books steeped in naughty jests not with a stern face but with an indulgent one. So perhaps tender Catullus ventured to send the *Passer* to great Vergil.)

In AD 88, when Martial published this book of epigrams,[29] Vergil had been dead for over a hundred years, Catullus for 140. Martial makes them contemporaries, conflating their two eras from the perspective of his own into a single undifferentiated past—in which, just as in Martial's time, the lesser poet sent verses to the greater. In both epigrams Martial ranks himself with Catullus, and sees both as minor poets. His criteria are social status and genre, with poetic worth a poor third. In his own poetry he seeks popularity, clarity, and simplicity, explicitly rejecting the Catullan categories—Callimachean poetics, learning, technical virtuosity—so dear to the neoterics and Augustans. To a writer of obscure poetry he says slightingly, 'in your opinion Cinna was greater than Vergil' (Mart. 10. 21. 6). And again, to the man looking for mythological poetry instead of Martial's home truths: 'you should read the *Aetia* of Callimachus' (Mart. 10. 4. 12). Among the neoteric topics Martial rejects in this epigram is Attis, the subject of what has been called 'perhaps the most remarkable poem in Latin'[30]—63, in which Catullus relates the crazed self-mutilation of Cybele's devotee Attis, his repentance, and ultimate slavery to the goddess. The poem is a metrical as well as a psychological tour de force, for it is the only extant ancient example of the exotic and difficult galliambic metre.[31] In another epigram Martial characterizes the *Attis* as an example of trivial metrical acrobatics, and finds its metre as distasteful as its subject:

> nec dictat mihi luculentus Attis
> mollem debilitate galliambon: (Mart. 2. 86. 4–5)

(nor does excellent Attis dictate to me his galliambic verse soft with effeminate weakness.)

By rejecting Alexandrian subjects and poetics Martial has both rejected Catullus' claims to poetic supremacy and created a model in his own image—Catullus the epigrammatist. He imitates specific poems and themes (a topic that we shall explore more fully in Chapter 5), but also—for over 200 of his 1,500 epigrams—he has taken over Catullus' metre, the hendecasyllable, and its characteristic vocabulary.[32] As a consequence, even his non-Catullan epigrams can have a distinctly Catullan flavour. His use of hendecasyllables is suggestive. For Martial the hendecasyllable and the elegiac couplet were both metres for epigram, and virtually interchangable ones at that. He treats the same subjects in both; his arrangement of the epigrams reflects no distinction between them. For Catullus it was presumably otherwise; whatever name he would have given to his hendecasyllables (most moderns call them lyrics),[33] he—or his editor—separated them and the other polymetrics from the elegiac epigrams.

The question is one of genre. Are hendecasyllables epigrams? Are short poems in elegiacs distinct somehow from those in other metres? What is an epigram? The categories are slippery, and perhaps we should join Martial's younger contemporary Pliny in resisting them. Pliny wrote and published at least two books of poetry, the second in various metres, the first in hendecasyllables alone. The hendecasyllables were a great success, for they were not only read and copied, but also sung to the lyre and cithara.[34] But he does not call them lyrics; indeed, he resists all generic labels—or rather, he leaves them to the reader:

> I plan to call these trifles (*nugas*) of mine hendecasyllables, and this title is defined by the metre alone. Therefore, you may call them epigrams or idylls or eclogues or *poematia*, as many do, or whatever else you like. I offer only the name hendecasyllables. (Pliny, *Ep.* 4. 14. 8–9)

Pliny's hendecasyllables have two things in common, their metre and their diversity:

> We jest in them, we play, love, grieve, complain, grow angry; we describe something now in low style, now in high, and with this very variety try to ensure that different things will be pleasing to different people—some things, perhaps, to all. (Pliny, *Ep.* 4. 14. 3)

Indeed, it was precisely the variety and versatility of the hendecasyllable, as well as its natural ease and elegance, that ensured its continued popularity. Martial and Pliny wrote in hendecasyllabics, but so did the encomiastic Statius and the obscene poet of the *Priapea*.[35] So, too, if we believe Pliny, did nearly every amateur poet in Rome. Thus, we hear that in publishing a separate book of hendecasyllables Pliny was following 'the example of many'.[36] His friend Pompeius Saturninus wrote verses 'like Catullus or Calvus'; another, young Sentius Augurinus, acknowledged Pliny himself as the model for his hendecasyllables:

> I sing songs in the tiny verses in which once my Catullus and Calvus and the old poets sang. But what is that to me? Pliny is all my forerunners rolled into one.[37]

The subjects of both poets sound like Pliny's description of his own verses. Thus, Pliny says of Saturninus: 'how much charm is in his verses, how much sweetness, bitterness, love!' (Pliny, *Ep.* 1. 16. 5.) Of Augurinus: 'He calls them *poematia*. He writes much in low style, much in high, much with charm, much tenderly, sweetly, with bile!' (Pliny, *Ep.* 4. 27. 1.) The poetry of Pliny and his friends is unabashed light verse, tossed off in an idle hour for the amusement of its author. Pliny introduces his poems: 'With this letter you will receive my hendecasyllables, with which I have happily spent my spare time—in my carriage, in the bath, at table.' (Pliny, *Ep.* 4. 14. 2.)[38] And he advises a busy friend: 'It is fine to relax with verse. I don't mean long, continuous poetry (this can be completed only in a period of leisure), but what is witty and short, which nicely punctuates the greatest business and cares.' (Pliny, *Ep.* 7. 9. 9.)

Catullus is not the only model for this verse. Whenever Pliny mentions forerunners in the hendecasyllable he links the name of Catullus with that of Calvus, and treats both as slightly old fashioned.[39] Augurinus listed his predecessors as 'meus Catullus et Calvus veteresque'. Saturninus was an archaizer in oratory and epistolography, but also in poetry:[40]

> he makes verses like Catullus or Calvus—really, like Catullus or Calvus . . . Sometimes he introduces (but intentionally) into his soft and light verses some slightly harsh ones (*duriusculos*)—and this, too, is like Catullus or Calvus. (Pliny, *Ep.* 1. 16. 5)

Pliny does not say what seemed harsh to him in Catullus and Calvus, but very likely it was the versification. Twenty years earlier his uncle had used the same word of Catullus (*duriusculus* appears in only these two places in Latin literature). In the dedication to his *Natural History* the elder Pliny quoted from 1, changing the word order of the fourth verse to secure a spondaic opening, since he considered that Catullus' iambic opening (*meas aliquid putare nugas*) made him 'a trifle harsher (*duriusculum*) than he wished to be considered by his darling Veraniuses and Fabulluses'.[41] It is not clear whether Calvus ever began his hendecasyllables with iambs or trochees (only two of his hendecasyllables survive—both spondaic), but the variation is common enough in Catullus; indeed, it may have been a neoteric experiment.[42] But whatever its origin, the variation seemed awkward and passé to later poets. The archaizer Saturninus may have affected it studiously, but Martial avoids it, and so, no doubt, did Pliny and the young Augurinus.

It was Catullus' short poetry that most appealed to the taste of the Silver Age. The comments of Martial and Pliny suggest as much, and the impression is confirmed by other testimonia. To take only a few examples: the elder Pliny and both Senecas mention only the polymetrics; polymetrics or epigrams are the subject of six of Quintilian's seven references to Catullus.[43] There are some favourites: the attack on Caesar and Mamurra (29), the dedication poem (1), the claim that the poet's life is separate from his poetry (16). Most popular of all, however, are the poems on Lesbia's sparrow (2 and 3). Martial imitates them several times, most notoriously in *Epig.* 11. 6:

> Da nunc basia, sed Catulliana:
> quae si tot fuerint quot ille dixit,
> donabo tibi Passerem Catulli. (Mart. 11. 6. 14–16)[44]

(Now give kisses, but Catullan-style, and if these be as many as he said, I will give you the sparrow of Catullus.)

Martial also seems to have called Catullus' book of polymetrics the *passer*, and perhaps the title was in general use (people often called literary works by their opening words, and—after the dedication—*passer* is the first word in Catullus' text).[45] But it may also be a jest on the precious Alexandrian habit of calling poems 'nightingales'—Martial, at any rate, would have enjoyed parodying Callimachean pretension.[46] Whatever its origin, the term became so well established that twenty years later Pliny was able to use not only *passer* but also *columba* as a cliché for poetry. Thus, he promised to send verses to his military friend, Pomponius Mamilianus:[47]

You will give wings to our little sparrows and doves [*passerculis et columbulis*] among your eagles [i.e. standards of the legion] if they please you as well as themselves. If not, please take care to keep them in their cage or nest. (Pliny, *Ep.* 9. 25. 3)

THE SECOND CENTURY AND BEYOND

Catullus came out of the Silver Age a minor poet, shorn of his Alexandrianism, a little old-fashioned, but still the model of choice for poets and poetasters of light verse. In the second century we find him even more diminished. He still has imitators. Thus, Lesbia's sparrow was remembered by an anonymous poet who used Catullus' verses as the model for an epicedion on a pet dog; the hendecasyllables are preserved in an inscription at Auch.[48] Another anonymous poet, the author of the *Ciris*, was a throw-back to the neoterics who steeped himself in Catullus' epyllion (64) and lifted large portions of it for his own strange and learned poem.[49] For the most part, however, the second century was an era, not of poets, but of grammarians and antiquarians, and it is to them that we owe our notices of Catullus.

Aulus Gellius (born *c.* AD 130) is our best representative of the age. His *Noctes Atticae* preserve a rag-bag of information, misinformation, and anecdote on all manner of subjects, including old authors and their manuscripts.[50] Gellius discusses Catullus in three passages. In 19. 9 he tells of the Greeks at a dinner party who thought that Rome had no poets to rival Sappho and Anacreon—'except . . . perhaps Catullus in a few poems and Calvus in a few'.[51] At 7. 16 he refutes a hostile critic who has attacked the use of *deprecor* in 92:

> Lesbia mi dicit semper male nec tacet umquam
> de me: Lesbia me dispeream nisi amat.
> quo signo? quia sunt totidem mea: *deprecor* illam
> assidue, verum dispeream nisi amo. (92)

The critic is typical of Gellius' straw men—'a conceited or affected or generally unseasonable individual whose delusions are exposed by the light of superior wisdom.'[52] The delusion in this case is the critic's belief that *deprecor* means only 'pray to' or 'beseech', whereas, says Gellius, Catullus uses it in the sense 'drive away' or 'remove' (with or without the help of prayers):

So then Catullus means that he is doing the same as Lesbia, in publicly speaking ill of her, scorning and rejecting her, and constantly praying to be rid of her, and yet loving her to madness.[53]

The passage is interesting as the earliest example we have of Catullan exegesis, but it is also typical of Gellius and his age in its narrow lexicographical focus on the sense of a single word. In 6. 20 Gellius' subject is euphony—specifically, the pleasing effect of hiatus in Vergil and Homer and also, he claims, in Catullus:

Catullus, too, the most graceful of poets, in the following verses,

Minister vetuli puer Falerni,
Inger mi calices amariores,
Ut lex Postumiae iubet magistrae
Ebria acina ebriosioris [27. 1–4, Gellius' text],

although he might have said *ebrio* and used *acinum* in the neuter gender, as was more usual, nevertheless through love of the melody of that Homeric hiatus he said *ebria*, because it blended with the following *a*. But those who think that Catullus wrote *ebriosa* or *ebrioso*—for that incorrect reading is also found—have unquestionably happened upon editions copied from corrupt texts.[54]

Modern editors disagree, printing *ebrioso acino ebriosioris*.[55] But the discussion is important for two reasons. It is based on an aesthetic argument that sheds some light on the taste and artistic criteria of the time, and it reminds us that even at this early period there were textual variations and disputed readings in Catullus.[56]

Gellius' flamboyant contemporary, Apuleius, is most famous for his novel, the *Golden Ass*, but he also wrote several other works, including the *Apologia* (AD 158–9), in which he defends himself against charges of magic, debauchery, and foppishness—as well as marrying his wife for her money. Part of the case against him arises from his composition of invective and erotic poetry, and he invokes Catullus three times in his defence. First, in response to the charge that he uses pseudonyms for the lovers addressed in his poems:

By the same token they should accuse Gaius Catullus, because he used the name Lesbia for Clodia, and likewise Ticidas because he wrote Perilla for Metella, and Propertius, who mentions Cynthia and conceals Hostia, and Tibullus, who has Plania in mind but Delia in his verse. (*Ap.* 10)

Then, to the related suspicion that his verses are a mirror of his conduct:

Haven't you read Catullus' reply to ill-wishers?
'nam castum esse decet pium poetam
ipsum, versiculos nihil necesse est [16. 5–6].' (*Ap.* 11)

Neither of these references is sure evidence that Apuleius was a serious reader of Catullus. The first must have been a standard morsel of literary history, and the second had already become a cliché by the time of Martial and Pliny.[57] But Apuleius' third reference to Catullus is more interesting. His accusers had read out some of his poems in court to embarrass him, beginning, as he says, 'with a little letter (*epistolium*) from my jests, written in verse to a certain Calpurnianus on the subject of tooth-powder' (*Ap.* 6). Apuleius quotes his poem (which seems only moderately offensive), and concludes that he has nothing to be ashamed of—except that perhaps he sent Calpurnianus the wrong dentifrice:

since it would have been much more appropriate for him in the filthy manner of the Spaniards, as Catullus says, to use his own urine 'to scrub his tooth and ruddy gums' (*dentem atque russam pumicare gingivam*, 39. 19 (Apuleius' text)).

Apuleius' citation is not quite right (he uses *pumicare* for Catullus' *defricare*), but he has the poem and its revolting hero Egnatius well in mind. He may also be thinking of 37, where Egnatius makes his first appearance:

Egnati, opaca quem bonum facit barba
et dens Hibera defricatus urina. (37. 19–20)

And acquaintance with another Catullan poem is suggested by his use of *epistolium*, which is found only in the *Apologia* and in Catullus.[58]

Clearly Apuleius and Gellius knew some, at least, of Catullus' poems; the anonymous poets of the *Ciris* and the Auch inscription imitated others. Together, the references substantiate the impression one has from Gellius that Catullus still had his readers in the second century and that texts (of various accuracy) were available. But the situation soon changed. To state the matter baldly, after Apuleius and Gellius and the poets of the *Ciris* and the Auch inscription, we know of only one person for the next millennium who surely read Catullus, and that is the anonymous scribe of a ninth-century florilegium containing poem 62. A few writers mention Catullus' name, quote a verse, or echo a collocation, and there are various scraps of evidence for the transmission of the text, but after the second century no one else displays clear and direct knowledge of so much as a single poem. The testimonia tell the tale. Festus (late second century) discusses some hard words in Catullus, but he was only epitomizing the *De significatu verborum* of the Augustan scholar Verrius Flaccus. Porphyrion (third century), Aelius Donatus (fourth century), and Nonius Marcellus (fourth century) quote single verses. The metricians Terentianus Maurus (late second century), Atilius Fortunatianus (fourth century), and Marius Victorinus (fourth century) cite verses from Catullus as examples; their source seems to have been the first-century poet and metrician Caesius Bassus. And so it goes among poets and philosophers as well. In the fourth century Ausonius uses 1 as a tag in his own dedications. Claudian echoes Catullan phrases. Martianus Capella in the fifth century, Boethius in the sixth, and Isidore in the seventh century quote single verses, all evidently from grammarians and other intermediate sources.[59]

Catullus' decline after the second century has parallels in the *fortunae* of other classical authors, but it surely also owes something to the fact that Martial and Pliny and their friends had admired and promoted him exclusively as a poet of light verse in the first century. When tastes changed again after the Silver Age there would have seemed little point in reading or copying his poetry. No doubt texts were already becoming scarce in the time of Gellius and Apuleius, and we can be sure that fewer still were preserved when the works of ancient authors were transferred from roll to codex in the fourth century.

CATULLUM NUNQUAM ANTEA LECTUM

After Isidore Catullus goes underground. We know that he made the journey from Antiquity to the Renaissance (he arrived, after all) but we do not know how or by what route. It is as if we were tracing a submarine or an underground stream—our evidence a faint blip of sonar or a tell-tale puddle. Such signs are often misleading, and there can be legitimate disagreement about their meaning.[60]

Catullus is listed in no medieval manuscript catalogue, and we have only two pieces of direct evidence for his transmission in the period between Isidore and the end of the thirteenth century. The first is a manuscript, BN Lat. 8071, called T after a sixteenth-century owner, Jacques-Auguste de Thou. T is a late ninth-century florilegium containing poem 62, various minor works, and selections from Martial, Juvenal, and Seneca's tragedies. For many years T was thought to have been copied from another florilegium, Vienna 277, which probably dates from the late eighth or early ninth century. In fact, however, the two manuscripts were copied from a common exemplar, as Otto Zwierlein has shown: they are sister manuscripts, rather than mother and daughter.[61] Unfortunately, it is not clear whether the scribe of T found Catullus in the common exemplar (Vienna 277 is now incomplete and lacks Catullus) or whether he imported it into his manuscript from another source, as he apparently did with his selections from Juvenal. Both T and Vienna 277 are French in script, and the latter, at least, may be connected with Tours.[62] The existence of these florilegia is interesting in itself, but does not take us very far. T belongs to the same tradition as our other surviving manuscripts, and we know nothing of its history before the late sixteenth century.[63] B. L. Ullman, drawn by the possible connection of Vienna 277 with Tours, speculated that perhaps the archetype of the two anthologies was a book sent by Bishop Gregory of Tours to the poet Fortunatus between 573 and 576, and saw evidence of Fortunatus' knowledge of Catullus in his use of a collocation (*agros hiulco*) found only in the two poets.[64] But the argument is less straightforward than it appears. Fortunatus' description of Gregory's gift seems to correspond not to an anthology of poems, but rather to a metrical treatise containing examples of the various metres:

> [a book] discussing at great length under various headings—and these things are related to rhythms and metres—how much the sweet epode enhances the sapphic or trimeter. It contains a great number of authors who speak of many things in tuneful measure[65]

Furthermore, as Ullman acknowledged, the combination *agros hiulco* appears not in 62, but in 68. We must conclude that if

Fortunatus knew Catullus, his source was not the archetype of T.[66]

Our second piece of direct evidence is contained in a sermon delivered by Bishop Rather of Verona in 966. Ullman paraphrases (the omissions are mine): 'What can I say about myself . . . if I meditate day and night on the law of God, while I read Catullus never read before or Plautus long neglected, while I explain music, though I know nothing about mathematics . . .?'[67] Rather's Latin is difficult, and it is hardly clear whether he is claiming to have read Catullus and Plautus himself or is simply adducing their study as an example of frivolous behaviour. The distinction is probably unimportant. It seems evident that someone in Verona was reading Catullus and that the action was not only frivolous but exceptional: *Catullum nunquam antea lectum*. The someone may have been Rather himself, for a sermon he delivered in 963 contains a possible echo of 58*b*. 2.[68]

It is tempting to suppose that Rather (if it was he who was reading Catullus) found a manuscript of Catullus in the Chapter library of Verona, where it lay undisturbed through most of the Middle Ages until it came dramatically to light at the end of the thirteenth century.[69] This hypothesis would fit with the identification of much earlier Catullan echoes in verses probably written in Brescia by the monk Hildemar, who was at S. Faustino in Brescia from 841 to 845—the safe presumption being that Hildemar had access to the nearby Chapter library in Verona.[70] On the other hand, there is no direct evidence for a Catullus manuscript in Verona either before or after Rather. Ullman argued that the rediscovered manuscript (which modern scholars call V, for 'Veronensis'), like its kinsman T, was probably French, and Clausen suggested that it was a ninth-century manuscript written in Carolingian minuscule.[71] One might also point out that Hildemar himself was French, perhaps from Corbie.[72] Rather left Verona for Lobbes in 968, but the fate of his Catullus manuscript (if he had one) is unknown. A Cologne manuscript of Priscian (Cologne 202) dated between the tenth and twelfth centuries contains a correct citation of 37. 18, which is corrupt in other Priscian manuscripts, and it is presumed that the scribe used a manuscript of Catullus for his reading. Cologne is not far from Lobbes itself or Aulne or Haumont, where Rather also lived in the last years of his life.[73]

The last medieval 'sighting' of Catullus is connected not with Italy or France, but with Britain. The echo is found in the twelfth-century *De gestis regum Anglorum* of William of Malmesbury. It is difficult to know what to make of this, as William apparently never left England, and there is no other evidence connecting Catullus with Britain before the fifteenth century.[74]

THE FOURTEENTH AND FIFTEENTH CENTURIES

After the frustrating effort to trace Catullus' nearly silent passage through the Middle Ages it is a great relief when he finally emerges into clear view with the discovery of V at the end of the thirteenth or the beginning of the fourteenth century. But clarity is a relative matter. We know that the manuscript was discovered, but the date and circumstances, as well as the identity of the finder, are obscure, and little light is shed by the riddling contemporary epigram (*c*.1303–7) of Benvenuto Campesani that commemorates the discovery.

Ad patriam venio longis a finibus exsul;
causa mei reditus compatriota fuit,
scilicet a calamis tribuit cui Francia nomen
quique notat turbe praetereuntis iter.
quo licet ingenio vestrum celebrate Catullum,
cuius sub modio clausa papirus erat.

(An exile, I come to my country from distant lands. A fellow-countryman was the cause of my return. Clearly France assigned him his name from the reeds, and the one who marks the journey of the passing crowd. With all your ability celebrate your Catullus, whose light[75] has been hidden under a bushel.)

From vv. 3–4 it seems that the finder may have been a notary (*a calamis*) named Francesco or that his name may be hidden in a punning reference to a French word for 'reed' or 'pen'. But whatever else it says, Benvenuto's epigram argues against the idea that the manuscript had remained through the Middle Ages in the Chapter library at Verona: Catullus after a distant exile has been returned to his homeland by a fellow countryman.[76]

The manuscript soon disappeared, but not before it had been copied at least once. D. S. McKie has demonstrated that the archetype of our three fourteenth-century manuscripts, O, G, and R (Oxford, Canon. Class. Lat. 30; Paris, BN Lat. 14137; and Vatican Library, Ottob. Lat. 1829), was not V itself but a copy of V. McKie does not name this copy, but Thomson calls it A. From A were copied O and X, the lost parent of G and R. G bears the date 1375, R was copied by 1390, and O at an undetermined date in the fourteenth century.[77] Benvenuto's epigram probably goes back at least to X, since it appears in R and G, though not in O.

Before its disappearance V seems also to have been studied in Verona by several anthologists. The most important of these was the Paduan judge, Geremia da Montagnone (*c.*1255–1321), whose *Compendium moralium notabilium* contains seven quotations from Catullus.[78] The *Compendium* was compiled between 1295 and 1310,[79] but Geremia added to his work over the years and perhaps incorporated Catullus as late as 1310–15. It seems, moreover, that the Catullus sections were not added all at once, for at least one manuscript contains only five of the seven.[80] Five of Geremia's seven passages are marked in R[81] and two in G. Hale concluded from the notations in R that the passages had been marked in V by Geremia himself as he was looking for suitable quotations, but (especially since none of the passages is noted in O) it is more likely that the notations were present in X, or that early readers of G and R noted in their manuscripts passages that they had found quoted in Geremia. The popular *Compendium* was no doubt readily available.[82]

Benzo of Alessandria (d. *c.* 1330) probably also consulted V in Verona around 1310, for he quotes 35. 1–4 in his encyclopaedic *Chronicle*. His error *occilio* for *cecilio* at 35. 2, found elsewhere only in O, confirms that Benzo took his quotation from V itself.[83] Another anthologist, the compiler of the *Flores* of 1329, quotes 22. 19–21.[84] His source was evidently a manuscript, perhaps V. Geremia had quoted from the same poem, but the selections are not identical (Geremia cites 18–20).[85] In the next generation, Guglielmo da Pastrengo (d. 1362) quotes Catullus directly (1. 5–7) in his *De originibus rerum*, and gives glosses nearly identical with those in O, which probably appeared also in V.[86]

On a visit to Verona in 1345 Guglielmo's friend Petrarch found and copied Cicero's Letters to Atticus.[87] It is possible that he saw V and perhaps even acquired a copy of it during the same visit, for he cites a verse from Catullus in a letter of 1347. Petrarch mentions or quotes Catullus on several other occasions, both in his letters and in the marginal glosses of his manuscripts. His quotations, like those of Geremia and the rest, tend to be gnomic *sententiae*, cited with little concern for their context; by themselves they show no great study of the poet. Some could have been taken from the compilations of the previous generation, but others he probably found for himself in a manuscript. Petrarch's knowledge of a manuscript seems guaranteed by a note in his manuscript of Apuleius, for he has glossed Apuleius' quotation of 16. 5–6 (*Apologia* 11) with the words, *Catullus ad Aurelium—Ad Aurelium* being the title of 16 in V.[88] Ullman believed that Petrarch owned and corrected X, the lost exemplar of G and R, and that it was from Petrarch's literary executors that the Florentine chancellor and humanist Coluccio Salutati acquired access to it. Recently, however, McKie has argued from the correspondence of Salutati that Petrarch was not the owner of X and that Salutati's source for it, Gasparo dei Broaspini, sent the manuscript to him from Verona in November 1375—only a month after it had been copied by Antonio da Legnago, the scribe of G. In any event, it is clear that Salutati did gain access to X, from which he commissioned the copying of G's sister manuscript R, and that R, corrected by Salutati himself, became the ancestor of most of the fifteenth-century manuscripts.[89]

Salutati's manuscript was copied more than once in the early years of the fifteenth century,[90] but Catullus was still hard to find. Thus, the poet Panormita (Antonio Beccadelli) in the *Hermaphroditus* (1425) asks a friend's help in finding a manuscript of Catullus for his importunate mistress:

> I am burning with eagerness, dear Galeazzo, to find tender Catullus so that I can please my mistress. The wanton girl loves to read sensuous poets, and prefers your measures, learned Catullus. Not long ago, coaxing, she begged me for them—thinking perchance that her poet was in my possession. 'I don't have this book', I said, 'my darling, my nymph, but still I'll bring it to pass. Perhaps you will have the work.' She insists, and demands the dear book continually, and now she is after me with terrible threats. Wherefore, by all the gods, I beseech you and beseech you again, my dear friend (may Venus be kind to your prayers), seek out that book for me so that I may become more pleasing to my goddess.[91]

We may be sceptical about the passion of Panormita's mistress for Catullus, but the interest of the poet himself would not be surprising. He owned a manuscript of Catullus' great imitator Martial, made corrections to the text, and imitated Martial studiously in his own scandalous epigrams in the *Hermaphroditus*.[92] It seems unlikely, however, that he managed to acquire a manuscript or studied Catullus, for although some Catullan echoes have been identified in his correspondence and in the *Hermaphroditus*, they do not demonstrate close familiarity with his poetry.[93]

The *Hermaphroditus* is obscene and sexually explicit, but Panormita excuses its licence by pointing to his classical predecessors, including Catullus:

> Hodus says my life isn't chaste; he imagines my character from my writings. Hodus must not have read soft Catullus and his like. He has not seen your penis, circumcised Priapus. Should I think that what suited Martial, Marsus, Pedo, and all the rest is base for me?[94]

In another epigram he uses Catullus' argument that the character of the poet is not revealed in his verses, though the sentiment and its expression have been filtered through Martial: 'Believe, please, that my life is separate from my book; if my page is naughty, my mind is without a stain.'[95] The same excuse appears in his correspondence—this time in Catullus' own verses, which he perhaps found in Catullus, but probably saw in Pliny, who had quoted them in defence of his own racy verses:

> nam castum esse decet pium poetam
> ipsum, versiculos nihil necesse est;
> qui tum denique habent salem ac leporem,
> si sunt molliculi ac parum pudici,
> et quod pruriat incitare possunt. (16. 5–9)

He might also have seen the verses in the letter in which his older contemporary, Guarino da Verona (1370–1460), had hailed and defended the *Hermaphroditus* soon after its appearance.[96] The defence was insufficient, for within a short time Panormita's work was generally condemned. In 1435 Guarino withdrew his praise in a feeble palinode, pretending to have admired the form, but condemned the content of Panormita's poems.[97] The defence was apparently insufficient also for Catullus, if we may judge from the contemporary reading list of Ugolino Pisano (1436 or 1437):

> Juvenal, Persius, Martial, Propertius, Tibullus, Catullus, the *Priapeia* of Vergil, Ovid's *Ars Amatoria* and *Remedia Amoris* should not be read in public, but left to the private study of those wanting to see them. Thus, knowledge may be gained and no inexperienced youth will be contaminated by reading them.[98]

Ugolino, like Panormita, knew enough about Catullus to include him in a list of scandalous ancient poets, but perhaps that was all he knew. Guarino, Panormita's defender and one of the most famous humanists of his time, no doubt at least saw a manuscript, for his correspondence contains several quotations from Catullus that he could not have found in the anthologies of the previous century. Like his predecessors from Geremia to Petrarch, Guarino culled the poems for quotable verses; he repeats his finds with embarrassing regularity. To patrons and admirers he quotes the deprecating words from Catullus' dedication to Nepos: *namque tu solebas / meas esse aliquid putare nugas* (1. 3–4); to absent friends: *amantes / non longe a caro corpore abesse volunt* (66. 31–2); to a son in Brescia: *Brixia Veronae mater amata meae* (67. 34).[99] He attributes the quotations sometimes to 'noster Catullus' or 'meus concivis', but most often to 'conterraneus meus' in imitation of the elder Pliny.[100]

As we look back from Ugolino, Guarino, and Panormita in the 1420s and 1430s to Salutati, Petrarch, and Geremia in the previous century, we must admit that although Catullus had been known in Italy for well over a hundred years, he had remarkably little to show for it. He was identified as an obscene poet in lists made to excuse or caution against scandalous poetry. His manuscripts were sought out and corrected by Salutati and others. Quotable verses were collected by anthologists or humanists eager to embellish their writing with classical tags. In contrast, his imitator Martial had been studied by every humanist from Boccaccio (*c.*1370) on, and his epigrams imitated by several poets.[101] To some extent Catullus was less accessible than Martial. His long poems were knotty and difficult; his epigrams no doubt seemed harsh and old fashioned to readers accustomed to the smooth elegiacs of the Augustan and Silver Ages. But the greatest obstacle was the text, which was corrupt and unmetrical, and sometimes utterly meaningless. As we shall see in Chapter 1, Catullus required emendation and explication—and sometimes both at once.

I

Emendatio: From the *Editio Princeps* to the First Aldine

> si ab inferis revocaretur Catullus carmina sua non esset agniturus.
>
> (Antonio Partenio)

AFTER being lost to sight for a thousand years Catullus came to light again in a single corrupt manuscript, the Veronensis, on the very eve of the Renaissance. An 'exile returning from a distant land', as Benvenuto Campesani describes him, he had narrowly survived the neglect and vicissitudes of the Middle Ages, and he was scarred and mutilated from his passage.[1] In 1375 Antonio da Legnago, the scribe of G, transcribed a copy of the Veronensis and appended the subscription lamenting the poet's condition that he saw in his exemplar:

> Reader, whoever you are, into whose hands this book may come, pardon the scribe if it appears corrupt, since he transcribed it from a most corrupt exemplar, for none other existed from which he could have the opportunity of copying this book. And that he might provide something from this rough source he decided to have even a corrupt text rather than to do without, still hoping to be able to correct it from another copy if one should come to light.[2]

This complaint, although first voiced by the scribe of X or A or even V itself, was equally valid for Antonio and his successors.[3] No good text existed, and the humanists did not wait for one. For the next hundred years they transcribed whatever copies they could find and corrected them as best they could, working enthusiastically and sometimes intelligently, but never systematically. They had little understanding of the relative age or merit of their manuscripts, and such understanding would have done little good in any case, since they were constrained to copy not the manuscripts containing the best texts, but the manuscripts that were available.[4] The humanists introduced new errors into the text as they either made mistakes in transcription or changed correct readings that they did not understand, and later scribes often ignored the legitimate corrections made by earlier ones. As the haphazard process continued, the text became both better and worse—better in the abstract, since among them the humanists in the period made over 400 corrections that have found their way into modern editions,[5] but worse in fact, because corrections and errors alike were scattered indistinguishably through the manuscripts, which had grown farther and farther away from their fourteenth-century ancestors. By 1470 or so, over a hundred manuscripts had been copied by humanists great and small, from the likes of Poggio Bracciolini, the famous papal secretary and manuscript hunter, and Pomponio Leto, founder of the Roman Academy, to the Perugian professor and pornographer, Pacifico Massimo (scribe of Scaliger's much vaunted *Cuiacianus*), to dozens of lesser known or anonymous figures.[6]

From one of these manuscripts, and surely not the best, the press of Wendelin von Speyer in Venice printed the first edition of Catullus in 1472.[7] We do not know why Wendelin's editor chose the manuscript he did, or even that an editor as such existed. Printers typically used the first text to hand, edited it perfunctorily if at all, and lost or destroyed it as soon as it had served its purpose; and presumably Wendelin did the same.[8] In any case, his Catullus is not a distillation of all the improvements that had been made on the text since its discovery, but only a printed version of an anonymous *codex deterior*. This undeserving text, now fixed in type and given relatively wide circulation, inaugurated a new era: throughout the fifteenth century the text had been transmitted heterogeneously from many unreliable sources, but now it would proceed from only one.[9] Venice 1472 was now the universal reference point, and within a decade of its publication manuscripts and the manuscript tradition would be all but irrelevant to correctors, editors, and interpreters.

THE FIRST EDITION

As he opened his copy of the *editio princeps* the Renaissance reader saw and handled something quite different from Catullus' 'charming new little book, just polished with dry pumice' (1.

1–2). He held a large quarto volume that contained not only Catullus, but also Tibullus, Propertius, and Statius' *Silvae*—all, like Catullus, making their first appearance (or, in the case of Propertius, first important appearance) in print.[10] This substantial volume of 189 folios, or 378 pages, printed in a run of several hundred copies, was one of nearly sixty books published by Wendelin within a three-year period and certainly contributed, however modestly, to his financial ruin.[11] The page that met the reader's eye was large and luxuriously arranged, with good-sized initial letters alternately coloured red and blue to mark the beginning of each poem, and wide margins that presented an irresistible space for annotation—or in some cases, illumination, since wealthy readers liked having their printed books adorned as expensively as their manuscripts.[12] At least one copy was not only richly illuminated, but even printed on vellum.[13]

The contents and appearance of the Catullus portion of the volume (bound sometimes at the beginning and sometimes after Tibullus and Propertius) shaped the reader's expectations and presented him with a way of reading Catullus before he encountered a single line of his poetry. The section begins on a verso with a short biography of Catullus composed by Gerolamo Squarzafico, a modest and ill-paid humanist who worked for Wendelin adding literary and occasional editorial touches to his books.[14] He culled his life of Catullus from two authors whose works must have served as general references in many printing shops, Jerome and the fifteenth-century biographer Sicco Polenton. Jerome provided the biographical details, Sicco the literary *color*:

> Valerius Catullus the lyric writer was born at Verona in the 163rd Olympiad, a year before Sallustius Crispus, in the terrible times of Marius and Sulla, on the day Plotinus first began to teach Latin rhetoric in Rome. He loved a girl of the first rank, Clodia, whom he called Lesbia in his poetry. He was very playful, and in his time he had few equals, and no superior, in versifying. In jests he was especially charming, but in sober matters very serious. He wrote erotic poems and an epithalamium to Manlius. He died in the thirtieth year of his life and was buried with public mourning.[15]

On the recto facing Squarzafico's biography appears Benvenuto's epigram celebrating the discovery of Catullus, but Benvenuto himself has been forgotten, for the epigram is here entitled: *Hextichum Guarini Veronensis Oratoris Clarissimi in Libellum*

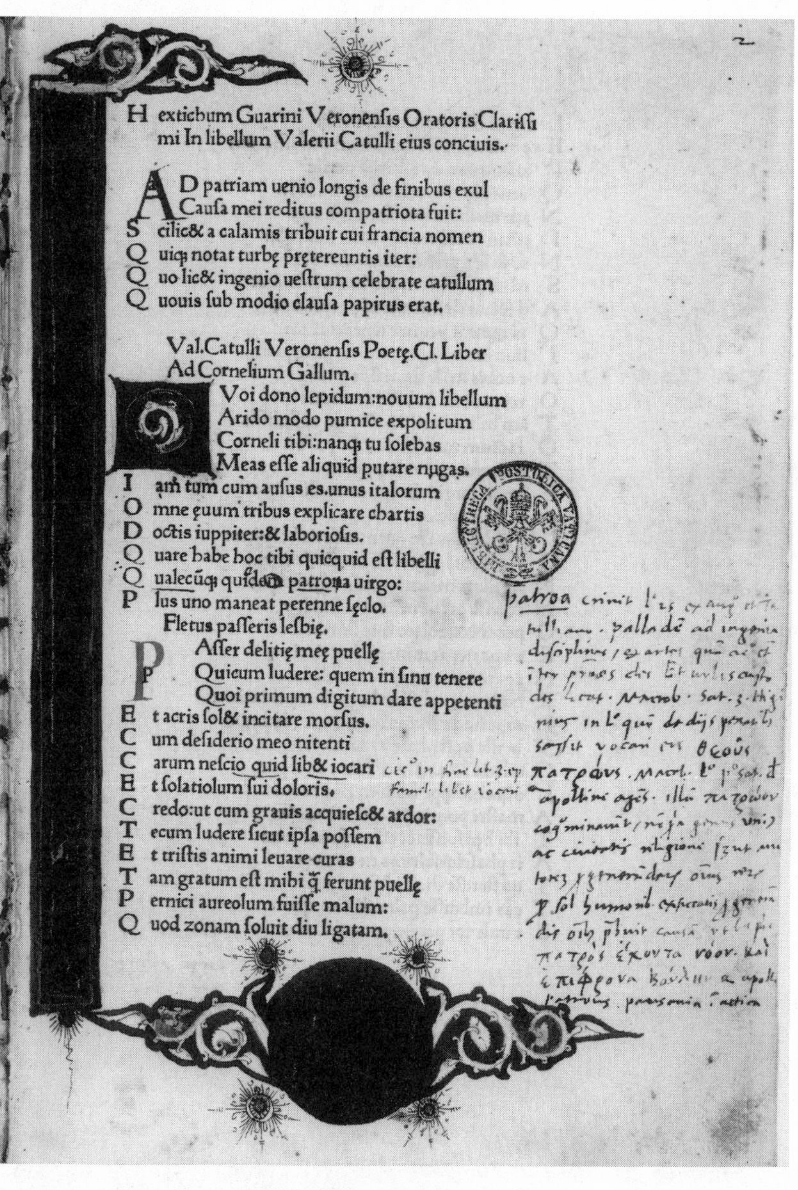
Hextichum Guarini Veronensis Oratoris Clarissimi In libellum Valerii Catulli eius conciuis.

AD patriam uenio longis de finibus exul
Causa mei reditus compatriota fuit:
Scilic& a calamis tribuit cui francia nomen
Quiq; notat turbę pretereuntis iter:
Quo lic& ingenio uestrum celebrate catullum
Quouis sub modio clausa papirus erat.

Val.Catulli Veronensis Poetę.Cl. Liber
Ad Cornelium Gallum.

Quoi dono lepidum:nouum libellum
Arido modo pumice expolitum
Corneli tibi:nanq; tu solebas
Meas esse aliquid putare nugas.
Iam tum cum ausus es.unus italorum
Omne ęuum tribus explicare chartis
Doctis iuppiter:& laboriosis.
Quare habe hoc tibi quicquid est libelli
Qualecūq; quidem patrona uirgo:
Plus uno maneat perenne sęclo.

Fletus passeris lesbię.

Passer delitię meę puellę
Quicum ludere: quem in sinu tenere
Quoi primum digitum dare appetenti
Et acris sol& incitare morsus.
Cum desiderio meo nitenti
Carum nescio quid lib& iocari
Et solatiolum sui doloris.
Credo:ut cum grauis acquiesc& ardor:
Tecum ludere sicut ipsa possem
Et tristis animi leuare curas
Tam gratum est mihi q̃ ferunt puellę
Pernici aureolum fuisse malum:
Quod zonam soluit diu ligatam.

Plate 1: The first page of Catullus in Venice 1472. The edition shown was owned and annotated by Angelo Colocci (Biblioteca Apostolica Vaticana, Inc. III. 18, fol. 2r).

Valerii Catulli eius Concivis. Immediately below is poem 1 (*Cui dono lepidum novum libellum*) with the title: *Val[erii] Catulli Veronensis Poetę Cl[arissimi] Liber ad Cornelium Gallum*. The distortions and anachronisms presented by the biography and titles inevitably influence the reader's understanding of the poet, dislocating Catullus from his historical context and foreshortening the recent history of the text. Squarzafico's dating is off by ten Olympiads, and he has both replaced Jerome's rhetor Plotius with the better known Plotinus (third century AD) and manufactured the interesting coincidence of Catullus' birthday with 'Plotinus'' teaching. The ascription of Benvenuto's epigram to the famous humanist Guarino da Verona (1370–1460) postpones the discovery of Catullus by almost a hundred years since it creates the false impression that it was Guarino who discovered the manuscript: the implication is that since Catullus is Guarino's fellow citizen (*concivis*) Guarino must also be the compatriot in the second verse of the poem ('a fellow countryman was the cause of my return').[16] Guarino and Catullus are further linked by the title of 1, which neatly balances that of the epigram, since 'the book of the most eminent poet Valerius Catullus Veronensis' nearly echoes 'the six-line poem of the most eminent orator Guarinus Veronensis'. According to the titles, both Catullus and Guarino are writing to fellow poets, Guarino to Catullus and Catullus to Cornelius Gallus (although in fact Catullus' addressee is the historian Cornelius Nepos, and Gallus would have been only about 10 years old at the beginning of Catullus' literary career).

The biography and titles are of recent pedigree, for the biography was composed for the *editio princeps*, and the two titles are only a few years older.[17] Other titles in the *princeps* have a longer pedigree and reinforce older problems and misunderstandings. Some may be traced as far as the lost Veronensis, others to A or X, and more still to Coluccio Salutati, who had embellished R with titles of his own invention.[18] Thus, the reader saw 36 (*Annales Volusi, cacata carta*) under the bizarre title *Ad Lusi Cacatam*, which arose from its corrupt first verse: *Annuale suo lusi cacata charta* (36. 1, Venice 1472).[19] As he read 29 he could see that the title *Ad Romulum Catamitum*[20] was derived from the addressee: *cinaede Romule, haec videbis et feres?* (verses 5 and 9); but he might not have been able to understand that Catullus was attacking Caesar and his crony Mamurra, since Caesar was not mentioned by name, and Mamurra's name was concealed in the ancient corruption of line 3, *nam murram*.

Sometimes in the *princeps* titles and poems do not correspond because the poems have not been correctly separated. For example, at some point in the tradition scribes lost sight of the fact that Catullus wrote two poems on Lesbia's sparrow—one celebrating its playful affection for its mistress (2: *Passer, delitiae meae puellae*), the other lamenting its untimely death (3: *Lugete, o Veneresque Cupidinesque*); and they began to run them together as a single poem. This unseparated block passed from the Veronensis to the fourteenth- and fifteenth-century manuscripts and on into the first edition, where the reader found it under Salutati's title *Fletus passeris lesbię*.[21] The Veronensis contained many blocks of this kind. Its descendants A and X broke up some of the blocks, R (corrected by Salutati) and its descendants, including the manuscript from which the *princeps* was printed, separated and retitled many more. Those that remained constituted the most obvious obstacle to the reader, whose first task, it seemed, was simply to discern the shapes of poems in the mass of Catullus' text. Appendix 1 shows the unseparated blocks and their titles both in R^2 (= Coluccio Salutati) and in the first edition. The reconstruction of R^2 is taken from McKie's dissertation.[22]

Several poems in Venice 1472 have been separated from their long blocks in R; the reader would see them titled with the names of their addressees. If the addressee was visible in the text the title was clear and specific (thus, *Ad Caelium* for 58 from the name in the first line); if not, the title was correspondingly vague, like *Ad Amicum* (24), *Ad Quendam* (103, 104), or *In Quendam* (108).[23] In several of the cases where the *princeps* shortens or breaks up a block without freeing all the poems textual corruption conceals the addressee or point of demarcation. Thus, the reader found Catullus' consolation to Calvus on the death of Quintilia (96) printed as a single poem with the obscene invectives of 97 and 98; the title, *De Aemylio*, was taken from the smelly protagonist of 97, and Calvus' name was concealed in *caule* at 96. 2. Thus, too, he read 83 and 84 together, even though the one is addressed to Lesbia's foolish husband (a 'mule' who does not see that she speaks ill of Catullus because she loves him) and the other mocks the pretentious Arrius who uses too many aitches. Several problems confuse the issue (including the disappearance of all the aitches in 84),[24] but it is the corruption *acrius* for *Arrius* in 84. 2 that makes it just possible to read the two poems together, taking Lesbia as the subject of the verbs in both:

Non solum meminit: sed quę multo acrior est res:
Irata est hoc est uritur: et loquitur:
Commoda dicebat: si quando commoda vellet
Dicere et insidias **acrius** insidias:
(83. 5–6, 84. 1–2, Venice 1472)

Loss of the addressee or the corruption of a proper name blurred the boundaries even of poems in different metres. Thus the reader found the last verse of Catullus' complaint that he caught cold reading a frigid speech (44, in choliambs) beginning the love idyll of Septimius and Acme (45, in hendecasyllables).[25] Most of Catullus' back-handed compliment to Calvus and his oratory (53) was printed as the conclusion to his attack on Nonius and Vatinius (52), although the one is in hendecasyllables, the other in iambic trimeter. The punch-line (53. 5) was printed as the first verse of 54, an attack on a pin-head named Otho. Here is what the reader saw (the corrupt words are in bold-face, and the text of 53 is italicized):

In Novium
Quid est catulle? quid moraris emori?
Sella in curuli struma **novius** sedet.
Per consulatum peierat vatinius:
Quid est catulle? quid moraris emori?
Risi nescio quem modo **et** *corona*
Qui cum mirifice vatiniana
Meos carmina salvus *explicasset.*
Admirans ait hęc manusque tollens.
De Othonis Capite
Dii magni **salapantium desertum**
Othonis caput oppido est pusillum
(52–54. 1, Venice 1472)

To put the epigram together again he would have had not only to find Calvus' name hidden in 53. 3 and to correct the rest of the verse (i.e. *meus crimina Calvos*) but also to recognize and understand the picturesque phrase *salaputium disertum* ('eloquent little squirt') hidden in 53. 5.[26]

He faced similar problems with the block entitled *Ad Egnatium* that extended from 37. 17 through 39. Catullus wrote two poems in choliambics about the Spaniard Egnatius who scrubbed his teeth with urine (37 and 39). In the first Egnatius appears as one of Lesbia's long-haired lovers in the low tavern she frequents; in the second Catullus celebrates his toothy smile. Between them, 38, in hendecasyllables, reproaches Cornificius for not sending the poet a consolation in his worsening troubles. At some point, however, scribes ran 38 and 39 together and attached them to the last verses of 37—so creating a single poem on the disgusting Egnatius and losing sight of Cornificius altogether.[27] Not only Cornificius but even Catullus' hendecasyllables were invisible in the printed text, since each of the first three verses contains an extra monosyllable (the corrupt words are in bold-face):

Male est: **si carnifici** tuo catullo
Male est: **si** me hercule et laboriose
Et magis **ac** magis indies et horas:

(38. 1–3, Venice 1472).

When the Renaissance reader put down his copy of the *princeps* he knew that he had encountered problems on every page that he could not identify or resolve, for the text was riddled with corrupt readings and impossible scansions, with historical anachronisms and unknown names and allusions, and, most obviously, with incomprehensible or even unidentifiable poems. Within a year two men of very different abilities and methods set themselves to the task of correction—Francesco dal Pozzo, called Puteolano, a hard-working and entrepreneurial humanist, and Angelo Poliziano, the greatest philologist of the age. It is characteristic of Catullus' fortunes in the fifteenth century that Puteolano's corrections made their way into an influential edition, while those of Poliziano lay unpublished in the margins of his book. Since Poliziano continued to annotate his book throughout the 1470s and '80s we will consider his emendations presently. For now we must turn to Puteolano and the successors of the first edition.

THE BUSINESS OF EDITING: FRANCESCO PUTEOLANO AND GIOVANNI CALFURNIO

One should not be too high-minded in considering Renaissance editions and editors. Printing was a business, and purely practical considerations, particularly those relating to money and time, influenced the production of every book. The pace of Wendelin's activities and a shortage of cash no doubt precluded any real editing of the *princeps*; Squarzafico produced biographies for it, and we can imagine that he, or someone like him, quickly assembled and proof-read the texts of Catullus and the other three poets. In the case of the second edition we can see a stronger editorial hand and infer a rather different financial arrangement between editor and printer. This edition, which contained only Catullus and Statius, was printed by Stefano Corallo in Parma in 1473.[28] It was prepared by Francesco Puteolano, as the colophon to Statius attests:

> Corrected by Master Francesco Puteolano, and indeed emended in three thousand places beyond the edition printed in Venice (that is, Catullus and the *Silvae*), as you the reader will be able to see for yourself in both texts, because they cannot be understood, etc. Printed in Parma by me, Stefano Corallo, in the year of Christ 1473, on the 31st of August.[29]

Francesco Puteolano was an energetic and successful humanist—lecturer in the Studio of Bologna (1467–77), protégé of the Sforza, and editor of the first edition of Ovid (Bologna, 1471).[30] He was also something of a businessman, for he entered into several partnerships connected with his educational and scholarly activities. In October 1470 he formed the first important printing firm in Bologna with Annibale Malpigli and Baldassare Azzoguidi. Azzoguidi and Malpigli were to provide the presses and to pay for ink, paper, and labour. Puteolano's responsibility was to provide correct texts for printing, to publicize the printed books, to lecture from them, and—to the best of his ability—to sell them. In return he was to have either a third of the books or a third of the profits after expenses.[31] It was under this agreement that Malpigli and Azzoguidi published the 1471 edition of Ovid and that Puteolano—if he kept his part of the bargain—lectured from it and sold it to his students at the Studio of Bologna. Since Puteolano entered into at least three other contracts with printers in Bologna in the 1470s, he probably also had a similar arrangement with Corallo in Parma even though we have no record of it and energetically promoted and sold his Catullus at the Studio.[32]

In April 1473 Puteolano was party to another business venture that had consequences for Catullus. This time we find him in a partnership to found a school with Giovanni Planza de Ruffinoni, called Calfurnio. Puteolano is to recruit students and outfit the establishment at his own expense, while Calfurnio is to teach, run the school, and keep accounts; the profits are to be divided and the agreement is to be in effect for two years.[33] The agreement is further evidence for the range of activities of a busy and enterprising humanist, but its real interest lies in the fact that Calfurnio, Puteolano's partner, soon went on to produce the 1481 Vicenza edition of Catullus, which was to be a monument in fifteenth-century Catullan studies. During their partnership Calfurnio published an edition of Ovid that was modelled on Puteolano's 'even down to the colophon'[34] When he turned to Catullus a few years later, naturally he consulted the edition of his former associate.[35]

The colophon of the 1473 Parma edition claims 3,000 changes from the first edition of Catullus and Statius, and, for Catullus at least, the claim is nearly justified. Puteolano had corrected Venice 1472 against a manuscript of another family. The manuscript Wendelin had used for the *princeps* was descended from X, one of the two fourteenth-century copies of A. Puteolano used a descendant of the other copy, O.[36] Our understanding of his method would be greatly enhanced if his manuscript were identified, but the important point is that it had a different pedigree from the source of Venice 1472 and could supply some of its deficiencies. Although Puteolano's manuscript furnished many new readings, two large-scale examples will suffice.[37] The first edition omitted 64. 334–7; Parma 1473 supplies them. The second couplet of 92 was omitted by Venice 1472 and by other descendants of X, but is preserved by O and its offspring. Puteolano prints the couplet, although in an idiosyncratic form.[38]

The reader turning from the *princeps* to Parma 1473 would be struck first by changes in the *dispositio carminum*, for Puteolano has broken up or shortened several of the blocks found in the first edition, as we can see from Appendix 2, which presents an overview of the *dispositio* in the fifteenth century. Sometimes he (or his source) has found and corrected a proper name at the point of demarcation. Thus, Catullus' kiss poem to the boy Iuventius (48) had appeared in the *princeps* at the end of the block 44. 21–48, with Iuventius himself lost in the corrupt line: *Mellitos oculos tuos niventi* (48. 1, Venice 1472). The change of *niventi* to *iuventi* in Parma 1473 makes everything clear, and 48 appears as a separate poem with the title *Ad Iuventium*.[39] At the beginning of the same block, Puteolano has separated 44. 21 (the last verse from the poem on the cold Catullus caught from a frigid speech) from the idyll of Septimius and Acme, printing the proper name *Agme* for *ac meminit* of the *princeps*.[40] (He still prints 45 itself in a block that extends through 47.) Similarly, he has rescued Catullus' *consolatio* to Calvus (96) from its obscene neighbours, although one cannot be sure who he thought was the addressee, for although he correctly prints *calve* for *caule* of the *princeps* at 96. 2 he entitles the poem *Ad Gallum*—perhaps from his manuscript.[41] Most of the time, however, Puteolano's separation of blocks or poems depends not on textual correction, but simply on intelligent observation. Thus, he (or his source) has noticed the change of topic between 32 and 33 (an obscene invitation to Ipsitilla and an obscene attack on the sticky-fingered thieves at the baths), 66 and 67 (the *Lock of Berenice* and the address to the door of an adulterous woman), 87 and 88 (an epigram on Lesbia and an attack on the oversexed Gellius).[42]

Anyone who had studied the first edition would agree with Puteolano's colophon that it was unintelligible in many places. In some of these his edition brings order and sense, as in 36 (*Annales volusi cacata charta*, 36. 1, Parma 1473), which is described aptly enough by its title *Ad Libellos Volusi*;[43] or at 10. 30, where he has emended the meaningless *Cumas: est gravis* of the *editio princeps* to *cinna est Caius*.[44] But there were also many problems he failed to solve or perhaps even to identify, like the Egnatius poems in the unmetrical block 37. 17–39. In one case at least, he made matters worse, for by joining the blocks 52–53. 4 and 53. 5–54. 5 he has buried Catullus' anecdote about Calvus' oratory (53) even deeper than it had been in the *princeps*.

Puteolano's edition was soon followed by three others. The 1475 edition probably printed in Milan was essentially a reprint of the *princeps*, which the editor apparently collated with a manuscript, introducing some small changes.[45] The first edition to contain only Catullus was printed in Rome probably in the same year; it was modelled less closely on the first edition, but its independence did not result in many improvements.[46] The 1481 edition printed in Reggio depends heavily on Puteolano's text but was not copied from it.[47]

Better and bolder than any of these was the edition of Puteolano's old partner, Giovanni Calfurnio (Joannes Calphurnius) which was printed in Vicenza in 1481.[48] Calfurnio was a well-known and successful scholar. He edited Ovid (1474), wrote a commentary on Terence's *Heautontimoroumenos* (1476), and edited Servius (1479) and Catullus, Tibullus, Propertius, and Statius (1481). In addition, he edited various works of other humanists, including the commentaries on Martial (1474) and Juvenal (before 1478) by Domizio Calderini.[49] In 1486 he became professor at the Studio of Padua, thereby incurring the enmity of his rival for the position, Raffaele Regio, who launched a lifelong vendetta against him. Regio cast the usual humanist aspersions on the origins, conduct, and learning of his enemy, but Calfurnio, apparently blameless on all counts, went on to lecture for many years to crowds of enthusiastic students at Padua.[50] Long after his edition of 1481 Calfurnio was regarded as an active authority on Catullus. The *Emendationes in Catullum* of Girolamo Avanzi (Hieronymus Avantius) were shown to him for his approval in 1493, and Avanzi tells us that he was still lecturing on Catullus and supplementing the work of his edition:

> But in every lecture he gives in the crowded Paduan Studio he corrects and explains daily (as they say) more meanings of Catullus that have been obscure and misunderstood until now. I ask and encourage you to get them all, for nothing emerges from his workshop that is not highly polished.[51]

Calfurnio died in 1503, and left his many books to the rich library of S. Giovanni di Verdara.[52]

Calfurnio is the first editor to discuss his work on Catullus. He explains the origins and circumstances of his edition in his dedication to Ermolao Barbaro:

> Men of our day who are enthusiastic students of literature, most eloquent Hermolaus, can rejoice to an astonishing degree because they

Plate 2: The funeral monument of Giovanni Calfurnio by Antonio Minelli (1512). The monument was originally placed in S. Giovanni di Verdara in Padua. It is now in the Chiostro del Noviziato of the Basilica di S. Antonio in Padua. (Photo. Thomas Gaisser)

have come upon a huge abundance of books, which both former ages and the era preceding our own lacked. And because of the number of printed books this supply indeed has grown so much that it must fill not whole libraries but whole houses. But, as the famous poet says, 'The rose is often closest to the thorn.' This divine gift, as usually happens in human affairs, could not be perfect in every respect, for I see that it lacks one thing: diligent and accurate correction of the books. Without this whatever is done must be done in vain. For confusion arises for students and an intolerable annoyance for scholars . . . Hear in a few words why I am writing this to you. When I was asked some days ago by some studious young men to comment on Propertius or (if I preferred) the *Silvae* of Statius in my daily lecture, I promised to do what they wanted in order not to disappoint them. And so I began to look over the work printed at Venice that contains these famous poets, Catullus, Tibullus, Propertius, and Statius' *Silvae*, and discovered that it was so filled with mistakes that far more was faulty and corrupt than had been corrected. No sense at any rate could be got out of them. At once I met with some printers and urged them to reprint it with the corrections that I promised. Therefore I can boast that I did not correct the work, but rather recopied almost the whole thing—as anyone can tell by comparing the two texts. Nevertheless, I have decided not to have any more dealings with printers because they habitually change and turn upside down the corrected works they have received. So if you find anything omitted or changed, please ascribe it not to me, but to the printers. For often, as I have said, they either transpose syllables or leave out a few letters or add what was supposed to be left out—just as in this place in Catullus: *famesque mundi* [47.2]. My correction was *memi*.[53] They printed both words. And in that verse, *deprendi modo pupullum puellae* [56.5], they left out *pupullum*. And in this verse, *Diverse variae viae reportant* [46.11], they left out *viae*. I am content to take notice only of these passages, lest anyone think that I have been careless in this work which is being published for the common convenience of scholars . . .[54]

Calfurnio is not the only humanist of his day to fulminate against the careless work of printers, but his outrage is real.[55] From only four pages of his Catullus he is able to cite three serious errors—one of which was to cost him credit for an emendation, for his correction *pupullum* in 56.5 (omitted by the printer) is attributed by modern editors to the 1485 edition of Partenio. The errors mentioned by Calfurnio are only a small fraction of the whole, and his annoyance is all the more understandable when we remember that he undertook his edition for the very purpose of correcting the mistakes in its predecessor.[56] Calfurnio's greatest success lay ahead of him, for at the time of his Catullus, the chair in Padua was still five years away; but, as far as we know, he kept to his resolve to have no more dealings with printers.[57]

Calfurnio embarked on his project because his students wanted him to lecture on Propertius and Statius, but Catullus, if only a parergon at the outset, soon became a major focus of his attention. It is the printers' mistakes in Catullus that draw his ire, and it is largely on Catullus that his reputation is based. Goold's census attributes 45 corrections to Calfurnio—more than to any other editor; and the number does not include other corrections that made just as much difference to contemporary readers—that is, improvements to the printed tradition that have also been found in manuscripts.[58] Avanzi, as he reviewed the state of Catullan studies in 1493, considered this edition its first landmark: 'For who could come into contact with the writings of Catullus without annoyance before Calfurnio's diligent correction?'[59] Calfurnio went to extraordinary lengths to produce a text that was more readable than its predecessors: 'I can boast', he says, 'that I did not emend, but recopied nearly the whole work.'[60] Indeed, he could almost claim to have rewritten it. In addition to many dozens of corrections to single words, he made major alterations in the *dispositio carminum*, correctly separating eight poems, several of which contain substantial, if not always correct, changes from earlier editions (see Appendix 2).[61] His most striking success is in 84, which he has separated from 83 and entitled *De Ario*; understanding that the epigram turns around Arrius and his aitches, he has supplied the appropriate aspirates: *Chommoda dicebat: si quando commoda vellet* (84. 1, Vicenza 1481).[62]

But we should not overestimate Calfurnio's achievement. In many places his text does not make sense, and all too often he seems either to have corrected only part of a problem or to have introduced a new difficulty along with his correction. In 4 he has made three corrections (italicized below) within two verses:

Phasellus ille: quem: videtis hospites
ait fuisse navium celerrimum:
neque *ullius* natantis *trabis* impetum.

(4. 1–3, Vicenza 1481)

Compare *aiunt*, *illius*, *tardum* in Venice 1472. But the combination *ait . . . celerrimum* is ungrammatical, and *trabis impetum* is unmetrical (the iambic metre requires *impetum trabis*, as Avanzi noted a few years later). At 10. 30 he reads *Cinna est gravis*, conflating Puteolano's correct *cinna est Caius* with *Cumas est gravis* of the *princeps*. In 38 he omits *si* from verses 1 and 2, thus mending the text and metre, but leaves the equally gratuitous and unmetrical *ac* of the *princeps* in line 3: *et magis ac magis in dies et horas* (38. 3, Vicenza 1481). He achieved even more mixed results in the hard case of 52–54, which had defeated both the *princeps* and Puteolano; for although he correctly separated 52, he misdivided 53–54 into two strange 'epigrams' (the corrupt words are in boldface):

Risi nescio quem modo **et** corona
Qui cum mirifice vatiniana
Meus **carmina** calvus explicasset.
Admirans ait haec manusque tollens.
Dii magni **solopycium** disertum
Othonis caput oppido est pusillum

(53–54. 1, Vicenza 1481)

Hoc iucunde tibi poema feci
Ex quo perspiceres meum dolorem:
At en rustice semilauta crura:
Subtile: et leve peditum **liboni est**
Si non omnia displicere vellem
Tibi et sufficio seni recocto.

(50. 16–17, 54. 2–5, Vicenza 1481)

Difficulties of several kinds have conspired against him: 54 is perhaps hopelessly corrupt;[63] the sense of *salaputium* (53.5) was lost; the verses that he used for the beginning of his second poem (*hoc iucunde tibi*, etc.) had in fact been wrongly repeated in the archetype from 50. 16–17. But Calfurnio himself added to the confusion; for although he saw that *salvus* in 53. 3 concealed *Calvus* and chose Puteolano's *disertum* over *desertum* at 53.5, he rejected his crucial improvement *crimina*, reverting to *carmina* of the first edition. Calfurnio does not interpret his creations for us, or even award them a title, but perhaps the commentary of Antonio Partenio preserves his intentions—at least for the first 'poem'. Partenio explains that after Calvus had interpreted

Catullus' poems against Vatinius in court, a foolish man, 'wishing to praise the poet's talent, blurted out some nonsensical words'– i.e. *solopycium disertum* in 53. 5.[64]

In two other cases it is somewhat easier to divine Calfurnio's interpretation from his results. In the first he wrongly manufactured two epigrams using the principles of balance and symmetry. The *princeps* had printed 85–88 in a block (see Appendix 2), thus lumping together three love poems and an epigram on the revolting Gellius (88). Puteolano sequestered Gellius and left the three love poems together, not noticing their differences: 85 treats the paradox that Catullus can love and hate at the same time, 86 acknowledges Quintia's individual good features but denies that they add up to Lesbia's charm, 87 asserts that no woman has ever been loved as much as Lesbia has been loved by the poet. But Calfurnio arrived at a different idea as he studied the block of poems in Puteolano's edition. He divided 85–87 into two poems which he entitled *De Quintia* and *De Lesbia*:

De Quintia

Odi et amo quare id faciam fortasse requiris
  Nescio: sed fieri sentio et excrutior.
Quintia formosa est multis mihi candida longa
  Recta est: haec ego singula confiteor:
Totum illud: formosa nego: nam nulla venustas
  Nulla in tam magno est corpore mica salis.

(85–86. 4, Vicenza 1481)

De Lesbia

Lesbia formosa est: quae cum pulcherrima tota est
  Tum omnibus una omnes surripuit veneres:
Nulla potest mulier tantum se dicere amatam
  Vere quantum a me lesbia amata mea lesbia est
Nulla fides ullo fuit unquam foedere tanta
  Quanta in amore tuo ex parte reperta mea est.

(86. 5–87, Vicenza 1481)

Instead of Catullus' three poems, then, Calfurnio saw two complementary and contrasting poems of equal length, the first on the theme of mixed emotions and Quintia's mixed and ultimately incomplete charms, the second on the complete beauty of Lesbia and Catullus' wholehearted devotion.

In our second case he ran into problems because he was

looking for an addressee. The *princeps* had printed 69–71 in a block (see Appendix 2)—sandwiching 70, the first in a cycle of serious epigrams on love and infidelity, between two poems on smelly characters whom the poet describes as having he-goats under their armpits. Puteolano or his source, noticing the first he-goat (*valle sub alarum trux habitare caper*, 69. 6), separated 69 from 70–71, which he left together under the title *De muliere sua*. The sphere of operations of the second goat, meanwhile, and hence the subject of 71, was concealed in the following verse (71. 1, Venice 1472: the corrupt words are in boldface):

> Si **qua viro bello sacrorum** obstitit hircus.

Compare Mynors' edition (71. 1, ed. Mynors):

> Si cui iure bono sacer alarum obstitit hircus.

Calfurnio, however, saw through the corruption, correctly separated the poems, and virtually rewrote the verse (71. 1, Vicenza 1481: the correct changes are italicized):

> Si *cui* virobon *sacer alarum* obstitit hircus

But what about the meaningless and unmetrical *virobon*? Calfurnio did not mean *viro bono*, as Zicàri assumed, but rather the vocative of a proper name, *Virobon* or *Virrobon*, whose provenance and scansion are obscure—either because Calfurnio had not yet worked them out or because they were misunderstood by the printers. In any case, however, *Virobon/Virrobon* is the intended addressee, for the newly separated poem is entitled *Ad .V.*[65]

This last case points up the difficulty of fully recovering either Calfurnio's text or his intentions in the mass of printing errors. Let us consider a few examples. Calfurnio is the first editor to separate 46 from its block (see Appendix 2). At 46. 1 Venice 1472 read *vero gelidos*, Parma 1473 *vere gelidos*. Calfurnio has *veregelidos*; does he want *vere gelidos* or the correct *ver egelidos*? In 46. 11 his text reads *Diversae variae reportant*. We know from the preface that the printers omitted *viae*, but in the preface the verse reads *diverse variae viae reportant*. Did he want *diversae* or *diverse*? At 4. 2, once having corrected to *ait*, did he mean to leave *celerrimum* and not the correct *celerrimus*? At 10. 30 did the printers record only half the correction, printing

Cinna but not noticing *Caius*? Certainly Calfurnio's printers were capable of anything, but he himself probably deserves some of the blame: like most Renaissance editors, he was in a great hurry, and he probably failed to enter a few corrections in his text or even to notice that they were required.[66]

Wherever we turn in considering Calfurnio and his text we run into the tangible and practical realities of printing, which included not only the fallible printers but also the printed book itself as a physical entity. When Calfurnio made his corrections he wrote in the margins and between the lines of his 'work printed in Venice', not merely emending individual words or verses, but recopying extensive passages.[67] The printers who were presented with this heavily corrected edition naturally made countless mistakes, like leaving the doublet *mundi memii* at 47. 2 that Calfurnio complains of in his preface—an error that could have resulted only from overlooking a deletion in a corrected text. Although Calfurnio's printers were probably worse than usual, his own procedure was typical, and probably essentially the same as that of his old partner, Puteolano—albeit with one very important difference: Puteolano corrected the text of the *princeps* against his manuscript, Calfurnio corrected it against Puteolano's edition. Calfurnio may have seen manuscripts of Catullus, and perhaps he even entered a manuscript reading or two in his book, but for him editions, not manuscripts, were the source of the text.[68] Catullus had already passed into a *lectio recepta* or base text or vulgate, as text critics call the current text that provides the basis for emendation and interpretation without being itself subject to fundamental re-evaluation or change. But Calfurnio's book and his method remind us that the base text is not an abstraction, for it has its concrete manifestation in the printed edition with corrections that moves from each editor to the next.[69]

THE EDITION THAT MIGHT HAVE BEEN: ANGELO POLIZIANO'S NOTES IN THE *EDITIO PRINCEPS*

While Calfurnio and Puteolano were negotiating with printers and producing editions for the marketplace, the young Angelo

Poliziano (1454–94) was quietly emending Catullus. He began to correct the *princeps* almost as soon as it appeared and continued to add to his notes at least until the mid-1480s, entering his own corrections and the readings he had found in manuscripts or other sources, and collating his text with each new edition as it appeared. Although Poliziano published a handful of his ideas on Catullus in the *Miscellanea*, as we shall see in Chapter 2, the vast majority of his emendations remained unknown to contemporary and later editors and exercised no influence on Catullan scholarship. But the book that contains them, now preserved in the Biblioteca Corsiniana in Rome, presents a valuable record not only of contemporary Catullan emendation and interpretation but also of Poliziano's own method and scholarly development.[70]

It is not easy to read Poliziano's annotations, for the binders have trimmed off some of his notes, and the ink in others has faded almost to the vanishing point; but by studying them carefully we can watch him at work as he set about reading Catullus. Although no one has ventured to establish a chronology, we can see from the various shades of his ink and slight differences in his handwriting that he annotated his book over a period of time. As he worked through the text he filled his margins with explanations of hard words and grammatical points, metrical comments, and a profusion of parallel passages from other authors, both Latin and Greek. He picked out words that he thought would be useful for his poetry, creating a sort of poetic lexicon of diminutives, compound words, and intriguing Catullan combinations of noun and epithet.[71] Sometimes he noted down words whose meaning escaped him in hopes of explaining them later.[72] Mostly, however, he emended Catullus—separating poems from their blocks with horizontal lines, and neatly entering dozens of tiny and now sometimes barely discernible corrections above the words and in the margins of his book.

Poliziano gives an account of his work in his subscription to Catullus, which is still legible although it has been lightly crossed out:

With much toil and many long nights, as far as was in me, I have corrected Catullus of Verona corrupted by the ignorance of scribes. Though I compared numerous texts of this poet I came upon none that was not as corrupt as my own. And so I have compared many Greek and

Latin authors and spent so much effort in correcting the text that I believe I have accomplished something achieved by no one else in these times of learned men. Here is Catullus of Verona, if not completely corrected, at least sound for the most part through my effort and toil and industry! Think as well of my work as you can, and out of kindness correct and emend what is still corrupt because of my ignorance or carelessness. And remember that when he completed this emendation Angelus Bassus Politianus was only eighteen years old. Farewell, dear Reader! Florence, August 12, 1473. Yours, Angelus Bassus Politianus.[73]

We find a more moderate assessment in the subscription to Propertius he wrote a dozen years later:

Even from boyhood, I, Angelus Politianus, began to work with the books of Catullus, Tibullus, and Propertius and to correct or explain them as well as I could at that age. As a result, today I myself no longer approve of many of my corrections. Please do not use them, Reader, to form an opinion or judgement of my intellect or learning or care. For there will be many things in them (to use Plautus' expression) that even in the judgement of their author deserve to be erased. 1485.[74]

His last mention of the annotations appears in a letter of 1486 to Alessandro and Lattanzio Cortesi:

After I had written this [the rest of his letter], it occurred to me that, since you have asked for some commentary of mine on Catullus, I once as a boy wrote something on Catullus, and that this, for what it was worth, I applied to the margins of my book.

And although perhaps I worked out some things rather usefully, nevertheless, I did not succeed so completely that we can read Catullus either fully emended or without some obscurities here and there. And some things there are childish and not sufficiently learned and worthy of sophisticated ears. Therefore, I have considered it not yet worthy of publication. But if you come upon some knotty passage that you cannot disentangle easily by yourself, write to me and, as far as is in me, I will make a good effort. Moreover, if some things have escaped me, you will not take it amiss—such is your kindness—to endure ignorance along with me. And yet I am afraid that you are teasing me when you ask for my foolish efforts, Alexander, especially since you can do more than I can say through your own ability and since you have Jovianus [Pontanus] with you—a single man who must be considered the equivalent of many scholars. Again, farewell.[75]

At 18 Poliziano made large claims for his accomplishments: he had surpassed all contemporary scholars, and he had essentially completed the correction of the text, offering the reader a Catullus *maxima ex parte incorruptus*. Even at this period he already had a clearly conceived critical method, which had as its cornerstone collation of manuscripts and study of the usage in parallel passages of other ancient authors.[76] When he wrote his subscription to Propertius at 30 he could afford to seem more modest, for he was no longer an impecunious young humanist in search of a patron, but a well-established scholar and poet who enjoyed both the economic security of Medici patronage and the professional dignity of a professorship in Greek and Latin at the Florentine Studio.[77] He was also more realistic, for as a mature scholar he could see that he had not solved all the problems in Catullus and that some were insoluble. But the second subscription also reflects a changed state of affairs in Catullan studies. In mid-August 1473 a young man could dream of making his reputation with Catullus simply by correcting the single corrupt edition before him, but in the next dozen years five more editions were published—six if we include the edition and commentary of Antonio Partenio.[78] The young Poliziano may also have thought of writing a commentary, for in the second subscription he says that he tried both to correct (*corrigere*) and to explain (*interpretari*) Catullus, and in his letter to the Cortesi a few months later he seems to consider his notes the basis for a commentary, although he rejects the idea of writing one.

Whenever Poliziano mentions his marginalia he treats them as a youthful endeavour. In 1473 he claimed to have put the finishing touches (*extremam manum*) on his corrections, and in the 1480s he implied that they had been long since completed and put aside. But his book itself tells a different, and more interesting, story. Appendix 3 shows Poliziano's corrections to the *princeps* under three headings: corrections also made in the *Miscellanea*, corrections found in other sources before 1494 (the year of Poliziano's death), and corrections attributed by modern editors to sources after 1494.

Two points are clear from our table: that Poliziano achieved a sizeable number of corrections now attributed to later sources, and that most of his corrections were current in his lifetime in editions or manuscripts.[79] The table seems to vindicate Poliziano's claim in his subscription of 1473 to have compared 'numerous texts [i.e. manuscripts] of the poet', for although the number of readings that could have come only from manuscripts or Poliziano himself is small, their distribution is impressive. Moreover, the number of readings he shares with the editions of Puteolano, Calfurnio, and Partenio strongly suggests that he continued his annotations well into the 1480s (and reminds us, as well, that the dates of his subscriptions are almost suspiciously close to those of the colophons of Puteolano and Partenio). The table cannot demonstrate, however, either that Poliziano derived all of his shared corrections from other sources (the number of his original corrections argues against it in any event) or that he had a source at all in any particular case. At 62. 7, for example, although Poliziano's correction *oeteos* appears in the ninth-century manuscript T (Paris, BN Lat. 8071), he surely did not find it there. He made very few corrections to 62. but if he had had access to T he would have made dozens, since it differed in nearly every line from the manuscripts and editions with which he was familiar.[80] Perhaps he found *oetheos* in the R^3 additions to R, which were made in Florence around 1475,[81] or perhaps he arrived at the correction independently, as he surely did in any number of other cases whose merits we know too little to judge.

Our table was designed to show Poliziano's successful corrections to the text (those accepted by modern editions) and to give some indication of his use of manuscript and printed sources, but it does not give a just picture of his complete *liber Catulli*, for it omits three types of corrections: unsuccessful corrections, corrections that appear to be merely restorations of the archetype, and separation and renaming of poems. Poliziano's unsuccessful corrections are very numerous. Of these, many never saw the light of day, and others appear only as variants in the *apparatus* of modern editions. But the unsuccessful corrections have their own interest for the history of emendation in the fifteenth century, and we will find them useful when we try to date and evaluate the contribution of Battista Guarino in the next chapter. Poliziano's restorations of the archetype, on the other hand, made the text of the *princeps* readable where before it was nonsense, and his *dispositio carminum* is the best in the fifteenth century, as we can see from Appendix 2.[82]

Let us see how Poliziano treated just one of the poems whose fortunes we have been following—Catullus' sombre little appeal to Cornificius (38), which he found sandwiched in the block

37.17–39 with the invectives on Egnatius and his repellent smile. He has correctly separated the block, indicating that 37. 17–20 should be taken with 37. Here is his text of 38, with his corrections indicated by italics (compare the first three verses with those of the *princeps* on p. 31 above):

Male est: [*si*] *cornifici* tuo catullo
Male est: **si** me hercule et laboriose
Et magis [*ac*] magis indies et horas:
Quem tu: quod minimum facillimumque est:
Qua solatus es allocutione:
Irascor tibi: sic meos amores.
Paulum quid lubet allocutionis
Mestius lachrymis simonideis

(38, corrected by Poliziano in Venice 1472)

Apart from punctuation Poliziano's text differs in only one detail from that in modern editions, and that detail is ambiguous, for it is not clear whether he intended to delete the unmetrical *si* in the second verse.[83] Two of his corrections appear in Appendix 3: his discovery of the addressee Cornificius, in which he anticipates Avanzi (1495), and his deletion of *si* (also in Calfurnio), both in the first verse. But although they were just as important if one was to make sense of the *princeps*, his deletion of *ac* and his correction of *mestus* to *mestius* appear neither in our table nor in the *apparatus* of modern editions, because they are restorations of the archetype—or, to put it another way, they are corrections of the base text rather than of the whole textual tradition.[84] His most important improvement of all is likewise unacknowledged—the discovery that 38 was an independent poem, first recognized elsewhere only in Avanzi (1495).

Every page of Poliziano's book reveals his achievement and makes one wish he had printed his own edition of Catullus, for with its new corrections and readings from manuscripts, readings from the recent base text of Partenio and Calfurnio and the good readings from earlier sources they had rejected—to say nothing of his improved separation of poems—his book presented a text of Catullus that was far better than that of the *princeps* and superior to any available before the first Aldine (1502), even if it was not *maxima ex parte incorruptus*.

THE ART OF EMENDATION: MARCANTONIO SABELLICO AND GIROLAMO AVANZI

In the 1480s Catullan studies took on a new air. Six editions had appeared in a decade, and in the fast-moving world of the humanists the *princeps* now seemed antique and far away. It was eclipsed by all its successors, but especially by the text of Calfurnio, which became the foundation for a new vulgate when Antonio Partenio used and corrected it for his popular commentary. Since everyone now had a text and there was no glory in producing a new one, the humanists turned their attention from editing to explication, presenting their emendations either in editions with commentaries or in brief lists or discussions of corrections without an accompanying text. Because their work properly belongs to the history of interpretation, we will consider the commentaries of Partenio (1485) and Palladio (1496) in Chapter 2, appealing to them in the present discussion only as witnesses to the work of other humanists. We must also postpone our discussion of Battista Guarino (Chapter 2) and Giovanni Gioviano Pontano (Chapter 3), since the best evidence for their lost emendations comes from the sixteenth century. For now we will turn to the emendations of Marcantonio Coccio, called Sabellico (1436–1506) and Girolamo Avanzi (*fl.* 1490–1535). The one was a man of broad culture and interests, good literary sense, and negligible concern for philological accuracy; the other a type more prominent in the next century—diligent and precise, narrowly focused, a born critic and editor. They approached Catullus with radically different purposes, methods, and results.

Marcantonio Coccio called Sabellico was the official historian of Venice, the custodian of Cardinal Bessarion's library, and the author of commentaries on various ancient authors. He was sometimes regarded as a careless scholar, and he took little care of Bessarion's precious library, but his books were popular, and he enjoyed the influence and prestige of a successful humanist.[85] In 1497, at the height of his reputation, he published a book of annotations on Pliny's *Natural History*, to which he appended twenty notes emending and interpreting the text of Catullus. He called his little work *Ex Catullo* and gave it the only modest introduction ever awarded to a work on Catullus in the fifteenth century:

I will now add a very few points from the poetry of most charming Catullus, nor are these (as I shall say openly) of very great moment, since right up to the present there has not been a lack of scholars to complete careful works on this most ancient poet. As a result, there are not so many problems left, and of those there are some that might seem to have been passed over deliberately. But, however trivial they are, since they pertain to the correction of the text, I shall add them as an appendix to the other *Century* [i.e. his *Annotationes in Plinium*], and this will be by way of alerting rather than instructing the reader, for I was aware that conjectures are not usually accepted quickly. For, if there is to be a dispute over opinions, everyone would more gladly rest on his own judgement (even if it is less likely) than on the excellent judgement of another. But may those who come upon these ideas be well disposed to them.[86]

Although Sabellico printed his notes in 1497, we can date them between Partenio (1485) and Avanzi (1493): Avanzi discusses most of his ideas in detail, and before Partenio's commentary no one, however modest, could have said that Catullus had already received plenty of attention.[87]

Sabellico no doubt composed *Ex Catullo* as an afterthought to fill up a page or so at the end of his *Pliny*, quickly gathering up notes from the margins of his Catullus text. Since his work is so short we can see it as a whole, to learn what one humanist, at least, found problematic or interesting in Catullus, what he looked for in a poem, and how he arrived at his corrections. Appendix 4 summarizes his discussion.

We can see from the table that Sabellico had his successes. Although modern critics give him credit for only one emendation (apparently *infecti* at 64. 243), he made several improvements to the current base text of Calfurnio and Partenio. His most important contribution is to separate the sparrow poems, 2 and 3—one of the few fifteenth-century improvements of the *dispositio carminum* not anticipated by Poliziano. At 64. 16 his suggestion *haudque alia* for *atque alia* is on the right track (modern editions print *atque* ⟨*haud*⟩ *alia*). His corrections at 64. 25 and 64. 106, though found in manuscripts, do not appear in any edition before Palladio's (1496).[88] At 14. 5 he restores *male*, a correction in the *princeps* dropped by Puteolano, followed by

Calfurnio and Partenio. Although Sabellico names no sources for these improvements, in other cases he refers airily to *codices* or *exemplaria* as it suits his argument, not specifying even whether he means manuscripts or printed editions. Thus, on 10. 30 he notes vaguely: 'instead of *gravis*, compelled by the metre, I gladly restored *Caius*, which certain less untrustworthy *codices* have.[89] Perhaps he saw Puteolano's reading *Caius* in Parma 1473 or Reggio 1481 (it had been changed to *gravis* in Calfurnio and Partenio), but he probably found it in a more recent and accessible work, the *Annotationes Centum* of Filippo Beroaldo (1488).[90]

His principal source, however, was Partenio. Sabellico disagrees with Partenio's interpretations on 34. 8 and 64. 159; all of the readings he rejects appear in Partenio, and he criticizes two that are found in no other edition. Thus, on 4. 24 he urges *novissime* against Partenio's *novissem*:

> I was amazed at the carelessness of scribes, still more at the laziness and thoughtlessness of learned men, because they had allowed that well-known place to stand in these verses contrary to the rules of metre . . . for I see *novissem* commonly written in them. But let others see whether *novissime* can be read more fittingly, with which reading neither sense nor quantity quarrels.[91]

If we had Sabellico as our only authority we might be persuaded that *novissime* was his own correction for the widespread corruption *novissem*. On the contrary: *novissime* is the reading of the archetype, the *editio princeps*, and Calfurnio, while *novissem* is an aberration in Partenio.[92] Similarly, at 31. 6: 'I find . . . *in tuo* . . . let the reader not be annoyed to consider if *in tutu* should be read instead . . .'.[93] Here *in tuto* (which he does not mention) is the general reading; *in tuo* is a misprint in Partenio.

Sabellico never hesitates to change a reading, for he is confident of his own powers and unimpressed by the text he finds in Partenio. Since he is generally ignorant of other texts, he relies only on his own instincts and literary judgement to identify and correct mistakes. He is usually wrong. In 50, for example, Catullus describes the evening he and his friend Calvus spent writing poetry together—*reddens mutua per iocum atque vinum* (50. 6). Accordingly, in 50. 2 (*multum lusimus in meis tabellis*), Sabellico thinks that *in meis* is flat and replaces it with *in vicem*.[94]

In 27 the poet calls for wine: *inger mi calices amariores* (27. 2). Sabellico, thinking *amariores* inappropriate, replaces it with *meratiores*, which, he argues, fits the context, finds an echo in *merus* (27. 7), and has parallels in Horace and Martial; but he ends his proposal half-heartedly: whichever reading suits everyone will be all right with him.[95] In 29 the poet attacks Caesar and Pompey for the excesses of their protégé Mamurra, whom he likes to call *Mentula*.[96] Sabellico, not noticing Pompey, makes two suggestions: that the poem contains 'two epigrams of similar form' attacking Caesar (apparently the sections 1–10 and 11–24, which are set off by repeated phrases), and that *vestra* is wrong in 29. 13 (*ut ista vestra diffututa mentula*):

> Since nothing could have been said less wittily and elegantly, so to speak, than if Catullus writing to Caesar alone had said *ista vestra* for *tua*, see whether he left instead the word *vesca*, i.e. *edax* . . .[97]

In 11 Sabellico is worried about metre, rewriting a whole line in the conviction that the fourth syllable in a sapphic verse must be long:

> In the sapphic hendecasyllable to Furius and Aurelius will anyone knowledgeable about metre so carelessly assent to the trustworthiness of scribes that he reads *seu saccas sagittiferosque parthos* [11. 6] as all the texts of Catullus have it or will he rather follow this: *seu sacas partosque feros sagittis*?[98]

On the same grounds he changes *nuntiate* to *nunc aite* in 11. 15 (*pauca nuntiate meae puellae*). But Sabellico is wrong, as Avanzi was to note a few years later: Catullus 'in conformity with the practice of the old poets' uses either a long or a short in the fourth syllable of his sapphics.[99]

Everywhere we look in Sabellico we find the same qualities of close reading and negligent philology—even in his greatest success, the separation of the two sparrow poems, whose argument perfectly epitomizes the man and his work:

> I would not hesitate to assert that the next epigram [2] is read too carelessly by most people together with what is certainly the beginning of a whole poem, *Lugete o iuvenes*, because the subject of each is different and the climax at the end of each is revealed to those who look more closely.[100]

This is vintage Sabellico: the successful literary discussion turns on the shape and subject of the two poems, but only in Partenio does 3. 1 begin *lugete o iuvenes*, and in Partenio *iuvenes* is clearly a misprint, since the commentary glosses the correct reading, *veneres*.

But Sabellico's qualities were shared by many Renaissance readers, and indeed many would have been able to produce a similar collection of *aperçus* that they had jotted down as they paged through this or that edition of the poet, not thinking about them too carefully or worrying overmuch about their validity. The principal difference is that since Sabellico was an important man his notes were published and enjoyed the publicity and respect surrounding their famous author. Avanzi discussed almost all of them, punctiliously crediting Sabellico's successes and carefully correcting his mistakes (without identifying their source).[101] Palladio, whose work (1496), like Avanzi's, was printed before *Ex Catullo*, was less scrupulous—perhaps hoping that Sabellico's emendations would remain unpublished and that his plagiarism would be unnoticed. Having the benefit of Avanzi's criticisms, he was able to print all of Sabellico's good readings (see Appendix 4), claiming four as his own.[102] But Sabellico's prestige was such that even his mistakes found their way into the baggage of variant readings that circulated in the next generation, particularly in the many copies of the notes of Francesco Pucci (1463–1512). Pucci was an early student of Poliziano and librarian for the Aragonese kings of Naples, as well as a friend of Pontano and a member of the Accademia Pontaniana. In 1502 he finished annotating his copy of an edition of Catullus, Tibullus, and Propertius, and his notes, as undeserving as Sabellico's, made their way into the margins of books all over Italy, picking up new material—including some of Sabellico's emendations—as they went.[103]

In spite of Sabellico's prestige, however, *Ex Catullo* was completely overshadowed by the work of its tactful critic, Avanzi. Girolamo Avanzi was younger by a generation than all of his Catullan predecessors, and a more careful text critic than any—with the obvious exception of Poliziano.[104] He was to become a professional editor of Latin poetry, principally for the Venetian printers Johannes Tacuinus and Aldo Manuzio, preparing *inter alia* editions of Ausonius (Tacuinus, 1496), Catullus, Tibullus, and Propertius (Tacuinus, 1500), Lucretius (Aldine, 1500), Statius (Petrus de Quarengiis, 1498/9), and the first and second Aldine editions of Catullus (1502; 1515).[105] He wrote his *Emendationes in Catullum* in the summer and autumn of 1493 when he was still a student of philosophy at the University of Padua and sent it to his senior colleague and friend, Augustinus Moravus Olomucensis, who circulated it among Paduan and Veronese scholars, including Calfurnio and Giacomo Conte Giuliari (Iacobus Comes Iuliarius), who had written a congratulatory letter and poem for Partenio's commentary. After thus testing the waters, Augustinus took the responsibility for publication, and the *Emendationes* was printed by Tacuinus in 1495. A spate of editions and philological works appeared over the next twenty years, and then, after a long silence, Avanzi's career ended as it had begun, with Catullus, in an edition printed in Venice by Trincavelli around 1535.

Avanzi's purposes were very different from Sabellico's, for he was not a famous humanist, but a young man with ambitions to become one. For him correcting Catullus was a serious business, since he was writing the *Emendationes* in order to make a name for himself and to launch his philological career. But Avanzi and his backers had a second motive as well. They were all Veronese or Paduan, and they intended the *Emendationes* to be a work of Veronese piety and polemic that would avenge Poliziano's attack in the *Miscellanea* on Verona's most famous humanist, Domizio Calderini, who was nearly a cult figure in Verona.[106] Soon after Calderini's death in 1478 his friends had put together a collection of poems in his memory, including one by Poliziano, which his father had had inscribed on a monument in his birthplace in the little town of Torri del Benaco on Lago di Garda.[107] His memory was still green in 1489 when Poliziano published the *Miscellanea*, and the Veronese humanists were surprised and angered by his treatment of their hero, which seemed a cynical reversal of his former professions of friendly esteem. Avanzi, young as he was, probably did not begin his work intending to attack Poliziano, but when Augustinus and the others heard that he was studying Catullus in the summer of 1493, they planned, and perhaps even commissioned, his *Emendationes* as their means of counterattack.

From Avanzi's letter of dedication (October 1493) and Augustinus' preface (March 1494) we can perhaps reconstruct the course of events. Avanzi opens his long letter with a reference to Augustinus' request for his corrections, though he says nothing of Calderini or Poliziano.[108] The *Emendationes* follow, and the work closes with a continuation of Avanzi's letter that includes the answers to specific questions about Catullus put to him by Augustinus:

At the end of your letter you ask about several places that should be interpreted not by me, since I devoted myself to these studies for barely three years and have put them aside for a long time, but by a man whose great heart and mind the Delian prophet inspires. . . . Therefore, when I had hastened to send you the things I have noted above, I decided to postpone this matter for a little so that I could satisfy more fully some of your questions (for you will find many of them explained above).[109]

From Avanzi's letter, then, we can infer that he had substantially completed the *Emendationes* before he received Augustinus' request and that he quickly dispatched the work to him before settling down to complete his commission, which seems to have included not only the discussion of Augustinus' Catullan questions, but also an encomium of Calderini. Although Augustinus composed his polemical preface a few months later, after circulating the work among its sponsors for their approval, Avanzi's book was not published until the end of 1495, over a year and a half later.[110] Perhaps the time was filled with strategy sessions and exchanges of correspondence between Avanzi and his sponsors over various details of the work. Perhaps, also, some of the Veronese humanists became nervous about taking on such an experienced controversialist as Poliziano or found the whole project less appealing after his death in September 1494. In the end, of course, they decided to publish, perhaps influenced by the fact that Poliziano himself, who had even contributed the *pièce de résistance* to Calderini's memorial collection, had not hesitated to attack him so long after his death.

The Veronese polemic against Poliziano is carefully ordered around its two focal points, Calderini and Catullus—with Avanzi elaborately eulogizing the one at the end of his dedication and Augustinus vindicating the other in his preface. Since Avanzi was too young to have known Calderini, he could not plausibly invoke personal connections or recollections in his tribute, but he does even better—describing a pilgrimage to Torri del Benaco and his uplifting encounter with Calderini's nephew Paolo, who seems to have been the official keeper of his memory and the custodian of his books. Only in Paolo's company, it seems, could Avanzi find the answers to the most taxing Catullan questions. Thus, he tells Augustinus:

Intent on the things you wanted to know, I arrived at Benaco, not because I wanted to see the lake, as delightful as it is, but to meet Paolo Calderini, whom indeed his uncle (a man no less undeserving of Angelo Poliziano's abuse than most worthy of the same Angelo's praises) had constituted the heir of his property and his abilities. . . . Here Paolo kept me with him for eight days just as if I had tarried at the cliffs of the Sirens.[111]

Together they saw the towns around Lago di Garda and climbed idyllic Mount Vilium, which Avanzi found more delightful than any of the beauty spots of fable:[112]

on the summit of this mountain, most fragrant with sweet-smelling herbs, with my dear Paolo I turned to many of the questions you had asked. Indeed, he saw many of the problems well and splendidly corrected most. But this did not surprise me greatly. He has acquired almost all of his uncle's books (if you exclude the seven buried with him), in both Greek and Roman letters, and when he looks at them he always finds a teacher.[113]

At last Paolo, 'weeping no more than was just',[114] revealed the *sanctum sanctorum*, Calderini's bookcases, stuffed with his precious unfinished works. 'Of what could Paolo be ignorant', Avanzi marvels, 'steeped in these teachings and outstanding monuments of learning . . .?'[115] Sanctified by their contact with the memorials of Calderini's great intellect, the two men study Avanzi's emendations of Catullus. When Paolo approves them, Avanzi feels that he has received a tremendous accolade: 'I showed him my trifling efforts on Catullus, and rejoice so greatly that they pleased him that someday I will undergo the judgement of others more boldly.'[116] At last, with a final assurance that they have the sanction of Calderini's heir, Avanzi presents his solutions to Augustinus' Catullan questions, and ends his work with an appeal to Augustinus:

It is for you to sponsor these writings (of whatever small value they may be) that we have hammered out most obediently to your orders . . . . Especially in these halcyon days, I beg you, revisit the most gentle Muses, once familiar and most delightful to us; and if we are making a worthy request, read carefully, examine, and correct as you think best our trifling efforts.[117]

Catullus was the ideal weapon for Augustinus and his friends to use in a Veronese offensive against Poliziano. He was a focus of intense local patriotism—indeed the Veronese were so proud of Catullus that they had erected a statue of him on the roof of their new Loggia del Consiglio only the year before Avanzi wrote his emendations.[118] He had been studied, as Avanzi points out, by several Paduan and Veronese humanists, including Calfurnio and Antonio Partenio, Avanzi's old teacher and one of the principal contributors to the collection of memorial poems for Calderini.[119] Best of all, however, the Veronese humanists could argue that Catullus had suffered a double injury: he lacked the restorative corrections of Calderini that had healed so many other poets, and he, too, had been mistreated by Poliziano. Thus, Augustinus in his preface:

> And in addition to the damage of the ages he could not even be saved from being branded with indelible stigmas by certain pedants. O pitiable fortune of the most charming poet! Who ought not to grieve more strongly that these delights of the human race are so beset with the dark errors of certain people and their trivial little interpretations that we can rightly and justly say against them what the most charming bard prophesied of himself: 'But damn you, evil shades of Orcus which devour all pretty things. Such a pretty sparrow you took from me! O badly done! Poor little sparrow!' [3. 13–16].[120]

The sparrow-maligning fiend, of course, was none other than the detestable Angelo Poliziano, who, as every Renaissance reader knew, had imputed an obscene meaning to Lesbia's sparrow in his *Miscellanea*.[121] Catullus must be rescued from his misfortunes, and fortunately Nature herself has provided the appropriate hero in the person of Girolamo Avanzi. Augustinus continues:

> But when for some time the most pleasing poet was squalid with neglect and decay, Nature the parent of things, no longer enduring such a loss, at last brought forth a way to bring him back to the light. That is, that some fellow citizen of his should be found to rescue him from barbarism and to emend, explain, and set in order whatever was corrupt or obscure. He is Girolamo Avanzi of Verona, whose labours and outstanding *pietas* to his fellow citizen have clearly succeeded in making him shining where before he was dark, sound where he was mutilated and Latin where he was barbarous.[122]

Plate 3: The statue of Catullus on the Loggia del Consiglio in Verona (1492) (Photo. Anita Moskowitz).

True to his mission, Avanzi attacks Poliziano repeatedly in the *Emendationes*. He refers to five of Poliziano's seven discussions of Catullus in the *Miscellanea*, disagreeing when he can and making snide remarks when he cannot.[123] His motives are transparent: 'if he had not blamed Calderini with too much license, I would not have attacked his writings unremittingly . . .'.[124] But in his polemical zeal he sometimes makes mistakes, as when he wrongly criticizes Poliziano's emendation *expernata* or *supernata* at 17. 19 on metrical grounds, boasting of his own superior knowledge:

I wonder why in two passages in Catullus noted by me, who have scarcely touched these studies, Poliziano has spoken so rashly—the man who brazenly wounds my fellow citizens and thinks that he alone speaks in accordance with the precepts of Apollo. Therefore I would read not *expernata* or *supernata* but *separata*.[125]

Cat. 17 is in priapeans. Avanzi rightly objects to *expernata* on the grounds that it would produce a pyrrhic after the first choriamb (17. 19):

in fossa Liguri iacet *expernata* securi.

He is wrong, however, to object that either *supernata* or *expernata* would produce a spondee before the second choriamb, since the metre allows it.[126] And he is so carried away by his desire to refute Poliziano that he emends the only other verse in the poem to show the same variation.[127]

Beneath its surface polemic, however, the *Emendationes* is a serious and careful scholarly work, as we can see from the first part of Avanzi's letter to Augustinus:

Before being initiated into the rites of the philosophers I tried very hard, to tell the truth, to understand most of the most difficult Catullan passages, and in particular to free this poet from the stigma of faulty metrics, with which he is especially charged. But at that time because of the slenderness of my talent I had found and carefully restored barely forty corrupt places or a few more, as I remarked in your presence on the day when Sebastiano Badoer (a renascent glory and outstanding ornament of our studies) embarked on his prefecture of Padua.[128] Now when in a respite from more taxing studies I was planning to withdraw to my little country place to be alone, Christopher Papallis (a youth versed no less in poetry than in the law) entrusted me with a very old Catullus. While I was mulling over and carefully scrutinizing every point in it and comparing exemplars and especially my own manuscript, which was written a long time ago, I restored some other places. I did this with such diligence that I do not at all regret my hard work. . . .[129] In the meantime, in order to comply with your wishes to the best of my ability, I will explain briefly whatever I have observed either with the aid of the old manuscripts or from my own continual weighing of the verses, for I will not include the reasons for everything. . . . I will run through each type of Catullan verse separately, and to satisfy your wishes more fully not only will I weigh the quantities of syllables, but at the same time I will write down the corrupt words. Catullus takes liberties with the first foot of the phalaecean hendecasyllable and the second foot of the sapphic verse. Otherwise (if you except a single corrupt poem), he was most observant of quantities.[130]

Avanzi has placed us in a different world from that of Sabellico and his casual insights, indeed, in a different world from that of any of his predecessors in Catullan studies—with the ironic exception of his imaginary adversary Poliziano. No other fifteenth-century Catullan critics even come close to articulating such a clearly conceived critical method. Poliziano's method, as we have seen, was to collate texts and to observe the usage of other ancient authors. Avanzi will rely on collating manuscripts and editions and on the careful study of Catullan metrics. Let us look more closely at his method and its results.

Avanzi used two manuscripts, his own and that of his friend, Christopher Papallis. He seems to cite their readings carefully enough, but we have little check on his accuracy, since neither manuscript has been identified. Like most Renaissance scholars he uses the word *codex* for both manuscripts and printed books. Generally his meaning is clear: for manuscripts he will say *utrique codices* or *codex meus* or *codex Papallis*, for books *codices impressi* or *codices alii*. The phrases *codices antiqui* and *antiqua lectio* (or *vetus lectio*) seem to refer to the manuscripts.[131] His precision is not wasted. Although neither Avanzi's nor Papallis' manuscript can be identified from his readings (most of the incorrect readings from his manuscripts are too common, while the correct readings merely vindicate the early editions against changes by Calfurnio and Partenio), his actual use of manuscripts (unlike that of Sabellico, for example) is never in doubt. Several of his manuscript readings are found in no printed source, and two have been identified as reproducing the original reading in R.[132] His undoubted use of a manuscript for these readings increases his credibility in cases where his manuscript citations might otherwise seem *too* good—that is, for corrections that modern editors attribute either to other fifteenth-century editors or to Avanzi himself.[133]

Avanzi's method shows to much better advantage in his use of the printed editions. His principal source is Partenio, or we might better say that he has corrected the text of Partenio, and that he has consulted most, if not all, of the earlier editions to do so. Appendix 5 lists, under the editions where he is most likely to have found them, the readings both right and wrong about which Avanzi is in agreement with modern editors.

Appendix 5 cannot tell us whether Avanzi studied every edition. But it does not matter whether he used Venice 1472, for example, or its virtual clone [Milan] 1475, or whether he used Parma 1473 or its descendant, Reggio 1481. He had a full and representative picture of the whole printed tradition—in contrast with all his predecessors, always excluding Poliziano (compare Appendix 3). Sabellico relied only on Partenio. Partenio, as is clear from their shared misprints, was correcting Calfurnio.[134] Calfurnio's source, in turn, was Venice 1472 or [Milan] 1475 corrected (not very systematically) with the aid of Parma 1473. Since Avanzi knew all these editions, as well as [Rome 1475], which the vulgate had not drawn on in its main line of descent, he was able to broaden the foundation of the vulgate text and to lay the groundwork for a new and more authoritative edition.

Collation, however, was only one part of Avanzi's programme. Close study of Catullus' metres was the other. Even in his student days, as he reminds Augustinus, he had endeavoured with some success to free Catullus of the charge of faulty metrics, and now he will attempt a full-scale analysis, studying the poems in metrical groupings rather than in their traditional order. He founds his analysis on two principles. The first, which he never explicitly states, is that understanding of the metre must proceed from Catullus' own metrical practice—not from rules derived from other sources. We have seen how he came to grief using this method in the case of 17. Careful scansion led him to the conclusion that the second choriamb in Catullus' priapeans must always be proceeded by a trochee. In the whole poem he found only one violation of this rule (17. 20). When Poliziano's emendation for 17. 19 produced a second, he both concluded that Poliziano was wrong and emended away the original anomaly. Polemical ardour hampered Avanzi's judgement, but he also had bad luck. A rule that worked for twenty-five of the twenty-six verses of the poem (excluding Poliziano's emendation) seemed good enough, but in fact it was not. Catullus wrote only one poem in priapeans, and the sample was too small.

In other cases, however, Avanzi's determination to judge Catullus by his own metrical practice succeeded brilliantly, enabling him to make necessary emendations and avoid unnecessary ones, and—even more important—to think of Catullan metre in historical terms. Thus, his understanding of Catullan sapphics allowed him to reject Sabellico's anachronistic criticisms, which were based on later metrical rules. So too Avanzi sees the occasional iambic and trochaic openings of Catullus' hendecasyllables, which had been criticized even in Antiquity, as a feature of archaic style. Although he is wrong (the licence seems to have been a neoteric affectation), his mistake does not invalidate the argument: the licence was appropriate to Catullus *in his time*.[135] Avanzi's whole discussion of the *Priapea*, at the end of the *Emendationes in Catullum*, is motivated by this point:

But, finally, since you ask whether in my opinion it is all right for us to take liberties with the first foot of the phalaecean hendecasyllable as Catullus does, I would say (though others disagree), 'not at all.' For no one will versify correctly when he adopts an Ennian licence. Granted that Ennius is celebrated with the venerable title, 'father of bards', for to Ennius and that sort of man many liberties were permitted. But the same things in our own time are so obsolete that the man who affects the smallest use of them offends the taste and ears of everyone. Now, as for the fact that our friend cites the authority of the *Priapea* . . . If he looks more closely not only will he find no foot other than a spondee in the first foot of the phalaecean in Vergil,[136] but in the whole of the *Priapea* (most offensive in other respects) he will discover not a syllable placed incorrectly unless Vergil (as generally happens) is being read from a corrupt text. And so that I might understand this matter fully, I have read this whole work of Vergil and have weighed the quantity of almost every syllable and have remedied the corruption and reversed order of all the words. And I have decided to explain all this to you . . .[137]

Avanzi has three periods in mind—the eras of Ennius and Catullus, of the *Priapea*, and his own—each with its appropriate stylistic requirements. His verdict is what we might expect: Augustinus' friend or any modern poet will commit a tasteless blunder if he adopts the practice of another time. Of course, Avanzi's historical sense is imperfect. He is able to distinguish the styles of different eras (although he lumps together Catullus and Ennius, who were separated by 150 years), but he cannot quite rid himself of the assumption that the standards of the later age are canonical and that deviations require explanation and forgiveness ('to Ennius and that sort of man many liberties were permitted'). We see something similar in his discussion of Catullan iambics, although here he uses the canonical practice to vindicate what he has observed in Catullus:

Moreover, in iambic verse Catullus attained this standard. For he never allows a foot other than an iamb in the second or fourth position. This is required by this sort of meter, as Horace teaches . . .[138]

Avanzi founds his discussion on his second metrical principle, which he treats almost as an article of faith: Catullus' poems are metrically correct, and where they are not, the fault lies not with Catullus but with a corruption in the text. He makes his point most trenchantly in his correction to the base text at 39. 12:

Among other things I ask, as I have said before, that everyone understand why Martial said, 'Verona loves the measures of her learned bard.' For Catullus was very observant of quantities—if his poems be written correctly, which is not the current practice. For who would not laugh at the ignorance, or at least the laziness of this age? All the printed texts have *aut Lavinius acer* although *Lanuvinus* should be read. Both old manuscripts had *Lanuvinus*, but this unsuitable and unmetrical word has been substituted—that is, *Lavinius*. And so in similar verses a slothful sort of man invokes Catullan licence—abuse, in fact—paying too little attention to scansion and content with any reading, however dissonant.[139]

Avanzi's indignation is not misplaced. The manuscript tradition had transmitted plenty of metrical problems, but many others were introduced by fifteenth-century editors, who had little understanding of Catullan metres—perhaps as Avanzi suggests, considering them so irregular that they did not even expect them to scan. Their lack of understanding is particularly evident in the iambics, which in fact hold few mysteries. Cat. 25 is iambic tetrameter catalectic, but for the rest Avanzi is right to maintain that the iambic poems are either all trimeters or all scazons (choliambs)—a simple fact that seems to have eluded his predecessors and contemporaries.[140] Although Avanzi receives credit from modern editors for several emendations in the iambics that improve the metre, his changes to the base text are more revealing since they show not merely his contribution but also the state of the problem. In several of these cases Avanzi is correcting the recent base text of Calfurnio and Partenio, who had introduced metrical problems into the correct verses of their predecessors.[141]

We must infer Calfurnio's metrical knowledge from his text, but for Partenio we have also the evidence of his commentary, which reveals that, in one case at least, just as Avanzi had charged, he failed to solve a straightforward problem because he was too willing to convict Catullus of metrical incomprehensibility. Here is his complaint about the unmetrical block 37. 17–20–39:

> The verses are unlike. For the first are scazons. Sometimes a hendecasyllable is inserted. But some lack the proper measure since they are faulty (as I believe) and corrupt.[142]

In fact, however, only two of the eight hendecasyllables in Partenio's text of 38 are unmetrical, and he has introduced one of the faults himself.[143] But Partenio, like earlier editors, was also misled by the ancient corruption *carnifici* for *Cornifici* at 38. 1, which allowed him to read 38 as part of the invective against Egnatius and his disgusting grin in 37 and 39. Thus he can say of 38. 1–2: 'Here the poet's anger against Egnatius flares up, since when he was in grief and sorrow Egnatius came up to him to console him and poured out laughs and guffaws.'[144] Avanzi, on the other hand, saw through *carnifici* and realized that different metres implied separate poems:

> the verses that are confused and forced together in a single poem should be rearranged thus: first, that verse *male est cornifici tuo Catullo* [38. 1] with the following seven verses. Catullus writes to Cornificius in a separate poem in phalaecean hendecasyllables.[145]

Because Avanzi was more systematic, thorough, and knowledgeable than his predecessors—and because he had the whole printed tradition to work with—he was able to make an enormous contribution to the text of Catullus in the *Emendationes*. In addition to a large number of emendations, he made dozens of corrections both to the printed tradition as a whole and to the recent base text of Calfurnio and Partenio.[146] He also made some improvements in the *dispositio carminum*, although this was becoming increasingly difficult, since the easy corrections had already been made (see Appendix 2).[147]

Avanzi continued to work on Catullus. In 1500 Tacuinus published an edition of Catullus, Tibullus, and Propertius that included commentaries on the three poets and a second edition of the *Emendationes*. Although Avanzi is advertised as the editor of the whole, the text of Catullus, at least, is nothing new, for it is virtually identical with the text of Partenio, and includes only a tiny handful of Avanzi's corrections.[148] But the second edition of the *Emendationes* contains many changes. Since Avanzi has greatly curtailed his personal and polemical comments, the work is more businesslike (and less interesting) than its predecessor. Poliziano is mentioned but not attacked; Calderini and his nephew, Papallis and his manuscript, have all disappeared. Avanzi includes most of the emendations from the first edition, makes some additions, and in a few places changes his mind.[149] Most important, however, he adds some readings from Palladio's edition, which he has clearly studied with care, although he never mentions Palladio by name.[150]

Avanzi's most important achievement was the first Aldine edition of Catullus, which appeared in 1502. The time and circumstances were right. The vulgate of Calfurnio and Partenio, though subject to criticism and corrections, had been essentially unchallenged for twenty years. Avanzi had the materials for a new text, and Aldo had recently begun to publish classical Latin poetry—in fact, his first such work was the Lucretius of 1500, edited by Avanzi. In their dedications to Marino Sanudo Aldo and Avanzi emphasize that their Catullus is new. 'Moreover, [our Catullus] will please you', Aldo writes to Sanudo, 'because he will seem not at all the same as he did before, because of many emendations and verses both added and restored to their original position.'[151] The novelty of the Aldine consists not only in its text, which is far superior to that of any previous edition and contains many changes even from Avanzi's *Emendationes*,[152] but also in the physical aspect of the book, for Aldo's handy octavo, with its almost unprecedented press run of 3,000 copies, made Catullus far more widely—and more conveniently—available than he had been in the unwieldy tomes of the fifteenth century.[153] None the less, the edition is not fundamentally new, for Avanzi, like his predecessors, was only correcting the vulgate that had been launched on its way by the *princeps*; and like them he wrote his changes for the printer in the margins of his printed book, as we can see by his comment to Sanudo: 'Our friend Aldo Manuzio . . . has used me as his colleague again for this work as he set out to print 3,000 copies from the text of Catullus once corrected by me with remarkable enthusiasm and incredible toil.'[154] He was able to achieve much of his success simply by studying the earliest texts and restoring their readings, since by his time the base text had become as remote from the *princeps* and its immediate successors as the later codices had been from the manuscripts of the fourteenth century.

2

Interpretatio: Making Sense of Catullus

> Catullus enim usque ad hanc aetatem in tenebrosis latebris iacuit nec adhuc ullas perlectionum illustrationes ullumve interpretationis lumen habuit.
>
> (Antonio Partenio)

ALTHOUGH his companions in the first edition had all received printed commentaries by 1475 and were well on their way to acquiring a modern critical tradition, it was to be another decade before anyone published a commentary on Catullus.[1] Renaissance readers could use Propertius and Tibullus to explain each other, and they found Statius' subjects well documented in Martial and Pliny, but they lacked contemporary *comparanda* and sources for Catullus. Because the poet had appeared in the Renaissance without any critical baggage from the past, they lacked even the dubious guidance of ancient scholia or medieval allegories to assist their interpretations. Thus, they had to confront Catullus directly, explaining his poetry either from the confusing and corrupt text itself or from clues scattered here and there in other ancient authors.

But the humanists were delayed rather than daunted by the difficulty of their undertaking. They set out eagerly to elucidate Catullus in lectures, editions, emendations, and even in public performances—each both jealously asserting the priority of his own interpretations and all too willing to plagiarize those of someone else. Catullus' interpreters were eager to bring the tottering and mutilated poet back to life, but they also wanted to acquire glory for themselves; for the successful exegete could be sure of prestige and acclaim wherever he went, and especially in Verona, where Catullus was an object of veneration and patriotic fervour.[2] Throughout the 1470s and early '80s the humanists raced to produce and publicize their ideas—some content with interpreting only one or two difficult passages, and others eager to produce a commentary—that is, the first commentary—on the poet.

In the sparsely documented period between the *princeps* and the first commentary three men in particular seem to have been engaged in interpreting Catullus. Angelo Poliziano was annotating his copy of the *princeps* (perhaps with the idea of writing a commentary), but he was also publicly interpreting Catullus in Florence and Verona, as he tells us in his *Miscellanea* (1489). Battista Guarino, son of the famous Guarino da Verona, was writing emendations or interpretations of Catullus in a manuscript or printed book, now lost; his work is preserved only in the much later commentary of his son, Alessandro Guarino, which appeared in 1521. Antonio Partenio, the least of the three and the only one to produce a surviving commentary, was lecturing on Catullus to his students in Verona.

POLIZIANO'S INTERPRETATIONS OF CATULLUS

In Chapter 19 of the first *Century* of his *Miscellanea* Angelo Poliziano recalls two scenes from the early days of excitement and competition in Catullan studies. As a very young man he had explained his ideas on Catullus when Domizio Calderini visited Florence in 1473, so impressing Calderini that he declared 'that he had learned more on that day from a single student than from any of his professors many years before.'[3] A few years later, in 1479 or 1480, Poliziano had an even more appreciative audience in Verona, so he tells us, when one rainy day a group of Catullan enthusiasts crowded into a shop to avoid the downpour and listened, enthralled, as he interpreted almost all of Catullus:

> taking in whatever we said so eagerly that again and again they shouted that an Angel had been sent down to them from heaven (for so they expressed it) to interpret their poet and countryman.[4]

The interpretation that dazzled both Calderini and his fellow Veronese was Poliziano's explanation of 84, a poem whose problems and solutions exemplify many of the elements of early Catullan criticism. The text below is that of the first edition, where it is printed together with 83 (see Appendix 1):

Ad Mullum

Lesbia mi prȩsente viro mala plurima dicit
Hoc illi fatuo maxima lȩticia est:

Mulle nihil sentis: si nostri oblita taceret
    Sana esset quod nunc gannit et obloquitur:
Non solum meminit: sed quę multo acrior est res:
    Irata est hoc est uritur: et loquitur: 6
Commoda dicebat: si quando commoda vellet 1
    Dicere et insidias acrius *insidias*:
Credo sic mater sic liber avunculus ei est: 5
    Sic maternus avus: dixerat atque avia:
Hoc misso in syria requierant omnibus aures
    Audibant eadem: hęc leniter: et leviter:
Nec sibi post illa metuebant talia verba:
    Cum subito affertur nuncius horribilis: 10
Et tum mirifice sperabat se esse locutum 3
    Cum quantum poterat dixerat *insidias*:
Ionios fluctus postquam illuc arctius isset 11
    Iam non ionios esse: sed *ionios*.

(83–84, Venice 1472)

Shapeless, corrupt and pointless, 84 required simultaneous interpretation and emendation—if not a *deus ex machina*. The epigram pokes fun at Arrius, the man who betrays his origins by misplacing his aitches, but the words essential to the point (italicized above) were transmitted without their aspirates, and the jest was lost—its point further obscured by the displacement of verses 3–4 after 10. Arrius himself was invisible in the corruptions *acrius* (84. 2) and *arctius* (84. 11), and without him, there was no change of subject and no clear line of demarcation from 83.[5] But the riddle was easily solved, since 84 happens to be one of the handful of Catullus' poems mentioned by an ancient critic.[6] Quintilian provides the clue in his discussion of aspirates:

> Other writers used it [h] but rarely even before vowels, saying *aedus* or *ircus*, while its conjunction with consonants was for a long time avoided, as in words such as *Graccus* or *triumpus*. Then for a short time it broke out into excessive use, witness such spelling as *chorona*, *chenturio* or *praecho*: the well-known epigram [*nobile epigramma*] of Catullus will be remembered in this connexion. (Quint. *Inst. Or.* 1. 5. 20)[7]

Once 84 was identified as Quintilian's *nobile epigramma Catulli*, everything fell into place: 'I think', says Poliziano, 'that this very epigram is meant . . . Thus, if you want the charm of Catullus' poem to be apparent to you, you will pronounce the aspirate itself in its place, as much as you can.'[8] He emends accordingly, presenting a text that is essentially identical with that of modern editions.[9]

The explication of 84 was a triumph, but the glow had faded by 1489, when Poliziano published his discovery in the *Miscellanea*: 'I see', he says sadly, 'that this has now become so well known that someone might think it was not my idea.'[10] Priority is the issue in *Misc.* i. 19, and Poliziano has designed his circumstantial account to demonstrate that he interpreted the poem in public on two separate occasions many years earlier—that is, long before the corrections and their explanation were claimed by anyone else. For the annoying fact was that they *were* claimed by others. In Vicenza 1481 Calfurnio correctly separated 84 from 83 and entitled it *De Ario*; he aspirated most of the relevant words and printed *arius* in verses 3 and 11.[11] In his *Liber de Aspiratione* (1481) Giovanni Gioviano Pontano identified 84 with Quintilian's *nobile epigramma* and added most of the appropriate aitches.[12] In 1485 Partenio provided the explanation and the reference to Quintilian in his commentary:

> Catullus wittily attacks Arius who barbarously aspirates Latin words and brings forth consonants and vowels with a full, thick breath and a great burst of air, to the unbearable annoyance of his hearers and beyond the bounds of grammar and Latin usage.[13]

Although neither Calfurnio nor Partenio recalled 84. 3–4 to their correct position, Battista Guarino may have done so, and the correction was later claimed for him by his son, Alessandro.[14] Thus, by 1489 no part of Poliziano's interpretation was new; the best that he could do was to broaden the discussion of 84 to include a general consideration of aspirates and to make it clear that most of his predecessors had had access to his interpretation. Battista Guarino was in the crowd in Verona ('a kinsman of Guarino was there, Giovanni Battista by name, if I'm not mistaken') and no doubt Partenio as well ('and also two not unlearned men who taught at that time in Verona').[15] Poliziano's reference to Calfurnio is indirect, but pointed, for he tells us that the poet Giovanni Aurelio Augurello (Aurelius Ariminensis), who witnessed his interpretation in Florence in 1473, astonished everyone with it when he later moved to Padua (1476).[16] His insinuation is clear: if the explanation of 84 was news to everyone in Padua, it was not the discovery of the Paduan professor, Calfurnio.

Priority is not the burning question for us that it was for the principals (and we should remember that in the first spurt of interpretation critics no doubt often arrived at the same ideas independently); but Poliziano does have one very important piece of evidence on his side, for his marginalia in the first edition of Catullus anticipate the argument in *Misc.* i. 19. In his marginalia Poliziano separated 84 from 83 with a horizontal line, added the appropriate aitches, and quoted Quintilian's chapter on aspirates. The two sets of interpretations are not identical, however, for several small but significant differences suggest both that he later refined and improved his original ideas and that he did not revise his notes to make them agree with the *Miscellanea*. Thus, in the marginalia his text at 84. 2 reads *insidias arrius hinsidias* (as in modern editions), instead of *hinsidias Arrius insidias* as in *Misc.* i. 19 and Partenio; he has not moved verses 3–4 to their correct position; and he has not changed *requierant* to *requierunt* in 84. 7 as in the *Miscellanea*.

We may observe a similar relationship between Poliziano's marginalia and other chapters of the *Miscellanea*. Poliziano devoted seven of the *Miscellanea*'s one hundred chapters to Catullus; in the list below an * marks the five for which there are clear precedents in the marginalia:

**Misc.* i. 2	98. 4
Misc. i. 6	2–3
**Misc.* i. 19	84
**Misc.* i. 68	66. 48
**Misc.* i. 69	66. 94
Misc. i. 73	17. 19
**Misc.* i. 83	74

In every instance Poliziano's argument in the *Miscellanea* presents a sharper and more complete interpretation than that in his notes. Not surprisingly, in every instance his comments also criticize or respond to Partenio's commentary. Thus, in *Misc.* i. 2 he adds to the list of Greek authors he had used in his notes to interpret the unusual expression *crepidas . . . carpatinas* ('shoes of undressed hide') in 98, not merely explaining Catullus'

Audes & neſcis quod facinus facias.

Ad Quintium.

q Vinti ſi tibi uis oculos debere catullum
Aut aliud ſi quid carius eſt oculis:
Eripere ei noli multo quod carius illi
Eſt oculis: ſeu quod carius eſt oculis.

Ad Mullum.

l Eſbia mi pręſente uiro mala plurima dicit
Hoc illi fatuo maxima lęticia eſt:
Mulle nihil ſentis: ſi noſtri oblita taceret
Sana eſſet quod nunc gannit & obloquitur:
Non ſolum meminit: ſed quę multo acrior eſt res:
Irata eſt hoc eſt uritur: & loquitur:
Commoda dicebat: ſi quando commoda uellet
Dicere & inſidias acrius inſidias:
Credo ſic mater ſic liber auunculus ei eſt:
Sic maternus auus: dixerat atq; auia:
Hoc miſſo in ſyria requierant omnibus aures
Audibant eadem: hęc leniter: & leuiter:
Nec ſibi poſt illa metuebant talia uerba:
Cum ſubito affertur nuncius horribilis:
Et tum mirifice ſperabat ſe eſſe locutum
Cum quantum poterat dixerat inſidias:
Ionios fluctus poſtquam illuc arctius iſſet
Iam non ionios eſſe: ſed ionios.-

De Quintia.

o Di & amo quare id faciam fortaſſe requiris
Neſcio: ſed fieri ſentio: & excrutior:
Quintia formoſa eſt multis mihi candida longa
Recta eſt: hęc ego ſic ſingula confiteor:
Totum illud: formoſa nego: nam nulla uenuſtas
Nulla in tam magno eſt corpore mica ſalis:
Leſbia formoſa eſt: quę cum pulcherrima tota eſt
Tum omnibus una omnes ſurripuit ueneres:
Nulla poteſt mulier tantum ſe dicere amatam

Plate 4: Poliziano's copy of Venice 1472 with his notes on Cat. 84 (Rome, Biblioteca Corsiniana 50 F 37, 34r).

expression, but vindicating it against Partenio's emendation, *crepidas . . . coprotinas* ('dung covered shoes').[17]

In *Misc.* i. 83 he discusses 74, printing the following text:

> Laelius audierat patruum obiurgare solere,
> Si quis delicias diceret, aut faceret.
> Hoc ne ipsi accideret, patrui perdespuit ipsam
> Uxorem, et patruum reddidit Harpocratem.
> Quod voluit fecit: nam quamvis irrumet ipsum
> Nunc patruum, verbum non faciet patruus.
>
> (74, *Misc.* i. 83)

This hair-raising epigram explains how Gellius[18] kept his uncle quiet while he seduced his wife, but its wit depends on the identification of Harpocrates, the Egyptian god of silence who is typically pictured with his finger to his lips. 'People wondered for a long time who this Harpocrates was . . . ',[19] Poliziano says, introducing a long and learned explanation that includes Plutarch, Ovid, Augustine, and the *Psalms* (complete with a quotation in Hebrew). He broadens the discussion from Catullus' epigram to a general account of Harpocrates, just as he had broadened the discussion in *Misc.* i. 19 from Arrius to the history of aspirates—and he does so for the same reason: Partenio had already printed the interpretation.[20] Once Harpocrates was identified and the point explicitly made (namely, that *fellatio* precludes conversation),[21] Poliziano could do little but display his superior learning and cry foul:

> But we explained this in public to some learned men about eight years ago both in Venice and in Verona (as we have said). And I call on their knowledge and trustworthiness if anyone thinks I am appropriating other people's ideas and not just claiming my own.[22]

In his marginalia on 74 Poliziano wrote only the lemmata *Harpocrates* and *perdespuit* with no discussion—as often with hard words that he wanted to remember and come back to.[23] But he wrote the lemma *Harpocrates* again on 102. 4 (. . . *et factum me esse puta Harpocratem*), this time with a long note referring to the *Isis and Osiris* of Plutarch and quoting from Plutarch's comments on Harpocrates.[24] He presents Latin translations of the same passages from Plutarch in *Misc.* i. 83. It is clear both that Poliziano wrote his note later than the lemma and that his citations in *Misc.* i. 83 depend on those in the note.[25]

In *Misc.* i. 68 and 69 Poliziano deals with textual problems in 66, Catullus' most learned production, which he aptly describes at the beginning of *Misc.* i. 68:

With marvellous elegance the celebrated poet Catullus translated into Latin Callimachus' elegy about the reception of Berenice's tresses among the constellations, although there are many corruptions, faults and mistakes in it because of the ignorance of scribes.[26]

In *Misc.* 68 Poliziano presents his famous correction for 66. 48: *Iuppiter, ut Chalybon omne genus pereat*. For *Chalybon* the manuscripts read *celitum* or *celerum* or *celorum*; Calfurnio and Partenio had printed *telorum*. Poliziano produces the correct *Chalybon* from a fragment of Callimachus' *Lock of Berenice* preserved in the scholia to Apollonius Rhodius, contemptuously dismissing the readings of his predecessors: 'And some ignorantly read *telorum*. Most texts keep *coelitum* even contrary to the metre'.[27] In *Misc.* i. 69 he produces not a new reading, but a vindication of the traditional text, this time of 66. 94: *proximus Hydrochoi fulgeret Oarion*. Partenio, not understanding the scansion of *Oarion*, had corrected to *Aorion*, which he explained as equivalent to *ensifer* or *ensiger*.[28] The title of *Misc.* i. 69 sets the tone of Poliziano's rebuttal: '*Oarion* is genuine in Catullus, which people who corrupt good books read as *Aorion*.'

In the same elegy of Catullus from Callimachus *Oarion* is read for *Orion*. Since some are now rashly beginning to attack this word which is still whole and uncorrupted, I must employ all my resources (as they say) against this perverse temerity of ignorant men—in particular, the authority of the same Callimachus, who speaks thus in the *Hymn to Diana*, which is still extant: 'not Otos, not Oarion wooed her successfully.'[29]

He continues with citations from Nicander, Pindar, and Eustathius.

Both of Poliziano's chapters on 66 have their genesis in the marginalia. Although his gloss on 66. 48 is very faint, it begins clearly enough with the words *Chalybum legendum*. Since his note goes on to mention Callimachus and Apollonius Rhodius, it is likely that its illegible portions contained the scholia on Apollonius given in the *Miscellanea*.[30] Poliziano's gloss on 66. 94 is also very faint, but one can read enough of it to see that he was arguing for *Uarion* instead of *Oarion* on the basis of a line from Nicander and its scholia.[31] In both cases, however, Poliziano's observations were to appear in a more developed form in the *Miscellanea*. In *Misc.* i. 68 he argues for the Greek genitive plural *Chalybon* rather than the Latin *Chalybum*. In *Misc.* i. 69 he vindicates *Oarion* (instead of *Uarion*) by recourse to Callimachus, treating the testimony of Nicander as secondary, and omitting the comment of the scholiast, so that we can infer that at the time of the gloss he knew the Greek word *Οὐαρίων* (*Uarion*) from the Nicander scholia, and only later found *Ὠαρίων* in Pindar, Eustathius, and (most important) Callimachus.

Not surprisingly, Poliziano knew more about Greek literature and Catullus' sophisticated use of it when he composed the *Miscellanea* than when he was writing the marginalia, and he had changed his mind about other matters as well. Since he did not revise his notes to make them agree with his later ideas, we can chart his progress and acknowledge the justice of his claims for priority. But it is equally important to note another implication of the differences between the *Miscellanea* and the corresponding marginalia: at some point before 1489 Poliziano had ceased to add new ideas to his notes. The reason is probably to be found in the publication of the edition and commentary of Antonio Partenio in 1485. Partenio was no match for Poliziano, but the appearance of his commentary laid to rest any plans Poliziano might have had for his marginalia. After Partenio had written the first commentary, Poliziano would not write the second. He entered some textual corrections from Partenio (see Appendix 3), and no doubt occasionally added a note or two, but the marginalia were no longer the principal forum for his Catullan ideas. Other evidence points to the same period—namely, Poliziano's subscription to Propertius (1485) and his letter to the Cortesi (1486), which we discussed in the previous chapter.

Final confirmation for the date is provided by the two chapters of the *Miscellanea* that have no parallels in the marginalia: *Misc.* i. 6 and 73. Both seem to have been inspired by a manuscript of Festus that Poliziano saw in the spring of 1485; but since he did not add to his marginalia accordingly, it is fair to assume that by this time he was no longer actively interested in them.[32] The manuscript that gave Poliziano his ideas for *Misc.* i. 6 and 73 is the famous Codex Farnesianus, then as now the sole witness to Festus' text apart from the eighth-century excerpts of Paul the

Deacon. It was a great find, and in *Misc.* i. 73 Poliziano tells in some detail how he was invited to study it:

Four years ago in Rome Manilius Rhallus (a Greek, but well-versed in Latin literature) showed me a certain fragment of Sextus Pompeius Festus (for so it was in the title)—extremely old, but mutilated in many places and chewed up by mice. . . . Pomponio Leto, a man most expert in literature and antiquity, had also kept some pages from the same fragment, which he likewise gave me to read and transcribe.[33]

In the tattered manuscript Poliziano found Festus' gloss on the rare word *suppernati*, 'hamstrung,' which the ancient grammarian had explained with citations from Ennius and Catullus. At once he saw how to correct 17. 19, which the archetype had transmitted thus: In fossas liguri iacet *separata* securi.

In this place in particular the old manuscript has the definition quite eaten away, but in such a way that from the barely coherent remains of the letters it appears that after Ennius Catullus, too, is invoked . . . Well, to make no claims about the rest of the verse, as I sniffed it out syllable by syllable, I seemed, at least, to be able to report for certain, that *expernata*, not *separata*, was to be read in it, as far as I could gather from the few scraps or rather scrapings, and as far as I could divine, too, from the nearly obliterated traces.[34]

In the same manuscript he found, if not the inspiration, certainly the confirmation for *Misc.* i. 6, in which he presents the most famous of all Renaissance ideas about Catullus, his obscene interpretation of the sparrow. Here is *Misc.* i. 6:

In what sense the sparrow of Catullus is to be understood, and a passage pointed out in Martial.

That sparrow of Catullus in my opinion allegorically conceals a certain more obscene meaning which I cannot explain with my modesty intact. Martial persuades me to believe this in that epigram of which these are the last verses:

> Da mihi basia, sed Catulliana:
> Quae si tot fuerint, quot ille dixit,
> Donabo tibi passerem Catulli. [Martial 11. 6. 14–16]

For he would be too inept as a poet (which it is wrong to believe) if he said he would give the sparrow of Catullus, and not the other thing I suspect, to the boy after the kisses. What this is, for the modesty of my pen, I leave to each reader to conjecture from the native salaciousness of the sparrow.[35]

Although no one in the Renaissance seems to have questioned his claim to it, this interpretation was not original with Poliziano. Forty years earlier Pontano had suggested it in one of his poems, using the same epigram of Martial as his starting point.[36] Poliziano certainly knew Martial's epigram long before writing the *Miscellanea*, for he quotes it in his marginalia on 5.[37] But although he probably also knew Pontano's poem and understood its innuendo, there is no sign in the marginalia that he applied it to Catullus. Perhaps he was unconvinced by the interpretation until he saw Festus' gloss on 'the sparrow':

In mimes especially they call the obscene male member 'the sparrow' [*strutheum*], evidently from the salaciousness of the sparrow, which is called *στρουθός* in Greek.[38]

Without Partenio, Poliziano no doubt would have continued his marginalia as before, but that is not to say that he would have written a commentary. He might have done so in the 1470s, when he was a very young man and printed commentaries were an exciting novelty. But a decade later such a project was less attractive for several reasons—among them an awareness of both the drudgery of commentary writing and the banality of the result, Poliziano's involvement in other projects, and the contemporary interest in developing a new genre that would allow a humanist to display his philological brilliance without plodding line by line through a text.[39] It was Poliziano himself who perfected the new form, in the *Miscellanea*.

We have been looking at Poliziano's Catullan interpretations historically, to establish his claims for priority and to observe the development of his ideas, but it is time to see them from another point of view. If Poliziano designed the *Miscellanea* as his philological showcase, what method and style of interpretation did he choose to display? The Catullan chapters, however diverse they are in other respects, are demonstrations of an identical method, which we may describe as looking for clues to an author's meaning in other ancient texts—Callimachus for Greek diction, Quintilian on aspirates, Plutarch etc. on Harpocrates. And, with one exception, they are examples of what is usually meant by the humanists when they speak of interpretation. The text is treated as a riddle to be solved. It has a single meaning that emerges once and for all when its points of difficulty have been explained or emended. Most often, of course, interpretation in this sense centres on text criticism, and the text is either vindicated or emended by the interpreter. The exception is *Misc.* i. 6, Poliziano's interpretation of the sparrow. The method is pure Poliziano: Catullus is explained by recourse to other ancient texts. But the interpretation itself is a far cry from the textual and philological ideas of the other chapters—not because it is obscene, or even because it is 'literary,' but because it is an allegory. For an allegory reveals not a single correct meaning (the answer to a riddle), but layers of meaning, discovered through clues not present or implied in the text itself.

Poliziano's interpretation of the sparrow unleashed a storm of controversy, and the dust has not yet settled.[40] But the question for us must be—not whether he was right—but what it was in his interpretation that so exercised and enraged his contemporaries. It was not primarily its obscenity. So far from being frightened by the obscene, Renaissance critics understood it and revelled in it—indeed, the obscene passages in Catullus were explained more frankly and explicitly in the period 1480–1520 than they would be for the next 450 years. Sentimental and methodological factors played an important role. Although the text of Catullus was difficult and obscure, everyone thought he understood the sparrow poems—even when they were in fact so little understood that they were treated as a single poem. Poliziano's intervention seemed to complicate and tarnish what had been straightforward and affecting, and readers who had shed a tear with Catullus over the death of Lesbia's sparrow were embarrassed and disgruntled to be told afterwards that they had really been feeling sentimental about the poet's impotence. Poliziano's allegory, moreover, seemed to typify the intellectual arrogance of its author, since almost by definition the allegorical interpreter claims to possess esoteric clues denied to others and to exist on a higher plane of exegetical competence. Thus, the young poet Jacopo Sannazaro could exclaim sarcastically: 'O gods, how clever you are, Poliziano, since you're the only one who understands poets!'[41]

The real objection, however, was to Poliziano himself. A master polemicist in a polemical age, he had many enemies and made new ones all the time. All of his Catullan chapters soon came under attack—most conspicuously by Michele Marullo, who attacked various chapters of the *Miscellanea* in his epigrams (although not the sparrow chapter), and by Girolamo Avanzi, whose *Emendationes* were motivated to a large extent by Poliziano's criticisms of Domizio Calderini in the *Miscellanea*.[42] The polemic outlived all of the principals: even sixty years after Poliziano's death Marc Antoine de Muret was still attacking his ideas in his own commentary on Catullus.[43]

ANTONIO PARTENIO AT THE FINISH LINE

Antonio Partenio da Lazise (1456–1506) was probably in the audience in Verona that rainy day in 1479 or 1480 when Poliziano explained 'almost all of Catullus', and no doubt joined his excited fellow citizens in hailing him as 'an Angel sent down from heaven'. Partenio was young, well-off, and already a part of the small but enthusiastic group of Veronese humanists who were just then putting together the memorial collection of poems in honour of Domizio Calderini. (Poliziano's poem headed the collection, but it was followed immediately by an epigram by Partenio.) In the years after Poliziano's visit Partenio taught Latin and Greek, dabbled in Latin verse, and, like his friends, remained steeped in local patriotism.[44]

In 1485 he published his commentary on Catullus. As we would expect, it is presented as a work of Veronese pride and *pietas*. It opens with a letter and an epigram to Partenio from Giacomo Conte Giuliari, leader of the Veronese circle: 'O poets, adorn the restored Catullus with laurel; / the civic crown is enough for my Parthenius'.[45] Next comes Partenio's dedication to Verona, 'the ancient and most holy temple of the divine Muses', in a letter to the leader of the Roman Academy, Giulio Pomponio Leto, who is to serve as its *pontifex maximus*.[46] In the long preface that follows Partenio emphasizes his patriotic duty to interpret Catullus:

> And indeed if . . . my fellow citizens Cyllenio and Domizio interpreted foreign authors with learned expositions—the one Tibullus, the other Juvenal, Martial, and Statius—how much more eagerly should I have interpreted my fellow citizen Catullus with my explanation, of whatever worth?[47]

Next comes a life of the poet, a short history of lyric poetry, and at last the text of Catullus, surrounded and nearly overpowered by Partenio's copious commentary. The book ends with a final letter from Partenio to the reader, in which he asks for corrections and promises another work on Catullus.

Patriotism and *pietas* notwithstanding, however, this first commentary on Catullus enters the scene, not with a fanfare, but with a harsh chord of dread, self-assertion, and apology. The same tone is everywhere—in Giuliari's letter, in Partenio's dedication, in his preface, in his concluding letter to the reader. Let us begin with the strange little poem that immediately follows the dedication:

Antonius Parthenius Lacisius to his Book

Dear book, on your way to the skies with my name,
Make sure to take care as you go.
Flee teeth that are stained with black mould of disdain,
And troops of grammarians low.
They are mighty in spite, with their nose in the air,
Self-appointed to carp at your page.
With teeth let them bite, with nails let them tear,
As long as your countryman's saved.
So may glory be yours, through long ages the same—
Long life, my dear book, and unperishing fame![48]

Giuliari's letter strikes the same defensive note:

You ask, Partenio, what I think of your study of Catullus' poetry, whether I think it does justice to the meaning of the poet in every detail. Although I think it not at all safe to express my opinion openly among the many spiteful critics of our age, I will say something none the less, but less to be sure than I think, lest I be thought to have indulged my affection for you too much. You have undertaken an especially difficult task and one attempted by no one before both because of the harshness of the poetry itself (which according to both Plinys the poet deliberately affected) and because of the corruption of the work mutilated by the carelessness of the past. Those who read your commentary will decide what you have achieved. To please everyone is a boundless task and almost beyond human strength. We consider you worthy of praise in this—that you have undertaken courageously what no one until now has either dared or been able to attain. In great undertakings (even if they are not accomplished) to have been willing is exceedingly fine and splendid. If you have anticipated any with your edition or if any have a disposition to find fault, I know that they will carp constantly until they

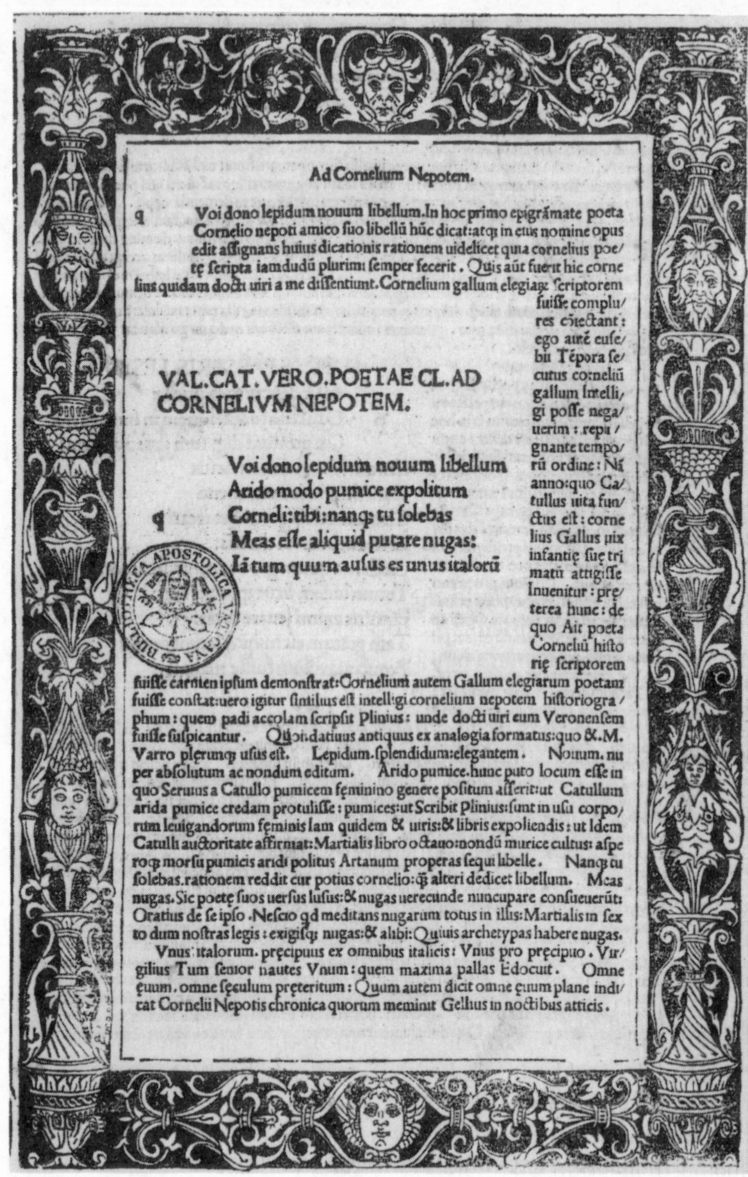

Ad Cornelium Nepotem.

q Voi dono lepidum nouum libellum. In hoc primo epigrãmate poeta Cornelio nepoti amico suo libellũ hũc dicat: atq; in eius nomine opus edit assignans huius dicationis rationem uidelicet quia cornelius poe/tę scripta iamdudũ plurimi semper fecerit. Quis aũt fuerit hic cornelius quidam docti uiri a me dissentiunt. Cornelium gallum elegiarũ scriptorem

VAL. CAT. VERO. POETAE CL. AD CORNELIVM NEPOTEM.

Voi dono lepidum nouum libellum
Arido modo pumice expolitum
q Corneli: tibi: nanq; tu solebas
Meas esse aliquid putare nugas:
Iã tum quum ausus es unus italorũ

fuisse complu/res coiectant: ego autẽ euse/bii Tẽpora se/cutus corneliũ gallum intelli/gi posse nega/uerim: repu/gnante tempo/rũ ordine: Nã anno: quo Ca/tullus uita fun/ctus est: cornelius Gallus uix infantię suę trimatũ attigisse Inuenitur: prę/terea hunc: de quo Ait poeta Corneliũ historię scriptorem fuisse carmen ipsum demonstrat: Cornelium autem Gallum elegiarum poetam fuisse constat: uero igitur similius est intelligi cornelium nepotem historiogra/phum: quem padi accolam scripsit Plinius: unde docti uiri eum Veronensem fuisse suspicantur. Quoi. datiuus antiquus ex analogia formatus: quo & M. Varro plerunq; usus est. Lepidum. splendidum: elegantem. Nouum. nuper absolutum ac nondum editum. Arido pumice. hunc puto locum esse in quo Seruius a Catullo pumicem fęminino genere positum asserit: ut Catullum arida pumice credam protulisse: pumices: ut Scribit Plinius: sunt in usu corpo/rum leuigandorum fęminis Iam quidem & uiris: & libris expoliendis: ut Idem Catulli auctoritate affirmat: Martialis libro octauo: nondũ murice cultus: aspero q; morsu pumicis aridi politus Artanum properas sequi libelle. Nanq; tu solebas. rationem reddit cur potius cornelio: q̃ alteri dedicet libellum. Meas nugas. Sic poetę suos uersus lusus: & nugas uerecunde nuncupare consueuerũt: Oratius de se ipso. Nescio qd meditans nugarum totus in illis: Martialis in sexto dum nostras legis: exigisq; nugas: & alibi: Quiuis archetypas habere nugas.

Vnus italorum. pręcipuus ex omnibus italicis: Vnus pro pręcipuo. Vir/gilius Tum senior nautes Vnum: quem maxima pallas Edocuit. Omne ęuum. omne sęculum pręteritum: Quum autem dicit omne ęuum plane indi/cat Cornelii Nepotis chronica quorum meminit Gellius in noctibus atticis.

Plate 5: The first page of Partenio's commentary (1485) (Biblioteca Apostolica Vaticana, Inc. II. 200, 1r).

understand on my testimony that you were brought to the interpretation of Catullus' poetry not because you wanted to be first and to snatch praise from others, but for the sake of duty to your fellow citizen, and that you might open to others the way of composing a more learned work. We on our own authority can assert this, safe from every criticism, that you are deserving of the true civic crown because you have lifted up and protected with the shield of your intellect your fellow countryman who was falling and almost undone by the injury of time—a thought we have put into verse in the following epigram.[49]

Giuliari praises Partenio (if we can call it that) for ambition, for good intentions, for trying hard—but not for succeeding ('In great undertakings, even if they are not accomplished, to have been willing is exceedingly fine and splendid'). His faint praise is apotropaic: perhaps the malevolent critics will be less harsh if they understand that little is claimed for Partenio's work and that he has been moved by civic duty rather than by hope of glory.

Partenio makes his dedication to Verona and Pomponio Leto in the same spirit—evidently not so much to honour them as to secure their protection:

For I was not unaware that the lot and condition of all writers has been subject to the insults of envy, and that no one from the foundations of literature to our own time has been able to escape the obdurate scorn of spiteful men. Warned by this unhappy fate, when I was seeking some safe refuge for my work I chose my homeland Verona, the ancient and most holy temple of the Muses, to which, with your support, my little book should be dedicated, hoping that by means of this vow it would be unviolated by the rashness of the mob.[50]

Mingled with all this apprehension is the acknowledgement of Partenio's inadequacy. Giuliari assumes that Partenio will not succeed and that the best he can do is to open the way for others to produce something better; and Partenio himself admits to a lack of competence:

Nor indeed do I fear very much what churlish spite may plot against me because with only moderate study and no very shining intellect I have boldly approached this work, which is lacunose in many places and corrupt in more and on that account left to obscurity by more learned professors of literature—like a corpse that can be revived by no human efforts or ability.[51]

This is a curious way to launch a new work that by rights should epitomize the pride and aspirations of Veronese humanism.

A man of Partenio's admittedly modest attainments had much to fear in the volatile and competitive world of the humanists. He was out of his depth, and he knew it. His worries were well founded, for he was to be sharply criticized by scholars of greater learning and reputation, including Poliziano. But though Partenio and Giuliari couch their apprehension in general terms (malevolent critics, or the slanders levelled at all writers since the beginning of literature), it clearly has a specific and immediate focus—not merely what Partenio might expect in several years from Poliziano or some other great man, but what he dreads here and now from a particular rival and critic known to be working on Catullus. Phrases like Giuliari's 'if you have anticipated any with your edition' and 'not because you wanted to be first and to snatch praise from others,' give the game away. Partenio has rushed his work into print to forestall someone else, and now he is afraid of the consequences.[52] Indeed, as we see in his final letter to the reader, the consequences may already be at hand:

> Why then did men of this sort, lying in ambush like drones hostile to other people's work, not undertake such an endeavour themselves before me? Why did they wait with their mouths open for someone else's discovery? Why did those who were equipped and supported by Herculean strength not dare to subdue the monstrous hydra of Catullus' poetry? Why were they such slothful dreamers before my sleepless nights? Why in short did the troublesome critics of other people's work not seek a name and reputation for themselves by commending rather than by disparaging honest labours?[53]

Partenio's rival was Battista Guarino (1435–1505), son of Guarino da Verona, from whom he inherited the chair of rhetoric in Ferrara and the patronage of the ducal family.[54] His principal patron was Ercole I—hence Partenio's jibe, 'equipped and supported by Herculean strength'. Twenty years older than Partenio, he was well known, not just in Ferrara but also in Verona and Bologna, and he moved in the highest intellectual and social circles. By comparison Partenio seemed a mere provincial dabbler, and, worse yet, one overshadowed even in his own city, since Guarino, though born in Ferrara, was considered by heredity a member of Verona's intellectual aristocracy.

In spite of Battista Guarino's importance and prestige, however, we know surprisingly little about his work on Catullus.

He seems to have studied the poet at two separate periods—first, briefly, in the 1450s, and again in the 1480s. The evidence for the first is an isolated remark by Battista himself in a dated but unsigned letter of 1456.)[55] For the later period we have not only the allusions in Partenio's commentary but also two poems of the 1490s—one by Battista (1496), presenting his emendations to the city of Verona, and the other by his friend and pupil, Ludovico Pittorio (1492), complaining that Battista has been too busy emending Catullus to read his verses.[56] Our principal source, however, is the edition and commentary that Battista's son, Alessandro Guarino, published a generation later (1521), using the manuscript emended by Battista as the basis for his text.[57]

Since Alessandro was eager to claim priority for his father's emendations, he naturally attempted to date them as early as possible. Thus, he says that Battista's manuscript had been emended 'many years ago'. He also reprints the poems of Battista and Pittorio, carefully including the date of the latter (1492), since a *terminus ante quem* of 1492, as any Catullan devotee could be expected to realize, would easily demonstrate Battista's priority over several competitors, e.g. Avanzi (*Emendationes*, 1495, 1500), Palladio Fosco (1496), Sabellico (1497), and Avanzi's Aldines (1502, 1515). Unfortunately, however, a *terminus* of 1492 could accomplish nothing against the claims of his most significant rival, Partenio. Worse still, Pittorio's poem represents Battista's emendations as still work in progress in 1492. There was no way out of the difficulty, but Alessandro does the best he can, asserting that Pittorio has told him that Battista had in fact completed his emendations some time before the publication of Pittorio's poem.[58] Pittorio does not say how long before, any more than Alessandro himself tells us how many years ago Battista emended his manuscript or when he presented his work to the city of Verona. Alessandro and Pittorio are vague just at the point where we want precision, and their vagueness is deliberate—to push back the date of Battista's emendations as far as possible without actually stating that he had completed them before Partenio's commentary. Their attempt is unconvincing, for everything in Partenio points the other way. He has had to hurry his work into print, to be sure, and perhaps it was a close race, but in the concluding letter we see him at the finish line, panting but indisputably victorious, and gloating (however apprehensively) over his slower rival. The epigram with which Battista presented his emendations to Verona tells the same story:

The Epigram of Battista Guarino to Verona
On Behalf of the Corrected Poetry of Catullus

O Verona who bore Catullus the poet,
Take, keep these verses now well corrected.
If their texts were corrupt before, did they know it?
Or is it just as I've always suspected?
Busybodies who try to get our attention,
Deaf to his verses down to this hour,
Miss the jests and the wit of the poet's intention,
Can't scan his measures, don't feel their power.
Though they'd praised him of old for verses cerebral
(Clear thought was his, and artful poetics)
Yet he spoke in a barbarous argot—medieval,
Spoiled through the fault of dim-witted critics.
Here's Catullus at last, all polished and witty,
Whom your citizens send as a gift to their city.[59]

Battista's words are those of a man who claims, not to have done the job first, but to have done it right. Every line in his epigram is designed to wound, and his confident presentation to Verona is a riposte to Partenio's apprehensive dedication.

It is not clear exactly what Battista was working on when Partenio forestalled him, but our sources imply either an edition or a collection of emendations like those produced a few years later by Sabellico and Avanzi—that is, corrections and interpretations of individual passages rather than a full-scale commentary. Although he surely intended to publish his work (for that is the whole point of the race with Partenio), he had to abandon his plans because no edition or emendations alone, whatever their merits, could compete with the first, long-awaited commentary—whatever its defects. He retaliated by presenting his own work as a pious gift to Verona, and he must have done so soon after the appearance of Partenio's commentary. Partenio's haste implies that his rival is not far behind, and Guarino's epigram would lose its sting if it did not appear close on the heels of the work it attacked.

But we should not be too quick to accept Battista's presentation at face value. The donation is attested in his epigram and in

Alessandro's quotation of it[60]—but not by any of his contemporaries. A few of Battista's readings (or rather, the readings claimed for him by Alessandro) were known in the period 1485–93, since they made their way into the emendations of Sabellico and Avanzi, as well as into Poliziano's marginalia.[61] But no one acknowledges Battista as his source. It is hard to imagine Sabellico and Avanzi stealing Battista's emendations if they were in the public domain; but it is harder still to explain why neither one celebrates Battista's pious donation to Verona if it actually took place. Sabellico introduces Battista as a speaker in his dialogue, *De latinae linguae reparatione* (1494), and praises his accomplishments, but he gives the credit for rescuing Catullus to Petrarch and Boccaccio, Guarino da Verona and Partenio.[62] Avanzi is punctilious about citing and congratulating his predecessors. Yet in the first edition of his *Emendationes* (1495) he mentions Battista Guarino only in a list of scholars said to be interested in Catullus, and in the second (1500) he omits him entirely.[63]

Thus, if Battista's donation of his emendations was not a fiction with its only existence in his epigram, it might as well have been, for it failed either to impress his contemporaries or to discredit Partenio, who was spared the ugly controversy he had expected. Although his commentary was criticized by Poliziano in the *Miscellanea* and by Alessandro many years after his death, Battista himself never refuted it. Partenio had indisputably won the race to produce the first commentary, and his work would remain unchallenged for another decade.

PARTENIO INTERPRETS CATULLUS

The need for a commentary was clear—indeed, Partenio's book proved so popular that it was reprinted five times in the fifteen years after its first publication.[64] Perhaps the very learned could enjoy Catullus' poetry without assistance even when much remained obscure or problematic, whetting their wits on textual problems or puzzles like those Poliziano was to take up in the *Miscellanea*; but most readers were unprepared to decipher Catullus by themselves. They were confused and discouraged not only by real difficulties with the text and its interpretation but also by the unfamiliar characters, place names, and mythological allusions they met on every page. It was largely for readers like these that Partenio conceived his commentary, and not without a sense of the enormity of his own task as he set out to produce the first complete and systematic interpretion of Catullus. He describes his mission thus in the Preface:

What then should seem to me worthy of as much joy as the possibility that Catullus might gain lustre by being known—not only to learned men but also to students and teachers—either through my lucubrations or through the studies of a number of men that have been set in motion in imitation of my labours? Therefore, since in all cities the surviving works of almost all poets were being read, and Catullus alone, both because his writings were most corrupt and because they lacked an interpreter, had remained unknown to the schools, I tried recently to the best of my ability to bring into schools and the hands of teachers this poet honoured by the most cultivated writers with the title of most learned and elegant poet. . . . Nor shall I much fear what inhuman envy may devise against me. . . . Moreover, I was and am so far removed from foolish fear of this sort of jealousy that I have hastened to complete my undertaking much more eagerly than I had planned. For since it is my purpose to restore Catullus to a place of light and honour, the more learned men are moved by rivalry of my interpretations, the more advantageously they will look after the interests of our poet, and where I have failed, held back by weakness of intellect, learned men, in their effort to speak more expertly and completely, will satisfy cultivated young men after I have taken the lead. In this way, under my auspices, little by little our poet will be assisted, and by the agency of many writers inspired by equal zeal he will recover his glory. . . . Indeed, if the most expert grammarian Servius, who followed Caper, Urbanus, Hyginus, Didymus, Probus, Asper, Donatus, and many other interpreters of Vergil in his Vergilian commentaries, is found to have erred in numerous matters and none the less does not lose the title and status of most learned grammarian, I too can and should hope for a bit of indulgence from cultivated readers, since with no guide in interpreting this exceedingly difficult work I have undertaken such a great burden of my profession and incurred such great danger of ill-will, both because of eagerness to fulfil my obligations to cultured young men and because of a special pious desire to assist my fellow citizen.[65]

Two important points emerge from Partenio's discussion. First, his goal is to make Catullus accessible, but to a rather surprising audience—not merely to mature scholars and university students, but to schoolboys and their teachers. His aspiration is an interesting comment both on his ambition (making an author of Catullus' difficulty accessible to schoolboys was no small undertaking) and on the moral climate of his period in contrast to that of the recent past and not so distant future. Partenio had been teaching Catullus in his school for years, and his commentary displays no inhibitions. In the previous generation, however, Catullus had been deemed unsuitable for schools; in the next, his obscenity was to be a problem for Pierio Valeriano and his university students.[66] Second, Partenio has a clear conception of the progress of scholarship and of his own place in it: 'little by little our poet will be assisted, and through the agency of many writers . . . he will recover his glory.' Partenio, standing at the beginning of the process, does not expect to have the last word. This conception fits neatly enough with the apologetic stance of the preface and dedication, but it is not merely defensive. Alone among Catullan interpreters of his century, Partenio understands what it means for an ancient author to lack a critical tradition and that one man cannot remedy the deficiency. The discussion of Servius is directly relevant, for his great commentary on Vergil (whose mistakes are useful enough for Partenio's defence) was the culmination of the ancient critical tradition, whose duration and richness are demonstrated by the long list of his predecessors. The contrast with the situation of the interpreter of Catullus is clear, and Partenio does not fail to emphasize it.

Partenio had undoubtedly set himself a formidable task, for in writing the first commentary on Catullus he had undertaken to give an intelligible account of every poem and to explain every separate point of difficulty in a corrupt and diverse corpus as long as three books of the *Aeneid*—all without the benefit of either a critical tradition or any of the lexica, concordances, encyclopaedias, or onomastica that later classicists would take for granted. The results were imperfect, for Partenio was a man of *mediocris doctrina*, as he says himself, and his ideas about Catullus are not sophisticated either as philology or as literary criticism. Like most Renaissance school commentators, he deals largely in the elementary and obvious, paraphrasing poems, spelling out details of grammar and usage, and explaining historical and mythological references. Often his basic information is wrong. None the less, his commentary is a precious document, for as we leaf through its pages we can observe Catullan interpretation at its starting point—not for just a few poems or passages as in Poliziano, but for all of Catullus.

By juxtaposing Partenio's ideas with those that we find both in Poliziano's marginalia and in the commentaries of his immediate successors, Palladio Fosco (1496) and Alessandro Guarino (1521), we can place his achievement in its context, seeing what problems the fifteenth-century reader faced, what he knew, and how he used his information to make sense of the text before him.

Partenio and his contemporaries encountered various pitfalls when they tried to identify the historical and mythological characters that not only populate Catullus' poems but often provide indispensable clues to their meaning. They usually made their identifications as Poliziano had identified Harpocrates to explain the obscenity of 74—by finding a reference in another ancient author. Accordingly, Partenio has one of his greatest triumphs in the very first poem, which he summarizes thus:

In this first epigram the poet dedicates this book to his friend Cornelius Nepos and publishes the work in his name, assigning the reason for this dedication—because Cornelius for a long time had valued the poet's writings highly.[67]

His comment seems obvious until we remember that every previous edition had followed the lead of the *princeps* in identifying Catullus' friend with Cornelius Gallus. Partenio discovered from Jerome's Eusebius that the identification was anachronistic.[68] He was able to rule out Gallus for the additional reason that he was an elegist,[69] whereas Catullus' allusion to his friend's literary endeavours (*cum ausus es unus Italorum / omne aevum tribus explicare cartis*, 1. 5–6) points to a work of history. He caps his discussion by producing the identity of the author and his book from Aulus Gellius, glossing 1. 6 as follows:

omne aevum: Each past age. Moreover, when he says, 'each age', he clearly indicates the *Chronica* of Cornelius Nepos, which Gellius mentions in the *Attic Nights* [Gell. 17. 21. 3].[70]

When he saw that Catullus' friend was a historian Partenio managed for once to surpass the young Poliziano, who had identified him with the poet Cornelius Cinna, thinking that the verse *doctis Iuppiter, et laboriosis* (1. 7) referred to Cinna's notoriously learned poetry.[71]

But information from ancient authors was not always so

helpful. It was all too often inapposite, incomplete, or confusing, and the humanists lacked the knowledge and experience to interpret it correctly. In 95 Catullus celebrated Cinna's epyllion on the incestuous heroine Smyrna, but Partenio thought Cinna's subject was the Amazon of the same name he had read about in Strabo.[72] His identification went unchallenged for nearly a century, since no one until Joseph Scaliger (1577) knew enough about the subjects of Alexandrian and neoteric poetry to correct him.[73] When Partenio tried to find out about the Calvus who had sent Catullus a mass of wretched verses as a Saturnalia present (14), he discovered a poet named Calvus in Horace and an orator of the same name in Quintilian. Not surprisingly, he came to the erroneous conclusion that there were two Calvuses in Catullus' time, and decided (perhaps because of the poem's traditional title, *Ad Calvum Poetam*) that the Calvus of 14 was the poet.[74] Palladio and Alessandro Guarino followed him, except that they identified Catullus' friend with the orator.[75] Sometimes the ancient sources provided material only for inference or guess-work. In 56 Catullus recounts an obscene jest to a certain Cato (*O rem ridiculam, Cato, et iocosam, / dignamque auribus et tuo cachinno*, 56. 1–2). But which one? Partenio learned from Aulus Gellius that there were many Catos, and inferred from Cicero that Cato Uticensis, the obvious candidate, would not have been amused. 'This cannot be said to Cato Uticensis', he concludes, 'for it is well known that he was very strait-laced, as Cicero clearly shows in his speech, *Pro Murena*.'[76] But although Partenio left the question open, the young Poliziano thought he had found the answer in Suetonius: 'Valerius Cato, as I suppose, a poet of Catullus' time.'[77] The matter is still unresolved.[78]

In his attempt to explain every detail, Partenio often purveyed irrelevant information, as in his gloss on *caprimulgus* ('goatherd') in 22, where Catullus mocks the urbane wit Suffenus, whose verses make him seem as cloddish as a ditch-digger or a goatherd:

caprimulgus [22. 10]: Here *caprimulgus* means goatherd. A *caprimulgus* is also a bird about which Pliny gives the following information: 'The birds called goat milkers, with the appearance of a good-sized blackbird, are night thieves, for by day they are sightless. They enter the pens of the shepherds and fly to the udders of the nannies to suck their milk. And because of this injury the udder withers away and blindness arises in the goats they have milked in this way.'[79]

Palladio and Alessandro Guarino faithfully pass on this nonsense from Pliny, and Guarino even gives it a literary significance:

> *caprimulgus* [22. 10]: a goatherd who milks goats, or he calls Suffenus a *caprimulgus* as a sneak-thief of other people's poetry, for a *caprimulgus* is a bird, which, as Pliny says . . .[80]

Sometimes Partenio's extraneous information has a touch of strange, unconscious humour, as on 15. 19, where, after explaining how adulterers were punished by having radishes thrust up their anuses, he adds irrelevantly: 'In Germany radishes grow as large as babies. They thrive on cold, but dislike manure. Read more in Pliny.'[81]

In trying to explain whole poems he sometimes produces detailed scenarios, which are most elaborate when he is standing on the shakiest ground. All the earlier editions had printed 40–42 as a single poem with the title *Ad Ravidum* (after the addressee of 40). Partenio separates 40, but prints 41–42 together under the title *De Acme Puella*. In 41 (*Ameana*[82] *puella defututa*) Catullus attacks an ugly girl who has asked too much for her services and avers that she needs psychiatric assistance. In 42 (*Adeste, hendecasyllabi, quot estis*) he calls on his verses to demand his writing tablets from some shameless hussy who won't give them back. The modern scholar, who has never read the two poems as a unit, sees nothing to bind them together, but to Partenio, who had never read them separately, the connection was obvious:[83]

> Catullus, enticed by the charms and flattery of the tart, Acme, had promised ten thousand sesterces through his writing tablets (as lovers in that situation often do). But the girl, believing that she had made her fortune, adduced the tablets as evidence and demanded ten thousand from Catullus by virtue of the promise. And so the poet bursts into a rage, shouting, 'Does that worn-out Acme demand a whole ten thousand from me? Let her give back my tablets!'[84]

Although neither the young Poliziano nor Avanzi (1495) would have agreed with Partenio's explanation (for both wanted to separate 41 and 42), it apparently pleased everyone else.[85] The two poems appear together in the first and second Aldines, as well as in the editions of Palladio and Alessandro Guarino, who pass on Partenio's interpretation.[86]

But if Partenio's account of 41–42 had a certain plausibility, his scenario for 35 can only be described as bizarre. The poem purports to be a letter to Catullus' friend Caecilius, urging him to hurry to Catullus in Verona even though his girl friend tries to detain him. (She's been madly in love ever since she read the poem he's writing on the Magna Mater, and Catullus can't blame her: she is a *docta puella*, and Caecilius has begun his poem charmingly.) Although Catullus, as often, is writing about poetry, Partenio believes that the subject is love—missing or misunderstanding every literary reference in the poem. His troubles are concentrated in the last six verses. (The text is Partenio's; readings that differ from those in modern editions are italicized.)

Nam quo tempore legit *entheatam*
Dindymi dominam: ex eo misellae
Ignes interiorem edunt medullam
Ignosco tibi saphyca puella
Musa doctior: est enim venuste
Magna *caecilii* inchoata mater.

(35. 13–18, Venice 1491)

A curious story emerges from Partenio's glosses:

Legit [35. 13]: 'Caecilius chose'.
Entheatam [35. 13]: 'full of divine spirit'. Others read *indotatam*, but wrongly.
Ignosco [35. 16]: The order and sense are: 'O girl, more learned than the Sapphic muse, you must be forgiven if you are consumed by love for Caecilius who is taking a wife. Indeed, so great is Caecilius' wisdom that his wife (who is pregnant by him) is now called Magna Mater, the name by which the mother of the gods was addressed.'
Doctior saphica musa [35. 16–17]: The poetess of Mytilene loved Phaon, an illiterate merchant, but Caecilius' girl friend acts more intelligently because she is madly in love with Caecilius, a learned and noble youth.
Invocata magna mater [35. 18]: because of the wisdom of her husband. *Invocata*: 'called'. Some read *Inchoata magna mater Caecilii*, i.e. now that she is pregnant, she has begun to be the mother of an infant (to be named Caecilius after his father).[87]

Not realizing that *Dindymi dominam* (14) and *Magna . . . mater* (18) refer to a poem, Partenio has ignored the obvious meaning, 'read', for *legit* in 13 and dreamed up a non-existent wife and baby for Caecilius. He knows the irrelevant story of Sappho and

Phaon from Ovid's *Heroides*, but since he is thinking in erotic rather than in literary terms, he overlooks the main point—that Sappho was a poet.

This tarradiddle, foolish as it undoubtedly is, is also a good demonstration both of the difficulties that faced the early commentators and of the lengths that they would go to make sense of a poem. But for once, Partenio had gone too far for his successors to follow him. Palladio, in what seems to be one of his few original comments, sees what Partenio had missed—the literary nature of the poem. 'For a long time I have wondered what Catullus means here', he says in his note on *Dindimi dominam*:

> But rejecting other people's ideas, which to be sure are many and various, I have finally been brought to the opinion that Caecilius had begun a poem about Cybele. And when the girl had read this, she began to love him more passionately—so great was the charm and learning of the poem.[88]

Alessandro Guarino follows Palladio, but his gloss on the last line deserves our attention. He prefers the reading: *Magna Caecilio invocata* (or *inchoata*) *mater*, but with typical piety prints his father's version:

> In my father's corrections I have found that this verse can be read as follows: *Caia Caecilia invocata mater*, with this meaning, as I believe, 'I forgive you if, learned yourself, you love a learned man, for you have been happily joined in marriage with Caecilius . . .'.[89]

Guarino bases his interpretation on the formula from the Roman marriage ceremony ('Tu mihi Caius et ego tibi Caia, tu mihi mater familias et ego tibi pater familias'), and supports it further with a reference in Plutarch to Tarquin's daughter-in-law, Caia Caecilia, who was held up as a model of feminine virtue in Antiquity.[90] He has had to find his own explanation for the emended verse—proof, if one were needed, that Battista Guarino's work on Catullus did not include a commentary—but it is likely that he was thinking along the same lines as his father. After all, what else can the collocation *Caia Caecilia* suggest, if not marriage and wifely virtue? All of this is a long way from the text and intention of Catullus, but it is strictly germane to the state of Catullan studies in the 1480s when Battista and Partenio were working their way through the poems. It is a further sign of the times that Poliziano entered Battista's far-fetched version of 35. 18 into his text.[91]

Since the text and its meaning were so poorly understood, it is not surprising that Partenio generally attempts interpretation only of the most basic kind and that he makes only sporadic and limited forays into anything that might be styled literary criticism. For the most part he confines his literary judgements to the short summaries that precede the notes to each poem. These tend to be quite superficial, as in the case of 51 (*Ille mi par esse deo videtur*):

> He praises the charm and the most pleasant love of Lesbia, indicating that through idleness [*otium*], which is the cause of almost all loves and troubles, he has been captured by the charming love of Lesbia.[92]

Sometimes they are a bit more ambitious. In 8 (*Miser Catulle desinas ineptire*) he is concerned with structure:

> First he encourages himself to desert the girl. Then he pronounces his rejection. Finally he rejoices in the sufferings of his deserted *amica*.[93]

He explains *odi et amo* in 85:

> He loves because of her beauty and the habit of sexual intercourse with her, but he hates her for her faithlessness, and the many lovers she receives.[94]

And he goes on to observe that the paradox is a rhetorical *color* later borrowed by Ovid in the *Amores*.

Partenio often identifies similes and other rhetorical devices, but seldom tries to explain them—content with such comments as 'apt and charming simile' or 'poetic digression'.[95] He takes more interest in the famous simile at the end of 11:

> nec meum respectet, ut ante, amorem,
> qui illius culpa cecidit veluti prati
> ultimi flos, praetereunte postquam
>   tactus aratro est. (11. 21–4)

'And it is a charming simile to show the dead beauty of his love.' Of the simile comparing a complaisant husband to a tree lying in a ditch (17. 18–19), he remarks oddly: 'Excellent comparison. For just as a submerged alder never rises to the surface, so this stolid and sluggish man does not stir himself, weighed down by marriage.'[96]

He is conscientious about pointing out the tone or nuance of a passage. Thus, he tells us that *meus* (17. 21, of the complaisant husband) and *boni* (37. 14, of Egnatius and his fellow lechers) are used ironically. Sometimes his comments become more elaborate and detailed, as when he produces almost a set of running stage directions to explain Catullus' attack on the unrealistically high-priced tart of 41:

[*Acme*] *an illa puella* [41. 1]: It is read interrogatively and with a question.
Defututa [41. 1]: He has spoken with strong anger, as if it is a reason why no promise should be kept to such a shameless woman or why she should not be trusted at all.
Ista turpiculo [41. 3]: All these insults are spoken with great spleen as reasons and arguments against the trustworthiness of the harlot so that she should not be believed, for it is not likely that anything so large is promised seriously to such an ugly woman.
Propinqui quibus est puella curae [41. 5]: He says this to lessen belief in her claim as if she were moved to make her demand not by reason but by insanity.[97]

Partenio is at his best in his discussion of 63. The poem describes the frenzy and repentance of the young Attis, who castrates himself in devotion to the goddess Cybele. Much is beyond him, and he makes his share of mistakes, but he is right on the essentials—the gender and psychology of Attis. The mutilated youth is effeminate and described with feminine adjectives, as Partenio notes in his gloss on 63. 8 (*niveis citata cepit manibus leve typanum*):

Citata [63. 8]: 'Atys stirred up by madness'. For the poet often describes him in the feminine gender because now he was deprived of his manhood, like a woman.[98]

He has similar notes on *Gallae* (11) and *vaga* (31).[99] He appreciates the force of the simile comparing Attis to a young heifer at 33 ('an apt simile to show his effeminate playfulness'[100]), and he sees why the eunuch priests are called *Maenades* (25):

Cleverly and elegantly he says Maenads for the priests of Cybele. For among the Greeks both women raging with madness and priestesses of

Bacchus are called Maenads. Such are the priests of Cybele because they are both like women and stirred up by madness.[101]

He thinks that the language of the repentant Attis shows both youth and distress. Thus on 50 (*patria o mei creatrix, patria o mea genetrix*), he says:

A boyish enough lament. *Creatrix* and *genetrix* mean the same thing, but the poet for the sake of poetic ornament has the boy repeat the same thing in different words when he weeps and laments—which is very fitting for those lamenting with excessive grief.[102]

And again on 59–60:

patria, bonis, amicis, genitoribus abero?
abero foro palaestro, stadio et gyminasiis? (63. 59–60)

Patria, bonis . . . [63. 59]: These things are mentioned in no order suitable for oratory, for the order that proceeds is not that of nature nor of importance nor of argument, but the clever poet has arranged these words in accordance with the poetic style most appropriate for afflicted characters and children . . .
Foro, palaestra . . . [63. 60]: These are all sights more pleasing to boys than to men, and for that reason the boy keenly feels their absence.[103]

Palladio and Alessandro Guarino picked up and extended Partenio's observations on 63 with more than their usual insight. On *ministra* in 68 (*ego nunc deum ministra et Cybeles famula ferar*) Palladio observes: 'He speaks of himself in the feminine gender since he knows that after losing his manhood he must be counted among women rather than men.'[104] Guarino comments still more acutely on the traditional reading *ipse* at 63. 45 (modern editions read *ipsa*):

Simul *ipse* pectore atys sua facta recoluit
(63. 45, Parthenius 1491)

Now he describes him in the masculine gender after he has regained his senses.[105]

That is, Guarino sees the feminines as belonging to Attis' delusion and frenzy, and the masculine as a sign of his return to reality.[106]

Partenio had set out to bring Catullus to a wide audience, and —to judge from the many editions of his commentary—he succeeded admirably. With the benefit of a text that was somewhat better than Calfurnio's and an explanation of every poem, readers of all kinds, including Partenio's fellow schoolmasters and their students, could now begin to enjoy and interpret Catullus for themselves. We should remind ourselves, however, that the text Partenio presented with his commentary was not a new edition in any modern sense of the word, but only a modified version of the vulgate, which he produced simply by studying and correcting the edition of Calfurnio. His procedure was even less scientific than that of his predecessors, for although Calfurnio had corrected his 'edition printed in Venice' against the text of Puteolano, and Puteolano had corrected the *princeps* against a manuscript, Partenio seems to have corrected Calfurnio against nothing at all—supplementing what he had picked up from his contemporaries or from ancient sources with intuition and guesswork. Although he was certainly capable of guessing wrong (witness his all too many gratuitous and even unmetrical changes), he was right often enough. Goold's census credits him with fifteen emendations—almost as many as Puteolano's seventeen, if only a third of Calfurnio's forty-five.[107] The last figure shows, not that Partenio was three times worse at intuitive editing than Calfurnio, but that the method itself was producing diminishing returns. (In the next decade Palladio Fosco produced only nine emendations, correcting Partenio's edition with his wits and by plagiarizing Sabellico and Avanzi.)[108]

Since he was determined to explain everything and inventive enough to do so, Partenio's interpretations were sometimes more ingenious than convincing. Although he lacked any particular method or point of view, he sometimes tried the strategy exploited so brilliantly by Poliziano, of interpreting Catullus by recourse to other ancient authors. Unfortunately. however, since (like most scholars in the fifteenth century) he lacked Poliziano's discrimination, he was no more likely to provide his readers with a genuine clue to Catullus' meaning (Quintilian on aspirates), than with a red herring (Pliny on radishes). But naïve and undiscriminating as he undoubtedly was, Partenio nevertheless achieved his principal goal, for he rescued his fellow citizen from neglect and oblivion and laid the foundation for the modern critical tradition.

CORRECTING PARTENIO

Partenio expected his work to be superseded, for in addition to his general understanding that neither he nor anyone else could interpret all of Catullus successfully at the first attempt, he had to admit that he had failed to solve several specific problems and that he had made omissions and mistakes in his haste to get ahead of Guarino.[109] Even as his book went to press he was making plans to supplement and revise it:

> But if it seems that I should change any of these interpretations (and perhaps I should change many), if fate does not stand in my way, I will inform you in my *Quaestiones*, which I have already begun in my spare time and will bring to light when they are ready.[110]

But Partenio's *Quaestiones* never materialized, and no one else attempted a major revision of his commentary. Three humanists who had the ability to do so—Poliziano, Filippo Beroaldo, and Ermolao Barbaro—published interpretations only of individual passages—Poliziano in the *Miscellanea*, Beroaldo in *Annotationes Centum* (1488), and Barbaro in *Castigationes Plinianae* (1492).[111] Palladio Fosco and Alessandro Guarino wrote full commentaries and managed to correct some of Partenio's mistakes, but neither criticized or re-examined his work systematically.

Palladio and Guarino were similar to Partenio in intellect and accomplishment—diligent rather than gifted, each of only modest repute among his contemporaries, each known to posterity principally for his commentary on Catullus. Palladio Fosco belonged to the same generation as Partenio. He began his career in Padua in the 1480s, and tried unsuccessfully for Sabellico's position in Udine (1483). He became friendly with the Dalmatian humanists in Padua, especially Donato Civalleli of Zara and Alvise Cippico of Trau, later bishop of Famagosta. With the encouragement of Civalleli he settled permanently in Dalmatia in 1493, teaching first at Zara (1493–1516) and finally at Capodistria, where he died in 1520.[112] He seems to have had no particular interest in Catullus that inspired him to write his commentary (1496).[113] Alessandro Guarino was born in 1486, at about the time that Partenio published his commentary. At 19 he inherited his father's position at the university and court of

Ferrara, where he lived out a long and successful life as courtier and professor.[114] His Catullus is a labour of love, inspired by the desire to preserve his father's work from neglect and oblivion. As much his father's work as his own, it bears the stamp of the 1480s and '90s much more than of his own generation.

Palladio made a few original contributions to Catullan interpretation (as when he made sense of 35 by realizing that its hero Caecilius had composed a poem on the *Magna Mater*), but more often he purveyed other people's ideas. Sometimes his borrowings are easily traced. The interpretations of Beroaldo and Barbaro appear in his commentary, for example, together with many of Avanzi's emendations—the former for the most part ostentatiously credited and the latter shamelessly plagiarized.[115] Often, however, his sources are less obvious, as in his explanation of *custos . . . Cretum* in 58*b*.1 (*Non custos si fingar ille Cretum*). Partenio had identified the *custos* as Daedalus, but Palladio knew better:

As Apollonius and Pausanias tell us, after Jupiter had seized Europa and carried her away to Crete, he set guards on the shore to fight off her father Agenor, and among them was Thalus, a man of great speed, who could circle the whole island on foot in a single day. Catullus is thinking of him, not of Daedalus, as many think.[116]

He had a better idea also at 63. 42–3, whose Alexandrian learning had defeated both Partenio and his predecessors. The verses describe the awakening of Attis ('Sleep fled swiftly away from Attis, now awakened, and the goddess Pasithea received him in her eager embrace'):

ibi Somnus excitam Attin fugiens citus abiit;
trepidante eum recepit dea Pasithea sinu.

But the traditional text was confused. Partenio printed the garbled version he found in Calfurnio:

Ubi *sonus excitum* atym fugiens citus abiit:
Trepidantem eum recepit dea *pasitheo* sinu.
(63. 42–3, Partenio 1491)

Misled by *sonus* in 42, he wrongly referred *trepidantem eum* to Attis and *dea* to Cybele and glossed *sinu pasitheo*: 'in her bosom holding all the gods, with room for all the gods. For Cybele is called in Greek Pasithea . . .'.[117] But Palladio prints *somnus* in

63. 42 and sees that it is the antecedent of *eum*. He prints *pasithea* in 43:

I emend, *pasithea*. For Pasithea was one of the nymphs, whom Juno in Book 14 of the *Iliad* promises as a bride to Somnus if he attacks the eyes of Jupiter who is aiding the Trojans against the Greeks. These are Homer's verses . . . [*Il.* 14. 267–9]. Therefore the goddess Pasithea received her trembling husband Somnus.[118]

Palladio's corrections in 58*b* and 63 are not original. He probably found *somnus* in Avanzi,[119] and he took his explanations of Thallus and Pasithea from Janus Lascaris, as Avanzi tells us in the second edition of his *Emendationes* (1500):

Read *pasithea sinu*. . . . From Lascaris we have learned that Pasithea in the fourteenth book of Homer was the one Juno promised to Somnus if he should close Jupiter's eyes in the Trojan war. Likewise Lascaris warns that Thallus is meant in Catullus in that verse *Non custos si ego fingar ille Cretum*.[120]

Although Palladio undoubtedly deserved the rebuke implied in Avanzi's punctilious footnote, his wide if unscrupulous research had its uses, for it allowed him to correct Partenio in more than a few places and to present his readers with helpful information from various and sometimes unlikely sources. Unfortunately, however, he was better at purloining other scholars' interpretations than at thinking of his own. If he found no help in his sources, he could do little except to paraphrase Partenio or keep silent.

Guarino had personal reasons to find fault with Partenio, but he is less critical than we might expect, and his corrections are sporadic and on the whole unimportant. Surprisingly, priority is almost never the issue. It was important to Guarino to claim credit for his father, and he is quick enough to do so against Avanzi, Sabellico, and even Poliziano, but his principal complaint against Partenio is ignorance.[121] Partenio was vulnerable to the charge, but Guarino himself did not have the learning to make it stick. At 10. 27 and 50. 18 Partenio saw that the last syllables in the second conjugation imperatives *mane* and *cave* must be short in order to scan. Not understanding the true explanation (iambic shortening), he wrongly imagined that the verbs belonged somehow to the third conjugation.[122] Guarino scornfully refutes him:

But when those who read *deferri mane* [10. 27] say that the last syllable in *mane* is shortened by the poet as if it descended from the third conjugation, let them look to what they say. For who has ever heard or seen or read *maneo*, *manis* of the third conjugation in the authors? Nor does the same thing happen in this word as in *caveo*, which is sometimes found in the second, sometimes in the third conjugation.[123]

The example is typical of Guarino's corrections in that it confuses as much as it clarifies. Both Partenio and Guarino are partly wrong. Partenio is right about the text and scansion, but gives the wrong explanation. Guarino correctly rejects the explanation, but misunderstands the scansion and argues wrongly for his father's drastically rewritten line: *ferri mane. mane inquio puellae* (10. 27, Guarino 1521).[124] The first *mane*, he explains, is the adverb, 'in the morning', the second, the imperative of *maneo*. No one seems to have cared much for Guarino's emendation, and it was heartily condemned by Pierio Valeriano in his lectures only a few months after the publication of the *Expositiones*:

Good god, how much the men of our time have allowed themselves! . . . One can scarcely tolerate those who have lopped off a third of *deferri*, the word a foot and a half long that is in all the texts, in order to make *ferri*. And then, as if in this they had committed too small a crime, they crammed in that nonsense, *mane, mane*, which I should have thought was ridiculous even to children.[125]

Filial piety moves Guarino to his greatest fury when he thinks that Partenio has slighted or overlooked Battista's corrections. Cat. 64. 278–301 contains a catalogue of the divine guests at the wedding of Peleus and Thetis. Second in the list is the river god Penios:

confestim Penios adest, viridantia Tempe,
Tempe, quae silvae cingunt super impendentes,
†Minosim linquens †doris celebranda choreis,
non vacuos: (64. 285–8)

The text was corrupt in the manuscripts at 287–8, and Partenio printed:

Mniosion linquens doris celebranda choreis
Nonacriis: (64. 287–8, Partenio 1491)

Although his interpretation is confused and inconsistent, he clearly believes that Doris is a third guest:

Doris: *adest* is understood from the previous line [285]. Moreover, Doris was goddess of the sea, daughter of old Ocean and Tethys and wife of Nereus, as Hesiod sings. *Chloris* (goddess of flowers) is also read, but if this reading should be approved *Mniosium* will have no explanation. And so I think these two words are corrupt and deserve vigorous complaint.[126]

Mniosium is a word of Partenio's own invention, a compound that he claims means 'god of the seaweed', hence Nereus.[127] He dismisses other possible readings: 'Some read *minosium*, that is, the Cretan Sea (from king Minos), but such a reading and explanation are utterly ridiculous . . . .'[128] He knows that *Nonacriis* means 'Arcadian', but cannot explain it in its context: 'Let others see why Catullus says Doris is to be celebrated by Arcadian choruses.'[129]

Neither Avanzi nor Palladio could explain 287–8, and the reaction of each is characteristic: Avanzi admits his ignorance,[130] and Palladio prints Partenio's text without comment. Guarino, however, had both his father's explanation and a hearty contempt for Partenio's neglect of it:

In this place certain people turning the poet's words upside down got stuck in such inextricable mire that they could by no means escape. For while they were undecided about whether to read *Doris* or *Chloris*, *Mniosion* or *Minosion*, they did not find what explanation to give. But they concluded that they should complain vigorously about these words, and while they thought that the explanation of others was utterly ridiculous, by their ridicule they made themselves laughable. But if they had understood the poet's true reading, which was pointed out earlier by my father, if they had not corrupted the order, they would not have left it to others to see 'why Catullus said Doris was to be celebrated by Nonacrian choruses'—which Catullus did not say anyway, but which they dreamed that he did by distorting Catullus' word order and the words themselves.[131]

Guarino banishes Doris and tidies up the syntax, arguing that the true text is:

Nessonidum linquens claris celebranda choreis,
Non vacuus, (64. 287–8, Guarinus 1521).

In spite of his air of scornful superiority, however, the fact is that Guarino's criticisms do not add up to very much. He is often petty, and seldom totally convincing; unlike his predecessors, he corrects no major mistakes. Seemingly content with the occasional petulant comment, he never undertakes a systematic reappraisal of either Partenio or Catullus.

FIRMANUS SALIUS AND THE *MENTULA* CYCLE

In his preface Partenio had imagined himself at the head of a critical tradition that would move step-by-step to a complete understanding of Catullus. He visualized a process in which his successors would find and correct his mistakes and recognize and build on his achievements, and their successors would do likewise. Instead, Catullan interpretation, like more ancient and venerable critical traditions before it, set out on a convoluted, crab-wise progress. Partenio, for all his faults, confronted Catullus directly, but Palladio and Guarino saw the text through Partenio's commentary, as through a veil or filter. Their commentaries are reactions to Partenio rather than to Catullus, and it is Partenio rather than Catullus who provides the genesis for their ideas; for just as the first edition had become the foundation for later editions, so Partenio's work became the base commentary, the source and foundation for the interpretations of his successors. The result was an accretion of information and misinformation, corrections well-taken and irrelevant. Partenio's errors were embellished, and new errors were introduced. This depressing process could be illustrated with dozens of examples, but let us see how it works out in four appropriately unedifying cases—the epigrams in which Catullus lampoons Caesar's henchman Mamurra, whom he attacks under the insulting sobriquet *Mentula* ('prick').

In 94 Catullus plays with the name *Mentula* ('Mentula is an adulterer, an adulterer is Mentula indeed. It is just as they say: the pot gathers its own greens.'). But the poem had been transmitted together with 93, and Partenio printed the two together thus:

In Caesarem

Nil nimium studeo tibi caesar velle placere
Nec si orem utrum sis salvus an alter homo.
Mentula moechatur: mechatur mentula certe
Hoc est quod dicunt ipsa olera olla legit.

(93–94, Partenius 1491)

His interpretation was the natural if mistaken result of the conjunction of the two couplets. Caesar's reputation did the rest:

As C. Julius Caesar entices the mind of the poet with flattery, Catullus castigates him with the stinging disgrace of his adulteries.[132]

He explains *Mentula* as '*Caesar mentulatus*', and takes the last verse as a proverb 'against adulterers and . . . pederasts'.[133] A few years later Filippo Beroaldo saw that 93 was the poem against Caesar that Quintilian had in mind when he said: 'some poet denies caring whether Caesar is black or white [*utrum Caesar ater an albus homo sit*].'[134] Accordingly, he corrected to *ater an albus homo* in 93. 2.[135] Palladio prints Beroaldo's correction (*Nec si orem utrum sis albus an ater homo*) and combines it with the interpretation he had found in Partenio:

Wishing to censure the adulteries of Julius Caesar the poet denies that he makes an effort to please him even if he asks whether he is white . . . or black.[136]

He calls the last verse 'an old proverb against adulterers'.[137] Guarino takes the process a step further, if not precisely forward. He prints 93. 2 as it appears in modern editions (*Nec scire utrum sis albus, an ater homo*), and makes it an integral part of his interpretation:

So Catullus says he does not want to know whether Caesar is white (that is gentlemanly and good) or black (evil and base), because if he wanted to ask this question, immediately (since he is prone to lust), Caesar's penis would become erect.[138]

Like his predecessors Guarino calls the last verse a proverb, but 'a proverb against those who are so inclined to some crime that they cannot help transgressing', and he takes it as a reference to Caesar and his incontinent behaviour.[139] Even though Guarino's interpretation is far-fetched and bizarre, it is still a recognizable descendant of Partenio's. Like Palladio he embellished and elaborated Partenio's original explanation and even modified it to incorporate new information (the emendation of 93. 2), but neither questioned the faulty premise supporting the entire structure—that 93 and 94 were a single poem and that Mentula was Caesar.

In 105 Catullus attacks Mamurra's literary pretensions ('Mentula tries to climb the Pipleian mountain; the Muses hurl him headlong with their pitchforks.'):[140]

Mentula conatur Pipleium scandere montem:
Musae furcillis praecipitem eiciunt. (105)

Partenio prints the text under the title awarded to it in the first edition, *De eius mentula*, but his own title, *De mentula sua*, appears in the commentary and shows us the direction his thoughts were taking:

> The poet attempted to deflower a certain virgin whom he had found, but was prevented both by the girl's reluctance and by the obstacles and barriers of her virginity. Humorously and wittily he says that he had tried to climb the Pipleian mountain of the Muses, but was thrown down by the Muses. By the Pipleian mountain he means the *eugium*, which is a certain part in the middle of the female pudenda . . .[141]

Palladio picks up this interpretation and adds a second: 'But some say that the poet is confessing that he had wanted to write obscene verses but was prevented by the Muses from doing so.'[142] Now Guarino:

> The Pipleian mountain was consecrated to the Muses by the Thracians . . . whence I think that the argument of this epigram is that the poet tried to debauch some learned girl or boy against his will—and thus by the Pipleian mountain he means the learned boy by a metaphor in which he persists, using the verb 'climb', by which he suggests 'enter' and 'have intercourse'. Moreover, he adds in jest: *musae furcillis eiiciunt praecipitem*, because he could not achieve his wish. He says this metaphorically . . . because the boy endowed with learning did not want to subject himself to lust and perhaps refused, writing an epigram to the poet. . . . We can interpret differently—that Mentula is a man's proper name or at least that someone was contemptuously called Mentula by the poet, and that the sense of the poem is that the poet says Mentula tried to climb the Pipleian mountain, that is, turn out to be a good poet, but that the Muses threw him down since he was of a perverse nature

and fat-headed, that is, thick-witted and ill-suited to composing verses. And perhaps he was the poet's rival in writing verses.[143]

Guarino closes his long paragraph with a criticism of Partenio:

But some think that he wanted to have intercourse with some virgin, but was unable to. . . . But let them explain by what argument they want the poet to mean hymen or *eugium* . . . by the Pipleian mountain, and why he said he was thrown down by the Muses.[144]

Guarino rejects Partenio's interpretation for the very good reason that it does not take all of the evidence of the poem into account. Why the Muses and the Pipleian mountain? But he has not banished Partenio as thoroughly as he thinks, since his own elaborate scenario of the learned and unwilling boy arises directly from Partenio's literal reading of *mentula*—a reading that he is not inclined to question. For him as for Palladio an erotic interpretation with its roots in Partenio is the first and presumably preferred explanation. His second interpretation, that Mentula is Catullus' pseudonym for a bad poet, may owe something to Palladio, but probably has its origin in Avanzi's trenchant comment in the second edition of his *Emendationes* (1500): 'he means nothing obscene, but Firmanus Salius, a bad poet.'[145]

We will return to Firmanus Salius presently, for he is an important shadow character in the Mentula poems, but first we must note another trait in the developing critical tradition, the tendency to present alternative and incompatible explanations. Sometimes, as in this case, it is possible to infer that one interpretation is preferred, but often the commentator seems unwilling or unable to choose among several possibilities. Such listing of alternatives was the method of ancient and medieval scholiasts, who were often epitomizing or cannibalizing the ideas of their predecessors—conflating but not reconciling their different opinions.[146] Although Palladio and Guarino had no long tradition of exegesis to draw on, they followed the conventions of the genre.

In our last examples, 114 and 115, Catullus satirizes Mentula's estate at Firmum. The two poems were transmitted together and were treated as a single epigram until the first Aldine edition. The difficulties arose from textual difficulties at the beginning of 114 and the end of 115. Mynors' text reads:

Firmano saltu non falso Mentula dives
fertur, qui tot res in se habet egregias (114. 1–2)
. . . .
omnia magna haec sunt, tamen ipsest maximus ultro,
non homo, sed vero mentula magna minax. (115. 7–8)

Partenio printed the traditional text of Calfurnio and the *editio princeps* (the principal differences from Mynors are italicized):

De Salio Firmano[147]

Firmanus salius non falso mentula dives
Fertur: qui tot[148] res in se habet egregias.
. . . .
Omnia magna haec sunt tamen ipse est maximus *ultor*
Non homo: sed vere mentula magna minax.[149]
(114. 1–2, 115. 7–8, Partenio 1491)

We may translate Mynors' text at 114. 1–2 thus: 'Mentula is rightly called rich because of his estate at Firmum which has in it so many fine things.' Now Partenio: 'Firmanus Salius who has so many fine things in his possession is rightly called a rich *mentula*.' Partenio drew the natural conclusion from his text:

With bitter jests he attacks Salius Firmanus who foolishly boasts that he is rich and prosperous thanks to his great *mentula*, and as a consequence haughtily threatens his enemies as if he were very powerful.[150]

Two more glosses in Partenio complete the picture:

Quicquam fructus [114. 4]: . . . For this man, being well-hung (*mentulatus*), attained much wealth by the adulteries and titillation of old women, but squandered everything as soon as possible by luxurious extravagance.
Ipse est maximus ultor [115. 7]: As he himself boasts that he can punish all injuries by this wealth of his *mentula*.[151]

Palladio embellishes the description of Firmanus, making him not merely *mentulatus* as in Partenio, but *bene mentulatus*, and explains his name Salius: 'The Salii were priests of Mars whom Numa founded.' He explicitly links his profits to prostitution, and expands his clientele to include 'bearded catamites' as well as 'sex-starved old women'. Firmanus now threatens to punish injuries 'with his *mentula* alone', which Palladio thinks is called 'an estate' (*saltus*) since it is the source of his riches.[152]

Guarino has yet another version of 114. 1–2 (*Firmani saltus non falso Mentula dives/fertur*), which I fear we must translate, 'The estate of Firmanus is rightly called *Mentula dives*.' Here is his explanation:

I think in Catullus' time there was a certain well-hung Firmanus, who because of the size of his *mentula* became so rich from adultery that he bought himself a farm, which from this very fact was called '*Mentula Dives*', but although he became rich he spent everything extravagantly. . . . But it must be noted that in some texts not *Firmani saltus*, but *Firmanus saltus* or *salius* is read, and then this will be the sense of the epigram, that Firmanus with the cognomen Saltus or Salius got rich from adulteries because of the size of his *mentula*, whence he was called 'Mentula Dives' . . .[153]

Guarino separates 114 and 115, and explains *mentula* in 115. 1 (*Mentula habet instar triginta iugera prati*) thus: '*Mentula*: i.e. Firmanus with the cognomen Mentula Dives . . .'.[154] This is the second explanation he had given above for 114; he seems to have forgotten the first, that Mentula Dives was the name of Firmanus' estate. He has two explanations for 115. 7–8:

> Omnia magna haec sunt. tamen ipse est maximus *ultor*
> Non homo, sed vere mentula magna Minax.
>
> (115. 7–8, Guarinus)

He is the greatest avenger [*ultor*], but not because he is feared as a man avenging but because it is his great *mentula* that threatens punishment, since everyone fears to injure him lest he punish them with buggery. There is another reading, *ultro*, not *ultor*, so that the sense is, 'all these things are great, but further . . .'[155]

But enough. It is easy to get caught up in the adventures of the nonexistent man from Firmum—Salian dancer, adaptable prostitute, big spender, and fearful possessor of a *mentula magna minax* with which he can confound and abuse his enemies. Each round of explanations is more complex and bizarre than its predecessor, and each owes its origin to Partenio's initial scenario. The original mistaken idea is like some hardy organism that evolves into stranger and stranger creatures without losing its distinctive, foolish identity. Good ideas, on the other hand, seem to be ephemera that produce no issue. While Partenio, Palladio, and Guarino were spinning their lays about the Mentula poems, Avanzi was making some shrewd observations. In the 1500 edition of his *Emendationes* he thought that 94 and 105 were both directed against Firmanus Salius insultingly called Mentula.[156] In the postscript, which contains a few afterthoughts, he banishes Firmanus Salius and corrects the text of 114. 1: 'Read *Firmanus saltus*, not *salius*. For he is talking about the estate at Firmum of a certain bad poet who was called Mentula.'[157] In the first Aldine (1502), Avanzi entitles 114 *De Saltu Firmano*, separates it from 115, and changes the first words of 114. 1 to read: *Firmano saltu*. He also correctly separates 94 from 93 and awards the appropriate titles.[158] But these ideas receive only passing notice in Guarino, and worse still, Avanzi himself seems to have lost confidence in them, for in the second Aldine (1515) he has reunited 93 and 94, 114 and 115, and resurrected the irrepressible Firmanus Salius:[159]

> Firmanus salius non falso Mentula, dives
> (114. 1, Venice 1515).

The case of Firmanus Salius seems to present us with a kind of Darwinism manqué or literary Gresham's law, but in fact the principle we have observed both in the interpretation of the Mentula poems and throughout the early commentary tradition is much simpler: the first explanation, whatever its merits, tends to survive and to form the core of subsequent explanations, even when it is explicitly rejected. Given the abilities of Partenio and the state of Catullan studies in the fifteenth century, the first idea is often wrong, but the process also produces its successes—for example, the sympathetic interpretation of 63. The difficulty is that successes and failures alike are fortuitous, and that the commentaries by their very nature amass information and ideas without evaluating them. With the exception of Poliziano, none of our interpreters had a consistent point of view or was directed by a single critical method. But Poliziano's method was more philological than literary; he worked on a small scale, and his chapters in the *Miscellanea* were designed to explicate individual passages, not the entire corpus. At the end of their first half century, then, Catullan studies still lacked an interpreter who could place his ideas within a general critical framework and who had either the philological and literary sense or the scholarly acumen to build on his predecessors' interpretations without being overwhelmed by them.

3

Praelectio: Pierio Valeriano at the University of Rome

> age, esto Catullus primus, qui profecturis in poetice discipulis proponatur.
>
> (Pierio Valeriano)

IN November of 1521 Pierio Valeriano began a series of lectures on Catullus at the University of Rome, at a moment when he was at the height of his success and Roman poetry and humanism were enjoying a golden age under the patronage of Pope Leo X.[1] Valeriano was well suited to his task: he was a poet as well as a philologist, he had an interpretative method, and, as we shall see, he was an entertaining and lively lecturer. His lectures are firmly grounded in their historical and cultural context and were affected, sometimes drastically, by outside events.

Valeriano was born Giovanni Pietro Valeriano dalle Fosse in Belluno in 1477 and spent his youth in relative poverty, although with the aid of his uncle, the famous traveller and antiquarian Urbano Bolzanio, he managed to acquire a humanist education under the best teachers in Venice and Padua.[2] It was Sabellico himself who changed his name from Pietro to Pierio in honour of the Pierian Muses.[3] In 1509 Valeriano came to Rome, where he found success and well-placed patrons almost at once, becoming the client of Egidio da Viterbo and of both Bartolomeo and Gian-Francesco della Rovere, and finally of his uncle's former pupil, Cardinal Giovanni de' Medici, who became Pope Leo X in 1513.[4] By 1521 he was both an intimate and an official of the papal court, as well as the holder of two lucrative sinecures and the tutor of the Pope's young nephews, Alessandro and Ippolito de' Medici.[5] He was a well-known Neo-Latin poet and a successful humanist. He had edited Lactantius (1502) and translated Lucian's dialogue, *De aulicorum aerumnis* (1516); in June of 1521 he published his important textual study of Vergil, *Castigationes et varietates Virgilianae lectionis*.[6] His greatest and most influential works were still to come—the short dialogue *De litteratorum infelicitate*, inspired by the destruction of books and the suffering of individual scholars during the Sack of Rome in 1527, and his life's work, the monumental *Hieroglyphica*, which catalogued and explained the signs and symbols of the Egyptians.[7]

In 1521 Roman humanism was flourishing, and Leo was its principal patron. His election in 1513 had been heralded generally as ushering in a new era of arts and letters. Even the 'talking' statue Pasquino voiced the prevailing optimism, saluting the new Pope as 'a lover of Peace and the Muses'. Pasquino had become the repository for the versified opinions of students and *litterati*. Verses were attached to the statue at any time, but especially on St Mark's Day (25 April), when Pasquino assumed the *persona* of an appropriate mythological character to comment on the year's events.[8] In 1513 he spoke in the character of Apollo:

I used to be an exile,
But I'm back in Leo's reign.
So burn your midnight oil, boys,
And follow in my train,
For no one leaves my Leo
Without a handsome gain.
Bards will sing for prizes,
And they'll not sing in vain.[9]

Leo lived up to Pasquino's expectations. He patronized not only the poets, but even Pasquino himself, for beginning in 1515 the considerable expenses of Pasquino's festival were financed from papal revenues.[10] Poets congregated at Leo's court, and were duly rewarded,[11] but they also enjoyed less formal gatherings—principally in the gardens of Valeriano's friends, Angelo Colocci and Johannes Goritz, called Coricius. Colocci was a wealthy antiquarian with literary interests.[12] Goritz was most famous for the annual gatherings of humanists at his celebration of the feast of St Anne (26 July), which focused on the altar of St Anne with the Madonna and Child that he had commissioned from Andrea Sansovino in the church of S. Agostino. The poets, including Valeriano, wrote verses in honour of the statue, Goritz, and one another.[13]

The Roman humanists enjoyed a life of patronage, poetry, and good fellowship, but their world was more fragile than they

Plate 6: Philippe Galle's engraving of Pierio Valeriano in *Imagines L. Doctorum Virorum* (1587). (Department of Special Collections, Van Pelt-Dietrich Library, University of Pennsylvania.)

knew. It was shattered abruptly with Leo's premature and unexpected death on 1 December 1521.[14] Valeriano had given only two of his Catullus lectures (an inaugural lecture and a general introduction to Catullus) before the catastrophe. The opening of the third lecture conveys the general mood of sorrow and desolation:

> Although my talent has been buried by long endurance of troubles and of the losses I have incurred in the death of my lord, Pope Leo X, who was snatched away so suddenly and so long before his time, I have not been too broken by so many misfortunes, so many difficulties, so many hardships, so many calamities (such is my affection for you, studious youths, and such my concern for your progress) to return at once to my studies, as soon as I observed, even in the absence of the new pope summoned from so far away and in the virtual desolation of letters, that the school was open, and when I saw that students were coming around the lecture halls. Therefore, whatever little bit of attention I have been able to pull together from my ruined and vanquished intellect I have turned entirely to a consideration of those matters I thought would be useful to you.[15]

Valeriano's lectures must have been suspended for the whole of December and at least the first two weeks of January, for the new pope was elected only on 9 January 1522. The man who had to be 'summoned from so far away' was Adrian VI, a Dutchman, and the last non-Italian pope for 450 years. He had been elected, almost in a fit of whimsy, by a conclave exhausted from weeks of wrangling and stalemate, as Valeriano laments in a contemporary poem:[16]

> Adrian is made Pope by everyone's vote.
> Yet (who would believe it?) against everyone's will.
> This is the might of the gods (of the gods!).
> This is the hidden will of the gods,
> that those who despise the ship of state's power
> may learn to obey the will of a viper,
> that the Cardinals who hated each other
> might have a leader hated by all.[17]

Adrian's election was a blow to Roman humanists, for he was known to be strict in his beliefs, ascetic by temperament, and unenthusiastic about art and secular letters. But in January of 1522 he was in Spain—many months from Rome—a small if ominous cloud on the cultural horizon. Meanwhile, Valeriano's lectures continued. They broke off for the summer, and resumed again in the autumn—a few weeks after Adrian finally arrived in August 1522 to find Rome in the grip of the terrible pestilence that Valeriano and his other detractors were to dub the *pestis Hadrianea*.[18] The new pope reacted sharply and puritanically to what he considered immoral and paganizing in Roman humanism; his possible influence on Valeriano's lectures will concern us presently. Adrian died barely a year after arriving in Rome, and was succeeded by Leo's cousin, Giulio de' Medici (Clement VII), whose clients and friends hoped for a new era of enlighted patronage. But in vain. Clement VII had acceded to a papacy crippled by debt and beset by the realities of politics and war. Rome was sacked and pillaged by the combined Spanish and German troops of Emperor Charles V in May 1527, and the humanists and their works were scattered to the winds.

Among the casualties was Valeriano's work on Catullus. Pietro Melini, a wealthy young poet and one of Valeriano's closest friends, had had the lectures transcribed as Valeriano delivered them, and he kept the manuscript in his library, which was largely dispersed or destroyed in the Sack of Rome.[19] Only a portion of the lectures survived, but Melini faithfully gathered the remnants together and sent them to Valeriano's former pupil, Ippolito de' Medici,[20] with the following letter:

Pietro Melini with greetings to Ippolito de' Medici.
When I returned home after the enemy had left my country and Clement was restored to his seat, it was my first concern, most magnificent Ippolito, to see again and gather up all the books (both my own and those of friends that were being kept at my house), so that I might array them in a safe harbour, so to speak, after such a foul and lengthy storm. And when I was turning them over solicitously and carefully and had learned from the Moorish serving boy, whom I had left at home by himself, that many had been torn apart, not only by the enemy but also by our own men (some were thrown into the fire, some were pulled apart by savage hands and torn to pieces, some, too, were lost), I was grief-stricken, since I rated the loss as worse by far than all the others and impossible ever to repair. Nevertheless, by good fortune some mementos of our friend Pierio turned up in the miserable destruction of this catastrophe—notes that he had jotted down on some small sheets of paper when he was lecturing on Catullus at the University of Rome. In addition to these there there was much other

material that we had ordered to be taken down and transcribed as he spoke; this was soon gathered together and placed in order. Although most of it has perished, lest it be lost completely someday, I wanted to send these transcriptions to you, (since now, as I have heard, he has been forced to go and see to his family affairs), so that in this most undeserved exile you might have at least pleasant reading matter to divert you, even though it is not yet complete, for I thought it much better to put this mutilated and disjointed work into your hands than to suppress it, in this matter following our example, and especially your own, since because you are gripped by a remarkable desire for ancient works you are accustomed to admire even a single foot or a hand or a head of some statue, nor do you seek these out with less diligence than you would the whole, since even from these you assess the talent, workmanship, and skill of the artist. I would like you to have these writings of your teacher published and not to be afraid to do so without his knowledge or consent. For he will surely accept what has been done both on my advice (for I am such a great friend of his) and on your authority (since he has enjoyed your patronage for so many years), and he will not reject our judgement of him. Farewell, and love us and him as you do.
Rome, 1 March 1528.[21]

Ippolito did not publish the lectures, but they are preserved in a manuscript (or rather, manuscript fragment) in the Vatican Library. The fragment is substantial. There are 249 folios, which contain two introductory lectures and detailed discussions of poems 1–22.[22] The manuscript contains no breaks except that the discussions of the obscene poems 15, 16, and 21 are missing—an important point that we will consider after looking at the lectures themselves.

PRODESSE ET DELECTARE: THE INTRODUCTORY LECTURES

Valeriano was not the first humanist to lecture on Catullus. It is likely, as we have seen, that Puteolano promoted the sales of his edition with a series of lectures at the University of Bologna; Calfurnio regularly lectured on Catullus in Padua at least up to 1493; Partenio lectured at his school in Verona in the 1480s.[23] But the lectures of Puteolano and Calfurnio are lost, and those of Partenio were revised to make his published commentary.

Valeriano's lectures have come down to us nearly as he delivered them, if we can believe their title:

> The Lectures on Catullus of Pierio Valeriano of Belluno, Professor of the University of Rome, Taken Down Word for Word as He Spoke, through the Care of Some of his Listeners.[24]

There is another difference as well. Partenio was a schoolmaster; Puteolano and Calfurnio, their university positions notwithstanding, were comparative small-fry. But Valeriano was a major figure. His professorial debut, in the last halcyon days of Roman humanism before the death of Leo X, was an important literary event. We could guess as much from his position at the papal court and from his poetic and philological achievements; the presence of a professional scribe, provided 'through the care of some of his listeners', confirms the impression. Valeriano was not unconscious of his own celebrity, and he designed his lectures accordingly. They were to be learned and instructive, to be sure, but also personal, literary, and witty. Thanks to the faithful amanuensis, who has recorded interruptions, asides, and digressions along with the central material of the lectures, we are able to catch some of the flavour of his performance.

By Valeriano's time the form for inaugural lectures was well established. The first lecture praised the liberal arts and encouraged the students to apply themselves; the second (sometimes omitted) praised the author under discussion and again exhorted the students.[25] Valeriano's opening lectures conform to the conventions of their genre. The first, in particular, is typical—a rhetorical set-piece on all the fields of human knowledge.[26] But Valeriano's focus is less on the arts than on the man who would study and interpret them—the *grammaticus*, who is expected to be master of all the arts:

> there is no discipline that anyone can understand completely, and yet the *grammaticus* alone is expected to accomplish everything. He alone must explain every type of writing, he alone must commit to memory all poets, historians and orators, he alone must investigate philosophers, mathematicians, lawyers, and even theologians. He is not to be pardoned or forgiven for anything, and they demand not only that he be instructed in the knowledge of matters both human and divine, but that he know something even of trivial things, so that not even the smallest detail can escape him. But I wonder why they do not add to these stipulations that the mortal *grammaticus* must be some kind of god.[27]

This infallible, impossible *grammaticus* is a straw-man, ultimately descended from the ambitious description in Quintilian (*Inst. Orat*. 1. 4. 3–4), but also meant to evoke Poliziano's famous account in the *Lamia*:

To study and interpret every type of writer—poets, historians, orators, philosophers, doctors, lawyers—this is the task of the *grammatici*.[28]

Valeriano's rejection of such a model for himself may be partly polemical (he has some harsh words for Poliziano later on in his lectures), but its main purpose is to highlight his own qualities and aspirations. He is not an austere polymath, but a teacher with a fatherly concern for his charges, whom he will educate 'in literature and in character' (*litteris et moribus*) to the attainment of virtue, by which he means both moral excellence and literary ambition:

But if these [intellectual qualities] are not found precisely in me, at least my dutiful concern for your progress will help you, and my watchfulness and care. I can be useful by admonition, advice, and encouragement. And I am persuaded of this by the progress of many young men who have hastened successfully on their way, stirred by my encouragement to virtue.

And so think of me thus: that today I must take on a parent's affection for you, and that I must succeed those who bore you and brought you up, and eagerly wish you to be educated in literature and character. Wherefore, my ambition will not limit itself to your understanding what the authors have written, but I will also strive to the best of my ability to get you to try to imitate them and to keep pace with the authors themselves.

I hope that those whom lively virtue arouses will first apply their talent to imitation and then begin to vie with the ancient writers themselves. And if I cannot help you in this by example, since I have not been trained much in speaking, I will at least perform the function of a whetstone, which although it cuts nothing itself, can sharpen steel.[29]

The emphasis on moral and literary teaching continues in the second lecture, where Valeriano sets out his method. It is conventional among the Greeks, so he says, to ask eight questions when one embarks on the study of any author—four before and four during the work:

Before the work: what is the intention of the writer, what profit will result if we set ourselves to reading it, what is its title, is the work authentic or false? In the work: what order of reading is established, into how many chapters or sections is it divided, what is its method of instruction (for all books teach), and finally, to what part of the encyclopaedia does it belong?[30]

He passes briefly over some of the questions: the title (*C. Valerii Catulli Poetae Lyrici Epigrammata*), authenticity of the work (indisputably genuine), the number of sections (three: lyrics, epithalamia, elegies and epigrams), the method of instruction (easy). But he treats the others more fully.

Thus, we learn that Catullus' intention is sometimes to benefit his readers, sometimes to delight them:

The poet is certainly useful when he celebrates virtues and does not allow the achievements of illustrious men to perish, by whose example others might be kindled to a desire for glory. He is useful when he chastises vice, criticizes evil ways, and attempts to deter mankind from imitating the wicked men he chastises in his poetry. He is pleasing when he expresses the emotions of love, dwells on charm, enticements, and delight, sings praises to the gods and composes epithalamia.[31]

Prodesse et delectare. The formulation is neither novel nor conspicuously appropriate, but Valeriano will find it surprisingly useful. Moral teaching is the issue also in his answer to the question: 'to what part of the encyclopaedia (or as we might say, "to what branch of knowledge") does the work belong?' The form of Catullus' poetry belongs to Music, but its content to Moral Philosophy:

since he expresses the emotions of love, since in his lamentation for his brother he concedes to nature the magnitude of his grief and does his duty to piety, since he recognizes the gods whose rites he sings, since he celebrates men worthy of praise, since he sets a limit to pleasure, since emerging from the whirling depths of the passions at times he pulls himself together and prudently embraces fortitude, justice, and temperance . . .[32]

Literary training is the focus in his answers to the remaining questions: what profit can the reader expect from Catullus, and when in the curriculum should he be studied (or in Valeriano's words, 'what order of reading is established')? Catullus is useful as a teacher of style,[33] and he is to be read when the student is best able to make use of him as a model:

I believe that the place for this book is immediately after the rudiments of philology (*grammatice*) have been instilled and understood or when the youth begins to compose something with his own talent—both because the subjects are short for the most part and accordingly easy for everyone to suit to his talent, and because they are varied and accordingly can imprint many forms of imitation on the minds of readers so that lively and fertile talents may attempt to express them now in one metre, now in another.[34]

Although the moral and the literary are Valeriano's essential categories, they tend to overlap throughout the lectures, as do the roles of poet, interpreter, and reader. Sometimes Valeriano attributes quite different purposes to the poet and to his interpreter. Thus, immediately after describing Catullus' aims (*prodesse et delectare*), Valeriano explains his own, which are mundane and clearly subject to personal and practical considerations:

I must explain with what purpose I have chosen Catullus to interpret rather than another author. The first reason was that a large number of highly talented young men who are taken with the charm and elegance of the Latin language, well aware of what they could gain from Catullus, beseeched me with daily requests to lecture on him. Then, because I had to lecture during the holidays and with that period as an interruption, a brief subject, which could be explained in a single lecture, seemed more useful for teaching. But most persuasive of all was the advice of outstanding men to begin with the best.[35]

For the most part, however, he conceives the roles of poet and interpreter as fundamentally similar: each is to be a teacher of both moral and stylistic excellence.

Valeriano emphasizes the similarities between poet and interpreter to further his literary purposes. In the first lecture he replaced the ideal of the infallible *grammaticus* with his own more humane and personal vision. The allusion to Quintilian and Poliziano surely did not escape his audience. In the second lecture he produces a more elaborate transformation—from Greek philological method to Greek and Neoplatonic theories of inspiration. Here too, much of his effect depends on literary allusion. The poet and his interpreter are similar, he explains, because of a bond that links them together, and the same bond extends both to the reader in one direction and to the poet's sources of inspiration in the other:

Or have you not read or heard from anyone, what the ancient philosophers say about possession and poetic madness? First, the most excellent and greatest god bestows his own wisdom of every kind on Apollo. Then Apollo shares it among all the Muses, who are distributed, each in her own sphere, through the nine celestial orbs. Each Muse according to her ability breathes the same power into the poets she favours, the poets transfer it into their interpreters, the interpreters distribute it to their hearers. And so, as if by a chain, the pupils hang from their teacher, the teacher from the poet he is lecturing on, the poet from the Muse, the Muse from Apollo, and Apollo is possessed by the god himself.[36]

Valeriano is borrowing from Plato's *Ion*, where Socrates uses a similar argument to explain Ion's affinity for Homer and his indifference to all other poets. As a magnet attracts iron rings and imparts to them the power to attract other rings in a long chain, a divine force has drawn Ion to interpret Homer:

Well, do you see that the spectator is the last of the rings . . . ? You, the rhapsodist and actor, are the middle ring, and the first one is the poet himself. But it is the deity who, through all the series, draws the spirit of men wherever he desires, transmitting the attractive force from one into another. . . . One poet is suspended from one Muse, another from another; we call it being 'possessed' . . .[37]

His more immediate source, however, is Marsilio Ficino's essay on the *Ion*, *De poetico furore*:

The steps by which this [poetic] madness descends are these. Jupiter possesses Apollo. Apollo illuminates the Muses. The Muses arouse and excite the mild and unconquerable minds of poets. The inspired poets inspire their interpreters. The interpreters move their hearers.[38]

And it is Ficino who supplies the astrological link (missing in the *Ion*) between a poet or interpreter and a particular Muse: each person is affected by different rhythms, depending on the planet and Muse that preside over his birth.[39] The Muses have different genres as their province, in accordance with the etymology of their names or their location among the planets or both. Valeriano's attribution of Muses to planets is identical to Ficino's (and different from the prevailing contemporary version), and he describes the Muses with similar phrases.[40] Appendix 6 juxtaposes Valeriano's discussion with Ficino's. It should be noted, however, that Valeriano's list exactly reverses the order in Ficino, beginning with Thalia and ending with Calliope.

Just as he corrected Poliziano in the first lecture, however, so Valeriano corrects Ficino in the second. He alters Ficino's allocation of poets to Muses, increases the number of poets, adds Latin poets to Ficino's predominantly Greek list, and changes some attributions—thus both asserting the importance of Roman poetry and revising Ficino's characterization of some of the poets.[41] In Ficino Clio inspires Homer, but in Valeriano Vergil; she offers not only the passion for glory but also love of immortality (see Appendix 6). In Ficino it was Thalia who inspired Vergil, but Valeriano changes her assignment; by emphasizing the derivation of her name from Greek *θάλλω*, 'bloom, be abundant', he makes her the source of poetic abundance and ease of composition and the natural patroness of Ovid. But his most important alteration is in the role of Calliope ('fair voice'), who is the best of the Muses because of her universality: she has no fixed abode in the planets but reechoes the voices of all the spheres.[42] In Ficino her protégé is Orpheus, but in Valeriano Catullus:

> They say that those poets are inspired by her who take delight in every poetic rhythm and in all kinds of metres and in every subject. And no one would deny that our Catullus is in this category . . .[43]

Valeriano's playful substitution explains both Catullus' variety and his general appeal. Since he is inspired by Calliope, Catullus too partakes of all the separate voices of the spheres. As a consequence, he exercises the attraction of all the Muses and their tutelary planets, making the birth signs of his interpreters and readers irrelevant: 'everyone may find in him a likeness of his own spirit'.[44] The conceit leads into the grand finale of the second lecture:

> come, let it be Catullus first who is set before students about to make their way into poetry, so that when each has fallen upon that rhythm which is well suited to his spirit, by which he feels himself moved and attracted as iron by a magnet or chaff by amber, he will gird himself up to imitate it and begin to practise with that type of poetry which he sees is proper to his ideal.[45]

METRICAL TEACHING

Rhythm was basic to Valeriano's budding poets, and Catullus' varied metres were to be their text. Valeriano had an active and professional interest in metre. His first collection of poetry, the *Praeludia* (1509), included poems in most of the Catullan metres; in the next decade he composed an exercise in galliambics and a reminiscence of 4 in iambics.[46] But Valeriano also wrote poems *about* metre. Thus, in the *Praeludia* we find not only discussions of general metrical questions (what subjects are appropriate to iambics? should poems in hendecasyllables be short?), but also specific technical treatments, including an attack on Pliny's criticism of Catullus' hendecasyllables and detailed instructions for composing in iambics and scazons.[47] Valeriano's metrical facility is in marked contrast with the discomfort of his predecessors. As we saw in Chapter 1, Catullus' fifteenth-century editors knew very little about metre; even the best of them, Girolamo Avanzi, treated it empirically, scanning every line and weighing every syllable in the hope of understanding the principles behind Catullan practice.[48] Valeriano's greater confidence and metrical proficiency no doubt arose from his own experience as a poet, but he derived his particular approach from an ancient metrical treatise not known to (or at least not exploited by) his predecessors, the *De Metris* of the famous second-century grammarian, Terentianus Maurus.[49]

Terentianus' treatise was discovered, together with some other ancient grammatical works, at Bobbio in 1493. The first edition appeared in 1497, and several other printings and editions followed in the period 1500–10.[50] The work was interesting because of its antiquity and the metrical lore it contained, but most of all because it was written in verse. Valeriano came into contact with it early, and he used Terentianus' treatment as the model for his poems on iambics and scazons in the *Praeludia*.[51] It was natural for him to remember Terentianus again a decade or so later as he prepared to lecture on Catullus, for both the content and the approach of the *De Metris* are ideal for his purposes.

Terentianus founded his treatise on the fact that the verse may be divided at different points, and that different metres can be achieved simply by omitting, adding, and transposing segments. He applied his principle to most of the main metrical types, but especially to the hendecasyllable, which he divided in seven different ways, rearranging and adding segments to form everything from hexameters to galliambics.[52] The demonstration provided Valeriano with the perfect opening for his lecture on Cat. 1 (in hendecasyllables) and vindicated his celebration of Catullus' metrical variety at the end of the second lecture. It had the added benefit of being appropriate to the diverse needs of his audience, which included both young students who required fairly elementary instruction and those like his friend Pietro Melini who expected entertainment and virtuoso display. Best of all, however, Terentianus' approach was active: he showed not how to scan, but how to create the various metres.

Valeriano turns Terentianus' discussion into a treatment of the metre of 1, mostly by substituting Catullan verses for Terentianus' examples, but also by abbreviating and simplifying his model. The first four verses are the basis of his discussion:

Cui dono lepidum novum libellum
arida modo pumice expolitum?
Corneli, tibi: namque tu solebas
meas esse aliquid putare nugas (1. 1–4)

He begins with the basic components of the hendecasyllable:

This metre has the particular distinction of being formed from the segments [*tomis*] of those verses considered the most ancient and celebrated, that is, from an epic *tome* and from an iambic one. Moreover, (so that the younger students may understand), a *tome* is a portion of a verse that is cut off from the rest in such a way that it either makes some type of verse by itself or creates a different form when joined to another segment.[53]

Thus, we may regard the first line of 1 as containing an epic segment, *Cui dono lepidum*, which is the first half of a hexameter verse, and an iambic segment, *novum libellum*, the first colon of an iambic trimeter. The hexameter may be completed by trimming the second segment and inserting words drawn from elsewhere in the poem. Thus: *Cui dono lepidum* | *Corneli docte* | *libellum*. Valeriano creates an iambic verse by completing the iambic segment with a phrase borrowed from 4. 1. Thus: *novum libellum* | *quem videtis hospites*. The argument that follows is technical but entertaining, as Valeriano turns the verses of 1 into alcaics, priapeans, asclepiadeans, and galliambics. (See Appendix 7.) 'If we have a thorough understanding of this rhythm', he concludes, 'we can exercise our talent through many kinds of verses.'[54]

Valeriano invokes Terentianus again in his discussion of iambic trimeter, which he says originally consisted of six iambs (i.e. with no substitutions) and was used for invective—'a bitter, furious, avenging metre', which was employed so effectively by Archilochus against his enemy Lycambes that he hanged himself.[55] As the metre mellowed and was used for other purposes, it admitted substitutions, but Catullus reverted to pure iambics for his fourth poem (*phaselus ille, quem videtis, hospites*):

He especially sought out a rhythm that could provide a pace of equal speed with the very swift yacht he was describing. And this was the reason that he wanted to compose this whole poem of iambics alone.[56]

We should pause here to note that Valeriano is not only the first Renaissance critic to characterize the curious rhythmical effect of 4, but also the first to see that it is composed in pure iambics. Terentianus does not explicitly identify the metre of 4, but his discussion of pure iambics and his use of 4. 1 among his other iambic examples surely helped Valeriano to make the connection.[57] Mere identification of a metre, however, interests Valeriano and his students less than learning how to use it:

And this would have been enough to say about the metre of this poem that we are considering today if some of you who are endowed with very elegant talent had not asked me yesterday to give a simple and detailed explanation of the way to compose this verse when the right time presented itself. Consider therefore. If you have a supply of words that would allow you to create this metre, go ahead and compose each verse with six iambs. But if you can't think of enough expressions to join together in succession, and other words come to mind that are fine-sounding, but are either spondaic or dactylic or anapestic, do not reject them.[58]

He continues with a detailed account of legitimate substitutions for iambs, their allowed positions in the verse, and the correct locations for caesurae. Throughout, the emphasis is on fluency of composition. If a rule proves difficult to follow, the poet should look for allowable alternatives: 'I would not wish you to check the course of your invention.'[59]

Valeriano wants his students to understand the technical details of metre, not for their own sake, but in order to appreciate and exploit their aesthetic and emotional effects. By taking the hendecasyllables of 1 apart and using the pieces to create other metres he showed that the same ideas and language can appear quite different in different metrical settings—a fact that his students surely appreciated as they listened to his various renditions of 1.1 (see Appendix 7). Most of the time, however, the object is not to convey the same idea in different metres, but to express a particular idea in the most appropriate metre, as we learn in his introduction to 8 (*Miser Catulle, desinas ineptire*):

It is worth pointing out that just as architects take care first of all not to make mistakes in decorum as would happen if shrines to Mars and Hercules were built in Corinthian style, because a style of this sort is suitable to effeminate subjects, or if shrines to Venus and the Nymphs were built in Doric, a style that is owed to masculine strength, so our poet is at great pains to preserve decorum and to adapt his metre to correspond with his subjects. And so when he treated kisses and endearments and jests of some kind, he used a gentle and languid metre—sapphic or phalaecian hendecasyllable. For since the three trochees in a row in this verse have been taken from the phallic type of poem sung in honour of Bacchus and Priapus, softness is necessarily present in it.[60] But when he wished to praise the agile speed of the yacht in which he had travelled from Bithynia to his homeland, he used the swiftest metre, the fleet and rapid iamb, unhindered by the weight of spondees to delay its hurried pace. But now on a serious and painful matter he uses the metre especially matched to the subject, the limping iamb [scazon], which is most suitable for expressing serious ideas and bitter circumstances. . . . For this verse seems somehow to limp, because in the last foot it stumbles against the obstacle of a spondee; but if that foot were an iamb the verse would run along quite freely. If you want to understand this more surely, come, ask your ears and say the verse, *Miser Catulle desinas ineptire*, this way: *Miser Catulle desinas ineptias*. Already you see the speed in the iambic senarius, but delay and a sort of impediment in the scazon.[61]

Iambs are swift, scazons halting, hendecasyllables soft and languid. The descriptions are helpful to prospective poets, to be sure, but equally so to critics, for Valeriano is concerned not only to characterize but also to vindicate Catullus' handling of metre. The most persistent criticism was that levelled against his admission of iambs and trochees in place of the usual spondee at the beginning of the hendecasyllable—a practice that even Avanzi, the strongest champion of Catullan metrics in the fifteenth century, had viewed as an archaic licence.[62] The question was interesting both because of the popularity of hendecasyllables with Renaissance poets and because it had been raised by no less an authority than the elder Pliny. Pliny criticized Catullus on aesthetic grounds, judging that the verse *meas aliquid putare nugas* (1. 4) made him a 'trifle harsher than he wished to be considered by his darling Veraniuses and Fabulluses', and he 'softened' the verse by rewriting it to secure a spondaic opening: *nugas esse aliquid meas putare*.[63] Although Valeriano certainly knew from Terentianus Maurus that Catullus' variations were deemed acceptable by ancient critics, he chose to vindicate him with technical and aesthetic arguments instead.[64] Catullus' variations, he argues, reflect the nature of the hendecasyllable, which may be considered a combination of hexameter and iambic elements (see Appendix 7. 3). The usual spondaic opening reflects the affinity of the first segment with the hexameter, but an iamb may be imported from the second segment. A trochaic opening, on the other hand, results naturally from the trochaic quality of the verse as a whole (Appendix 7. 2).[65] To refute Pliny's charge that Catullus was 'a little too harsh' (*duriusculus*), he adduces ancient testimonia characterizing him as soft (*mollis*), playful (*lascivus*), and delicate (*tener*), and argues that in fact his trochaic and iambic variations enhance rather than detract from his elegance. Short syllables, Valeriano claims, are lighter and softer than long ones, and iambs and trochees smoother than spondees.[66] 'I would not have believed that anyone was so foreign to the Muses, so tone-deaf, that he could not tell the difference . . .'.[67]

'Consult your ears!' Valeriano exhorts his audience again and again.[68] The verbal music of the poet can be apprehended easily, if one has the patience to listen and the knowledge to understand. His defence of Catullus' metrics proceeds ultimately from the conviction that the poet is right and that it is the obligation of the modern critic to understand why. 'Grammarians ought to establish their rules from the practice of ancient poets; the old poets, moreover, ought not to be blamed because of the ignorance of modern grammarians.'[69]

VALERIANO AND THE TEXT

Valeriano defends the traditional text in a similar spirit. The scholars of the fifteenth century claimed the authority of manuscripts (often disingenuously, as we have seen), but emended and altered the text using their own instincts and judgement. Valeriano takes no such liberties; rather, he is concerned to vindicate the received text and to defend it from modern improvements. Manuscripts and early editions are authoritative; readings from other sources are suspect. The formulation is simplistic, but for the purposes of his lectures Valeriano is not interested in systematic collation or even in distinguishing between the testimony of early editions and that of manuscripts.[70] He wants to show that there is a traditional text, and that it can be recovered from early sources. Corruptions and variants are a part of the tradition; later corrections must be rigorously scrutinized.

Some are accepted. Thus, at 3. 11 (*qui nunc it per iter tenebricosum*) he defends Partenio's' correction, *tenebricosum*: 'Some read *tenebriosum*, which is found also in a number of manuscripts; but *tenebricosum* is a Latin word and a common one for that learned age.'[71] And he admires 3. 4, which had been added by the first Aldine to the announcement of the death of Lesbia's sparrow:

> Passer mortuus est meae puellae,
> *Passer, deliciae meae puellae* (3. 3–4)

> This little verse, *passer deliciae meae puellae*, repeated in this place from the previous epigram [2. 1], is not contained in most manuscripts. But the repetition has such charm and elegance and inspires such pity that, even if Catullus did not make it, I would have to give my highest approval to the diligence and judgement of those who have decided that it should be repeated here.[72]

In Valeriano's opinion, however, most later corrections are not redeemed by literary merit or Latin usage, but fly in the face of both. So, in 3. 16 (*o factum male! o miselle passer!*), he approves the hiatus *male o* of the traditional text as charming and appropriate to Catullus' sorrowful theme,[73] and castigates Battista Guarino's 'correction' *proh* for *o*. It is unnecessary and unmetrical, he claims,[74] but, worst of all, it is ugly: 'if you read *o factum male proh miselle passer*, you will produce something thick and discordant and offensive to the ear, which is most foreign to Catullus' naturalness and simplicity.'[75]

Guarino's correction, however misguided, was at least made in response to a difficulty in the text, but other readings crept in gratuitously. In Catullus' poem on the napkin thief (*Marrucine Asini, manu sinistra*, 12. 1) Avanzi had unnecessarily changed *Marrucine* to *Inter cenam*.[76] Valeriano argues that the reading originated in a marginal gloss, *inter cenam*, paraphrasing *in ioco atque vino* in the next verse. Later the gloss was taken as the correct reading and substituted for *Marrucine*. His conclusion is acerbic: 'But come, let us follow the advice of Timon of Phlius who said that if we want correct exemplars we must seek out old ones that no one has laid a hand on; and let us read *Marrucine*, as it appears in the ancient manuscripts.'[77]

The most important gratuitous reading mentioned in the lectures is Pontano's revision of 1. 9—not because the reading itself has any merit, but because Valeriano's discussion provides new evidence about Pontano's notes on Catullus. Pontano (d. 1503) certainly studied Catullus; he owned a manuscript, imitated the hendecasyllables and other lyrics, and made some emendations in the text.[78] He also left notes on Catullus, which his friend and editor, Pietro Summonte, discussed in a letter to Angelo Colocci in 1509:

> I also plan (since our friend Pontano is well known everywhere, and his reputation has been placed out of any danger) to bring to light some of his youthful trifles, if Sannazaro agrees. The fact that he never mentioned it while he lived shows that he was a little ashamed of them. They are choice jottings on Valerius Catullus, in whom it is well known he took a great interest in his youth. But if harm should be done to him after his death by publishing these things that he disdained and that might seem completely foreign to his dignity, let our boldness be weighed against the benefit of the reader. For they are of such a kind that no one would regret having read them.[79]

Summonte tried repeatedly and unsuccessfully to acquire Pontano's notes, both for his own purposes and on behalf of Colocci in

Rome; but although they seem to have survived until at least 1548,[80] they are lost, and their nature is unknown. Although Pontano himself, according to Summonte, was ashamed of his notes and never mentioned them, and none of his associates or successors seems to have had access to them, nevertheless a few of his emendations were well known—the most famous being his suggestion for 1. 9.

Pontano's idea is not entirely gratuitous, for the text of 1. 9 (*qualecumque; quod* ⟨*o*⟩ *patrona virgo*) presents some difficulties, principally the introduction of a second addressee, *patrona virgo*, in a poem already dedicated to Cornelius Nepos, and the fact that in the archetype the line was a syllable short (a deficiency remedied by the fifteenth-century supplement ⟨*o*⟩).[81] Pontano banished these difficulties by changing the last part of the verse to *ora per virorum*,[82] so that Catullus' dedication would end:

> quare habe tibi quidquid hoc libelli
> qualecunque, quod ora per virorum
> plus uno maneat perenne saeclo. (1. 8–10, *Pontanus*)

So written, the verses evoke another claim for poetic immortality, the famous epigram of Ennius:

> Nemo me lacrimis decoret nec funera fletu
> faxit. Cur? Volito vivus *per ora virum*.
> (Ennius, *Epigrams* 9–10, Warmington)[83]

Pontano's revision is cited approvingly several times in the fifteenth century;[84] it appears in the first Aldine and in most of the apographs of the notes of Francesco Pucci, which were written in 1502 and circulated for the next fifty years;[85] and it is mentioned in the commentary of another Neapolitan humanist, Aulo Giano Parrasio, which was written between 1512 and 1517:

> Nor shall I omit the emendation of Pontano, a poet of keen intellect and authoritative judgement: *qualecunque quod ora per virorum*, which (even if it is not his) Catullus would gladly acknowledge as his own.[86]

Parrasio's comment echoes the last verse in an epigram of Pontano's friend and fellow poet, Jacopo Sannazaro:

> *To Iovianus* [*Pontanus*] *on the Emendation of Catullus*
> If learned Catullus should return from the Elysian vale and his only Lesbia should bring her ungrateful chorus, he will not grieve so much

for the damage of his blemished book as he will rejoice in your kindness, Iovianus. He would repay you with embraces and grateful kisses, and he would rather remember these verses than his own.[87]

The comments of Sannazaro and Parrasio suggest that perhaps Pontano did not produce a commentary or emendations at all, but rather a creative rewriting of troublesome passages, and that his purposes were more poetic than philological. Some evidence for his work on Tibullus points in the same direction, for the annotator of an early edition in Florence has glossed several lacunae with verses attributed to him.[88] Valeriano, himself, however, is our best witness:

It is worth the effort to run through the various opinions of the many who attack this passage [1. 9] in various ways, who change and turn it upside down—to say nothing of those who have so shamelessly perverted, not to say violated, the pure reading, when they have blotted out the legitimate words and published the suppositious half-line, *ora per virorum*; and in order to defend their impudence they claim falsely that Iovianus Pontanus presented it as Catullus' text. But I know from reliable sources that Iovianus Pontanus, the most illustrious literary man of our age, did not write *qualecumque quidem ora per virorum* or *qualecumque quod ora per virorum* in the margins of his book to pass it off as Catullus' reading, but because he was in the habit of playing with authors in this way for the sake of his intellect, to test his ingenuity and to practise his style. Thus we will pass over this reading *ora per virorum* as patently false on the evidence of those who heard the matter from Pontanus himself.[89]

Valeriano confirms the hints of Parrasio and Sannazaro, and his description of Pontano's literary approach is consistent with the account of Summonte, who described the notes as youthful trifles,[90] now a little embarrassing to the dignity of their author, but worth publishing if the poet Sannazaro should agree.

Given Valeriano's conservative attitude, it is not surprising that his numerous textual notes evaluate and select readings but almost never propose them. At 22. 13 he argues for *tritius* instead of the traditional *tristius*, but claims to have taken the reading from the manuscript of Ermolao Barbaro.[91] According to Achilles Statius, Valeriano and Gabriele Faerno suggested *ilia et emulso* at 80. 8.[92] Although this tantalizing remark seems to indicate some knowledge of the lost portion of the lectures, Statius cannot have been very well informed. The reading appears in the edition of Alessandro Guarino, and although Valeriano might have reported it, he would not have claimed it for his own. Valeriano does propose an emendation, however, for the defective verse at 8. 9 (*nunc iam illa non vult; tu quoque impote⟨ns noli⟩*), where after discussing other solutions, he announces his own with a flourish:

What shall we do? Is it not permitted for the Roman Academy to attempt something in a controversial matter? Let us be given permission, too, I pray, so that where there is an obvious fault in the text we can devise something on the same conditions as they have done. Therefore, without crossing off a letter, or transposing a word, without recourse to an unrelated expression, but preserving the reading of the old manuscripts and restoring only a single word, which seems broken off to me, I would read, instead of *tu quoque impotens es, tu quoque impotens esto*.[93]

DELECTARE ET PRODESSE: THE INTERPRETER AND THE POET

Valeriano was a sounder text critic and a better metrician than his predecessors, but he was also a more sophisticated interpreter. He was able not only to explain Catullus, but to do so elegantly, using as the leitmotif of his lectures the idea he had suggested at the outset, that the aims of the poet and his interpreter were identical—to amuse and to benefit their audience.

Thus, he seasons his lectures with verse to entertain his students, but also to remind them to practise writing their own Latin poetry. Poetry is everywhere—not just the verse of Catullus, or of other Roman poets adduced as parallels, but also Greek poetry, quoted and translated (often into verse), and even the poetry of Valeriano himself. He weaves these poetic scraps now loosely, now tightly, into the fabric of his interpretations. Sometimes he uses one as the centrepiece. Thus, in his lecture on 13 (*Cenabis bene, mi Fabulle, apud me*) he uses some verses of his own as a starting point. He interprets Catullus' witty dinner invitation to his friend Fabullus as part of a lighthearted exchange of verses. Fabullus, he imagines, had invited himself to dinner at Catullus' house in hopes of hearing his love poetry.

Naturally, he wrote to Catullus in hendecasyllables, which Valeriano kindly supplies:

> I'm planning to dine at your house, Catullus,
> In a few days, if the gods are on my side
> (When I am free of business and court cases)
> So that you can read your love poems to me.[94]

Thereupon, Catullus, 'not forgetting the wit and playful humour that he scattered everywhere through all his work', responded with his own verses.[95] On this interpretation the love poems so interesting to Fabullus are promised in the *meros amores* of 13. 9 (*sed contra accipies meros amores*). But Valeriano also uses *meros amores* for poetic purposes of his own, as the pretext for a digression on the genealogy of love that he has taken from the scholia to Apollonius Rhodius. The connection of the digression to Catullus is negligible, but he wants to include verse translations of two fragments of Greek poetry quoted by the scholiast.[96]

Like other Renaissance commentators Valeriano discourses at length on people and places mentioned only briefly in the poems, packing his digressions with nuggets of more or (usually) less relevant information; but his digressions are self-conscious and purposeful, and tend to be integrated into the lectures in a lively and entertaining fashion. His discussion of 11 (*Furi et Aureli, comites Catulli*) is a case in point. The poet imagines that his friends Furius and Aurelius would be willing to accompany him to the ends of the earth; Valeriano uses his pleasing[97] catalogue of exotic places and peoples as an excuse for digressions: why does Catullus call the Arabs *molles* (11. 5), the Nile *septemgeminus* (11. 7), the Britons *horribiles* (11. 11)?[98] He treats each explanation differently. The softness of the Arabs is only a pretext to include a quite unrelated discussion from Stephanus of Byzantium about the proverbial long-windedness of Arabian fluteplayers, and the witticism about the Arab flautist 'who would pipe for a drachma, but stop only for four'.[99] The epithet *septemgeminus* ('sevenfold'), referring to the seven mouths of the Nile, occasions a whole geographical and etymological excursus, starting with the names and etymologies of the seven mouths, and moving on to the meaning of the word 'Nile' and ancient accounts of the river's source. The digression, which consumes most of a lecture, is surely included for its own sake, but when it has finally run its course, Valeriano carefully re-attaches it to his discussion. Thus, in his comments on the next verse (*sive trans altas gradietur Alpes*, 11. 9):

In the last lecture we were worn out by our long journey up the Nile and could not arrive at the end of our epigram, especially since we were frightened off by the steep and difficult journey along the ridges of the Alps between. Today, therefore, refreshed after three days' rest, let us hasten on our way to Gaul and Britain.[100]

But it was in connection with the combination *horribiles . . . Britanos* that Valeriano created his greatest effect, either by good luck (as he would have us believe) or by good management. For just as he arrived at the verses, *Gallicum Rhenum horribilesque ultimosque Britanos* (11. 11–12), two English envoys entered the lecture room—Richard Pace and a companion whose name eluded the scribe.[101] Their appearance allowed Valeriano to turn his explanation of *horribiles . . . Britanos* into an elaborate compliment to Pace, to his king, Henry VIII, and to the British nation:

I should think, rather, that Catullus said '*horribiles . . . Britanos*' for the same reason that Horace said, 'I shall go to see the Britons, fierce to strangers'. . . . But lest you be convinced that their character or nature has persisted in this way, the Britons are now as civilized and hospitable as they were savage in the past, although they have by no means put aside their warlike ferocity. Yet now they are also considered outstanding in intellect and for study of the fields of knowledge, famed for eloquence, most eminent in the study of Greek and Latin literature. I could name many men of this kind for you—More, *** and the one educated in your city whom you see sitting on the benches with you today to honour me, Pace. Because he is present, I shall keep to myself (lest I seem to fawn upon him) the many things that could be said in his highest praise, postponing their rehearsal to another time and place; and I shall change my tack, so that I may leave their King Henry by no means unpraised. This is the man the fates of a kindlier nature have bestowed on our times, so that he might be the king (and a young one at that) from whom almost all of Europe might take its example of just and moderate rule, from whom we might learn to judge by the standard of piety the study of the liberal arts and the disciplines themselves, and also the training of talent and eloquence. For the most pious writings of this king are in the hands of all—so learned, so devout, so ardent—by which he has most successfully demolished the most vile enterprises of the Lutheran faction (or should I say, pestilence?) which had begun to overthrow the laws, religion, and all secular things; so that you may understand from this one man what hope exists for the future if, as Plato argued, citizens will be of the same quality as their kings.[102]

Valeriano finds it easy enough to be both amusing and instructive, but fitting Catullus into the same mould presents certain obvious difficulties. The poet is certainly lively and entertaining, and Valeriano can show again and again that he is useful as a teacher of style, but there is little to support the assertion in the second lecture that he 'chastises vice, criticizes evil ways, and attempts to deter mankind from imitating the wicked men he chastises in his poetry.'[103] In 10, however, Valeriano finds a way to make a case (of sorts) for Catullus in a discussion that nicely blends learned digressions and useful (if not necessarily moral) advice. In this poem (*Varus me meus ad suos amores*) the poet's friend Varus has taken him to see his girlfriend, and the conversation turns to Bithynia, where Catullus has just been serving on the staff of the provincial governor. 'You must know', says Valeriano, introducing his first digression, 'that there were many things they could have said about Bithynia . . .'.[104] And a folio later: 'This and much more about Bithynia could have been said in answer to *Quid esset iam Bithynia* [10. 5–6], but the tart's whole interest was to find out the part pertaining to riches.'[105] Catullus at first admits that he made nothing out of his sojourn in Bithynia, but then foolishly (and quite falsely) claims to have brought back eight litter bearers, whereupon the girl asks to borrow them so that she can be carried next day to the temple of Serapis. The next verse provides Valeriano's opening for another digression:

Mane tum inquio puellae [10. 27][106]: . . . In saying these words he seems to be trying to think of something with a thoughtful gesture and to be rubbing his head to stimulate his power of memory. But while Catullus is looking for something to say, come now, let us recall some things about Serapis that perhaps you will not mind hearing . . .[107]

The long discussion that ensues treats the etymology of Serapis, the bull Apis, Joseph in Egypt, and an emendation and verse translation of an oracle of Serapis from Macrobius, and concludes by identifying Serapis with Pluto, the god of wealth:[108]

No wonder then if the greedy tart is so anxious to be carried to Serapis to address her prayers to him in her quest for money and wealth. . . . And so she says, *Volo ad Serapin deferri* [10. 26–7]. And Catullus, when he has been stuck for an answer for some little time, finally answers her . . .[109]

The answer, when it finally comes, is feeble. It seems that Catullus has been a little careless: the bearers are not actually his, but his friend Cinna's, which (he assures her) is almost the same thing. Valeriano sees this little vignette as a cautionary tale:

I began these lectures with the premise that the task of the poet is both to delight and to be useful. This has been borne out so amply in the discussion of the first nine poems that it requires no further demonstration. But this tenth epigram consists completely of utility, so that it may advise us how we can take the opportunity to escape the shameless behaviour and greed of harlots, and after we have perceived their wicked and troublesome nature, that we should not be afraid to look out for our property in every possible way, in order (as the proverb says) to knock out one nail with another.[110]

This strange view is unique to Valeriano, but it is based on an assumption that goes back to Palladio: that Catullus emerges triumphant from his encounter with Varus' girl and has cleverly foiled her greedy designs.[111] Thus Valeriano can say of the poem's dénouement:

And as for what he said he had before—unblushingly, to give her tit for tat, he says he had absentmindedly made a mistake, for the slaves were not his, but Cinna's. . . . And when he had thus escaped by cleverly pretending insanity, he attacked the wantonness of the harlot herself since she was so shameless that she would not allow anyone to say anything carelessly or foolishly. And so he teaches others when they have fallen into a business of this kind to take a stand and to suspect the harlots of readiness to make demands, despoil and impoverish them.[112]

Valeriano takes the programme *delectare et prodesse* in still another direction in his discussions of the sparrow poems, 2 and 3. Predictably enough, he begins the lecture on 2 (*Passer, deliciae meae puellae*) with an attack on Poliziano's obscene interpretation of the sparrow:[113]

you will find no manuscript that is not corrupt, no interpreter who has the same opinion as another—so much do they distort both the language and the meaning to suit their whims. But it would have been better (and less wicked) if every one of them had wilfully mutilated the sense, reversed the words, mixed up the structure, and pulled it apart this way and that—if only they had spared the meaning and not thought up an unchaste interpretation and so basely served up to Catullus filth that is found nowhere in such a refined poem. Good god! Had his body not been treated cruelly enough without their planning to quench his spirit? . . . We know that sparrows are so salacious that they mate seven times an hour; we know from medical writings that eating sparrows (or even their eggs) has an aphrodisiac effect. We know what filth the term *στρουθοὶ* (that is, 'sparrows') signifies in mimes; . . . we know from the writings of the Egyptian priests that human lust is symbolized by the picture of a sparrow. . . . We know these things, I say, but we neither know nor wish to know that in Catullus or perhaps even in Martial the male genitals (if you'll pardon the expression) ought to be understood under the word 'sparrow'.[114]

Like his predecessors, Valeriano finds Poliziano's allegory repellent and unnecessary, but his main objection is that it is impossible. If Poliziano is right, he argues, the allegory must be applied to both 2 and 3–that is, to the dead sparrow as well as to the living one. And therein lies the difficulty:

But if they wish to understand by the dead sparrow that his ardour has cooled and that with these veiled words Catullus wants to show that he is no longer capable of sex, the idea is far-fetched and over-elaborate, especially since Catullus wrote this poem when he was in the very flower of youth . . .[115]

The argument hardly appears cogent to the modern reader, but Valeriano thinks it decisive. Once impotence is ruled out as the meaning for the dead sparrow, we must either abandon Poliziano's reading or confront a term that is symbolic in one poem and not in the next—a clear impossibility as far as Valeriano is concerned.[116]

The lecture continues with the usual line-by-line discussion, accompanied by digressions—on Love the child of Plenty and Want from Plato's *Symposium*, on the story of Atalanta, on the *Amores* described by Philostratus—and concludes with an account of the erotic symbolism of apples and poppies and the promise of a fuller discussion 'in the commentary I am producing on the symbolism of Egyptian literature'.[117] The lecture on 2 was evidently a success, whether for this rag-bag of information, the refutation of Poliziano, or Valeriano's serious philological analysis, for twice as many came to hear him on 3 (*Lugete, o Veneres*

Cupidinesque).[118] It is only at the end of the discussion that he returns explicitly to his programme *delectare et prodesse*:

> Now I will add one thing as a corollary, which we can apply to these rites of a dead sparrow. For they can both amuse you in the listening and benefit you greatly by their example. The life of a sparrow is very short. For, as those who write of these matters tell us, the males can live no more than a year, and they say that the reason is unrestrained lust—which also wears out so many men before their time and hands them over to old age. The crow, on the other hand, is very long-lived, since it copulates most seldom. Wherefore, young men, if the sweetness of life delights you, nothing will be more useful to you than to reject Venus and the goads of blind passion . . .[119]

We are surely entitled to question the seriousness of this advice, but it is perhaps more important to note its incongruity, for the very discussion of the sparrow poems that began by rejecting a sexual meaning for the sparrow ends by assuming one. It would be wrong to place too much weight on the inconsistency—after, all, Valeriano is speaking in jest; but it seems that we have discovered yet another example (or at least a variant) of the principle of interpretation noted in the last chapter: that the first explanation (here Poliziano's obscene suggestion), whatever its merits, tends to survive and to form the core of subsequent explanations, even when it is explicitly rejected.[120]

NOT AN IVORY TOWER

Valeriano's lectures, conceived as they were in the last happy days of Roman humanism under Leo X, provide an occasional glimpse of the literary and convivial life so dear to the humanists. Thus, on 12. 13 (*verum est mnemosynon mei sodalis*):

> No form of association produces a greater bond of friendship than dining together, than being nourished and fed together—whence the terms 'close friends' (*sodales*) and 'fellowship' (*sodalitium*) for a gathering of those friends who often dine together. You know this sort of fellowship at Rome, the *sodalitia* of Sadoleto and of Giberti, Coricius, Colocci, Melinus, Cursius, Blosius, and others.[121]

But they were delivered in a different and harsher world, whose various intrusions are sometimes recorded—thus, Leo's death, the embassy of Richard Pace, the Sack of Rome; thus, too, even a snow-ball fight, which broke up the lecture that had begun with a reference to Leo's death.[122]

The most drastic intrusion, however, is not explicitly chronicled. At the end of August 1522, many months after his election, Pope Adrian VI finally arrived in Rome. He had been characterized by the Romans as a barbarian almost from the moment of his election. Thus Pasquino, quoted by Sanuto in a letter of 13 January 1522:

Sonnet on the Election of the Pope

O traitor of Christ's blood—thief!
College of traitors! You have betrayed
Our beautiful Vatican to German rage.
Why does your heart not burst with grief?
O ruined world, o age past all belief!
Vain thought, through false longing strayed!
Rome's fair name, name fair in every age,
Is dust—barbarians' booty. A fief![123]

Pasquino's invective was little more than uninformed but predictable xenophobia, but it seemed to find confirmation in Adrian's conduct. Once in Rome, he was immediately anathema to the humanists and they to him. Contemporary accounts vie with each other in producing examples of his dislike of the greatest treasures of Italian and classical art. He loathed the Laocoon ('*sunt idola antiquorum*!' was his famous comment); and he was alleged to be planning to destroy Michelangelo's frescoes in the Sistine Chapel ('a bath house of naked bodies').[124] But his greatest dislike was reserved for the poets. 'He suspected the talent of poets', writes his contemporary biographer Giovio, 'since they were said not to have sincere feelings about the Christian religion, and to cultivate eagerly the damned names of false gods in imitation of the ancients . . .'.[125]

It was in this climate that Valeriano resumed his lectures, after a break of some months over the summer and fall of 1522.[126] As luck would have it, he was faced with the first obscene and pederastic poems in the collection, 15 (*Commendo tibi me ac meos amores*) and 16 (*Pedicabo ego vos et irrumabo*). He begins:

I had decided last year, young men and most honourable youths, to lecture to you on Catullus in such a way as to conceal what seemed unworthy to be expounded from this place because of the shameful nature of its argument. And with that in mind, I was not at all sorry to stop (since summer was already pressing in, in any case), when I was called home by family business, because I had come to those epigrams that could not be explained without baseness.[127]

He had planned, so he claims, to substitute Horace's *Epistles* on his return, recognizing that 'nothing was more suited to good character, nothing more useful for living a courtier's life with dignity, nothing more suited to the balanced system of an upright and happy life.'[128] The lecture continues with an account of the students' reactions—a passage that we shall examine presently.

It is hard to be sure of Valeriano's real intentions. His hesitation to deal with the obscene is in surprising contrast to the frankness (not to say salacious pleasure) exhibited by his predecessors, but it is consistent with the role he claimed for himself as a teacher in the first lecture ('I must take on a parent's affection for you, and . . . I must succeed those who bore you and brought you up, and eagerly wish you to be educated in literature and character').[129] It is also consistent with a certain discomfort with homosexual innuendo that he has shown earlier in the lectures. His rejection of the reading *meos amores* at 13. 9 (*sed contra accipies meros amores*) is a case in point. Most of those who favour *meos amores*, he explains, argue that Catullus is offering his boy to Fabullus, and they support their interpretation by referring to 15. 1 (*Commendo tibi me ac meos amores*), where *meos amores* clearly refers to a boy. Others think ('more decently', according to Valeriano) that Catullus is offering a girl.[130] (The preference for heterosexual over homosexual innuendo is characteristic, as we shall see presently.) Valeriano himself argues for *meros amores*, because it has manuscript authority and is paralleled in Martial, and concludes: 'it seems impious to me to twist the sense to inchastity and immorality when it is possible to interpret something decently and with modesty intact.'[131]

On the other hand, he is by no means squeamish about heterosexual material. He is explicit about the nature of the cuckolded husband's inactivity in 17:

Nec se sublevat ex sua parte, sed velut alnus
In fossa Liguris iacet separata securi
[17. 18–19, Vat. lat. 5215, fol. 226]:[132]

Nor in the wrestling of marital intercourse does he know how to play his part (that is, to assist things by moving, which is the man's role), although the woman for her part (I mean, one who wants to conceive) ought not to move at all. . . . But he is so slow and inexperienced that, like a tree trunk, he clings unmoving to his wife.[133]

He glosses *latera ecfututa* in 6. 13 ('loins spent and exhausted by frequent intercourse') and explains *ilia rumpens* in 11. 20 ('breaking, weakening, unmanning . . . the loins of all, who as a consequence of having been challenged to battle so often, are exhausted by excessive combat and can no longer perform their duty. . . .').[134] Valeriano's language is discreet—in the explanation of 6. 13, for example, he avoids uttering the obscenity *ecfututa*[135]—but his meaning is perfectly clear. Moreover, whatever his distaste for homosexual material, there is some evidence that he was willing to treat it and in fact was planning to do so, for he concludes his discussion of *ilia rumpens* with this comment: 'by such constant [intercourse] she goes on to render so many men impotent (*elumbes*). But on another occasion we will have a full discussion of *lumbi*, *renes*, and *ilia*.'[136] *Renes* does not appear in Catullus; *ilia* occurs three times: 11. 20, 63. 5 (of Attis), 80. 8 (obscene and homosexual);[137] *lumbus* appears once, at 16. 11—that is, in one of the obscene pederastic poems that Valeriano is now ostensibly refusing to discuss. There is a further piece of evidence to suggest that, in spite of his present protestations, he perhaps did go on to treat passages that contained explicit homosexual obscenity—for we must remember Statius' comment that Valeriano read *ilia et emulso* at 80. 8 (which is one of the most obscene verses in all Catullus).[138]

It is clear that Valeriano's pious disclaimer deserves to be treated with caution, but does it merit our disbelief? Let us reserve judgement for a moment, while we examine his account of the students' reactions:

But you urge me to complete the task once it has been undertaken, and a good number of you complain of being cheated of a text that you think most learned of all. But as for my plan of at least suppressing many things, many say that Catullus has appeared in their dreams at night, angry because I want to castrate his books. Others lament that we have fallen back into the times of the Goths and the Vandals because it seems that just as they used to cut off the genitals of all the statues, so now anything titillating is taken out of books, too. Others accuse me (quite unjustly) of trying to avoid work, or allege that I am afraid of exposing my ignorance, since perhaps I do not understand what sophistication is concealed in these matters. Some say that I am a hypocrite, others that I am pretending to be more virtuous than I am, others fabricate still harsher things. To these [I reply] . . .[139]

But we will never know what he replied, for the text breaks off here. The whole discussion is on two pages, the *recto* and *verso* of folio 194. Both pages are filled, and each has been lightly crossed out with a single transverse stroke. At the bottom of 194v the scribe has noted, 'Desunt multa usque ad *O Colonia* [17] 209'—'much is missing until *O Colonia* on 209.'

As we consider this passage, it is important to remember that Valeriano was speaking to an audience, and a sympathetic one at that. Surely everyone in the room—friends, contemporaries, students—was both hostile to Adrian and well versed in the language of invective against him. Vandals, Goths, mutilation of statues—all evoke the oppressive puritanism of the pope and suggest the threat, at least, of censorship. Looking back on Adrian's papacy seven years later in *De litteratorum infelicitate*, Valeriano sketches the era in similar terms:

For when he had succeeded Leo X, a cultured prince (around whom, naturally, a large number of literary men had congregated), while each was entertaining the same hopes of Adrian, lo, he appeared—a most bitter foe of the Muses, of eloquence, of all elegance. For he threatened all men of letters with his hostility, since they were 'followers of Terence', as he used to say, and when he had begun to hate and even to persecute them, they went to ground—some seeking voluntary exile, others various hiding places—until by the grace of God he died in the second year of his reign. He seemed likely (if he had lived any longer) to revive the time of the Goths in his onslaught against literature.[140]

But if the tone and context of Valeriano's lecture are clear, his intentions are not. Was he preparing to defy the 'foe of the Muses' or to yield to the times? Perhaps the condition of the manuscript can suggest some answers. The contents of fols. 194r–249v are as follows:

194r–v	Praelectio xxii: Cat. 15
209r	Blank
209v–221r	Lecture not numbered: Cat. 17
221v–231v	Praelectio xxv: Cat. 17

232r–241r	Praelectio xxvi: Cat. 22
241v–249v	Praelectio xxvii: Cat. 22

That is, lecture xxii is incomplete, lecture xxiii is missing, lecture xxiv (the first lecture on 17) is unnumbered. Discussions of the obscene poems 15, 16, 21 are lacking.[141] In his prefatory letter Melini implied that all the absent portions of the manuscript disappeared in the Sack of Rome, but the random and senseless destruction of the Sack (though no doubt responsible for the loss of the end of the manuscript) cannot account for the internal lacunae, coinciding exactly as they do with the obscene poems.

Let us look at the manuscript more closely, remembering that Melini had it bound (or rebound) after much of it had been lost in the Sack.[142] Some of Melini's work is obvious. Thus, he has inserted a short gathering including end papers and his letter to Ippolito de' Medici (fol. I r–v) at the beginning of the manuscript, and he has had a few small sheets of Valeriano's own notes sewn into the centre of the original first gathering (between fols. 7v and 8r). The original gathering had seven leaves (fols. 1–14). He has split the outside leaf, which contained fol. 1 and fol. 14, and the two folios are sewn in separately. After this point, however, it becomes more difficult to distinguish his handiwork. The numeration of folios and gatherings (the former with arabic numbers at the upper right-hand corner, the latter with letters in the lower right corner) seems to be the work of Valeriano's amanuensis, although one might imagine that Melini numbered the gatherings himself after the Sack as he put them in order for his binder. The lectures were numbered by the original scribe (*Praelectio* i, ii, etc.), who also used the first word or so of each poem as a heading for the folios of the corresponding lecture.

Beginning with fol. 15, the manuscript is bound in gatherings of 12, intact until 194v, which ends a gathering. The whole of the next gathering (195–206v) and three folios of the one following (207–9) have been removed, leaving raw edges in the gutter. A new folio 209 has been glued to the raw edges of the missing folios. Folio 209r is blank, 209v begins the unnumbered lecture on 17. The hand on 209v is different from that in the bulk of the manuscript (and it is not the hand of Melini). The text on 209v ends in the middle of the last line, but the sentence continues without a break on 210r, and the continuation is indicated by matching sigla on 209v and 210r. There is a long scar in the gutter between 209v and 210r. The hand on 210r and the following folios is the same as that in the bulk of the manuscript. After 210 the only oddity is that the number on fol. 211 has been changed to 212; the next folio is numbered 213 and so on. Otherwise, the manuscript continues without a break until it ends on fol. 249v.

It is evident that the manuscript has suffered deliberate alteration as well as loss. The two missing lectures occupied 194r–209r; the removal of 195–209 made it necessary to insert a new sheet and to recopy the first page of the next lecture, which had occupied the verso of 209. But since there is no sign of tampering with subsequent lectures, we must infer either that Valeriano did not lecture on 21 or that the lecture was not recorded if he did, inasmuch as there is no gap either in the binding or in the numbering of folios or lectures between the discussions of 17 and 22.[143] Perhaps it was Melini who removed Lectures xxii and xxiii (he certainly could have done so easily enough), but the total absence of a lecture on 21 makes it more economical to suppose that the mutilation of the manuscript and the decision to omit 21 were related and roughly contemporary events.

In the censored lectures Valeriano surely discussed the obscene poems 15 and 16. Had he lectured on the *Epistles* of Horace or on any other safe and acceptable topic, there would have been no need to alter the manuscript. At the other extreme, the general tone and restraint of his other lectures makes it unlikely that he indulged in salacious or obscene discussion. He probably gave a short lecture on each poem (if our analysis of the manuscript is correct, the two lectures together occupied only 16 folios), explaining its contents clearly but discreetly.

We may perhaps be able to guess at the tenor of his remarks from three passages in the *Hieroglyphica*, for he sometimes used the same material in both works, as we have had occasion to note.[144] In a section of the *Hieroglyphica* entitled *Titillatio* Valeriano discusses the role of the *renes* and *lumbi* in sexual arousal. The context is not homosexual, and there is no mention of Catullus. The tone is dry and scientific, the examples drawn from scripture and the medical writers. It is tempting to imagine that this account appeared in a slightly different version in the discussion of 16. 11 (*qui duros nequeunt movere lumbos*), especially since when he lectured on 11. 20 Valeriano promised a full discussion of *renes*, *lumbi*, and *ilia*, and since 16. 7–11 concern sexual excitement and would fit neatly as an *exemplum* in the following passage in the *Hieroglyphica*:

the Egyptians refer to sex with the *lumbi*. And so in the comic poets and epigrammatists there is frequent mention of *lumbi* when they want to say something *risqué* . . . Persius alludes to this, when he attacks the recitation of playful poems, saying *cum carmina lumbum intrant* . . .[145]

Compare Catullus:

qui [sc. *versiculi*] tum denique habent salem ac leporem,
si sunt molliculi ac parum pudici,
et quod pruriat incitare possunt,
non dico pueris, sed his pilosis
qui duros nequeunt movere lumbos. (16. 7–11)

The second passage is a short section *De pudendis*, in which Valeriano sets out his approach to the obscene. The ancients, he notes, tended to be free and unembarrassed in their treatment of indecency, and the task of the modern interpreter is serious explanation for those 'who, having been educated scrupulously, probe the heart and inmost marrow of things, not the surface of words'.[146] And finally, a section entitled *De perdice*, 'On the Partridge'. The partridge is an emblem of *amor turpissimus*, i.e. homosexuality: 'These vices are expressed so that they might be condemned and so that mortals, hearing of what seems loathsome, might be frightened away from it.'[147]

Such a discussion as we have suggested would have attempted to treat the homosexual obscenity of 15 and 16 clearly and soberly—and with a strong measure of moral disapproval. Perhaps Valeriano thought that such an approach would be acceptable to the new pope, but it is likely that he soon changed his mind. He did not do so immediately—certainly not before the first lecture on 17, which was written before the mutilation of the manuscript (witness the need to recopy fol. 209v), but perhaps before coming to 21, which he either omitted or did not allow to be recorded.

We must also ask how long the lectures continued, and whether Valeriano in fact discussed the whole text of Catullus.

The lectures were copious and leisurely, as we have seen. In 19 lectures in the winter and spring of 1522 Valeriano covered only 14 poems, the longest of which, 10, contains only 34 verses. Returning to his task in the late autumn of 1522, he discussed 4 more poems in 6 lectures—that is, from Praelectio xxii to Praelectio xxvii, where the manuscript breaks off. Ninety-four poems remained to be discussed—a task that would require something like 130 or 140 additional lectures, if we base our estimate on his rate of about one and a third lectures per poem for 1–22 and ignore the great length of 61–68, which surely would have required far more (3 or 4 lectures for each is a conservative estimate). Even if Valeriano omitted all the obscene poems he would not have been able to cover the rest in fewer than 100 lectures—still a formidable undertaking. Even more important, however, it is hard to imagine that he could have found time to deliver 100 lectures between September 1522 and April or May of 1523. Too many difficulties intervened—the plague, which did not begin to abate until December, the Christmas season, and (above all) the very harsh climate for poets and humanists that seems to have set in in earnest in the spring of 1523.

In the early months of 1523 Adrian embarked on a plan to abolish or reduce the positions held by the humanists under Leo.[148] In March the prominent humanist Jacopo Sadoleto (papal secretary under Leo), left Rome for his bishopric in Carpentras: 'and most important people envy him', says Girolamo Negri, reporting on the event,

> since they would like to do the same thing themselves, because truly Rome is no longer Rome. Having emerged from one plague, we have entered into a greater one. This pope recognizes no one, no favour is shown. All things are full of despair.[149]

In April Adrian forbade the festival of Pasquino and threatened writers of pasquinades with terrible punishments.[150] Examples could be multiplied, but the point is clear. A Rome that had room neither for Sadoleto at one end of the humanist spectrum nor for Pasquino at the other, was certainly no place for Valeriano and his lectures on Catullus. It is likely, then, that Valeriano himself was a part of the exodus of humanists he described in *De litteratorum infelicitate* ('they went to ground, some seeking voluntary exile, others various hiding places . . .'), and that Adrian's papacy, even before the Sack of Rome, cut short the most sophisticated treatment of Catullus yet produced in the Renaissance.

4

Commentarius: Marc-Antoine de Muret, Achilles Statius, and Joseph Scaliger

Divin Muret, tu nous liras Catulle.

(Pierre Ronsard)

As we saw in Chapter 2, the first generation of Catullan commentators laboured mightily just to make sense of Catullus' poems—often with little success. None of the three was a famous or distinguished scholar. Partenio and Palladio were schoolmasters; Alessandro Guarino, though of a famous humanist family, was himself primarily a courtier. Each, to the extent that he is known at all, is known almost exclusively for his work on Catullus. There is nothing to link them with one another, and, except for Partenio, almost nothing to link their work to its time and place. With the second generation it is quite otherwise. Marc-Antoine de Muret, Achilles Statius, and Joseph Scaliger were all renowned and prolific scholars, and the work of each is firmly bound to its intellectual and cultural milieu. Muret's *Catullus* reflects contemporary French poetic theory and the philological polemics of Muret's publisher and friend, Paolo Manuzio. Statius' *Catullus*, presented as a work of Christian humanism, belongs to Rome after the Council of Trent. Scaliger's *Catullus*, designed as a model of Italian philological method, also reveals the austere Calvinism of its author. The three men knew each other's work, and in some cases each other, all too well; for Statius and Scaliger had both once considered Muret their friend, and both were driven by a spirit of personal, as well as professional, rivalry and emulation—restrained and largely suppressed in Statius, but overt and unbridled in Scaliger. The work of each, and particularly that of Scaliger, was written in reaction to Muret.

MURET, THE BRIGADE, AND PAOLO MANUZIO

Thirty years after the lectures of Pierio Valeriano discussed in the previous chapter another poet lectured on Catullus to an audience of real and aspiring poets, but with a very different outcome. Marc-Antoine de Muret had arrived in Paris in 1551 at the age of 25, already a famous and brilliant professor. He was at once taken up by the new school of French poets who called themselves the Brigade—especially Du Bellay, Baïf, and Ronsard—and his lectures attracted large and enthusiastic crowds.[1] 'He seemed to have risen up as a new Demosthenes in a Christian Athens', boasts his student and biographer, Francesco Benci:

> Crowds came to hear him from the whole city, and the lecture room was packed with a mass of people. The seats themselves were filled up, the entrances were blocked. Because of the huge audience not even a foot was left for the teacher to set down his foot, and so on their shoulders as if on the waves he made his way to the podium, from which they all listened to him in eager silence—their greatest fear that he would stop speaking too soon. But when he had finished, they carried him off with universal shouting and applause.[2]

Muret's celebrity in Paris was short-lived, for at the end of 1553 he was driven from the city by charges of heresy and sexual immorality. A few months later he was burned in effigy in Toulouse, and by May of 1554 he had taken refuge in Venice. There, befriended by Paolo Manuzio, he set to work on a commentary on Catullus, which was printed by the Aldine press in October of 1554.

Muret's hasty departure from Paris effectively ended his association with the Brigade, but he had already played his part in their literary programme and made his own contribution to one of the most remarkable chapters in the literary history of the Renaissance. The poets of the Brigade sought nothing less than the creation of a new French poetry, which was to integrate the French literary tradition with classical learning on the one hand and with Neo-Latin and Italian poetry on the other.[3] Aspiring to a fusion of poetry and philology, they found in Muret the ideal collaborator. He was enormously learned, he was a poet, and (surely not least important) he was a contemporary. All were still

Plate 7: Philippe Galle's engraving of Marc-Antoine de Muret in *Imagines L. Doctorum Virorum*, 1587 (Department of Special Collections, Van Pelt-Dietrich Library, University of Pennsylvania)

in their twenties, friends as well as fellow-poets, and the young Muret easily became both a companion and a guide of their activities. His Paris years, although they included various philological projects,[4] must be seen principally as a literary dialogue with the poets of the Brigade.

In 1552 Muret lectured at the Collège de Boncourt on Horace and the elegists (including Catullus), and perhaps on Greek poets as well. His learning was celebrated in Antoine de Baïf's sonnet, *A Marc Antoine de Muret*, which appeared in December 1552:

> O learned Muret, is it your design
> To turn away from Greek, from books that bare
> Their secrets—lore and monuments so fair
> To those who seek true nature there enshrined?
> Now gaze at these laments, Muret, and find
> Cruel madness, pain, to prick and scar and tear.
> Love plants my troubled heart with thorny care.
> Grief forces bitter sighs. Regret is mine.[5]

Baïf's poem neatly compliments Muret's Catullus lectures, for one of its verses ('Love plants my troubled heart with thorny care') is a striking echo of Catullus' *spinosas Erycina serens in pectore curas* (64. 72).[6] At the end of 1552 Muret published the *Iuvenilia*, a collection of his own Latin poetry, which included pieces of various dates arranged by genre. 'I have done what the rich winesellers sometimes do', he says in the *Preface*, 'for they set out many types of wine for their guests to taste, to choose what suits their palate best.'[7] Thus, the work contains his tragedy, *Iulius Caesar*, elegies, satires, epigrams, epistles, and odes. Muret's comments on French poetry in the *Preface* echo the literary manifestos of the Brigade; the Brigade poets and their friends are prominently represented both in the complimentary epistles and odes that end the collection and in the verse testimonials that precede it.[8]

Muret's lectures continued. He seems to have treated the *Anacreontea* and perhaps also the *Greek Anthology* in the winter of 1552–3.[9] In April of 1553 Ronsard anonymously published his *Livret de folastries*, a collection of poems heavily indebted both to Muret and to Catullus.[10] The familiar verses from Cat. 16 appear on the title page as an announcement, a warning, and a justification of the contents:

Nam castum esse decet pium poetam
Ipsum, versiculos nihil necesse est. (16. 5–6)

Ronsard's dedication, 'A Janot Parisien' (i.e. Jean-Antoine de Baïf), is a *contaminatio* of 1 (*Cui dono lepidum novum libellum*) and a dedication by the Neo-Latin poet, Marcantonio Flaminio. It is Catullus, however, that one thinks of first and last. 'To whom do I give these trifles and these dainty little verses?' asks Ronsard. 'To you, my friend Janot. . . . Take it then, Janot, such as it is . . . so that you and I and my book may live more than a single age.'[11] The *Folastries* were conceived as French counterparts of the Catullan hendecasyllable, and their title, 'Folastries', ('little follies') recalls Catullus' names for his own verses: *nugae*, *ineptiae*, *lusus*.[12] The second major section of Ronsard's *Livret* is devoted to a collection entitled *Traduction de quelques epigrammes grecz, à Marc Antoine de Muret*, and its first poem is dedicated to Muret.[13]

In the *Livret de folastries* Ronsard embarked on a new poetic programme, turning from the elaborate Pindaric style of his earlier poetry to the lighter, less overtly complicated mode of the Catullan hendecasyllable and Greek epigram.[14] Du Bellay had called for the adoption of the hendecasyllable into French poetry as early as 1549, but Muret and his lectures provided the essential stimulus, inspiring not only Ronsard but other French poets as well to write in the Catullan manner.[15] Only a month after the publication of the *Folastries* Muret played a still more active role in another literary event—the second edition of Ronsard's *Amours* (May 1553). The work is a collaboration: Ronsard's poems are presented with a full scholarly French commentary by Muret (complete with preface).[16] Muret is acknowledged on the title page, his portrait appears at the beginning of the volume, along with those of Ronsard and his Cassandre, and he is honoured in the ode *Les Isles fortunées à Marc Antoine de Muret*. In this poem, Ronsard, like Horace in the sixteenth *Epode*, urges his friends to abandon their corrupt and war-torn world for a mythical realm of peace and plenty—*les îsles fortunées*. Muret will be their Orpheus: 'There, venerable in a white robe and crowned with a branch of laurel or twisted olive, guiding our steps, . . . divine Muret, you will read to us Catullus . . .'.[17] Ronsard's Orpheus is not a poet but a teacher of poetic lore, and the account of his repertoire, which includes not only Catullus but also Anacreon and the elegists and above all Homer,[18] pays tribute to the varied learning Muret has brought to the interpretation of Ronsard's own poetry.

But in the spring of 1553 Muret was already under fire. He composed his notes on Ronsard in haste and under constant pressure to leave Paris, as he says in the preface to his commentary:

> But being urged daily to withdraw from this city by the authority of those to whom, after God, I owe the greatest obedience, and so pressed that at almost every moment I must think of departing, I could undertake nothing, with my spirit troubled and ill-suited to bring forth fruit that was worthy of coming to light. So finally, I have taken a chance, hoping that my toil will find some excuse among those who know that I have been brought to such a pass that I have had to write as much each day as the printers could put in production.[19]

His troubles soon came to a head, and he fled from Paris before the end of the year. By May of 1554 he was in Italy, on the eve of a still more brilliant career than he had enjoyed in Paris.

In Paris Muret's success had been assured by his association with the Brigade and their literary programme. In Venice he walked into the waiting arms of Paolo Manuzio: 'it happened as if by a magic wand', he claims, 'that no sooner had I set foot in this city than I was received into his friendship and intimate circle . . .'.[20] Muret was indeed lucky in Venice, for his interests perfectly complemented those of Manuzio. Manuzio had a programme of his own—to publish readable texts and to attack and discredit the Florentine scholar Pier Vettori, with whom he had a long-standing personal feud.[21] Muret, eager to make a name for himself in Italy, needed support and an outlet for his philological works. Their first venture was Muret's commentary on Catullus.

Although Muret's commentary was published scarcely five months after his arrival in Italy, we find him already well launched in his new alliance. In the *Preface* he disingenuously invokes Manuzio as a reason for his presence in Italy:

> But when I had come recently into Italy both to see this country—those who miss it without regret seem to me to care too little for the memory of Antiquity—and (to tell the truth, by Hercules!) in order to make the acquaintance of other learned men, but especially of Paolo Manuzio,

because in his writings I thought I discerned clear signs of excellent learning and outstanding character . . .[22]

Manuzio is named twice in the commentary in announcements of future publishing ventures: the first edition of Servius' commentary on Terence ('not that counterfeit Servius, of whom some nonsense on Terence is commonly circulated, but the ancient Servius'), and the first edition of Longinus, with the Greek text edited by Manuzio and Muret's Latin translation.[23] Muret also heralds Manuzio as the author of various emendations; since his improvements are negligible it seems likely that Muret introduced his name principally to advertise their partnership.[24] Manuzio's target Vettori is even more prominent in the commentary. Vettori's *Variae Lectiones* were published in September, 1553. Muret probably did not have time to study them closely in the last troubled months before his flight from Paris, but he certainly did so before publishing his own commentary, which responds in some way to nearly every one of Vettori's observations on Catullus.[25] Although his responses are ostensibly even-handed (sometimes he accepts Vettori's ideas, sometimes he even attributes them to him by name), in fact Muret takes every opportunity to represent Vettori as inept and lacking in judgement. Thus, Vettori had quoted some verses from Plautus' *Pseudolus* in his interpretation of the notoriously corrupt Cat. 54; Muret (without mentioning Vettori) uses a quotation from the *Pseudolus* to deny that any interpretation is possible: 'I believe that no one except the Sibyl could interpret these verses, as that well known Pseudolus in Plautus says.'[26] Vettori quoted some verses from the Greek comic poet Alexis as a parallel to 39. Muret corrects them: 'and I am sure that I will do so with the good will of Vettori himself.'[27] And unkindest cut of all: in a long and elaborate discussion Vettori had attributed one of the *priapea* to Catullus; Muret does the same, makes no mention of Vettori, and ostentatiously corrects the text:

Moreover, since Terentianus tells us that Catullus sang verses of this sort to the god of gardens, and there are some verses extant among Vergil's jests that learned men have attributed to Catullus (and we, too, have never thought otherwise) we will set them down both so that they may be restored to their rightful author and so that we may note quickly some points in them that have escaped others.[28]

Muret also comes at Vettori indirectly, by attacking his model Poliziano.[29] He does so to the detriment of the text, since he spitefully rejects three correct readings in the process.[30]

But the commentary is as much French as Italian. Though oriented towards Muret's new life and the world of Manuzio with its publishing projects and philological polemic, it looks back also to Paris and the Brigade. We get brief glimpses of the past—Lazare Baïf and his library, Muret's Horace lectures in Paris and a day he spent with Adrien Turnèbe studying Pierre Galland's ancient manuscript of Horace, the objections made by Muret's great friend, Memmius Fremiot, to a reading in 61 as 'frigid' and 'alien to the charm of the poet'.[31] The *Preface* is dominated by the poetic theory of the Brigade, as Muret resumes the discussion of the scarcity of outstanding poets that he had begun in the *Preface* to the *Iuvenilia* two years earlier. In the *Preface* to the *Iuvenilia* he was concerned specifically with contemporary French poetry, whether in French or in Latin. In the *Preface* to Catullus, however, his theme is ancient poetry, although he begins with an observation about poetry in general: 'There has never been any great abundance of outstanding poets . . . and their praise has always been great.'[32] In the *Preface* to the *Iuvenilia* Muret explained that although all poets must possess 'excellence of intellect, skill in language, and extensive knowledge of many important matters',[33] these qualities alone are not sufficient to produce great poetry. Although he identified a specific essential ingredient for French poetry (the ability to bring the riches of classical literature into the vernacular), his prescription for success in contemporary Latin poetry was vague: perhaps great poets arise at 'some proper season' or 'somehow by the fixed revolutions of the heavens'.[34] The argument is similar in the *Preface* to Catullus. In other endeavours, says Muret, a person who is not actually stupid can be confident of at least modest accomplishment if he applies himself, but it is otherwise with poetry:

> In this nothing can be accomplished by toil, diligence, or long hours except by those whom nature herself has somehow fashioned for it. This very fact created admiration for poets in the minds of mankind—evidently because people were astounded when they saw that some, spontaneously and with a natural inclination, effortlessly poured out what was marked by every ornament of style and adorned in many

places with signs of varied learning, and that their verses not only charmed the ear with their pleasing sound, but also stirred the inmost thoughts and feelings of their audience with every kind of emotion. But they saw that others, though thoroughly polished by knowledge of the liberal arts, could never achieve a reputation or rank among the poets no matter how hard or long they studied.[35]

Muret is speaking the language of the Brigade, but he is also alluding to a specific work, Ronsard's *Ode à Michel de l'Hospital*, which sets out in detail the theories of the Brigade on poetry and the nature of poetic inspiration.[36] His contrast between the practised art of other professions and the inspired genius of the poet echoes Ronsard's lines:

By art the helmsman in the sea guides and turns the bridle of his ship, by art the orator makes his case, by art kings are warriors, by art craftsmen are created. But if you do not have the unprofitable experience of that mistake, straightway my divine furor will polish your skill.[37]

Ronsard's ode continues with a literary history, which traces a process of degeneration from the early Greek poets ('*poëtes divins*'), who were directly inspired by the Muses, to the classical and Alexandrian Greeks ('*poëtes humaines*'), farther from the Muses' furor, and to the Romans, still farther removed, but so adept at the lyre that 'even today one hears the murmur of their voices sounding.'[38] The movement is similar in the *Preface* of Muret's *Catullus*:

As in every treatment of elegant learning, so in the excellence of this quality too the talents of the Greeks flourished far beyond the rest. The Romans not only came into contact with poetry later but cultivated it with less care, and in a short time they strayed from the path of writing poetry well. Thus, when poetry, setting out from its rude beginnings among them, at last through many stages had reached Vergil (and I am convinced that nothing more divine than this man could have been created), their abilities afterwards so began to deteriorate that it is remarkable how great a change followed, and in how short a time. It was especially the Spanish poets who both sullied the purity of Roman speech and—when they had imported an inflated and swollen style (and one suited to the character of their race)—turned others away by their example from the direct and simple imitation of nature, in which is placed the special glory of poets and to which earlier poets had devoted themselves with every effort.[39]

Muret has borrowed from the theories of the Brigade in order to establish a literary and poetic tone for his commentary, but he also has a polemical purpose—to attack two modern day 'Spaniards' who are so deluded by 'painted beauty' and 'counterfeit elegance' that they prefer the Spanish poets Lucan and Martial to their superior Roman predecessors Vergil and Catullus:

> I think there is as much difference between the writings of Martial and Catullus as between the words of some wag on the street-corner and the well-bred jests of a gentleman, seasoned with sophisticated wit. . . . In Martial there is none of that innate and totally unvarnished genuineness of Latin style, but it is outstanding in Catullus. Therefore, although I have always disliked the other somehow, there has never been a time in which I did not wonderfully love Catullus.[40]

The opposition of Martial and Catullus would be familiar enough to Muret's old friends in Paris, since they disdained the one as much as they admired the other.[41] But Muret's reference to 'two Spaniards of the present day' seems to point rather to Venice and the polemics of Manuzio, although the specific targets have not been identified.

POETRY AND PHILOLOGY IN MURET'S *CATULLUS*

The time was right for a new commentary on Catullus. It had been over thirty years since the appearance of the last full commentary, the *Expositiones* of Alessandro Guarino (1521). But the *Expositiones* had been obsolete even at the time of their publication, since Guarino derived most of his ideas from the work of his father Battista Guarino (d. 1505) and from the commentary of Partenio (1485). The lectures of Guarino's contemporary, Valeriano, for all their learning and sophistication, lay unpublished and unknown.[42] Although commentaries on individual poems were beginning to appear in the late 1540s,[43] and Vettori had devoted two dozen chapters to Catullus in his *Variae Lectiones* (1553), scholarship had not kept pace with Catullus' growing popularity. Eighteen editions of Catullus were published in the period between 1521 and 1554 (fourteen of them outside Italy).[44] Italian Neo-Latin poets had imitated Catullus from the early days of the Renaissance, but from around 1530 on he also became a favourite model for French Neo-Latin poetry, and in the early 1550s, as we have seen, the Catullan style was naturalized into French poetry.[45]

Although Muret is generally silent about his debts to recent scholars (with the exception of Vettori), he undoubtedly drew on much of the material from the past thirty years, for his commentary bears a very different aspect from those of his predecessors. Between the commentary of Guarino and that of Muret many of the grossest problems and confusions in Catullus had been solved—or we might better say that they had simply vanished. In Muret the *dispositio carminum*, with few exceptions, is identical to that in modern editions.[46] The Mentula poems, so problematic for Partenio, Palladio, and Guarino, are properly separated and interpreted. The elaborate scenarios used to explain them (and poems like 35, 41, and 42) have been banished in favour of straightforward summaries.[47] The trivial and irrelevant information that abounded in the first generation of commentaries is gone, for Muret is not generally disposed to traffic in the unnecessary or the obvious.[48] That is not to say, however, that all of the problems have been solved. Cruces and mysteries remain. But Muret, unlike his predecessors, refuses to manufacture complicated explanations in the face of difficulty. He states his refusal as a matter of principle in his remarks on 113 (*Consule Pompeio primum duo, Cinna, solebant*):

> Here, too, I am not ashamed to admit that I do not understand these four verses. I could refute other people's ideas. I could also, if I liked, make up something on their example. I prefer to make a simple statement of the case and not to do the same thing as those who, while they explain without hesitation the sound, the corrupt, the easy, the difficult without distinction, appear learned perhaps to the ignorant, but ignorant and rash to the learned and intelligent.[49]

The distance that separated Muret from his predecessors allowed him a certain freedom from their interpretations. Moreover, since he has the capacity and the learning to read the commentaries of all critically and to profit from their mistakes, we might expect him to fulfil the hopes expressed by Partenio when he published the first commentary—that other scholars would make use of his work and constantly improve on it to the better understanding of the poet. Partenio's hopes were not realized by his immediate successors, for, as we have seen, they allowed his commentary to set the terms for their own, and so read Catullus, not directly, but as though through a filter of someone else's ideas.[50] Muret does much better, for he is able to interpret Catullus for himself. His independence is far from complete, however, because although he is largely free of the interpretations, or at least of the mind-set, of his predecessors, he is not free of their text. His principal source is either the second Aldine or one of the Gryphianae, which he has compared—not very systematically—with the texts of Partenio, Palladio, and Guarino.[51] But none of these texts was based on a collation of manuscripts, and of the previous editors, only Avanzi had undertaken a systematic study of the early editions.[52] Muret, then, like all editors from the time of the *editio princeps*, used the base text with its various corrections and accretions; both his own text and to a large extent its interpretation resulted from the inherited amalgam. Since the base text generally improved as it went along, Muret's text (which of course incorporates his own improvements) is better than those of the earlier commentators.[53] But we must remember that the base text picked up errors as well as improvements in its progress, and that these often enough passed unremarked into the tradition—all the more easily since no one was attempting to reconstitute the text on the basis of a fresh and independent study. Thus, although Muret's text and commentary benefited from the overall improvement of the base text, they were equally vulnerable to its accumulated mistakes.

Muret claims, of course, that his text is based solidly on the witness of *veteres libri*, by which he apparently means the pre-Parthenian texts of the previous century, and he makes occasional half-hearted appeals to the authority of the manuscripts, which we need not take very seriously.[54] He invokes the early editions to clear away some of the mistakes of his predecessors, and piously protests against their additions and gratuitous improvements.[55] Thus, on Partenio's supplement for the lacuna at 95. 4:

> We cannot heal these wounds, for we are not seers or fortune-tellers. Moreover, far from us be such madness as to imitate what certain others have done with their bad example—men who had no scruples, when something was lacking, about polluting with intolerable rashness these sacrosanct remnants of the venerable past with their own feeble efforts. Perhaps when Minerva had consumed the shoulder of Pelops (as the

story goes), it was allowed for the gods to attach an ivory shoulder in place of the real one. But it is not allowed for us, when time has destroyed the real verses of poets, to substitute others made up by ourselves in their place. I explained earlier that this had been done by Parthenius in the sapphic verses [51]. He did the same thing in this place, too (since he knew no limit once his rashness was incited, and since for many people having sinned once is argument enough for them to dare to sin a second time), and he mixed his own pentameter in with Catullus' verses. If he had not admitted it, today perhaps the verse would have been attributed to Catullus without any hesitation.[56]

But this respect for the past should not deceive us, for in fact Muret was all too often ignorant of the readings of the early editions he so conspicuously reveres. He attributes *utrum ne* at 97. 2 and *guttis abstersisti* at 99. 8 to 'the old books'; modern editors credit both readings to the Trincavelli edition of 1535. At 116. 4 he prints *Tela infesta meum mittere in usque caput*, claiming to have read the verse *in veteris libris*, but in modern editions he receives credit for both the correction *tela* and the supplement *meum*. At 66. 94 and 98. 4 he attacks Poliziano for corrupting the text of the *veteres libri*, although in both cases Poliziano was vindicating rather than changing the traditional text.[57]

In his ignorance Muret sometimes unwittingly admires the style or discusses the literary qualities of a predecessor's erroneous innovation. Two examples will suffice. In 10 Varus' naughty *amica* asks Catullus for the loan of his (nonexistent) litter bearers, much to the poet's discomfort:

> 'quaeso', inquit 'mihi, mi Catulle, paulum
> istos commoda: nam volo ad Serapim
> deferri.' 'mane', inquii puellae, (10. 25–7)

For line 27 Guarino had urged his father's *Ferri mane. Mane inquio puellae*. Valeriano, as we have seen, ridiculed and demolished the reading,[58] but Muret was not to know that. He prints Guarino's version with the enthusiastic gloss: '*Mane. Mane*. The first is an adverb, the second a verb. It is, moreover, an extremely pleasant paronomasia.'[59] Muret should have known that the reading was an innovation since Guarino says as much in his commentary, but he has silently incorporated it as if it belonged to the traditional text. In 28 (*Pisonis comites, cohors inanis*) the poet compares the bad luck of his friends Veranius and Fabullus with their praetor Piso to his own ill-treatment by Memmius—and he does so with his usual vivid obscenity. The first Aldine had divided the poem into two—28. 1–8 (on Veranius and Fabullus) and 28. 9–15 (on Memmius).[60] Muret, seemingly unaware of its comparative novelty, persists in the division, and worries about the propriety of the first verses of the 'Memmius poem':

> O Memmi bene me, ac diu supinum
> Tota ista trabe lentus irrumasti (28. 9–10).

Unless I am badly mistaken, the poet is not speaking here in his own person, but is imitating the voice of someone who had suffered this filth from the praetor Memmius. For it is not to be believed either that a man of character and good family would have endured such vileness to his person, or that (if he had proceeded to such a pitch of shamelessness) he would have been so phenomenally stupid as to brand himself willingly in his own verses.[61]

We can easily convict Muret of editorial carelessness—and indeed he was found guilty by his contemporaries as well[62]—but the truth of the matter is that he was primarily interested, not in the text, but in the poetry of Catullus. Catullus' qualities (a deceptively unassuming elegance of style and a prodigiously learned Alexandrianism) appealed to his own; for Muret was a poet and a formidable stylist himself, and in Paris, where the primacy of Greek studies was almost an article of faith, he had acquired a taste for the Alexandrian poets.[63]

Not surprisingly, 68 is one of his favourite poems. The elegy is one of Catullus' most difficult and recherché productions—an elaborate thank-you to his friend Allius (or Manius—the point is important, and we shall return to it presently) for providing a rendezvous for Catullus and his mistress. In a concentric series of digressions the poet takes us from his mistress on the threshold of Allius' house, to the bride Laodamia burning with love for Protesilaos, to Troy (*commune sepulcrum Asiae Europaeque* [68. 89]), and finally—at the very heart of the poem—to a lament for his brother, who also died at Troy. Muret is lavish in his praise:

This elegy is altogether very beautiful, and perhaps none more beautiful can be found in the entire Latin language. For the style is most pure, and the narration is compounded of a remarkable diversity of emotions, and so many highlights of language and thought are scattered everywhere, that one may see from this single poem how greatly Catullus could have surpassed all others in this genre if he had applied the force of his talent to its cultivation.[64]

The qualities he singles out are virtually the same as those he had attributed to the inspired poet in the *Preface*—variety of emotions and ornamentation of language and style.

Although he has left out erudition, treated in the *Preface* as the necessary but not sufficient characteristic of fine poetry, he soon goes on to discuss it as the pre-eminent virtue of his favourite simile (68. 107–18):

Seeking the opportunity to mingle different myths and to ornament his work by scattering (as it were) the seeds of his learning, he says that Laodamia's love was deeper than a certain marsh, which used to be in Thessaly, but was afterwards drained by the effort of Hercules. And having taken the opportunity, he digresses to touch lightly on the deeds of Hercules.[65]

And Muret takes the opportunity to sow some of the seeds of his own learning by giving Pausanias' account of the Stymphalian birds (*Stymphalia monstra*, 68. 113). But his effect is marred by a small inaccuracy: Hercules' marsh is not in Thessaly, but in Arcadia. The mistake, which arises from Muret's uncritical use of the texts of his predecessors, provides another example of his ignorance or carelessness of the tradition.[66] The point is a small one, but another is far more important—the question of the poem's addressee. The addressee is named six times: at 68. 11, 30, 41, 50, 66, and 150. At 11 and 30 a name beginning with a consonant is required (the archetype read *Mali*); but elsewhere the name seems to be *Allius* (it must begin with a vowel at 50). Are Manius/Mallius and Allius the same man? Is 68 one poem or two? These are complicated and still controversial matters, which clearly have great relevance to the interpretation of Catullus' poem—or poems.[67] The interesting point here is that Muret was not even aware of the problem. He entitles the poem *Ad Manlium* and prints *Manli* or *Manlius* everywhere except at v. 150, where he follows the traditional reading *aliis*. At v. 50 (where an initial vowel is required) he innocently prints *Deserto in Manli*, an expedient introduced by Calfurnio for the traditional reading, *in deserto ali* (rendered as *indeserto aliis* by the editions before Calfurnio). It was left for his successors Statius and Scaliger, who actually consulted manuscripts, to notice the discrepancies.[68]

Although Muret's literary talents could accomplish little when they were tripped up by editorial negligence, he was an excellent interpreter if the text was not at issue. Cat. 64 is the poet's longest and most elaborate work, a miniature epic (or epyllion) in the Alexandrian style. It tells two stories, one framed within the other. The frame is the marriage of Peleus and Thetis, the insert the tale of Ariadne and Theseus, depicted as an ecphrasis on the coverlet of the marriage bed. Muret notices Alexandrian details—a bilingual pun, a translation of a verse from Theocritus—and glosses Catullus' verses with an abundance of well-chosen Greek parallels.[69] He perceives the emotional effect of Catullus' similes. When Ariadne awakes and sees that Theseus has left her, she stands on the shore 'like a stone statue of a maenad' (*saxea ut effigies bacchantis*, 64. 61) and watches him sail away. 'There is very great power in this comparison', Muret remarks:

> First, the comparison of Ariadne to a bacchante signifies that both in her expression and in the attitude of her whole body she displayed a certain violent excitement of mental disturbance. The addition, 'stone likeness', shows that her grief was so violent that for a long time she could neither move nor burst forth into utterance. For any excessive passion tends to take away the use of one's voice and to impede for a time the functions of every part of the body. No wonder, then, that the poets say that Niobe hardened into stone when she saw her children pierced by the arrows of Apollo and Diana.[70]

Catullus' comparison of Ariadne at her first sight of Theseus to the myrtle on the banks of the Eurotas (64. 89–90) reminds Muret of the comparison of the bride to flowering myrtle in the epithalamium for Manlius (61. 21–25), and he traces its source to Odysseus' comparison of Nausicaa to a young palm (*Od*. 6. 162–3), providing a metrical translation—one of several in the commentary.[71] He is also the first critic to see how Catullus' account of Theseus' faithlessness both depends on and is explained by his Alexandrian sources. The story opens with Ariadne standing on the shore in the first realization that she has been abandoned. Of Theseus at the same moment Catullus says:

> immemor at iuvenis fugiens pellit vada remis,
> irrita ventosae linquens promissa procellae. (64. 58–9)

Modern readers, like Ariadne herself, condemn Theseus for his unfaithfulness, but Muret has an explanation. Thus, on *immemor at iuvenis* at 64. 58:

> He seems to be alluding to the opinion of those who say that it came to pass by the power of Bacchus that Theseus completely forgot Ariadne as he cast off. And so his leaving her was brought about only by forgetfulness (which was sent upon him by divine power), and not by an ungrateful heart. See Theocritus' *Pharmaceutria* [Theoc. 2] and the commentaries on it.[72]

The passage that Muret remembers in Theocritus is another curse of an abandoned woman: 'Whether woman or man lies beside him, may his forgetfulness be as great as they say Theseus' once was when he forgot fair-haired Ariadne in Dia' (Theoc. 2. 45–56). The scholia ad loc. explain:

> When Theseus had carried off Minos' daughter Ariadne and sailed away to the island of Dia (now called Naxos), he suffered forgetfulness in accordance with the will of Dionysus and left her as she slept.[73]

Dionysus, of course, made Theseus forget so that he could marry Ariadne himself, and the story in Catullus ends with the arrival of Bacchus with his train of Satyrs and Maenads: 'te quaerens, Ariadne, tuoque incensus amore' (64. 253).

Some of Muret's observations on 64 had been anticipated by his predecessors,[74] but he is the first to bring them together and to demonstrate both the Alexandrianism and the emotional force of Catullus' poem. To take only the comparison of Ariadne to the myrtle: the link with other similes of the same kind emphasizes Ariadne's youth, innocence, and readiness for marriage, and establishes her as a kind of bride—an essential element both of the Ariadne myth[75] and of the design of the poem, in which Ariadne's unions with Theseus and Bacchus provide a foil to the marriage of Peleus and Thetis.

MURET DISPLAYS HIS WARES

Given Muret's interests it was natural for him to pay special attention to Catullus' translations of Greek poetry. Cat. 66 had been identified as a translation of Callimachus' *Lock of Berenice* by the earliest commentators, and Poliziano had been able to correct one of its verses from a fragment of Callimachus that he had found in the scholia on Apollonius Rhodius.[76] But Callimachus' poem was lost, and no substantial fragment of it was recovered until the twentieth century.[77] Muret was frustrated by the loss, for he knew that Callimachus' Greek would be invaluable for understanding and correcting Catullus' corrupt text. His regret, however, was as much literary as philological:

> It would be pleasing to confront the Greek with the Latin, to observe not only in individual words, but in figures and ornaments of style, in the very pattern of the verses, and finally in the whole structure of the poem, how neatly and skilfully the Latin poet (indisputably the most elegant of all) emulated the force and charm of the poet who is easily foremost in this style among the Greeks.[78]

Muret knew only the three and one half verses of Callimachus that Poliziano had recovered from the scholia on Aratus and Apollonius (Call. fr. 110, 7–8, 48–9), but he did his best to compare the two poems. The results are not impressive. The only literary observation he can make is a comment on 66. 7 that Catullus has translated two verses of Callimachus with four of his own—a remark that the fragmentary state of Callimachus' text still will not allow us to corroborate. His philological efforts are spoiled by his interest in outdoing Poliziano. Poliziano had corrected 66. 48 from Callimachus fr. 110. 48; Muret ostentatiously corrects Poliziano's Greek text, and rewrites Callimachus' verse on the model of Catullus'.[79] And at 66. 94, where there was no corresponding verse from Callimachus, Muret discarded the correct reading (which Poliziano had vindicated) in favour of a verse of his own composition that he falsely characterized as the traditional reading.[80]

In the case of 51, however, Muret was in a position to make a more substantial contribution. Cat. 51 (*Ille mi par esse deo videtur*) is a creative translation of Sappho 31, which is preserved only in the essay *On the Sublime* by pseudo-Longinus. Longinus' essay had been known in the fifteenth century (there are several manuscripts from the period 1450–1500), but it attracted little interest. In the middle of the sixteenth century, however, the work received a sudden flurry of attention. Paolo Manuzio had access to Cardinal Bessarion's manuscript, corrected by his friend the Cretan scholar Francesco Porto, and he planned to publish the first edition with a Latin translation by Muret—a project announced by Muret in his commentary on 51. But Manuzio and Muret were anticipated by Francesco Robortello, who published Longinus from another manuscript only a few weeks before the publication of Muret's *Catullus*, and their projected edition never appeared, although Manuzio printed the text alone in 1555.[81] But even though Muret and Manuzio did not have their triumph with Longinus, Muret must be recognized as the first to identify 51 as a translation of Sappho, whose text he prints in his commentary. He makes his disclosure with a just if scarcely modest sense of its importance:

> It is a pleasure in this place to earn the particular gratitude of all who are fascinated by the study of Antiquity and the charm of tender and sensuous poetry. For when I had begun to translate Dionysius Longinus' work *On the Sublime* into Latin . . . I noted many other things in it indeed . . . but also the most charming lyric of the poetess Sappho, which Catullus has largely translated in the preceding verses.[82]

The possession of Sappho's poem gave Muret the opportunity to do what he had longed to do in the case of 66 and Callimachus—to confront and compare Catullus' poem with its Greek model:

> Is there anyone (at least of those who have some sense of literature and culture) who would not take the greatest pleasure in comparing in turn the verses of the most outstanding woman in this genre in human history and those of the tenderest of all the Latin poets?[83]

But Muret himself makes no such comparison. His only literary comment on either poem is a summary of 51:

> Happy the man, he says, who can enjoy the sight and address of Lesbia. Afterwards he chastises himself, asserting that such notions arise only from idleness, and he adds the serious thought that idleness has caused the destruction of many kings and many cities.[84]

It is not clear why Muret neglected the opportunity for a close comparison of Sappho and Catullus. Perhaps he expected the texts to speak for themselves or thought that detailed comments would detract from the effect of his great announcement. Or perhaps he did not have time (we must remember that his commentary appeared only a few months after his arrival in Italy and that he claims to have spent less than three months on its composition).[85] Muret's omissions were not repaired by his immediate successors Statius and Scaliger.[86] Indeed, no truly comparative treatment of the two poems appeared before the discussion of Janus Dousa the younger in 1592—nearly forty years after Muret's publication of Sappho with Catullus.[87]

Although Muret promised more than he delivered in the case of 51, he had accomplished his real purpose—to make a striking and memorable addition to his commentary, which was conceived largely as a means of promoting his new career in Italy and his partnership with Manuzio. By including Sappho's poem he intended both to create an immediate sensation and to advertise the publication of Longinus, a joint venture of even greater interest. His discussions of 63 and 17 were directed to similar purposes.

Cat. 63 had attracted attention even in the fifteenth century. Although the commentators with their limited understanding of metre had wisely concentrated on the psychology and sexual identity of Attis, the poets were bolder, and the strange and difficult rhythms of the galliambic inspired a series of fifteenth- and sixteenth-century poems.[88] Muret adds his own to the series, using his *Galliambus in Bacchum* to introduce his commentary on 63. It is likely, as Morrison suggests, that Muret composed this poem too late for it to be included in his *Iuvenilia*,[89] but the *Galliambus* is ideally suited for his present purpose. Muret uses it to demonstrate what he has said about the intricacies of the galliambic metre, but also to rival the galliambic poems of three famous predecessors, Michele Marullo, Giorgio Anselmo, and Marcantonio Flaminio—better than average poets, he observes patronizingly, who none the less made metrical mistakes because they had only a corrupt text of Catullus as their model.[90] Thus, with a single stroke Muret attempts both to present himself as a better poet than his forerunners on the grounds that he is a better philologist, and to outshine previous commentators with a display of poetic virtuosity.

The priapean metre of 17 provided him with an even better opportunity—to add to the corpus of Catullus. From the time of Partenio scholars had speculated that some of Catullus' poetry was lost, since they believed from a comment in the elder Pliny that Catullus wrote love charms like those in the bucolics of Theocritus and Vergil (Theoc. 2; Vergil, *Ecl.* 8).[91] But there was evidence that Catullus had also written priapea, or poems to the fertility god, Priapus, as Valeriano had discovered from the metrical treatise of Terentianus Maurus. After discussing the metre of 17 with Terentianus as his guide, Valeriano told his students: 'you should know . . . that other poems of this metre were composed by Catullus which have perished through the ravages of time.'[92] He was thinking of the four previously unknown verses in priapeans that Terentianus had quoted as Catullus' (i.e. Cat. fr. 1), and perhaps also of Terentianus' tantalizing postscript: 'and we know that Catullus wrote many similar [verses].'[93] Terentianus' words encouraged other scholars to seek more priapean poems that could be attributed to Catullus, and Pier Vettori thought he had found one, as he announced in a chapter of the *Variae lectiones* entitled, 'An elegant poem, whose author is now incorrect or uncertain, is shown to be by Catullus'.[94] Vettori's candidate was one of the three priapea in the *Appendix Vergiliana (Hunc ego, o iuvenes, locum villulamque palustrem*, Buecheler 86). He argued that its style was redolent of Catullus, pointed out that it belonged to the same genre as the verses quoted by Terentianus Maurus, recalled Terentianus' assertion that Catullus wrote other verses in the same metre, and produced an additional priapean fragment quoted by Nonius Marcellus (Cat. fr. 2).

Muret managed not only to exploit and expand Vettori's ideas but to deprive him of the credit as well. In a metrical appendix to his commentary on 17 he quotes Terentianus and follows his account of the priapean, emphasizing its softness and supposed affinity with the hexameter—all as preamble to his real business, which is ascribing new priapeans to Catullus. He easily outdoes Vettori. As we have seen, he corrects the text of Vettori's poem. But he does more. He finds another priapean in the *Appendix Vergiliana* to ascribe to Catullus (*Ego haec, ego arte fabricata rustica*, Buecheler 85) and prints both poems in the same format as the rest of the text—complete with commentary. Muret's discovery (appropriated from Vettori) was designed to be a high point of his commentary, but it seems to have had little immediate effect, if we can judge from the work of his closest successors. Statius prints the four verses from Terentianus at the end of his commentary on 17 and says nothing of Muret's two priapea. Scaliger accepted the attribution in his edition of the *Catalepton* (1572), only to reject it a few years later in his commentary on Catullus.[95] Later editors were less cautious, and the poems inserted by Muret (Terentianus' verses and the pseudo-Vergilian priapea) were regularly printed after 17 until they were excluded by Lachmann in 1829. By that time the numbering of the poems had become canonical, and removal of the three priapea (poems 18–20) left the anomalous gap between 17 and 21 that is still found in modern editions as the only legacy of the attempt to find new poems for Catullus.

Muret and Manuzio intended the publication of their *Catullus* to be an important literary event, and there is no reason to doubt that it lived up to their expectations. It was, after all, the first major work on the poet in over a generation, and its brilliant and controversial author had made his greatest reputation with Catullus. But there is little evidence for its immediate reception except that Muret rose quickly to prominence in Venice after its publication. In October 1554 he seems to have secured a professor's chair in Venice, and in the next year he published editions of Terence and Horace (both with commentaries), as well as three lectures *De studiis litterarum* that he had delivered in connection with his candidacy for a professorship.[96] All were printed by Manuzio. Although now well situated, however, Muret was apparently not content. At the beginning of 1558 he left Venice to teach privately in Padua, but the move was only a stopgap, for he was already negotiating to secure the patronage of the francophile Cardinal of Ferrara, Ippolito II d'Este.

Unfortunately, we do not know when Muret and Manuzio first began to think of a second edition, but their plans were already well advanced by the time of Muret's move to Padua, as we learn from their almost daily correspondence on the subject. In the earliest mention of the new edition the deadline is almost at hand. 'I expect you in any event on 1 April,' Manuzio writes to Muret at the end of March 1558, 'but if not, I expect your Catullus. It is inconvenient to have a single day's delay.'[97] Muret responds, somewhat lamely, on 29 March: 'About Catullus, allow me a little time, and I shall work hard to satisfy you.'[98] In the correspondence that follows various details are arranged. The edition is to include Tibullus and Propertius as well as Catullus, and on 12 April Muret writes to make sure of Manuzio's intentions:

But I ask, what do you plan to do? Do you perhaps mean to publish Catullus with my commentary at the same time with Tibullus and Propertius without any commentary, and to bind these three into a single volume? I am beginning to suspect something of the sort. If that is the case, I do not criticize or disapprove—I think the book will even sell better—but it will seem odd to many people, I think.[99]

'You've got it!' Manuzio responds. 'It will be excellent to join the three poets—the one ELUCIDATED BY THE COMMENTARY OF MARCUS ANTONIUS MURETUS, the other two . . . EMENDED BY THE SAME.'[100] Muret finished his revisions of Catullus and was reading the proofs by mid-April, even as Manuzio was encouraging him to press forward with Tibullus and Propertius.[101] A few weeks later Manuzio was reminding him of their next project, the second edition of Terence.[102] Given Muret's many projects in 1558 and the constant pressure he was under from Manuzio (to say nothing of his negotiations with Cardinal d'Este or of his teaching responsibilities in Padua), it is hardly surprising that the edition of Catullus that appeared in the autumn of 1558 was little different from the first—except that it was accompanied by Muret's hasty editions of Tibullus and Propertius.

ACHILLES STATIUS: PHILOLOGY AND CHRISTIAN HUMANISM IN POST-TRIDENTINE ROME

From the appearance of the *editio princeps* in 1472 the editing and interpretation of Catullus had followed a single course. Each editor derived his text from the one before; each commentator read the poet through the eyes of his predecessor. Muret was a better and more sophisticated literary critic than the commentators of the previous era, and the quality of his work benefited accordingly, but at bottom his commentary (in either edition) was a hasty, commercial production, and its considerable literary merits were undermined by editorial weakness. The base text had become an increasingly elaborate and flimsy house of cards that could not support another ramshackle addition. It was time to knock it down and to rebuild it on the foundation of the manuscripts. Systematic collation in the modern sense of the word was too much to hope for, but Muret's successor, Achilles Statius (Aquiles Estaço), was to come remarkably close in the commentary on Catullus that was published by Manuzio in 1566.

Like his contemporary, Muret, Statius was a foreigner in Italy.[103] The son of a Portuguese aristocrat (and named for his father's favourite hero, Achilles), the young Statius had travelled briefly as a child to Brazil, then newly conquered by Portugal. Apparently unmoved by the charms of the New World, he turned at an early age to scholarship, and by the late 1540s he had completed theological studies in Paris and was studying Latin literature in Louvain. By 1555 he was in Padua, trying, as it seems, to cultivate Muret and Manuzio in Venice. The evidence for his friendship (if such it was) with Muret and Manuzio is contained in a letter written to Muret in July 1555. Statius' tone is affectionate and effusive; he longs to see Muret and Manuzio, to know what they are doing, to have Muret's *Terence* and Manuzio's *Longinus*, and above all to receive an answer to his letters and inquiries. The letter closes with a poem in hendecasyllables, *Ad Paulum Manutium, et M. Antonium Muretum*:

> Now tell me, what are you doing? Are you both well? Are you both playing with verses, and trying to surpass Calvus or Catullus? Or is it more pleasing to vie with great Cicero, matching his very rhythm and elegance? Whatever you are doing now, whatever you have published, whatever you both are thinking, I am eager to know from your letters. Do you love me at all, or have I, your comrade, slipped out of your mind?[104]

Statius' letter seems to have gone unanswered, but its enthusiasm is understandable.[105] He and Muret were much of an age, they had both spent time in Paris, both were newly arrived in Italy. Too little is known of the details of Statius' early career, but it is clear that his intellectual interests matched Muret's. By 1555 he had already published a book of poems (1547), a commentary on the *Ars Poetica* (1553), and (a sign of French influence?) a translation of two *Hymns* of Callimachus (1549), as well as commentaries on rhetorical and philosophical works of Cicero.[106] But the paths of the two men were soon to diverge. By the early 1560s both were in Rome, but Muret, now by papal appointment a professor at the University of Rome, was increasingly interested in prose writers and was taking his own role in the polemics of the partisans of Ciceronianism and anti-Ciceronianism.[107] He maintained his close friendship with Manuzio, now also in Rome, and the two continued their attacks on Vettori.[108] Statius, on the other hand, devoted himself to poetic and theological projects. He was a member of the papal commission charged with editing the works of the Church Fathers, and he annotated Tibullus, Vergil, Horace, and Lucretius in addition to Catullus.[109] Moreover, his friends in Rome were the friends of Vettori rather than of Muret, principally the distinguished philologist Gabriele Faerno (a severe critic of Muret's Terence) and the bibliophile Fulvio Orsini.[110] In method, too, he allied himself with Vettori and his followers. Not for Statius, as we will see, was Muret's blithe reliance on the base text and his own powers as a literary critic; rather, he practised Vettori's laborious consultation and collation of manuscripts.

Statius never mentions Muret by name in his commentary, but at least one reference reveals the distance that existed between them in the mid 1560s. In the second edition of his commentary (1558) Muret had proposed the emendation *meus venter* at 44. 8, claiming to have been inspired both by a manuscript reading reported to him by Denys Lambin and by a reading in his own manuscript.[111] Statius accuses him of plagiarizing from Faerno:

> Around nine years ago Gabriele Faerno was the first of all to write, 'Quam mihi meus venter' [44. 8]. And since he had shared his discovery quite readily with many people (as he was a man with an open and generous nature), someone published it as his own. Before he died he called on me at great length to testify on his behalf.[112]

Philological polemic, however, plays very little part in Statius' *Catullus*, and it is completely absent from the preface, which Statius uses, not to explain or defend his method, but to justify his writing a commentary on Catullus at all. It seems that long ago he had undertaken to translate the poetry of the Old Testament into Latin lyrics, hoping to represent its metrical variety with appropriate diversity in his own verses.

> And so before I embarked on this work, in order that I might more readily furnish it with polished and ornamented verses, I carefully studied the Latin poets, each the best in his own genre. In my reading, as often happens, I had noted so many things that they seemed almost to

make a complete volume. Since these notes pleased my friends, they urged me again and again not to keep them from others or begrudge them to the public. And so, won over, I have begun with Catullus—whom every earlier age valued highly enough to judge that he easily surpassed all poets in elegance. St Jerome, in fact, considered his name worthy of inclusion in the *Chronica* of Eusebius, which he translated into Latin. For, as to the fact that he wrote somewhat racily and effeminately, this was the habit of those times, or rather the licence and defect, although he says of himself as if in embarrassment: 'Nam castum esse decet pium poetam / ipsum, versiculos nihil necesse est' [16. 5–6].[113]

The *apologia* of Statius' preface is in sharp contrast to the sophisticated poetic theorizing of Muret, but it reflects the Rome of the 1560s as surely as Muret's preface evoked Paris and the world of the Brigade. Rome after the Council of Trent was not entirely hostile to the study of ancient poets, even those as transparently unedifying as Catullus, but it preferred its humanism to have a Christian *color*.[114] Statius, recently named secretary for the Latin correspondence of the newly elected Pope Pius V, and dedicating his work to another papal secretary, needed to set his work firmly, if somewhat incongruously, in a religious context.[115] Catullus' obscenity was not a stumbling block like Boccaccio's (it did not reflect on the religious or on the Church), but it still required an excuse.[116] Not surprisingly, Statius' language reflects the terms in which the Council of Trent had excluded ancient authors from its ban on obscene literature: elegance of style and the general licentiousness of paganism were precisely the mitigating circumstances allowed by the Council.[117] Jerome's stamp of approval and Statius' claim that Catullus himself had the grace to be self-conscious about his obscenity provide additional legitimacy. The strongest justification, however, is Statius' plan to versify the *Psalms* and other Biblical poetry using Catullus and other ancient poets as metrical models, for nothing could be more in the spirit of the age than to make the study of pagan poetry the handmaid of Christian humanism.

There is no reason to doubt Statius' sincerity. He did indeed write verse paraphrases of the *Psalms* and other *carmina sacra*, and he was to edit, annotate, and translate many of the Church Fathers.[118] But there is also no escape from the facts that Catullus is an unlikely subject for Christian humanism, and that the tone of the preface is not sustained in the commentary. In the beginning Statius does his best to invoke parallels from Christian writers for Catullan usage, but such references become less frequent as the work proceeds. Catullus is too remote from the Christian world for even stylistic comparisons. But if the Christianity of the commentary is barely skin-deep, the work reflects the social and intellectual life of Statius' Rome in its constant references to other humanists and to the great churchmen who patronized them, to their gardens, inscribed gems, and manuscripts, and to the Roman churches with their ancient inscriptions—all invoked, in Statius' austere way, to defend readings and elucidate points of Catullan usage. Statius cites his friends Jacopo Corbinelli and Fulvio Orsini ('Ursinus meus') on Greek parallels, and presents the readings of Faerno and Vettori with appropriate *pietas*. He quotes inscriptions from the house of Angelo Colocci and the gardens of Cardinal Rodolfo Pio and of his own earlier patron, Cardinal Francesco Sforza.[119]

We should perhaps attribute another characteristic of Statius' commentary to its time and place—the fact that Statius, unlike his predecessors from Partenio to Muret, expresses so little personal enthusiasm for the poet. Partenio hailed Catullus as his fellow citizen and described his commentary as an act of *pietas* and patriotism. Valeriano made him the protégé of Calliope, greatest of the Muses. Muret boasted, 'there has never been a time in which I did not wonderfully love Catullus.' Statius, by contrast, firmly situates Catullus' praise in the past, describing him merely as the poet 'whom every earlier age valued highly enough to judge that he easily surpassed all poets in elegance'. And again in the preface: 'Of Catullus himself, that most highly praised poet, I shall say no more by way of commendation.'[120] The Christian humanist in the post-Tridentine era will study and annotate Catullus, but evidently deems it prudent to distance himself from the praise of his subject. Statius characterizes his work on Catullus with similar restraint. He concludes his preface thus:

> As for this work of mine, I think I can truly say that it was begun with this intention and attempt (which I admit I have not accomplished, since many things have escaped me and I have no doubt erred in many more, being a person of scarcely moderate intellect)—to improve at

least a little, if I could not restore completely, a fine poet much corrupted by the neglect of ages.[121]

Statius' careful preface is a document of its era, but it introduces a work that was written over a long period of time and with more ambitious purposes than its author admits. For, as we will see, Statius began to work on Catullus while he was still in Padua, and he probably intended to produce nothing less than a newly constituted edition of Catullus based on collations of all the manuscripts available to him. The nature of his work is clear from the first lines of the commentary, as is the fact that his method and purpose will be fundamentally different from those of Muret. Let us see how each approaches Cat. 1:

Cui dono lepidum novum libellum
arida modo pumice expolitum?
Corneli, tibi: namque tu solebas
meas esse aliquid putare nugas
iam tum, cum ausus es unus Italorum
omne aevum tribus explicare cartis
doctis, Iuppiter, et laboriosis.
quare habe tibi quidquid hoc libelli
qualecumque; quod, ⟨o⟩ patrona virgo,
plus uno maneat perenne saeclo.

Muret is polemical and literary from the beginning. His first gloss provides the occasion for a diatribe against those who have corrupted texts with unwarranted improvements:

If only the scrupulous care that is necessary in treating the monuments of the ancients both had been preserved by earlier generations and were being preserved today! Undoubtedly everything we read would be simpler and sounder. Now while each one according to his own whim adds, deletes, makes changes, the printed books, from not very sound manuscripts, become entirely corrupt.[122]

Muret's indignation is intended to sound an impressive note of philological responsibility, but it is empty. He has no specific offender in mind and knows too little of the textual tradition he disparages to identify one. A few lines later he criticizes Pontano's version of 1. 9 in an elaborate literary discussion:

Ora per virorum was added by Gioviano Pontano . . . . Palladio says so, and it is known openly from this epigram of Sannazaro's to Pontano: 'If learned Catullus came back from the Elysian vale . . . he would give you embraces and grateful kisses, and he would rather remember these verses than his own.' Sannazaro writes with affection and charm, but in my opinion Catullus would surely prefer his own verses. Although I do not see what could be added more aptly, still I consider it better for lacunae to exist in good books than for them to be filled in by someone's ingenuity.[123]

Again, typical Muret, and the elegant literary argument betrays its author's ignorance of the basic information; for, if he had looked carefully at any edition before the first Aldine he would have seen that Pontano was not filling a lacuna, but rewriting an existing line.[124]

Statius' first gloss, like Muret's, deals with the first verse of the poem, but there the resemblance ends:

Cui dono lepidum novum libellum [1. 1]: In two manuscripts, *cui*, as it is also printed. In one *quoi*. In the second Paduan [manuscript] *quin*, which reading comes closer to the convention the ancients maintained, if you just take away the letter *n* from the end. The authority for this matter is Donatus, commenting on the *Andria* of Terence . . .[125]

There are no vain generalities here. In a single note Statius has given the readings of four manuscripts and footnoted Donatus on archaic spelling. The same concern for manuscript and historical evidence is apparent in the rest of his discussion. Thus he rejects *arida* (for *arido*) in 1. 2, a reading that Muret and most of his predecessors had espoused on the testimony of Servius, on the grounds that 'it is contrary both to the evidence of the manuscripts and to the authority of all the ancients.'[126] He counters Servius' claim that Catullus wrote *arida . . . pumice* by citing Plautus to demonstrate that *pumex* was masculine in archaic Latin and by arguing that Pliny the elder, Martial, and the grammarians Victorinus and Atilius Fortunatianus all read *arido* in Catullus' verse.[127] On 1. 4 he discusses the elder Pliny's criticism that Catullus was 'a little too harsh' (*duriusculus*) in using an iambic opening instead of the usual spondee, and correctly concludes that Pliny was simply unaccustomed to the variation, since it had fallen into disuse by his time. At 1. 9 he prints Pontanus' *Qualecumque quidem ora per virorum*, but notes, '*Qualecumque quod patrona virgo* was in all the manuscripts'.[128] He then gives a number of variants from the printed tradition before presenting his own reading: 'I wanted to show what I have seen written, but I read *qualecumque quod est, patrona virgo*.'[129] At the end of the same note he identifies Minerva as Catullus' *patrona virgo*, pointing out that Ennius had called her *patrona*, *era*, and *domina* as well as *virgo* and quoting Greek inscriptions to show that her Greek counterpart Athena was called *κόρα*.

Statius is factual and historical where Muret is uncritical and literary, but it is in his use of manuscripts that he differs most from his predecessor—and in fact from all his predecessors. Statius used manuscripts more carefully and consistently, and he consulted and cited more manuscripts, than any previous student of Catullus. His citations are so specific and detailed that it is possible not only to see that he used seven different manuscripts, but to identify four of the seven, as Ullman demonstrated long ago.[130] Statius put his manuscripts to good use. According to Goold's census he achieved 17 corrections to the text, almost as many as the 18 ascribed to the first Aldine (1502), and more than either Muret (9) or Scaliger (14).[131]

Sometimes Statius tells us how he arrived at a correction with the aid of his manuscripts. Thus, he glosses the traditional reading *directa* at 22. 8, in the description of Suffenus' book, 'all ruled with lead and polished off with pumice':

> *Detecta*, not *directa*, is in all the manuscripts. It seems that we should read *derecta*, for thus the ancients wrote *derigere* and *derectus*, which one can see in my very old exemplar of Caesar's *Commentaries*, and in the ancient inscription at Rome in St Peter's Basilica, in which appears the name of a horse, 'Derector'. And so from *derecta* [the reading] became *detecta*.[132]

And again, in the epithalamium for Manlius, where the poet asks the bride to look upon her new husband (61. 164):

> Aspice, unus ut accubans
> Vir tuus Tyrio in thoro,
> Totus immineat tibi. (Cat. 61. 164–6, Venice 1566)
>
> Since I had long thought that there was a corruption in the first verse, for [I could not see] what *unus* meant in that place nor what wit and charm it had, I investigated it, and when I consulted the manuscripts I found written both *unus* and *unius*. And so I thought *intus* was to be

read, and this I proved still more afterwards, when I noticed that *imus* was written in a third manuscript.[133]

In the course of the tradition scribes and editors had filled in lacunae with verses of their own composition, but with the help of his manuscripts Statius was able to recognize and expel spurious verses like 68. 47 (*omnibus inque locis celebretur fama sepulti)*, which goes back at least to the *editio princeps*:

This verse was not in the manuscripts, and in all there was just enough space left to contain a single verse. And in one it was noted in the margin, 'this verse was missing in the exemplar.' Thus, any verse that is read in this place is spurious.[134]

There are undoubted deficiencies and weaknesses in Statius' work. Perhaps the greatest is that unlike his models, Vettori and Faerno, he seems not to have understood the importance of weighing, as well as comparing, his manuscripts.[135] Thus, he treated all his witnesses as of equal merit, and this despite the fact that one was the fourteenth-century manuscript, R (Vatican Library, Ottob. lat. 1829), which modern editors recognize as one of the most important sources of the text.[136] Nor did Statius provide full collations of his manuscripts. He used them unevenly, reporting many readings from four (designated by Ullman 'the inner circle of Statius' manuscripts'), but noting readings only from single passages in the others.[137] The composition of his 'inner circle' (two Paduan manuscripts; R, then also in Rome; and his own, now lost), suggests that he consulted his manuscripts at different times, and perhaps also with varying degrees of precision. He no doubt studied the Paduan manuscripts early in his Italian career and saw R only a few years later, after he had come to Rome. Under the circumstances it is not surprising that he is occasionally inaccurate in his citations or imprecise in identifying their source.[138] Even when his citations are correct, moreover, Statius often incorrectly assesses their value. He sometimes wrongly vindicates manuscript readings against corrections in the printed tradition, just as he sometimes wrongly sides with the printed tradition against the manuscripts or proposes wrong-headed corrections of his own.[139]

Neither mistakes in editorial judgement, however, nor deficiencies in method can detract from Statius' greatest achievement, the fact that by his collations he provided the means for a fresh look at the text as a whole. Not since Avanzi had anyone studied the text so thoroughly and in such detail. Indeed, Statius and Avanzi are very much alike in their methods and accomplishments. Neither reconstituted the text systematically by seeking out the oldest and most reliable witnesses, and neither achieved a systematic collation that would survive modern scrutiny. But each compared every word, or at least every line, of his source with all the available versions. Although he accomplished little with his manuscripts, Avanzi, as we have seen, controlled the whole printed tradition, and was thus able to get behind the dominant base text of his period, that of Calfurnio/Partenio, to the readings of the early editions. He also found and corrected dozens of errors simply by scanning Catullus' verses. Statius cared little for the early editions, and they would have been of scant help to him in any event, since by his time the base text was rooted in Avanzi's Aldines. But just as Avanzi had used the editions to see behind the text of Calfurnio and Partenio, so Statius with the aid of his manuscripts was able to look behind the Aldines, and sometimes even behind the entire printed tradition. Appendix 8 demonstrates his contribution to the vulgate for a single poem, Cat. 61. Statius attributes all of his corrections, including his emendation in 61. 164, either to the readings or to the inspiration of his manuscripts.

It is clear in spite of the claims of his preface that Statius' principal interest lay in the text rather than in the content or even the metre of Catullus, and that in his laborious collations he had the raw material from which a new text (and not merely another version of the base text) could be constructed.[140] Yet he did not produce an edition of Catullus. The text that accompanies his commentary shows little sign of his labours: not a single reading, for example, from Appendix 8 appears in his text of 61.[141] The omission is surprising, but perhaps Statius' other interests in the 1560s seemed more pressing than the additional labour involved in editing a pagan poet. Statius had several Christian philological projects in hand after the Council of Trent, and he was no doubt busy as papal secretary. It is easy to imagine that he simply published his notes as they were and hastened on to more laudable projects. But we should also remember that it was not necessary for textual labours to culminate in an edition. It is true that Avanzi's *Emendationes* were the prolegomenon for the first

Aldine, but some of the most important textual studies stood alone: Valeriano's *Castigationes* of Vergil, for example, might well have provided Statius with a model.[142]

Statius' readings did not remain buried in the notes of his commentary for long. Within a few years they were being studied carefully by the Belgian humanist, Victor Giselinus, as he prepared his edition of Catullus for the press of Christopher Plantin in Antwerp.[143] Incorporating some of Statius' readings into his own text and entering the rest in its margins, Giselinus provided in his 1569 Plantin edition a neatly arrayed collation of Statius that would prove invaluable to Joseph Scaliger a few years later as he set to work on his own edition of Catullus.

JOSEPH SCALIGER CASTIGATES CATULLUS

Joseph Scaliger's *Catullus* enjoys an exalted position in the history of textual criticism, for in learning and historical sense—and above all, in method—it has been seen to anticipate the triumphs of the great nineteenth-century philologists.[144] In fact, it is not going too far to say that Scaliger is the first Catullan critic to have any method at all. All of his predecessors—from Puteolano to Statius—corrected the base text either by conjecture or by comparing it with manuscripts or other editions (usually the latter, as we have seen). No one before him seems to have thought about the history of the text or tried to construct a theory that would account for its errors. Scaliger, in contrast, realized that all the manuscripts were descended from a single exemplar, which he reconstructed (to his own satisfaction, at least) down to its place of origin and the peculiarities of its script—so creating a model that explained the genesis of errors in Catullus' text and showed the way to their correction. And yet there is a wonderful paradox in Scaliger's *Catullus*. Scaliger is a greater editor than any of his predecessors, and his method is a landmark in Catullan studies—but the two facts are essentially unrelated. As we shall see, Scaliger's method was largely irrelevant to his improvement of the text. Furthermore, although his *Castigationes in Catullum* soared intellectually and methodologically above earlier studies, it was not free of their influence, nor was Scaliger himself unmoved by the work and the personalities of his predecessors.

The laborious collations of Statius provided the groundwork, if not the backbone, of his edition, and Muret seems to have stimulated him to work on Catullus in the first place.

Our story begins in 1559, when the young Joseph Scaliger came to Paris, like Muret and Statius before him, and, like Muret, at least, soon became friendly with the poet-scholars of the Brigade.[145] He immersed himself at once in the study of Greek, which he mastered quickly—even if we doubt the fabulous speed he was later to claim in his autobiography. By 1561 he was translating Latin poetry into Greek—influenced by the general climate of literary Alexandrianism in Paris or perhaps inspired directly by Muret. Scaliger undoubtedly knew Muret's work, and he was no doubt acquainted with Muret himself at this period, for Muret had returned to Paris in August 1561 with his patron, Cardinal Ippolito d'Este, and he remained in France until March 1563.[146] Scaliger surely met Muret when he visited his old friends in Paris, and both men would have remembered that in his own youth Muret had been on close terms with Scaliger's father, Julius Caesar Scaliger.[147] The best token of their friendship, however, is Scaliger's dedication of his Greek translation of 65 and 66 to Muret in September 1562—and his use of Muret's text of the poems.[148]

When Scaliger came to Rome in 1565 and again in 1566 with his own patron, Louis Chasteigner, Muret was his mentor and guide. It seems also to have been at this time that Muret played his notorious trick on Scaliger.[149] He gave Scaliger two poems of his own composition, passing them off as the work of the archaic poets, Accius and Trabea. Scaliger was deceived, and printed them with some fanfare a few years later as genuine examples of early Latin verse in his notes on Varro's *De re rustica* (1573). Muret, of course, could not resist exposing his own cleverness, and in 1575 he claimed his handiwork, virtuously asserting that he had decided to reveal the truth in order to avoid further confusion.[150] Clearly, the next step was for Scaliger to retaliate. He did so, as Grafton has shown, in the edition and *Castigationes* of the *tresviri amoris* (Catullus, Tibullus, and Propertius) that he published in Paris in 1577.[151] Scaliger began to work almost immediately after Muret's revelation, for in November 1575 we find him writing to ask his friend François Vertunien for an edition and commentary of the three poets.[152] In December he

Plate 8: Joseph Scaliger at 35 (1575), by Hendrik Goltzius from a portrait (courtesy of the Bryn Mawr College Library).

wrote to Claude Dupuy for a copy of Statius' *Catullus*, and in February 1576 he wrote again to Dupuy to report his progress and to express concern about a rumour of Muret's death: 'I should be very sorry if he died before I had settled accounts for his verses of Attius and Trabea.'[153]

Scaliger's intentions seem clear enough, but in the event he did not produce a sustained, all-out attack on Muret in his *Catullus*, and probably he never meant to. His feelings for Muret were always complicated—even in the epigram he wrote to celebrate Muret's trick. This poem, of uncertain date, was not published until after the death of both principals. It contains a mixture of chagrin, spite, and ferocious good humour characteristic of Scaliger's remarks on Muret: 'Rumetus escaped the flames of strict Toulouse and sold the smoke to me.'[154] His *obiter dicta* in the *Second Scaligerana* have a similar tone. As in the epigram, he loves to dwell on Muret's shady past. Thus: 'Muret fled Toulouse and came to Venice, but because he wanted to tup the sons of the highest nobility, he fled to Rome.'[155] And again: 'He was a learned man; they didn't want to put up with him in Venice because of his pederasty.'[156] But there is praise, too. Often it is undermined by sarcasm ('Muret used to call me brother since my father called him son. He wrote as well as any of the ancients. He wished to imitate the Italians—to say little in many words.').[157] And yet sometimes his compliments seem sincere:

> After Cicero there was no one who spoke and wrote in Latin more readily than Muret. Lipsius could do nothing in comparison with him, and envied him; he stole his emendations. In this business I can judge the ability of this one or that quite well. He had been a schoolmaster and generally they don't rise unless they have an unpedantic mind, like Muret, who was truly royal.[158]

Scaliger was capable of unqualified, vicious attack when he chose, but that was not his purpose in the *Castigationes*. The work was not a means of destroying Muret; rather, Muret's trick had provoked him into studying Catullus. Scaliger was angry, and what better way to spite Muret than to outdo and eclipse his *Catullus*, the work with which he had achieved his greatest reputation? Scaliger's superior achievement would be revenge enough. Of course, he would not miss the opportunity to get in a few licks at Muret, in passing as it were—or at anyone else, for that matter (for, as we shall see presently, the egotistical and spiteful polemic of the *Castigationes* has no single target); but he was principally interested in applying his critical method to Catullus and in the glory he was sure would result.

The polemical nature of Scaliger's work is clear from the beginning. Thus, in his dedication to Dupuy:

> I know that men of great learning have contributed not a little to the elucidation of these authors. For my part I do not begrudge them their glory. But they can neither snatch mine from me if I have employed my labour well nor disparage my effort, at least, if I have done badly. In these brief and nearly unadorned notes I have adhered to this method—to injure no living person by even the slightest reference and never to name the dead except with the greatest respect, even when I disagree with them. For it is an ignoble act to place at risk the learning of such great men, and so their whole name and reputation, because of some worthless words or for some error, which flesh is heir to.[159]

Scaliger's remarks are both formulaic[160] and transparently disingenuous, for both he and his readers were well aware that no humanist ever asserted that he was going to be generous to his predecessors unless he planned to attack them.

His attack on Muret takes two forms. In the first, he employs the familiar convention of philological polemic, in which the writer attacks his (usually unnamed) victim by referring to some detail of his life or work that he counts on the reader to recognize. Thus, long ago Partenio had attacked 'those equipped and supported with Herculean strength', knowing that his readers would recognize his target as Battista Guarino, who enjoyed the patronage of Ercole I, Duke of Ferrara. Thus, Muret himself attacked Vettori by censuring his model Poliziano and by quoting lines from the same play Vettori had cited to support his interpretation of a vexed passage.[161] Scaliger uses this technique only sparingly: the important examples discussed by Grafton do not find many parallels.[162] But he also relies on a second device, which is a logical, if disagreeable, extension of the first. Frequently in his *Catullus*, but especially in the notes on 61 and 66, we find references to whole tribes of fools who have destroyed and misinterpreted the text—'dullards, mutton heads', 'sciolists', 'insignificant schoolmasters', 'inept pedagogues', and their ilk.[163] The reader expects the details to fit a particular, identifiable individual—presumably Muret—because of the emphasis on schoolmasters, or possibly Statius, Scaliger's immediate predecessor. Generally, however, these clues lead neither to Muret nor to Statius nor to anyone else, and the attack has no target. But this important point can be discovered only by those who take the trouble to check. If one is content to match the attack with the obvious target, as no doubt Scaliger expected many of his readers to be, the innuendo is as good as the fact: Muret had been a schoolmaster, and Scaliger's polemics must refer to him—or if not, to some other recent student of Catullus. By this slanderous expedient, Scaliger can even remain true, in his fashion, to the rule he has established so piously at the outset: 'to injure no living person with even the slightest reference.'

Taken together, however, Scaliger's polemics against Muret do not add up to much—some small-arms fire, to be sure, but not a rocket attack. Scaliger did not even take the trouble to attack Muret where he was most vulnerable, in his ignorance of the textual tradition, although a little close reading of Muret's commentary would have provided plenty of ammunition. But in fact there is nothing in Scaliger's *Catullus* to suggest a recent and detailed study of Muret. The examples discussed by Grafton deal with well-known passages; the attacks on dolts and schoolmasters apply to no one in particular. Neither required much research on Scaliger's part. He certainly did not read Muret as Muret had read Vettori—to launch a full-scale attack on every vulnerable point and to plagiarize the rest.

It was Statius, rather, who received his close attention. Scaliger was in possession of Dupuy's copy of Statius' *Catullus* and *Tibullus* by February 1576 and kept it for six or seven months while he worked on the *Castigationes*.[164] He professed to find nothing in it, and nearly every letter to Dupuy in this period contains some reference to Statius' folly and stupidity. Thus in February 1576: 'I find that our poor Statius is a great fool, and I cannot keep from laughing when I read the commentaries on Catullus and Tibullus. Still, he is not always wrong, and that is when he is most unlike himself.'[165] And in May 1576: 'I am sure that if I have done my duty, at least I won't make as big a fool of myself as Messer Achille Statio has, to whom may God give a good, long life—for if he does not obtain this through our kind prayers, he will hardly acquire it through his own good understanding.'[166]

These pleasantries should not deceive us, for even as Scaliger was deriding Statius in public, he was quietly helping himself to his ideas.[167] Or it may be that he had already helped himself, for his own working copy of Catullus was the 1569 Plantin edited by Victor Giselinus, which displayed dozens of clearly labelled variant readings from Statius in its margins.[168] One suspects, in fact, that some of Scaliger's derision of Statius stemmed from relief. Knowing Statius' merits from Giselinus' edition, he may have expected (or feared) to find in his commentary something more than he had already seen in Giselinus—perhaps even some anticipation of his own historical and analytical method. For, after all, Statius was no Muret. There is no evidence that Scaliger had met Statius in Rome, but he probably knew that he was a friend of Orsini and Faerno, and thus likely to be a follower of Vettori. But whatever worries he might have had evaporated when he saw Statius' *Catullus*, which was learned and acute, but contained no sign of a method like Scaliger's own. He settled down to learn what he could from it and went back to his 1569 Plantin, which soon (thanks to Giselinus and Statius, and to his own manuscript collations which he entered in the margins) provided not a recension of the text, to be sure, but at least an overview of its modern history.

Scaliger never mentions Statius in his *Catullus*, but the extent of his debt is clear. Appendix 9 shows the readings found in both Statius and Scaliger, but not in the Aldines, Guarinus, or Muret.[169] Virtually all of the fifty-five readings appear also in either the text or the margins of the Plantin edition. Scaliger attributes twenty readings to his manuscript, but it is quite likely that he saw most of them first in either Giselinus' edition or Statius' commentary. We shall consider the implications of this point presently, when we turn our attention to the important matter of Scaliger's method.

Although the list contains only a handful of emendations and a good number of unsuccessful corrections (Appendix 9c), it demonstrates the extent to which Statius and Scaliger jointly improved the base text—Statius by mentioning the readings in his commentary, and Scaliger by incorporating them into his edition. The base text had been modified for a hundred years by a process of internal correction—by conjectures and changes made on the evidence of the text itself or by *ad hoc* comparison with an occasional manuscript or early edition, but the edition published by Scaliger in 1577 is the first to exploit evidence gathered systematically from outside the printed tradition.

Scaliger used the manuscript of Catullus, Tibullus, and Propertius owned by his friend, the legal scholar, Jacques Cujas. He saw it first when he was studying in Valence between 1570 and 1572, and probably again in 1576 when he collated it in preparation for his edition of the three poets.[170] The manuscript is of no particular consequence, but Scaliger valued it highly, as he says at the beginning of his *Catullus*:

> Furthermore, the manuscript we used and which we have already mentioned seems to me to surpass by far other manuscripts of this poet, although they were all copied, in any event, from a single exemplar. This exemplar, which was found in France by somebody from Verona, is the parent of all the manuscripts of this poet that exist in Italy.[171]

Two points are important here—the French manuscript and its discovery and the assertion that it was the source of all the existing manuscripts. Scaliger's evidence for the first was the epigram of Benvenuto Campesani, which he had found in Cujas' manuscript.[172] The epigram supports the second point, too, but Scaliger no doubt arrived at his theory as he studied Giselinus and Statius and saw the similarities between his own manuscript (or rather, Cujas') and Statius' seven: such close agreement could come about only if all the manuscripts were descended from a single exemplar. From the errors he discovered in Cujas' manuscript, as well as from those he detected at second hand in Statius', he believed he could deduce the nature of the exemplar: it employed archaic spelling, and it was written in 'a wretched Lombardic script'.[173] The errors produced by these factors were predictable and could be easily reversed by a scholar who understood them. Thus, *a* and *u* looked nearly alike in the 'Lombardic exemplar', as did *c* and *t*, and *l* and *i*. Scribes confused the similar shapes and introduced errors into the text, as, for example, at 68. 52 where they read *corruerit* for the correct *torruerit*.[174] Archaic spelling caused errors like *laedere* at 17. 1, where the exemplar read *loedere* (= *ludere*).[175]

It is reasoning like this that has earned Scaliger much of his glory as a father of modern philology. He concludes the introduction to his *Catullus* thus:

> Indeed you will marvel, studious reader, that such a crop of mistakes has attacked this most polished author. And if I do not root it out completely, nevertheless I will leave no great gleaning behind me.[176]

But do Scaliger's results live up to his method? Grafton lists sixteen places where Scaliger thought he detected errors derived from the script of the exemplar.[177] In only one did he produce an original correction that has found its way into modern editions.[178] Five more corrections belong to his predecessors.[179] Ten are wrong.[180] His reconstruction of the spelling of the archetype fared no better. Thus, in 61 he thought he could trace six errors to spelling confusion. Two of his proposed readings are old corrections, and four are wrong.[181] Some of his strangest proposals result from his lifelong preoccupation with archaic Latin. Scaliger was the man who had commented on Festus, translated Sophocles' *Ajax* into the Latin of Accius and Pacuvius, and been gulled by Muret's archaic counterfeits;[182] and he was convinced—quite wrongly—that Catullus wrote in archaic Latin and that successful correction would naturally produce archaic forms and diction. At 95. 7 (*at Volusi annales Paduam morientur ad ipsam*), for example, his manuscript read: *At Volusi annales paduam portentur ad ipsam*:

> First, I do not hesitate to read *apuam* for *paduam*, and then *porcentur* for *portentur*: *c* for *t*, by the custom, or rather by the usual mistake, of scribes, which I remember mentioning so often earlier. *Porcentur* at that time used to be read for *porgentur*, which is read even now in the majority of manuscripts. And the change of *c* to *t* is very common. Everyone knows that *apua*, *ἀφύη*, is a little fish, as the Glossarium notes.[183]

And similarly at 61. 68 and 61. 99, where he scornfully rejects correct readings in favour of his own archaizing solutions.[184]

Clearly, Scaliger's method, notwithstanding its importance to the history of textual criticism, proved an indifferent tool for the correction of Catullus: it produced a relatively large number of wrong answers and confirmed old corrections more readily than it achieved new ones. This is not to detract from Scaliger's achievement. His successes, however—and they are many—

result, not from his method, but from a combination of great natural ability, judicious use of his predecessors, and the knowledge of the manuscripts that he had gained from his own collations and Statius'. In 61, for example, where his method showed itself to little advantage, he nevertheless made no fewer than three emendations.

At 61. 213 the vulgate (i.e. the Aldines, Guarinus, and Muretus) and Scaliger's Plantin edition read Avanzi's *sed micante labello*, but knowing both from his own manuscript and from Statius that the exemplar read *sed mihi ante*, he concluded: 'By taking away only one letter we can elicit the true reading, *Semihiante labello* . . .'.[185] Here for once we can hardly begrudge him his customary crow of triumph: 'Who will hesitate about the emendation of this place rather than admiring its elegance?'[186] His other emendations are still more impressive. In the three stanzas of 61. 184–98 the poet addresses the bridegroom of his epithalamium, describing the bride in the first stanza, the groom in the second, and the help of Venus in the third. In the course of transmission, however, the second and third stanzas had become transposed, and the resulting confusion had inspired prodigies of imagination and interpretation.[187] At 61. 189 the base text read *At marita tuum tamen*: 'a most corrupt place', Scaliger remarks, 'which Partenio has patched up as it is read today. I wish he had left the old corrupt reading instead of giving us an interpretation of his fantasy.'[188] From Cujas' manuscript and Statius' reports he saw that the exemplar at 61. 189–91 had read:

> At maritum tamen iuvenem
> Caelites nihilominus
> Pulcre res . . .

> A monstrous reading, as you see, but on this alone hinges the corruption and the correction of this passage. For this strophe must be transposed and change places with its predecessor, and thus we place everything in order and then we will easily remove these mistakes.[189]

Thus:

> At, marite, ita me iuvent
> Caelites, nihilominus
> Polcher es, . . . [61. 189–91, *Castig.*, 52–3]

Scaliger's solution is brilliant, but it owes nothing to the elaborate reconstructions of his method. Through his own labour and Statius' he was able to see behind Partenio's confusing correction to the reading of the exemplar at 61. 189, and from Robortello's commentary he knew the reading *pulcher es* for the traditional *pulcre res* at 61. 191.[190] His powerful intellect accomplished the rest. It is precisely a passage like this, in fact, that points up the distance between Scaliger and Statius, for Statius, after all, had the same information as Scaliger, and yet he failed to see that the stanzas had been reversed, and he emended 61. 189 to read *Admetum iuvenem tamen*, identifying 'Admetus' as the *puer delicatus* of the bridegroom.

Scaliger trusted in his superiority and was confident that he could perceive the intentions of the poet and rise above the blunders and stupidity of his predecessors; but his instincts were not always perfect—particularly in the matter of the structure and logic of the poems. His brilliant success at 61. 184–98 is matched by several mistaken efforts to rearrange poems and verses, and as a consequence the *dispositio carminum* of his edition is worse than those of Statius and Muret.[191] He is outraged by their separation of 59 (*Bononiensis Rufa Rufulum fellat*) and 60 (*Num te leaena montibus Libystinis*):

> Here dirty men have substituted a dirty word, and I criticize them not only in that but because by the same rashness with which they soiled this passage, two fragments have been created from one epigram. And yet this epigram is an integral whole if you restore the old reading in its place, for it is clearly written:
>
> Bononiensem Rufa Rufulum fallat.[192]

The 'dirty word' he objects to is *fellat*, which he wants to replace with *fallat*, from *fallare*, a rare verb that he defends on the analogy of vocabulary from his old friend Accius.[193] He declares 87 (*Nulla potest mulier tantum se dicere amatam*) to be a fragment, which he completes with 75 (*Huc est mens deducta tua mea, Lesbia, culpa*), concluding smugly: 'I think there is no student of this poet who would not thank me for the rearrangement of this golden epigram.'[194] He ignores Statius' separation of 95 (*Zmyrna mei Cinnae nonam post denique messem*) and 95*b* (*Parva mei mihi sint cordi monimenta . . .*), and misunderstands Catullus' argument, maintaining that Catullus dislikes Cinna's poem.

The treatment of these poems is typical of Scaliger's approach.

In joining 59 and 60 he is misled by two sentiments: his usual enthusiasm for archaic diction and his deeply ingrained distaste for the obscene, which we shall consider presently. In the case of 75 and 87 he has so much confidence in his own critical powers that he disregards the order of the poems in the manuscripts (as well as the integrity of the two epigrams). In interpreting 95 and 95*b* he assumes that Cinna's *Zmyrna*, since it was nine years in the making, must be a massive composition like the cyclic poetry of the flatulent Antimachus, whom Catullus criticizes (95*b*. 2). Although he quotes Callimachus, he does not seem to understand Callimachean (and Catullan) poetics. Here, as often on poetic matters, Muret did much better, observing on 95. 1: 'He praises the poem of Cinna, which he had entitled *Smyrna* and toiled for nine whole years in polishing to perfection.'[195] And again, on 95*b*. 1: 'Vettori's objection is not important—that verses laboured over with such effort over such a long time can scarcely be called "parva monimenta". We know that books are valued for their excellence, not for their size, and that small jewels are often preferred to huge colossi.'[196]

But in general Scaliger does not present himself as an interpreter or literary critic. The text of Catullus' poetry interests him more than its frivolous and often embarrassing content, and like Statius he must find excuses for studying it. Statius, we recall, had needed to study the metres of Catullus as an aid to his translations of the Psalms. Scaliger, so he tells Dupuy in his preface, was recovering from a debilitating illness and still too weak to undertake the study of serious authors. He took up Catullus first, then Tibullus and Propertius—correcting all three poets, he claims mendaciously, in less than a month. The boast advertises his philological prowess and emphasizes that studying the likes of Catullus, Tibullus, and Propertius, though justifiable enough, is properly a spare-time activity:

> Since I know that these three poets are glorified by all, so that the man who can understand one of them boasts of considerable literary accomplishment, why should I think I have wasted a few hours if I have brought it about that any moderately learned man can understand the three at once?[197]

The difficulty, of course, is that the *tresviri amoris* are not only unedifying but also improper. The obscenity of Catullus (for we must leave the raciness of the elegists out of consideration) had evoked a wide range of approaches—from the total frankness of the first commentators to the nervousness of Valeriano and the tact of Muret. For Statius and Scaliger, papal secretary and Calvinist alike, the dry winds of religious orthodoxy and sexual prudery produced a harsher climate. Statius responded by excusing Catullus' licence in his preface and explaining the details in his commentary, so remaining well within the boundaries of the Tridentine Index.[198] Perhaps predictably, Scaliger takes a more austere position:

> we shall never leave off from devoting all the (time) we have left from more serious studies to helping good authors, as we have demonstrated in these three ornaments of Roman poetry—in which we have not passed over any place worthy of notice except for those that chaste ears cannot endure. For it is neither for me to touch them nor for anyone else who has any modicum of chastity. Not a syllable exists in these little notes of ours that it would have been better for me to have passed over than to have written. I wish, indeed, that the ancients themselves had taken some account of chastity and not handed themselves down to mankind in so many disgraceful writings; but since we see that it happened otherwise, for now we shall be content with the standard of that time—for from what springs shall we drink in Latinity if not from these? And yet these three poets speak no more outrageously than even a single comedy of Aristophanes—and yet it is handed down that Chrysostom read many plays of this sort over and over. What a great man! No subsequent age has produced his equal in eloquence, virtue, piety. I compare the reading of poets to the sea. There are reefs in it, but the experienced sailor never runs his ship aground on them. In poetry there are some indecent words on which the virtuous mind does not stumble, but briskly sails past unconcerned. Just as I ask certain poetry fanciers to keep their ears, eyes, tongue, and spirit from those unseemly words, so I think others should be censured, who consider a whole work filthy on account of one or two, or several, blemishes scattered here and there.[199]

Scaliger is more prolix than Statius but he invokes the same excuses—the general licence of Antiquity, the need to study ancient texts to understand Latin style, a saint whose example legitimizes the reading of obscene authors. He differs in his conception of the duty of the commentator, preaching not moderation but abstinence in the face of obscenity. Accordingly, he omits one or two lewd poems from his discussion, and he refrains—most scrupulously—from uttering obscenities, even in his lemmata.[200] In other cases, he denies that obscenity exists, either by emending it away as he did at 59. 1, or by denying that an obscene word means what it says.[201] But total abstinence proves too hard. At least two of Scaliger's emendations are key words in obscene contexts, and he occasionally finds it necessary to explain an obscene allusion.[202] Sometimes he skirts the reefs of obscenity by gliding around them with delicate periphrasis or glossing them in Greek.[203]

Scaliger's response to the obscene is a mark of his times, but in other respects his work is abstract and impersonal. Here he differs radically not only from Statius but from the other sixteenth-century interpreters we have been discussing. The notes of Muret, for example, express his own literary enthusiasm and evoke the world of the Brigade. Valeriano's lectures show us a dynamic and charismatic teacher active in the circle of literary humanists around Leo X. Statius moves in the world of post-Tridentine Rome. All present themselves as part of a social world in whose atmosphere the poet is read and interpreted—whether we want to think of Valeriano's linking the word *sodalis* in Catullus with the literary and convivial circles of his own friends or of Statius' love of citing Fulvio Orsini's ideas with the Catullan-sounding attribution, 'Ursinus meus', or of Muret's references to the readings of his friend and partner, Manuzio. Scaliger, on the other hand, presents us with no coterie of humanists, but only with his own solitary and ungenerous intellect. In his notes we find only a few references to the readings of Vettori and Turnèbe (usually identified as mistakes) and a paragraph on the genealogy of the Scaligers.[204]

Scaliger's *Catullus* provoked an immediate storm of controversy, but no one produced a commentary to challenge it.[205] Indeed, it was only in 1608 that the next complete commentary appeared—the posthumous work of Jean Passerat, who probably had not even intended his notes for publication.[206] Scaliger was an intimidating opponent, and his work was so authoritative that no one wanted to launch a detailed rebuttal. Indeed, no serious challenge was possible without a greater knowledge of the sources of the text and a more sophisticated literary approach to ancient poetry than the Renaissance possessed.

Equally important, however, is the fact that the times were not favourable for Catullan studies. Catullus' subjects are poetry and personal emotions. The poet places himself in the centre of a world of friends, enemies, lovers, and other poets, where the highest values are personal and aesthetic—the bonds of trust and obligation between individuals, and a poetic credo founded on learning, craftsmanship, and—above all—charm and wit. There is no room in his poetic landscape for moral or national themes, no reference to ideals or claims beyond those of the individual. Such poetry serves, and can be made to serve, no utilitarian purpose except the one we have so often seen claimed for it—that of teaching elegant Latin style. It was Catullus' lack of moral utility—even more than his obscenity—that discouraged study in the later sixteenth century. Martial, after all, is often much more obscene than Catullus, but his epigrams (with some judicious surgery) were regarded as suitable school texts.[207] The difference is that Martial is a satirist and that he is interested not in his own emotions but in the foibles of society. Suitably censored and selected, his epigrams have interesting and amusing moral—or at least social—lessons to teach. Catullus, in contrast, offers nothing to moralists and pedagogues, and for those gripped by serious spiritual or philosophical interests he can be justified only as a diversion or a model of style. He can be taken seriously only by those for whom poetry and poetics are serious. It is no accident that our three commentators all began their careers in Paris in or near the orbit of the Pléiade poets or that Muret, the most perceptive of the three (although not the best or most skilful editor), studied Catullus as a member of their inmost circle.

5

Imitatio: Catullan Poetry from Martial to Johannes Secundus

Huc huc, hendecasyllabi, frequentes,
huc vos quicquid habetis et leporum,
iocorum simul et facetiarum,
huc deferte, minutuli citique.

(Giovanni Pontano)

CATULLUS' first Renaissance readers searched his text for tags to ornament their own writings and correspondence, but their successors were more ambitious. By the first decade of the fifteenth century poets (or would-be poets) were attempting to write their own versions of Catullus' poems; by mid-century, Giovanni Pontano, the major poet of the age, had produced two remarkable collections of poetry in the style of Catullus, and within a few years Catullan poetry was established as a recognizable and popular genre. The Renaissance poets naturally favoured some of Catullus' poems and themes over others. Although they sometimes wrote epithalamia modelled on 61 or 62 or tried to reproduce the galliambics of 63, they generally preferred short poems to long, and playfulness and direct expression to Alexandrian *doctrina*.[1] They took great interest in metrical technique—hence their interest in 63, and hence also, as we shall see in Chapter 6, the many parodies of 4, which is written in another rare and nearly intractable metre, pure iambic trimeter. They argued about the ideal length for hendecasyllabic poems and debated such details as the propriety of following Catullus' habit of opening hendecasyllabic verses with iambs or trochees as well as spondees.[2] Above all, however, they tried to imitate the manner of Catullus, and to reproduce the tone of youth and freshness that attracted them most to the newly discovered poet.

Indeed, it was the Catullan manner, and the *persona* it represented, that made Catullus the natural model for the personal poetry of the Renaissance. The poets looked into his poems as into a mirror and saw the young Catullus, with his loves, his enemies, and his circle of fellow poets, all coming to life in verse that was, by turns, affecting, obscene, or sentimental, but always elegant and urbane—and of such liveliness and immediacy that the young poet might almost be a contemporary. Thus, they wrote love poems in imitation of Catullus, but also poems about poetry and friendship, and they attacked their enemies with the witty obscenities Catullus had used for rivals, bad poets, and great men. In Naples Pontano wrote an invitation poem in the Catullan style to Panormita, Marullo chided Sannazaro for his harshness to bad poets, and Sannazaro celebrated the fall of Cesare Borgia in a *contaminatio* of 56 and 58 that branded Cesare and Lucrezia Borgia as the modern counterparts of Catullus' incestuous pair, Publius Clodius and his sister Clodia (Lesbia):

O dulce ac lepidum, Marine, factum,
dignum perpetuo ioco atque risu,
dignum versiculis facetiisque,
nec non et salibus, Marine, nostris.
Ille maximus Urbis imperator,
Caesar Borgia, Borgia ille Caesar,
Caesar, patris ocellus et sororis,

(Sannazaro, *Ep.* I. 56.1–7)[3]

(O sweet and charming deed, Marino, worthy of joy and eternal laughter, worthy of jests and verses—and of our wit, as well, Marino. That greatest general of the city, Caesar Borgia, that Borgia Caesar, Caesar, darling of his father and his sister . . .)

The Venetian poet Navagero sent greetings in Catullan style to his young fellow poets, Canal and Bembo—and fifty years later Achilles Statius borrowed his verses for his own greetings to Muret and Paolo Manuzio.[4] Here is Navagero:

Canale optime, tuque Bembe, nostri
Amantissimi utrique, amati utrique
A me non minus atque utrique ocelli,
Quid rerum geritis? valetis? atque
Absentis memores sodalis estis

(Navagero, *Lusus* 30. 1–5)[5]

(Excellent Canal, and you, too, Bembo—both most fond of me, and both loved by me not less than both my eyes—what are you doing? Are you well? And are you mindful of your absent friend?)

In Rome the poets saw their sodalities as counterparts of Catullus' circle, and used Catullus as a standard for praise or blame. Thus, Flaminio praised Blosio Palladio's verses as 'worthy not of the bad poet Flaminio, but of your Catullus', and Angelo Colocci ridiculed a sermon of Pope Adrian VI (*Sermo de sacculo pertuso sive de superbia*) with Catullus' verse: 'plenus sacculus est aranearum' (13. 8).[6] Similar examples abound among the poems of Muret and his friends in Paris in the middle of the sixteenth century and in the literary circle of the elder Janus Dousa in Antwerp in the 1570s.[7]

The poets imitated Catullus in many metres, but above all in hendecasyllables—which were so strongly associated with Catullus that they immediately identified their user as a Catullan poet even when he was not imitating a particular Catullan poem. The hendecasyllable conveyed precisely the qualities of *lepos* and *lascivia* the poets most admired in their model, and it also had the advantage of being the most imitable of metres. The short eleven-syllable line with its regular but not inevitable break after the fifth or sixth syllable naturally attracts certain word shapes and favours a characteristic kind of diction (diminutives, comparatives, genitive plurals).[8] Memorable words like *beatiorum*, *basiationes*, *Cupidinesque*, *venustiorum*, or formulae like *meae puellae*, *tuos amores*, *meus sodalis* gravitate to the end of the verse.[9] By imitating and exaggerating these and other Catullan mannerisms the Renaissance poets soon found themselves in possession of a vehicle or language for a whole style of poetry. 'Catullan' hendecasyllabic poetry became so popular, in fact, that a full account of it would amount to a history of Renaissance epigram and lyric. The account would have to deal with vernacular poetry as well, which often tried to approximate the effects of the hendecasyllable, and it would have to take into account cross-fertilization and imitation between languages.[10]

The aims of this chapter are more modest, and the account below is intended to be suggestive rather than exhaustive. We will focus on a few Catullan themes and poems of particular interest to the Renaissance, and on a rather small number of Renaissance poems, which will be treated in some detail with attention both to their literary qualities and to the interaction and influence of contemporary interpretations and scholarly debate. The literary discussion is grounded in several important ideas that have emerged from modern studies of imitation, which we must now consider briefly.

Since the time of Giorgio Pasquali's seminal essay, '*Arte allusiva*', it has been recognized that imitation and allusion function as an essential element of meaning whereby the context of the imitated passage is evoked and made present in the later work.[11] More recently, Gian Biagio Conte, though continuing in the tradition of Pasquali, has rejected Pasquali's emphasis on authorial intention to concentrate on intertextuality itself.[12] For Conte, imitation functions like a figure or trope in classical rhetoric. The imitated word or phrase is a pivot that links the separate realms of meaning in the original and secondary texts:

> The gap between the letter and the sense in figuration is the same as the gap produced between the immediate, surface meaning of the word or phrase in the text and the thought evoked by the allusion. . . . In both allusion and the trope, the poetic dimension is created by the simultaneous presence of two different realities whose competition with one another produces a single more complex reality.[13]

Conte illustrates his point with an example from Catullus, showing that the opening line of Catullus' lament for his brother in 101 (*Multas per gentes et multa per aequora vectus*) is an allusion to the beginning of the *Odyssey*, and that Anchises' greeting to Aeneas in the underworld in *Aeneid* 6 is an allusion to both.[14] Catullus' allusion brings the voyage of Odysseus into his own journey to Troy; Vergil's both reminds us of the parallels between Aeneas and Odysseus and evokes the funerary context in Catullus. For Conte, as for Pasquali before him, the competence of the reader is indispensable to the effect:

> And just as no figure exists until the reader becomes aware of the twofold nature of figurative language, so too allusion only comes into being when the reader grasps that there is a gap between the immediate meaning ('after *I* have sailed through many peoples and on many seas') and the image that is its corollary ('as Odysseus sailed').[15]

The modern discussions of intertextuality remind us, however, that not all echoes are significant, or, as Pasquali puts it: 'The poetic language is like a stream that combines in itself the taste of the rock from which it springs and of the soil through which it has passed.'[16] The literary tradition develops a set of conventions, themes, laws, and expressions appropriate to a genre or form, and the system may be seen as a 'language' (*langue*) employed by the practitioners of the genre. The tradition, like Pasquali's stream, is cumulative, but it may have an authoritative source. Thus Homer provided the *langue* of epic.[17] So too, in its style, diction, subject matter, and affect, the Catullan hendecasyllable provided the language for a certain type of Renaissance lyric; and even as the tradition acquired new and non-Catullan (or even anti-Catullan) elements, it identified itself—often explicitly—as Catullan, and the poets—even at their farthest from the Catullan sensibility—saw themselves as devotees of Catullan poetry.

There are different kinds of imitation. The Renaissance theorist, Bartolomeo Ricci, speaks of three in *De imitatione* (1541): following, imitating, and emulating;[18] although in practice his three categories generally collapse into two, to make a broad distinction between following and imitating on the one hand and emulating or rivalling on the other. Ricci's examples include both ancient and Renaissance imitations of Catullus. As a follower he adduces Navagero, whose lament for the puppy Borgettus imitates Catullus' lament for Lesbia's sparrow:[19]

> The subject is very similar (which indeed we said was a property of imitation), since the one presents a dead sparrow, the other a puppy, the one a pitifully weeping mistress, the other a master. Likewise their games are very similar—in jumping, biting, cheeping, barking, and recognition of the master—but just as everything is similar, so also the evocation of pity is not at all different: at the end, instead of the continual weeping with which Catullus complains that 'his girl's poor little swollen eyes were red' Navagero has substituted: 'a long mourning for the puppy has been left to its master . . .'.[20]

Such an imitation is typical, Ricci concludes, of those who 'have rightly decided that they must look to the invention of others for their own invention, and follow, as it were, in someone else's footsteps . . .'.[21] As an example of emulation, on the other hand, he adduces Dido's rebuke to Aeneas in *Aeneid* 4, which rivals and surpasses Ariadne's lament in 64: 'Indeed, if you read Catullus alone it seems that nothing better could be desired, but when you compare him with Vergil you will scarcely go back to Catullus for a second taste, so much has Vergil overshadowed him and blocked all his light.'[22] Ricci concludes with a resounding description of Vergil's *aemulatio*:

What milk is more like milk, or what water like water, than this whole imitation of Vergil from beginning to end? But I do not think that you are waiting for me to explain how much more splendidly, abundantly, seriously, the imitator handles it. The one tells, the other sings—and on the most noble and serious trumpet ever blown—so that finally these [critics of imitation] can see that an imitator is not so imprisoned that he is not able sometimes to outstrip with ease the one whom he is following.[23]

The type of imitation chosen reflects not only the talent and goals of the imitator but also his perception of the distance of time and circumstance between himself and his model. Thus, recently Thomas Greene has identified four strategies of humanist imitation 'each of which involves a distinct response to anachronism and each an implicit perspective on history.'[24] Greene's categories are: the reproductive or sacramental, the eclectic, and—most important for our purposes—the heuristic and dialectical. The heuristic imitation acknowledges and advertises its distance in sensibility and world view from its model and creates a bridge between them. The dialectical (or emulative) imitation, on the other hand, creates not a bridge, but a conflict or dissonance between the world of the imitator and that of his model, with the result that: 'anachronism becomes a dynamic source of artistic power.'[25] The force of anachronism in imitation was noted by earlier scholars,[26] but Greene has treated it most fully, and in terms that are fundamental to our discussion. Greene bases his treatment of imitation on the existence of a *mundus significans*, a universe of signs and symbols underlying every work of literature and assumed in it:

I want to argue that the meaning of each verbal work of art has to be sought within its unique semiotic matrix, what might be called a *mundus significans*, a signifying universe, which is to say a rhetorical and symbolic vocabulary, a storehouse of signifying capacities potentially available to each member of a given culture.[27]

The *mundus* of the literary work, bound as it is to its own time and place, is ephemeral and passes away, even though the work itself may be preserved. The words remain, but their meaning and context change—subtly or drastically—depending on the degree of alteration in the world they describe.[28] The imitator, who of course lives in his own *mundus significans*, may ignore or exploit the gap between it and the lost world of his model, but the gap exists in any event and inevitably directs both his interpretation of the earlier work and the way in which it appears in his imitation.

The distance between Catullus' *mundus* and those of his Renaissance imitators is obvious and will loom large in our discussion. Indeed, for the first Renaissance poets the gulf was too great to be bridged at all. Catullus' world and his learning (much of it derived from lost Alexandrian poets) were inaccessible, and his text was so corrupt that often even the subject of his poems was unclear. His first imitators, Leonardo Bruni and Cristoforo Landino, tried to imitate him directly, but with only indifferent results. Bruni produced a single abortive pastiche, while Landino wrote only a handful of imitations that enjoyed little reputation or influence. Successful imitation became possible only when Giovanni Pontano found an intermediary in Martial, Catullus' most famous ancient imitator. Other poets followed Pontano's lead, and Martial was quickly established as the favourite model for Renaissance Catullan poetry. His smooth and racy epigrams, untroubled by excessive learning or emotional complexity, were accessible and appealing. Moreover, since his manuscripts were common in the crucial first decades of the fifteenth century when Catullan manuscripts were still scarce, most poets had read Martial first and so found it natural to imitate the Catullus they saw in Martial and to read his poetry through Martial's imitations.[29] Thus they tended to read and imitate their model at one remove, just as editors read him through the vulgate and commentators through the interpretations of their predecessors.

In doing so, however, they generally disregarded the differences between Martial and Catullus. Since they were perceiving both poets across the space of almost a millennium and a half, it was easy to overlook the relatively short span of 140 years or so that separated them. But though short, the distance was crucial, for Martial, too, inhabited a different *mundus* from that of Catullus. His sensibility, social position, and personal circumstances reflect the new political and social realities of early imperial Rome, a world subtly and dangerously altered from the time of Catullus. In imitating Catullus Martial transported his poetry into this new world, leaving behind what did not interest him and translating the rest into silver Latin epigram.

Thus, while Renaissance readers viewed both poets with Renaissance eyes, they also saw Catullus through the additional lens provided by Martial. Both lenses magnified and distorted some elements of his poetry while failing to register others, and the image they produced was not that of Catullus himself, nor yet of Martial's Catullus, but rather of a different poet altogether, the Renaissance Catullus. To understand this image and its reflections in Renaissance poetry, we must begin with Martial.

MARTIAL AND HIS WORLD

Sometime in AD 85 or 86 Martial completed the first of his twelve books of epigrams.[30] The first poem, in which he introduces himself and his work to the Roman literary scene, is in hendecasyllabics, Catullus' most characteristic metre:

Hic est quem legis ille, quem requiris,
toto notus in orbe Martialis
argutis epigrammaton libellis:
cui, lector studiose, quod dedisti
viventi decus atque sentienti,
rari post cineres habent poetae. (Mart. 1. 1)

(He, unto whom thou art so partial,
O reader, is the well-known Martial,
The epigrammatist; while living,
Give him the fame thou wouldst be giving
So shall he hear, and feel, and know it:
Post-obits rarely reach a poet.
George Gordon, Lord Byron)[31]

Martial was to write many other presentation poems (around forty, by one count),[32] but few are farther away from the content or spirit of Catullus' dedication (1: *Cui dono lepidum novum libellum*). In fact, in this epigram we are as far away from Catullus as Martial can take us, for he has produced almost a reversal of Catullus' dedication, using hendecasyllables to invite comparison and emphasize the distance between himself and his model. The theme is not, as it is in Catullus, the gift of a book to a friend, but rather the presentation of a celebrity to his public. The issue is not eternal or posthumous fame (cf. *plus uno maneat perenne saeclo* 1. 10) or even the desire for fame (here Byron's witty translation spoils the point of Martial's fourth verse), but rather present popularity, which has been granted by no supernatural agency but only by an appreciative audience. Catullus' *cui dono?* is challenged by Martial's *cui . . . dedisti*; his interrogative is replaced by a relative, his present tense by Martial's perfect: the only recipient in the epigram is Martial himself, and celebrity is his prize. The Alexandrian poetic stance of Catullus is conspicuously absent. In its place is barefaced self-promotion, which Martial happily underlines in the next poem with directions to the nearest bookshop.

Martial claims Catullus as his principal model throughout the *Epigrams*—by invoking his name, by imitating his themes and turns of phrase, and by his frequent use of the hendecasyllable to lend a Catullan flavour to his verse.[33] Yet Martial's poetry is very different from Catullus', and its very Catullan *color* emphasizes the sense of distance and disjunction. Part of the difference lies in the *personae* of the two poets. This is what Muret felt when he remarked: 'there is as much difference between the writings of Martial and Catullus as between the words of some wag on the street-corner and the well-bred jests of a gentleman, seasoned with sophisticated wit.'[34] But their two worlds differ as well. Catullus was a young man whose property and social position allowed him to move in the highest (if most morally lax) levels of Roman society. He could afford to be in the literary avant-garde, to live for his poetry, and to insult anyone he liked—from Caesar and Pompey to the demagogue Publius Clodius, the brother and lover of his Lesbia. Martial enjoyed no such licence.

Martial's Rome to a large extent preserved the forms and trappings of social and political life under the Republic, and it was as violent, dirty, and dangerous as it had been in Catullus' day.[35] But the city itself was greatly changed: the building programmes of the Caesars and the influx of new inhabitants from every corner of the empire had transformed it into a grandiose and polyglot metropolis.[36] Martial himself had come to Rome from Spain in AD 64. He lived by his wits on the fringes of society, without independent means, social prestige, or a steady patron, hoping to reap some profits from his poems and dependent on small patrons and occasional gifts from the Emperor. With his fellow citizens he witnessed the downfall of Nero, the dreadful year of the four emperors (AD 69), the relative tranquillity of Vespasian and Titus, and the long cruelty of Domitian (AD 81–96), poignantly evoked in Tacitus' contemporary account:

> Rome of old explored the limits of freedom; we have plumbed the depths of slavery, robbed even of the interchange of ideas by the secret police. We should have lost our memories as well as our tongues had it been as easy to forget as to be silent. . . . Think of it. Fifteen whole years—no mean fraction of our human life—taken from us. Many have died a natural death, all the most irrepressible have fallen victims to the cruelty of the Emperor. Even we few that survive seem to have outlived, not only our fallen comrades, but our very selves, in those years stolen from our manhood that have brought us from youth to age, from age to the far end of life's journey—and no word said.[37]

In such times only very brave or very careful voices break the silence. Martial was not brave, but he published ten of his twelve books of epigrams between AD 85 and 96.[38] He survived political dangers just as he earned his livelihood—by flattery and caution. His epigrams, however offensive, are designed to offend no one in particular: the butts of his satire and obscene jests are types; real people receive pleasantries and compliments.[39]

In Martial poetry is a commodity that may be commissioned, bought, or stolen (or even counterfeited or produced on speculation), and its value is determined on a scale of popularity, not art. The poetry book in this new world is personified as a *puer*, indeed, a *puer delicatus*, his master's agent, slave, and darling—a characterization absent from Catullus, who occasionally addresses, but hardly personifies, his verses.[40] It is Horace, rather, who provides the image. The runaway book in *Epistles* 1. 20, explicitly personified as a *puer delicatus* with ambitions to sell himself downtown, is the model for the book in Mart. 1. 3 ('You want to fly through the air, naughty one—go on, run away, but you could be safer at home').[41] Martial's book is less explicitly depicted as a 'sex-object', being merely determined to be off to the bookshops in spite of the poet's warnings, but for the attentive reader it is bound to share the same erotic nature.[42] A similar transfer of meaning takes place in Mart. 1. 52:

> Commendo tibi, Quintiane, nostros—
> nostros dicere si tamen libellos
> possum, quos recitat tuus poeta:
> si de servitio gravi queruntur,
> adsertor venias satisque praestes,
> et, cum se dominum vocabit ille,
> dicas esse meos manuque missos.
> Hoc si terque quaterque clamitaris,
> impones plagiario pudorem. (Mart. 1. 52)

(I entrust my books to you, Quintianus—if, that is, I can call those books mine, which your poet recites. If they complain about their harsh servitude, I ask you to appear as their champion and provide guarantees, and, when he calls himself their master, to say that they are mine and have been given their freedom. If you shout this out three or four times, you will make the plagiarist feel shame.)[43]

This time it is an allusion to Catullus that provides erotic *color*. Martial is citing 15 (*Commendo tibi me ac meos amores, / Aureli*), in which the poet entrusts his darling boy to the untrustworthy Aurelius and promises obscene punishments for any misbehaviour. Martial's echo leads us to expect the same scenario, and the illusion is preserved until the end of the second verse when Martial substitutes *libellos* for Catullus' metrically equivalent *amores*. Martial's poem now moves away from 15, but Catullus' *puer delicatus*—not mentioned, but summoned up by allusion—is still a presence in it, as we watch Martial seek redress, not for seduction, but for plagiarism—the appropriate violation of the *liber* as *puer*. The Catullan allusion complements the principal metaphor of the epigram, by which Martial depicts his book as a manumitted slave, unjustly claimed by his rival. (The metaphor is maintained even more strongly than the English translation reveals, since in classical Latin *plagiarius*, translated 'plagiarist', always refers to a thief of *human* property.)[44]

In many epigrams Martial's personified book is given directions or instructions and dispatched to a patron. In 1. 70 it is sent on an errand, to appear in Martial's place at a patron's *salutatio*. (In contrast, when Catullus sends a poem on an errand—and the only time he does—it is dispatched to an equal, and the subject is neoteric poetry.)[45] Sometimes Martial's book appears in dedications that advertise their Catullan pedigree. Thus, in Martial 3. 2:

> Cuius vis fieri, libelle, munus?
> festina tibi vindicem parare,
> ne nigram cito raptus in culinam
> cordylas madida tegas papyro
> vel turis piperisve sis cucullus.
> Faustini fugis in sinum? sapisti.
> cedro nunc licet ambules perunctus
> et frontis gemino decens honore
> pictis luxurieris umbilicis,
> et te purpura delicata velet,
> et cocco rubeat superbus index.
> illo vindice nec Probum timeto. (Mart. 3. 2)

(Whose gift do you want to be, little book? Hurry up and get yourself a protector so that you won't be snatched away into a dark kitchen to cover young tuna fishes with moist paper or to be a cone for incense or pepper. You're fleeing to Faustinus' bosom? You've got good taste. Now you may walk around anointed with oil of cedar and indulge yourself in painted bosses, handsome with the twin decoration of your brow; and fine purple may clothe you, and your title may glow proudly with scarlet. With him as your protector, do not fear even Probus.)

The first verse sends us to Cat. 1 (*Cui dono lepidum novum libellum*). (For the text see p. 173 above.) But almost in the same breath Martial departs from his model: not he but his book will select an appropriate recipient. The focus is all on book and patron, while the poet has nearly effaced himself, speaking not as the book's creator, but merely as its scarcely disinterested adviser. In Catullus the poet's role is uppermost, his pride in his creation apparent; the book and its recipient Cornelius Nepos, both closely linked to the poet, receive nearly equal attention. But there is no sign of a bond of friendship or shared literary interests between Martial and Faustinus (although Faustinus' poetry is mentioned in Mart. 1. 25), and there is no address to the muse or prayer for long-lasting fame. Martial's hopes are pinned on present survival, and he operates in the here and now where there is no room for supernatural intervention.[46]

Martial's two descriptions of his book in this epigram have Catullan antecedents, but as often he has conflated and reinterpreted motifs from several poems. The germ of the description of the successful book in verses 7–11 is probably Catullus' 'charming new little book, just polished with dry pumice' (1. 1–2): the book description, like the initial question and the choice of dedicatee, is an essential element in Catullus' dedication, and it is likely to find a place in any imitation.[47] But the two descriptions have nothing else in common, and Martial's resplendent book owes more to the account of Suffenus' book in Cat. 22:

> . . . cartae regiae, novi libri,
> novi umbilici, lora rubra membranae,
> derecta plumbo et pumice omnia aequata. (22. 6–8)

Catullus' descriptions play on the relationship between the physical appearance of the book and the nature of its contents. His own book in 1 is a neoteric literary production; each element in its description is a byword of Alexandrian poetics: 'new', 'charming', 'highly polished'. Suffenus' poems in 22, on the other hand, are at odds with their elegant and careful packaging, just as their author's talent falls short of his charming manner: when one reads his verses, 'the smart and urbane Suffenus seems a common goat-milker or ditch-digger' (22. 9–11). Martial has emptied his description of literary-critical overtones, not because he has not understood Catullus' meaning,[48] but to replace it with his own; he uses the punning description not to define the literary qualities of his book but to personify it. He establishes the personification, familiar by now from other poems in the first two books, in the opening verse with an address to his book (*Cuius vis fieri, libelle, munus?*) and reinforces it by having the book choose Faustinus as its patron (Mart. 3. 2. 6). The personification continues in the description in verses 7–11. The well-kept book roll is treated with cedar-oil as a preservative, its edges (called *frontes*, 'brows') are brightly painted, the rod around which it is wrapped is finished off at either end with a painted finial or boss (*umbilicus*), and the whole is protected by a purple cover with a brightly coloured label. Each element (perfumes, garlands,[49] expensive purple garments) is equally appropriate for the well-kept boy about town as he strolls around haughtily in his finery (cf. *ambules*, 7; *luxurieris*, 9). The strutting, successful book has been outfitted not by the poet but by its new-found protector (and here again Martial departs from his model, for the books of Catullus and Suffenus were adorned by their authors). Martial, in the background, gives advice and rejoices in the good fortune of his protégé, his role that of an agent or go-between, not unlike the *lena* in Roman elegy who tells her girl how to make the most out of her suitors.[50]

The parts sketched for poet, book, and patron reflect the realities of literary patronage in Martial's Rome, for the poet's success depended not only on the outright gifts of a patron, but also on his willingness to support, circulate, and publicize his client's work—or (if we use the imagery of our epigram) to dress it up and show it off.[51] Several epigrams demonstrate this aspect of patronage, but Mart. 7. 97 nicely displays the personification with erotic nuances that we have been discussing. Again, Martial addresses his book, which he expects to be the toast of the town:

> O quantum tibi nominis paratur!
> o quae gloria! quam frequens amator!
> te convivia, te forum sonabit,
> aedes, compita, porticus, tabernae.
> uni mitteris, omnibus legeris. (Mart. 7. 97. 9–13)

(O what a name is in store for you! What glory! How many admirers! Banquets and the forum, houses, street-corners, porticoes, and shops will sound your name! You are being sent to one, but will be read by all.)

A book without a patron or promoter, however, must suffer the fate sketched in Mart. 3. 2 as the counterpart to that of the successful book—dehumanized drudgery in the kitchen as wrapping paper (Mart. 3. 2. 3–5). Here Martial's starting point is Cat. 95 (*Zmyrna mei Cinnae nonam post denique messem*). Indeed 95 may also have suggested the structure of Martial's epigram, for it too is organized around contrasting descriptions; the second half of the poem contrasts the fate of Cinna's neoteric poem, *Zmyrna*, destined to be read in distant parts of the world for many generations, with that of Volusius' wretched *Annales*, which will meet an early end as fish-wrap:

> Zmyrna cavas Satrachi penitus mittetur ad undas,
>   Zmyrnam cana diu saecula pervolvent.
> At Volusi annales Paduam morientur ad ipsam
>   et laxas scombris saepe dabunt tunicas. (95. 5–8)

Again, Martial has omitted Catullus' literary judgements.[52] Volusius' *Annales* deserve their fate, but artistic merit is irrelevant to the survival of Martial's book: without a patron it will perish; with Faustinus it will flourish even beyond the reach of fault-finding critics (*illo vindice nec Probum timeto*, Mart. 3. 2. 12). The support of the patron plays a similar role in Mart. 4. 86: if Apollinaris likes Martial's book it can brave its detractors and avoid a fishy fate:

si te pectore, si tenebit ore,
nec rhonchos metues maligniorum,
nec scombris tunicas dabis molestas.
si damnaverit, ad salariorum
curras scrinia protinus licebit,
inversa pueris arande charta. (Mart. 4. 86. 6–11)

(if he keeps you in his heart and on his lips, you'll neither fear the jeers of spiteful people nor supply painful wrappings for mackerel. If he condemns you, you'll have to run to the boxes of the salt-fish sellers, with your page turned over for the boys to scratch on.)

The failed book will be torn up for scratch paper (dare we say 'dismembered'?), and like the books in 95 and Mart. 3. 2, it will provide sheets of paper for cooking fish.[53] But the image in the present passage is stronger and crueller. In 95. 8 Volusius' book will supply *laxas . . . tunicas*; the wrappings can be loose because the odious Volusius is so prolific, and the adjective, as often in Catullus, also carries an aesthetic judgement. Martial, though closely imitating, substitutes *molestas* for *laxas*—not carelessly.[54] The *tunica molesta* was a garment smeared with pitch (and sometimes elaborately decorated) in which criminals were burned; since fish were often roasted in wrappings, Martial's adjective is appropriate. But the phrase retains grim overtones. The most famous use of the *tunica molesta* is one that Martial himself might well have witnessed—Nero's torture of the Christians in AD 64. Tacitus describes the scene:

And in their deaths they were also made the subjects of sport, for they were covered with the hides of wild beasts, and worried to death by dogs, or nailed to crosses, or set fire to, and when day declined, burnt to serve for nocturnal lights. (Tacitus, *Annales* 15. 44)[55]

Martial's presentation poems derive from and shed light on his own world of signs and symbols (Greene's *mundus significans*), which, though it overlaps in many ways with that of Catullus, nevertheless contains new elements and generates a new kind of poetry. Compared with their Catullan models Martial's dedications reveal both a new aesthetic and a different status for poetry and the poet; Catullus' élitism has been replaced by Martial's popularity, his independence by Martial's social marginality; and both ideas are conveyed in the image of the poetry book as a fragile *puer delicatus* in search of a patron and protector. Imitation is the means by which Martial secures much of his effect, for the evocation of Catullus' world places the qualities of his own in stronger relief. He imitates a theme, a verse, a phrase or collocation, but does not model a whole poem on one of Catullus', preferring (when he draws deeply from his model) to conflate elements from several different poems. He may echo or cite a previous poem, whose context (like that of 15 or Horace *Epistle* 1. 20) adds an essential element of meaning to the new epigram. Often he empties a Catullan image of its original content and fills it with a meaning from the semiotic store of his own world.

The same distance from his model and the same techniques of imitation and allusion are apparent in Martial's defences of his obscene poetry. The defence is based on the assertion that light poetry requires a *mentula*—i.e. that it must be racy and titillating in order to please. Thus, in Mart. 1. 35:[56]

Versus scribere me parum severos
nec quos praelegat in schola magister,
Corneli, quereris: sed hi libelli,
tamquam coniugibus suis mariti,
non possunt sine mentula placere.
quid si me iubeas thalassionem
verbis dicere non thalassionis?
quis Floralia vestit et stolatum
permittit meretricibus pudorem?
lex haec carminibus data est iocosis,
ne possint, nisi pruriant, iuvare.
quare deposita severitate
parcas lusibus et iocis rogamus,
nec castrare velis meos libellos.
Gallo turpius est nihil Priapo. (Mart. 1. 35)

(You complain, Cornelius, that I write verses not sufficiently serious and not of the sort that a schoolmaster might dictate in school; but these poems, like husbands with their wives, cannot please without a prick. What if you were to order me to celebrate the wedding song in words not of the wedding song? Who dresses the Floralia and allows the modesty of the matron's dress to harlots? This law has been established for playful poems: that they cannot please unless they titillate. Therefore, put away your seriousness, I ask, and spare my sport and jests—and don't wish to castrate my poems. Nothing is more disgusting than a eunuch Priapus.)

Martial's model is Cat. 16, later invoked incessantly by the Renaissance poets to justify writing obscene verse:

> Pedicabo ego vos et irrumabo,
> Aureli pathice et cinaede Furi,
> qui me ex versiculis meis putastis,
> quod sunt molliculi, parum pudicum.
> nam castum esse decet pium poetam
> ipsum, versiculos nihil necesse est;
> qui tum denique habent salem ac leporem,
> si sunt molliculi ac parum pudici,
> et quod pruriat incitare possunt,
> non dico pueris, sed his pilosis
> qui duros nequeunt movere lumbos.
> vos, quod milia multa basiorum
> legistis, male me marem putatis?
> pedicabo ego vos et irrumabo. (16)

Martial uses formal parallels to evoke Catullus: Cornelius' complaint recalls that of Furius and Aurelius, the cadence *parum severos* echoes Catullus' *parum pudicum* and *parum pudici*, Martial's poetic law (*ne possint, nisi pruriant, iuvare*) invokes Catullus' (16. 7–11). In typical fashion, he has banished all the personal and affective elements of his model, for he makes no attack on the critic and no reference to the character of the poet. Less characteristically, however, he has not replaced the banished elements with elements of his own. The result is a radically simplified, and greatly distorted, version of Catullus' argument, which Martial states (and restates) as a principle of artistic decorum: the 'law', *ne possint, nisi pruriant, iuvare*. Contravening this pleasure principle is wrongheaded and incongruous, indeed an assault on the *mentula* itself, its embodiment and necessary instrument—and the dominant image in the poem, which concludes with the crowning paradox (Martial would say, perversion) of a castrated Priapus. But in fact Martial has not departed so thoroughly from Catullus as one might think, for the *mentula* of his epigram has its origins in 16 (for what else is represented in Catullus' opening and closing verse, *pedicabo vos ego et irrumabo*?). The difference is not that Martial utters an obscenity while Catullus does not (*mentula*, *pedicabo*, and *irrumabo* would all have about the same value on a Richter scale of obscenity);[57] it is rather that he has changed the function of the image. In Catullus the *mentula* is the poet's, and by using it in a sexual attack on his critics he will rebut their slur on his masculinity; in Martial it is depersonalized and transformed into a symbol of sensuality. The change is typical of Martial, who likes to substitute the abstract and impersonal for the emotional and subjective; and it is largely responsible for the difference between his argument and Catullus'. Martial is justifying the obscenity of his verse; Catullus is denying a connection between the character of the poet and the nature of his poetry.

Martial does use Catullus' point, or rather, a version of it, as the conclusion of 1. 4, another defence of obscene poetry: 'my page is naughty, my life is pure.'[58] But his model is Ovid's excuse to Augustus in the *Tristia* ('my life is chaste, my Muse is playful'):[59] his antithesis echoes Ovid's, and, like Ovid, he is addressing the emperor (Domitian). The defence was already a cliché by Martial's time,[60] and it was trotted out and ascribed to Catullus with shameless regularity in the Renaissance. We should note, however, that the formulation in Ovid and Martial is a simplification and a distortion of 16. 5–6. Catullus does not claim, as his imitators do, that he is *castus* though his verses are not, but rather makes a more subtle and quite different point. We may translate: 'it is *appropriate* (*decet*) for the upright (*pius*) poet to be free of filth (*castus*),[61] but his verses need not be.' By using the ambiguous *decet* rather than a simple indicative Catullus presents not an easy antithesis between the chastity of the poet and the obscenity of his verse but rather a general statement of propriety that leaves his own character unrevealed. Such ambiguity was not desired by Ovid and Martial in their apologies to their dangerous and straitlaced emperors, and it was probably lost on the younger Pliny, who quotes 16. 5–8 as the 'truest law' of light poetry in a defence of his own not very racy verse.[62] Pliny's treatment was decisive: as we shall see presently, verses 5–8, quoted out of context and termed a law, became the basis of Renaissance imitations of 16 and the justification for 'Catullan verse'.

FIRST STEPS IN RENAISSANCE IMITATION: LEONARDO BRUNI AND CRISTOFORO LANDINO

It seems to have been Leonardo Bruni (1370?–1444) who produced the first Catullan imitation of the Renaissance. Recently James Hankins has published a poem in hendecasyllables ascribed to Bruni in three manuscripts.[63] The earliest manuscript was copied in 1421, but Hankins dates the composition of the poem between 1405 and 1415. At first sight Bruni appears an unlikely candidate for the title of Catullan poet, for he was a moralist, an orator, an historian—a devotee of Cicero, to be sure, but hardly, one imagines, of Cicero's frivolous contemporary.[64] But even Bruni was young once. As Hankins reminds us, he is not only the translator of Plato and Plutarch and the author of the *Historiae Florentini populi* but also the perpetrator of the ribald *Oratio Heliogabali ad meretrices*, which was probably written in the same period as his Catullan poem and appears as its companion piece in the oldest manuscript.[65] Still more to the point, however, Bruni was also a protégé of Coluccio Salutati and a colleague and friend of Poggio Bracciolini—the two most important Catullan enthusiasts of the period. Coluccio, as we have seen, owned R, one of the three fourteenth-century manuscripts now extant; and Poggio was the scribe of M, the next oldest manuscript, which he copied from R, probably between 1398 and 1400.[66] In the years between 1405 and 1415 Bruni, like Poggio, was part of the papal court as it was shunted from one city to another in northern Italy, and he maintained close ties with Florence and contemporary humanists. He would have had ample opportunity to study Poggio's manuscript or Salutati's, and he was humanist enough, especially given the comparative novelty and rarity of Catullus, to have done so.

The poem that resulted from these studies is hardly a masterpiece, and its flagrant obscenity would scarcely have enhanced the reputation of the mature Bruni, statesman and moralist that he was. Its preservation may result from this very fact, for Hankins suggests that the earliest manuscript may have been circulated to embarrass him as a hypocrite.[67] However that may be, neither the poem nor Bruni's authorship of it became well known, for some years later—perhaps in the last half of the fifteenth century—an unknown forger made a few changes in it and tried to pass it off as the work of Cornelius Gallus. The 'Gallus' redaction was edited by Scevola Mariotti, who, unaware of Bruni's version, dated the poem to the second half of the century.[68] The text that follows is that of Professor Hankins:

Incipiunt endecasyllabi Leonardi Aretini
O mei procul ite nunc amores,
ite nunc Veneres Cupidinesque
quicquid et fuit antea iocundum!
Galla me, o superi, impie fefellit,
Galla, proh superi, impudica mechos
pretulit mihi clanculum trecentos.
O scelesta, potes pati hec nefanda?
nec videre pudet diem atque lucem
nec vero metuis truces iambos?
Surgite, endecasyllabi, repente!
impudentia percitemur ora!
clamate! audiat ista mecha turpis.
'Scortum vulgare, putidum lupanar,
publice stabulum et cloaca gentis,
vas urine olidum, vorago penum,
sordido meritorie taberne
scorto putidior lutosiorque,
ten ego aspiciam? te amare possim?
Bella tu amplius mihi videare,
nec pares oculos habens nec ora
munda nec faciem, ut prius, venustam,
mala, quin etiam abstinente lingua
nec mundo pede nec manu pudenti?
Novit Aretium tuum pudorem,
cum tu concubias vagata noctes
custos impavida trementis arcis,
tonsorem tuum adusque ventitabas
atque inter socios pudore misso,
ardens et nimium impudica mecha,
illius inguina turpe palpitasti.
Salve Penelope et pudica Dido
ac Lucretia castitatis instar!
Te Diana suis cupit magistram

dare virginibus tuumque Vesta
nomen predicat omnibus sacellis.'
Sed nil verba facit neque his movetur;
heret mentula nanque fixa cordi
auresque obstruit. Ergo colloquamur
suis qui rabiem domare possunt:
'Agnati, quibus imminet propinque
cura, quid facitis? furit puella
effrenis neque iam tenetur ullo
pudore in patria provintiaque.'
O tonsoris amica sordidosi,
sola qui tibi mentula probatur,
recte nos alios nil esse ducis,
quos tanta inguina haud habere nosti.
Desine aspicere ac videre lucem!

(The hendecasyllables of Leonardo Aretino begin: Now get ye hence, o my loves, go now, Venuses and Cupids, and all my former pleasure! Galla (o gods above!) has deceived me disloyally, unchaste Galla (o gods!) has slyly preferred three hundred adulterers to me. O wicked woman, can you endure these crimes? Aren't you ashamed to see the light of day, and don't you fear scathing iambics?

Rise up at once, hendecasyllables! Let us smite[69] her shameless face! Shout! Let the base hussy hear this!

'Cheap harlot! Stinking brothel! Whorehouse and sewer of the common herd, foul pot of urine, sink hole of penises, filthier and more stinking than an unclean harlot of the whore shop, could I look at you? Could I love you? Would you seem pretty to me any longer, with your mismatched eyes and dirty face and no charming appearance as before, with an evil tongue even when you keep it in your head, and with dirty foot and unchaste hand?

'Arezzo knows your modesty, when you—fearless guardian of the trembling citadel!—roaming the sleepy nights, used to go back and forth to your barber, and shamelessly among his cronies—o hot and too unchaste adulteress—basely fondled his loins. Hail, Penelope and chaste Dido and Lucretia, model of chastity! Diana wants to give you as teacher to her virgins and Vesta proclaims your name to all her shrines.'

But she doesn't utter a word and she isn't moved by these things, for the penis sticks fast in her heart and blocks her ears. Therefore, let us address her family and friends who can tame her madness:

'Kinsmen who are charged with the care of your relative, what are you doing? The girl is raging out of control and she is restrained by no modesty in her homeland and province.'

O girlfriend of the filthy barber, whom you approve for his penis alone, you rightly despise the rest of us, knowing that we have no such great members. Cease to view and see the light!)

Bruni's poem is less important as a work of literature than as a reflection of the state of Catullan studies at the beginning of the fifteenth century. Although it contains borrowings—one cannot call them echoes or allusions—from other poems, for the most part it is a pastiche of 41–43, which were transmitted as part of a longer block of poems that extended from 40 through 48. The poems remain unseparated in the extant manuscripts that might have been available to Bruni (that is, O, R, G, and M), and he should probably have the credit for being the first to separate 41–43 from 40–48.[70] In doing so, he undoubtedly considered that he had isolated a single poem—not three. It is not difficult to follow his line of reasoning. A clear line of demarcation separates 41–43 from the poems on either side, for both 40 and 44 are on different subjects, and 44 is in a different metre, limping iambics. Cat. 41–43, moreover, have a certain affinity with each other. All are invectives against a woman, and 41 and 43 both attack the same woman, 'the girlfriend of the bankrupt from Formiae' (*decoctoris amica Formiani*, 41. 4 and 43. 5). Whether Bruni understood more than this, however, is unclear, for his imitation departs substantially from Catullus. In 41 (*Ameana puella defututa*) the poet complains of the girl who has asked too much for her services; in 42 (*Adeste, hendecasyllabi, quot estis*) he calls on his verses to attack a girl who will not return his writing tablets; in 43 (*Salve, nec minimo puella naso*) he is astonished that anyone could compare the bankrupt's ugly girl-friend with his Lesbia. Bruni, on the other hand, merely addresses his invective to an unfaithful girl, omitting all reference to money, writing tablets, or comparisons of beauty—details that he probably failed to recognize or at best vaguely understood in the corrupt text of Catullus' poems. (We should remember in this connection that seventy or eighty years later Partenio (1485) thought that Catullus wanted his writing tablets back because they contained a promissory note to the girl for ten thousand sesterces, and that no commentator before Muret (1554) printed the three poems separately or explained them correctly.)[71] Bruni's grasp of metre is equally tenuous—not surprisingly, since his seem to be the first hendecasyllables of the Renaissance. Some of his more glaring faults were recognized or corrected by 'pseudo Gallus'. Thus, 'Gallus' changed *haud* to *non* in verse 47, and omitted the impossible verse 19 altogether: *Bella tu amplius mihi videare*. But other difficulties were too subtle or too intractable for "Gallus'" own modest powers, and even the later redaction has a high proportion of prosodical mistakes.[72]

Bruni's poem, in short, is exactly what we would expect after reviewing the history of the text and interpretation of Catullus in the fifteenth century—a kind of metrical equivalent of Partenio or Palladio. But the comparison is unfair, for Bruni and Partenio were operating at opposite ends of the century. As we shall see presently, the poets learned their trade much faster than the critics: by the time that Partenio and the rest were writing lame scenarios to explain poems they could not understand and trying with imperfect success to scan Catullus' metres, the poets were producing sophisticated and metrically perfect imitations that often revealed a subtle understanding of their models. Part of the difference was talent, for, at least in the fifteenth century, one cannot deny that Catullus' imitators were more gifted than his critics; but the poets had another advantage as well: unlike the commentators, they could omit the poems they did not understand. Not surprisingly, we will see that the poets tended to imitate a small number of Catullus' poems, and that the poems they chose were for the most part short and free from serious textual problems. Cat. 41–43, so disastrously attempted by Bruni, did not become a regular part of their repertoire.

If Bruni's example inspired other poets, history—so far, at least—has been silent about the results. It was to be another generation before Catullan imitation began in earnest. The imitator was a young Florentine, Cristoforo Landino (1424–1504).[73] In 1443–4 Landino completed a collection of poems he called the *Xandra* and sent it to his friend Leon Battista Alberti:[74]

> Ibis, sed tremulo libelle gressu,
> nam cursus pedibus malis negatur;
> verum ibis tamen et meum Leonem
> Baptistam, Aonidum decus sororum,
> antiqua Aeneadum videbis urbe.
>
> (Landino, *X.* 1 (= A 1. 13), 1–5)

(You will go, little book, but with trembling step (for running is denied to bad feet); but you will go just the same, and you will see my Leon Battista, the ornament of the Aonian Muses, in the ancient city of the Aeneidae.)

Landino's hendecasyllables, though not the first of the Renaissance, are still early enough to have been an interesting novelty, and their use in Landino's opening poem, as Walther Ludwig suggests, is an announcement of the poet's affinity with Catullus.[75] It is characteristic of early Renaissance imitation that it is Martial who provides the form of the announcement—a dedication poem in which the personified book is admonished and sent on its way to an addressee.[76] But unlike Martial's books, which tend to be in a hurry, Landino's must hobble along on 'bad feet'—a modest (or perhaps, mock modest) reference to the difficulty of reviving hendecasyllabic poetry.[77] (No one who has read Bruni's verses can doubt that the difficulty was real.) The poem concludes with the book's reception by Alberti:

> Hic te, parve liber, sinu benigno
> laetus suscipiet, suisque ponet
> libris hospitulum. Sed, heus, libelle,
> audin, nequitiae tuae memento!
> Quare, si sapies, severiores,
> quos ille ingenuo pios pudore
> multos composuit, relinque libros,
> et te Passeris illius querelis,
> doctis sive Canis iocis Hiberi,'
> argutae lepidaeque sive Muscae
> extremum comitem dabis: superque est
> istis si potes ultimus sedere.
>
> (Landino, *X.* 1 (= A 1. 13), 25–36)

(He will receive you gladly, little book, in his kindly protection, and will place you as a small guest among his books. But, hark, little book (are you listening?), think of your naughtiness! Therefore, if you're wise, leave the more serious books (which are many and virtuous) that he has composed with noble modesty, and make yourself the last companion to the complaints of his *Passer* or the learned jests of the Spanish *Dog* or the witty and charming *Musca*. It is too much if you can sit last among these.)

The final verses announce the character of Landino's book and neatly compliment Alberti at the same time by naming some of his own light writings: his *Passer* is unfortunately lost (it sounds tantalizingly like an imitation of 3); the *Canis* is an encomium of his dog, inspired by Theodore of Gaza; the *Musca*, a diversion in the manner of Lucian, was dedicated to Landino.[78] The passage also recalls and refashions Martial's dedication to Domitian's librarian (Mart. 5. 5). There Martial asks that his books be placed next to those of Pedo, Marsus, and Catullus in the imperial library; Vergil's shall be shelved beside the great epic of Domitian.[79] Landino has simplified Martial's social and literary *schema* both by substituting the criterion of seriousness for Martial's hierarchy of genres and by measuring himself against Alberti alone; but Martial's poets (Catullus, Vergil, and the rest) still remain a presence in Landino's poem—both increasing the compliment to Alberti (whose versatility seems enhanced by the implied comparison) and granting Landino a place in the genealogy of poets as a descendant of Catullus and Martial.

In fact, however, Landino is interested in the whole line of poets inaugurated by Catullus, and particularly in Propertius. In the fifty-three poems of the *Xandra* of 1443–4 there are only four imitations of Catullus himself, and these are modelled on only two poems, 8 and 11.[80] Landino's work, like Bruni's, differs significantly from later Renaissance imitations: his imitations are based on poems of little interest to later imitators, and they are imitated directly from Catullus without Martial as an intermediary. Most uncharacteristic of all, however, his imitations are not in hendecasyllables.[81] We shall see again and again that Renaissance imitators in general tended to bypass the emotional complexities of the Lesbia poems in favour of their erotic playfulness—a preference related as either cause or effect to their predilection for the hendecasyllable, which Catullus uses for many purposes, but hardly ever to convey deep emotional involvement or to explore his own contradictory feelings. Landino, however, student and imitator of Roman elegy that he was, wrote three different versions of 8 (*Miser Catulle, desinas ineptire*), one of Catullus' most serious and powerful poems. Not surprisingly, in all three versions he transposed its limping iambs into his own elegiac couplets.

Cat. 8 is a soliloquy in which the poet calls on himself to cut his losses (*quod vides perisse perditum ducas*, 8. 2) and leave his girl. He reminds himself that his happiness is over, urges himself to be firm, and bids her 'goodbye', imagining how sorry she will be that he no longer wants her. But soon his picture changes to a jealous fantasy:

> quis nunc te adibit? cui videberis bella?
> quem nunc amabis? cuius esse diceris?
> quem basiabis? cui labella mordebis? (8. 16–18)

The poem ends with an attempt to return to his resolution: *at tu, Catulle, destinatus obdura* (8. 19). Landino's *X.* 6 follows a similar pattern:

> Dum licuit tecum gratissima gaudia sumpsi,
> laetitia pleni dumque fuere dies:
> nunc vertis mores: sic et vertenda voluntas.
> Esto quoque. Iam nobis, iamque puella vale!
> (*X.* 6 (= *A.* 1. 6) 9–12)

(I took most welcome pleasures with you while it was allowed and while the days were full of joy. Now you change your ways. Thus, my will must also change. All right then. Now, girl, as far as I'm concerned, farewell!)

Like Catullus, Landino imagines that his girl will be sorry, but he has replaced Catullus' jealous fantasy with another picture: Xandra will weep and beg him to return—and he will not take her back: *Iamque puella vale*! (*X.* 6. 20). In structure and style *X.* 6 is close to Cat. 8,[82] but there are major differences in content. Landino addresses not himself, but Xandra, throughout, and when he does refer to himself, it is in the first person, not in the second as in Catullus. Consequently, the dialogue or drama, so far as there is one, is not internal, but rather between himself and Xandra: the poet is not in conflict with himself, and his resolve never falters. Landino imitates 8 again in *X.* 35, this time addressing himself: 'What are you doing, unhappy man? . . . Cease now to nourish empty pain for yourself. . . . Put an end to tears and consider lost what you see is lost, and repent.'[83] Landino's self-apostrophe makes his epigram sound like 8, but again there is no internal conflict: the poem contains only one point of view, that of the voice that addresses the apparently unresisting poet. Landino's third version of 8, *X.* 34, is addressed to the Muses:

> Hactenus o lusi, satis est, lasciva Camenae
> carmina, iamque satis me malus ussit amor!

Nunc meliore lyra, divae, meliora canamus,
nam satis atque super me malus ussit amor.
Dicamus coelum, belli dicamus honores,
sitque mihi lacrimas promere posse pias.
Et tandem pigeat tantos sumpsisse labores
in cassum; pigeat paeniteatque mei. (*X*. 34 = *A*. 1. 16)

(Up to now I have played light songs—it is enough!—o Muses. And now wicked love has burned me enough. Now, goddesses, let us sing better songs on a better lyre—for wicked love has burned me enough and to spare. Let us speak of heaven, let us speak of the honours of war, and may I have the power to send forth pious tears. And may it disgust me at last to have taken up such great labours for nothing; may I feel disgust and regret.)

The poem is farther away from Catullus than Landino's other imitations, but it is surely a companion piece to *X*. 35, whose relation to 8 is clear. In the second edition of the *Xandra* both epigrams are entitled *Ad se ipsum*, the title awarded to 8 in the archetype.[84] The poems are of the same length and were placed next to each other in both editions of the *Xandra*. They are both on the theme of renunciation and repentance, and they are linked by their final cadences: *paeniteatque tui* (*X*. 35. 8) and *paeniteatque mei* (*X*. 34. 8). But there are differences, too. In *X*. 35 Landino tries to renounce love, which he does not contemplate replacing with another emotion or way of life; in *X*. 34 he renounces love poetry (or tries to do so), but in favour of a better kind of verse—indeed, just as he rejected Xandra in *X*. 6 in hopes of finding another, more faithful girl.[85]

Landino's three versions constitute a set of variations on the theme of 8, each more distant from the source as the poet introduces more permutations of the original elements. The constant theme is renunciation of vain and avoidable suffering, but all else is subject to variation and substitution—including the addressee and the object of renunciation. As a consequence the imitations differ from their model and from each other in tone and emotional force, and in all of them the conflict (and most of the pain) of 8 has disappeared. *X*. 35 is the darkest of the three: like 8, it is addressed to the poet himself, and it presents no goal or hope beyond that of renunciation and repentance. *X*. 6 bears the strongest formal resemblance to 8, but unlike its model assumes a chastened *puella* and the possibility of a new love. *X*. 34, linked to 8 principally by its relation to *X*. 35, shows the influence of Augustan elegy as well as the imprint of Landino's own historical and spiritual *Weltanschauung*. Like the elegists, Landino ponders a different and more worthy subject for his verse, but the subject he contemplates is not only martial and patriotic, but also religious: 'let us speak of heaven, let us speak of the honours of war, and may I have the power to send forth pious tears.' Each of the important elements (*coelum*, *lacrimas . . . pias*) inevitably carries the weight placed on it by over a millennium of Christianity, just as *paeniteat* in the last verse of both *X*. 34 and *X*. 35 inevitably carries overtones, at least, of Christian penitence. Landino's poem, then, like other imitations (although perhaps more obviously than most), is an artefact of both literary and historical intertextuality; and we find not only that Catullus' theme has been transposed into an Augustan *recusatio*, but that by a second transposition the epic of Augustan aspiration has been replaced by a genre appropriate to Landino's own changed world, the penitential hymn—a change that appears still more clearly in the second edition of the *Xandra*, where *belli* of *X*. 34. 5 has been replaced by *coeli*. The interweaving of Christian and erotic elements (i.e. elements from Roman erotic elegy) is characteristic of Landino, who elsewhere in the *Xandra* transfers the flirtation scene of the elegists from its usual ancient setting, the dinner party, to church and morning mass.[86] The religious element by itself, of course—divested of erotic frivolity, and suitably buttressed by serious study of the Neoplatonists—was to manifest itself in the work of the mature Landino, especially in his commentary on the *Divine Comedy*.[87]

GIOVANNI PONTANO AND THE CATULLAN PROGRAMME

Landino's imitations of Catullus, though of undoubted historical and literary interest, exercised only a limited influence; and they were soon overshadowed by the work of one of the most important of all Renaissance Latin poets, Giovanni Gioviano Pontano (1429–1503), who was to set the course of subsequent Catullan poetry.[88] In 1448 Pontano, not yet 20, arrived in Naples at the behest of King Alfonso of Aragon, aptly surnamed

'Magnanimo' for his patronage of poets and scholars. He soon became a friend and disciple of another poet in Alfonso's service, Panormita (Antonio Beccadelli), whose obscene *Hermaphroditus* had scandalized and delighted the previous generation.[89] Not surprisingly, Panormita and his models, Martial and the *Priapea*, were to be the formative influences on the work of the young Pontano. Thus the scene was set at the outset for Pontano to produce a different kind of Catullan poetry from Landino, whose principal models in the *Xandra* were not the *nugae* of Catullus, Martial, and the *Priapea*, but the emotional and serious (or at least relatively serious) poems of the Roman elegists. Although Catullus is the father of both traditions, his contribution to elegy was overshadowed even for Landino by the poetry of his successors in the Augustan age, and he had but little influence on Renaissance elegy, which was to move instead in the direction of melding the Petrarchan sonnet with Propertian and Tibullan poetry.[90]

For Pontano, however, Catullus was a major influence, and an influence not confined to his youth and earliest poetry. He produced three collections of Catullan poetry: the *Pruritus* (1449), the *Parthenopeus sive Amores* (*c*.1457), and the *Hendecasyllabi sive Baiae*, written throughout the 1490s and completed a year or so before his death in 1503.[91] Although all the collections follow in the footsteps of Catullus' erotic *nugae*, they differ in character and approach. The *Pruritus* is more explicitly obscene than the later collections and closer to Panormita and the *Priapea*. The *Parthenopeus*, which incorporates much of the *Pruritus*, excludes its most obscene poems and embarks on a more sophisticated literary programme. The *Hendecasyllabi*, erotic poems of Pontano's old age, have moved farthest from imitation of Catullan subjects to an almost elegiac celebration of the enfeebled and fragile, but enduring, *Eros* of old men. Most of Pontano's imitations are in hendecasyllables;[92] indeed, he created the particular version of the hendecasyllable that was to predominate in subsequent Catullan poetry. Pontano's metre is recognizably Catullan, for it reproduces Catullan tricks of style and achieves a lightness and delicacy generally absent in earlier imitators like Martial and the poet of the *Priapea*; but it also exaggerates Catullan features (particularly assonance, diminutives and the use of internal repetitions or refrains) to create an effect that is unmistakably new—sensuous, lyrical, and sometimes almost hypnotic.[93]

All three collections are frankly sensual (indeed, more so than Catullus himself, as we will see), and all have as their point of departure the idea—ultimately derived from 16, but filtered through Martial and Pliny—that poetry is an aphrodisiac whose purpose is to arouse and titillate the reader.[94] Thus, in the opening poem of the *Pruritus* ('Titillation'):

Pruritum feret hic novus libellus
Ad rubri luteum dei sacellum,
Qui semper puerisque furibusque
Minatur gladioque mentulaque.
At tu, si sapias, cave, libelle.

(Pontano, Soldati, *App.* 9)[95]

(This new little book will bring excitement to the mud shrine of the ruddy god who always threatens boys and thieves with his sword and penis. But, you, little book, if you're smart, watch out!)

The short poem is full of programmatic allusions: to Catullus (*hic novus libellus*), to the *Priapea* (the 'ruddy god' is Priapus), and to Martial (whose book so often takes on the character of a *puer delicatus*). Its first word, *pruritum*, announces the theme and title of the collection, but also alludes to 16. 9 (*et quod pruriat incitare possunt*) and Martial's restatement of it (*ne possint, nisi pruriant, iuvare*, Mart. 1. 35. 11). The last poem of the *Pruritus* is similar in spirit:

Leonti Tomacello sodali suo

Leon, delitium tui poetae,
Nostrum dum legis arrige ad libellum
Cuius nequitiae procaxque lusus
possunt herniolam senis voracis
Samarrae patris irrumationum,
Vel siquid mage languidum, incitare.

(Pontano, Cortona, Biblioteca comunale, MS 84, 37v, verses 1–6)[96]

(To his friend, Leonte Tomacelli: Leonte, darling of your poet, as you read, be aroused at our book, whose naughtiness and wanton play can stir up the ruptured limb (and nothing can be more limp than that) of insatiable old Samarra, father of fellation.)

Leonte Tomacelli is the brother of Pontano's lifelong friend, Marino Tomacelli (1429–1515), and so presumably a near contemporary of the poet.[97] Samarra is otherwise unknown, but certainly old. Thus, the poem, which at first sight is not so very close to 16, is in fact a demonstration of one of its central themes: that light poetry should arouse not just boys but also sexually exhausted old men (*his pilosis / qui duros nequeunt movere lumbos*, 16. 9–10).[98]

The explicit and rather shocking programme poems of the *Pruritus* were excluded from the *Parthenopeus sive Amores* in favour of subtler and more complicated statements, but 16 is still Pontano's starting point. In *Am*. 1. 1, like Martial (and Landino) before him, he sends off his book with an admonition: 'Go, little book, (without too harsh a face) as a gift to my charming friend . . . .'[99] The friend is Lorenzo Bonincontri, and the book will find him making love to his wife, Cecilia, whose naked beauty Pontano lovingly describes—ostensibly to the book, but mostly, of course, for the reader and for Bonincontri. The poem closes with a nice riposte both to Martial's request to Domitian's librarian (Mart. 5. 5) and to Landino's dedication to Alberti (Landino, *X*. 1):

Festina Miniatum adire nostrum,
Qui te tam facili videbit ore,
Ut post millia basiationum
Dignum te faciat sinu Cicellae.
Hanc tu malueris, libelle, sedem,
Quam si scrinia regis ampla dentur.

(Pontano, *Am*. 1. 1. 28–33)

(Hasten to approach our friend Miniatus,[100] who will be so glad to see you that after thousands of kisses he will judge you worthy of Cecilia's lap. You will like this place better, little book, than if the king's fine bookcases were given.)

Domitian's bookshelves and Alberti's lie behind King Alfonso's, and Pontano's choice challenges the literary programmes of Martial and Landino. Any shelves at all are inferior to the home that Pontano seeks for his own book, for only the lap of a beautiful and desirable woman is suited to his own brand of

Catullan poetry. Pontano describes his new poetry earlier in the poem in an evocation and reworking of 16:

> Legem versiculis dedere nostris
> Aetas et male sobrius magister,
> Ut tantum teneras ament puellas,
> Ut sint virginibus nihil molesti,
> Ut molles, lepidi, leves, iocosi;
> Quos uxor canat in sinu mariti,
> Quos coniux legat in sinu puellae,
> Quos discant pueri, senes et ipsi,
> Siqui sunt pueris ineptiores,
> Et castos fugiunt timentque versus.
>
> (Pontano, *Am.* 1. 1. 6–15)

(Youth and the scarcely sober master have laid down the law for our little verses: that they love only susceptible girls, that they be not troublesome to maidens, that they be soft, charming, light, playful, the kind of thing that a wife croons in the embrace of her husband, or a husband reads in the embrace of his bride, that boys learn—and old men, too, if there are any who are more foolish than boys and fear and flee chaste verses.)

The 'law' that governs Pontano's verses is the pleasure principle of Cat. 16 in the familiar codification of Martial: *ne possint, nisi pruriant, iuvare* (Mart. 1. 35. 11);[101] but its purview has been greatly altered and expanded beyond the predominantly homosexual obscenity of his ancient models (and of Pontano himself in the programme poems of the *Pruritus*) to a sensual heterosexual romanticism that includes even the married love of Bonincontri and Cecilia. Pontano's innovation not only rewrites the old law of Catullus and Martial, but it also—and this is still more important—reverses the conventions of ancient erotic poetry, which celebrates illicit love, but never marriage.[102] The love sung by Catullus and the elegists was outside the conventions of society and at odds with them. Catullus tries to apply Roman values (*fides*, *pietas*, love of family) to his affair with Lesbia, and the elegists often use the language of marriage to describe their liaisons; but their attempts only emphasize the conflict of values that is both at the root of their poetry and one of its principal subjects.[103] Pontano has removed the conflict, and by depicting Bonincontri and Cecilia in a scene more intimate than that of any elegiac lover and his mistress he announces a new direction for Catullan poetry.

In spite of his innovations, however, and the distance between himself and his model, Pontano sees himself as following, not revising, Catullus. In the last poem of his book, also addressed to Bonincontri, he asks for an opinion of his poetry:[104]

> . . . Nunquid a Catullo
> Quenquam videris esse nequiorem,
> Aut qui plus habeat procacitatis,
> Non dico tamen elegantiorem?
> Sed certe meus hic libellus unum
> Doctum post sequitur suum Catullum
> Et Calvum veteremque disciplinam.
> Non multo minor est novis poetis.
> Saltat versiculis canens minutis
> Hoc, quod non sonuere mille ab annis
> Musarum citharae et Lyaei puellae.
>
> (Pontano, *Am.* 1. 28. 4–14)

(Surely you won't have seen anyone naughtier since Catullus, or anyone who has more wantonness—to say nothing of being more elegant? But certainly this book of mine is second to its learned Catullus alone, and Calvus and the ancient discipline. It is not much less than the modern poets. It dances, singing in tiny verses a strain that the Muses' lyres and the girls of Bacchus have not sounded for a thousand years.)

'A strain not sounded for a thousand years.' Pontano's claim is arresting and correct, except that, properly speaking, his melody has never been sung before at all, and certainly not by Catullus; for in *Am.* 1. 28 the Catullan strain has become a chord, transposed into a modern key. Pontano's claim to be second to Catullus alone is drawn from Martial's famous wish: *uno sed tibi sim minor Catullo* (Mart. 10. 78. 16); the 'tiny verses' and 'Catullus and Calvus and the ancient discipline' recall the younger Pliny, or rather his friend, the poetaster Sentius Augurinus.[105] The notion mentioned a few verses later that his pages might be hauled into a smelly kitchen for fish wrapping comes from Mart. 3. 2, which was to be a favourite model for later Catullan poets; and the poem closes with a programmatic nod to Propertius 3. 3 and his rejection of epic for love poetry.[106] Only the reference to Propertius is an allusion; the rest are simply part of Pontano's poetic vocabulary—the language, largely forged in the Silver Age, for Catullan poetry. Pontano knew Martial (and probably Pliny) before he knew Catullus—nearly everyone in the early Renaissance did; almost inevitably, he imitated Catullus in Martial's words and saw him through Martial's eyes and from the perspective of Martial's world. But his own perspective is different still—the view of a modern man looking over a gulf 'of a thousand years' to a foreshortened past in which Catullus and Martial might almost be contemporaries. At the end of the first century AD Pliny's friend Augurinus looked back at Catullus and Calvus as 'old poets', and perhaps smiled at the thought of Catullus' 'new little book, just polished with dry pumice'. Pontano saw only a great divide separating himself and the other moderns (*novi poetae*, all) from an undifferentiated *vetus disciplina*.

Almost forty years after the *Parthenopeus* Pontano embarked on his last and most ambitious Catullan poems, the *Hendecasyllabi*, or *Baiae*, so called after the famous resort on the Bay of Naples where Pontano and his friends, like the ancients before them, sought girls and pleasures.[107] Baiae's revivifying springs provide the setting, but also symbolize the possibility of recovering the lost joys of *Eros*, for Pontano and most of his addressees are now old men. A strange subject for Catullan poetry, one thinks—for Catullus himself died young, and the subjects of his poetry are quintessentially youthful. But Cat. 16 is still Pontano's subtext, this time as the springboard for an exploration of the power of poetry—specifically, the *Hendecasyllabi* of his title—to create erotic adventures and to arouse and please old men. In *Hend*. 1. 1 Pontano calls Catullus' Muse from Sirmio to Baiae, along with Catullus' verses:

> Huc huc, hendecasyllabi, frequentes,
> huc vos quicquid habetis et leporum,
> iocorum simul et facetiarum,
> huc deferte, minutuli citique.
> Quod vos en pretium, aut manet voluptas?
> Inter lacteolas simul puellas,
> inter molliculos simul maritos
> ludetis simul atque prurietis.
>
> (Pontano, *Hend*. 1. 1. 10–17)[108]

(Here, here, hendecasyllables, in crowds, bring here whatever charms you have, and jests and wit at the same time—bring them here, you tiny ones and swift. What reward or pleasure waits you? Among the milk-white girls, among their amorous husbands at the same time, you too will play and grow wanton.)

The verses are not only reporters as we learn below ('how many kisses and love bites, how many quarrels you'll count . . . how many sighs, whispers, and laughs',[109] but also wanton participants in the lovemaking. The poem ends with a warning to the addressee, Marino Tomicelli, to avoid the hendecasyllables as companions in Baiae: they will tell all his erotic adventures and reveal him to be 'a sexy old man' and impotent from exhaustion.[110] But the power of both Baiae and the hendecasyllables is limited and equivocal. In *Hend*. 1. 7 the baths promise that the girl who comes with an old husband will leave with a young one: 'such is the strength of the spring';[111] but the epilogue (addressed again to Tomacelli) reveals that the miracle is achieved not by rejuvenation but by substitution. In *Hend*. 2. 1 Tomacelli is warned to avoid the baths and love altogether in favour of wine ('for the baths are suited to youths, but wine-shops to weak old men');[112] and poetry—represented not by the playful and garrulous hendecasyllables but by the 'ashes of Catullus'—provides only a drinking song:

Amabo, puer, hos minutiores
irrora calices. Marine, sume:

. . . . .

Hae sunt deliciae, haec senum voluptas.

(Pontano, *Hend*. 2. 1. 32–3; 38)

(Please, boy, bedew these little drinking cups. Drink, Marinus. . . . This is the delight, this is the pleasure of old men.)

In *Hend*. 2. 38, the last poem of the collection, Pontano bids farewell to the hendecasyllables, aphrodisiac as they are, and companions of his old age: 'there must be an end even to laughter.'[113] His valediction is also a farewell to life; the hendecasyllables cannot confer immortality on him any more than Baiae could revive the impotent Tomacelli. Rather, he looks forward to a time when he shall be ashes—like Catullus—and young men will read his verses:

Ergo qui, iuvenes, meas legetis
nugas, qui tenerae iocos Thaliae,
optetis cineri meo quietem:

(Pontano, *Hend*. 2. 38. 8–10)

(Thus, may you youths who read my trifles and the jests of slender Thalia wish rest for my ashes.)

In his three collections of Catullan poetry, but especially in the *Amores* and the *Hendecasyllabi*, Pontano established himself as the modern heir of Catullus, overshadowing both Bruni's youthful obscenities and the more substantial imitations of Landino. Henceforth Catullan poetry would speak in the language of Martial, but with the Renaissance voice and accent of Pontano; and subsequent poets would see Catullus in Pontano's terms, which they could imitate or react to or reject outright, but never escape or ignore. Pontano himself clearly understood his place in the literary continuum, and expressed it with the emphasis on time and process characteristic of his Catullan collections. The young Pontano of the *Pruritus* applied the aphrodisiac properties of poetry to his young friend Leonte Tomacelli and old Samarra or Aurispa; the old Pontano reassigned the parts, replacing Leonte with the anonymous youths of Baiae and casting himself and Marino Tomacelli as the worn out old men. In the *Parthenopeus* he looked over a void of a thousand years to claim Catullus as his model. In the programme poems of *Hendecasyllabi* 2 he linked himself in his death with the dead Catullus, seeing both as ashes but with the power to please and inspire men in the future.

The basis of Pontano's Catullan poetry was the idea from 16 that light poetry should arouse and titillate the reader. Cat. 16 remained the basis of the Catullan programme, but Pontano's successors also included (and found more interesting) the other half of Catullus' statement—his denial of a connection between the character of the poet and the nature of his verses: 'nam castum esse decet pium poetam / ipsum, versiculos nihil necesse est' (16. 5–6). This excuse, or rather the distortion of it promulgated by Martial and Pliny ('my verse is naughty, but my life is chaste'), had its most obvious use as a justification for obscenity. Indeed, a generation before the *Pruritus*, Panormita and Guarino da Verona had both invoked 16 in defence of the *Hermaphroditus*.[114] Obscenity required excuse, since apart from offending individual sensibilities, it flouted the moral teaching of the Church; but the Catullan denial could not answer serious moral objections, and no one expected it to. (The *Hermaphroditus*, one recalls, was banned by an angry pope after a decade of extravagant popularity, and its readers were threatened with excommunication.) The real functions of the excuse were literary. Throughout the Renaissance, it identified its user as a Catullan poet and a subscriber to the principles of Catullan poetry established by Pontano. Thus, Pierre Ronsard could announce the Catullan programme of his French *Folastries* (1553) merely by citing 16. 5–6.[115] So, too, Salmon Macrin (1490–1557), one of the earliest Catullan poets in France, used 16 in the programme poem of his first collection of erotic verse:

Nam legem tulit hanc Catullus olim,
Princeps Hendecasyllabôn Catullus,
Ut castus foret, integerque vates,
Vatis carmina non item, lepore
Quae tum praecipue suo placerent
Si essent mollicula, et parum severa.
(Macrin, *Carminum libellus* 1528
1. 9–14)[116]

(For Catullus once passed this law—Catullus, prince of hendecasyllables: that the bard be chaste and pure, but not his songs, since these please most with their charm if they be wanton and not too strict.)

Macrin's 'wanton poems' (which celebrate his betrothal and marriage) are sentimental rather than sensual—*parum severa* only in comparison to his earlier devotional subjects.[117] In fact, however, the degree of licence is immaterial. Pontano had defined Catullan poetry as lascivious and titillating. Sometimes it was so in fact (as in the case of Ronsard's *Folastries*), but where it was not, the excuse from 16 provided the requisite racy, 'Catullan' *color*. But the Catullan programme and its excuse did not go unchallenged, even in Pontano's lifetime. In the late 1480s it was attacked twice in short succession, first by the Carmelite Battista Spagnoli, better known as Mantuan (1447–1516), and then by Pontano's own friend and student, Michele Marullo (1453–1500), who criticized the positions of both Pontano and Mantuan.[118]

Mantuan's poem, *Contra poetas impudice scribentes carmen*, is a diatribe against not only obscene poetry but erotic poetry of any kind, and it rejects the Catullan excuse out of hand:

Vita decet sacros et pagina casta poetas:
Castus enim vatum spiritus atque sacer.

Si proba vita tibi lascivaque pagina, multos
Efficis incestos in veneremque trahis.
(Mantuan, *Contra poetas*, 19–22)[119]

(A chaste life and a chaste page befit holy poets, for chaste and holy is the inspiration of bards. If your life is upright and your page lascivious, you make many unchaste and draw them into venery.)

Not surprisingly, Mantuan speaks of sin and damnation, arguing that the erotic poet, even if chaste himself, leads others to sin and death. Chastity is not for him, as it was for Catullus, a matter of avoiding degrading encounters, but rather of absolute sexual purity: 'Chaste is the mother of God, chaste the Master of Olympus. The unchaste soul cannot taste the ambrosial feast.'[120] It is also the property of the Pierian Muses, Helicon, and the Castalian spring, which is not to be tainted by the lips of the 'bard of Venus'.[121] The chaste waters of Helicon, moreover, are to be the only drink of the poet ('true poets drink not wine but the Castalian spring'),[122] since the pleasures of Bacchus bring one all too close to the odious Venus:

Qui bibit assidue gelidis de fontibus undam
Et vitrio siccam diluit amne sitim
Carmina casta facit. Veneris commertia vitat,
Nec movet ad versus ora pudica leves.
Vina iocosque canunt veneris bacchique poetae.
Quod latet in vapido pectore carmen olet.
(Mantuan, *Contra poetas*, 85–90)

(The man who constantly drinks water from the icy springs and washes away his dry thirst with the clear stream creates chaste poems. He avoids the commerce of Venus and does not move his modest lips to frivolous verses. The poets of Venus and Bacchus sing of wine and jests. The poem that lurks in the wine-soaked[123] breast has a stench.)

A poet deserving of the name will spurn such trivia in favour of worthy subjects, which Mantuan lists in loving detail: the triune God, creation, the stars and their courses, Hell and its punishments, the world and its creatures, philosophy, law, mathematics, history, martyrdoms of the Saints, agriculture, and seafaring (*Contra poetas*, 117–46). Mantuan ends his poem with the conditions for poetic initiation and consecration:

Tunc helicona bibes castisque rigabere lymphis
Si venus in versu non erit ulla tuo.

(Mantuan, *Contra poetas*, 155–6)

(Then you will drink of Helicon and be moistened with the chaste waters if there shall be no Venus in your verse.)

If Mantuan's harsh verses were directed against Pontano's *Pruritus* or *Parthenopeus*, they had little effect, for in the next decade, Pontano resumed his Catullan poetry with the *Hendecasyllabi*, casting himself more strongly than ever as a 'poet of Venus and Bacchus' and singing of 'wine and jests'. By Mantuan's standards Pontano was unfit to taste the waters of Helicon, but he had already disdained them: even in the *Parthenopeus* he had rejected the Castalian spring and its association with serious poetry.[124] In the *Hendecasyllabi*, perhaps in response to Mantuan, he suggested a competing *locus* for poetic inspiration, presenting amorous Baiae as a rival of cool and virginal Helicon:

Et fontis calidos amant Camenae
et Musae calidis aquis lavantur

(Pontano, *Hendecasyllabi*, 2. 1. 1–2)

(The Camenae love warm springs, too, and the Muses bathe in warm waters . . .)

Pontano's friend Michele Marullo, however, had a still different view of the love poet and his sources of inspiration and authority. In *Ep.* 1. 62 he answers both Pontano and Mantuan, rejecting the Catullan excuse but also claiming, even as a love poet, to have a right to the Castalian waters. *Ep.* 1. 62 opens by recalling—and reversing—Mart. 1. 35.[125] Martial's adversary had objected to the indecency of the poet's verses, Marullo's objects to their chastity:

Quod nimium castus liber est nimiumque pudicus,
Displicet; ingenium, Quintiliane, probas.

(Marullo, *Ep.* 1. 62. 1–2)[126]

(Because it is too chaste and too modest, my book displeases. My talent you approve, Quintilianus.)

The allusion is only the first of three polemical references to Martial, each either refuting or inverting one of his arguments for obscene poetry. Thus, in vv. 9–12 Marullo asserts that an appeal to Martial's list of obscene models will not induce him to write for low tastes,[127] and in vv. 21–2, as we shall see presently, he reverses Martial's poetic 'law'. Marullo's attack is not directed against Martial himself, however, but against Martial as the authority for the modern poetic programme of his critic, 'Quintilianus'—who may be Pontano himself[128] or Sannazaro (both poets teased him for the modesty of his verses) or perhaps only a straw man who favours Pontano's Catullan poetry. Marullo's own chaste poetry, in contrast, claims a different—and higher—authority:

Gratulor ingenio quantum sinis, heus age, sed dic:
 Cur tibi non adeo carmina casta placent?
Casta placent Phoebo, castissima turba sororum est,
 Casta pios vates Pieriosque decent:
Nos quoque casta movent, quamvis distamus ab illis,
 Et vetat ingenuus verba inhonesta pudor.

(Marullo, *Ep.* 1. 62. 4–8)

(Thank you for crediting so much to my talent, but tell me: why do chaste poems not please you still more? Chaste things are pleasing to Phoebus, most chaste is the crowd of sister Muses, chaste things are fitting for pious bards and those dedicated to the Pierian Muses. Chaste things move us, too, although we are far distant from them [Apollo and the Muses], and noble modesty forbids indecent words.)

Marullo is quoting Mantuan's appeal to the Muses in *Contra poetas* 39–42 ('chaste are the Pierian Muses, chaste the Libethrian waters . . .'), but the chastity he insists upon is as remote from Mantuan's as Mantuan's had been from that of Catullus—not the superhuman purity of the Virgin Mary, but merely the absence of 'obscene licence'.[129] Such a definition, unlike Mantuan's, does not exclude love poetry, which Marullo claims as a legitimate subject in a *recusatio* in the manner of the Augustan poets. In his *recusatio* he refuses both the subjects suggested by Mantuan (or a list very like them) and the 'Catullan programme', reversing and reformulating Martial's old poetic law:

Utque nec arma virum nec magni orientia coeli
 Signa nec immensum mundi aperimus opus—
Quid pluat, unde homines, quae vis maria inficit alta,
 An Deus, an Manes, an Flegethontis aquae—,

Sic iuvat in tenui legem servare pudori
Et quae non facimus dicere facta pudet.

(Marullo, *Ep.* 1. 62. 17–22)

(And just as we recount neither the arms of men nor the rising constellations of the great heaven nor the unbounded structure of the world—why it rains, the origin of mankind, what power imbues the deep seas, whether god or the shades or the waters of Phlegethon—so we are pleased to keep the law in delicate modesty and ashamed to speak of things we do not do.)

The *recusatio* concludes with a brief summary of his chosen themes (Neaera's golden hair, her cruelty, the birth of savage *Amor* from the Scythian rock)—all capable of treatment, as he demonstrates, in accordance with his newly constituted law. His chaste love poetry earns the approval of Apollo himself ('Phoebus nodded and moistened my lips with his sacred waters'),[130] a consecration that echoes and answers the promise at the end of Mantuan's *Contra poetas*: 'you will be moistened with the chaste waters if there shall be no Venus in your verse.'

But Marullo's effort to reform the Catullan programme was as ineffective as Mantuan's attempt to eliminate it, and Catullan poetry continued on its way unregenerate and unimpressed by the authority of Helicon and its chaste Muses. But the debate was not over. Poets continued to argue the limits of sensuality and obscenity poem by poem and theme by theme, using as ammunition either their own poetry or their interpretations of Catullus', and deriving their motives from a mixture of moral, philological, sentimental, and polemical considerations.

KISSES AND SPARROWS

A modern reader who knew Catullus only through his Renaissance imitators might well imagine that he had written on but two subjects—kisses and sparrows—for these topics exercised a fascination bordering on obsession for the later poets. There are literally hundreds of kiss poems by poets great and small and dozens of poems on sparrows or doves—almost as many altogether as the very stars and sands invoked as images of innumerability by the poets.[131] Often sparrows and kisses are brought together in amorous, obscene, or polemical contexts, and it is with this link that we shall be primarily concerned. For the origins of the connection we must turn again to Martial.

Catullus wrote several poems about kisses, but it was 5 and 7 that appealed most to his imitators:

> Vivamus, mea Lesbia, atque amemus
> rumoresque senum severiorum
> omnes unius aestimemus assis!
> soles occidere et redire possunt:
> nobis cum semel occidit brevis lux,
> nox est perpetua una dormienda.
> da mi basia mille, deinde centum,
> dein mille altera, dein secunda centum,
> deinde usque altera mille, deinde centum
> dein, cum milia multa fecerimus,
> conturbabimus illa, ne sciamus,
> aut ne quis malus invidere possit,
> cum tantum sciat esse basiorum. (5)

> Quaeris, quot mihi basiationes
> tuae, Lesbia, sint satis superque.
> quam magnus numerus Libyssae harenae
> lasarpiciferis iacet Cyrenis
> oraclum Iovis inter aestuosi
> et Batti veteris sacrum sepulcrum;
> aut quam sidera multa, cum tacet nox,
> furtivos hominum vident amores:
> tam te basia multa basiare
> vesano satis et super Catullo est,
> quae nec pernumerare curiosi
> possint nec mala fascinare lingua. (7)

For Martial, as for many later imitators, counting kisses is the essential point in 5 and 7, but he translates Catullus' amatory arithmetic into a calculus of his own. Thus, in Mart. 12. 59 we hear of the returning traveller to whom Rome gives 'more kisses than Lesbia gave Catullus'.[132] These countless kisses are dispensed, not as one might first imagine, by a personified *Roma* who corresponds somehow to Catullus' Lesbia, but rather by the whole rogue's gallery of Martial's Rome, invoked in order of their increasing undesirability as kissers—from the farmer as bristly as a he-goat to the *fellator* and *cunnilingus*. Martial's coarseness undermines the delicacy and sentiment of Catullus—indeed, that is part of the jest (the rest consists in the substitution of many kissers for Catullus' one, a twist made possible by the false formal parallel between *Roma* and Lesbia); but the starting point is the kissing theme in general rather than a particular poem. In contrast, Mart. 6. 34 more specifically recalls its models. We should note that it contains both scenes from Catullus' little drama (the request for kisses from 5 and the answer to the question, 'how many?' from 7).

Basia da nobis, Diadumene, pressa. 'Quot' inquis?
   Oceani fluctus me numerare iubes
et maris Aegaei sparsas per litora conchas
   et quae Cecropio monte vagantur apes,
quaeque sonant pleno vocesque manusque theatro
   cum populus subiti Caesaris ora videt.
nolo quot arguto dedit exorata Catullo
   Lesbia: pauca cupit qui numerare potest.

(Mart. 6. 34)

(Give me close-pressed kisses, Diadumenos. Do you say, 'how many? You are asking me to count the waves of Ocean and the shells scattered on the shores of the Aegean sea and the bees that range on the Cecropian mount, and the hands and voices that sound in the packed theatre when the people catch sight of Caesar's face. I don't want as many as Lesbia, under persuasion, gave to witty Catullus: the man who can count his kisses wants too few.)

Here as in 12. 59 Martial undermines his model: it seems to be the boy Diadumenos rather than the poet who likes the images of number, and Catullus' counting is rejected as passionless. Catullus' images belong to his own romantic and literary world: the stars are those that look down on lovers; the sands are located with Callimachean precision in a Callimachean landscape with intimations of mortality (*Batti veteris sacrum sepulcrum*, 7. 6) that recall the opening verses of 5. Martial's images are barefaced clichés, until the last—the applause for Domitian in the theatre. Here, characteristically, Martial has replaced the content of Catullus' imagery with a picture from his own crass world, but he has also achieved a *tour de force* of the flatterer's art: by the blandness of the preceding images he highlights the applause for Domitian, and by placing it among clichés he implies that it too is an obvious simile for the uncountable.

Mart. 12. 59 and 6. 34 display many of the same imitative techniques that we observed in his presentation poems, but the poet is no longer merely alluding to or echoing his model, but actively challenging him. As before he juxtaposes Catullus' world with his own, but now its qualities are undermined and dismissed.[133] In 6. 34 he criticizes Catullus' kiss-counting as banal and lacking in ardour, and attributes the desire for it to the *puer delicatus* (who evidently likes clichés). In 12. 59 he replaces Lesbia as the kiss-giver with the manifold and revolting *Roma*. In both poems Lesbia's kisses seem grudging and ambiguous; indeed, Martial's phrasing leaves it in doubt whether she ever kissed Catullus at all.[134] In his kiss poems, then, Martial casts himself as a rival and almost a detractor of his model; his treatments of Catullus' sparrow demonstrate a similar critical and emulative spirit.

Catullus' two poems on Lesbia's sparrow, like the kiss poems, form a pair: Cat. 2 describes the sparrow at play with Lesbia, and 3 laments his death:

Passer, deliciae meae puellae,
quicum ludere, quem in sinu tenere,
cui primum digitum dare appetenti
et acris solet incitare morsus,
cum desiderio meo nitenti
carum nescio quid lubet iocari,
et solaciolum sui doloris,
credo, ut tum gravis acquiescat ardor:
tecum ludere sicut ipsa possem
et tristis animi levare curas! (2)

Lugete, o Veneres Cupidinesque,
et quantum est hominum venustiorum:
passer mortuus est meae puellae,
passer, deliciae meae puellae,
quem plus illa oculis suis amabat.
nam mellitus erat suamque norat
ipsam tam bene quam puella matrem,
nec sese a gremio illius movebat,
sed circumsiliens modo huc modo illuc
ad solam dominam usque pipiabat;
qui nunc it per iter tenebricosum
illud, unde negant redire quemquam.
at vobis male sit, malae tenebrae

Orci, quae omnia bella devoratis:
tam bellum mihi passerem abstulistis.
o factum male! o miselle passer!
tua nunc opera meae puellae
flendo turgiduli rubent ocelli. (3)

Martial imitates the sparrow poems in Mart. 1. 109; here, as in 6. 34, he compresses Catullus' two poems into one. He replaces Lesbia's sparrow (or rather, Catullus') with the puppy of a certain Publius:

Issa est passere nequior Catulli,
Issa est purior osculo columbae,
Issa est blandior omnibus puellis,
Issa est carior Indicis lapillis,
Issa est deliciae catella Publi.
(Mart. 1. 109. 1–5)

(Issa is naughtier than Catullus' sparrow, Issa is purer than the kiss of a dove, Issa is softer than all the girls, Issa is dearer than Indian pearls, Issa is the darling, the puppy of Publius.)

Martial follows the outline of 2 by presenting an account of the puppy's charms, then immediately averts the death and lament of 3 with a neat compliment to her owner:

Hanc ne lux rapiat suprema totam,
picta Publius exprimit tabella,
in qua tam similem videbis Issam,
ut sit tam similis sibi nec ipsa.
(Mart. 1. 109. 17–20)

(Lest her final day snatch her away completely, Publius is portraying her on a painted tablet, in which you will see an Issa so like her that even she is not so like herself.)

The sentiment of 3 is washed away, and Catullus' *epicedion* gives way to a poem of a genre more appropriate to Martial's world, the praise of a patron's *objet d'art*.[135] In two *epicedia* of his own, however, Martial recalls 3 without distortion. In Mart. 5. 34 he laments the little slave girl Erotion; although Catullus is not quoted directly, Erotion's status as a pet (*deliciasque meas*, Mart. 5. 34) and the reference to her dark journey evoke Catullus' sparrow.[136] In 11. 13 Martial cites the first verse of 3 in his epitaph for Paris, the famous pantomime dancer murdered by

Domitian: all charm and grace, 'and all the Venuses and Cupids (*atque Veneres Cupidinesque*, Mart. 11. 13. 6) are buried in the tomb with Paris'.[137] The quotation strikes a note of uncharacteristic pathos and at the same time manages to outdo Catullus. The sparrow's death was to be lamented by the Venuses and Cupids; Paris' death destroys them.

In other poems Martial refers to Catullus' poetry as the *passer*.[138] Thus, in Mart. 4. 14 he sends his poetry as a Saturnalia gift to the epic poet Silius Italicus with the excuse: 'so perhaps tender Catullus ventured to send the *passer* to great Vergil.' And in Mart. 1. 7 he compares the *columba* of his patron Stella (presumably a poem or poems) to Catullus' *passer*: 'The darling dove of my Stella (I may say so even in Verona's hearing) has surpassed, Maximus, the sparrow of Catullus.'[139] The character of Stella's poetry has been much disputed, although most would agree that it was light erotic verse in the Catullan style. The poems sent to Silius Italicus were no doubt also obscene: Martial presents them at the licentious Saturnalia, describes them as 'little books steeped in naughty jests' (Mart. 4. 14. 12), and asks Silius to read them with the indulgence appropriate to the season. It is often thought that Stella's *columba* was an *epicedion* for his wife's pet dove; recently scholars have asserted that it, too, was obscene.[140] Their arguments depend on the interpretation of two additional sparrow poems: Mart. 11. 6 and Mart. 7. 14.

Mart. 11. 6, another poem for the Saturnalia, is the most notorious and controversial evocation of Catullus' *passer*:

Unctis falciferi senis diebus,
regnator quibus inperat fritillus,
versu ludere non laborioso
permittis, puto, pilleata Roma.
Risisti; licet ergo, non vetamur.
Pallentes procul hinc abite curae;
quidquid venerit obvium loquamur
morosa sine cogitatione.
Misce dimidios, puer, trientes,
quales Pythagoras dabat Neroni,
misces, Dindyme, sed frequentiores:
possum nil ego sobrius; bibenti
succurrent mihi quindecim poetae.

Da nunc basia, sed Catulliana:
quae si tot fuerint quot ille dixit,
donabo tibi Passerem Catulli. (Mart. 11. 6)

(On the festive days of the old scythe-bearer [Saturn], which the dice box rules as king, you allow jesting in frivolous verse, I think, o Rome in your freedom-cap.[141] You smiled. Therefore, it is allowed; we are not forbidden. Get ye hence, pale cares! Let us speak whatever comes our way without tedious reflection. Mix the measures by halves, boy, like those Pythagoras gave to Nero. Mix them, Dindymos, but more frequent. I can do nothing sober, but when I drink fifteen poets will come to my aid. Give kisses now, but Catullan-style. And if these be as many as he said, I will give you the sparrow of Catullus.)

Mart. 7. 14 invokes both Cat. 3 and Stella's *columba*:

Accidit infandum nostrae scelus, Aule, puellae;
amisit lusus deliciasque suas:
non quales teneri ploravit amica Catulli
Lesbia, nequitiis passeris orba sui,
vel Stellae cantata meo quas flevit Ianthis,
cuius in Elysio nigra columba volat:
lux mea non capitur nugis neque moribus istis
nec dominae pectus talia damna movent:
bis denos puerum numerantem perdidit annos,
mentula cui nondum sesquipedalis erat. (Mart. 7. 14)

(A terrible misfortune has befallen our girl, Aulus. She has lost her plaything and her pet—not like the one Lesbia, the girlfriend of tender Catullus, lamented, bereft of the wanton tricks of her sparrow, and not like the one Ianthis, sung by my Stella, wept, whose black dove flies in Elysium. My darling is not taken by trifles or by such humours, and losses like these don't move the heart of my mistress. She has lost a 20-year-old slave boy, whose penis was not yet a foot and a half long.)

In Mart. 11. 6 there can be no doubt that *passer Catulli* in the last line is obscene.[142] Indeed, everything in the poem conspires to guarantee it: the setting (Saturnalian and sympotic), Martial's request to *pilleata Roma* to allow playful verse, the reference to Nero's boy Pythagoras (whom the Emperor married in a full-dress wedding ceremony),[143] and finally the kisses themselves. After all this, Martial would surely be 'too inept as a poet' (the phrase is Poliziano's) if he presented the boy only with a pet bird. A third meaning was proposed by Alessandro Guarino, who pointed to Martial's use of *passer* to mean poem in 4. 14 and argued for the same sense here ('he promises . . . to write a poem in the boy's honour like the one Catullus wrote about Lesbia's sparrow . . .').[144] This view has found modern advocates and receives some support from the literary references in the poem (symposia were occasions for poetry as well as sex, we must remember), but by itself it is almost as flat as 'pet bird'.[145] Clearly what works best is a *double* (or rather *triple*) *entendre*, bird, poem, penis, with the last sense dominant.

The case is somewhat different with Mart. 7. 14. The poem itself is obscene, but the references to Lesbia's sparrow and Ianthis' dove *could* be innocent, forming a contrast rather than a parallel with the lost pet of Martial's girlfriend. By itself, too, Mart. 1. 7 on Stella's *columba* might be innocent. Taken together, however, the two poems present the same *triple entendre* that we have noted in 11. 6. The common thread in the two epigrams is the idea of size. In 1. 7 Stella's *columba* beats Catullus' *passer*: 'my Stella is as much greater than your Catullus as a dove is greater than a sparrow.'[146] In 7. 14 there are three terms in the comparison, arranged in ascending order: *passer*, *columba*, *mentula . . . sesquipedalis*.[147] According to Martial, then, Lesbia, Ianthis, and his own unnamed girlfriend all experienced the same bereavement (taking into account the differences of scale), and the poems of Catullus and Stella, just like 7. 14, commemorated the loss. Whether this was really the case is a separate question: Martial surely felt free to pretend what he liked about the meaning of Stella's and Catullus' poetry, and it would be quite characteristic if he had replaced a sentimental image in his source with a crude one of his own. His innuendo is not inherently improbable (ancient poets *did* write about their own impotence, and the erotic tendencies of sparrows and doves were notorious).[148] But there is no proof for it either. Stella's poem is lost, and whether one reads Cat. 2 and 3 as allegorical is in the end a matter of taste. Sustained allegory is not a technique used elsewhere in Catullus; if it is present in his sparrow poems it is so skilfully integrated as to hide its presence. (Here the contrast with Martial may be instructive: his sparrow poems, as we have seen, are so transparently ambiguous that they nudge the reader to look for meanings beneath the surface.) On the other hand, the allegorical reading seems to fit every detail of

Catullus' poems, and no one has argued convincingly against it. In the face of such a dilemma it may be appropriate, if craven, to fall back on the old Scottish verdict that brands its victim for life—neither 'innocent' nor 'guilty', but 'not proven'.

But there is more to be said about Mart. 11. 6, for the sparrow is only one part (although admittedly the climax) of what is a meticulously structured imitation and emulation of Catullus. The poem contains two sections of equal length (verses 1–8 and 9–16), each of which consists of a question or address, followed by a reaction from the poet, which is expressed with a quotation from Catullus. Thus, in the first section Martial's question to *Roma* ('may I jest in easy verse?') and the answer ('you smiled, therefore I may') are followed by the poet's resolution to say whatever comes to mind, and the resolution begins with an echo of Cat. 27, another drinking poem (cf. *hinc abite curae*, Mart. 11. 6. 6, and *hinc abite, lymphae*, 27. 5). Since the context in Catullus is an address to the wine-steward (*Minister vetuli puer Falerni / inger mi calices amariores*, 27. 1–2), Martial's echo nicely anticipates or perhaps even triggers his own orders to Dindymos in the second section. There Martial calls for wine with an excuse that begins with both sexual and literary overtones, but ends with the literary note predominating ('I can do nothing when I'm sober, but when I drink fifteen poets will come to my aid'). The sequel to this request, of course, is the notorious conclusion of the epigram (*da nunc basia*, etc.), which cites Cat. 2 and 5. The effect of Martial's tight formal structure is to create the impression of spontaneity—of casual sympotic verse composed 'without tedious reflection' as one thought leads to another; but of course the impression is false. The epigram is as carefully wrought—and as literary—as any neoteric production; and all of its elements are artfully disposed to lead up to the last three verses, which constitute a separate (or at least separable) epigram that Martial pretends to be composing on the spot, a little drunk, and under the inspiration of the fifteen poets. Its subject is obvious and familiar (can a topic suggested by fifteen poets be anything else?), but the sudden appearance of Catullus' sparrow at the end of the last verse explodes the cliché with its surprise *contaminatio* of Catullan themes—surely Martial's most influential, if least heralded, contribution to the annals of Catullan kiss poetry.

Even if fifteen poets before him *had* imitated Catullus' sparrow and kisses (and, perhaps mercifully, we can never know),[149] Martial must have the credit for linking the two themes (for that is the point and punch line of 11. 6). Was he also the first to call a poem *passer* or *columba*? It hardly matters. He is the first we know of, and his treatment alone would have been enough to make them near technical terms for indecent poetry. In the next generation the younger Pliny coyly called his own verses *passerculi* and *columbuli*,[150] and the Renaissance imitators took up the conceit, as we shall see presently.

The young Pontano was the first to seize on Martial's *triple entendre*. In *Am*. 1. 5, originally part of the *Pruritus* of 1449,[151] he selects a recipient for his 'snow-white dove'. By echoing the opening verses of two dedication poems, Cat. 1 and Mart. 3. 2, he alludes to the use of *columba* to mean 'book' or 'poem'.[152] Thus:

> Cui vestrum niveam meam columbam
> Donabo, o pueri? (Pontano, *Am*. 1. 5. 1–2)

(To which of you, o boys, shall I give my snow-white dove?)

And, a few lines later:

> Sed cuinam cupis, o columba, munus
> Deferri? (Pontano, *Am*. 1. 5. 10–11)

(But to whom, o dove, do you wish to be taken as a gift?)

It is evident from the first, however, that the *columba* is not a book. The boys mentioned as possible recipients in line 2 are dismissed as 'wretched catamites, unworthy of such an elegant gift', and in line 11 the poet awards the *columba* to his girl.[153] It will frolic in her lap in the approved manner of the Catullan sparrow, but, as always, Pontano is more sensual and explicit than his model:

> Huius tu in gremio beata ludes,
> Et circumsiliens manus sinumque
> Interdum aureolas petes papillas.
>
> (Pontano, *Am*. 1. 5. 17–19)

(You will play happily in her lap, and you will hop about, pecking her hands and bosom and sometimes her golden breasts.)

The poet warns the *columba* not to harm her breasts (the lovely apples in Venus' garden), but approves other play:

> Impune hoc facies, volente diva,
> Ut, cum te roseo ore suaviatur
> Rostrum purpureis premens labellis,
> Mellitam rapias iocosa linguam,
> Et tot basia totque basiabis,
> Donec nectarei fluant liquores.
>
> (Pontano, *Am.* 1. 5. 26–31)

(You may do this without fear, if the goddess wishes: when she kisses you with her rosy mouth, pressing your beak with purple lips, you may playfully snatch her honey-sweet tongue and you will give kisses and kisses again, until the streams of nectar flow.)

There could hardly be a better example of the Renaissance tendency to read Catullus through Martial. The poem is a *contaminatio* of Mart. 11. 6 and Cat. 2–3 (which Pontano undoubtedly read as a single poem), and its ostensible movement is from Martial to Catullus—repudiating Martial's homosexual context (*non vobis dabimus, mali cinaedi*, Pont., *Am.* 1. 5. 4) for Catullus' pretty vignette of the girl at play with her sparrow. But of course Martial has not been repudiated. Rather, Pontano has rewritten Cat. 2–3 to spell out and show off Martial's interpretation of Catullus: *donabo tibi passerem Catulli* (Mart. 11. 6. 16). Placed in Martial's frame, Catullus' picture loses its affective and sentimental elements. Pontano's playful dove is not Catullus' *passer* 'who chirped for his mistress alone' (3. 10), but only the sexual toy Martial promised to Dindymus at the Saturnalia.[154]

Although Pontano anticipated Poliziano's application of Mart. 11. 6 to Cat. 2–3 by forty years, it was always Poliziano rather than Pontano who received the credit—or rather, the blame—for the discovery, even among the Neapolitan humanists.[155] Indeed, the most vicious attack on Poliziano's interpretation was launched by Pontano's friend and protégé, Jacopo Sannazaro (1458–1530),[156] who certainly knew *Am.* 1. 5 and clearly understood its all but explicit obscenity. Sannazaro begins his attack with a restatement and parody of Poliziano's argument in *Misc.* 6 (the metre, naturally, is hendecasyllabic):

> Ait nescio quis Pulicianus
> Ni pulex mage sit vocandus hic, qui

Unus grammaticus, sed his minutis
Vel longe inferior, minutiorque est;
Divinum sibi passerem Catulli
Haudquaquam bene passerem sonare;
Nec iam id esse, quod autument legentes,
Sed quod versiculis parum pudicis
Ludens innuat ipse Martialis:
Da mi basia, sed Catulliana:
Quae si tot fuerint quot ille dixit;
Donabo tibi passerem Catulli:
Ut sit, quod puero poeta possit
Post longas dare basiationes
Quod salvo nequeat pudore dici.

(Sannazaro, *Ep.* I. 61. 1–15)[157]

(A certain Pulicianus says (unless he should be called a flea instead, who is a unique *grammaticus*, but far worse and smaller than these insignificant creatures) that the divine sparrow of Catullus does not sound like a sparrow to him, and isn't what its readers think, but what Martial hints playfully in his naughty verses: 'Give me kisses, but Catullan-style, and if these will be as many as he said, I'll give you the sparrow of Catullus'—so that what the poet can give to the boy after long kissings is a thing which he cannot name and preserve his modesty.)

In the unkind reflection of Sannazaro's parody Poliziano's interpretation is presented as the work of the most insignificant, pettifogging creature in the world—a flea, or (even worse) a *grammaticus*, the very title that Poliziano had claimed for himself with philological pride;[158] and the elegant circumlocution of *Misc.* i. 6 now seems mincing and affected—just what one would expect from the low species *grammaticus pruriens*. Here is Poliziano:

That sparrow of Catullus in my opinion allegorically conceals a certain more obscene meaning which I cannot explain with my modesty intact. . . . For he would be too inept as a poet (which it is wrong to believe) if he said he would give the sparrow of Catullus and not the other thing I have in mind to the boy after the kisses.[159]

The second half of Sannazaro's poem is a mirror image of the first. Again Poliziano is ironically presented as the supreme arbiter of poetry, and again his ability to divine obscene meanings lost on lesser readers is demonstrated with a quotation and interpretation of a sparrow poem of Martial. This time, however, it is Sannazaro who has selected the quotation (Mart. 4. 14. 13–14), and his interpretation obscenely demolishes Poliziano's argument:

> Proh dii, quam vafer es Puliciane;
> Solus qui bene calleas poetas.
> Nimirum, et quod ab omnibus probetur
> Mutandum quoque suspicaris illud,
> Quod nunc illepidumque et infacetum
> Mendosis epigrammaton libellis
> Insulse legit imperita turba:
> Sic forsan tener ausus est Catullus
> Magno mittere passerem Maroni:
> Cum sit simplicius rectiusque,
> Mitti, dicere, mentulam Maroni.
> Sed quid vos Aganippides puellae
> Ridetis? meus hic Pulicianus
> Tam bellum sibi passerem Catulli
> Intra viscera habere concupiscit.
>
> (Sannazaro, *Ep.* 1. 61. 16–30)

(O gods! how clever you are Pulicianus, since you're the only one who understands poets. Indeed, and what is approved by everyone, you suspect should be changed—the now inelegant and stupid thing the ignorant crowd reads in its unsophisticated fashion in the faulty books of epigrams. Thus, I suppose, delicate Catullus ventured to send a sparrow to great Vergil, although it would be simpler and more correct to say, a penis is sent to Vergil. But why are you laughing, Muses? My friend Pulicianus longs to have the pretty sparrow of Catullus within his own flesh.)

Sannazaro's malicious wit is grounded in an interesting methodological objection—that a symbol can have only one meaning: if Martial uses *passer* in one poem to refer to a poem, he cannot use it in another to refer to a penis. But Sannazaro's interest in methodological consistency is specious, and so is his sentimental concern for 'the divine sparrow of Catullus'. In Naples the obscene interpretation of Catullus' sparrow was nothing new, and Sannazaro's outrage is belied by one of his own poems, as we shall see presently. The real target is Poliziano himself, with whom Sannazaro's friend, Michele Marullo, was engaged in a literary vendetta.[160] One wonders why Marullo did not write a polemic of his own, as he did in the case of some of Poliziano's other Catullan interpretations.[161] Given his distaste for obscenity on the one hand and his quarrel with Poliziano on the other, the sparrow would seem an obvious point of attack. However that may be, Marullo seems to have been engaged with his friends Sannazaro and Pontano in a more amicable debate on the subject that has left its traces in three contemporary poems. The ostensible subject of each is kisses, but both Sannazaro and Pontano also allude teasingly to the sparrow. Although there is no external evidence for the exact chronology, we can place the poems in a probable sequence. Marullo wrote *Ep.* 3. 31 before January 1494; Sannazaro's *Ep.* 1. 6 responds to it; Pontano's *Hend.* 1. 29 was written before June 1496.[162]

In *Ep.* 1. 62, as we have seen, Marullo set out the programme for his Catullan poetry, asserting his determination to write only chaste love poems. True to his vow, he treated Catullus' kiss poems with almost ostentatious restraint—counting sighs rather than kisses in 1. 49 and snatching a single kiss from a chaste and unwilling Neaera in 2. 4.[163] In *Ep.* 3. 31 his kisses are more passionate ('darling little lips, is there any reason I cannot press and suck you and bring a hundred kisses?'), and they cause a conflagration: 'I have burnt you with the raging breath of my heart.'[164] But in fact he has kissed not the girl herself, but only the painted lips of her portrait, and it is the painting that has gone up in flames. Sannazaro rebukes Marullo and his one-sided and symbolic kisses in *Ep.* 1. 6 ('Give me six hundred kisses, Nina, when I ask'),[165] and he explicitly rejects the premise of Marullo's epigram:

Nolo marmora muta, nolo pictos
dearum, Neaera, basiare vultus.

(Sannazaro, *Ep.* 1. 6. 9–10)

(I don't want to kiss mute marble, Nina. I don't want to kiss the painted countenances of goddesses.)

Sannazaro goes on to describe what he does want in a picture that is clearly indebted to that in Pont. *Am.* 1. 5, including even Pontano's 'flowing streams of nectar'.[166] The lovers are to engage in erotic play 'like doves' (*columbulorum in morem*)—an allusion, not itself obscene, to the obscene *columba* in Pontano, and a further hint that Sannazaro, like his model, is talking not only about kisses but about sexual intercourse. Our third poem, Pontano's *Hend.* 1. 29, thanks Marullo for two gifts, some cheese and some charming verses ('the kind the Muses sing').[167] It is tempting to suppose that Marullo's poetic gift was *Ep.* 3. 31, and that *Hend.* 1. 29 is Pontano's reply, but in any case Pontano is teasing Marullo for his whole position on Catullan poetry:

Par est versiculis referre versus:
quid pro caseolis referre par est?
Oranda est mihi blanda Septimilla,
ut pro caseolis velit referre
centum basiola et Catulliana,
centum suaviola atque Lesbiana.

(Pontano, *Hend.* 1. 29. 7–12)

(It is right to pay back verses with verses. What is fair payment for the cheeses? I must ask charming Septimilla to be willing to pay for the cheeses with a hundred Catullan kisses and a hundred more like Lesbia's.)

The *basiola Catulliana* that Pontano wishes for Marullo are not to be found in Marullo's poetry nor yet in Catullus'. They are the kisses of Sannazaro's *Ep.* 1. 6 and Pontano's *Am.* 1. 5—but above all of Mart. 11. 6—the erotic, explicit kisses associated with the sparrow of intercourse:

Da nunc basia, sed Catulliana:
quae si tot fuerint quot ille dixit,
donabo tibi Passerem Catulli.

(Mart. 11. 6. 14–16)

The obscene sparrow remained a fixture in Neapolitan humanism and was still alive and well nearly a generation later. In 1514 the young Marcantonio Flaminio (1498–1550) visited Naples and became a fast friend of Sannazaro's.[168] The next year he published his poem *Ad Septimillam*:

En nunc Flaminius tuus rediens
Urbinum mea chara Septimilla
Secum millia multa basiorum,
Secum illum quoque passerem elegantem
Ferens, quem in manibus tuis tenere
Qui cum ludere saepe gestiebas.

(Flaminio, *Ad Septimillam*, 8–13)[169]

(See, my dear Septimilla, your Flaminio is coming back now to Urbino, bringing with him many thousands of kisses, and with him too that elegant sparrow, which you used to be eager to hold in your hands and play with.)

In all of these poems the obscene meaning of the sparrow or dove is hinted at rather than explicitly stated. Thus, in *Hend.* 1. 29 Pontano's phrase *basiola Catulliana* evokes the notorious passage in Martial and so (appropriately enough in a poem for the fastidious Marullo) conjures up the sparrow without mentioning it. Flaminio's *passer* is not explicitly obscene, but is made so by his context—the thousands of kisses and the echoes of Cat. 2–3. In *Ep.* 1. 6 Sannazaro has moved away from the dove as allegory (an awkward device even in Pont. *Am.* 1. 5) to the dove as a kind of metonymy for the lover—a conceit that became very common in later Catullan poets—and not only because it avoided obvious obscenity.[170] In their brief appearance Sannazaro's doves function as an emblem or symbol of the sexual act, a shorthand indication of the basic premise of the poem that still provides the poet with space to develop his other themes.

It was this emblematic function of the sparrow or dove that Catullan poets found so useful. Sometimes the other theme they wished to explore was the *carpe diem* from Catullus:

> soles occidere et redire possunt:
> nobis cum semel occidit brevis lux,
> nox est perpetua una dormienda. (5. 4–6)

Thus, in one of the epigrams of his *Iuvenilia* (1552) Marc-Antoine de Muret used both *passer* and *columba* as erotic emblems ('I will call you *columba* and you, my sweet, will call me *passer*'):[171]

> Sic nos, sic age, dum viremus ambo,
> Dum res ad Veneris valemus ambo,
> Ne frustra melior teratur aetas,
> Ludamus, mea Margari, et iocemur.
> Tergo debilis imminet senectus.
> Quae cum venerit, a dolor, columba,
> Nos tussis mala viriumque languor
> Pro ludisque iocisque consequentur.
>
> (Muret, *Ep.* 23. 25–32)

(Then come now, let us (while we both are young and strong enough for Venus' business)—lest the better part of our life be wasted—let us sport and play, my Margaret. Weak old age is close behind us, and when it comes (o woe, my dove!) a bad cough and weakness will attend us instead of play and sport.)

More often, however, Catullus' theme was joined or replaced by a somewhat different approach to Eros and mortality that has its source in a Greek epigram of Pseudo-Plato and its Latin paraphrase (both preserved in Aulus Gellius, *AN* 19. 11). According to 'Plato' the lover's spirit (breath of life) can depart with the kiss, entering into and animating the loved one. Thus, in the Latin paraphrase:

Tum si morae quid plusculae
Fuisset in coetu osculi,
Amoris igni percita
Transisset et me linqueret
Et mira prorsum res foret,
Ut fierem ad me mortuus,
Ad puerum ut intus viverem.
(Anon. in Aulus Gellius,
AN 19. 11. 11–17)[172]

(Then, if we had dallied a little longer in the union of our kiss, my spirit, urged on by the fire of love, would have crossed over and left me. And there would have been a wondrous thing: I should have been dead to myself and lived within my darling boy.)

These soul kisses can bring the lover to the brink of death, as when Marullo snatched his kiss from Neaera ('unwitting, I left my soul on your lips')[173] or they can bring him to such happiness that he can despise both earthly wealth and the immortality of the gods. It was this version of the theme that Sannazaro developed in *Ep.* 1. 6 under the aegis of his erotic doves:

Quae si contigerint mihi tuisque
admovere sinas manum papillis,
quis tunc divitias, quis aurum et omneis
assis me putet aestimare reges?
Iam non maluerim mihi beatas
Aurorae Venerisque habere nocteis;
non Hebes thalamos beatiores,
non, si deserat haec suum maritum,

non, si roget usquequaque, non si
aeternam mihi spondeat iuventam.

(Sannazaro, *Ep.* 1. 6. 21–30)

(If I might attain these kisses and you let me move my hand to your breasts, would anyone imagine that I would care a whit for riches, gold, and all the kings? I would not rather have for myself the happy nights of Aurora and Venus, nor the still happier marriage chamber of Hebe—not if she deserted her husband, not if she pleaded with me continually, not if she promised me eternal youth.)

The 'Platonic' kiss has a rich and complicated history from the Neapolitan poets to Johannes Secundus (1511–36) and Joachim du Bellay (1522–60) and on into European lyric, where we cannot follow it.[174] We must content ourselves instead with a brief discussion of one of its finest manifestations, *Basium* 16 of Johannes Secundus. Unlike the other kiss poems we have seen, *Basium* 16 is written neither in hendecasyllables nor in elegiacs, but in Asclepiadeans—a complex lyric metre not used by Catullus, but a favourite in Horace's *Odes*. The choice of metre is significant, for, as we shall see, Horace is almost as much a presence in this poem as Catullus. Secundus begins with the familiar request for kisses:

Latonae niveo sidere blandior,
Et stella Veneris pulchrior aurea,
Da mi basia centum,
Da tot basia, quot dedit
Vati multivolo Lesbia, quot tulit:
Quot blandae Veneres, quotque Cupidines
Et labella pererrant
Et genas roseas tuas:[175]

(You, more alluring than Latona's snow-white moon and more beautiful than the golden star of Venus, give me a hundred kisses, give me as many kisses as Lesbia gave to her poet who wanted so many, give as many as she got—as many as the charming Venuses and as many as the Cupids that wander over your lips and rosy cheeks.)

How many kisses? The stars from Catullus' calculation ('aut quam sidera multa cum tacet nox / furtivos hominum vident amores', 7. 7–8) have been transferred to a different object, the girl herself, glowing with the contradictory radiances of chaste Diana and amorous Venus.[176] Instead, the poet enters into a complex accounting that invokes not only the number of

Catullus' kisses but also the erotic emblem of the dove/sparrow. The Venuses and Cupids of line 6 are a familiar and almost banal quotation from 3. 1 (*Lugete, Veneres Cupidinesque*), but line 5 evokes the dove more subtly, by alluding to a simile in Cat. 68 that describes Laodamia's passion for Protesilaus. A single word, *multivolo*—used in classical Latin only at 68. 128—establishes the allusion:[177]

non tantum niveo gavisa est ulla columbo
  compar, quae multo dicitur improbius
oscula mordenti semper decerpere rostro,
  quam quae praecipue *multivola* est mulier. (68. 125–8)

The counting proceeds, and, as before, the images of innumerability express more than numbers. The girl's kisses must be as many as the lives and deaths, hopes and fears she carries in her eyes, and 'as many as the joys mixed with eternal cares, and as many as the sighs of lovers' ('quotque perennibus / mista gaudia curis, / et suspiria amantium', *Basium* 16. 10–12). The images establish her as Venus or Love incarnate, for mixing joys with cares (a quality of Love at least since the time of Sappho) is a special property of Catullus' erotic deities.[178] From kisses it is on to love-play, presided over and summed up by the emblematic dove:

Adde et blanditias, verbaque publica,
Et cum suavicrepis murmura sibilis,
    Risu non sine grato,
  Gratis non sine morsibus:
Quales Chaoniae garrula motibus
Alternant tremulis rostra columbulae,
    Cum se dura remittit
  Primis bruma Favoniis.
      (Secundus, *Basium* 16. 17–24)

(And add endearments and explicit words and murmurs with sweet-rustling whispers, not without a pleasing laugh, not without pleasing bites—as Chaonian doves interchange cooing beaks all a-flutter when harsh winter lets loose its grip atthe first spring breezes.)[179]

Secundus' vignette draws from the spring poems of Horace and assumes both their basic analogy between the human and natural seasons (spring and youth on the one hand, winter and old age on the other) and their basic contrast, between the inexorable cycle of the seasons and the linear course of human life.[180] In Secundus' closest model, the Soracte ode (Horace *C.* 1. 9), Horace moves from winter (the snow and ice on Mt. Soracte) to *carpe diem* ('don't scorn sweet love and dances as a boy, while harsh frost is far from your green youth')[181] to the scene recalled by Secundus:

nunc et Campus et areae
  lenesque sub noctem susurri
    composita repetantur hora,
nunc et latentis proditor intimo
gratus puellae risus ab angulo
  pignusque dereptum lacertis
    aut digito male pertinaci.

(Horace, *C.* 1. 9. 18–24)

(Now before nightfall, seek the Campus Martius and the temple squares and soft whispers at the appointed hour, and now seek the girl's pleasant laughter from the farthest nook, betrayer of her hiding place, and the pledge snatched from her arm or unresisting finger.)

To Horace's elements (spring, whispers, the girl's pleasing laughter) Secundus has added the Chaonian doves, which transpose the scene from mere flirtation into lovemaking and anticipate the reciprocal action of the next section, in which the lovers exchange 'Platonic' kisses, in turn dying and restoring each other to life:

Stringam nexilibus tete ego brachiis,
Frigentem calido pectore comprimam,
    Et vitam tibi longi
  Reddam afflamine basii.
Donec succiduum me quoque spiritus
Istis roscidulis linquet in osculis,
    Labentemque lacertis,
  Dicam, collige me tuis.
Stringes nexilibus me, mea, brachiis,
Mulcebis tepido pectore frigidum.
    Et vitam mihi longi af-
  flabis rore suavii.

(Secundus, *Basium* 16. 29–40)

(I shall hold you tight in my embracing arms. I shall press you to my warm breast as you grow cold and bring back your life with the breath of a long kiss, until the breath leaves me, too, collapsing in those dewy kisses, and I shall say, 'Gather me up, fainting, in your arms.' You will hold me tight in your embracing arms, my own. You will warm me—already cold—with your warm breast, and you will breathe life into me with a long kiss.)

But the power of the kisses is only transitory (hence the need to multiply their numbers), and they can only revive swooning lovers—not reverse the course of time. The poem closes with the familiar admonition:

> Sic aevi, mea lux, tempora floridi
> Carpamus simul, en, iam miserabileis
> Curas aegra senectus
> Et morbos trahet, et necem.
>
> (Secundus, *Basium* 16. 41–4)

(So, my life, together let us enjoy the season of flowering youth. Lo! soon sick old age will bring wretched cares and disease and death.)

In *Basium* 16 Secundus has woven together many strands from earlier poetry—from Catullus and Horace, to be sure, but also from the Neapolitan poets, particularly Pontano, whose interpretations of Catullus' sparrow and 'Plato's' kiss were by now part of the Neo-Latin poetic vocabulary. But although Secundus is indebted to Pontano and the rest, he has produced a poem utterly different from the work of his Neapolitan predecessors. Part of the difference is that between lyric and epigram, or—if one thinks these categories too ill-defined—between Horace and Martial as mediators of Catullan themes. The earlier poets either filtered Catullus through Martial or (like Marullo) quarrelled with Martial's treatment, but in either case Martial remained a presence in their Catullan poetry. In Secundus Martial's influence has all but disappeared; all that remains is the erotic dove like a sort of Cheshire cat's smile, disembodied and dislocated from its original context and marked by its recent encounters with Pontano and Sannazaro. Instead, Secundus has paired Catullus with Horace, using a Horatian metre and linking Catullus' kisses with Horace's spring poems through their common theme of *carpe diem*, enhanced and complicated by the life-giving but ephemeral 'Platonic' kiss. We are far away from the self-conscious voyeurism of Martial and Pontano. But genre and models do not account for all the differences between Secundus and his predecessors. The Neapolitan poets were humanists as well, and much of their poetry can be read as a debate—on obscenity, on the correct way to write Catullan poetry, on the merits of this or that interpretation. Secundus, at least in *Basium 16*, is non-polemical and ahistorical, neither looking back at ancient models over a gulf of a thousand years nor asserting a literary-critical position on particular issues, but dealing directly with his inherited material, taking earlier interpretations for granted and seemingly feeling no more distant from Catullus and Horace than from his models in the previous generation.

6

Parodia: Catullus and the *Res Publica Litterarum*

difficile nimirum esse, quod in una aliqua re, concinne et venuste dictum est, pari argutia ac venustate ad aliam detorquere.

(Andreas Senftleben)

Phaselus ille, quem videtis, hospites,
ait fuisse navium celerrimus,
neque ullius natantis impetum trabis
nequisse praeterire, sive palmulis
opus foret volare sive linteo.
et hoc negat minacis Hadriatici
negare litus insulasve Cycladas
Rhodumque nobilem horridamque Thraciam
Propontida trucemve Ponticum sinum,
ubi iste post phaselus antea fuit
comata silva; nam Cytorio in iugo
loquente saepe sibilum edidit coma.
Amastri Pontica et Cytore buxifer,
tibi haec fuisse et esse cognitissima
ait phaselus: ultima ex origine
tuo stetisse dicit in cacumine,
tuo imbuisse palmulas in aequore,
et inde tot per impotentia freta
erum tulisse, laeva sive dextera
vocaret aura, sive utrumque Iuppiter
simul secundus incidisset in pedem;
neque ulla vota litoralibus deis
sibi esse facta, cum veniret a mari
novissimo hunc ad usque limpidum lacum.
sed haec prius fuere: nunc recondita
senet quiete seque dedicat tibi,
gemelle Castor et gemelle Castoris. (Cat. 4)

Even if the rest of Catullus' poetry were lost, 4 by itself would entitle him to the title 'doctus poeta', for it is an Alexandrian *tour de force*. It lavishly employs Greek prosody, morphology, and syntax, as well as Alexandrian and neoteric poetic techniques, and it is written in pure iambics, a rare and nearly intractable metre.[1] The poem purports to be the self-description of a yacht (*phaselus*) now retired and musing on its history and accomplishments. Moving through time and space, the *phaselus* takes us on a journey back to its origins—from the Adriatic to the Cyclades and Rhodes, and on to the Propontis and the Black Sea and the leafy forest it once was (lines 10–11). Arrived at this furthest point, it reverses course and returns, now bearing its master, to a final safe haven, where it dedicates itself to Castor and Pollux, patrons of seafaring.

Personifications and 'speaking objects' are not infrequent in ancient dedications: the *Greek Anthology* contains several examples, including at least two in which ships speak in their own person (*AP* 9. 34 and 36). In Catullus, however, the device is different, for the boat never speaks directly; rather, its words are reported by the poet in indirect discourse frequently punctuated with verbs like *ait*, *negat*, or *dicit*—a technique that distances both poet and reader from the *phaselus*. There are two voices in the poem (the voice of the *phaselus* and that of the poet), and Catullus never assumes responsibility for the validity of the utterance he claims to report. As a consequence the *phaselus* is cut off from our sympathy and made to seem loquacious and self-important.

The distinctive qualities of 4 inspired the only parody of a whole poem that survives from Antiquity, the *10th Catalepton*.[2] No one knows the author of *Catal*. 10, but in the Renaissance he was most often identified with the young Vergil; and the Vergilian aura and authority prevailed in spite of the caution or protests of individual scholars. Vergil (as we shall call him) produced a parody so close to the original that the texts of the two poems have been used to correct each other. He used Catullus' metre, artfully abused his language, and exploited his devices of transformation, suggesting a journey by a series of place names, and reporting the speech of the speaking object:

> Sabinus ille, quem videtis, hospites,
> ait fuisse mulio celerrimus,
> neque ullius volantis impetum cisi
> nequisse praeterire, sive Mantuam

opus foret volare sive Brixiam.
Et hoc negat Tryphonis aemuli domum
negare nobilem insulamve Ceryli,
ubi iste post Sabinus, ante Quinctio
bidente dicit attodisse forcipe
comata colla, ne Cytorio iugo
premente dura volnus ederet iuba.
  Cremona frigida et lutosa Gallia,
tibi haec fuisse et esse cognitissima
ait Sabinus; ultima ex origine
tua stetisse ⟨dicit⟩ in voragine,
tua in palude deposisse sarcinas
et inde tot per orbitosa milia
iugum tulisse, laeva sive dextera
strigare mula sive utrumque coeperat,
neque ulla vota semitalibus deis
sibi esse facta praeter hoc novissimum,
paterna lora proximumque pectinem.
  Sed haec prius fuere: nunc eburnea
sedetque sede seque dedicat tibi,
gemelle Castor et gemelle Castoris.

(*Catalepton* 10)[3]

(That Sabinus you see, my friends, says he was once the fastest muledriver, and that there was never any speeding gig whose pace he could not outdo, whether he had to rush to Mantua or Brescia. And this, he says, the noble house of his rival Trypho does not deny, or the apartment block of Cerylus, where that erstwhile Quinctio (afterwards Sabinus) says he cropped hairy necks with two-bladed shears lest the coarse mane produce a sore under the pressure of the Cytorian yoke.

O chill Cremona and muddy Gaul, Sabinus says this was and is well known to you; he says that from his earliest beginnings it was your mire he stood in and your swamp in which he unloaded his packs and went on bearing the yoke through so many miles of rutted roads, whether the mule on right or left or both at once began to give up, and that he never made any vows to the gods of the roads except this last one, his ancestral reins and the curry-comb next to it.

But these things are past; now he sits in an ivory seat and dedicates himself to you, twin Castor and Castor's twin.)[4]

Vergil's speaking object is Sabinus, transformed from mule-skinner to magistrate and now recalling his past—not a voyage like that of Catullus' *phaselus* to distant places sanctified by literary and mythical associations, but instead a banal commercial itinerary on the muddy roads of northern Italy.[5] At the poem's end he hangs up the tools of his former trade to the gods of the back roads he used to frequent and dedicates himself in his ivory chair to Castor and Pollux, horse-tamers and patrons of horsemen.

Part of the fun of Vergil's parody is its application of Catullus' learned Alexandrianism to such an ostentatiously unexalted Italian subject, and we might remind ourselves of Greene's comment: 'superior parody always engages its subtext in a dialectic of affectionate malice. Parody proper is intensely time-conscious and culture-conscious . . .'.[6] More important, however, the poet has realized and exploited the satiric possibilities in Catullus' use of reported speech. Whether the Sabinus whose words we hear at second hand is the parvenu magistrate or only his statue (and the poet does not care to make the point perfectly clear), he is debased and dehumanized by his treatment as a speaking object. Reporting the claims of the *phaselus* created an ironic distance between the poet and reader on the one hand and the inanimate object on the other; reporting the claims of Sabinus discredits him entirely, aligning the poet and reader in a conspiracy to despise his shabby past and upstart pretensions. His stature is diminished not only because he is not allowed to speak for himself but by the fact that his life story parodies the saga—not of another man, but of an inanimate thing.

But Vergil had only revealed—not exhausted—the parodic possibilities of Catullus' poem. Cat. 4 was to become a favourite subject for parody in the Renaissance both for its own qualities and because Renaissance poets and scholars could not resist imitating and parodying Vergil parodying Catullus.

PHASELUS CATULLI

In 1579 the learned world was presented with a curious and pedantic work bearing the following title:

Phaselus Catulli and All the Existing Parodies on It, with the Notes of the Most Learned Men (and with the Addition of Some Other Things of the Same Sort), Edited by Sixtus Octavianus, at York, at Joannes Marcantius'.[7]

The *Phaselus* contains discussions of the nature of parody by Julius Caesar Scaliger and Henri Estienne, 4 with the commentaries of Muret, Statius, and Joseph Scaliger, *Catal.* 10 with Scaliger's commentary, and ten Renaissance parodies—as well as the editor's own notes to Catullus and some of the parodies.[8] True to its title, the volume continues with 'other things of the same sort', including Cat. 57 and 3, Horace *C.* 3. 9 and 1. 35, and the Hylas elegy of Propertius (1. 20), all with contemporary imitations or parodies. It concludes with two short epigrams attacking a critic ('Zoilus') and a verse dedication in hendecasyllables to 'the most eminent and erudite N. Ascanius':

O excellent Catullus and you bards closely following the footsteps of excellent Catullus, who, as Thalia sees, have followed on a like journey the yacht of the best and greatest poet (in an unequal contest and with unequal art)—you, o you most charming poets, go and with your delight and charm hold fast your Ascanius, whom now the Senate keeps totally occupied in strict and serious affairs . . .[9]

Although the printer of this remarkable volume has not been identified (there seems to have been no printer Joannes Marcantius of York), Henri van Crombruggen demonstrated that 'Sixtus Octavianus' was the *nom de plume* of two Belgian humanists, Victor Giselinus (Victor Giselin, 1539–91) and Janus Lernutius (Jean Lernout, 1545–1619), and argued persuasively that the 'N. Ascanius' to whom their work is dedicated was Janus Dousa the Elder (Jan van der Does, 1545–1604).[10] The three men were old friends, linked by their literary interests and especially by their study of Catullus, whom they edited, imitated and annotated, dedicating their works to each another in a series of affectionate if sometimes obscure poems and prefaces.

Giselinus was a philologist by inclination, although he began the study of medicine as a young man and later became a physician to support himself. In the middle 1560s he edited Prudentius and Ovid and worked as a proofreader for the printer Plantin in Antwerp. He met Dousa a few years later, found a printer for Dousa's first collection of poems, and saw it through the press.[11] In the late 1560s he began to work on an edition and commentary on Catullus which he planned to dedicate to Dousa, but Plantin rushed the work into print in 1569 omitting Giselinus' notes and dedication, although including the variant readings from Statius that were to be so useful to Scaliger a few years later.[12] In the 1570s Giselinus resumed his medical studies and settled down in Bruges, largely losing contact with his old friend Dousa during the turbulent years of the Dutch revolt against Spain (1571–6). After the revolt Dousa and Giselinus enjoyed several brief reunions, including a visit by Giselinus to Leiden in 1578.[13]

Lernutius—more poet than philologist, and rich enough to pursue his literary interests as he liked—was nearly the perfect complement to Giselinus; their mutual friend Justus Lipsius liked to refer to him as Pollux to Giselinus' Castor.[14] Giselinus introduced Lernutius to Dousa in 1570, and the two embarked on an enthusiastic correspondence that seems to have lapsed during the Dutch revolt. But Lernutius was part of Giselinus' reunion with Dousa in 1578, and dedicated his elegies and epigrams to Dousa in 1579. The same volume included a series of *Ocelli*, modelled on Catullus and the *Basia* of Johannes Secundus.[15]

Dousa was the most important of the three. Squire of the North Sea village of Noordwijk near Leiden, he became a leader in the Dutch revolt and was military commander of Leiden during the Spanish siege of 1574. After the liberation of Leiden he was among the three men chosen to found Leiden University (1575), to which he was able to attract some of the greatest scholars of the age, including Lipsius (1578) and Joseph Scaliger (1592).[16] In spite of his successes as a commander and university administrator, however, Dousa was first and foremost a poet and philologist. As a very young man (1564–6) he went to Paris, that Mecca of poets, and became friends with Muret's old friends, Jean Dorat and Antoine de Baïf, and probably made the acquaintance of Scaliger as well.[17] Between 1569 and 1576 he published three collections of poems, the last of which, *Nova poemata* (1576), contained a group of *Savia* or *Basia* in imitation of Secundus and Catullus. In 1570 he promised to dedicate the *Basia* to Lernutius, although in the event he dedicated the edition to Daniel Rogers instead.[18] But if he did not keep his word with the *Basia*, a few years later he made amends with an elaborate thank-you for both the *Phaselus* and Lernutius' *Ocelli* in the dedication to his philological work on Catullus, the *Praecidanea pro Q. Valerio Catullo* (1581):

And so that you won't be annoyed any longer to be in unpaid service and continue to judge us by the natures of those who (lest I fail to obtain my usual privilege from you of quoting Plautus) 'bestow largess only with their tongue, but disappoint in effort and action', in return for those twin brothers (I mean your delightful books), here are these *Praecidanea* of ours, *Plena ruris, et inficetiarum*.[19]

A work on Catullus was the obvious thank-you gift for Lernutius' twin books—the *Phaselus* with its Catullan parodies, and the *Ocelli*, in which Dousa professed to see 'the image of Catullan merriment'.[20] But Dousa also responded in kind in the *Praecidanea*, including a Catullan parody of his own modelled on Lernutius' *Ocelli*.[21]

Given the shared interests of Giselinus, Dousa, and Lernutius, it was natural if not inevitable that their friendship should find its literary expression in Catullus. They surely remembered, too, that Catullus and his friends had been invoked as the model for poetic and humanist sodalities since the time of Pontano. Their choice of parody as a medium, however, was influenced by three more recent literary works—the chapter on parody in Julius Caesar Scaliger's *Poetics* (1561) and Henri Estienne's *Homeri et Hesiodi Certamen* (1573) and *Parodiae morales* (1575).[22]

In Chapter 42 of the *Poetics* (quoted almost in its entirety by Giselinus and Lernutius in the *Phaselus*) Scaliger argues that parody originated as a means of amusing the audience after the epic recitations of the Homeric rhapsodes: 'Parody therefore is an inversion of *rhapsodia* that makes the sense ridiculous by changing the words.'[23] Its characters, he decrees, are riff-raff or fools: amorous or drunken women, wastrels and their fathers, and charlatans.[24] Its content may be 'jests against bad poets in the character of innkeepers or bakers, or derision of a bad doctor in the account of his gouty patient.'[25] Not surprisingly, Scaliger's examples treat low subjects of a similar kind. Thus, the parody of 'the divine Vergil' that he claims to have composed during Carnival:

> Praela merumque cano: Cretae quod nectar ab oris
> Italiam cyathis profugum, potoria venit
> Littora. (J. C. Scaliger, *Poetices Libri Septem*, 46)

(The wine-press and strong wine I sing, the nectar that has come as a refugee from the shores of Crete in cups to Italy, to the bibulous coasts.)

So too, Vergil's parody of Catullus with its upstart muleskinner and Scaliger's parody of both:

> Boletus[26] ille qui necavit hospites,
> Ait fuisse carnifex sacerrimus.
>
> (*Poetices Libri Septem*, 46)

(That Boletus who killed his friends says he was the most accursed murderer.)

Scaliger's recipe for parody would have its influence on subsequent poets, some of whom dutifully filled their parodies of Cat. 4 with drunkards and criminals. His choice of examples, however, was to be far more important, for it firmly established two essential characteristics of Neo-Latin parody. Following the example of *Catal.* 10 and *Boletus ille*, Renaissance parodies tended to reproduce and distort whole poems, parodying their models nearly line for line.[27] Following the example of *Boletus ille*, they inevitably recalled both the model and previous parodies. Scaliger regarded this inevitability as an obstacle, as he says in the introduction to *Boletus ille*: 'it was so much harder because I could represent neither the model of Catullus nor what had been brought out by Vergil, but had to look for very different things that would still be suitable.'[28] Other poets, however, exploited the unavoidable intertextuality of their genre, as Dousa used the *Ocelli* as the model for his own Catullan parody in the *Praecidanea* in order to compliment Lernutius.

The French printer Henri Estienne (1528–98) took a somewhat different line from Scaliger in his two works on parody, arguing not that parody inverts its model by presenting base characters and situations but merely that it alters the themes of its model in unexpected ways. Thus in a passage quoted by Giselinus and Lernutius from the preface to his collection of parodies on Homer (*Homeri et Hesiodi certamen . . . Matronis et aliorum Parodiae*), Estienne maintains that: 'parodists must only take care to convert the words they have stolen to another use that is so remote from what they had in their author . . . that no such idea could have occurred to him while he was using them.'[29]

In the first section of *Parodiae morales* he presents parody as a game of theme and variations, telling how he had amused himself during a long journey on horseback by refashioning a single verse of Horace in so many different ways, 'that I forced it, like some

Proteus, to put on many different faces one after the other.'[30] The fact that each succeeding parody of the same verse had more models than its predecessors was a prime source of the game's amusement, for one parody suggested the next 'until I multiplied a few maxims or sayings of the old authors into many, or (if you will allow me to speak thus) grafted them like shoots into old trees into each one of the verses I had chosen from the old poets.'[31] He goes on to discuss his various versions with attention to their stylistic and artistic merits and concludes with a series of unannotated examples, placing a verse from an ancient author on the verso of each page and listing below it his parodies in order of increasing variation. But only on the verso: the recto is left blank to encourage the reader to write in his own parodies.

In the second section Estienne proceeds from moralizing parodies of single lines to parodies of whole poems, but still applying the same principles of variation and transformation. Here he spells out what Scaliger had only implied—that it is desirable for the parodist to preserve the shape and sequence of as many verses as possible:

> in parodies it is not only allowed but admired if someone (applying whatever variation is appropriate) can make it appear that verses from one and the same place and in the same order are not dragged in but rather follow of their own accord.[32]

As in the first section Estienne encourages the reader to write his own parodies, arguing that both pleasure and profit will result, since although parody is amusing it requires the highest degree of poetic skill:

> I think that a person can train his muse in this kind of poetry not only with considerable enjoyment but also with good results, because it is sometimes forced (being hindered by too little space) to make a path by force, or rather to find a path where there is none.[33]

He concludes with some parodies of Catullus and Horace, again leaving a few blank pages for the reader.[34] Included is his own parody of Cat. 3 (*Lugete o veneres cupidinesque*), a *parodia moralis* that exemplifies the qualities of surprise, variation, and reversal he attributes to the genre:

Ad Catulli Versus Parodia Henrici Stephani de morte ebriosissimi cuiusdam iuvenis

Lugete o calices capedinesque,
Et quantum est hominum bibaciorum.
Vester mortuus est sodalis ille,
Quem plus quisque oculis suis amabat.
Nam rex vester erat, suumque norat
Bacchum tam bene quam puella matrem.
Nec sese a Bromio suo movebat;
Sed circumspiciens modo huc, modo illuc,
Ad sola illius arma gestiebat.
Qui nunc it per iter siticulosum,
Illuc, vina negant ubi videri.
At vobis bene sit bonae tenebrae
Orci, quae haec cito monstra devoratis:
Tam foedum barathrum meri abstulistis.
O factum bene! O bonae tenebrae!
Vestra nunc opera, improbo biboni
Vini pernicie haud rubent ocelli.

(Estienne)[35]

(A parody by Henri Estienne on the verses of Catullus, about the death of a young drunkard: Grieve, o cups and wine bowls, and all topers everywhere. Your companion is dead, whom each one loved more than his own eyes. For he was the leader of your drinking parties and knew his wine as well as a girl knows her mother. And he never left his wine god Bromios, but looking around—now this way and that—was eager to do battle with the god alone. And now he goes along the thirsty path to that place where they say wine is not seen. But bless you, good shades of Orcus, which quickly devour this monster. Such a foul sink for wine you have carried off. O well done! O good shades! Thanks to you, the wicked tippler's eyes grow red not at all with the ruination of the wine.)

The *Phaselus* of 1579 is the natural sequel of Estienne's *Parodiae morales*. Giselinus and Lernutius took over Estienne's collection of parodies, imitated his idea of assembling and discussing parodies of a single model, and accepted his invitation to take up parody writing for themselves.[36] They conceived their collection as an ensemble (one hesitates to say, 'artistic unity') that would include all the parodies of Catullus' *phaselus* yet written, and they hoped, quite reasonably, to inspire even more.[37]

Predictably enough, six of their ten parodies follow J. C.

Scaliger's prescription, presenting us with a rogue's gallery of murderers, thieves, quacks, cooks, drunks, and schoolmasters.[38] At least some of the rogues are real people, thinly disguised or not at all, for the humanists found Catullus' *phaselus* a handy tool for ridiculing their enemies. Scaliger's 'Boletus/Doletus' was the unfortunate French printer Étienne Dolet, hanged and burned for blasphemy in 1546. (He had offended Scaliger, however, by entering into his dispute with Erasmus over Ciceronianism.)[39] Giselinus' 'Tricongio' and 'Lavernio' are pseudonyms for Ludovicus Carrio, generally regarded among his contemporaries as a plagiarist and a thief.[40] Missing from the line-up, however, is Florent Chrestien's 'Muretus', obscenely and savagely ridiculed in order to avenge Muret's famous trick on Chrestien's friend Joseph Scaliger:[41]

> Muretus ille, quem videtis hospites,
> Ait fuisse paederasta pessimus[42]

Chrestien's parody was in circulation by September 1578,[43] but perhaps Lernutius and Giselinus were unaware of it. More likely, they regarded it as too scurrilous and indecent for their collection.

The other four parodies in the *Phaselus* are more varied in tone and content: Anselmi's tribute to Vergil (*Libellus iste*), Melissus' soldier turned farmer (*Colonus iste*), Lernutius' *Ocellus iste*, and Giselinus' epicedion for a puppy (*Melissa Lipsii illa*), which was inspired by a letter to Ludovicus Carrio in Lipsius' *Epistolicae Quaestiones*:

> Will you laugh or will you be indignant? But be indignant, rather, or by Hercules *I* will be indignant. My Melissa, my darling puppy, is lost to me by a terrible theft. In comparison with her intelligence and loyalty the dogs of Ulysses, Lysimachus, and Sabinus were mere trifles. Please tell Lernutius, tell Modius to provide hendecasyllables.[44]

All of the parodies follow the Catullan pattern: the poet reports the story of the 'speaking object', telling of its journey, transformation, and final dedication. The poems are of necessity derivative and formulaic, and the more so as their numbers increase, but that is part of the game. Thus the authors note that J. C. Scaliger's *Maranus ille* is a 'parody of a parody', and Giselinus' two parodies against Carrio contain enough similarities to identify them as a pair even if one did not know that they were directed against the same person.[45] The game does have its rules, however, as we can see from the authors' notes on the parody of the unfortunate Joannes Matthaeus Toscanus, whom they criticize for incomprehensibility, false quantities, bad Latin, and, worse yet, for misunderstanding the basic pattern of his model: 'He has departed from Catullus farthest of all, for he has made the same person an agent, a brigand, a robber, an eloquent speaker, a schoolmaster, and a voluptuary.'[46]

Apart from *Catal.* 10, the oldest poem in the collection is that of Giorgio Anselmi (d. 1528) written long before Scaliger and Estienne had defined the terms of Neo-Latin parody, but already obeying the laws of the genre:[47]

In P. Virgilii opera

Libellus ille, quem videtis hospites,
Ait voluminum fuisse maximus.
Neque ullius canentis impetus fidis
Nequisse praeterire, sive fistula
Opus foret sonare, sive classico.
Et hoc negat superba Romuli iuga
Negare, vatibusque claram Achaidem,
Rhodonque nobilem, horridamque Thraciam,
Sicana saxa, aquaeve Sisyphi vadum.
Ubi iste, post libellus, ante vox fuit
Deorum amica: namque Delphico in specu
Loquente saepe verba condidit Deo.
Ilisse flumen, et Lycaee pinifer,
Tibi haec fuisse et esse cognitissima
Ait libellus: enthea ex origine
Tuo stetisse dicit in cacumine,
Tuo imbuisse tibias in aequore:
Et inde tot per ora docta cursitans
Phrygas tulisse, laeva sive dextera
Vocaret aura, sive utramque Pythius
Simul secundus incidisset in manum.
Neque ulla vota provehentibus Deis
Sibi esse facta, cum veniret a Iove
Novissimum hunc adusque candidum diem.
Sed haec prius fuere; nunc Poetico
Tumet favore, gratiasque agit tibi
Gemelle Cynthia, et gemelle Cynthiae.

(Giorgio Anselmi, *Ep.* 1.5)[48]

(On the works of Vergil: That book you see, my friends, says it was the greatest of volumes, and that it was not unable to surpass the force of any playing lyre whether it was necessary to sound on shepherd's pipe or soldier's trumpet. And it denies that the haughty Romulan ridges deny this, and Greece famous to poets, and celebrated Rhodes and savage Thrace, Sicilian cliffs, or waters of Sisyphus' streams—where that one, afterwards a book, was first the kindly voice of the gods. For in the Delphic cave it often fashioned its words while the god spoke. O river Ilissus and pine-covered Lycaeus, the book says these matters were and are well known to you. From an inspired source it says it stood on your peak and dipped its pipes in your stream. And from there, racing through learned mouths, it brought the Trojans, whether the breeze called on right or left, or whether favouring Apollo fell on both hands at once. Nor did it make any vows to the gods who carried it along when it came from Jupiter right down to this most recent shining day. But these things went before. Now it swells with poetic acclamation and gives thanks to you, twin Cynthia, and Cynthia's twin.)

Anselmi's poem is the earliest known Renaissance parody of Catullus' *phaselus*.[49] By the time that Lernutius and Giselinus were assembling their collection both poem and poet were nearly forgotten. The parody had escaped the notice of both Scaliger and Estienne, and Giselinus seems to have known of it only by report as late as March 1579 when he wrote to a friend urgently asking him to look for a copy.[50] Contemporary critics condemned Anselmi's 'dried-up style of writing', but he was also, as Giselinus and Lernutius observe, 'a poet . . . of rare erudition.'[51] For he not only imitated Catullus' use of learned Grecisms but perfectly reproduced the pure iambics of 4, even though he was writing at a time when every published commentary was quite oblivious to its metre.[52]

Anselmi, like J. C. Scaliger in the next generation, was faced with the challenge of writing a parody with two models and not merely copying one or the other, but finding 'very different things that would still be suitable'.[53] Scaliger's solution was simply to find a modern substitute for Vergil's Sabinus and to follow the invective mode of *Catal*. 10. Anselmi's is more ambitious—to exploit the intertextual nature of his task by paying tribute to both Catullus and Vergil. Vergil, or rather Vergil's *Aeneid*, is the subject of his poem, but *Catal*. 10 is also a presence in it—for that is the point of choosing a poem parodied by Vergil as the vehicle of his praise. Catullus is the major subtext, for Anselmi closely follows the structure and language—and especially the tone, of the *phaselus* throughout. His intention is clear from the start. The first word—*libellus*—inevitably sends the reader to Catullus, as well as reminding us that Anselmi, like many early readers, read *phasellus* at 4. 1 and probably thought of it as a diminutive.[54] But irony, even the gentle irony of Catullus, is lacking. Anselmi's speaking object is a book, perhaps the only inanimate object whose words can be repeated at second hand without distance and loss of sympathy, since the poet seems to be reading rather than reporting them to us. The transformation of the *libellus* is from the divine utterance of Apollo (verses 10–11) to the *Aeneid*; it journeys from Greek inspiration to Roman actuality (6–7), and, by the various stages of Aeneas' voyage (8–9), from Troy to Rome, but also from Antiquity to the present, as—both book and boat—it carries the Trojans from Juppiter down 'to this most recent shining day'.

Unfortunately, however, Anselmi's poetic reach exceeded his grasp, or, as Giselinus and Lernutius observe: 'Even with his talent he was not able to avoid leaving some points deserving of criticism.'[55] He has too many ideas working at once for the close confines of his parody, and occasional obscurity is the result. His three images (book, boat, voice of the gods) are sometimes muddled or confusing, as in line 23 where he presents the book as coming from Jove, although he had just told of its inspiration by Apollo, or in 14–17 where he presents it 'dipping its pipes' in the Ilissus and standing on the peak of Lycaeus. 'Let it be said with the kind indulgence of a good poet', Giselinus and Lernutius complain: 'The "friendly voice of the gods or divine voice of the Delphic cave" could not have stood on the "peak of pine-covered Lycaeus" as the "leafy forest stood on the ridge of box-covered Cytorus".'[56]

Anselmi's poem, virtually forgotten before its prominent appearance in the *Phaselus*, soon influenced other parodists, helping to launch a friendly, 'Catullan' style of parody to stand beside the prevailing invective, 'Vergilian' mode popularized by J. C. Scaliger. Since parody is hardly a subtle genre, the two styles are easily distinguished: 'Catullan' parodies generally (though not invariably) begin with a diminutive, 'Vergilian' parodies with a word with a long open vowel in the second syllable. The only 'Catullan' parodies in the *Phaselus* are those of its authors (Lernutius' *Ocellus ille* and Giselinus' *Melissa Lipsii illa*), both of which might just have been inspired by Anselmi, although the chronology is tight. The type is well represented, however, in the great 1642 omnium-gatherum of Catullus parodies of Andreas Senftleben and Nicolaus Henelius: *Phaselus Catulli and Five Decades of Parodies on the Same Written by Various Authors*.[57] Among the many examples there are Rocasius' praise of Dousa's epodes (*Libellus iste, Lector aeque, quem vides*), Heinsius' praise of an ass (*Asellus iste, quem videtis, hospites*), and Caspar Barthius' *In Molossum*, whose first word, though not a diminutive in fact, still creates the effect of one:[58]

Molossus iste, quem timetis hospites,
Ait, fuisse quadrupes fugacior.
. . . . . .
Et hoc negat voracis Albidos latus
Negare, et actam, et Insulas Bratensium
Ubi iste, post molossus, antea fuit
Latrans catellus, hinc Berolino in iugo,
Loquente saepe baubitum dedit hero.

(Barthius, *In Molossum*, 1–2, 6–10)

(That Molossian you fear, my friends, says it was the fleetest quadruped. . . . And he denies that the shore and strand of the raging Elbe deny this, and the isles of the Bratensii, where that Molossian-to-be was first a yapping puppy, and then on the ridge of Berlin often barked when his master spoke. . . .)

The most curious mutation of the 'Catullan' strain, however, is to be found in the Christian parodies in the collection of 1642, where the speaking object is Christ. Of the three beginning *puellus ille* or *puellus iste*, that of the Jesuit Joannes Niess is most interesting:[59]

Invitatio Adolescentum ad Pueri in Stabulo Bethlehemitico, a Virgine Matre nobis nati, imitationem

Puellus iste, quem videtis Aemuli,
Ait fuisse Coelitum tenerrimus:
Neque ullius volantis impetum Angeli
Nequisse praeterire, sive plantulis
Opus foret volare, sive plumulis.
Et hoc negat Parentis illa Olympici
Negare siderea, incolasve siderum,
Polumve stelleum, globumve terreum.

Ubi iste, post-Pusillus, antea DEUS
Fuit verendus: ipse namque fulmine
Crepante saepe territavit impios.
Pater supreme, rheda Solis aurea,
Tibi haec fuisse, et esse cognitissima,
Ait puellus: ultima ex origine,
Tuo stetisse dicit in cacumine,
Tuo imbuisse corculum sub aethere:
Et inde corpus induisse terreum:
Crucem paratus, ardua atque stipitis
Obire fata pollicetur omnia.
Quid ergo, o Aemuli, iuvat reponere?
Amo, iuvat. Quid hoc daretis aptius?
Capesse dona, dona digna Numine,
Et hos tuere: bis tenelle parvule,
Tenelle Patris, et tenelle Virginis.

(Joannes Niess, SJ, in Alphabeto Christi)

(An Invitation to young people to imitate the child born to us of the Virgin Mary in the stable at Bethlehem: That baby boy you see, imitators, says he was the youngest of the heavenly beings, and that he was not unable to surpass the rushing speed of any flying Angel, whether he had to fly with his little feet or wings. And he denies that those constellations of his heavenly father deny this, or the inhabitants of the constellations, or the starry sky, or the terrestrial sphere, where that one, the babe-to-be, was first awful God. For he often terrified the impious with his crackling thunderbolt. O supreme Father, golden chariot of the sun, the babe says these things were and are well known to you. From his first origin he says he stood on your peak, and instructed his small heart under your ether, and then put on an earthly body. Prepared for the cross, he promises to undergo all hard fates, even that of the tree. What recompense then, my imitators, is pleasing? 'I love' is pleasing. What could you give more fitting than this? Take the gifts, gifts worthy of Divinity, and watch over these children, twice tender little child, tender child of the Father and tender child of the Virgin.)

Niess' version amply fulfils Estienne's stipulation that good parodies 'should convert the words they have stolen to another use that is so remote from what they had in their author . . . that no such idea could have occurred to him while he was using them.' But it also manages to ring some other changes on the *phaselus* and its sixteenth-century parodies. The poet's tone is loving and reverent, with no touch of irony, as he reports and explains the words of the Christ child, who is treated not so much as a speaking object as an icon. The poet's audience are not his friends and equals (*hospites*), but his pupils (*aemuli*), whom he urges to imitate the infant Jesus. Thus, whereas in other versions the poet and his friends are allied against the speaking object, or at least share a common ground with respect to it, Niess presents a threefold hierarchy in which the poet is an intermediary between the divine 'object' and his young worshippers. The *aemuli*, moreover, unlike the *hospites* of other versions, are an active presence throughout the poem. They are urged to respond to the story they have heard (20–1) and commended to Christ's care (22–3); and their interests and point of view are central—from the racing angels of 3–5 to the simple response ('I love') that they are asked to make to Christ's suffering. The poem closes with a prayer, not to fostering deities, but to the speaking object or icon himself.

Sed haec fuere postea. We must leave the Jesuit schoolroom and return to Lernutius and Giselinus and their friends. The northern humanists liked to think of themselves as citizens of a *res publica litterarum* that transcended regional and national boundaries. Although their conception of humanism and its purposes had a serious political side that cannot concern us here, it also bore a festive and convivial aspect that had as its centre their shared interests in philology and poetry. Learned play was the passport into their world and the hallmark of their friendships, which involved personal as well as intellectual ties. Dousa's dedication of his *Praecidanea* to Lernutius typifies this world, with its affectionate tone, self-conscious gaiety and learning, and personal news at the end: 'Please note that I have been blessed with a son and the mother is well. And do you see that you now owe me a birthday poem?'[60] The *Epistolicae Quaestiones* (1577) of Justus Lipsius represent it even better. The work is a collection of Lipsius' fictional letters to his friends, praising their poetry and quoting his own, sharing news of family and friends, and discussing textual problems in ancient authors – all with ponderous charm and levity. The *Phaselus* of Lernutius and Giselinus is from the same mould, using the humanists' shared enthusiasms for poetry and style to create a learned parlour game with almost infinite possibilities. Anyone can play the game of 'Parodies'—that is, any citizen of the *res publica litterarum* with both the requisite philological knowledge and skill and the ability to allude to and incorporate earlier versions in his own.

Conclusion: *The Renaissance Catullus*

AROUND 1300 Catullus washed up on the shore of the Renaissance after being lost for a thousand years, with only the poor manuscript he stood up in and a few laudatory testimonia from Antiquity. Although his first readers greeted the new arrival with excitement, they were frustrated not only by the condition of his text but also by their own ignorance—of Catullus' contemporaries, of his language and metres, and of his Alexandrian sources. They believed that Catullus was *lascivus*, *tener*, *mollis*, and (above all) *doctus*, because they had read it in the testimonia, but for their own part they could do little more for the next hundred years than produce a handful of manuscripts and cull quotable verses for their anthologies and correspondence.

The poets were Catullus' first successful interpreters. Landino wrote several imitations of Catullus in the early 1440s, but it was Pontano a few years later who launched Catullan poetry firmly on its way, reading Catullus through Martial, his most famous ancient imitator, and imitating the Catullus he saw reflected in Martial's verses. The first edition appeared a generation after Pontano's earliest imitations, and the first commentary (the naïve but influential work of Antonio Partenio) was later still. Both made Catullus more widely accessible, and both were followed by derivative successors that led readers farther and farther away from the manuscripts. By the end of the fifteenth century Catullus and his readers were in a hall of mirrors. Poets imitated Pontano and other poets imitating Martial's Catullus. Editors corrected previous editions, writing their corrections in the margins of their predecessors with hardly a thought of the manuscripts. Commentators corrected the interpretations of previous commentators, interpreting Catullus through the filter of someone else's ideas.

Little by little, however, they improved the text and learned to read it more intelligently. The first Aldine edition (1502) fittingly inaugurated Catullus' third century in the modern world. With a text far superior to those of its fifteenth-century predecessors, and with its handy octavo format and extraordinary press run of 3,000 copies it made Catullus more widely and more usefully available than ever before. Since the new generation of readers (poets and poetasters alike) enthusiastically devoted themselves to writing Catullan poetry, Alexander Guarino's commentary of 1521 was less in the spirit of the age than Pierio Valeriano's little-known Catullan lectures of the same year. Guarino's book, written in an effort to preserve his father's work on Catullus, is a relic of the fifteenth century. Valeriano, a poet himself, urged his students to read Catullus actively, to hear his rhythms, to study his diction so that they could write their own Latin verse.

The same active poetic interest characterized the work of Marc-Antoine de Muret a generation later, as he lectured on Catullus to the poets of the Brigade in Paris, wrote his own Catullan poetry, and finally produced an edition and commentary. His successors, Achilles Statius and Joseph Scaliger, though philologically more acute, came from the same literary background, spending their formative years in Paris in the vicinity if not in the orbit of the new French poets. Unlike Muret, however, and indeed unlike all of their predecessors, both Statius and Scaliger systematically studied manuscripts in order to improve the text. Scaliger produced the best text seen or possible in the Renaissance and set out a brilliant philological method regarded as a landmark in the history of textual criticism—although his method, paradoxically, was largely irrelevant to his improvement of the text. Scaliger's authority discouraged successors, but he did not have the last word. That, as always, belonged to the poets. Demonstrating their mastery of Catullan technique, their affinity with Catullus himself, and their membership in a company for whom poetry and style were the guiding principles even in times of war and religious upheaval, they began to write parodies—playing a rigidly structured intellectual game that continued on its imitative, intertextual way well into the seventeenth century.

Renaissance readers created their own Catullus. In the picture that emerges from their interpretations and imitations we see the features of neither the tormented Romantic nor the self-conscious Alexandrian so dear to the twentieth century, but of someone else entirely—a figure part sensualist, part *sodalis* and patron of poets. The sensualist is the Renaissance descendant of Martial's Catullus, his paternity evident in his preference for short poetry over long, his lack of interest in Alexandrian *doctrina*, and above all in his predilection for sexual pleasure and obscene licence without emotional complexity. The patron of poetic sodalities has his origin in the poems Catullus wrote to or about his fellow poets, in which the humanists found both a pattern and a way of legitimizing their social and convivial approach to poetry. As Catullus moved through the Renaissance—from Pontano's Naples, to Valeriano's Rome, Muret's Paris, Statius' and Scaliger's post-Tridentine Italy and France, and on to the Leiden of Janus Dousa and his friends—his readers retouched the portrait, highlighting and elaborating some features, and leaving others in shadow. Martial's features became less prominent in the mid-sixteenth century, both because of literary taste (Martial was out of fashion in the ambit of the Pléiade poets) and in deference to the century's increasing discomfort with explicit obscenity. Some versions of the Renaissance Catullus began to look more like Horace, but even these retained traces of the distinctive physiognomy he had acquired from Martial by way of his fifteenth-century readers. Whatever the circumstances, however, the literary and convivial aspect of Catullus' portrait remained essentially unchanged throughout the Renaissance, for in it Catullus' readers thought—or hoped—they recognized themselves.

NOTES

NOTES TO THE INTRODUCTION

1. Jerome, *Chronica* 150 H (Ol. 173. 2) and 154 H (Ol. 180. 3); Suetonius, *Iulius* 73 (the scurrilous poems are no doubt 29 and 57). For the testimonia see L. Schwabe, *Catulli Veronensis Liber*[2] (Berlin, 1886), pp. vii–xxiv. The ancient testimonia have been recently collected again by T. P. Wiseman, *Catullus and his World* (Cambridge, 1985), 246–62.
2. *Catullus' brother*: 65, 68, 101. *Lesbia*: *passim*, but especially 58:

   Caeli, Lesbia nostra, Lesbia illa,
   illa Lesbia, quam Catullus unam
   plus quam se atque suos amavit omnes,
   nunc in quadriviis et angiportis
   glubit magnanimi Remi nepotes.

   Here and elsewhere Catullus is quoted from the text of R. A. B. Mynors (Oxford, 1958). Exceptions will be noted in the text.
3. See Apuleius, *Apologia* 10: 'Eadem igitur opera accusent C. Catullum quod Lesbiam pro Clodia nominarit . . .'. For Lesbia as the Clodia Metelli attacked by Cicero see R. G. Austin (ed.), *M. Tulli Ciceronis Pro Caelio Oratio*[3] (Oxford, 1960), 148–50. T. P. Wiseman suggests that Lesbia may not have been Clodia Metelli but her younger sister: *Catullan Questions* (Leicester, 1969), 50–60; *Cinna the Poet* (Leicester, 1974), 104–18.
4. For these and other historical figures see C. L. Neudling, *A Prosopography to Catullus*, Iowa Studies in Classical Philology, 12 (1955).
5. For a balanced discussion of the problem of writing Catullus' biography from his poems and a typical attempt to do so see K. Quinn, *Catullus: An Interpretation* (London, 1972), 131–203. The best recent biographical discussion is that of M. Rambaud, 'César et Catulle', in *Actes du Colloque L'Élégie romaine: Enracinement, Thèmes, Diffusion (16–18 mars 1979)*, Bulletin de la Faculté des Lettres de Mulhouse, fasc. 10 (Paris, 1980), 37–50.
6. A modern poet's warning may be salutary. Thus Robert Pack, quoted in the *New York Times Book Review*, 28 Sept. 1986, p. 47:

'Having just given a reading of one of my own poems, I was delighted when a woman from the audience came to the podium and took my hand in both of hers, in what I assumed was a warm gesture of appreciation and approval. "I feel so sorry for you," she said; "believe me, I understand." At first I thought she was commiserating with me for an unsuccessful performance, and then I realized that she must be referring to a poem I had read about the death of "my brother" in a hunting accident. . . . I apologized to her, explaining that I never had a brother, that I invented the brother for the sake of my poem. If my hand could have been detached at the wrist, she would have thrown it on the floor, so violent was her disgust with me. "You mean you lied," she said; "you took advantage of my sympathy."

'I didn't have the wit then to say that is exactly what poems ought to do. Poems tell personal lies in order to express impersonal truths. And even if I had so replied, I doubt that she would have been convinced and not felt cheated. The intimacy of lyric poetry seems to invite a response that assumes an autobiographical revelation has been made, that the poet has offered a confession to his reader.'

7. For the historical milieu see Wiseman, *Catullus and his World*; for the picture in Catullus see also D. O. Ross, Jun., *Style and Tradition in Catullus* (Cambridge, Mass., 1969), 80–95; Quinn, *Catullus*, 204–77.

8. For Parthenius see W. Clausen, 'Callimachus and Latin Poetry', *GRBS* 5 (1964), 181–96; Wiseman, *Cinna the Poet*, 44–58. A more cautious position is taken by N. B. Crowther, 'Parthenius and Roman Poetry', *Mnemosyne*, 29 (1976), 65–71.

9. Cicero, *Att.* 7. 2. 1. On the term 'neoteric' see N. B. Crowther, '*OI ΝΕΩΤΕΡΟΙ*, Poetae Novi, et Cantores Euphorionis', *CQ*, 20 (1970), 322–7; R. O. A. M. Lyne, 'The Neoteric Poets', *CQ* 28 (1978), 167–87.

10. The fragments of the neoterics have been conveniently assembled by A. Traglia, *Poetae Novi*[2] (Rome, 1974); see also J. Granarolo, 'L'Époque néotérique ou la poésie romaine d'avant garde au dernier siècle de la République (Catulle excepté)', *Aufstieg und Niedergang der römischen Welt* i. 3 (Berlin, 1973), 278–360.

The Phalaecean hendecasyllable takes its name from the obscure third-century (?) Greek poet, Phalaecus, of whom one poem in Phalaeceans survives (*A.P.* 13. 6). See A. S. F. Gow and D. L. Page (eds.), *The Greek Anthology: Hellenistic Epigram* (Cambridge, 1965) ii. 458–64. Four other Greek examples are listed by M. L. West, *Greek Metre* (Oxford, 1982), 151. In Latin only Laevius (early first century BC) before the neoterics seems to have used hendecasyllables. See Traglia, *Poetae Novi*, for his surviving two verses.

11. Wilamowitz attributed Catullus' success with the hendecasyllable to his ancestry: 'cuius [sc. Catulli] admirabilis facilitas, quam Gallico sanguini deberi credo . . .': (U. von Wilamowitz-Moellendorf, *Griechische Verskunst* (Berlin, 1921), 139).
12. A. L. Wheeler, *Catullus and the Traditions of Ancient Poetry* (Berkeley, Calif., 1934), 20–1; W. Clausen, 'Catulli Veronensis Liber', *CP* 71 (1976), 38.
13. D. F. S. Thomson, *Catullus: A Critical Edition* (Chapel Hill, NC, 1978). Thomson prints 6 verses of fragments; these have not been counted.
14. T. Birt, *Das antike Buchwesen* (Berlin, 1882), 291–3.
15. F. G. Kenyon, *Books and Readers in Ancient Greece and Rome*[2] (Oxford, 1951) 54–5.
16. The calculations are rough and require some assumptions, principally about the height of the papyri. According to Kenyon (*Books and Readers*, 51) 10 inches (25 cm.) is common, although books of poetry might be 9 inches (22.5 cm.) or less. The Gallus papyrus could accommodate about 27 lines in a 25 cm. column; for the sake of argument we will assume the same number for PHerc 817 even though the script is demonstrably larger. At that rate Catullus' text of 2,289 verses would require 85 columns (making no allowance for lost verses or spaces between poems). The width of the columns in the Gallus papyrus is 13.5 cm., in PHerc 817 19.5 cm. Taking into account the varying length of Catullus' verses, we assume 46 columns of 13.5/19.5 cm., 30 columns of 9/13 cm., and 9 columns of 6.75/9.75 cm. (The 1,239 verses of Cat. 17 and 62–116 contain around 43–6 letters; the 798 verses of Cat. 1–60, excluding 17 and 34, contain around 30–32 letters; the 252 verses of Cat. 34 and 61 contain around 20–4 letters.) Thus, written in the style of the Gallus papyrus, our 85 columns would require 9.52 m.; the same text in PHerc 817 would require 13.75 m. With space allowed for intercolumniation (2.5 cm. in the Gallus papyrus) the total rises to 11.62 m. and 15.85 m.

    For PHerc 817 see CLA III. 385 (with bibliography) and the facsimiles in W. Scott, *Fragmenta Herculanensia* (Oxford, 1885), plates A–H. For the Gallus papyrus, R. D. Anderson, P. J. Parsons, and R. G. M. Nisbet, 'Elegiacs by Gallus from Qaṣr Ibrîm', *JRS* 69 (1979) 125–55.

    Many years ago and using very different assumptions, Wheeler calculated a minimum length for Catullus of 38 feet (11.58 m.). Wheeler, *Catullus*, 16.
17. Clausen, 'Catulli Veronensis Liber', 39–41. Clausen suggests that

poems 51–60 are fragments and poetic experiments gathered by the editor from Catullus' papers. See also Wiseman, *Catullan Questions*, 1–31; and M. Skinner, *Catullus' Passer: The Arrangement of the Book of Polymetric Poems* (New York, 1981), 21–3.

18. But it has been argued that the opening poem in each group contains a programmatic reference to Callimachus, and that the repeated phrase *carmina Battiadae* (65. 16, 116. 2) links the beginning and end of the third book. Wiseman, *Catullus and his World*, 183–4.

19. Terentianus (*Grammatici Latini* vi. 406); Nonius vol. 1, p. 195 (Lindsay) s.v. *ligurrire*; Porphyrion, *ad Horati carmen* 1. 16. 22. The verses are printed as *Fragments* 1–3 in Mynors and Thomson.

Other claims have been made. It has sometimes been argued (e.g. by Birt, *Das antike Buchwesen*, 404–5, and Wheeler, *Catullus*, 11–12) that Catullus wrote an imitation of Theocritus' *Pharmaceutria*; their evidence is Pliny *Nat.* 28. 19: 'Hinc Theocriti apud Graecos, Catulli apud nos, proximeque Vergilii incantamentorum amatoria imitatio.' F. Della Corte used Pliny's comment, together with the fact that the text cited in ancient sources sometimes differs from that of our tradition, to argue for a much larger corpus and a second tradition. ('L'altro Catullo', in *Due studi catulliani* (Genoa, 1951)). He was refuted on both counts by M. Zicàri ('A proposito di un "altro Catullo"', *Scritti Catulliani* (Urbino, 1976), 29–42 (=*Rendiconti dell' Istituto Lombardo*, 85 (1952), 246–58)). Zicàri argues that Pliny is probably referring to a brief love charm, perhaps contained in one of the *priapea*. Most recently, Wiseman has revived the idea of a Catullan *Pharmaceutria* and used it in his argument that Catullus is to be identified with Catullus the mimographer (*Catullus and his World*, 183–98).

20. Especially the epyllia of Calvus and Cinna. See Traglia, *Poetae Novi*², 145–52.

21. Clausen, 'Callimachus and Latin Poetry', especially 188–93.

22. See, for example, Wheeler, *Catullus*, 153–82; Ross, *Style and Tradition*, 115–75; F. Cairns, *Tibullus: A Hellenistic Poet at Rome* (Cambridge, 1979), 214–30. For references to Catullus in the elegists see the testimonia collected by Schwabe, *Catulli Veronensis Liber*², vii; and by Wiseman, *Catullus and his World*, 246–62.

23. E. Fraenkel, *Horace* (Oxford, 1957) s.n. Catullus in index; C. J. Fordyce, *Catullus: A Commentary* (Oxford, 1961), p. xxiii. Influence is most obvious in c. 1. 22, which uses the structure and language of Cat. 11 and 51. Horace's only reference to Catullus by

name is slighting: 'neque simius iste nil praeter Calvum et doctus cantare Catullum' (*Serm* 1. 10. 19).

24. Dido has some characteristics in common with Catullus' Ariadne, as Renaissance scholars observed. See pp. 197–8 for the discussion of Bartolomeo Ricci (1490–1569). For Catullus and the *Fourth Eclogue* see W. Berg, *Early Virgil* (London, 1974), 158–67. Some other Vergilian echoes are listed by Fordyce, *Catullus*, p. xxii.
25. R. E. H. Westendorp Boerma (ed.), *P. Vergili Maronis Catalepton* (Assen, 1963), ii. 28–48. For 4 and *Catal.* 10 see pp. 255–8.
26. For Martial's imitations see pp. 200–11.
27. Domitius Marsus was an Augustan epigrammatist. Albinovanus Pedo lived in the next generation; although Martial cites him here as a writer of short poems, only fragments of an epic survive. For the fragments of both see W. Morel (ed.), *Fragmenta poetarum latinorum*[2] (Stuttgart, 1975). Domitian apparently wrote an epic on the battle of the Capitoline in AD 69: '. . . Capitolini caelestia carmina belli' (Mart. 5. 5. 7). See L. Friedlaender (ed.), *M. Valerii Martialis Epigrammaton Libri* (Leipzig, 1886), ad loc.
28. Here and elsewhere Martial's text is quoted from the edition of W. M. Lindsay (Oxford, 1929, repr. 1981).
29. Friedlaender, *Martialis*, 55–6.
30. K. Quinn (ed. and comm.), *Catullus. The Poems*[2] (London, 1973), 282.
31. Some galliambic fragments are preserved: Hephaistion 12. 3; Varro, frr. 131–2 (Büch.); Maecenas, frr. 5–6 in Morel, *Fragmenta*.
32. R. Paukstadt, *De Martiale Catulli imitatore*, diss. (Halle, 1876), 29–34.
33. But see Quinn, *Catullus*, 26–37.
34. Pliny, *Ep.* 8. 21. 4; 7. 4. 8–9. See F. Gamberini, *Stylistic Theory and Practice in the Younger Pliny* (Hildesheim, 1983), 84–91.
35. Statius wrote four poems in hendecasyllables in the *Silvae*, ranging in length from 55 to 160 verses. Only one, a mock serious complaint about a gift of poems, can be characterized as an imitation of Catullus (Stat. *Silv.* 4. 9, cf. Cat. 14). Of the other three, one (*Silv.* 2. 7) is a lament for the poet Lucan, and two praise the generosity of Domitian (1. 6 and 4. 3). The poet of the *Priapea* used hendecasyllables for about 30 of his 80 poems, thereby provoking Quintilian's strictures against letting young people read verses in that metre (*Inst. Or.* 1. 8. 6). On the reasons for dating the *Priapea* after Martial see V. Buchheit, *Studien zur Corpus Priapeorum* (Munich, 1962) Zetemeta 28, 108–23.

36. 'Postremo placuit exemplo multorum unum separatim hendecasyllaborum volumen absoluere, nec paenitet' (Pliny, *Ep.* 7. 4. 8).
37. For Saturninus See Pliny, *Ep.* 1. 16. 5; for Augurinus *Ep.* 4. 27. Augurinus' hendecasyllables are quoted from 4. 27. 4: 'Canto carmina versibus minutis, / his olim quibus et meus Catullus / et Calvus veteresque. Sed quid ad me? / Unus Plinius est mihi priores . . .'.
38. Similarly, Augurinus sees Pliny's verses as the proper relaxation for a busy man: 'mavolt versiculos foro relicto' (Pliny, *Ep.* 4. 27. 4, verse 5). On Pliny's view of his own poetry see Gamberini, *Stylistic Theory*, 97–103.
39. Catullus and Calvus are treated as a pair as early as Horace (*Sat.* 1. 10. 19). See testimonia 2, 3, 13–17 in Wiseman, *Catullus and his World*, 246–8. The association persists into the Silver Age, but, curiously enough, does not appear in Martial.
40. A. N. Sherwin-White, *The Letters of Pliny: A Historical and Social Commentary* (Oxford, 1966), 123–4.
41. 'namque tu solebas / nugas esse aliquid meas putare [cf. 1. 3–4] ut obiter emolliam Catullum concerraneum meum . . . (ille enim, ut scis, permutatis prioribus syllabis duriusculum se fecit quam volebat existimari a Veraniolis suis et Fabullis) . . .' (Pliny, *Nat.*, Praef. 1). The translation is from H. Rackham, *Pliny, Natural History* i (London, 1979).
42. O. Skutsch, 'Metrical Variations and Some Textual Problems in Catullus', *Bulletin of the Institute of Classical Studies of the University of London*, 16 (1969), 38. Skinner, *Catullus' Passer*, 21–3.
43. See Schwabe's testimonia in *Catulli Veronensis Liber*², pp. viii–ix. Pliny may also refer to the *priapea* (see n. 19 above).
44. See also Mart. 1. 7; 1. 109; 4. 14; 7. 14; 14. 77. For the *fortuna* of the innuendo in Mart. 11. 6 see pp. 238–54.
45. For *passer* as 'poem' in Martial, see Mart. 1. 7 and 4. 14 (quoted above) and pp. 239–43.
46. For 'nightingales' see Call. *Ep.* 2. 5 and *Aetia* fr. 1. 16 with Pfeiffer's note ad loc. (R. Pfeiffer, *Callimachus* (Oxford, 1949–53)).
47. Martial published Book 1 in 85/6. See Friedlaender, *Martialis*, 52–4. Pliny, *Ep.* 9. 25 is dated to 107/8 by Sherwin-White, *The Letters of Pliny*, 500.
48. *CEL* 1512. See K. R. Walters, 'Catullan Echoes in the Second Century A.D.', *Classical World*, 69 (1976), 353–60. The identical lines 4 and 7 of this inscription have been used to emend 3. 16: G. P. Goold, 'Catullus 3. 16', *Phoenix*, 23 (1969), 186–203.

49. The date of the *Ciris* is unknown, but it probably belongs to the second century—perhaps even to the third. See R. O. A. M. Lyne, *Ciris* (Cambridge, 1978), 48–56.
50. For a good account see J. E. G. Zetzel, *Latin Textual Criticism in Antiquity* (Salem, NH, 1981), 55–74.
51. Gellius' Greeks have a less favourable opinion of Catullus' predecessors and other contemporaries: 'Nam Laevius inplicata et Hortensius invenusta et Cinna inlepida et Memmius dura ac deinceps omnes rudia fecerunt atque absona' (Gellius 19. 9. 7).
52. H. Nettleship, *Lectures and Essays* (Oxford, 1885), 253.
53. Gellius 7. 16. 13. The translation is that of J. C. Rolfe, *The Attic Nights of Aulus Gellius* (London, 1927; repr. 1967).
54. Gellius 6. 20. 6, translated by Rolfe, *The Attic Nights*.
55. For criticism of Gellius see Fordyce, *Catullus*, ad loc. But in his forthcoming text and commentary D. F. S. Thomson is now inclined to accept Statius' *ebriosa acino* and to follow R. G. C. Levens in reading the same in Gellius. (According to this reconstruction the readings Gellius cited as incorrect were *ebrios* and *ebriosos*.) Thomson points out that Gellius does not say that Catullus *used* Homeric hiatus, only that he liked its blending (*concentus*) of identical vowels—an effect produced by elision as well as hiatus.
56. As in other authors. For the difficulty of getting accurate copies of texts in Antiquity see E. J. Kenney, 'Books and Readers in the Ancient World', *Cambridge History of Classical Literature* (Cambridge, 1982), ii. 23–37.
57. e.g. Mart. 1. 4. 8; Pliny, *Ep.* 4. 14. 5.
58. Cat. 68. 2; *Ap.* 6 and 79. See H. E. Butler and A. S. Owen (ed. and comm.), *Apulei Apologia* (Oxford, 1914), 18.
59. There are other citations of the same sort. See the testimonia in Schwabe, *Catulli Veronensis Liber*², pp. xi–xiii. For a good discussion see A. Manzo, 'Testimonianze e tradizione del "Liber" Catulliano nella letteratura esegetico-scolastica antica', *Rivista di Studi Classici*, 15 (1967), 137–62.
60. The best account of the medieval *fortuna* of Catullus is that of B. L. Ullman, 'The Transmission of the Text of Catullus', in *Studi in onore di Luigi Castiglioni* (Florence, 1960), ii. 1027–57.
61. O. Zwierlein, *Prolegomena zu einer kritischen Ausgabe der Tragödien Senecas*, Abhandlungen der Geistes- und Sozialwissenschaftlichen Klasse der Akademie der Wissenschaften und der Literatur (Mainz, 1983), Nr. 3, 15–23. For earlier discussions of the manuscripts see Ullman, 'The Transmission', 1028–9;

Thomson, *Catullus*, 10; B. Richardson, 'Pucci, Parrasio and Catullus', *IMU* 19 (1976), 285–7.

62. Vienna 277 closely fits Summonte's description of the trophies brought by Sannazaro from France to Naples in 1502. The description (which does not mention Catullus) appears in Summonte's preface to Pontano's *Actius* (1507). See M. Haupt, *Ovidii Halieutica Gratii et Nemesiani Cynegetica* (Leipzig, 1838), pp. xxiii–xxiv; Richardson, 'Pucci, Parrasio and Catullus', 285–7. Summonte says Sannazaro brought his prizes 'ex Heduorum usque finibus atque e Turonibus . . .'.

63. In 1577 Pierre Pithou used it for the first edition of the *Pervigilium Veneris*. See Richardson, 'Pucci, Parrasio and Catullus', 285–7.

64. 'This of course is pure speculation and perhaps not worth mentioning, but the temptation to explain the coincidence about Tours is one that no researcher can resist' (Ullman, 'The Transmission', 1029). According to Ullman the verb *hiulco* is also rare: it occurs only in Catullus, Fortunatus (6. 10. 6) and Pseudo-Augustine.

65. disputans multum variante milto
quaeque sunt rythmis vel amica metris,
Sapphicum quantum trimetrumve adornet
dulcis epodus.
multus auctorum numerus habetur
plura dicentum modulo canoro

(Fortunatus 9. 7. 41–6, in *MGH*, *Auct. Ant.* 4. 1)

I owe this interpretation of Fortunatus to my colleague, Myra Uhlfelder.

66. The same must be true of Heiricus of Auxerre in the ninth century, in whose poems Ullman identified several close echoes ('The Transmission', 1030–1). For here, too, the passages imitated are not confined to 62 (Ullman found echoes of 1, 40, 63, 67, 68). If Heiricus read Catullus, his manuscript was not T or its exemplar, but probably a full text of the poems.

67. 'quid de me dicere, quid valeo cogitare (et ut turpia subsidens honesta solum, prohibita licet, depromam), si in lege Dei, ut debitorem me fore non nescio, die meditor et nocte, Catullum nunquam antea lectum, Plautum quando iam olim lego neglectum, musicam quando sepe rogatus expono, cum nequeam (primo aritmetico scilicet cassatus auxilio) . . .' (*Sermo de Maria et Martha* 4. 9–13, in *Sermones Ratherii Episcopi Veronensis*, ed. B. Reece (Worcester, Mass., 1969), 86). See Ullman, 'The Transmission', 1031.

68. R. Ellis, *Catulli Veronensis Liber* (Oxford, 1878), p. viii; Ullman, 'The Transmission', 1032–3. Rather, *Sermo I de Ascensione* 2. 7–8 ed. Reece, *Sermones*, 30: 'non pennigero, ut poeticus ille noster . . . volatu . . .' (cf. 58*b*. 3–2: non Ladas ego pinnipesve Perseus / non si Pegaseo ferar volatu). But a more likely source for Rather is Jerome: 'et quasi *pennigero volatu* petulcam animal aufugit' (*Vita Pauli* 8). I am indebted to Paul Harvey for this reference.
69. Giuseppe Billanovich, 'Dal Livio di Raterio al Livio del Petrarca', *IMU* 2 (1959), 164–5; 'Terenzio, Ildemaro, Petrarca', *IMU* 17 (1974), 58–9; 'Livio e Catullo nella Catedrale di Verona', in *La tradizione del testo di Livio e le origini dell' umanesimo* (Padua, 1981), i. 273–7; 'Il Catullo della Cattedrale di Verona', in *Scire Litteras* = Bayerische Akad. der Wissenschaften Philosophisch-Historische Klasse Abhandlungen 99 (Munich, 1988), 35–57.
70. Billanovich, 'Terenzio, Ildemaro, Petrarca', 43–60.
71. Ullman, 'The Transmission', 1031–2; Clausen, '*Catulli Veronensis Liber*', 42–3.
72. Billanovich, 'Terenzio, Ildemaro, Petrarca', 52.
73. Schwabe, *Catulli Veronensis Liber*[2], p. xiv; Ullman, 'The Transmission', 1033.
74. *De gestis regum Anglorum* ii. 159: 'virginem sane nec inelegantem nec illepidam', cf. 6. 2 and 10. 3. See Ellis, *Catulli Veronensis Liber*, p. ix; Ullman, 'The Transmission', 1033–4.
75. For *papirus* as both 'paper' and 'light' or 'lamp', see O. Skutsch, 'The Book under the Bushel', *Bulletin of the Institute of Classical Studies of the University of London*, 17 (1970), 148.
76. For Benvenuto see R. Weiss, 'Benvenuto Campesani (1250/55?–1323)', *Bollettino del Museo Civico di Padova*, 44 (1955), 129–44. On the riddle: e.g. T. Frank, 'Can Grande and Catullus', *AJP* 48 (1927), 273–5; H. Levy, 'Catullus and Cangrande della Scala', *TAPA* 99 (1968), 249–53; O. Skutsch, 'The Book under the Bushel'; E. Zaffagno, 'L'epigramma di Benvenuto de Campesani: *De resurectione Catulli poetae Veronensis*', *I classici nel medioevo e nell' umanesimo*, Università di Genova Pubblicazioni dell' Istituto de filologia classica e medievale, 42 (Genoa, 1975), 289–98.

The evidence of the epigram was termed a 'fairy tale' by Giuseppe Billanovich (see n. 69 above), who argued that the archetype was discovered in Verona and that the discovery should be placed a generation earlier. This second point depends on the argument by Guido Billanovich that the Paduan poets Lovato Lovati (d. 1309) and Alberto Mussato (d. 1329) read Catullus, and that there are some echoes in Lovato that can be dated as early as

1268. (Guido Billanovich, '*Veterum vestigia vatum* nei carmi dei preumanisti Padovani', *IMU* 1 (1958), 155–243, esp. 155–70 and 191–9.) In spite of Ullman's scepticism ('The Transmission', 1055–6), the suggestion was widely and uncritically accepted (see e.g. L. D. Reynolds and N. G. Wilson, *Scribes and Scholars: A Guide to the Transmission of Greek and Latin Literature* (Oxford, 1974), 110–11); but Ludwig has demonstrated that the passages in Lovato adduced by Billanovich do not demonstrate knowledge of Catullus, and that most can be traced to other, more familiar models. If Lovato knew Catullus, the fact is not reflected in his poetry. (W. Ludwig, 'Kannte Lovato Catull?' *RhM* 129 (1986), 329–57.)

For further arguments that the archetype remained in Verona and an elaborate solution to Benvenuto's epigram see Billanovich, 'Il Catullo della Cattedrale di Verona'.

77. For the intervention of 'A' see the invaluable work of D. S. McKie, *The Manuscripts of Catullus: Recension in a Closed Tradition*, diss. (Cambridge University, 1977), 38–95. For the manuscripts see Ullman, 'The Transmission', 1038–55; Thomson, *Catullus*, 3–38; 'A New Look at the Manuscript Tradition of Catullus', *Yale Classical Studies* 23 (1973), 113–29; Zicàri, *Scritti catulliani*, 79–104 (= 'Ricerche sulla tradizione manoscritta di Catullo', *Bollettino del comitato per la preparazione dell' edizione nazionale dei classici greci e latini*, 6 (1958), 79–89).
78. 22. 18–20; 39. 16; 51. 15–16; 64. 143–8; 66. 15–16; 68. 137; 76. 13.
79. R. Weiss, 'Geremia da Montagnone', in *Il primo secolo dell' umanesimo* (Roma, 1949), 26.
80. B. L. Ullman, 'Hieremias de Montagnone and his Citations from Catullus', in *Studies in the Italian Renaissance* (Rome, 1955), 83–5. Oxford, Bodleian Library Canon. lat. class. 212 contains no Catullus; Rome, Bibl. Casanatense 312 (C.IV.II) lacks 66. 15–16 and 76. 13. McKie has used Geremia's method of citing Catullus by *capitula* to demonstrate the existence of 'A': Geremia's source was higher in the tradition than the archetype of OGR. *The Manuscripts of Catullus*, 80–93.
81. W. G. Hale, 'Benzo of Alexandria and Catullus', *CP* 5 (1910), 62.
82. Ullman counted thirty manuscripts of the fourteenth and fifteenth centuries: 'Hieremias de Montagnone and his Citations from Catullus', *CP* 5 (1910), 79–80. Weiss ('Geremia da Montagnone', 29–30) lists a dozen more. Unfortunately, Ullman's census of the library of Coluccio Salutati, the first owner of R, lists no manuscript of the *Compendium*: *The Humanism of Coluccio Salutati* (Rome, 1958), 129–212.

Half a dozen fifteenth-century Catullus manuscripts also indicate some of Geremia's selections with braces or pointing fingers, perhaps because the scribe or annotator was remembering Geremia or perhaps only by coincidence, since Geremia's passages all have a moralizing or proverbial air and since most of these manuscripts also distinguish other verses in the same way. The following designate at least two of Geremia's selections: Brussels IV.711 (= Schlägl 143); Edinburgh, National Library, Adv. MS 18.5.2; Florence, Bibl. Laurenziana. Plut. 33.11; London, British Library, Egerton 3027; Milan, Bibl. Ambrosiana I.67. sup; Paris, BN Lat. 7989; Vatican Library, Barb. lat. 34. I have not checked all the manuscripts.

83. Milan, Bibl. Ambrosiana. B. 24. inf; Catullus is cited on f. 94. R. Sabbadini, *Le scoperte dei codici latini e greci ne' secoli xiv e xv* (Florence, 1914), ii. 128–50; Hale, 'Benzo of Alexandria', 56–65. Conceivably Benzo could also have used A, but since he saw Catullus at nearly the same time as Geremia (i.e. *c.*1310), his source was probably V.

84. Verona, Bibl. Capitolare, CLXVIII (155); Catullus is quoted on f. 10 v. Sabbadini, *Le scoperte*, 90–7.

85. R. Ellis, *Catullus in the XIVth Century* (Oxford, 1905), 6. McKie argues that the compiler did not find his title for *22* (*Ad Varum*) in his manuscript, but invented it himself from the name of the addressee in *22*. 1. McKie, *The Manuscripts of Catullus*, 69.

86. Ed. 1547 (Venice) pp. 16a, 18b. Ellis, *Catullus in the XIVth Century*, 16; Ullman, 'The Transmission', 1041–2.

87. My account of Petrarch and Catullus largely follows Ullman, 'The Transmission', 1043–50. See also Ellis, *Catullus in the XIVth Century*, 16–23. Petrarch's quotations are listed by U. Bosco, 'Il Petrarca e l'umanesimo filologico', *GSLI* 120 (1942), 108–16. Bosco and Zicàri ('A proposito di un "altro Catullo"', 35–6) believed that Petrarch saw not a complete manuscript, but a florilegium that included the Ariadne episode of 64. But see Ullman, 'The Transmission', 1043, and 'Petrarch's Acquaintance with Catullus, Tibullus, Propertius', in *Studies in the Italian Renaissance* (Rome, 1955), 195–200.

88. See C. Tristano, 'Le postille del Petrarca nel Vat. lat. 2193', *IMU* 17 (1974), 414–15. For the title, see Mynors, *Catulli Carmina*, p. xiv.

89. For Coluccio and the manuscripts see: Ullman, 'The Transmission', 1040, 1045–51; McKie, *The Manuscripts of Catullus*, 178–86; Thomson, *Catullus*, 3–38; 'A New Look'; 'The Codex Romanus of Catullus: A Collation of the Text', *RhM*, 113 (1970),

97–110. The second hand in R (R^2) is that of Salutati. For Antonio da Legnago see Giuseppe Billanovich, 'Dal Livio di Raterio al Livio del Petrarca', 163–9.

90. M (Venice. Bibl. Marciana 12. 80 [4167]) was copied by Poggio, probably *c.*1398–1400. (A. C. de la Mare and D. F. S. Thomson, 'Poggio's Earliest Manuscript?' *IMU* 16 (1973), 179–95.) Other manuscripts belonging to the period 1400–20 are Bologna, Bibl. Univ. lat. 2621 (1412), written by Hieronymus Donatus and subsequently owned and corrected by Ermolao Barbaro; BN Lat. 7989 (1423), which is apparently the earliest manuscript in which Catullus, Tibullus, and Propertius are brought together, and contains later annotations indebted to the 1496 commentary of Palladio Fosco (see pp. 97–9); and Siena, Bibl. Comunale H.V. 41 (*c.*1425). (For BN 7989 see A. C. de la Mare, 'The Return of Petronius to Italy', in J. J. G. Alexander and M. T. Gibson (eds.), *Medieval Learning and Literature: Essays Presented to Richard W. Hunt* (Oxford, 1976), 240–51.) See also Florence, Biblioteca Laurenziana Laur. 36. 23 and Laur. 33. 13, and Vatican Library Vat. lat. 1630 (nos. 23, 22, and 109 in Thomson's list of manuscripts); Thomson, *Catullus*, 44–63.

91. Ad Galeaz, quem orat ut sibi Catullum inveniat.

Ardeo, mi Galeaz, mollem reperire Catullum,
Ut possim dominae moriger esse meae.
Lectitat illa libens teneros lasciva poetas,
Et praefert numeros, docte Catulle, tuos.
Nuper et hos abs me multa prece blanda poposcit,
Forte suum vatem me penes esse putans.
'Non teneo hunc,' dixi, 'mea lux, mea nympha, libellum,
'Id tamen efficiam, forsan habebis opus.'
Instat, et omnino librum me poscit amicum,
Et mecum gravibus nunc agit illa minis.
Quare ego per Superos omnes, o care sodalis,
Sic precibus lenis sit Cytherea tuis,
Te precor atque iterum precor, id mihi quaere libelli,
Quo fiam nostrae gratior ipse deae.'

(Panormita, *Hermaphroditus* 2. 23, quoted from *Antonio Beccadelli, L'Ermafrodito, e Pacifico Massimo, L'Ecatelegio*, ed. A. Ottolini (Milan, 1922), 74.)

92. On Panormita see G. Resta, 'Beccadelli, Antonio', *DBI* 7 (Rome, 1965), 400–6. Panormita was given a manuscript of Martial by Giovanni Aurispa (*c.*1369–1459). The manuscript, which contains Panormita's autograph corrections, is preserved in the Herzog

August Bibliothek in Wolfenbüttel (Cod. Wolfenbüttel Aug. 50. 5). See F.-R. Hausmann, 'Martial in Italien', *Studi medievali*, 17. 1 (1976), 186–8.

93. Schwabe, *Catulli Veronensis Liber*², pp. xvii–xviii; Ellis, *Catulli Veronensis Liber*, 353–5. Schwabe lists four Catullan quotations in Panormita's correspondence. For 16. 5–9 see p. 21; 35. 7, *viam vorabit*, (twice in Panormita) and 66. 32 (*amantes / non longe a caro corpore abesse volunt*) appear also in Guarino's correspondence. See n. 99 below.

94. Hodus ait nostram vitam non esse pudicam:
E scriptis mentem concipit ille meis.
Non debet teneros Hodus legisse Catullos,
Non vidit penem, verpe Priape, tuum.
Quod decuit Marcos, quod Marsos, quodve Pedones,
Denique quod cunctos, num mihi turpe putem?

(Panormita, *Hermaphroditus* 1. 18. 1–6, quoted from *Antonio Beccadelli, L'Ermafrodito*, 28)

95. Crede velim nostra vitam distare papyro;
Si mea charta procax, mens sine labe mea est.

(Panormita, *Hermaphroditus* 2. 11. 3–4)

cf. Martial 1. 4. 8: 'Lasciva est nobis pagina, vita proba'. Note also Ovid, *Tristia* 2. 354: 'Vita verecunda est, Musa iocosa mea'.

96. 'Enimvero, ut Horatius in poeticis institutionibus scriptum reliquit, semper Poetis, atque pictoribus concessum fuit quodlibet audere, licere. Cum vero lasciviam delegerint, ea lex est Poetis et verissima illa quidem, quam Catullus dixit "Nam castum decet . . . incitare possint" [16. 5–9]' (Panormita, *Epist. gallic* 4. 12 in *Antonii Bononiae Beccatelli Cognomento Panhormitae Epistolarum Libri V* (Venice, 1553), 81).

cf. Pliny, *Ep*. 4. 14. 5: 'Scimus alioqui huius opusculi illam esse verissimam legem, quam Catullus expressit: "Nam castum esse . . . parum pudici" (16. 5–8).' Also Guarino (in a letter to Johannes Lamola in 1426): 'Plus valet apud me conterranei mei vatis non illepidi auctoritas quam imperitorum clamor, quos nil nisi lacrimae ieiunia psalmi delectare potest, immemores quod aliud in vita aliud in oratione spectari convenit. Ut autem ad meum conterraneum revertar, ille hunc in modum ait: "Nam castum esse . . . incitare possint" [16. 5–9]' (R. Sabbadini, *Epistolario di Guarino Veronese* (Venice, 1915), ii. 505–6 (no. 346)).

97. Sabbadini, *Epistolario*, ii. 209–14 (no. 666). For contemporary reactions to the *Hermaphroditus* see J. A. Symonds, *The Renaissance in Italy* (New York, 1881), ii. 254–8.

98. 'Publice non legantur Iuvenalis, Persius, Martialis Cocus, Propertius, Tibullus, Catullus, Priapeia Virgilii, Naso de arte amandi et de remedio amoris, sed relinquantur studio camerario videre eos volentium, ut plurima sciantur, non ut quisquam adolescens tyro eorum lectione contaminetur' (Milan, Bibl. Ambrosiana F 141 sup., fo. 68v, quoted from Sabbadini, *Le Scoperte*, ii. 201).
99. Of the 27 citations of Catullus listed in Sabbadini's index (*Epistolario*, iii. 572) 14 are quotations of 1. 4 or 66. 32 (seven times each); 16. 5–8/5–9 is quoted twice. Guarino urged his pupils to note down useful material as they read; no doubt his Catullan quotations come from such a notebook. For Guarino's methods see A. Grafton and L. Jardine, *From Humanism to the Humanities* (London, 1986), 1–28.
100. Pliny, *Nat.*, Praef. 1. *conterraneum* is a variant for *concerraneum*.
101. See Hausmann, 'Martial in Italien', especially 173–88; 'Enea Silvio Piccolomini "Poeta" und die Rezeption der heidnischen Antike', *BHR*, 35 (1972), 454–61; 'Untersuchungen zum neulateinische Epigramm italiens im Quattrocento', *Humanistica lovaniensia*, 21 (1972), 1–35.

NOTES TO CHAPTER 1

1. The text of Benvenuto's epigram is given on p. 18.
2. 'Tu lector quicumque ad cuius manus hic libellus obvenerit scriptori da veniam si tibi coruptus videbitur, quoniam a corruptissimo exemplari transcripsit; non enim quodpiam aliud extabat, unde posset libelli huius habere copiam exemplandi. Et ut ex ipso salebroso aliquid tantum sugger⟨er⟩et, decrevit potius tamen coruptum habere quam omnino carere, sperans adhuc ab alliquo alio fortuite emergente hunc posse corigere' (Paris, BN Lat. 14137, 36r). See Mynors, *Catulli Carmina*, p. vi. For Antonio da Legnago see Giuseppe Billanovich, 'Dal Livio di Raterio al Livio del Petrarca', 160–5.
3. Antonio's somewhat perfunctory methods do not seem consistent with the scholarly distress of the subscription. Ullman argued that the author was the scribe of V, the notary Francesco celebrated in Benvenuto's epigram ('Transmission', 1047). In his forthcoming commentary Thomson suggests that the author was A. McKie argues for X (*The Manuscripts*, 171–7). Billanovich maintains it was Antonio himself ('Dal Livio di Raterio al Livio del Petrarca', 160–5).
4. Later scholars had better opportunities but not better judgement:

indeed, it was not until the twentieth century that editors finally agreed on the identity of the most important manuscripts. See Thomson, 'A New Look'. We should also remember the lapses of two famous sixteenth-century scholars. Achilles Statius used R, the important sister-manuscript of G, but failed to recognize its value, while Joseph Scaliger, the greatest scholar of his age, founded his edition on a late and unimportant manuscript. See pp. 175–6 and 185.

5. The number is taken from the chronological list of the originators of corrections that Goold compiled from the *apparatus* of Mynors' edition. G. P. Goold, 'A New Text of Catullus', *Phoenix*, 12 (1958), 98–9.

6. See the list of manuscripts in Thomson, *Catullus*, 44–63. For the fifteenth-century manuscript tradition see the important articles of M. Zicàri, now collected in *Scritti catulliani* (Urbino, 1976). For Pacifico Massimo see A. Grafton, *Joseph Scaliger: A Study in the History of Classical Scholarship* (Oxford, 1983), i. 166.

7. The manuscript has not been identified. According to Zicàri it was similar to British Library Add. MS 11915. M. Zicàri, 'Calfurnio, editore di Catullo', *Atene e Roma* 2 (1957) 157 (= *Scritti catulliani*, 106). Kenney's discussion of the texts of first editions is particularly apt for Catullus: 'it was nearly always the mongrel texts produced by the activities of humanist copyists, scholars and critics . . . that served as printer's copy for the *editiones principes*.' E. J. Kenney, *The Classical Text* (Berkeley, Calif., 1974), 3.

8. For the activities of early editors see Kenney, *The Classical Text*, 12–20 and M. Lowry, *The World of Aldus Manutius* (Cambridge, 1979), 26–41.

9. For the unilinear or monogenous descent of texts after printing see Kenney, *The Classical Text*, 18–19.

10. For a description of this edition see *BMC* v. 161–2; HC 4758. There were two editions of Propertius in 1472 in Venice, but although the other seems to be earlier, ours was 'the source of all the other fifteenth-century editions of Propertius except the *princeps*.' J. Butrica, *The Manuscript Tradition of Propertius* (Toronto, 1984), 160.

11. For Wendelin and his fortunes see *BMC* vol. v. p. ix and V. Scholderer, 'Printing at Venice to the End of 1481', in *Fifty Essays* (Amsterdam, 1966), 74–89.

12. Like the handsomely illuminated copy in the Vatican Library (Inc. III. 18) owned and annotated by Angelo Colocci (see Plate 1 p. 27). For a description of the volume see *Atti del Convegno internazionale di studi su Albio Tibullo* (Rome, 1986) 405.

13. British Library IB 19549. See the description in *BMC* v. 162.
14. Squarzafico also composed a poem celebrating the Italian Bible published by Wendelin in 1471 and joined in editing Leonardo Bruni's letters for Wendelin in 1472. See J. Allenspach and G. Frasso, 'Vicende, cultura e scritti di Gerolamo Squarzafico, Alessandrino', *IMU* 23 (1980) 233–92.
15. 'Valerius Catullus scriptor lyricus Veronae nascitur Olympiade Clxiii anno ante natum Salustium Crispum diris Marii Syllaeque temporibus quo die Plotinus latinam rhetoricam primus Romae docere coepit. Amavit hic puellam primariam Clodiam quam Lesbiam suo appellat in carmine. Lasciviusculus fuit et sua tempestate pares paucos in dicendo frenata oratione, superiorem habuit neminem; in iocis apprime lepidus, in seriis vero gravissimus extitit. Erotica scripsit et epithalamium in Manlium. Anno vero aetatis suae xxx Romae moritur elatus moerore publico' (Venice, 1472, 3v, quoted from Rome, Biblioteca Corsiniana 50. F. 37). Cf. Jerome *Chronica* 150 H (Ol. 173. 2) and 154 H (Ol. 180. 3). For Sicco see B. L. Ullman (ed.), *Sicconis Polentoni Scriptorum Illustrium Latinae Linguae*, Papers and Monographs of the American Academy in Rome, 6 (Rome, 1928), 63. 13–22.
16. Thus, in 1465 Johannes von Rabenstein, the scribe of Brussels IV. 711 (formerly Schlägl 143), glossed the epigram: 'Guarinus Veronensis in Francia repperit Catullum et portavit in Italiam ac publicavit sibique haec fecit carmina' (fol. 77).
17. They are not found in many manuscripts antedating Venice 1472, but both appear in Brussels IV. 711 (= Schlägl 143).
18. See McKie, *The Manuscripts of Catullus*, 38–95. McKie's discussion and *dispositio carminum* (95a–95c) supersede the reconstruction in Mynors, *Catulli carmina*, pp. xiv–xv.
19. The title is a descendant of Salutati's *Ad lusicacatam*. See McKie, *The Manuscripts of Catullus*, 71 and 95*a*.
20. The title is a descendant of Salutati's *In Romulum cathamitum*. See McKie, *The Manuscripts of Catullus*, 71 and 95*a*.
21. See McKie, *The Manuscripts of Catullus*, 65 and 95*a*. Salutati: *lesbie*.
22. McKie, *The Manuscripts of Catullus*, 95*a–c*. McKie's table shows his reconstruction of the titles in V, A (which he calls the archetype), X, and 'R etc.' (= R^2, G^2, and M). Since our interest is to show Salutati's *dispositio carminum* against that of the *princeps*, I have included in Appendix 1 only unseparated blocks and titles and I have not followed McKie in distinguishing between Salutati's contributions and those of the higher tradition.
23. In 24 the addressee Iuventius was not recognized in the corruption

iuvenculorum (24. 1, Venice 1472). In 103 Silo (*Sylo*, Venice 1472) was not recognized as a proper name. In 104 the addressee is not named. In 108 (*Si, Comini*, . . .) the addressee Cominius was lost in the corruption *Sic hominum* (108. 1, Venice 1472).

24. See pp. 38 and 67–71.

25. 'Qui nunc vocat me cum malum librum **legit**: / **Ac meminit septimos** suos amores' (44. 21–45. 1, Venice 1472). The corrupt words are in bold-face. As in the case of 83–84, the mismatched lines can be read together, even though the match depends on a series of misunderstandings: with its twelve syllables 45. 1 is not easily identifiable as a hendecasyllable; *ac meminit* (for *Acmen*) seems parallel with *vocat*; *septimos* (for *Septimius*) can modify *amores*.

26. *Salaputium* appears only in this passage and in one in the elder Seneca that refers to it (*Con.* 7. 4. 7). It is probably obscene; see J. N. Adams, *The Latin Sexual Vocabulary* (London, 1982), 65.

27. Part of the confusion seems to have been caused by Salutati. According to McKie the division in A and X was *37*. 1–16, *37*. 17–20, *38–9*. Salutati, seeing that *37*. 17–20 did not constitute a poem, joined the four verses to *38–9*. McKie, *The Manuscripts of Catullus*, 57–8.

28. For a description of this edition see *BMC* vii. 939; HC 4756; GW 6386.

29. 'Correctum per d. Franciscum Puteolanum: et vere ultra impressionem venetiis factam in iii milibus locis emendatum. s. Catullum et Sylvas, ut tu lector ambobus exemplaribus experiri poteris ita quod nullo modo intelligi possunt et caetera.

'Impressum Parmae per me Stephanum Corallum Anno Christi M.cccclxxiii. secundo cal. septembris' (Parma 1473, quoted from New York, Pierpoint Morgan Library 1258, 77r).

30. R. Contarino, 'Dal Pozzo, Francesco', *DBI* (1986), xxxii. 213–16; I. Affò, *Memorie degli scrittori e letterati parmigiani* (Parma, 1789), ii. 292–316; L. Sighinolfi, 'Francesco Puteolano e le origini della stampa in Bologna e in Parma', *Bibliofilia*, 15 (1913), 263–467.

31. Puteolano's part of the agreement was as follows: 'Nam quidem primo dictus dominus Franciscus promissit eisdem magistro Hannibali et Baldassari dare et tradere exemplum librorum imprimendorum seu stampandorum, que sint correcta et corrigere teneatur ipse dominus Franciscus pro posse suo et etiam pro posse suo arbitrio boni viri cum honestate dictos libros sic stampatos publicare et legere publice et conabitur quantum poterit dictos libros vendere seu vendi facere . . .' (Archivio Notarile di Bologna,

Rogito di Giovanni Antonio Castagnoli, 25 ottobre 1470). Quoted from Sighinolfi, 'Francesco Puteolano', 455. See also C. F. Bühler, *The University and the Press in Fifteenth Century Bologna* (Notre Dame, Ind., 1958), 15–16.

32. Puteolano had agreements with Bolognese printers in 1474 and 1476; see Sighinolfi, 'Francesco Puteolano', 457–60. After Parma 1473, Corallo is next found engaged in a contract with two Bolognese lawyers and with his presses in Bologna. *BMC* vol. vii. p. xlvii.

33. 'Franciscus Puteolanus debet conducere domum honestam et aptam idoneam arbitrio boni viri omnibus suis impensis et ad quam possint homines, iuvenes et pueri convenire et dare operam litteris et si forte acciderit quod velint dicti socii alere domi scolares in duodena teneatur idem Franciscus conducere omnibus suis impensis domum aptam in qua possint habitare arbitrio boni viri . . . Item dominus Franciscus promittit curare et facere quantum poterit ut multi scolares conveniant et similiter duodenantes.

'Ex altera parte Calphurnius promittit attente et diligenter arbitrio boni viri edocere legere et ludum regere et examinare in bonis litteris et fungi officio boni preceptoris et habere libros rationum in quibus scribet receptas pecunias et dividere omnia cum dicto Francisco' (Archivio Notarile di Bologna, Rogito di Pellegrino Caraviti, 17 aprile 1473). Quoted from Sighinolfi, 'Francesco Puteolano', 456.

34. G. Steiner, 'Source Editions of Ovid's *Metamorphoses*', *TAPA* 82 (1951), 227. See also Steiner, 'The Textual Tradition of the Ovidian Incunabula', *TAPA* 83 (1952), 312–18.

35. Zicàri demonstrates Calfurnio's use of Puteolano but does not mention the personal link between them. For his comparison of the texts of 1–5 in Parma 1473, [Milan] 1475, and Vicenza 1481 see 'Calfurnio', 157–8 (= *Scritti*, 106–7).

36. For the manuscript tradition see pp. 18–19 above. On Puteolano's manuscript as a member of the same group as the Vicentinus [Bibl. Bertoliana G 2 8 12 (216)], see Zicàri, 'Ricerche', 95–6 (= *Scritti*, 99).

37. Zicàri lists some correct readings as well as some errors stemming from Puteolano's manuscript. 'Ricerche', 95–6 (= *Scritti*, 99).

38. Thus, for 92. 3: 'Cui ego quasi eadem totidem mox deprecor illi' (Parma 1473). According to Zicàri, this version of 92. 3 appeared first in Parma 1473, but was later copied into a few manuscripts, notably Cesena, Bibl. Malatestiana 29 *sin*. 19. 'Ricerche', 90, 96 (= *Scritti*, 92, 100). Also see Appendix 3.

39. The archetype read *inventi*, which was corrected by manuscripts

of the γ family to *iuventi* (see Thomson's *apparatus*). But the γ family does not seem to be descended from O (compare Mynors, *Catulli Carmina*, pp. ix–x and Zicàri, 'Ricerche' 80 (= *Scritti*, 80–1)). Professor Thomson suggests that perhaps Puteolano also consulted a non-O type manuscript.

40. For 45 in the *princeps* see n. 25 above.
41. Although the only manuscripts I know of that entitle 96 thus postdate Puteolano's edition: British Library Add. MS 10386 (given a probable date of 1474 by Thomson, *Catullus*, 48–9) and its direct copy, Florence Laurenziana Ashb., and cf. Butrica *The Manuscripts of Propertius*, no. 51. 260.) Both read Galle at 96. 2 and call the epigram *Ad Gallum poetam*.
42. So also with 9 and 10, 58 and 58*b*, 69 and 70, 77 and 78, 78*b* and 79, 94 and 95. Salutati had separated 67, followed by G[2] and M, although the separation did not appear in the *princeps*. (See McKie, *The Manuscripts of Catullus*, 47, 59, 95b.) If Puteolano did not make the separation independently, perhaps it is another indication of his seeing a non-O manuscript. See note 39.
43. The correction was made in manuscripts of the η–θ group (see Thomson's *apparatus*). For these manuscripts see Thomson, *Catullus*, 71–2 and Zicàri, 'Ricerche', 80 (= *Scritti*, 80–1)).
44. The correction seems to have originated in Parma 1473.
45. HC 4759; *BMC* vi. 702–3; *GW* 6387. Its colophon reads: Catulli Tibulli Propertii et liber Silvarum Statii Papinii in isto volumine continentur. Et impressi sunt opere et impensa Iohannis de Colonia et Iohannis Manthen de Ghersem qui una Veneciis fideliter vivunt ([Milan] 1475, 93v). But the colophon does not say the book was printed in Venice, and Phillipus de Lavagnia was a Milanese printer (*BMC* vi. 702–3). Three slight changes in 1–3 are discussed by Zicàri, 'Calfurnio', 157 (= *Scritti*, 106).
46. Copinger 1539; *BMC* iv. 26; *GW* 6388. Goold credits it with only six ('A New Text', 99), but his count does not include corrections of the vulgate text. This is the first edition, for example, to print *Acmen septimius* at 45. 1.
47. HC 4757; *BMC* vii. 1087. This edition contains Tibullus, Catullus, Propertius; its colophon (105v) is dated xix Kal. Octobris 1481.
48. HC 4760; *BMC* vii. 1041; *GW* 6389.
49. A. Albertini, 'Calfurnio Bresciano. La sua edizione di Catullo (1481)', *Commentari dell' Ateneo di Brescia* (1953), 69–72.
50. For Calfurnio and Regio see G. Tiraboschi, *Storia della letteratura italiana* (Florence, 1805) vi. 1049–59 and V. Cian, 'Un umanista bergamasco del Rinascimento. Giovanni Calfurnio', *Archivio*

storico lombardo, 4: 14 (1910), 221–35. Some of the details are given in Mazzuchelli's unedited article on Calfurnio (Vatican Library: Vat. lat. 9263 ff. 192–7v). Calfurnio's younger contemporary Pierio Valeriano sums up the prevailing contemporary view: 'Joannes autem Calphurnius rarissimae vir eruditionis, qui Patavii, me puero, bonas litteras perquamdiu docuerat, nullo umquam tempore non expositus invidorum obtrectationibus, et iniuriis, dum omnia fortiter ferens adversa, uni studet immortalitati . . .' (*De litteratorum infelicitate* (Geneva, 1821), 21).

51. 'At singulis lectionibus quas in frequentissimo Gymnasio Patavino profitetur plures Catulli sensus latentes atque ad hoc aevi non praeceptos in dies (ut dicitur) recognoscit ac edocet. Quae omnia ut habeas et hortor et rogo. Nihil enim ex eius officina non excultissimum prodit' (Hieronymus Avantius, *Emendationes* (Venice, 1495) a 2, cited from Harvard University Inc. 5435). The volume is described in *BMC* v. 530.

52. Cian publishes the inventory made only a few days after Calfurnio's death. It lists 229 volumes: 71 Greek authors (some in Latin translation), 80 classical Latin authors, fewer than a dozen religious works, and the rest humanist writings. Oddly enough, no Catullus appears, but there are two volumes of Statius and one of Propertius that perhaps contained Catullus. The ungrateful monks allowed Calfurnio's library to become dispersed, and by the first half of the seventeenth century Tomasini was able to find only five volumes (J. P. Tomasini, *Bibliothecae patavinae manuscriptae* (Udine, 1639), 21, 25, 26, 27.) See Cian, 'Un umanista bergamasco', 228–31, 236–48.

53. The text of Vicenza 1481 at 47. 2 reads *fauesque mundi memii*.

54. 'Homines aetatis nostrae, Hermolae facundissime, qui litterarum perquam studiosi sunt, mirifice laetari possunt quia in immensam librorum copiam inciderint qua et prisca aetas et ea quae nostram praecessit caruerit. Quae quidem ex impressorum numero tantum crevit ut iam necesse sit non bibliothecas totas sed domos implere. Verum ut inquit poeta ille clarissimus: et urticae proxima saepe rosa est. Non potuit hoc divinum munus ut in humanis accidere solet ex omni parte esse perfectum. Huic enim unum deesse video, diligentem et accuratam librorum castigationem. Sine hac quicquid fit frustra fieri necesse est. Nam et discentibus sensus obscurus et doctis tedium minime tollerandum insurgit . . . Cur autem haec ad te scribam paucis accipe. Superioribus diebus a quibusdam adolescentibus studiosis rogatus ut Propertium aut si nollem hunc Papinii Sylvas lectione quotidiana interpretarer, ne desiderium eorum frustrarer promisi me facturum quod vellent. Quapropter

cum percurrere coepissem id opus quod Venetiis impressum est quod hos poetas clarissimos continet, Catullum, Tibullum, Propertium et Sylvas, tot mendis refertum esse deprendi ut longe plura essent vitiosa et depravata quam quae emendata. Nullus certe sensus ex his elici poterat. Confestim conveni nonnullos impressores et eos cohortatus sum ut iterum id opus imprimerent ea correctione quam pollicitus sum. Possum igitur gloriari me non id emendasse sed fere totum exscripsisse ut quivis deprendere poterit collato utroque exemplari. Statueram tamen nihil negotii cum impressoribus habere quia et ipsi ea quae emendata acceperunt invertere et permutare soleant. Quare si qua praetermissa vel immutata inveneris non mihi ascribito sed impressoribus. Nam plerumque ut dixi vel invertunt syllabas aut aliquas omittunt litteras vel addunt quod relinquendum. Sicut eo loco Catulli, "famesque mundi". Ego "memi" emendaveram. Utramque dictionem impresserunt. Et in eo carmine, "Deprendi modo pupullum puellae", "pupullum" omiserunt. Et in eo versu, "Diverse variae viae reportant", "viae" reliquerunt. Haec tantum notasse contentus ne quis me negligentem fuisse existimet in eo quod ad comunem litteratorum commoditatem editur . . .' (Vicenza 1481 a iv, quoted from Vatican Library, Inc. Ross. 587).

55. For the problem of printers' errors see Lowry, *The World of Aldus Manutius*, 24–47. Calfurnio seems to have had a low opinion of printers in general, for in the postface of his commentary on the *Heautontimoroumenos* (1476) he attacked them for falsifying the authorship of their products to bolster sales; see J. Monfasani, 'Calfurnio's Identification of Pseudepigrapha of Ognibene, Fenestella, and Trebizond, and His Attack on Renaissance Commentaries', *RQ* 41 (1988), 32–43.

56. Calfurnio does not bother to mention, for example, the misprint *fauesque* for *famesque* in the same verse with *mundi memii* (47. 2). Albertini has collected others ('Calfurnio bresciano', 61).

57. No work by Calfurnio after 1481 is listed in Albertini's bibliography ('Calfurnio bresciano', 69–72).

58. Goold, 'A New Text', 99.

59. 'Quis enim ante laboriosissimam Calphurnii castigationem Catulli scripta non stomachosus attingebat?' (Avantius, *Emendationes* 1495, a 2).

60. 'Possum igitur gloriari me non id emendasse sed fere totum exscripsisse . . .' (Vicenza 1481, a iv). For the sense of *exscribo*, 'copy a text', see S. Rizzo, *Il lessico filologico degli umanisti* (Rome, 1973), 181, 200–2.

61. He has separated 45, 46, 47, 52, 70, 71, 83, 84. His important

changes are (corrections printed in modern editions are in boldface): 46. 1 *ver egelidos*; 46. 11 *diverse variae*; 47. 2 *famesque memi*; 54. 5 ***seni recocto***; 71. 1 ***cui***; *virobon*; ***sacer alarum***; 83. 3 ***mule***; 84. 1 ***chommoda***; 84. 2 *hinsidias*; 84. 11 *arius*; 84. 12 ***Hionios***.

62. For the interpretation of 84, see pp. 67–71.

63. Mynors remarks: 'Carmen vix integre traditum' (*apparatus* ad loc.).

64. 'Quum enim Licinius Calvus superius scriptum Catulli in Vatinium carmen in caetu et Corona forensi explicasset quidam fatuus Libo volens poetae ingenium laudare exclamans insulsissima verba effutivit' (Parthenius, ed. 1491, g 6v, quoted from Harvard University Inc. 5029). Partenio divides the poems differently, but prints substantially the same text. He treats 53–54. 3 as a single poem, *Ad Rusticum*, with three textual changes: *e* for *et* (53. 1); *solopechyum* for *solopycium* (53. 5); *suffecio* for *sufficio* (54. 5).

65. This is certainly how Partenio read Calfurnio. He entitles the poem *Ad Virrobonem* and prints *virrobon* in 71. 1, glossing: 'Virrobonem alloquens eum iocose consolatur . . .' (Parthenius, ed. 1491, k 2v). Zicàri argued that Calfurnio imported *viro bon⟨o⟩* into his text from a manuscript. 'Calfurnio', 159 (= *Scritti*, 107–8). The metre requires a phrase of the shape – ∪ ∪ – or – – –; *viro bon⟨o⟩* (∪ – ∪ –) does not do the job.

66. Calfurnio says he was in a hurry to dedicate the work to Ermolao Barbaro and that his friend, the poet Bartolomeus Paiellus, was eager to have it: 'Quod et mentem nostram tibi iampridem dicaverim eo maiori celeritate hoc opus properavimus. Quod Bartolomeus Paiellus vicentinus eques clarissimus et nostri temporis poeta cultissimus ingenti aviditate id perlegere cupiebat' (Vicenza 1481, a 1v). As often, however, the printers may be the source of the haste: 'Hic [Calphurnius] porro quantum humani vires ingenii passae sunt uno mense elaboravit . . . dum quattuor illa poetarum volumina impressoribus festinantibus emendaret' (Avantius, *Emendationes* 1495, a 2).

67. It is not clear whether Calfurnio used the *princeps* or its near double, Milan 1475, often wrongly attributed to Venice. See n. 45 above.

68. The evidence for Calfurnio's use of manuscripts is exiguous. See n. 65 above.

69. For the base text see Kenney, *The Classical Text*, 18–19. On the perpetuation of errors when editors correct and print the text of previous editions see A. Severyns, *Texte et Apparat: Histoire*

critique d'une tradition imprimée (*Mémoires* Acad., Royale de Belgique 66. 2 (1962)) 79: 'Lorsqu'il recopie préalablement son text, l'auteur perpétue deux fois moins de fautes qu'il n'en laisse passer en corrigeant préalablement les feuillets imprimées qui serviront de copie.'

70. The shelf number of Poliziano's copy is Rome, Biblioteca Corsiniana 50. F. 37. See the descriptions of A. Perosa, *Mostra del Poliziano nella Biblioteca Medicea-Laurenziana: manoscritti, libri rari, autografi e documenti. Firenze, 23 Settembre–30 Novembre 1954* (Firenze 1954) 13–16; and I. Maïer, *Les manuscrits d'Ange Politien*, (Geneva, 1962) 361–2. The Catullan annotations are discussed by Maïer, *Ange Politien: la formation d'un poète humaniste* (Geneva, 1966), 116–20, 124–9. The discussion below is largely based on J. H. Gaisser, 'Catullus and his First Interpreters: Antonius Parthenius and Angelo Poliziano', *TAPA* 112 (1982), 83–106. I have made a few additions to the list of Poliziano's corrections, and one deletion (99. 8 *abstersisti*) as a result of a recent inspection of the marginalia.

71. Maïer, *Ange Politien*, 125–9.

72. See p. 72.

73. 'Catullum Veronensem librariorum inscitia corruptum, multo labore multisque vigiliis, quantum in me fuit emendavi, cumque eius poetae plurimos textus contulissem, in nullum profecto incidi qui non itidem ut meus esset corruptissimus. Qua propter non paucis graecis et latinis auctoribus comparatis, tantum in eo recognoscendo opere absumpsi ut mihi videar consecutus quod nemini his temporibus doctorum hominum contigisse intelligerem. Catullus Veronensis, si minus emendatus, at saltem maxima ex parte incorruptus mea opera meoque labore et industria in manibus habeatur! Tu labori boni consule in quantum in te est, quae sunt aut negligentia aut inscitia nostra nunc quoque corrupta, ea tu pro tua humanitate corrige et emenda. Meminerisque Angelum Bassum Politianum, quo tempore huic emendationi extremam imposuit manum annos decem et octo na(tum). Vale iucundissime Lector. Florentiae, MCCCCLXXIII, pridie idus sextiles. Tuus Angelus Bassus Politianus' (Rome, Bibl. Corsiniana 50. F. 37, f. 37).

74. 'Catulli Tibulli Propertiique libellos coepi ego Angelus Politianus iam inde a pueritia tractare, et pro aetatis eius iudicio vel corrigere vel interpretari. Quo fit ut multa ex eis ne ipse quidem satis (ut nunc est) probem. Qui leges, ne quaeso, vel ingeni vel doctrinae vel diligentiae nostrae hinc coniecturam aut iudicium facito. Permulta enim infuerint (ut Plautino utar verbo), me quoque qui

scripsi iudice digna lini. Anno MCCCCLXXXV.' (Rome, Bibl. Corsiniana 50. F. 37, f. 127v.).

75. 'His scriptis, rediit in mentem quod, cum in Catullum commentarium aliquod nostrum petieris, quondam non nihil pueri in Catullum scripsimus; idque tamen qualecumque fuerit marginibus libelli nostri affiximus.

'Et quamquam nonnulla fortasse non inutiliter eruimus, non tamen plane perfectum a nobis est, ut Catullum aut omnino emendatum, aut non alicubi obscurum legere possimus. Sunt et nonnulla puerilia, neque satis erudita tritisque auribus digna. Quapropter nondum editione dignum putavi. Siquis tamen inciderit nodus quem tu non ita per te facile solvere potueris, scribito ad nos ubique quantum in nobis erit, bonam operam exhibebimus. Siqua autem nos fugerint patiere, quae tua est humanitas, non iniquo animo et te nobiscum ignorare. Atque tamen vereor ne cum nostras ineptias petis, nos illudas, Alexander, utpote qui et per te ipsum quidem tantum ingenio valeas quantum non facile dixerim et domi Jovianum habeas qui unus multorum instar doctorum hominum sit habendus. Iterum vale' (L. D'Amore, *Epistole inedite di Angelo Poliziano (Lettere latine estratte dal codice Vaticano-Capponiano 235)* (Naples, 1909) 32–3 (= I. Maïer (ed.), *Angelus Politianus Opera Omnia* (Torino, 1971), iii. 502–3.

76. Rizzo, *Lessico*, 262–3.

77. For chronology and a biographical summary see E. Bigi, 'Ambrogini, Angelo, detto Poliziano', *DBI* (Rome, 1960), 691–702; Maïer, *Ange Politien*, 419–38. Rizzo discusses Poliziano's development as a textual critic; see especially *Lessico* 263.

78. Parma 1473 (Puteolano); [Milan] 1475; [Rome 1475]; Vicenza 1481 (Calfurnio); Reggio 1481; Brescia 1485 (Partenio). Partenio's colophon appears dated variously: 6 April 1485, 6 April 1486, 21 April 1486, 21 May 1485. It is impossible to know if Poliziano could have seen the edition before writing his subscription in 1485, since he does not mention the month.

79. There is an element of doubt in the case of Avanzi. Since the *Emendationes* (published in 1495) were completed in October 1493 and certainly in circulation for several months before his death in September 1494, Poliziano could have seen or heard of some of Avanzi's corrections and added the ones he approved to his text. On the other hand, he was very busy in the last year or so of his life, and, since Avanzi and his friends were angered by his attacks on Domizio Calderini in the *Miscellanea*, he might not have been informed of Avanzi's work. For Poliziano's activities in 1493–4 see Maïer, *Ange Politien*, 436–8. For Avanzi and the *Emendationes* see pp. 52–65.

80. On the availability of T in Italy in the fifteenth century see Richardson, 'Pucci, Parrasio and Catullus', *IMU* 19 (1976) 285–6.
81. On R and the R³ additions see Thomson, 'A New Look', 35.
82. Among his restorations of the archetype is that of 3. 4, present in O, G, and R, but omitted from all the editions before the first Aldine. He adds the verse thus: *passer delicium meae puellae*.
83. He has drawn a line not through *si* but under it.
84. Partenio is the first to print *maestius* (Brescia 1485/6). Palladius first deletes *ac* (Venice 1496), although Avanzi toys with the idea (*Emendationes* 1495, a 2v).
85. F. Tateo, 'Coccio, Marcantonio, detto Sabellico', *DBI* 26 (Rome, 1982), 510–15; C. Nauert, 'Plinius,' *CTC* iv. 344–8. For Sabellico and Bessarion's library see Lowry, *The World of Aldus Manutius*, 36–8.
86. 'Subtexam nunc ex lepidissimi Catulli carmine quam paucissima, nec ipsa ut aperte dicam magni admodum momenti, quoniam ad hunc diem non defuerunt qui sedula in vetustissimum poetam opera consecuti sint, ut non adeo multa in eo desiderarentur, atque ex illis ipsis quaedam quae consulto praeterita videri possint; sed sint illa quantumlibet levia, quia ad lectionis emendationem attinent, pro apendice alteri centuriae adiiciam. Eritque hoc ipsum admonere lectorem non docere, etenim quae in coniectura posita sunt, sciebam non temere recipi solere. Nemo enim non libentius si opinione certandum sit suo et si minus sit probabile quam alterius optimo acquiescit iudicio. Sed qui in haec inciderint boni consulant' (Sabellicus, *Annotationes* [1497], 10, quoted from Rome, Biblioteca Angelica Inc. 43).
87. Nauert has dated Sabellico's dedication and notes on Pliny between 1487 and 1493. Nauert, 'Plinius', *CTC* iv. 344–5.
88. 64. 25 *taedis* (*tedis* is read in O). 64. 106 *conigeram*. Palladio prints both readings without acknowledging Sabellico. Poliziano's marginalia include the correction *tedis* (in manuscripts of the θ group).
89. 'pro *gravis* carminis lege compulsus *Caius* libens reposueram, quod et fidei minus profligatae codices quidam habent' (*Annotationes* [1497], 10).
90. Contrast Beroaldo's precision with Sabellico's woolly explanation in the previous note: 'Namque in hendecasyllabo claudicat ille versus clauditione secundi pedis manifestaria: *Cinna est gravis, is sibi paravit*. Igitur legendum: *Cinna est Caius* . . . Quod autem *Caius* trisyllaba sit, et faciat dactylum, etiam pueri sciunt . . .' (*Annotationes centum in varios auctores* (Bologna, 1488) c 2v).
91. 'Mirabar quae tanta librariorum fuisset incuria, immo quae peritorum seu ignavia seu negligentia, quod locum insignem passi

essent contra metri rationem diutius versiculis illis haerere . . . *Novissem* enim vulgo in his notatum video, sed videant alii an *novissime* aptius legi possit, cui sane lectioni neque sensus neque syllabae repugnat natura' (Sabellicus, *Annotationes* [1497], 10).

92. Parma 1473 and Reggio 1481 read *novissimo*.

93. '*in tuo* . . . reperio . . . Quare ne gravetur lector advertere an *in tutu* sit potius dicendum . . .' (Sabellicus, *Annotationes* [1497], 10).

94. 'apparet Catullum poetam non *in meis* sed *invicem* potius scripsisse' (Sabellicus, *Annotationes* [1497] 10v).

95. 'Num tam secure et ociose aliquis Catulli carmen adierit ut *amariores calices* arbitretur vetustissimum poetam a pincerna sibi misceri in resoluta voluptate petierit quasi amarum pro suavi aut fumoso metri necessitate coactus sit scribere? Ego quia neque Flaccum Horatium neque Martialem aut alium quempiam urbanorum eiusmodi usurpatione usum reperio aut inepte ut mihi videor ausim *meratiores* inibi pro *amariores* reponere, tum quia vocis ratio est frequentior apud illos quorum modo memini, tum etiam ob ea quae e vestigio subiiciuntur *ad vos quolibet habite lymphae vini pernities* [27. 5–6]. Caeterum id quoque admonere sit non legem cuiquam scribere. Integrum erit per me omnibus utrumlibet tenere' (Sabellicus, *Annotationes* [1497], 10).

96. As in 94, 105, 114, 115. For the interpretation of these poems, see pp. 102–8 below.

97. 'Quum nihil minus salse et ut sic dicam eleganter dici potuisset quam si ad unum Caesarem scribens *ista vestra* pro *tua* dixisset, vide igitur ne ille vesca (ed. *nesca*) potius quasi edax scriptum reliquerit et illud *παραινέσεος* vim habuerit. Videri eodem loco duo epigrammata simili figura et in unius invidiam perfecta librariorum inscitia in unum convaluisse' (Sabellicus, *Annotationes* [1497], 10).

98. 'Num metricae rationis gnarus quispiam in sapphico illo endecasyllabo ad Furium (ed., *Turium*) et Aurelium tam leviter librariae fidei accesserit ut *seu saccas* legat *sagittiferosque parthos* quemadmodum omnia habent Catulli exemplaria an potius illud sequetur: *seu sacas partosque feros sagittis*?' (Sabellicus, *Annotationes* [1497], 10).

99. 'Subest carmen Saphicum in quo Catullus ex veterum more ter admisit Trocheum in secunda sede. At viri alioquin et eloquentia et summa eruditione praecellentes veronensium omnium amantissimique reformant versum illum . . . et illum versum . . . Caeterum quum *aite* sit dictio non quadrans, quum item alii eadem sede abusi fuerint, quumque inferius passim legatur, *otium*

Catulle tibi molestum est, nec a quopiam hactenus iste versus secus legatur, labori parcant admonerem, immo utrosque priores versus loco suo restituerem. Hanc enim licentiam [ed., *licetiam*] prius usurparunt Graeci et in primis Saphos Pindarusque' (Avantius, *Emendationes* 1495, a 3v). See also Raven, *Latin Metre*, 143–4.

100. 'illud affirmare non dubitarim parum accurate a plerisque coniunctim legi proximum epigramma cum eo quod tutius est summae principium, *Lugete o iuvenes*, quod et materia utraque ab altera diversa et suum in utriusque calce acumen altius intuentibus demonstrat' (Sabellicus, *Annotationes* [1497] 10).

101. *Credit* (e.g., on 16, 25, 106): 'Aliter reponitur istud emistichium, *illaque haud alia*, et tunc intellectus illustrior est. Huius lectionis auctor est Marcus Antonius Sabellus, non poetice minus quam historia praecellens, qui etiam plaeraque alia probe reformat, ut *teque adeo eximie taedis foelicibus aucte*, non autem *tethydis*. idem legit ibidem *Conigeram pinum*, non *cornigeram*' (Avantius, *Emendationes* 1495, a 4).

Correction: '[on 10. 16] cave ne legas ut nuper impressum legimus *ad lecticam hominum* c. ii. deficeret enim syllaba et sensus esset puerilis' (*Emendationes* 1495 a 2v). For another example see n. 99 above on 11. 6 and 15.

102. Palladio prints only the readings approved by Avanzi. He claims *male* (14. 5), *thedis* (64. 25), *conigeram* (64. 106), and *infecti* (64. 253)—each time with the formula *emendo*. He also paraphrases Sabellico's explanations of 34. 8 and 64. 159. Palladius, *In Catullum Commentarii* (Venice, 1496) *ad loc*. Palladio and Sabellico were old acquaintances, and some of their correspondence is preserved. See M. A. Sabellicus, *Epistolae familiares* in *Opera* (Venice, 1502), 10r–v, 32r–v, 48. The tone is cordial, but Sabellico, at least, was capable of being disingenuous: even as he claimed to be supporting Palladio to succeed him as professor of rhetoric in Udine (1483), he was writing to the citizens of Udine on behalf of another candidate. *Epistolae familiares*, 5r–v. See also J. H. Gaisser, 'Catullus', *CTC* vii, 242.

103. Pucci's autograph has not been identified. Eighteen apographs of his notes have been identified, and no doubt more remain to be discovered; they were still being copied in the middle of the sixteenth century. See Gaisser, 'Catullus', pp. 243–9. For his notes see F. Calonghi, 'Marginalia', *Miscellanea Pandiani* (Genoa, 1921), 97–114; Richardson 'Pucci, Parrasio and Catullus'; J. Butrica, 'Pontanus, Puccius, Pocchus, Petreius, and Propertius', *Res Publica Litterarum*, 3 (1980), 5–9. At least two of Sabellico's readings are found in one apograph, Göttingen, Universitäsbiblio-

thek, MS philol. 111 (a copy of Vicenza 1481): *meratiores* (27. 2) and *vesca* (29. 13).

104. Surprisingly little is known about Avanzi apart from the information to be gleaned from his prefaces. He was born in Verona, and became a professor of moral philosophy at Padua, and a doctor of arts and medicine. He edited various Latin poets and died sometime after 1534. For the fact that he took his doctorate *in artibus* at Padua in July 1494 see B. Nardi, *Saggi sull'aristotelismo padovano dal secolo XIV al XVI* (Florence, 1958), 159. The most complete source is still Cosenza, *Dictionary of Italian Humanists*, i. 349–50, v. 162–3. For further references see R. Avesani, 'Doctos viros tu aliis gentibus dedisti', in *Verona e il suo territorio* (Verona, 1984) IV. ii. 195–6, n. 1. Avanzi is not mentioned in *DBI*.

105. For a brief discussion of Aldo and Avanzi see C. Dionisotti, *Aldo Manuzio Editore* (Milan, 1975), vol. i. pp. xxxv–xxxvi.

106. See the important study of C. Dionisotti, 'Calderini, Poliziano e altri', *IMU* 11 (1968), 151–79.

107. See R. Weiss, 'In memoriam Domitii Calderini', *IMU* 3 (1960), 309–21.

108. 'Scribis Augustini eruditorum humanissime tibi renunciatum esse quemadmodum hac publica studiorum remissione sepositis altioribus studiis Valerii [*ed.* Vallerii] Catulli lusus retractem, rogasque ut tibi Catullianas dictiones mancas aut inversas seu epigrammata incautius congesta transverso calamo illinire velim' (Avantius, *Emendationes* 1495, a 2).

109. 'In calce epistolae tuae pleraque inquiris loca non a me qui vix per triennium in haec studia incubuerim ac eadem iam dudum sequestraverim, sed depromenda a viro magnam cui mentem animumque Delius inspiret vates. . . . Quare quom quae supra annotavimus ad te mittere maturuissem decrevi rem hanc paululum differre ut aliquibus quaesitis tuis (nam eorum multa superius enarrata invenies) a me uberius satisfactum iret' (Avantius, *Emendationes* 1495, a 5).

110. 'The absence of woodcut capitals . . . suggests that the tract belongs to the latter part of 1495' (*BMC* v. 530). Tacuinus suspended his use of the capitals from August 1495 until April 1496 (*BMC* v. 527).

111. 'Tuis igitur optatis inhiens Benacum accessi non studio visendi lacum alioquin amoenissimum sed ut convenirem Paulum Calderinum quem certe avunculus eius non minus Angeli Politiani probris indignus quam eiusdem Angeli laudibus dignissimus et rerum et virtutum heredem constituit. . . . Hic Paulus octo diebus

haud secus me detinuit ac si syrenios scopulos immoratus fuissem' (Avantius, *Emendationes* 1495, a 5).

112. 'Nescio cur Pheacum cur Hesperidum hortos cur Elisios campos cooptet qui iuga haec incolat' (Ibid.).

113. 'in eius montis olentissimis herbis fragrantissimo vertice cum Paulo meo ex his quae cunctabaris multa una advertimus. Ipse quidem plura probe vidit, plurima optime recognovit. Quod tamen nec multa me admiratione afficit: hic avunculi fere omnes libros (si septem cadaveris comites excipias) tam graecis quam nostris litteris nactus est, quos quom intuetur quasi praeceptorem semper invenit' (Ibid. a 5v).

114. 'nihil ultra sed iure illachrimans' (Ibid.).

115. 'Iis igitur institutionibus ac praeclaris monumentis Paulus imbutus quid ignorabit . . .' (Ibid.).

116. 'Nostras has in Catullum meditiunculas huic ostendimus ac placuisse sic gratulamur ut aliorum iudicium aliquando subiturus sim' (Ibid.).

117. 'Tua enim interest iis scriptis (qualiacunque sint) patrocinari quae tuis praescriptis obsequentissime cudimus . . . Revise precor his praesertim quasi halcyonidum diebus mansuetissimas ac nobis quondam familiares amoenissimasque musas, nostrasque has meditatiunculas (si digna deposcimus) perlegas recognoscas atque pro arbitrio castiges' (Ibid. a 6v).

118. For the Loggia see M. T. Cuppini, 'L'arte a Verona tra i secoli xv e xvi' in *Verona e il suo territorio*, iv. 1 (Verona, 1981), 261–75.

119. Avanzi itemizes the Veronese contribution to Catullan studies in *Emendationes* 1495, a 2. For the contributors to Calderini's collection see Weiss, 'In memoriam Domitii Calderini'.

120. 'Cui ad temporum iniuriam ne id quidem defore potuit, quominus a litteratoribus quibusdam stigmatibus ineluibilibus inureretur. O miserandam lepidissimi poetae fortunam! Quis enim indolere vehementius non debeat eas humani generis delitias tenebrosis quorundam erroribus interpretatiunculisque adeo obductas ut contra eos iure ac merito dicere possimus id quod de se vates ipse lepidissimus vaticinatus est: "At vobis male sit malae tenebrae Orci quae omnia bella devoratis. Tam bellum mihi passerem abstulistis. O factum male, o miselle passer [3. 13–16]"' (Avantius, *Emendationes* 1495, a 1v).

121. For Poliziano's interpretation of the sparrow see pp. 75–8.

122. 'Verum enimvero rerum natura parens diutius tantam iacturam non sustinens quom aliquandiu poeta iucundissimus situ marcoreque squaleret quo modo tandem hunc etiam in lucem reduceret enixa est. Idest ut civium ipsius inveniretur aliquis, qui eum et a

barbarie vindicaret et ubi aliqua vel mendosa vel abstrusa essent, emendaret explicaret atque digereret. Is est Hieronymus Avantius Veronensis cuius vigiliae eximiaque in civem suum pietas id tandem effecisse perspiciuntur ut ex obscuro nitidum ex lacero solidum et ex barbaro denique Latinum denuo efficeret' (Avantius, *Emendationes* 1495, a 1v).

123. Poliziano discussed poems 2–3; 17. 19; 66. 48; 66. 94; 74; 84; 98. 4. See pp. 67–77. Avanzi does not mention his discussions of 74 and 98. 4.

124. 'nisi Calderinum nimia libidine damnasset eius scripta non sedulo animadvertissem . . .' (Avantius, *Emendationes* 1495 a 4v). And again in the discussion of 92, where he contrasts the generosity of Filippo Beroaldo with Poliziano's ingratitude: 'quo magis pudeat virum illum qui quom iam quindecim annis plurimis doctis viris se editurum centuriam ut ipse dictitabat (per egregiam) pollicitus fuerit, hanc nuper emisit, in qua eum potissimum mordet ac lacerat cuius tamen annotationibus in achademia Romana publice dictatis centuriam suam faleratam (ut sic dicam) reddidit' (Ibid. a 5).

125. 'Miror cur in duobus locis Catullianis a me qui vix haec studia delibaverim animadversis adeo inconsulte locutus sit Politianus ille, qui cives meos nulla adhibita modestia laceret seque unum ex Apollinis praescriptis profari censeat. Non igitur *expernata* nec *supernata* sed *separata* legerem' (Avantius, *Emendationes* 1495, a 3v). In *Misc.* 73 Poliziano suggested only *expernata*, but by 1492 *supernata* also seems to have been associated with him. See Marullo's *Epig.* 3. 39 quoted in n. 126. *Suppernata* is found, as Thomson reminds me, in the marginal notes of Poliziano's student, Pucci (see Thomson's *apparatus criticus* ad loc.). See also pp. 74–5 and Chapter 2 n. 34. The second passage Avanzi refers to is 2–3, where he has disagreed with Poliziano's obscene interpretation of the sparrow.

126. Raven, *Latin Metre*, 140. Avanzi's metrical objection may have been inspired by Marullo's epigram, *In Ecnomum* [= Politianum]: 'Quid separatam, vane, supernas, rogo, / Alnum Catulli nobilem,/ Plebi otiosae scilicet risum parans, / Oblitus ut soles pedis?.' Michele Marullo, *Epig.* 3. 39. Marullo wrote his epigrams against Poliziano before April 1492. See A. Perosa (ed.), *Michaelis Marulli Carmina* (Turici, 1951), p. x; and A. Perosa, 'Studi sulla formazione delle raccolte di poesie del Marullo', *Rinascimento* 1. 2 (1950–1), 137.

127. 'Quare in sequenti versu lege *quasi* . . . unica dictione non autem *quam si* . . .' (Avantius, *Emendationes* 1495, a 3v). He adds the

explanation in the second edition – the *i* in *quasi* may be long or short: '*quasi* enim indifferens est' (Avantius *Emendationes* 1500, a 2v).

128. Avanzi thus dates his first efforts with Catullus at least as early as 1490, since by that date Badoer was already governor in Padua. See G. Cracco, 'Badoer, Sebastiano' *DBI* (Rome, 1963), v. 126.

129. At this point Avanzi launches into a catalogue of Paduan and (mostly) Veronese scholars who have improved the text of Catullus (or have the ability to do so), beginning with Calfurnio and ending with Partenio, who rushed his commentary into print, and is now repairing the damage.

130. 'Priusquam philosophorum sacris initiarer, impensissime (haud vera tacebo) conatus sum Catulliana plaeraque loca abstrusissima percipere ac potissimum vatem hunc a syllabarum praevaricatione qua maxime notabatur vindicare. Caeterum tunc tenuitate ingenii vix quadraginta loca aut paulo plura perversa offenderam ac anxius restitueram, ut coram te annotavimus eo die quo patavinam praefecturam inivit Sebastianus Baduarius nostrorum studiorum recidivum decus ac singulare ornamentum. Nunc quum intermissis severioribus studiis in agellum meum (ut apud me essem) secedere vellem, Christoforus Papallis iuvenis nonminus poetice quam legum peritus Catullum satis bonae vetustatis mihi sub certa fide commendavit; inibi dum singula regustarem ac diligentius perscrutarer conferremque exemplaria et meum praesertim iamdiu manu exaratum, nonnulla alia restitui loca. Qua industria id effeci ut me haud laboris poeniteat. . . . Ego interim ut pro viribus nostris tibi mos geratur, quicquid vel ex veterum codicum praesidio vel ex assidua nostra versuum libratione observaverim brevibus explicabo. Non enim omnium rationes subiiciam. . . . Omne Catulliani carminis genus seorsum percurram atque ut plenius optatis tuis obtemperem non modo syllabarum quantitatem pensitabo verum pravas descriptiones [corrected to *dictiones* in 1500 edn.] simul exarabo. Prima sede phaleutii hendecasyllabi ac secunda sede saphyci versus Catullus abutitur. Alias si unum tantum corruptum epigramma excipias syllabarum fuit observantissimus' (Avantius, *Emendationes* 1495, a 2).

131. Rizzo, *Lessico*, 69–71, 211–12. Several of the readings so identified appear in none of the editions, e.g. 2. 9 *ipse*, 2*b*. 3 *negatam*, 63. 31 *animo egens*, 64. 139 *calasti*. One, however, seems to have originated with Venice 1472: 14. 5 *male*.

132. Of the readings Avanzi credits to one or both of his manuscripts, the following (and perhaps others as well) appear in no earlier printed source (an * marks those accepted by Mynors): 2. 9 *ipse*;

2*b*. 3 *negatam*; 3. 17 *vestra* (accepted by Thomson in his forthcoming edition); *3. 18 *rubent*; 9. 4 *sanamque*; 29. 8 *an ydoneus*; 35. 18 *Caecilia*; *39. 12 *Lanuvinus*; 63. 31 *animo egens*; 64. 319 *calasti*; 66. 94 *fulguret*. The R readings are 2*b*. 3 *negatam* and 3. 18 *rubent* (see McKie, *The Manuscripts of Catullus*, 5–6).

133. The corrections are: the separation of 2 and 3; *male* for *malis* at 14. 5; *Cornifici* for *carnifici* at 38. 1; separation of 42 from 41; *qui* for *quid* at 81. 5. Thus: 'Imprimis codex meus carmen passeris . . . seiungit . . . ut agnovit Sabellus noster' (Avantius, *Emendationes* 1495, a 2); 'lege . . . *male* [14. 5] pro *malis*. Sic habent codices et antiqui et sine commentariis impressi' (a 2v); 'Idem error [*Carnifici* for *Cornifici* at 38. 1] omnes codices quos adhuc viderim si meum excipias invasit . . .' (a 2v); 'Sequens versus [42. 1] in codice meo est principium seiuncti epigrammatis' (a 2v); 'Inde unus codex meus habet *qui* [81. 5] . . .' (a 5v). As far as we know, however, the sources are Sabellico, Venice 1472 (14. 5), Avanzi (38. 1, separation of 42), and Calfurnio (81. 5).

134. e.g. the omissions of *fallere* in 30. 3 and *sic* in 86. 2.

135. 'Nec tamen postliminio habendus est Catullus quod hac licentia abusus fuerit. Nam tempori hoc tribuendum est' (Avantius, *Emendationes* 1495 a 6v). For Catullus' licence and the ancient reactions to it, see pp. 10–11.

136. Vergil was often identified as the author of the *Priapea*, but Avanzi disagrees: 'meo quidem iuditio fuit multorum poetarum farrago' (Avantius, *Emendationes* 1500, o 3).

137. 'At quom postremo quaeras an me iudice liceat nobis in faleucio endecasyllabo abuti primo pede ut Catullus solet, pace aliorum dixerim, nequaquam decet. Cui enim non iure illudetur quom hic sibi enianam licentiam usurpet. Esto veneranda nuncupatione vatum pater cantitetur Ennius, Ennio namque atque id genus viris tunc multa licebant. At eadem temporibus nostris adeo desueta sunt ut qui eorum minimum abusum affectet omnium aures simul et stomachum offendat. Quod autem noster ille citet Priapeiarum auctoritatem . . . Caeterum si perspiciet intimius, non modo in prima sede falecii apud Maronem pedem alium a spondeo non reperiret, sed in toto Priapeiarum opusculo alioquin obscenissimo nullam syllabam perperam positam inveniet, nisi Maro (ut vulgo fit) ex prava inscriptione legatur. Ego enim ut hanc rem penitus perciperem totam hanc Maronis paginam perlegi ac fere omnium syllabarum quantitatem ponderavi omniumque dictionum inversionem depravationemque accommodavi, quae omnia tibi explicare constitui . . .' (Avantius, *Emendationes* 1495, a 5v–a 6).

138. 'In iambico autem carmine hanc dignitatem consecutus est

Catullus. Nunquam enim recepit pedem alium ab iambo in secunda et quarta sede, quod hoc carminis genus maxime requirit, ut docet Horatius . . .' (Avantius, *Emendationes* 1495, a 3).

139. 'Inter alia quaero ut praedixi ut omnes intelligant cur Martialis dixerit, *Verona docti syllabas amat Vatis*. Syllabarum enim observantissimus fuit Catullus si recte eius carmina scribantur, quod hodie non observatur. Quis enim non rideat huius aevi inscitiam vel saltem segnitiem? Omnes codices impressi habent *aut Lavinius acer*, quom legendum sit *Lanuvinus* [*ed*. Lanuvinis, corrected to Lanuvinus in *Emendationes 1500*]. Antiqui utrique codices habebant *lanuvinus*, sed contra suppositum est hoc importunum nec quadrans verbum, s. *Lavinius*, itaque in similibus versibus tunc Catulli licentiam immo abusum adducit ignavum hominum genus parum pensitans, ac omni quantumlibet absona lectione contentum' (Avantius, *Emendationes* 1495, a 3r–v).

140. One Catullan refinement seems to have eluded Avanzi. Cat. 4 and 29 are in *pure* iambic trimeters. See Chapters 3 and 6, pp. 123–4 and 255–71.

141. *Emendations*, e.g. 4. 3 *impetum trabis*; 8. 9 ⟨*noli*⟩; 44. 20 *mi*; 59. 1 *Rufulum*. *Corrections to the base text*. e.g.: *8. 3 *candidi tibi*; 8. 9 *nunc iam*; *29. 16 *helluatus est*; *29. 22 *uncta*; 37. 13 *mihi sunt*; 39. 3 *orator excitat*; 39. 12 *Lanuvinus*; *59. 2 *sepulchretis*. An * marks readings found earlier in the printed tradition, but not in Calfurnio or Partenio.

142. 'Versus dissimiles sunt. Nam primi sunt scazones. Interdum interponitur hendecasyllabus. Non nulli vero depravati ut opinor ac corrupti dimensione carent' (Parthenius 1491, g 3v).

143. The faulty verses are 38. 3 and 7. He has created the problem in 38. 7 by changing the traditional and correct *paulum* to *paululum*.

144. 'Hic poetae in Egnatium iracundia excandescit, quia quum esset in luctu ac moerore Egnatius ad ipsum accedens consolandi gratia risus et cachinnos effudit' (Parthenius 1491 g 3v).

145. 'versus qui et confunduntur et unico epigrammate congeruntur sic reponendi sunt. Primo versum illum *male est cornifici tuo Catullo* cum septem sequentibus versibus. Scripsit Catullus ad Cornificium seposito carmine phaleucio endecasyllabo' (Avantius, *Emendationes* 1495, a 3). Avanzi should have stopped there, but he goes on to place 37. 17–20 after 39. 9—an arrangement that was to prevail until the edition of Muret (1554).

146. Goold's census credits him with 37 emendations, but the number includes emendations made in the second edition of the *Emendationes* and in the 1535 edition of Catullus. Goold, 'A New Text', 99.

147. Although he did not know what to do with 53–55, he saw at least

that the extra verses after 54. 11 should be removed: 'Utinam scirem liberare Catullum a carminum sequentium confusione. Reor omnino corruptos codices' (Avantius, *Emendationes* 1495, a 3). He divides into 3 poems: 53–54. 1, 54. 2–5 (corrupt and incomplete), 54. 6–55.

148. 'Haec omnia sunt ex exemplaribus emendatis domini Hieronymi Avancii' (Venice, 1500, f. 1). The edition is described in *BMC* v. 535. It includes the commentaries of Partenio and Palladio on Catullus. The number of corrections from the *Emendationes* is surely under ten. I have counted three: 4. 24 *novissime*, 61. 196 *iuverit*, 64. 25 *thedis*.

149. *Additions*: e. g. *62. 9 *par est*; 63. 18 *herae*; 64. 96 *golgos*; *64. 108 *radicitus*; 68. 109 *Phenum*; 93. 2 *scire* (Avanzi attributes to Partenio); 106. 1 *cum puero bello*. (An * marks corrections to the base text; the rest are emendations.) *Changes*: e. g. 63. 55 omits *in* (insisted on in 1495); 66. 63 *deum me* (vs. *decume* read in his manuscript); 66. 79 *quas* (vs. *quae* of his manuscript). His most interesting change is at 64. 178: 'Parthenius legit *ideos ne petam montes* . . . legebam olim ut scis *Isthmiacos ne petam pontes*. Nunc haereo' (Avantius, *Emendationes* 1500, o 2v). But *Isthmiacos . . . pontes* is not mentioned in the first edition.

150. e.g. 63. 34 *propero pede* (not in modern editions); 64. 75 *gortynia*; 71. 1 *iure*, 72. 7 *qui*. Avanzi frequently corrects Palladio, but is harsh only in a long note on 68. 99: 'In hoc versu *obscoena* ultimam producit non tantum per pentimemerin quam ratione consonantium sequentis dictionis, unde miror quosdam me carpentes quod in priori editione ego ut inquiunt syllabarum librator non emendarim *propontida trucemve ponticum sinum* [4. 9], *propontidem* . . .' (Avantius, *Emendationes*, 1500, o 3). On *Propontida* Palladio had said: 'Sic habent exemplaria. Ego autem emendo *propontidem*. Nam si aliter legas versus non stat cum in secunda sede non ponatur nisi iambus' (Palladius, 1496 a 4).

151. 'Delectabit te praeterea quod longe alius, quam qui erat, videbitur ob multas emendationes, et versus, tum additos, tum in pristinum locum restitutos' (Aldus in Venice 1502, a 1v). cf. Avanzi: 'Quam industriam nostram qui alios codices contulerit, agnoscet' (Venice, 1502, f 2v).

152. Goold's census credits Venice 1502 with 18 emendations ('A New Text', 99). There are also some changes in the *dispositio carminum*: e.g., 41 and 42 are printed together (*De Acme*); 66 is separated (*De Coma Berenices*); 53–54. 5 are printed together (*De quodam et Calvo*), but in *Emendationes* 1500, Avanzi had abandoned any attempt to divide 53–55.

The edition also includes some of Avanzi's bad ideas from the *Emendationes* and abandons some of his good ones. *Bad ideas included*: e.g. 11. 1 *inter coenam Asini*; 17. 20 *quasi*; 22. 11 *nutat*; 37. 17–20 placed after 39. 9. *Good ideas abandoned*: e.g. 8. 9 ⟨*noli*⟩; 9. 2 *antistans*; 10. 15 *esse*; separation of 42 from 41. Avanzi and Aldo placed an asterisk beside controversial readings, promising to provide variants, but the list of variants was not included in the edition. An asterisk is found in some of the places where Avanzi's reading from the *Emendationes* has not been used.

153. For Aldus' editions generally see Lowry, *The World of Aldus Manutius*, 141–51. For the size of the press run, cf. 'Idem et in Tibullo et in Propertio fecimus, quos ad tria millio voluminum, et plus eo hac minima forma excusos, in manus tuas, et caeterorum, commode, assidueque una cum Catullo et ire et redire speramus' (Venice 1502, a iv). See also Lowry, *The World of Aldus Manutius*, 174 n. 96, 257; and H. G. Fletcher III, *New Aldine Studies* (San Francisco, 1988), 100–2.

154. 'Aldus Manutius noster . . . ex codice Catulliano per me miro studio et incredibili labore olim emendato tria exemplorum millia politis typis impressurus, me iterum ad hanc operam socio usus est' (Venice 1502, f 2v).

NOTES TO CHAPTER 2

1. Commentaries on the other three poets appeared in 1475: Tibullus, by Bernardinus Cyllenius (HC 15522); Statius and Propertius, by Domitius Calderinus (HC 14983).
2. For the language used to describe Catullus' condition, cf. the remarks of Augustinus Olomucensis quoted on p. 56 and Parthenius: 'Catullum nostrum miserabiliter disiectum et exanimem . . . vix spirantem ac male pedibus innixum . . .' (Parthenius, 1491 f. 1). On the necromantic imagery see T. Greene, *The Light in Troy* (New Haven, Conn., 1982), 92 and *passim*. For the importance of Catullus in Verona see p. 56.
3. 'ut ingenue fateretur, se plus eo die ab uno scholastico didicisse, quam multis ante annis a quopiam professorum' (Poliziano, *Miscellanea* i. 19, in *Opera omnia* ed. I. Maïer (Torino, 1971), i. 243). For the date see Maïer, *Ange Politien*, 122. For Poliziano and Catullus see Gaisser, 'Catullus and his First Interpreters'.
4. 'ita pronis auribus nostra illa qualiacunque accipientes, ut identidem clamarent demissum coelitus Angelum sibi (sic enim aiebant) qui poetam conterraneam interpretaretur' (Angelo Poliziano,

Miscellanea i. 19, in *Opera* i. 243). For the date see Maïer, *Ange Politien*, 423.

5. For 83 and 84 in the *princeps* see pp. 29–30.
6. See Introduction, p. 11.
7. 'Parcissime ea veteres usi etiam in vocalibus, cum *aedos ircos*que dicebant; diu deinde servatum, ne consonantibus aspirarent, ut in *Graccis* et in *triumpis*; erupit brevi tempore nimius usus, ut *choronae*, *chenturiones*, *praechones* adhuc quibusdam in inscriptionibus maneant, qua de re Catulli nobile epigramma est.' The text and translation are those of H. E. Butler in the Loeb edition (London, 1921).
8. 'Putamus autem epigramma citari hoc potissimum . . . Quare si constare tibi Catulliani epigrammatis leporem voles aspirationem ipsam suo loco, quantum poteris, pronunciabis' (Poliziano, *Miscellanea* i. 19, in *Opera* i. 242.
9. *Differences*: 84. 2 *hinsidias Arrius*; 84. 7 *requierunt*; 84. 9 *post illa*.
10. 'Sed ista video iam sic innotuisse, ut aliena fortasse cuipiam videri possint' (Poliziano, *Miscellanea* i. 19, in *Opera* i. 242–3.
11. 84. 1 *Chommoda*; 84. 2 *hinsidias arius*; 84. 12 *hionios*.
12. 'Catulli enim veronensis ac Ciceronis temporibus erupit abusus quidam aspirandi. Nam et *praechonem* et *chenturionem* et *chenturiam* et *choronam* quidam malebant. Cuius enim rei etiam meminit Quintilianus: idque damnasse Catullum suo quodam epigrammate tradit. Quod et si integrum apud nos hodie non extat ex uno tamen atque altero illius versiculo facile potest intelligi. Reprehenditur enim quidam qui *chommoda dicebat si quando commoda vellet dicere*, et *insidias acrius insidias*, et de eodem: *et tum mirifice sperabat se esse locutum cum quantum poterat dixerat hinsidias*. Vides igitur quosdam contra omnem rationem voluisse *chommodum* cum aspiratione pronuntiare necnon et *hinsidias* et *hionium*, ut hic idem poeta eodem irridet epigrammate: *Ionios fluctus postquam illuc appulit ipse non iam ionios esse sed hionios*' (J. Jovianus Pontanus, *Liber de Aspiratione* (Naples, 1481), quoted from BL IB.29419, e5 r–v). Although *De aspiratione* was printed in 1481, it was in circulation from 1469 on: see R. Fabbri, 'Approcci umanistici a Catullo', *Materiali e Discussioni per l'analise dei testi classici*, 19 (1987), 176–9.
13. 'Arium verba latina barbare aspirando pronunciantem ac consonantes et vocales literas pleno ac crasso spiritu magnoque aspirationis afflatu praeter grammatices rationem praeterque latinitatis usus cum intolerabili audientium fastidio proferentem ioco risuque Catullus insectatur' (Parthenius, 1491, k 1).

14. I am not convinced by Fabbri's argument that Pontano recalled the verses ('Approcci umanistici', 178–9). The verses Pontano cites are in the right order (see note 12), but they would be in any event, since the tradition had wrongly placed 3–4 after 9–10, not after 11–12. For Guarino: 'Cum hic versus et subsequens in fine epigrammatis perverso ordine legerentur pater meus illos loco suo restituit' (*Alexandri Guarini Ferrariensis in C. V. Catullum Veronensem per Baptistam Patrem Emendatum Expositiones cum Indice* (Venice, 1521) *ad* 84. 3–4). For the date of Battista Guarino's emendations, see pp. 82–5.
15. 'Cum quidem illic adesset [*ed.* adesse] etiam Guarini propinquus, Iohannes Baptista (ni fallor) nomine, . . . neque non duo, qui tum Veronae non indocti homines profitebantur . . .' (Poliziano, *Miscellanea* i. 19, in *Opera* i. 243).
16. 'Scit Aurelius Ariminensis (ut alios omittam) qui nunc Patavii degit, praestanti iuvenis et ingenio et literatura, quam multos abhinc annos, istam de nobis enarrationem Florentiae tum quidem agitans acceperit, quamque sit (ut idem postea Patavii narrabat) nova prorsus, ignotaque iam tum visa omnibus ad quos de ea' (Poliziano, *Miscellanea* i. 19, in *Opera*, i. 243). Augurello was in Padua from 1476 until at least 1485; see *DBI* iv. 578–80.
17. 'Quidam autem plani, et tenebriones in literis, vetere expuncto vocabulo, nescio quas supponunt aut Cercopythas aut Coprotinas ex hara productas, non schola, vocabula nuda, nomina cassa, et nihili voces. Nos de graeco instrumento, quasi de cella proma, non despicabilis, nec abrogandae fidei proferemus autoritates, quibus et lectio praestruatur incolumis, et interpretamenti nubilum discutiatur' (Poliziano, *Miscellanea* i. 2, in *Opera* i. 228).
18. Venice 1472 read *Lęlius*, which Poliziano corrected to *Gęlius* in his notes.
19. 'Quaesitum diu qui nam is foret Harpocrates . . .' (Poliziano, *Miscellanea* i. 83, in *Opera* i. 296).
20. Although with a pointless addition, for he imports into the poem a human character named Harpocrates. '*Reddidit Harpocratem* [74. 4]. mutum fecit, silere coegit. Harpocrates Catulli temporibus fuit mutus quidam denominatus ab Harpocrate deo aegyptiorum. Nam ut Plutarchus in oratione de Serapidis numine scribit Harpocrates ab Aegyptiis colitur deus silentii cuius numinis simulacrum digito labiis admoto figuratum indicat silentium' (Parthenius 1491, k 2v–k 3).
21. *Parthenius, ad* 74. 5: 'Nam qui irrumatur et fellat tacere cogitur' (Parthenius 1491, k 3). *Poliziano*: 'ipsum iam coepit irrumare patruum, eoque pacto tacere coegit, quoniam loqui fellator non potest' (*Miscellanea* i. 83, in *Opera* i. 297).

22. 'Nos tamen et Venetiis, et etiam Veronae (quod diximus) abhinc annos octo ferme de eo studiosis aliquot publice responsitavimus, quorum nunc testor fidem, conscientiamque sicui forte aliena adscribere, ac non mea potius mihi videor vindicare' (Poliziano, *Miscellanea* i. 83, in *Opera* i. 296).
23. He did not come back to *perdespuit* (the correction *perdepsuit* first appears in Statius). Parthenius explained *perdespuit* as meaning *contempsit*, and Poliziano evidently had a similar idea: 'posthabita illius [sc. patrui], quam comprimebat uxore . . .' (Poliziano, *Miscellanea* i. 83, in *Opera* i. 297).
24. Plutarch, *Isis and Osiris* 358e, 377b–c, 378c.
25. The lemma appears in the margin in the middle of the page next to the word *Harpocratem* at the end of 102. 4, but the quotation is placed above it, extending from the top of the page down to and past the lemma. Corresponding reference marks are placed next to the quotation and *Harpocratem* in the text, but none is near the lemma *Harpocrates*. Moreover, both in the marginalia and in *Misc.* i. 83 the quotation from *Isis and Osiris* 377b–c ends in mid-sentence: *διὸ καὶ φακῶν αὐτῷ φυομένων ἀπαρχὰς ἐ[πιφέρουσι* (Corsiniana 50.f.37, p. 34); *quo circa etiam lentis primitias illi offerri* . . . (*Miscellanea* i. 83). There are only nine words in the rest of the sentence, but since space was at a premium in the note, they were easily omitted. Since he had no such reason for omission in the *Miscellanea*, we may infer that he was translating from the Greek in his note and simply forgot that it was incomplete.
26. 'Elegiam Callimachi de crinibus Berenices inter sidera receptis mira elegantia vertit in linguam latinam nobilis poeta Catullus, quamvis pleraque sint in ea corrupta mendosaque, et temere scripta librariorum inscitia' (Poliziano, *Miscellanea* i. 68, in *Opera* i. 281).
27. 'Atque hoc inscite legunt quidam *telorum*. Vulgatissimi codices *coelitum* retinent contra etiam metri rationem' (Poliziano, *Miscellanea* i. 68, in *Opera* i. 282. For *vulgatissimi codices* as synonymous with *plerique codices, sic vulgo legitur*, etc. see Rizzo, *Lessico*, 74.
28. '*Aorion* [68. 94]. Haec est vera huius loci lectio. Alii autem legunt oyrion divisa diphthongo imperite. Penultima enim fieret brevior quum apud omnes poetas producatur, sed legendum est Aorion nulla diphthongo divisa. Non enim ab orione deducit quamquam idem est signum sed aorion ensiger dicitur. *ἄορ* enim significat ensem, inde aorion quasi *ensifer*' (Parthenius 1491, i 6v).
29. 'Oarion synceriter esse apud Catullum, quod Aorion isti legunt, qui bonos violant libros.

'In elegia eadem Catulli ex Callimacho, Oarion legitur, pro eo quod sit *Orion*. Quam quoniam integram adhuc, inviolatamque dictionem nonnulli temere attentare iam incipiunt, contra hanc sinistram imperitorum audaciam standum mihi est omni (quod aiunt) pede, vel Callimachi eiusdem autoritate, qui sic in hymno in Dianam, etiam nunc extante ait: *οὐδὲ γὰρ Ὦτος / οὐδὲ μὲν Ὠαρίων ἀγαθὸν γάμον ἐμνήστευσαν* [Callimachus, *Hymn to Artemis* 264–5]' (Poliziano, *Miscellanea* i. 69, in *Opera* i. 282).

30. The words after *chalybum legendum* are *puto id ex Callimachi*. The object of *ex* is too faint to read, as are the next two lines, which contain perhaps eight to ten words in all. Then it is possible to make out rather clearly *Apollonius Rhodius* (or *Apollonii Rhodii*), which is followed by half a dozen lines that have nearly vanished from the page.

31. The word *Nicander* is legible, followed by: "*Βοιωτῷ τεύχουσα κακὸν μόρον Οὐαρίονι* [Nic. *Ther.* 15]. Uarion puto scribendum quod *ἀπὸ τῶν οὔρων,* id est ab urina Iovis, Apollinis, et Neptuni sit natus." The reference to the curious story of Orion's birth is a close translation of the scholia on the same verse of Nicander: *Οὐαρίων δὲ, ἐπειδὴ ἀπὸ τῶν οὔρων τοῦ Διὸς καὶ Ἀπόλλωνος καὶ Ποσειδῶνος ἐγένετο* (H. Keil, *Scholia in Nicandri Theriaca*, in O. Schneider, *Nicandrea Theriaca et Alexipharmaca* (Leipzig, 1856)).

32. Poliziano's marginalia also lack Festus' other citations of Catullus (63. 38 *rabidus*, and 97. 6 *ploxeni*). For the date, see Maïer, *Ange Politien*, 426; R. Sabbadini, *Le scoperte dei codici latini e greci ne' secoli xiv e xv* (Florence, 1914), i. 153–4.

33. 'Ostendit mihi Romae abhinc quadriennium Manilius Rallus, graecus homo, sed Latinis literis apprime excultus, fragmentum quoddam Sexti Pompeii Festi (nam ita erat in titulo) sane quam vetustum, sed pleraque mutilatum, praerosumque a muribus. . . . Nonnullas quoque ex eodem fragmento, Pomponius Laetus, vir antiquitatis, et literarum bonarum consultissimus sibi pagellas retinuerat, quas itidem legendas mihi, describendasque dedit' (Poliziano, *Miscellanea* i. 73, in *Opera* i. 284).

34. 'Hoc utique loco vetus codex circunrosam plane habet expositionem, sed ita tamen, ut appareat ex reliquiis literarum male cohaerentibus, Catullum quoque post Ennium adduci . . . Nam ut de carminis residuo nihil mihi arrogem temere, videbar sane tum syllabatim quoque olfactans, etiam pro explorato afferre posse, expernata legendum in eo, non separata, quantum ex paucis illis poteram veluti minutalibus, aut ramentis colligere, quantumque etiam vel ex obliteratis pene iam vestigiis ariolari' (Poliziano, *Miscellanea* i. 73, in *Opera* i. 284).

The Codex Farnesianus of Festus (Naples IV.A.3) has sustained still more damage since Poliziano's time. The right column is further eaten away, so that little remains of the Catullus citation (Festus 396L): *et Catu*[*llus . . . in*] *fossa ligari ia*[*cet suppernata se*]*curi* (*Codex Festi Farnesianus*, ed. A. Thewrewk (Budapest, 1893) plate xxix). The loss is particularly maddening since Poliziano illogically and unmetrically reads *expernata* instead of *suppernata* as we would expect. For the metrics see Chapter 1, p. 58. For the manuscript see Thewrewk, pp. i–v, and the editions of Festus by C. O. Mueller (Leipzig, 1839) and W. M. Lindsay (Leipzig, 1913).

35. 'Quo intellectu Catullianus passer accipiendus, locusque etiam apud Martialem indicatus.

Passer ille Catullianus allegoricôs, ut arbitror, obscoeniorem quempiam celat intellectum, quam salva verecundia, nequimus enunciare. Quod ut credam, Martialis epigrammate illo persuadet, cuius hi sunt extremi versiculi:

> Da mihi basia, sed Catulliana:
> Quae si tot fuerint, quot ille dixit,
> Donabo tibi passerem Catulli. (Martial, 11. 6. 14–17)

Nimis enim foret insubidus poeta (quod nefas credere) si Catulli passerem denique ac non aliud quidpiam, quod suspicor, magis donaturum se puero post oscula diceret. Hoc quid sit, equidem pro styli pudore suae cuiusque coniecturae, de passeris nativa salacitate relinquo' (Poliziano, *Miscellanea* i. 6, in *Opera* i. 230–1). (Poliziano has slightly misquoted Martial; Mart. 11. 6. 14 begins 'Da *nunc* basia.')

36. See pp. 242–3.

37. On 5. 7 under the heading *Martialis de basiis* he quotes two extracts from Martial: 6. 34. 7–8 and 11. 6. 14–16 (the same verses cited in the *Miscellanea*). See Gaisser, 'Catullus and his First Interpreters', 103.

38. 'Strutheum in mimis praecipue vocant obscenam partem virilem, ⟨a⟩ salacitate videlicet passeris, qui Graece στρουθός dicitur' (Festus 410L). A portion of Poliziano's transcription of the Festus manuscript is preserved (Vat. lat. 3368). It contains both *suppernati* (f. 11) and *strutheum* (f. 11v)—the latter with the marginal gloss *passer Catulli*, probably in the hand of Poliziano himself. (I wish to thank A. C. de la Mare for her confirmation of this point.) For Vat. lat. 3368 see P. de Nolhac, *La bibliothèque de Fulvio Orsini* (Paris, 1887), 212–15; and 'Le *Festus* d'Ange Politien', *Revue de philogie*, 10 (1886), 145–8; Lindsay (ed.), *Festus: De verborum significatione*, pp. xii–xiv; Maïer, *Les manuscrits*, 358; Rizzo, *Lessico* 178–80.

39. Calderini, Sabellico and Beroaldo all tried their hand at such a work. See Dionisotti, 'Calderini, Poliziano e altri,' 165–9; A. Grafton, 'On the Scholarship of Politian and its Context,' *JWCI* 40 (1977), 152–6.
40. Compare, for example, H. D. Jocelyn, 'On Some Unnecessarily Indecent Interpretations of Catullus 2 and 3', *AJP* 101 (1980), 421–41; and R. W. Hooper, 'In Defence of Catullus' Dirty Sparrow', *Greece and Rome*, 32 (1985), 162–78. See also Chapter 5, pp. 242–54.
41. 'Proh dii, quam vafer es Puliciane: / Solus qui bene calleas poetas' (*Ep.* 1. 61. 16–17. For Sannazaro see pp. 243–5.
42. For Marullo see p. 304, n. 126 and p. 392, n. 161; for Avanzi see pp. 52–9. See also L. A. Ciapponi, 'Bartolomeo Fonzio e la prima centuria dei "Miscellanea" del Poliziano', *IMU* 23 (1980), 165–77.
43. See p. 158.
44. For Partenio's biography see V. Cavazzocca-Mazzanti, 'Due illustri lazisiensi', *Pro Verona*, nos. 8–10 (1911), 13–27; C. Perpolli, 'L'*Actio Panthea* e l'umanesimo veronese', *Accademia di agricoltura, scienze e lettere, Verona, Atti e memorie* S. iv. 16 (1915), esp. 35–40. For his contribution to the collection for Calderini see Weiss, 'In Memoriam Domitii Calderini', 310–13.
45. 'Vos reducem lauro vates ornate Catullum: / Parthenio satis est civica sola meo' (Iuliarius, vv. 11–12 in Parthenius 1491, k 8). The text of the commentary and prefatory material in Parthenius 1491 is the same as that of the first edition (Parthenius 1485), although the prefatory matter appears in a different order. The following discussion refers to the order in the 1485 edition.

    Giuliari wrote two epigrams for the Calderini collection (see Weiss, 'In Memoriam Domitii Calderini', 310–13). He was the editor, if not the guiding spirit, of the *Actio Panthea* (1485). See G. C. Giuliari, *Della letteratura veronese al cadere del secolo XV* (Bologna, 1876), 20–1, 120–3; Perpolli, 'L'*Actio Panthea*', 94–6.
46. 'veronensem patriam meam pervetustum atque sacratissimum divinarum musarum templum' (Parthenius 1491, f 1). There is no evidence that Partenio knew Pomponio Leto, but Pomponio had visited Verona between 1479 and 1483, and apparently Giuliari and Partenio hoped they could count on his support. For the visit to Verona see R. Avesani, 'Studies in Pietro Donato Avogaro of Verona,' *IMU* 5 (1962), 58–9. The members of the Roman Academy called Pomponio *pontifex maximus*. For the significance of the title and bibliography see R. J. Palermino, 'The Roman Academy, the Catacombs, and the Conspiracy of 1468', *Archivum Historiae Pontificiae*, 18 (1980), 117–55.

47. 'Etenim si . . . cives mei Cyllenius atque Domitius doctis enarrationibus suis interpretati sunt, alter Tibullum, alter Iuvenalem, Martialem, atque Papinium externos scriptores, quanto studiosius debui Catullum civem meum quantulacunque mea declaratione interpretari?' (Parthenius 1491, f 1).

48. '*Antonius Parthenius Lacisius libello suo*. Chare liber superas tecum lature per auras / Nomina nostra vide cautius ut sit iter. / Effuge sordidulos atra rubigine dentes / Et vulgum audacem grammaticasque manus. / Lividius nihil est, nihil est nasutius illis, / Pagellae criticum se tibi quisque geret. / Infestos morsus et acutos fortius ungues / Perfer, dum civis stet tibi tuta salus. / Sic tibi perpetuum decus et per longa superstes / Saecula sit vivax gloria chare liber' (Parthenius 1491, k 8).

49. 'Quaeris Partheni quid sentiam de tua in Catullianum carmen lucubratione, an existimem in omnibus ad poetae sensum satisfacere? Ego etsi palam afferre iudicium meum inter tot malivola obtrectatorum ingenia quos nostra videt aetas, haud quaquam arbitror tutum, dicam tamen aliquid, sed minus certe quam sentio, ne meo in te amori nimium credar indulsisse. Adortus es rem in primis arduam et a nullo antehac tentatam tum carminis ipsius duritie quam affectasse de industria poetam uterque auctor est Plinius, tum mutilati operis vetustatis incuria, depravatione; in quo quid effeceris, iudicabunt qui commentarios tuos legent. Omnibus placere immensum et supra vires prope humanas est. In hoc te dignum laude ducimus, quod ingenti id tu animo, quod nemo hactenus aut ausus est aut potuit attingere. In magnis etiam non assecutis voluisse abunde pulchrum atque magnificum est. Oblatraturos tantisper scio si quos aut editione praevenisti aut quibus suopte ingenio calumniandi animus est, donec intelligent nostro testimonio te non ea causa ad Catulliani carminis interpretationem adductum, ut aliis praereptam laudem velles, sed simul et officii in civem tuum gratia et ut aliis excultius fortasse aliquid elucubrandi viam aperires. Nos iure nostro id possumus vel ab omni calumnia tuti affirmare, te vera civica dignum, quod labentem iam et a vetustatis iniuria pene obrutum civem ingenii tui clypeo sublevasti protexistique, quod huiusmodi epigrammate lusimus' (Iuliarius in Parthenius 1491, k 8).

50. 'Non enim ignorabam quantis invidiae iniuriis esset obnoxia sors atque conditio scriptorum omnium, quorum nemo a conditis litterarum monumentis usque ad aetatem nostram malivolorum hominum difficilem nasum effugere valuit. Qua ego adversa sorte monitus quum tutum aliquod operi meo profugium inquirerem, Veronensem patriam meam pervetustum atque sacratissimum

divinarum musarum templum cui libellus meus te authore dedicetur delegi, sperans fore ut hoc voto sit a vulgi temeritate inviolatus' (Parthenius 1491, f 1).

51. 'Nec vero multum reformidabo quid in me inhumana invidia sit machinatura quod opus hoc multis in locis diminutum et in pluribus depravatum atque ob id ab eruditioribus bonarum litterarum professoribus tanquam cadaver quod nullis humanis opibus nullove ingenio excitari possit obscuritati relictum ego mediocri studio nec claro admodum ingenio audaci conatu sim aggressus' (Parthenius 1491, f 1).

52. There are several references to his haste. *In the Dedication*: 'Plerique cives mei . . . me coegerunt ut tandem ederem . . . meas in lepidissimum poetam Catullum interpretationes . . . Ego etsi noveram nullo pacto editionem esse praecipitandum . . .' (Parthenius 1491, f 1). *In the Preface*: 'Tantum autem a me abfuit et abest huiusmodi vanus invidiae metus ut multo avidius quam statueram susceptum opus maturaverim' (f 1). *In the Final Letter*: 'Si quid est a me vel praetermissum vel ignoratum . . . atque si quid erratum est . . . non tantum mihi vitio des quantum amicis meis honori meo nimis cupide studentibus, per quos non licuit mihi scripta mea in nonum comprimere annum. Est praeterea quaedam alia editionis festinatae causa non minor nonnullis hominibus invidis qui enarrationes meas superiore anno quarto discipulis meis dictatas et in commentarium sine nomine meo redactas dum inique intercipiunt meum operis maturandi consilium everterunt' (k 7v). (Nothing else is known of the pirating of Parthenius' lectures.)

53. 'Cur igitur huiusmodi homines tanquam fuci operi alieno infesti insidiatores ipsi ante me tales conatus non sunt aggressi? Cur alienam inventionem oscitantes expectarunt? Cur herculea virtute instructi ac freti immanem Catulliani carminis hydram non sunt ausi conficere? Cur ante vigilias meas tam desidiosi hallucinatores fuere? Cur denique molesti alieni operis critici benedicendo potius quam obtrectando honestis laboribus nomen ac famam sibi non quaesivere?' (Parthenius 1491 k 7v).

54. For Guarino see L. Cittadella, *I Guarini: famiglia nobile ferrarese oriunda da Verona* (Bologna, 1870), 44–55; S. Maffei, *Verona illustrata* (Milan, 1825), iii. 162–6; A. Luzio and R. Renier, 'La coltura e la relazioni letterarie di Isabella d'Este Gonzaga', *GSLI* 35 (1900), 212–20; Cosenza, *Dictionary of the Italian Humanists* ii. 1718–20.

55. Guarino's remark appears in a letter to Ottavio Ubaldini: 'Catullum ubi meliorem fecero ad proprios lares remeare compellam.'

The letter is attributed to Battista and published by Sabbadini, *Epistolario di Guarino Veronese*, iii. 465–79.

56. For Battista's poem see below. *Pittorio*: '. . . . Si nondum sibi dixerit fuisse / Nostris versibus otium vacandi / Quod pro viribus explicare tentet / Quos pridem petii mihi resolvi / Arguti dubios locos Catulli / Sive aenygmata verius vocarim, / Dic saltem lubeat supersedere / Tres vel quattuor hoc dies labore, / Nec te id propterea tamen Catulle / Contristet, nec enim tibi nocebit . . .' (Ludovicus Pictorius Bigus, *Baptistae Guarino* vv. 8–18, in *Tumultuariorum carminum libri* (Mutina, 1492), quoted from BL IA. 32264, p 2v–3).

57. 'Cum abhinc multis annis . . . Baptista . . . corruptissima Catulli docti et elegantis poetae carmina emendasset . . . mendosumque et mutilatum ipsius codicem divino (ut affirmare non vereor) ingenio in pristinum redegisset, quod ad communem rei publicae litterariae utilitatem spectabat minime occultandum ratus, nitidum et tersum opus edidit . . . His igitur meis qualescumque fuerint elucubraciunculis profiteor me Catulliano codici secundum paternam emendationem impresso lucem attulisse . . .' (Alexander Guarinus, *Expositiones*, a 2).

58. 'hos subscripsimus endecasyllabos, quos Ludovicus Pictorius parentis mei delicium ultimos Tumultuariorum suorum typis Mutinae impressos edidit anno mcccclxxxxii et ut ipse mihi rettulit post annos multos antea opus pater absoluerat' (A. Guarinus, *Expositiones* a 10).

59. '*Baptistae Guarini ad Veronam: pro emendato Catulli poemate Epigramma:* Accipe facundi genitrix Verona Catulli / Iam bene correctos quos tueare locos. / Nam seu mendosos habuerunt ante libellos / Seu fuit in causa dicere quod vereor, / Hactenus in multis errarunt versibus illi / Qui se opponendos omnibus esse putant. / Quippe iocos alii non percepere disertos, / Carminis ast alii non tenuere pedes. / Cumque vocent doctum priscorum scripta Catullum / Quod docte norat lucida sensa loqui / Barbarico ritu quidam fecere locutum, / Tantae illorum animis obstiterant tenebrae. Nunc vero exibit tersus nitidusque Catullus. / Haec tibi dant cives munera grata tui' (*Baptistae Guarini Poema Divo Herculi Ferrariensium Duci Dicatum*, HC 8127 (Mutina, 1495) 1 2v—1 3). The text is cited from Vatican Library, Inc. Ross 528.

60. 'Cum . . . mendosumque et mutilatum ipsius codicem divino (ut affirmare non vereor) ingenio in pristinum redegisset, quod ad communem rei publicae litterariae utilitatem spectabat minime occultandum ratus, *nitidum et tersum opus* edidit. Atque Veronae

patriae epigrammate suis inserto carminibus . . . *gratum munus* donavit' (A. Guarinus, *Expositiones* a 2).

61. A full collation of Battista's readings with those of his contemporaries (which I have not undertaken) might be instructive. The following sample includes only readings specifically claimed for Battista by Alessandro Guarino. An * marks readings that appear in Mynors. *Sabellicus*: *64. 25 *taedis*; *64. 243 *infecti*. *Avantius 1495*: *separation of 14, 14*b*; 72, 73; rearrangement of 37–39 (see p. 63 and p. 307, n. 145); *17. 6 *suscipiantur*; *17. 14 *cui cum*. *Poliziano's marginalia* (see Appendix 3): 3. 16 *pro miselle passer*; *17. 14 *cui cum*; 35. 18 *Caia*; *93. 2 *scire*. None of the readings in Appendix 3 (B.12) is claimed by Alessandro for his father.

62. *Guarinus Veronensis*: 'Catullum [Catulum, *ed.*] municipem suum situ et squalore confectum lucemque ex diuturnis tenebris reformidantem ita abstersit ut sine maiore rubore in publicum exire non dubitaverit' (M. Antonius Sabellicus, *Opera* (Venice, 1502), 111). *Petrarch and Boccaccio*: 'vindicarunt servitio quidem Ciceronem Fabium Catullum . . .' (111v). *Parthenius*: 'pari paene laude nominandi sunt Cyllenius et Partenius Veronensis Catulli hic, ille Tibulli interpres: sed alter civica ut sic dicam corona paene dignus qui civem servarit suum. Servavit enim quem multis nodis vinctum soluerat' (114).

63. 'Audio etiam Matheum Ruffum ac Pantheum non minus sincerae latinitatis quam religionis cui praesident acerrimos custodes simul et virum singularem Benedictum Prunulum ac litteratissimum Baptistam Guarini filium conterraneos nostros omni praeconio meo praestantiores mirum in modum ad legitimam Catulliani operis lectionem anelhare' (Avantius, *Emendationes* 1495, a 2).

64. Partenio's text and commentary were reprinted in 1487 (HC 4762 [I]); 1491 (HC 4763*); 1493 (HC 4764); 1497 (HC 4765); 1500 (HC 4766). For the edition of 1500, see p. 64.

65. 'Quid deinde tanto gaudio meo mihi dignum videri debet, quam si aut per meas lucubratiunculas aut per nonnullorum virorum studia mearum vigiliarum aemulatione mota cum doctorum hominum tum scholarum, atque praeceptorum ulla familiaritate Catullus illustrabitur? Quum igitur in omnibus civitatibus omnium fere poetarum quae supersint scripta legerentur, ac solus Catullus tum quia eius scripta corruptissima erant, tum quia carebant interprete, scholarum familiaritate orbatus esset, hunc poetam ab eruditissimis scriptoribus nomine doctissimi elegantissimique poetae honoratum in scholas atque magistorum manus quoad potui nuper inducere tentavi. . . . Nec vero multum reformidabo quid in me inhumana

invidia sit machinatura. . . . Tantum autem a me abfuit et abest huiusmodi vanus invidiae metus ut multo avidius quam statueram susceptum opus maturaverim. Nam quum sit consilium meum luci et honori suo restituere Catullum, quanto plures docti viri mearum interpretationum aemulatione movebuntur, tanto utilius consulent poetae nostro, et in quibus ego inbecillitate ingenii detentus defecero, studiosi homines cura peritius perfectiusque dicendi litteratae iuventuti me duce satisfacient. Hoc modo auspiciis meis paulatim adiuvabitur poeta noster atque per multos scriptores pari studio motos decus suum reparabit. . . . Etenim si Servius peritissimus grammaticus in Virgilianis expositionibus Caprum Urbanum Hyginium Didimum Probum Asprum Donatum multosque alios Virgilii enarratores secutus in plurimis errasse deprehenditur, et nihilo minus doctissimi grammatici nomen et dignitatem non amittit, ego quoque a lectoribus non inhumanis aliquantulum veniae sperare possum et debeo; quum in hoc perquam difficili opere interpretando ducem nactus neminem et studio satisfaciendi litteratis iuvenibus et singulari adiuvandi civis mei amore ac pietate tantum meae professionis onus tantumque invidiae periculum susceperim' (Parthenius 1491, f 1 r–v).

66. See p. 22 and pp. 137–45.

67. 'In hoc primo epigrammate poeta Cornelio Nepoti amico suo libellum hunc dicat atque in eius nomine opus edit assignans huius dicationis rationem videlicet quia Cornelius poetae scripta iamdudum plurimi semper fecerit' (Parthenius 1491, f 2).

68. 'Ego autem Eusebii tempora secutus Cornelius Gallum intelligi posse negaverim, repugnante temporum ordine. Nam anno quo Catullus vita functus est Cornelius Gallus vix infantiae suae trimatum attigisse invenitur' (Parthenius 1491, f 2). Although Jerome's dates are wrong (by his reckoning Gallus was born in 60 rather than in 69 and Catullus died in 57 rather than after 55), Partenio's point is still valid.

69. 'Cornelium autem Gallum elegiarum poetam fuisse constat' (Parthenius 1491, f 2).

70. '*Omne aevum*: omne saeculum praeteritum. Quum autem dicit omne aevum plane indicat Cornelii Nepotis chronica quorum meminit Gellius in noctibus atticis' (Parthenius 1491, f 2).

71. In Venice 1472 poem 1 has the title *Val. Catulli Veronensis Poetae Cl. Liber ad Cornelium Gallum*, which Poliziano glosses: 'magis puto ad Cornelium Cinnam cui fuit convictio ut in epigrammate . . . Smyrna mei Cinnae [95. 1].' He glosses 1. 7: 'Hic etiam Smyrnam composuit quam nono anno ex quo illam incepit edidit' (Biblioteca Corsiniana 50 F. 37, p. 4).

72. 'Smyrna fuit amazon quae Ephesum tenuit' (Parthenius 1491, k 2). He is quoting Strabo 14. 1, p. 633.

73. Alessandro Guarino passes on Partenio's identification, but Palladio, Muret (1554), and Statius (1566) do not attempt to identify her. Scaliger identifies Smyrna, but misunderstands 95: 'Hoc igitur ridet Catullus in Cinna, qui videtur historiam Cinarae, et Myrrhae, quam Smyrnam vocat, altius, quam poetam decet, repetisse . . .' (Joseph Scaliger, *Castigationes in Valerii Catulli Librum* (Paris, 1577), 100). For Scaliger and 95 see p. 189.

74. '*Iucundissime Calve* [14. 1]: duos ea aetate Calvos nomine fuisse comperio, alterum Licinium Calvum poetam cuius meminit Horatius . . . De poeta hic intelligit Catullus. Alterum vero Calvum fuisse oratorem apud Quintilianum legimus' (Parthenius 1491, f 5v). For the title, which seems to have been awarded by Salutati, who added *poetam* to X's *Ad Calvum* (McKie, *The Manuscripts* of Catullus, 52), see Appendix 1. Poliziano may also have thought of two Calvuses, since he refers to *hic Calvus* in his marginalia on 14. Thus: 'huius Calvi adducit versum Priscianus libro 9 his verbis . . .' And again: 'hic Calvus amavit Quintiliam . . .' (Biblioteca Corsiniana 50 F 37, p. 7v).

75. Palladius, *Commentarii*, b 1; A. Guarinus, *Expositiones*, 14v.

76. *Gellius*: 'Plurimos autem fuisse Catones diligenter scribit Gellius.' *Cicero*: 'Hoc Uticensi Catoni dici non potest. Constat enim illum rigidissimum fuisse, ut Cicero in oratione pro Murena plane indicat' (Parthenius 1491 g 7).

77. 'Vale]rium Catonem ut puto suae aetatis poetam' (Biblioteca Corsiniana 50 F. 37, p. 15v). The gloss continues with quotations on Valerius Cato from Suetonius, *De Grammaticis* xi.

78. Nearly a hundred years later Achilles Statius thought of Valerius Cato again: 'Hic est forte Valerius Cato Grammaticus, de quo sunt illi versus Bibaculi apud Suetonium de Illustribus Grammaticis . . . . Intellegerem de Catone Censorio, si ratio temporum conveniret; nam iocis illum delectatum scribit Macrobius in II Saturn.: "M. etiam Cato, ille Censorius, argute iocari solitus est," . . .' (*Catullus cum Commentario Achillis Statii Lusitani* (Venice, 1566), 152). Although Valerius Cato was the preferred candidate for the next 300 years, modern criticism tends to favour Cato Uticensis—because of the very strictness for which Partenio had excluded him. See Ellis, *A Commentary*, ad loc.; V. Buchheit, 'Catull an Cato von Utica (c. 56),' *Hermes*, 89 (1961), 345–56. See also W. C. Scott, 'Catullus and Cato (c. 56),' *CP* 64 (1969), 24–9.

79. '*Caprimulgus*: *Caprimulgus* hic aepolum significat. *Caprimulgus* item avis est de qua Plinius haec tradit: "Caprimulgi appellantur

grandiores merulae aspectu fures nocturni. Interdiu enim visu carent. Intrant pastorum stabula, caprarum uberibus advolant suctum propter lactis. Qua iniuria uber emoritur, caprisque caecitas quas ita mulsere oboritur." [Pliny, *NH* 10. 56. 115]' (Parthenius 1491, f 7v).

80. 'Caprimulgus, aepolus qui capras mulget, vel caprimulgum [-us, *ed.*] Suffenum appellat tanquam aliorum carmina sufurantem, nam caprimulgus avis est quae ut Plinius . . .' (A. Guarinus, *Expositiones*, d 4).

81. 'Raphani in Germania ad infantum magnitudinem excrescunt. Frigore gaudent, fimum oderunt. Apud Plinium plura legito [Pliny, *NH* 19. 26. 83]' (Parthenius 1491 f 6).

82. The name is uncertain. Parthenius prints 41. 1 thus: *Acme an illa puella defututa*.

83. As it seems to have been also to the young Leonardo Bruni. See pp. 211–15.

84. 'Catullus Acmes meretriculae blandiciis ac deliciis pellectus illic ut amantes solent promiserat per codicillos decem milia nummum. Puella vero credens sibi rem factam allatis codicillis iure promissionis a Catullo decem milia poposcit; poeta itaque in iracundiam exit exclamans: illane Acme totiens fututa poscit a me tota illa decem milia? Reddat mihi illos codicillos' (Parthenius 1491, g 4).

85. For Poliziano and Avanzi see Appendix 2.

86. Palladio's explanation differs slightly: Acme has the tablets and won't give them back unless Catullus gives her ten thousand sesterces (Palladius 1496 c 1). Guarino gives both explanations without choosing between them (A. Guarinus *Expositiones*, F 2v).

87. '*Legit*: elegit Caecilius. *Entheatam*: divino spiritu plenam; alii *indotatam* legunt, sed male. *Ignosco:* ordo et sensus: o puella doctior musa saphica ignoscendum est tibi si Caecilii uxorem ducentis amore carperis. Etenim tanta est Caecilii sapientia ut eius uxor ex eo gravida iam magna mater vocetur, quo nomine deorum mater appellabatur. *Doctior saphica musa*: poetica mulier mitilenaea Phaonem mercatorem indoctum adamavit; haec Caecilii amica prudentius facit quae Caecilium perdoctum ac generosum iuvenem deperit. *Invocata magna mater*: propter sponsi sui sapientiam. *Invocata*: appellata; alii legunt: *Inchoata magna mater Caecilii*, i.e. iam facta [*ed. 1485*; factam *ed. 1491*] praegnans incepta est mater infantis Caecilii patre nominandi' (Parthenius 1491, g 2v).

88. 'Ego diu et multum quaesivi quid hic sibi vellet Catullus, sed repudiatis aliorum sententiis quae sane plures et diversae fuerunt, in eam tandem adductus sum opinionem ut credam Caecilium poema quoddam de Cybele inchoasse. Quod forte cum legisset

puella eum ardentius amare caeperat, tanta erat poematis ipsius tum venustas tum eruditio' (Palladius 1496, b 5v).

89. 'In paternis correctionibus sic etiam carmen istud legi posse comperi, *Caia Caecilia invocata mater*, eo ut arbitror sensu, ignosco tibi si docta doctum amas, foeliciter enim iuncta es matrimonio cum ipso Caecilio . . .' (A. Guarinus *Expositiones*, E 6v).

90. Plutarch, *Roman Questions*, 30.

91. Venice 1472 read *Nagna caecilia incohata mater*. Poliziano has written in *Caia* and *invocata*.

92. 'Venustatem atque suavissimum Lesbiae amorem laudat significans se per ocium quod est omnium fere amorum et malorum causa venusto Lesbiae amore captum esse' (Parthenius 1491, g 6).

93. 'Primum seipsum ad deserendam puellam hortatur. Deinde repudium indicit. Postremo amicae destitutae miseriis insultat' (Parthenius 1491, f 4).

94. 'Amat autem propter pulchritudinem atque rei Venereae cum ea consuetudinem, sed eandem odit ob eius perfidiam et multos quos accipit amatores' (Parthenius 1491, k 1).

95. 'apta et lepida similitudo' (on *ferream ut soleam*, 17. 26), Parthenius 1491, f 7. 'digressio poetica' (on 64. 52), h 7.

96. *On 11. 21–4*: 'Et est lepida similitudo ad demonstrandam sui amoris pulchritudinem extinctam' (Parthenius 1491, f 5). *On 17. 18–19*: 'Commoda comparatio. Nam quemadmodum alnus summersa nunquam emergit ita hic stolidus atque segnis se matrimonio pressum non sublevat' (f 7).

97. '[*Acme*] *an illa puella* [41. 1]: Interrogativae et cum percontatione legitur. *Defututa* [41. 1]: Cum vehemente iracundia dixit quasi sit ratio cur tam impudicae mulieri nullum servetur promissum aut nihil illi omnino credatur. *Ista turpiculo* [41. 3]: Hae omnes vituperationes cum ingenti felle dicuntur tanquam rationes et argumenta contra fidem meretriculae, ut omnino nihil illi sit credendum. Nam tam deformi mulieri quicquam tam grande serio promitti non est verisimile. *Propinqui quibus est puella curae* [41. 5]: Haec dicit ut eius petitioni fidem deroget quasi non ratione sed insania moveatur ad poscendum' (Parthenius 1491, g 4 r–v).

98. '*Citata* [63. 8]: Atys furore concitatus. Nam eum poeta genere foeminino appellat saepe quia virilitate iam privatus erat ut foemina' (Parthenius 1491, h 4v).

99. '*Gallae* id est o vos sacerdotes castrati. Gallae autem dixit genere foeminino quia erat effoeminati . . .' (Parthenius 1491, h 4v). '*Vaga* [63. 31]: Atys. Iterum atque iterum foeminam vocat Atym eviratum' (h 5).

100. 'Apta similitudo ad effoeminatam lasciviam ostendendam' (Parthenius 1491, h 5).
101. 'Eleganter et ingeniose dixit maenades pro Cybelis sacerdotibus. Nam Maenades apud Graecos dicuntur mulieres furore insanientes et Bacchi sacerdotes. Tales igitur sunt Cybelei qui et tanquam foeminae sunt et furore concitantur' (Parthenius, 1491, h 4v).
102. 'Satis puerilis lamentatio. *Creatrix* et *genitrix* idem significat, sed poeta pro poetico decoro facit ut puer flens et conquerens idem diversis verbis repetat, quod satis convenit ex nimio dolore lamentantibus' (Parthenius 1491 h 5).
103. '*Patria bonis* . . . [63. 59]: Haec nullo oratorio dicuntur ordine. Nam neque naturae neque dignitatis neque argumenti ordo procedit, sed pro poetico decoro pueris et afflictis personis accomodatissimo ingeniosus poeta haec verba disposuit.' (Parthenius describes the *ordo dignitatis* as *patria parentibus amicis bonis*; the *ordo argumenti* is the reverse.) '*Foro, palaestra* . . . [63. 60]: Haec omnia spectacula sunt magis pueris quam viris grata, ideo puer horum privationem moleste fert' (Parthenius 1491, h 5).
104. 'De se loquitur in genere foeminino ut qui scit se post amissam virilitatem foeminis potius quam viris esse annumerandum' (Palladius, *Commentarii*, d 3v).
105. '*Simul ipse* [Cat. 63.45]: iam genere masculino appellat postquam resipivit' (Guarinus, *Expositiones*, G 8v). (The edition reads *primoquam* for *postquam*, but Guarinus makes the correction in his *errata*.) The manuscripts had masculine forms also at *42 *excitum*, 51 *miser*, 78 *hunc*, 80 *qui*, *88 *tenerum*, *89 *ille*. (An asterisk indicates that the feminine is printed in Mynors.) On the gender of Attis see P. Oksala, 'Das Geschlecht des Attis bei Catull', *Arctos*, 6 (1969), 91–6.
106. Ironically, most modern editors read *ipsa* and credit Battista Guarino. Although *ipsa* appears in Alessandro Guarino's text, it is surely a misprint since he glosses *ipse* and mentions no other reading. If Battista had wanted *ipsa* Alessandro would have told us, as he does in the few cases where he disagrees with his father's ideas. For example, at 17. 19 he prints and glosses *separata*, 'sequtus parentem et codices omnes manu scriptos . . .', although he leans towards Poliziano's *expernata* or *supernata* (Guarinus, *Expositiones*, D 2v). For a similar discussion on 35. 18 see pp. 92–3.
107. Goold, 'A New Text', 99.
108. Ibid.
109. 'Nonnulla tamen confiteor esse loca de quibus adhuc valde quaerendum esse arbitror, ut *Salipentium* sive *Solopechyum*

disertum [53. 5] et bona pars epigrammatis in Egnatium intercepta [37–39] et illud *idmaeneos ne petam montes* [64. 178], tum *Peneum prope Cylleneum* [68. 109] et quaedam alia pauca, de quibus ego nihilominus tam probabiles ut opinor attuli sententias, ut a lectoribus sperem me si non magnam laudem bonam tamen iudicii mei veniam consecuturum' (Parthenius 1491, *Preface*, f 1v). For Partenio's haste see pp. 82–3 and n. 52.

110. 'Sed ex his interpretationibus si quae mihi mutanda quae fortasse non pauca erunt videbuntur, fato mihi non adversante faciam te certiorem in quaestionibus meis quas iam exorsus succisivi [successivi, *ed. 1491*] temporis textura in lucem maturo partu deducam' (Parthenius 1491, *Final Letter*, k 7v). According to Avanzi, he was still working on Catullus in 1493: 'Parthenius quoque (ne longe abeam) plura loca in suis commentariis reformat et multis aliis locis lucem daturus erat nisi amicorum assiduis et precibus et adhortationibus editionem paene praecipitare coactus fuisset. Verum nunc ut accepi festinationis iacturam mora ac diligentia resarcire nititur' (Avantius, *Emendationes* 1495, a 2).

111. Beroaldo interpreted 93. 2 (see p. 103) and 41. 7–8. For the punch-line of 41 Partenio had printed:

> Non est sana puella: nec rogate
> Qualis sit: solet haec imaginosum. (41. 7–8, Parthenius 1491)

He glossed: '*Qualis sit*: an insana an aegrota an phraenetica an cerita.
Imaginosum: larvarum imaginationes.
Solet: scilicet videre' (Parthenius 1491, g 4v).

Beroaldo printed *rogare*, explaining: 'Quibus venuster et festiviter poeta significat, puellam utpote sanae mentis minime compotem, nusquam speculum contemplari, ut ex eius inspectione cognoscat, qualis ipsa sit . . . *Speculum* novo quidem sed eleganti vocabulo, *imaginosum* Catullus appellat ab imaginibus scilicet, quae in speculo numerose visuntur' (Philippus Beroaldus, *Annotationes Centum in Varios Auctores* (Bologna, 1488) c 3).

Barbaro explained 26. He realized that the villa in the poem was beset not only by a windy situation (Partenio's idea) but also by debt: 'Non enim praecium id aut sumptum videri, sed aeris alieni summam, qua futurum esset, ut nominibus dissoluendis villa divenderetur et quasi licitaturis opponeretur' (Hermolaus Barbarus, *Castigationes Plinianae et Pomponii Melae* (Rome, 1492) r 4). See also the important edition of G. Pozzi, *Hermolai Barbari Castigationes Plinianae et in Pomponium Melam* (Padua, 1973), ii, 549–50.

112. The principal biographical information is given in A. Zeno,

Dissertazioni vossiane (Venice, 1752–3), ii. 49–56. See also B. Scardeone, *De antiquitate urbis Patavii et claris civibus patavinis libri tres* (Basle, 1560); G. Praga, 'Un poemetto di Alvise Cippico sulla guerra di Ferrara nel 1482', *Archivio storico per la Dalmazia*, 10 (Oct. 1930), 318–20. For Palladio's relations with Sabellico see their correspondence in M. A. Sabellico, *Opera* (Venice, 1502), 5–5v, 10–10v, 32–32v, 48. Cippico's family owned one of the earliest fifteenth-century Catullus manuscripts, Paris BN Lat. 7989, which contains abridgements of the summaries of the poems from Palladio's commentary (see p. 286, n. 90 and Gaisser, 'Catullus', 241). Civalleli's poem celebrating the Catullus commentary is printed in Palladius, *Commentarii*, a 2.

113. Apart from poetry (of which little survives) Palladio wrote historical and geographical works; he is best known for *De situ orae Illyrici* (Rome, 1540). In the dedication of his *Commentarii* he says that he is writing a commentary on Pliny's *Letters*, but the work is otherwise unknown.

114. Lorenzo Barotti, *Memorie istoriche di letterati ferraresi* (Ferrara, 1792–93), ii. 74–9; Hieronymus Baruffaldi, *Dissertatio de poetis ferrariensibus* (Ferrara, 1698), 27; Ferrante Borsetti, *Historia almi Ferrariae gymnasii in duas partes divisa* (Ferrara, 1735) ii. 107–11; Cittadella, *I Guarini*, 58–60, 100–2.

115. *Palladio and Beroaldo*. On 41. 7: 'Catullus novo sed eleganti vocabulo speculum appellat imaginosum . . .Hoc autem referimus acceptum Philippo Beroaldo' (Palladius 1496, c 1 r–v). On 93. 2 Palladio gives the interpretation without mentioning Beroaldo (Palladius, f 4). *Palladio and Barbaro*. On 26. 5: 'Hermolaus Barbarus vir seculi huius eruditissimus cuius immaturo obitu litterae tum graecae tum latinae maximam iacturam fecerunt in plinianis castigationibus hoc epigramma ad verbum exponit . . .' (Palladius b 3v). *Palladio and Avanzi*: see p. 301, n. 102.

116. 'Iuppiter ut Apollonius et Pausanias tradunt, cum Europam rapuisset eamque in Cretam avexisset, ad repellendum Agenorem eius patrem per littus custodes disposuit, inter quos Thalus fuit vir maxime pernicitatis, ut qui uno die totam insulam pedibus circuiret. De hoc intelligit Catullus non autem de Dedalo, ut plurimi existimant' (Palladius 1496, c 4v).

117. 'gremio suo deos omnes continenti, deorum omnium capaci. Nam Cybele [*Pasithea*] graece appellatur' (Parthenius 1491, h 5).

118. 'Emendo *Pasithea*. Fuit enim Pasithea una nympharum quam Iuno apud Homerum lib. xiv Iliados Somno promittit uxorem si is Iovi Troianis contra Graecos auxilianti oculos invaserit. Versus

Homeri sunt . . . [*Il.* 14.267–9]. Dea ergo Pasithea recepit Somnum maritum suum trepidantem' (Palladius 1496, d 3v).

119. *Somnus* is also read in Parma 1473 and Reggio 1481, but Avanzi is Palladio's usual source.

120. 'Lege *Pasithea sinu* . . . Ex Lascari edocti fuimus Pasitheam in xiiii Homeri eam fuisse quam Somno Iuno despondit, si Iovi oculos clausisset in bello troiano. Idem Lascari monuit apud Catullum de Thallo intelligi eo versu, *Non custos si ego fingar ille Cretum*' (Avantius 1500, o 2v). Avanzi may be referring to Lascaris' editions of the Greek Anthology (1494; *BMC* v. 666)—Pasithea appears at 9. 517; and Apollonius Rhodius (1496; *BMC* v. 667). But since the editions do not contain notes ad loc., perhaps Lascaris made the observations in lectures (he was at the Florentine Studio from 1492 to 1495). See A. Grafton, 'Janus Lascaris', in *Contemporaries of Erasmus*, ed. P. Bietenholz and T. B. Deutscher (Toronto, 1986), ii. 292–4. I wish to thank G. N. Knauer for his counsel on this point.

121. *Avanzi*. On 60. 5 *Ah nimis fero corde*: 'hoc ultimum carmen pater primus sic emendavit, licet quidam tanquam foetum suum emittere non erubuerint' (Guarinus, *Expositiones* G 5v). On 66. 63 *deum me*: 'sic pater primus ut multa alia loca quibus posteriores gloriati fuerunt, locum istum correxit . . .' (Guarinus, N 2. See also n. 61 above. *Sabellico* and *Poliziano*: see n. 61 above. *Partenio*. In the very few cases where priority is the issue Guarino's tone is mild, e.g. on 57. 1 'Hoc est alterius endecasyllabi initium quod ante paternam emendationem coniunctim cum praecedenti legebatur' (Guarinus, G 4v).

122. '*mane* brevi posteriore dixit a tertia coniugatione ut ipse alibi *cave* a tertia brevem protulit' (Parthenius 1491 f 4v).

123. 'Qui vero legunt *deferri mane*, cum dicant ultimam in *mane* breviari a poeta tanquam a tertia descendat coniugatione hi quid dicant ipsi viderint. Quis enim unquam *maneo*, *-nis* tertiae coniugationis vel audivit, vel vidit, vel legit, apud auctores? Neque idem fit in hoc verbo, quod in *caveo* quod aliquando secundae, aliquando vero tertiae reperitur coniugationis' (Guarinus, *Expositiones*, C 3).

124. Guarino's text reads *ferri mane inquio puellae*, but it is clear from the commentary that *mane* is to be repeated.

125. 'Bone deus quantum sibi mortales aetate nostra permisere . . . Illos minime ferre possis qui tertiam partem sexquipedali locutioni quae in omnibus exemplaribus *deferri* est partem absciderunt ut *ferri* facerent. Inde ac si parum in hoc sceleris admisissent, nugas illas intrusere, *mane mane*, quod quidem ego vel pueris ipsis ridiculum

esse iudicarim' (Vat. lat. 5215, 137v–8v). For the date of Valeriano's lectures see Chapter 4, pp. 109–14.

126. '*Doris*. subauditur *adest* a superiore. Doris autem maris dea Oceani senis et Thethyos filia. Nereique uxor fuit ut canit Hesiodus. Legitur et *Chloris* dea florum quae lectio si probetur *Mniosium* non habebit expositionem. Itaque arbitror has duas dictiones corruptas ac de iis valde querundum' (Parthenius 1491, i 2).

127. '*Mniosium* Nereum, i.e. mare. Mniosius autem dicitur quasi algae deus. Nam *ὁ μνίος* alga et *σιός* deus dicitur lingua (ed. *longa*) dorica' (Parthenius 1491, i 2).

128. 'Sunt qui legant *minosium*, i.e. mare cretense a minoe rege, sed lectio talis et expositio perquam ridicula est . . .' (Parthenius, 1491, i 2).

129. 'Cur dorida choreis nonacriis celebrandam (ed. *celebranda*) dixerit Catullus alii viderint' (Parthenius 1491, i 2).

130. 'non praecipio intellectum eorum versuum nec etiam syllabarum quantitatem' (Avantius 1495, a 4). In 1500 he makes a half-hearted suggestion for 287: 'Forte legendum est *annosum linquens doris* ubi omnino corruptus est codex ut in prima editione sexto superiori anno impressa praefati fuimus' (Avantius 1500 o 2v). Avanzi's *aporia* strongly indicates that he did not have Battista Guarino's corrections.

131. 'Hoc loco quidam poetae verba invertentes adeo inextricabili coeno haeserunt, ut neutiquam egredi potuerint. Nam dum incerti sunt utrum *Doris* an *Chloris*, *Mniosion* (*Mnision*, ed.) an *Minosion* legendum sit, quam expositionem darent non invenerunt, sed de verbis istis denique valde querendum concluserunt, et dum aliorum expositionem perquam ridiculam existimarunt, isti ridendo ad risum caeteros provocaverunt. Sed si veram lectionem poetae a parente meo praemonstratam percepissent, si ordinem non depravassent, aliis videndum non reliquissent cur Catullus Dorida choreis Nonacriis celebrandam dixerit, quod tamen non dixit Catullus, sed quod dixerit ordinem catullianorum verborum et verba ipsa pervertendo somniarunt' (Guarinus, *Expositiones*, L 4v).

132. 'C. Iulium Caesarem blanditiis poetae animum allicientem mordaci adulteriorum infamia distringit' (Parthenius 1491, k 5).

133. '*Ipsa olera olla legit* (94. 2): proverbium erat in adulteros moecharum sectatores ac pedicones puerorum aucupes' (Parthenius 1491, k 5).

134. Quint., *Inst. Orat.* 11. 1. 38. The translation is from Butler's Loeb edition, ad loc.

135. *Annotationes Centum*, c 3. Beroaldo claimed as his authorities

probatissimi codices as well as the passage in Quintilian. Interestingly enough, Avanzi claims the correction for Partenio: 'Immo et Parthenius dum nobis pueris Quintilianum ennarreret, memini eum . . . nos admonuisse ut versum hunc . . . sic legeremus: *albus an ater homo*, ut non diu post advertit Philippus Beroaldus . . .' (Avantius 1495, a 5). Alessandro Guarino claims it for his father: 'Locum istum multi quidem sed pater prior omnibus animadvertit' (Guarinus, *Expositiones* p 3v).

136. 'Volens poeta insectari Iulii Caesaris adulteria negat se dare operam ut illi placeat et si roget utrum idem Caesar sit albus . . . an ater . . .' (Palladius 1496, f 4).

137. '*Ipsa olera olla legit* (93. 2): vetus est in adulteros proverbium' (Palladius 1496, f 4).

138. 'Sic ergo Catullus dicit se nolle scire utrum Caesaar sit albus, i.e., bonus et liberalis, an ater, i.e., malus et sordidus, quia si vellet hoc inquirere, statim illi ut est ad libininem pronus mentula arrigeretur' (Guarinus, *Expositiones* P 3v). And again: 'Mordet Caesarem in mares pronum cui se nolle placere dicit, quia sola una interrogatiuncula ipsa mentula arrigitur et per se sperma effundit' (P 3).

139. '*Ipsa olera olla legit*: . . . proverbium est contra eos qui ad scelus aliquod inclinati sunt, ita, ut non possint facere quin peccent. Ideo hoc loco contra Iulium Caesarem proverbio usus videtur qui ita fuit ad libidinem in masculos proclivis ut per se sola alloquutione semen effunderet . . .' (Guarinus, *Expositiones* P 3v).

140. V. J. Rosivach has traced the interpretation of 105 from Partenio to Voss (1691), in 'Sources of Some Errors in Catullan Commentaries,' *TAPA* 108 (1978), 203–5.

141. 'Conabatur poeta cuiusdam virginis quam erat nactus primitiis potiri, sed naturae virginalis claustris et obstaculis atque puella reluctante prohibebatur. Iocose atque facete ait se conatum fuisse pipleum musarum montem ascendere, sed a musis inde praecipitatum esse. Per pipleum montem intelligit eugium, quod est quaedam pars media inter muliebria genitalia . . .' (Parthenius 1491, k 6v).

142. 'Non poterat Catullus virginem irrumpere. Cum maxime cuperet obstabat ei firmitas pelliculae quae virginibus obtenditur. Hanc Catullus appellat montem pimpleum . . . Alii vero dicunt poetam confiteri se obscaena scribere voluisse sed a musis quominus id faceret prohibitum' (Palladius 1496, f 5).

143. 'Pipleus mons a thracibus musis consecratus fuit . . . inde existimo epigrammatis huius argumentum esse, quod poeta tentaverit doctam aliquam puellam vel puerum subagitare et ille noluerit, et sic per montem pipleum [pimpleum, *ed.*] puerum doctum

intelligit per metaphoram in qua persistens utitur verbo scandere per quod inire et rem habere innuit. Iocose autem subiungit *musae furcillis eiiciunt praecipitem*, quia scilicet non potuit fieri compos voti. Ideo metaphorice inquit . . . quia puer doctrina praeditus noluit se libidini subiicere, et fortassis epigrammate ad poetam scripto hoc recusaverat . . . Aliter intelligere possumus mentulam esse viri proprium nomen vel saltem in contemptum mentulam appellatum a poeta et esse talem epigrammatis sensum, ut poeta dicat mentulam conari ut ascendat montem pipleum [pimpleum, *ed.*], i.e. evadere in bonum poetam, sed musas illum inde reiicere, tanquam sit genio sinistro et pingui minerva, i.e., ingenio crasso et minime ad versus componendos idoneo. Et fortassis erat aemulus poetae in componendis versibus' (Guarinus, *Expositiones*, P 7v–P 8).

144. 'Alii vero existimant, voluisse cum quadam virgine rem habere sed eum non potuisse . . . sed quo argumento velint poetam per pipleum montem vel hymen vel eugium . . . intelligere et cur a musis inde se eiectum dixerit ipsi viderint' (Guarinus, *Expositiones*, P 8).

145. 'nil obscoenum intelligit, sed Firmanum Salium malum poetam' (Avantius, *Emendationes* 1500, o 3).

146. 'it seems, for example, that virtually all commentators, from Alexandrian times down to the fifteenth century, preferred when they had two conflicting explanations of a given point to provide both of them rather than to decide between them' (Grafton, 'Politian,' 154, n. 12). Medieval commentators apparently considered it their duty to provide, 'not a single true explanation, but a wide range of possible ones' (Grafton, 188).

147. The title in Partenio's commentary is *In Salium firmanum*.

148. At 115 the *princeps* reads *quot*.

149. The *princeps* reads *et* for *est*. The *princeps* and Calfurnio read *vero* for *vere*.

150. 'Salium Firmanum se magnae mentulae beneficio beatissimum atque locupletissimum ridicule iactantem ac propterea tamquam plurimum posset superbe minantem inimicis amaris iocis insectatur' (Parthenius 1491, k 7).

151. '*Quicquam fructus*: . . . Nam hic mentulatus adulteriis atque vetularum subagitationibus multum divitiarum consequebatur, sed omnia luxuriosis sumptibus quam primum absumebantur. . . . *Ipse est maximus ultor*: ut ipse iactat se hac mentulae opulentia posse omnes iniurias ulcisci' (Parthenius 1491, k 7v).

152. 'Irridet Firmanum, qui cum bene mentulatus esset et ob id partim a vetulis prurientibus partim a barbatis Cynedis conductus

magnum lucrum faceret. . . . *Salius* [114. 1] : erant salii sacerdotes Martis quos Numa primus instituit. . . . *Uno in saltu* [115. 4]: appellat saltum eiusdem Firmani mentulam. . . . *Mentula magna minax* [115. 8]: Firmanus enim minabatur se sola mentula omnes iniurias ab inimicis sibi illatas facile posse vindicare' (Palladius 1496, f 5v–f 6).

153. 'existimo, Firmanum quendam temporibus Catulli fuisse bene mentulatum, qui ob mentulae magnitudinem ex adulteriis multa lucraretur adeo ut agrum sibi comparaverit qui ex re ipsa mentula dives appellaretur. Sed Firmanus, etsi multa lucraretur tamen etiam profuse omnia exponebat . . . Notandum tamen quod in quibusdam codicibus non Firmani saltus, sed Firmanus saltus sive salius legitur, et tunc is erit epigrammatis sensus, quod Firmanus cognomento saltus sive salius propter mentulae magnitudinem ex adulteriis multa lucrabatur, unde mentula dives cognominabatur . . .' (Guarinus, *Expositiones* Q 2–Q 2v).

154. 'Mentula, i.e. Firmanus cognomento Mentula Dives . . .' (Guarinus, *Expositiones*, Q 2v).

155. 'Est inquit maximus ultor sed non quia tamquam homo ultor timeatur sed quia eius mentula magna est illa quae minatur ultionem, quoniam omnes timent ei facere iniuriam ne ipse pedicando eos puniat. Legitur etiam ultro non ultor ut sit sensus, omnia haec magna sunt sed ultro . . .' (Guarinus, *Expositiones*, Q 2).

156. On 94. 1: 'Firmanum cognomento Mentulam intelligit.' On 105. 1: 'nil obscoenum intelligit, sed Firmanum Salium malum poetam' (Avantius, *Emendationes* 1500, o 3).

157. 'Lege *Firmanus saltus, non salius*. Loquitur enim de saltu firmano cuiusdam mali poetae qui dicebatur Mentula' (Avantius, *Emendationes* 1500, o 4v).

158. 93: *In Caesarem*; 94: *De Mentula;* 114: *De Saltu Firmano*; 115: *In Mentulam*.

159. 93–94: *In Caesarem*; 114–115: *In Firmanum*.

NOTES TO CHAPTER 3

1. For Leo X and the Golden Age, see C. L. Stinger, *The Renaissance in Rome* (Bloomington, Ind., 1985), 296–9 and references ad loc. For the biography of Valeriano (1477–1558) see V. Lettere, 'Dalle Fosse, Giovanni Pietro (Pierio Valeriano)', *DBI* (Rome, 1986), xxxii, 84–8; S. Ticozzi, *Storia dei letterati e degli*

artisti del dipartimento del Piave (Belluno, 1813) i. 85–150; K. Giehlow, 'Hieroglyphenkunde des Humanismus in der Renaissance', *Jahrbuch der kunsthistorischen Sammlungen des allerhöchsten Kaiserhauses*, 32 (1915), 113–29; L. Alpago-Novello, 'Nuove notizie intorno a Pierio Valeriano con documenti inediti', *Archivio storico di Belluno, Feltre, e Cadore*, 6 (1934), 477–84, 497–504; G. Bustico, 'Pierio Valeriano, poeta bellunese del sec. XVI', *Atti della R. Accademia roveretana degli Agiati*, 11 (1905), 155–76; G. Lucchetta, 'Contributi per una biografia di Pierio Valeriano', *IMU* 9 (1966), 461–76. For the lectures see L. Alpago-Novello, 'Spigolature vaticane di argomento bellunese. I. Un' opera inedita ed ignorata di Pierio Valeriano', *Archivio Veneto Tridentino*, 9 (1926), 69–96; J. H. Gaisser, 'Catullus', 255–9; 'The Catullan Lectures of Pierius Valerianus', in *Acta Conventus Neo-Latini Guelpherbytani* (Binghamton, NY, 1988), 45–53.

2. For Bolzanio see L. Gualdo Rosa, 'Dalle Fosse (Bolzanio), Urbano', *DBI* (Rome, 1986), xxxii. 88–92.
3. Sabellico commemorated the event in an epigram. See Valerianus, *Amorum Libri V* (Venice, 1549) 17v: 'M. Ant. Sabellicus Ioannis Petri Valeriani Nomen in Pierium vertit hoc Epigrammate. Petrus eras, cum te tot Norica Saxa tenebant; / Pierus ad Venetae dictus es Urbis aquas. / At postquam Cyrrha superato Antra illa subisti, / Adscribi Aoniis ut mereare choris, / Iam mihi nec Petrus, neque Pierus; ista facessant, / Sed fueris vero nomine Pierius.'
4. Egidio became a Cardinal in 1517; Gian-Francesco della Rovere was Bishop of Turin and Governor of Castel S. Angelo.
5. Valeriano fits almost perfectly the model of the curial humanist described by J. D'Amico, *Renaissance Humanism in Papal Rome* (Baltimore, 1983), 38–60. For his sinecures see Alpago–Novella, 'Nuove notizie,' and Lucchetta, 'Contributi'.
6. For the importance of the *Castigationes* see V. Zabughin, *Vergilio nel Rinascimento italiano*, (Bologna, 1923), ii. 72–5 and Grafton, *Joseph Scaliger*, 48–51.
7. *De litteratorum infelicitate* was written in 1529, but first published only in the Venice edition of 1620. Two editions of the *Hieroglyphica* were published in 1556. The first, containing only eight books, was published in Florence; the second, published in Basle, contains the complete work.
8. On Pasquino see R. and F. Silenzi, *Pasquino: Cinquecento Pasquinate* (Milan, 1932), and D. Gnoli, *La Roma di Leon X* (Milan, 1938), 164–84, 300–29.
9. 'Exul eram: redii tandem, regnante Leone. / Nunc iuvenes studiis vigilate meis. / Namque Leone meo nemo indonatus abibit. /

Carminibus vates munera magna ferent.' The verses, from *Carmina apposita Pasquillo anno MDXIII*, are quoted from Gnoli, *La Roma di Leon X*, 178. The phrase *Musarum et pacis amator* is from the same poem. The frontispiece showing Apollo from the collection of 1513 is reproduced in Gnoli, p. 179.

10. Gnoli, *La Roma di Leon X*, 180.
11. Ibid. 133–4; Pastor, *The History of the Popes*[2], viii. 183–220.
12. For Colocci see especially Federico Ubaldini, *Vita di Mons. Angelo Colocci*, ed. V. Fanelli (Città del Vaticano, 1969).
13. For Goritz see L. Geiger, 'Der älteste römische Musenalmanach', *Vierteljahrsshrift für Kultur und Literatur der Renaissance*, 1 (1886), 145–61; Gnoli, *La Roma di Leon X*, 151–60; and V. Bonito, *The Saint Anne Altar in Sant' Agostino, Rome*, Ph.D. diss. (New York University, 1983). A collection of the commemorative poems was published in 1524 by the poet Blosio Palladio: *Coryciana* (Rome, 1524). See J. Ruysschaert, 'Les Péripéties inconnues de l'édition des "Coryciana" de 1524', in *Atti del Convegno di studi su Angelo Colocci: Jesi, 13–14 settembre 1969* (Jesi, 1972), 45–56; P. P. Bober, 'The "Coryciana" and the Nymph Corycia', *JWCI* 40 (1977), 223–39; V. De Caprio, 'L'Area umanistica romana (1513–1527)', *Studi romani*, 29 (1981), 321–35. For a literary discussion of the *Coryciana* see J. IJsewijn, 'Poetry in a Roman Garden: The *Coryciana*', in *Latin Poetry and the Classical Tradition: Essays in Medieval and Renaissance Literature*, ed. P. Godman and O. Murray (Oxford, 1990), 211–31. Three poems on Sansovino's statue are found in P. Valerianus, *Hexametri, odae, et epigrammata* (Venice, 1550) 104v–5v; two of these appear in the *Coryciana*.
14. The Pope was only 46 (Pastor, *The History of the Popes*[2], viii. 65).
15. 'Quamvis obruit ingenium patientia longa malorum, earumque iacturarum, quas in Leone Decimo Pontifice Maximo Domino meo tam repente, tam ante diem erepto feci, non sum tamen tot casibus, tot difficultatibus, tot aerumnis, tot calamitatibus ita fractus, ut qui meus est erga vos amor, quae vestri profectus cura, studiosi adolescentes, non statim ad studia me contulerim, ubi primum in novi pontificis tam procul accersiti absentia, bonarum artium propemodum desolatione, aperiri ludum intellexi, et gymnasia frequentari conspexi. Tantillum igitur illud mentis, quod ex fusa lapsaque acie colligere potui, totum id ad earum rerum meditationem converti, quae vobis usui fore iudicarem.' (Biblioteca Apostolica Vaticana, Vat. lat. 5215, fol. 26r).
16. Pastor, *The History of the Popes*[3] ix. 1–33.
17. 'votis Hadrianus omnium / Fit Pontifex, sed omnibus / Quis

credat? invitis. Deum vis haec Deum / Deum abditum hoc arbitrium est. / Ut, qui natantis dispuunt regnum trabis, / Parere discant Viperae. / Ut invicem qui se oderant Patres, ducem / Invisum haberent omnibus' (*Hadriano Pont. Max. designato*, vv. 19–26, in P. Valerianus, *Hexametri Odae et Epigrammata*, 71v). See also *Sodalium Convictus Die Bacchanalium*, in the same volume, 74–5.

18. P. Valerianus, *De litteratorum infelicitate* (Geneva, 1821), 17. And again: 'pestilentia illa . . . quae cum Adriano Sexto advecta Romam invasit' (*De litteratorum infeliciate*, 13). The plague is discussed by Adrian's contemporary biographer, Paolo Giovio, 'Vita Hadriani Sexti Pont. Max.', in *Elogia virorum bellica virtute illustrium* (Florence, 1551), ii. 135–7.

19. Melini (or Mellini) was the brother of Celso Mellini, famous for his dispute with the Belgian humanist, Christophe Longueil; the family was among the richest and most noble in Rome. See D. Gnoli, 'Un giudizio di lesa romanità sotto Leone X', *Nuova Antologia*, 115 (1891), 691–6. According to Gnoli (p. 696), Valeriano had taught the young Melini before becoming tutor to Alessandro and Ippolito de' Medici. *De litteratorum infelicitate* is set at Pietro's house; Book XXVI of the *Hieroglyphica* is dedicated to him.

20. Ippolito de' Medici (1511–35) was an illegitimate son of Giuliano de' Medici. In 1523 Clement VII established him and his cousin Alessandro as puppet rulers of Florence, but they were driven into exile in May 1527 by revolutionaries who had taken advantage of the Sack of Rome to oust the Medici and re-establish the Florentine republic. See Pastor, *The History of the Popes* ix. 426; G. Moretti, 'Il cardinale Ippolito dei Medici dal trattato di Barcellona alla morte (1529–1535)', *Archivio storico italiano*, 98 (1940), 137–78.

21. 'Petrus Melinus Romanus Hippolyto Medicae s.p.d. Post relictam a publicis hostibus patriam suisque sedibus Clementem restitutum, ubi domum me recepi, nihil mihi prius curae fuit, magnificentissime Hippolyte, quam libros revisere omnesque tum meos tum amicorum qui apud me asservabantur colligere, ut eos ex tam foeda et diuturna tempestate velut certo in portu collocarem, quos dum sedulo et diligenter evolverem, multosque partim in ignem coniectos partim efferatissimis manibus dilaceratos et in frusta concerptos [*conscerptos*, MS], partim etiam deperditos, et non ab inimicis tantum, sed etiam a nostris distractos ex Mauro puerulo quem solum domi reliqueram, comperissem, magno afficiebar dolore, ut qui iacturam sane longe aliis omnibus graviorem et nullo

sarciendam tempore aestimarem. Accidit tamen bono certe fato ut inter miserabilem huiusce stragis ruinam apparerent nonnulla Pierii nostri monumenta, quae is dum publice in Ro. gymnasio Catullum interpretaretur brevibus quibusdam scedulis adnotarat. Accedebant hu[c] pleraque alia quae nos ex legentis ore excepta [excerpta, MS] describi iusseramus, mox in unum collecta et suis reddita partibus. Licet pleraque interierint, ne quo tamen tempore funditus pessum irent, volui ea sic descripta ad te mittere, ut quando nunc ut accepi coactus est ille domesticas res suas invisere, haberes in indignissimo hoc exilio iucundam sane quare te oblectares lectionem, tam et si eam nondum absolutam, longe enim satius putavi luxatum hoc atque mutilum tuas in manus tradi quam supprimere, exemplum in hac re secutus nostrum et praecipue tuum, qui cum miro antiquorum operum desiderio tenearis, soles vel unum statuae alicuius pedem aut manum aut caput admirari nec minore cum diligentia ista perquiris quam faceres integra, quippe cum vel ex illis artificis ingenium artemque et solertiam perpendas. Tu velim haec praeceptoris tui scripta publicanda cures, neque quicquam vereare id eo inscio et inconsulto facere. Nam aequo animo ferat necesse est quod et meo qui illi amicissimus sum consilio, et auctoritate tua, cuius ille patrocinio tot annos fruitur factum fuerit, neque est ut nostrum de se iudicium sit unquam aspernaturus. Tu vale et nos atque illum quod facis ama. Romae. Kal. Martiis MDXXVIII' (Vat. lat. 5215, fol. Ir–v).

22. The manuscript is Vat. lat. 5215. For a survey of its contents, see Alpago-Novello, 'Spigolature', 78–9.
23. For Puteolano see Chapter 1, pp. 32–3; for Calfurnio, Chapter 1, p. 35; for Partenio, Chapter 2, pp. 86–7.
24. 'Pierii Valeriani Bellunensis Ro. Gymnasii Professoris Praelectiones in Catullum Auditorum Quorumdam Diligentia Dum Profiteretur Ad Verbum Exceptae' (Vat. lat. 5215, fol. 1). For *excipio*, 'take dictation', see Rizzo, *Lessico*, 95.
25. R. Sabbadini, *Il metodo degli umanisti* (Florence, 1920), 35–8. Some fifteenth-century lectures are given in K. Müllner, *Reden und Briefe italienischer Humanisten* (Vienna, 1899). Reprint with introduction, summaries, bibliography, and indexes by B. Gerl; Munich: Wilhelm Fink, 1970; see especially the summary analyses on pp. lxv–lxxviii.
26. 'L'elogio delle arti liberali dava agio agli oratori di far pompa di ornamenti rettorici e di sfoggiare dottrina, tanto che a quei discorsi si accorreva più per solleticar gli orecchi che per imparare . . .' (Sabbadini, *Il metodo*, 35).

27. 'nullam esse disciplinam, quam quis absolute callere possit, et tamen hi grammaticum unum omnia praestare compellunt, uni illi omne scriptorum genus evoluendum, uni illi poetas, historicos, oratores omnes ediscendos, uni illi philosophos, mathematicos, iurisconsultos, atque etiam theologos excutiendos, nihil illi condonandum, nihil indulgendum; quem non modo coelestium et mortalium cognitione institutum efflagitant; sed eorum etiam quae parva existimantur non ignarum, ut nihil denique (fols. 11v/12) sit, ne in minimis quidem quod eum possit fallere. At miror cur non his legibus illud etiam addiderint oportere grammaticum mortalem esse quendam deum' (Vat. lat. 5215, fols. 11v–12).

28. 'Grammaticorum enim sunt hae partes, ut omne scriptorum genus, poetas, historicos, oratores, philosophos, medicos, iureconsultos excutiant atque enarrent' (Poliziano, *Lamia* in *Opera Omnia* i. 460). See also Angelo Poliziano, *Lamia*, A. Wesseling, ed. and comm. (Leiden, 1986) 16 and 99–101; A. Scaglione, 'The Humanist as Scholar and Politian's Conception of the *Grammaticus*', *Studies in the Renaissance*, 8 (1961), 49–70.

Earlier in the first lecture Valeriano states the duty of the *grammaticus* in the form of a 'law' that echoes the language of Quintilian and Poliziano: 'Grammaticus quicunque es omne scriptorum genus excutito, argumenta omnia suone an alieno elocutionis genere sint elaborata iudicato. In auctoribus non modo versus sed libros etiam qui falso videantur inscripti tanquam subditicios familia summoveto. Alios ex iudicii tui (fols. 3v/4) censura in ordinem redigito, alios omnino numero eximito. Addis etiam sanctionem: qui se talem praestare desperassit ab omni cathedra etiam triviali excidat' (Vat. lat. 5215, fols. 3v–4).

29. 'In me vero si non illa exacte reperientur, certe vos iuverit officiosa quaedam vestri profectus cura, vigilantia, sollicitudo. Potero admonitione, potero consilio, potero adhorta- (fols. 13v/14) tionibus prodesse. Quod ut mihi persuadeam multorum adolescentium profectus in causa est, qui meis ad virtutem stimulis incitati cursum felicissime corripuere.

'De me itaque sic habetote, parentis erga vos animum hodie mihi desumendum esse, et in eorum loco succedendum, qui vos genuere, qui vos educarunt, qui vos litteris et moribus maxime cupiunt erudiri. Quocirca meum non in eo tantum se studium continebit, ut quae auctores scripserint intelligatis, sed id etiam pro viribus adnitemur, ut vos quoque similia facere, et cum auctoribus ipsis gressum conferre parem contendatis.

'Spero enim futurum, ut quos vivida virtus excitabit, ingenium primum ad imitationem adcommodent, mox cum antiquis ipsis scriptoribus certare aggrediantur; in quo si non exemplo vos iuvero, quippe in dicendo non admodum exercitatus saltem fungar vice cotis, acutum reddere quae ferrum valet exsors ipsa secandi' (Vat. lat. 5215, fols. 13v–14). Valeriano's linking of literary accomplishment with moral development belongs to the rhetoric of humanist education. See Grafton and Jardine, *From Humanism to the Humanities*, 1–28.

30. 'Ante opus quidem quae scriptoris intentio fuerit, si lectioni nos accingamus, quae inde utilitas emersura, quae feratur inscriptio, legitimumne opus sit, an adulterinum. In opere (fol. 15/15v) lectionis ordo qui statuatur, in quot capita vel partis dividatur, qui modus institutionis, nam libri omnes docent. Demum ad quam encyclopaediae partem referatur' (Vat. lat. 5215, fol. 15r–v). For parallels to Valeriano's eight questions see Iohannes Argyropulos' lectures on Aristotle in Müllner, *Reden und Briefe*, 13–14 and 53–4.

31. 'Prodest utique quum virtutes celebrat, illustrium virorum adoreas interire non sinit, quorum exemplo reliqui subinvitati ad gloriae cupiditatem accendantur. Prodest dum vitia carpit, malos mores exsecratur, et mortales omnes a sceleratorum quos carminibus proscindit imitatione conatur avertere. Delectat quum amatorios affectus exprimit, lepores, delicias, illecebras meditatur, divis laudes canit, epithalamia modulatur' (Vat. lat. 5215, fol. 18).

32. 'quippe quum affectus exprimit amatorios, quum, in fratris luctu naturae concedit doloris magnitudinem, et suas dat partes pietati, quum deos agnoscit, quibus sacra canit, quum viros laude dignos celebrat, quum modum voluptatibus statuit, (fols. 22v/23) quum e perturbationum voraginibus emergens sese interdum colligit et fortitudinem, iustitiam, et temperantiam prudenter amplexatur . . .' (Vat. lat. 5215, fols. 22v–23). Valeriano sees the encyclopaedia as an organic whole, likening it to a body whose members are the several parts of learning (grammar the feet, music the teeth, philosophy the heart, etc.) (Vat. lat. 5215, fol. 17v). For more on the encyclopaedia see J. Seznec, *The Survival of the Pagan Gods*, trans. B. F. Sessions (Princeton, 1972), 122–47.

33. 'Quantum vero utilitatis ex poetae huius lectione consequi possimus, superfluum est recensere, quum non minus vobis quam mihi innotuerit, quantum is prodesse possit, quem uno omnes ore doctum, uti dicebamus, suo quodam proprioque nuncuparint elogio, qui eo floruerit tempore, quo latini sermonis puritas atque elegantia maxime vigebant, quem praestantissimi quique mox secuti pro exemplo sibi proposuerint ad imitandum. Neque hoc tantum pro utilitate quae phrasin faciat dictum accipiatis, verum

etiam quae inventionem iuvet, dispositionem doceat, elocutionem variis carminum generibus in sua quamque specie luculentam, ornatam, cultam, et elegantem ostentet' (Vat. lat. 5215, fol. 18v).

34. 'Ordo autem huic libro esse mihi videtur statim post imbuta, perceptaque grammatices rudimenta vel quum adolescens suo aliquid ingenio meditari ceperit. Tum quia argumenta ipsa plurimum brevia sunt, et ob id facilia, ad quae unusquisque suum accomodet ingenium. Tum quia varia, atque ideo multas imitationis formas legentium animis imprimere possint quas vegeta fertiliaque ingenia numero modo hoc modo illo exprimere conentur' (Vat. lat. 5215, fol. 20v).

35. 'quo scilicet consilio Catullum potius quam scriptorem alium interpretandum desumpserimus causae reddendae sunt. Ea vero prima fuit quod ingeniosissimi plerique adolescentes, qui Latini sermonis nitore et elegantia capiuntur, non ignari quid ex Catullo assequi possent, ut eum praelegerem cotidiano convicio flagitarunt. Inde quia festis diebus mihi profitendum erat, eoque dierum interiecto spatio, breve aliquod argumentum, quippe quod una praelectione expediri posset, facere magis ad institutionem videbatur. Sed illud potissimum persuasit, quod ab optimis incipiendum praestantium virorum admonitione praecipitur' (Vat. lat. 5215, fol. 18r–v).

36. 'An non legistis vos, vel ab aliquo audistis, quae philosophi vetustiores de poetico furore, deque occupatione loquuntur? Deum quippe optimum maximum suam illam omnifariam sapientiam Apollini primum elargiri. Apollinem mox Musis omnibus, quae per novem caelorum orbes singulae singulis dispositae sunt, impartiri. Illas pro se quamque quibus faverint vatibus vim eandem inspirare, vates eadem in interpretes transfundere, interpretes auditoribus erogare, atque ita quadam veluti catena discipuli a praeceptore pendent, praeceptor a poeta, quem praelegit, poeta a musa, musa ab Apolline, Apollo a deo ipso occupatur' (Vat. lat. 5215, fol. 21).

37. Plato, *Ion*. 535e–36a, trans. Lane Cooper, in *The Collected Dialogues of Plato*, ed. E. Hamilton and H. Cairns (Princeton, NJ, 1978), 219–20.

38. 'Gradus autem quibus furor ille descendit, hi sunt. Iupiter rapit Apollinem. Apollo illuminat Musas. Musae suscitant et exagitant lenes et insuperabiles vatum animas. Vates inspirati interpretes suos inspirant. Interpretes auditores movent' (Marsilio Ficino, *De poetico furore* in *Opera Omnia* (Turin, 1959), ii. 1283).

39. *Valeriano*: 'Evenire vero ut alii aliis afficiantur numeris, pro ut quisque hunc vel illum ex planetis, ac perinde hanc vel illam ex

Musis originationis suae dominam sortitus fuerit' (Vat. lat. 5215, fol. 21). *Ficino*: 'Ab aliis vero Musis aliae animae rapiuntur, quia et aliis sphaeris sideribusque aliae attributae sunt animae, ut in Timaeo traditur' (*De poetico furore in Opera Omnia* ii. 1283). For Ficino and the Muses see especially A. Chastel, *Marsile Ficin et l'art* (Geneva and Lille, 1954), 129–40; M. J. B. Allen, *The Platonism of Marsilio Ficino* (Berkeley, Calif., 1984), 28–30.

40. M. Ficino, *De poetico furore* in *Opera Omnia* ii. 1283–4; Vat. lat. 5215, fols. 23–4v. The scheme of Ficino and Valeriano follows that of Macrobius, (*Somn. Scip.* 2. 3), at least for Urania and Calliope, the only Muses Macrobius names. Franchinus Gafurius presented a different scheme in his *Practica music*e (Milan, 1496), following the arrangement of Martianus Capella i. 27. Among other differences, in Martianus and Gafurius Thalia is on Earth, while in Ficino and Valeriano she is associated with the moon. For Gafurius, see Seznec, *Survival*, 140–2 and plate 48; E. Wind, *Pagan Mysteries in the Renaissance* (New York, 1968), appendix 6 (= pp. 265–9).

41. *Calliope*: Orpheus (Ficino); Catullus (Valeriano). *Urania*: Musaeus (F); Musaeus, Manilius (V). *Polyhymnia*: Pindar (F); Empedocles, Lucretius (V). *Terpsichore*: Hesiod (F); Hesiod, Phocylides, Theognis (V). *Clio*: Homer (F); Vergil (V). *Melpomene*: Thamyras (F); Horace (V). *Erato*: Sappho (F); Tibullus, Propertius (V). *Euterpe*: Ovid (F); Plautus, Terence, Martial (V). *Thalia*: Vergil (F); Ovid (V).

42. See Appendix 6 and Macrobius, *Somn. Scip.* 2. 3.

43. 'Afflari hac poetas eos dicunt, qui omnibus poeticis numeris, metrorum generibus omnibus, argumentis omnibus delectantur, in qua classe Catullum nostrum esse negarit nemo . . .' (Vat. lat. 5215, fol. 24 v).

44. 'quum denique hinc genii sit unusquisque sui similitudinem inventurus . . .' (Vat. lat. 5215, fol. 25).

45. 'age esto Catullus primus, qui profecturis in poetice discipulis proponatur, ut quum unusquisque in eum ex numeris inciderit, qui genio suo sit accomodatior, quo scilicet se non aliter moveri atque attrahi sentiat quam ferrum a magnete, paleam a succino, se ad eius imitationem accingat, eoque carminis genere sese exercere incipiat, quod magis ideae suae proprium esse animadverterit' (Vat. lat. 5215, fol. 25).

46. Both are printed in *Hexametri, odae, et epigrammata*. The reminiscence of Cat. 4 (*Diana Venatorem ignaviter facientem ornatu spoliat, consortioque abdicat*) advertises its paternity in the first verse: *Venator ille quem videtis Naiades*. *Hexametri* 65v–

66v). For the occasion of the poem see Gnoli, 'Le cacce di Leon X', in *La Roma di Leon X*, 217–65, and Chapter 6 n. 49 below. *Galliambum* appears on 70v–71.

47. General: *Ad Hieronymum Bononium Tarvisinum. Iambum unicuique materiae iam aptum esse* (*Praeludia*, I 4). *Prolixitatem non incongruam hendecasyll.* (*Praeludia, E 1*). Specific: *In Plinianum Illud: duriusculum se fecit. Ad Petr. Aleandrum ex Corneliano* (*Praeludia*, K 4). *De decoro iambici carminis. Ad Paulum Dandulum* (*Praeludia*, K 2v–K 3). *De scazonte. Ad Annib. Phaethonta* (*Praeludia*, K 3v).
48. For Avanzi see pp. 60–3.
49. Terentianus receives a bare mention in the commentary of Alessandro Guarino. See n. 64 below.
50. For the discovery and early editions of Terentianus Maurus see H. Keil, *Grammatici latini* (Leipzig: 1874), vi. 245, 315–17. The treatise *De ratione metrorum* of the fourth-century grammarian Marius Victorinus, which was based on Terentianus, was printed in 1473, but seems not to have been used by Catullus' fifteenth-century editors. For Victorinus see Keil vi. xviii–xxii.
51. *Iambics*: *De decoro iambici carminis* (*Praeludia* K 2v–K 3); Ter. Maur. 2181–212 (Keil, vi. 390–1). *Scazons*: *De scazonte* (*Praeludia* K 3v); Ter. Maur. 2398–418 (Keil, vi. 397). Valeriano mentions Terentianus in *De decoro iambici carminis*, 10–11: 'Terentianus hocce carmen approbet / Quod alterius indiget pedis nihil.' (cf. Ter. Maur. 2184.)
52. Ter. Maur. 2539–912 (Keil, vi. 401–11). Terentianus based his account on Caesius Bassus (first century AD), whose work was also discovered in Bobbio in 1493. See Keil, vi. 258–63.
53. 'Id vero potissimum dignitatis habet carmen hoc, quod constat ex tomis eorum versuum, qui antiquissimi omnium ac celeberrimi censentur. Ex heroica quippe tome, atque ex iambea. Est autem tome ut iuniores intelligant, pars alicuius carminis [*the following words are crossed out*: uno plus pede numerosa] quae ab reliquo dissecatur, ita ut vel ipsa per se genus aliquod carminis adstruat vel sectioni alteri copulata diversam efficiat speciem' (Vat. lat. 5215, fol. 28v).
54. 'ut hoc uno recte percepto numero facile possemus per multa versuum genera ingenium exercere' (Vat. lat. 5215, fol. 36).
55. 'Sena- (fol. 64/64v) rius Archilocheus ex sex continuis iambis. Hoc numero usus Archilochus, quum Lycamben, quia ille filiam quam ei desponderat, postea negavit acerrime proscindere aggressus est; quumque in Lycamben ea profudisset, quae in profligatissimum quenque ingeri possunt, tanti ille dedecoris impatiens, laqueo

vitam finivit. Hic igitur versus amarus, impotens, ultor furibundus clamosus, impetuosus et rabie propemodum efferatus apud veteris fuit' (Vat. lat. 5215, fol. 64r–v). Cf. Ter. Maur. 2181–204 (Keil vi. 390–1). (The story of Lycambes' suicide does not appear in Terentianus.)

56. 'In primis genus carminis exquisivit quod pari celeritate cum velocissimo, quem scribit, fasello gradum conferre posset. Atque ea causa fuit, cur totum hoc poemation ex solis iambis struere voluerit' (Vat. lat. 5215, fol. 66v).

57. See Terentianus' comments at 2277, 2279, 2283, 2311 (Keil vi. 393–4).

58. 'Atque haec de numero huius epigrammatis quod hodie prae manibus est dixisse sufficeret, nisi quidam ex vobis, ingenio admodum eleganti praediti, heri ex me petiissent, de huius carminis conficiendi ratione, quum tempus incideret, apertius atque simplicius dissererem. Sic igitur habetote. Si vobis liceat per vocabulorum copiam quae numerum hunc efficiat, agite versus singulos senis iambis pangite. (fol. 65/65v) Sin locutiones tot minime succurrent, ut continuare possitis, et alia dictu speciosa, sed vel spondaica, vel dactylica, vel anapaestica in mentem venerint ea minime repudiate' (Vat. lat. 5215, fol. 65r–v).

59. 'nolim vos inventionis impetum retardare . . .' (Vat. lat. 5215, fol. 66.

60. For three trochees in the hendecasyllable see Appendix 7. 2. For phallic trochees see Ter. Maur. 1845–8, 2551–5 (Keil vi. 380, 401).

61. 'Est enim illud observatione dignum, quod veluti architecti primum omnium cavent, ne in aedifiicis excitandis, in decore peccetur, quod fieret si Marti atque Herculi, Corynthio opere, phana erigerentur, quod eiusmodi genus mollibus conveniat, aut si Veneri et Nymphis Dorico, quod genus masculae virtuti debetur, ita poeta noster id diligenter cavit, ut decorem servaret, et genus carminis pro argumentorum ratione adcommodaret. Itaque quum basia et blandicias, atque iocationes nescio quas describeret, molli et enervulo carminis genere usus est, sapphico quidem aut phalaecio hendecasyllabo. Nam quod tris in hoc versu continui trochei ex phallico genere cantilenae, quae Baccho et Priapo decantabatur, desumpti sunt, ideo necesse est ei inesse molliciem. Quum vero expeditissimam faselli, quo ex Bithynia in patriam vectus fuerat celeritatem (fol. 108v/109) commendare vellet, genere carminis usus est velocissimo, iambo quippe praepete ac celerrimo, nulla eum spondeorum gravitate impediente, quae gradum adeo concitatum moraretur. Nunc vero in re gravi atque acerba carminis

genere utitur rei maxime adcommodato, iambo s. scazonte, quod quidem genus et sententiis gravibus et rerum acerbitatibus explicandis maxime congruit. . . . Videtur enim versus hic, quia sede ultima spondei offenditur impedimento, quodammodo claudicare, qui si iambus esset, expeditissime decurreret. Id si cognoscere vultis exploratius agite ipsi aures vestras consulite, et versum qui est *Miser Catulle desinas ineptire* ita enuntiate *Miser Catulle desinas ineptias*. Videtis iam in iambeo senario velocitatem, in scazonte moram et quoddam quasi impedimentum' (Vat. lat. 5215, fols. 108v–109.

62. See pp. 61–2.
63. For Pliny's criticism see pp. 10–11 and Introduction, n. 41.
64. Terentianus explicitly discusses the opening of the hendecasyllable, using three verses from 1 as his model: 'verum mobilis hic locus frequenter / non solum recipit pedem, ut loquebar, / spondeum, sed et aptus est trochaeo, / nec peccat pede natus ex iambo. / exemplis tribus hoc statim probabis, / docti carmine quae legis Catulli, / "*cui dono lepidum novum libellum, / arido modo pumice expolitum?*" / "*meas esse aliquid putare nugas*"' (Ter. Maur. 2556–64 (Keil vi. 401)). Alessandro Guarino refers to this passage in his introduction to 1: 'Terentianus variationem istam tribus huius epigrammatis versibus annotavit. In quorum primo spondeo, in secundo trocheo, in tertio qui quartus est iambo usus fuit' (Guarinus, B 1).
65. 'trocheum ea ratione primam huius carminis sedem occupare, quod hic numerus maxima sui parte trochaicus est. . . . Iambum autem recipit non indecenter ob cognationem quam cum iambo dimidia sui parte contraxit. Nam spondeum ideo appetere manifestum est, quod veluti (30v/31) praefati sumus, versus hic plurimum incipit ab heroico' (Vat. lat. 5215, fols. 30v–31).
66. 'In rebus molle id appellare solemus, quod rarius, quod solutius, quod tenue magis, neque ulla asperitate aut pertinacia tactui resistit, eaque similtudo ad aures etiam transfertur, et quod illae liquidius et sine soni litterarumve, aut productorum temporum scabricie vel asperitate admittunt molle esse diiudicent. Durum autem quod densius atque compactius est, soliditateque praeditum tactui resistit, cedere nescium. Syllabam autem longam densiorem esse, quam brevis sit, nemini dubium crediderim. Ea enim ex duobus temporibus sub uno accentu compacta soliditatem prae se fert, quum brevis uno et perexili admodum constet tempore, eaque de causa sit magis tenuis et soluta magis, ac perinde mollior' (Vat. lat. 5215, fol. 32).
67. 'Profecto neminem ego tam a Musis alienum, tam obturatis

auribus esse crediderim qui rationem hanc non internoscat . . .' (Vat. lat. 5215, fol. 32).

68. e.g. 'agite ipsi aures vestras consulite . . .' (Vat. lat. 5215, fol. 109). 'quae si cui minus percipitur, age exemplum proponamus, ex quo aures unusquisque suas consulere poterit.' fol. 32v. And see n. 61.

69. 'debere grammaticos canonas suos ex antiquorum poetarum usu conficere, non autem veteres poetas ex iuniorum grammaticorum imperitia culpari' (Vat. lat. 5215, fol. 30v).

70. e.g., to defend *patrona* (vs. *patroa*) at 1. 9 he invokes 'manu scripti codices et qui primis impressionibus vulgati sunt . . .' (Vat. lat. 5215, fol. 42v). On 2. 1: 'invenio tamen in codicibus manu scriptis et in veteribus impressis, *deliciae* . . .' (fol. 47v). On 3. 12: 'Sed codices manu scripti quotquot vidi *illuc*, ad locum, habent' (fol. 59v). Valeriano does not say which editions he considers 'early', but evidently Vicenza 1481 is not among them, since it reads *patroa*.

71. 'Sunt qui *tenebriosum* legant, quod etiam in plerisque codicibus manu scriptis habetur. Sed *tenebricosum* est Latina locutio, et erudito illi saeculo frequens' (Vat. lat. 5215, fol. 59v).

72. 'Versiculus hic *passer deliciae meae puellae* loco hoc repetitus ex epigrammate superiore, in plerisque manu scriptis codicibus non habetur. Repetitus tamen tantum venustatis habet et elegantiae, tantum miserationis movet, ut si etiam Catullus hoc non fecisset, non possim tamen non summo opere probare eorum diligentiam atque iudicium, qui loco hoc repetendum censuere' (Vat. lat. 5215, fol. 56v). Although the verse is found in O, G, and R, it was omitted from all the editions before the first Aldine. See also Chapter 1, n. 82.

73. 'Quum tamen emendatiores codices habeant *o factum male* (fols. 61v/62) *o miselle passer*, et hiatus ille vocalium, absque synalaepha in locutionibus *male, o* in maesto praecipue argumento plurimum habeat venustatis, non ego aliam lectionem magis castam et legitimam esse crediderim' (Vat. lat. 5215, fols. 61v–62).

74. Unnecessary, because the Latin poets sometimes used hiatus in the Greek fashion; unmetrical, because in the collocation *male proh* the second syllable of *male* is lengthened before the two consonants in *proh* (Vat. lat. 5215, fol. 62). On the hiatus, see Goold, 'A New Text', 109; and Zicàri, 'Some Metrical and Prosodical Features of Catullus' Poetry', in *Scritti Catulliani*, 213–14.

75. 'si legas *o factum male, proh miselle passer*, nescio quid spissum et absonum, quodque aures offendat protuleris, quod denique sit a candore et puritate catulliana alienissimum' (Vat. lat. 5215, fol.

62). For Valeriano's criticism of Guarino's rewriting of 10. 27, see p. 100.

76. 'Infra legit Christoforus Papallis *inter caenam asini*, non autem *Marucine*, quae lectio mihi mirum in modum placet' (Avantius, *Emendationes* 1495, a 2v). He makes a different claim in 1500: 'Lege *inter coenam asini*. Fere omnes codices bene habent' (*Emendationes* 1500, o 2). The reading appears in the first Aldine.

77. 'In codicibus quidem manu scriptis nusquam ego *inter cenam* scriptum inveni, sed vel *Matrucine*, vel quod in pluribus atque his ipsis antiquioribus habetur *Marrucine*. Quare putarim omnino *inter cenam* suppositiciam esse lectionem, quum praesertim quod in subsequenti versu est *in ioco atque vino*, idem significet, quod intercenandum. Facile vero evenire potuit ut ex aliqua docti omnino hominis paraphrasi, quae uti fit, in margine adscripta esset, crediderint isti *inter cenam* poetae verba esse debere, atque ut novi aliquid atulis- (fol. 167v/168) se in medium viderentur, casta lectione expuncta adulterinam intruserint. Id vero qua ratione tueantur ipsi viderint. Nos Timonis Phliasii admonitionem secuti, qui vetera exemplaria, in quae nemo manus iniecisset perquirenda respondit, si castigata ea cuperemus; legamus age *Marrucine*, ut in vetustis codicibus habetur' (Vat. lat. 5215, fols. 167v–168). For Timon see Diogenes Laertius 9. 113. He is supposed to have given this advice to Aratus, who had asked how to find a good text of Homer.

78. Pontano's manuscript of Catullus and Tibullus is included in the inventory of his books presented in 1501 to S. Domenico Maggiore in Naples. E. Pèrcopo, *Vita di Giovanni Pontano* (Naples, 1938), 120–1. For Pontano and Cat. 84 see p. 69. For his imitations of Catullus, see Chapter 5. He is credited with two emendations in Goold's census ('A New Text', 99).

79. 'Est mihi praeterea in animo, cognito iam ubique Pontano nostro atque ipsius fama extra omne periculum posita, iuveniles quosdam eius lusus (si Actio nostro ita videbitur) in lucem proferre. Quorum quidem suppuduisse hominem illud declarat, quod eius rei nullam dum vixit mentionem unquam fecerit. Hi sunt exquisiti quidam commentarioli in Valerium Catullum, cuius illum constat iuvenem studiosissimum fuisse. Quod si iniuria mortuo fiat edendis iis quae ille contemnebat quaeque a viri gravitate aliena omnino videri possint, audacia haec nostra legentium utilitate compensetur. Sunt enim talia ut neminem omnino ea legisse poeniteat.' The letter is printed in Summonte's edition of Pontano's *De immanitate* (Naples, 1512), verso of title leaf.

In a vernacular letter to Colocci in 1515 Summonte despairs of getting the notes: Vat. lat., Reg. lat. 2023, fol. 352v; published in E. Pèrcopo (ed.), *Le rime del Chariteo* (Naples, 1897), p. ccxcvi. The evidence for Pontano's notes is discussed in detail in Gaisser, 'Catullus', 209–11.

80. Summonte's pupil, Traiano Calcia, writing to Colocci in 1548, says that he acquired the notes during the siege of Naples (1528), and promises that he will have them published by Paolo Manuzio. See Pèrcopo, *Vita di Giovanni Pontano*, 294.

81. The problems are summarized by Zicàri, 'Sul primo carme di Catullo', in *Scritti catulliani* 147–50 (= *Maia* 17 (1965), 236–9).

82. Pontano's version of 1. 9 is variously reported: *qualecumque quod ora per virorum*; *qualecumque quidem ora per virorum*; *qualecumque per ora quod virorum*. The first is reported by his fellow Neapolitans Pucci and Parrasio. The second is a variant (*quidem* was introduced by Venice 1472; scholars who had that reading in their editions kept it in their report of Pontano). The third is given by Ermolao Barbaro, Avanzi, and Palladio. See nn. 85–7 below.

83. Quoted by Cicero, *Tusc. Disp.*, 1. 15. 34.

84. e.g. by Ermolao Barbaro, *Castigationes Plinianae* (Rome, 1492), XIV. 24; Avanzi, *Emendationes* 1495, a 5v; Palladio, 1496, a 3. The fact that Barbaro, Avanzi, and Palladio cite Pontano's line as *qualecunque per ora quod virorum* supports Pozzi's suggestion that Avanzi and Palladio are quoting from Barbaro (Pozzi (ed.), *Hermolai Barbari Castigationes Plinianae* vol. i. p. cxxi.

85. For Pucci's notes see p. 52 and Chapter 1 n. 103.

86. 'Nec omittam quae acri ingenio gravique iudicio poeta Pontanus emendabat: *qualecunque quod ora per virorum*. Quod ipse Catullus etiam si suum non sit pro suo libenter agnoscat' (Naples, Biblioteca Nazionale, MS. XIII. B. 12, fol. 4). For Parrasio's unfinished commentary (abandoned at 4. 20–1) see Richardson, 'Pucci, Parrasio, and Catullus', and Gaisser, 'Catullus', 249–50.

87. 'De emendatione Catulli ad Iovianum: Doctus ab Elysia redeat si valle Catullus / ingratosque trahat Lesbia sola choros / non tam mendosi moerebit damna libelli / gestiet officio quam Ioviane tuo. / Ille tibi amplexus, atque oscula grata referret; / mallet et hos numeros quam meminisse suos' (Iacopo Sannazaro, *El.* I. 13). Muret, commenting on 1. 9 fifty years later, disagreed: 'Amice Sannazarius, et venuste. Sed Catullus mallet profecto, ut opinor, suos. Ego, etsi non video, quid aptius appingi potuerit, satius tamen duco, esse lacunas in bonis libris, quam easdem ex cuiusquam ingenio expleri' (M. A. Muretus, *Catullus et in eum commentarius* (Venice, 1554), 2r–v).

88. B. Soldati, 'Un emistichio di Manilio e quattro lacune di Tibullo', *Rivista di filologia e d'istruzione classica*, 28 (1900), 287–90.
89. 'Verum hic operae precium est varias multorum opiniones percurrere, qui locum hunc diversimode capiunt, mutant, invertant. Ut vero eos missos faciam qui tam impudenter castam lectionem ausi sunt pervertere, ne dicam vitiare dum legitimis verbis expunctis adulterinum hemistichium imprimendum curavere, *ora per virorum*; quoque impudentiam tueantur suam falso Iovianum Pontanum hoc pro Catulliano publicasse obiectant. Sed enim scio ego ex fide dignis hominibus Iovianum Pontanum virum in re litteraria aetate nostra summum, non eo consilio in sui codicis margine scripsisse *qualecumque quidem ora per virorum*, vel *qualecumque quod ora per virorum*, ut eam pro Catulliana lectione venditaret, sed quia solebat animi gratia cum au- (fol. 42 r–v) ctoribus ita iocari, quo ingenium ipse suum experiretur et stilum exerceret. Quare iam eam lectionem, quae est *ora per virorum*, eorum confessione qui ex Pontano ipso rem acceperunt, nimirum adulterinam praeteribimus' (Vat. lat. 5215, fol. 42r–v).
90. The expression 'iuveniles . . . lusus' strongly suggests poetry. For *lusus* of poetry see H. Wagenwoort, '*Ludus Poeticus*', in *Studies in Roman Literature, Culture, and Religion* (Leiden, 1956), 30–42.
91. 'Quam lectionem ex Hermolai Barbari codice desumpsi' (Vat. lat. 5215, fol. 245). Statius attributed *tritius* to Pontano, as do modern editors.
92. 'Itaque doctissimi viri, Pierius Valerianus, et Gabriel Faernus, coniecturam fecerant valde probabilem, legendum, *Ilia et emulso*' (Statius, *Catullus*, 371).
93. 'Nos igitur quid faciemus? An non licebit Academiae Romanae in re quae sit in medio posita, aliquid attentare? Detur obsecro nobis etiam venia, ut ubi manifestum est mendum possimus eadem qua illi fecerunt lege aliquid excogitare. Ego igitur nulla dispuncta littera, nulla transposita dictione, nulla aliena locutione accersita, conservata veterum codicum lecti- (fol. 113 r–v) one, una tantum dictione, quae mihi curta videtur resarcita legerem pro *tu quoque impotens es, tu quoque impotens esto*' (Vat. lat. 5215, fol. 113r–v).
94. ['Fabullus, qui maxima poetae nostro necessitudine copulatissimus erat, quum audivisset Catullum amatoria quaedam poemata elucubrasse, cupidissimus ea audiendi forte Catullo significaverat, velle se, quando alias otium non dabatur, apud eum cenare die quodam, quo scilicet aut negotiis aut litibus ex-(fols. 177v/178) peditus esset; quare et pararet, et amicum expectaret. Forte autem ita quoque scripserat:] "Cenare institui Catulle apud te / Paucis si mihi dii favent diebus / Lite iam vacuus negotiisque / Ut mihi ipse

legas tuos amores." [Aut aliquid huiusmodi.'] (Vat. lat. 5215, fols. 177v–178).

95. 'Catullus autem nihil oblitus facetiarum, iocosaeque illius festivitatis, quam per universum opus passim inspergit respondet' (Vat. lat. 5215, fol. 178). Valerianus' interpretation might find some agreement among modern critics. See D. Burgess, 'Catullus C. 50: The Exchange of Poetry', *AJP* 107 (1987), 576–86.

96. The scholia on Apollonius Rhodius 3.26 preserve Simonides 70 (see D. L. Page (ed.), *Poetae Melici Graeci* (Oxford, 1967), 575) and a verse of 'Orpheus' (frag. 37 Kern). C. Wendel, *Scholia in Apollonium Rhodium Vetera* (Berlin, 1935), 216. Valeriano translates the latter into a hexameter ('At Saturnus Amorem, animorum et flabra propagat') and the former into glyconics: 'Infelix Veneris genus, / Astu et insidiis potens / Quem cuiusque doli arbitro / Gradivo peperit dea' (Vat. lat. 5215, fol. 182v).

97. 'delectat insuper ode haec Catulliana, pulcra ea, et usque adeo brevi totius fere terrarum orbis descriptione, delectat epithetorum proprietate, splendoreque atque elocutione apprime eleganti' (Vat. lat. 5215, fol. 146).

98. At 11. 11–12 the traditional text read: . . . *horribilesque ultimosque Britannos*. Cf. Mynors: *horribile aequor* etc.

99. Vat. lat. 5215, fol. 148v. cf. Stephanus Byzantinus, *Ethnikon*, ed. A. Westermann (Leipzig, 1839), s.v. *Arabia*, p. 48.

100. 'Superiore praelectione longa per Nilum navigatione fatigati ad inchoati epigrammatis finem pervenire non potuimus, quum praesertim ardua et perdifficilis via per obiectarum Alpium iuga nos absterreret. Hodie itaque facti ex tridui quiete alacriores in Gallias et Britannias iter arripiamus' (Vat. lat. 5215, fol. 156v).

101. 'Hic evenit ut oratores duo Britaniarum Regis, Hier . . . et Ricardus Paceus, ex improviso auscultatum ingrederentur. Quare professor ad eos inspectans ex improviso sermonem ita convertit' (Vat. lat. 5215, fol. 158v). The scribe has circled these sentences and added a marginal note (for a possible printer?): 'Haec in margine scribenda sunt uti glosa.'

Pace had been sent to Italy after Leo's death to win support for Cardinal Wolsey in the papal election, but arrived on January 12, three days after the election of Adrian VI. He arrived in Rome on January 27. (J. S. Brewer, J. Gairdner, and R. Brodie (eds.), *Letters and Papers of Henry VIII* (London, 1920), iii. 1995.) He could accomplish little in Rome, but remained through the spring, occupying himself with humanist pursuits, including a translation of Plutarch. For Pace see J. Wegg, *Richard Pace, A Tudor Diplomat* (London, 1932); and Richard Pace, *De Fructu qui ex doctrina percipitur*, ed. and trans. F. Manley and R. Sylvester (New York, 1967), ix–xiii.

102. 'HORRIBILES itaque Britanos ea potius de causa dictum a Catullo crediderim, qua dixit Horatius: "Visam Britanos hospitibus feros [*Odes* 3.4.33]". (fol. 161v) . . . Sed ne mores aut naturam eorum ita perseverasse persuasum habeatis, quanto olim immaniores fuere Britani, eo nunc mansuetiores, et hospitaliores inveniuntur, quamquam bellicosam ferocitatem minime unquam exuerint. Iidem tamen ingenio et disciplinarum cognitione insignes, facundia celebres, Grecarum et Latinarum litterarum studiis florentissimi nunc habentur. Cuiusmodi multos vobis recensere possem, Moros, [*here the scribe has left the space of about half a line, presumably for additional names*] et quem in urbe vestra educatum, nunc in subselliis vobiscum hodie honoris mei causa sedentem conspicitis Paceum, de quo quia praesens est, ne adulari videar, quae multa summa cum eius laude dici possent dissimulabo, alio loco et tempore ea repetiturus, eoque me convertam, ut eorum Regem Henricum minime illaudatum relinquam. Quem fata temporibus nostris benignioris naturae munus favendum obtulere ut Rex esset, atque idem admodum iuvenis, a quo omnis fere Europa iusti moderatique imperii exemplum sibi desumeret, a quo bonarum artium studia disci- (fols. 162v/163) plinasque ipsas, tum ingenii et eloquentiae exercitationes ad pietatem referre disceremus. Versantur enim in manibus omnium Regis huius castissimae lucubrationes, tam doctae, tam piae, tam vehementes, quibus profligatissima Luterianae factionis ne an pestilentiae dicam incepta, quae leges, sacra, profanaque omnia evertere aggressa erat felicissime demolitus est ut ex uno hoc quid spei sit reliquum cognoscatis si ut Platonis est sententia, tales futuri sunt cives, quales fuerint eorum reges' (Vat. Lat. 5215, fols. 162v–163).

103. See p. 117.

104. 'sciendum multa omnino eos de Bithynnia loqui potuisse . . .' (Vat. lat. 5215, fol. 129).

105. 'Haec et alia multa fuerant, quae de Bithynia dici potuerunt, *quid esset iam Bithynia*, sed meretriculae eius intentio eo tota ferebatur, ut partem eam quae ad divitias pertineret sedulo pervestigaret' (Vat. lat. 5215, fol. 130).

106. Mynors: *'mane,' inquii puellae*.

107. 'In quibus verbis enuntiandis videtur gestu quodam cogitabundo nescio quid secum meditari et forte etiam manu occipitium confricare ad memoriae vim excitandam. Sed dum interim Catullus quid responsurus sit exquirit age nos de Serapi quae forte vos audisse non pigeat referamus' (Vat. lat. 5215. fol. 139).

108. Valerianus used much of the same material verbatim in the *Hieroglyphica*: Joseph in Egypt, *Hieroglyphica* 1602, p. 28; Macrobius, p. 320; Serapis and Pluto (including quotations from the passage cited in n. 109) p. 320.

109. 'Non mirum igitur si meretrix avarissima, adeo sollicita est, ut ad Serapin deferatur, cui preces alleget, divitias et opes petitura . . . . Atque ideo ait (fols. 143v/144) *volo ad Serapin deferri*. Cui Catullus, quum aliquantulum, quid responsurus esset, haesitasset, demum dixit . . .' (Vat. lat. 5215, fols. 143v–144).

110. 'Quod initio proloquiorum nostrorum praefati sumus officium esse poetae vel prodesse, vel delectare, ita hactenus verum esse, ex novem epigrammatum (fol. 125 r–v) praelectionibus apparuit, ut nulla id ulterius indigeat probatione. Decimum autem hoc epigramma totum in utilitate consistit, ut scilicet nos admoneat, quo pacto possimus per occasionem impudentem meretricum petulantiam atque rapacitatem eludere, neque quicquam ubi malum molestumque earum ingenium deprehenderimus, rebus ipsi nostris quocumque modo consulere vereamur ut ita, quod proverbio fertur clavum clavo excutiamus' (Vat. lat. 5215, fol. 125r–v).

111. 'sed cum puella magis instaret non se sed C. Cinnam servos habere dixit et ita meretriculae elusit petulantiam' (Palladius, *Commentarii* a 5v). Cf. Guarinus: 'poeta . . . narrat quo puellam Varri amicam . . . in petitione servorum quos e Bithinia advexerat eluserit' (*Expositiones* C iv).

112. 'Et quod se paulo ante habere dixerat, nullo rubore perfusus, ut par pari referret, aberrasse ait se ex mentis alienatione, servos enim eos non esse sibi, sed Cinnae sodali suo . . . Quumque ita per insaniae simulationem sapiens evasisset meretricis ipsius petulantiam incessit quae adeo sit impudens ut non patiatur quemquam negligenter aut imprudenter quidpiam effari. Atque ita alios docet, ut quum in mores inciderint huiusmodi sibi constent, et eas semper ad petendum, ad spoliandum, et exhauriendum paratas esse suspicentur' (Vat. lat. 5215, fol. 126).

113. For Poliziano's interpretation and its critics see pp. 75–8.

114. 'nullum pene codicem invenias, qui non in damno sit, nullum interpretem qui idem cum altero sentiat, usque adeo omnes tam verba quam sensa pro animi sui libidine detorquent. Sed enim minus incommode actum esset, immo minus improbe, si contextum tantum arbitrio unusquisque suo lancinasset, vocabula invertisset, structuram implicasset, et modo in hanc modo in illam partem abstraxisset, si modo sententiae pepercissent, neque impudicum intellectum excogitassent ac tam prave Catullo turpitudinem, quae

nusquam in tam mundo epigrammate reperitur oggessissent. Bone Deus, an non satis in corpus saevitum erat, nisi animum ipsum etiam extinguere cogitassent? . . . (fol. 45 r–v) . . . At scimus quidem nos passeres adeo salaces esse, ut vel septies una hora saliant. Scimus ex medicorum dictatis passeribus in cibo datis, vel eorum ovis, venerem concitari. Scimus quid turpitudinis in mimis significet *τῶν στρουθῶν* hoc est passerum nomen. . . . Scimus (fols. 45v/46) ex sacerdotum Aegyptiorum commentationibus per passeris picturam prolificam hominis salacitatem significari. . . . Haec inquam scimus, sed quod apud Catullum, forte etiam apud Martialem, pudenda pace vestrarum aurium dixerim, virilia sub nomine passeris intelligi debeant, neque scimus, neque scire volumus' (Vat. lat. 5215, fols. 45–6).

115. 'Quod si volunt hi per mortuum passerem refrigeratum libidinis ardorem intelligere, et Catullum voluisse hoc verborum involucro se ad rem veneream non amplius idoneum ostendere, longe accersitum et ingeniosum nimis erit, quum praesertim Catullus haec in flore ipso iuventutis scripserit' (Vat. lat. 5215, fol. 46v).

116. 'numquid in uno de (fol. 46r–v) re turpi, in altero de vero passere loquitur? Atqui neminem tam stupidum esse crediderim, qui unum utriusque epigrammatis intellectum non fateatur' (Vat. lat. 5215, fol. 46r–v). Sannazaro made a similar argument in his attack on Poliziano. See pp. 245–6.

117. ['Sed enim haec vobis latius et copiosius disputabuntur] in commentariis quae de litterarum Aegyptiarum significatis parturimus' (Vat. lat. 5215, fol. 52v). Cf. *Hieroglyphica* 574 (apples), 609–10 (poppies).

118. 'et quando hodie sunt duplo magis subsellia repleta eorum concursu, qui alteri praelectioni non interfuerunt . . .' (Vat. lat. 5215, fol. 53).

119. 'Nunc unum addam pro corollario, quod ad has extincti passeris inferias conferamus. Nam et vos delectare possunt audiendo et exemplo plurimum iuvare. Passeribus vitae brevitas angustissima. Eorum enim mares anno diutius durare non posse tradunt, qui rerum huiusmodi historias conscripsere; cuius rei causam esse aiunt, incontinentissimam salacitatem; quae tot hominum etiam ante diem effoetos tradit senectuti. Contra vero corvinum genus, quia rarissime coit vivacissimum. Quare si vos vitae dulcedo capit adolescentes nihil vobis magis praestiterit quam venerem et caeci stimulos avertere amoris . . .' (Vat. lat. 5215, fol. 63). cf. *Hieroglyphica*, 207.

120. See p. 108.

121. 'Nulla enim commercia maiorem conciliant amiciciae coniunctionem

quam convictus, quam simul ali, et enutriri, unde sodales et sodalitium, pro amicorum eorum collegio qui saepe simul cenitant. Cuiusmodi Romae habetis (fol. 176 r–v) Sadoletium, Gyberticum, Coritianum, Colotiacum, Melineum, Cursiacum, Blosianum, et alia' (Vat. lat. 5215, fol. 176r–v).

A fuller picture is given in a nostalgic letter that Sadoleto wrote to Colocci in 1529: 'Ac mihi recordanti spatium praeteriti temporis et vetera animo repetenti, cum et plures convenire soliti eramus una, et erat aetas nostra ad omnem alacritatem, animique hilaritatem longe aptior; quoties venire in mentem putas eorum coetuum, conviviorumque, quae inter nos crebro habere solebamus? cum aut in hortis tuis suburbanis, aut in meis Quirinalibus, aut in Circo Maximo, aut in Tyberis ripa ad Herculis, alias autem aliis in urbis locis conventus agebantur doctissimorum hominum: quorum unumquemque et propria ipsius virtus et communis cunctorum praedicatio commendabat. Ubi post familiares epulas, non tam cupedia multa conditas, quam multis salibus, aut poemata recitabantur, aut orationes pronuntiabantur, cum maxima omnium nostrum, qui audiebamus, voluptate; quod et summorum ingeniorum in illis laus apparebat, et erant illa tamen, quae proferebantur, plena festivitatis et venustatis. . . .' (Jacopo Sadoleto, *Epist*. 5. 18 in *Opera omnia* (Verona, 1737), i. 118).

122. Thus, at the end of his discussion of 1. 2 (*arida modo pumice expolitum*): 'Haec sunt quae hactenus veluti in cavernosi pumicis latebris mihi delitescere videbantur. Nunc vero domini mei videtis petulantium adolescentium manum, qui lapsae nivis occasione nacta Como sacra facturi corticibus horrenda cavatis ora induxere. Satius itaque nobis fuerit, priusquam illi huc irrumpant vosque omnes nive conspargant hodiernae praelectioni finem facere' (Vat. lat. 5215, fol. 35v). He refers to the incident again in the next day's lecture: 'quumque circa aridam hanc, exustam, porosam cavernosamque pumicem nobis negotium esset, humidae, frigidae, solidaeque et compactae nivis lusu, lascivientium manu iuvenum adventante praelectionis nostrae series interrupta est' (fol. 37).

123. 'Soneto per la creatione dil Papa: O del sangue di Christo traditore, / Ladro Colegio che 'l bel Vaticano / A la todescha rabbia hai posto in mano, / Come per doglia non ti scoppia el cuore? / O mondo guasto, o secol pien di errore / Per fallace desir, o pensier vano! / Caduto / è a terra il bel nome Romano / E dato in preda al barbaro furore . . .' (Marino Sanuto, *I Diarii* 32 (Venice, 1892), 383). For this and other pasquinades on Adrian see Silenzi, *Pasquino. Cinquecento Pasquinate*, 217–22; V. Marucci, A.

Marzo, A. Romano, *Pasquinate Romane del Cinquecento* (Rome, 1986), i. 291.

124. *On the Laocoon*: Girolamo Negri, writing to Marc' Antonio Micheli on 17 March 1523, in G. Ruscelli (ed.), *Lettere di Principi* (Venice, 1581), i. 113. A similar account is given by Paolo Giovio, 'Vita Hadriani Sexti', 148. *On the Sistine Chapel*: 'una stufa d'ignudi', G. Vasari, 'Antonio Sangallo', in G. Milanesi (ed.), *Le Opere di Giorgio Vasari* (Florence, 1973), v. 456. Pastor considers Vasari's story a fiction (*History of the Popes*[3] 9, 73 n. 3).

125. 'Suspecta enim habebat poetarum ingenia utpote qui minus syncero animo de Christiana religione sentire, et damnata falsissimorum Deorum nomina ad veterum imitationem studiose celebrare dicerentur . . .' (Giovio, *Vita Hadriani Sexti*, 144–5).

126. There is no internal evidence to fix the times precisely. Valeriano broke off 'quum aestas omnino iam appeteret' (Vat. lat. 5215, fol. 194). One would expect him to resume in the autumn, but the plague broke out again in September and did not abate until December. See Pastor, *History of the Popes*[3] ix, 100–6.

127. 'Decreveram anno superiore iuvenes et adolescentes honestissimi Catullum ita vobis praelegere, ut ea dissimularem, quae propter impudicam argumentorum licentiam indigna videbantur, quae ex hoc loco exponerentur. Atque eo tunc consilio, quum in haec epigrammata incidissem, quae sine turpitudine enuntiari minime poterant, domesticis negotiis in patriam avocatus, quum aestas omnino iam appeteret, haud gravate finem feceram . . .' (Vat. lat. 5215, fol. 194).

128. 'nihil ad bonos mores aptius, nihil ad vitam hanc aulicam cum dignitate degendam utilius, nihil ad temperatam quandam rectae beataeque vitae rationem adcommodatius . . .' (Vat. lat. 5215, fol. 194v).

129. For the text and Valeriano's first lecture, see p. 116. On obscenity in his predecessors, see, for example, pp. 102–8. Compare Valeriano's insistence on chaste poetry in his preface to the *Amores*: 'Quod vero ad argumentum pertinet, eam in amoribus nostris modestiam, eumque pudorem secuti sumus, ut longe a multorum procacitate et impudentia recesserimus, darique locum, ut de amore, pudice et caste scribi possit, ostenderimus, quippe qui inductam in scena huiusmodi ante hac paucissimis admodum poetis Pudoris ipsius personam in his exhibuerimus' (*Amores* iiir–v).

130. 'Interpretes nonnulli malunt *meos amores* legere, quod quidam ita intelligunt ut si ipse bonam atque magnam cenam attulerit cum puella, Catullus contra amores suos, scilicet quicquid illud esset,

quod in deliciis haberet, exponere se polliceatur, atque huc trahunt illud *commendo tibi me ac meos amores*. Alii verecundius de puella intelligunt' (Vat. lat. 5215, fol. 181v).

131. 'Impium mihi videtur, ubi quid honeste et verecundia salva interpretari potest intellectum ad impudicitiam et mores malos distorquere' (Vat. lat. 5215, fol. 182).

132. Mynors: *Liguri iacet suppernata*.

133. 'Neque in congressu palaestraque coniugali suas agere scit partis, rem scilicet motu iuvare, quae quidem sunt viri partes, quum mulier alioqui ea inquam cui sit concipiendi cura minime motari debeat. . . . (fol. 226 r–v) . . . Hic autem adeo stolidus et rerum imperitus est, ut veluti truncus immobilis uxori inhaereat' (Vat. lat. 5215, fol. 226r–v).

134. *latera ecfututa* (6. 13): 'latera coitu frequenti tam exhausta et debilitata' (Vat. lat. 5215, fol. 95v). cf. 'latera tam frequenti rei veneris usu consumpta et liquefacta' (fol. 96v). *rumpens* (11. 20): 'confringens, debilitans, enervans . . . cunctorum latera qui tam frequenter ad palaestram provocati nimio certamine delassati labori ferundo amplius sufficere non possunt' (fol. 164v).

135. Thus, in quoting 6. 13 he says only, '*Cur non tam latera* et quae sequuntur' (Vat. lat. 5215, fol. 95).

136. 'tali assiduitate pergat viros tot elumbes reddere. Sed enim de lumbis, de renibus, et iliis alias copiose disputabimus' (Vat. lat. 5215, fol. 164v).

137. But Valeriano would have known of only the occurrences in 11 and 80, since the reading *ili* at 63. 5 was introduced by Bergk in the nineteenth century.

138. For Statius see pp. 129–30 and n. 92.

139. 'Vos autem ut susceptum semel opus absoluam efflagitatis bonaque pars vestrum queritur fraudari se lectione, quam omnium doctissimam existimetis. Quod vero meum fuerat consilium ut saltem multa dissimularem, plerique Catullum aiunt per nocturnam imaginem indignari visum, quod castrare velim suos libellos. Alii recidisse nos iterum in Gottica et Vandalica tempora lamentantur, quod videatur, veluti statuis omnibus illi virilia decutiebant, nunc quoque e libris, siquid pruriat, tolli. Alii laborem me, quod obiicitur, indignissime subterfugere incusant, aut vereri me, ne palam faciam imperitiam meam, qui forte in illis quid eruditionis lateat non intelligam. Alii hypocrisin, alii Curios me simulare, alii quaedam his acerbiora comminiscuntur. Quibus—' (Vat. lat. 5215, fol. 194v). (cf. Juvenal's remark on the worst sort of hypocrites, 'qui Curios simulant et Bacchanalia vivunt' (Juv. 2. 3).

140. 'Nam cum is Leoni Decimo suffectus esset, ad quem utpote litteratum Principem magnus litteratorum numerus confluxerat, dum non minora de Hadriano sibi quisque pollicetur, ecce adest Musarum, et eloquentiae totiusque nitoris hostis acerrimus, qui litteratis omnibus, inimicitias minitaretur, quoniam ut ipse dictitabat, "Terentiani" essent, quos cum odisse, atque etiam persequi caepisset, voluntarium alii exilium, alias atque alias alii latebras quaerentes, tamdiu latuere, quo ad Dei beneficio altero Imperii anno decessit, qui si aliquanto diutius vixisset, Gottica illa tempora adversus bonas litteras videbatur suscitaturus' (P. Valerianus, *De litteratorum infelicitate*, 69–70).

141. Poems 18, 19, 20 were not in Valerianus' text and do not appear in modern editions. They are Cat. frag. 1 and *Priapea* 36 and 35 in the *Catalepton*, which were inserted by Muret in 1554 and excluded by Lachmann in 1829. See pp. 166–7.

142. I wish to thank Professors Virginia Brown and G. N. Knauer for their expert examination of the manuscript. My discussion has greatly benefited from their comments and suggestions.

143. It is just conceivable that an additional whole gathering has been removed either after 194v or between 231v and 232r after Praelectio xxv, which ends a gathering. In this case, Lectures xxii and xxiii would have occupied 28 folios instead of 16, and the lecture on Cat, 21 would have occupied a whole gathering. But this hypothesis forces us to assume that the lectures as well as the folios were numbered after the alteration. The folios could have been numbered after the fact, but the lecture numbers and titles are part of the design of the pages where they occur.

144. See nn. 108, 117, 119.

145. 'Aegyptii per lumbos Venerem innuebant: hinc apud Comicos et Epigrammatarios Poetas, ubi quid lascivius enunciandum fuerit, frequens adeo de lumbis mentio . . . et Persius hoc, ubi lascivorum Poëmatum recitationem incessit, dicens: *Cum carmina lumbum intrant* [Persius 1. 20–1] . . .' (*Hieroglyphica*, 347–8).

146. 'qui sanctius instituti, rerum viscera et intimas medullas, non verborum superficiem, examinarent' (*Hieroglyphica*, 349).

147. 'Sed enim vitia ideo ponuntur, ut reprehendi possint, quodque abominabile videatur mortales audientes ipsi absterreantur' (*Hieroglyphica*, 245).

148. Pastor, *The History of the Popes* ix. 106–8. Cf. V. Fannelli, 'Adriano VI e Angelo Colocci', in *Ricerche su Angelo Colocci e sulla Roma cinquecentesca*, Studi e Testi 283 (Vatican City, 1979) 34: 'Invece di sovvenzionare poeti e buffoni preferiva soccorrere poveri e infermi.' For a detailed account of Adrian's attempts at

economizing and reform see R. E. McNally, SJ, 'Pope Adrian VI and Church Reform', *Archivum Historiae Pontificiae*, 7 (1969), 253–86.

149. 'e maggiore parte de gli huomini grandi gli hanno invidia, che vorriano poter fare il medesimo ancor essi, perchè in verità Roma non è più Roma. Usciti d'una peste, siamo entrati in una maggiore. Questo pontefice non conosce nissuno, non si vede una gratia. Omnia sunt plenissima desperatione' (Negri in *Lettere di Principi* (Venice, 1581), i. 113).

150. Pastor, *The History of the Popes* ix. 119. Cf. Negri in *Lettere di Principi* i. 114–15. Sanuto, *Diarii*, 34. 194.

NOTES TO CHAPTER 4

1. For the biography of Muret see C. Dejob, *Marc-Antoine Muret: Un professeur français en Italie* (Paris, 1881). For his teaching and relations with the Brigade poets, see P. de Nolhac, *Ronsard et l'humanisme* (Paris, 1921) 17–18, 92–100, 146–62; P. Laumonier, *Ronsard, poète lyrique*[2] (Paris, 1923) 95–6, 106–15; M. Morrison, 'Ronsard and Catullus: The Influence of the Teaching of Marc-Antoine de Muret', *Bibliothèque d' humanisme et renaissance*, 18 (1956), 240–74; I. Silver, 'Marc-Antoine de Muret et Ronsard', in R. Antonioli, R. Aulotte, *et al.* (eds.), *Lumières de la Pléiade* (Paris, 1966), 33–48.
2. 'Novus videbatur exortus Demosthenes Christianis Athenis. . . . concursus audiendi caussa ex tota urbe fiebant, magna hominum frequentia gymnasium celebrabatur, loci ipsi in gymnasio occupabantur. Aditus complebantur, ne pes quidem relinquebatur prae maxima auditorum multitudine, ubi pedem doctor ipse ponere posset, ita per illorum humeros, quasi per undas, gradiebatur ad suggestum, e quo, etsi magno ab omnibus audiebatur studio ac silentio, nihil magis timentibus, quam ne cito faceret dicendi finem, ubi tamen fecerat finem, mirifico omnium clamore et plausu excipiebatur' (Franciscus Bencius, 'Oratio in funere M. Antonii Mureti' in M. Antonii Mureti, *Scripta Selecta* (Heidelberg, 1809), vol. i. pp. xxiii–xxiv).
3. Silver, 'Marc-Antoine de Muret et Ronsard', 36.
4. Dejob, *Marc-Antoine Muret*, 20–1.
5. Voudroys tu bien apres les livres Grecz
   Que tu discours, recherchant la nature
   Aux monumentz de l'antique ecriture,
   Pour eclercir les plus divins segretz:

Voudroys tu bien oeillader ces regretz,
savant Muret, que la folle pointure,
Qui seme aux cueurs mainte epineuse cure,
Me fait pousser en ces soupirs aigretz?

(Antoine de Baïf, *A Marc Antoine de Muret*, 1–8, in *Les Amours* (Paris, 1552), 53).

I wish to thank my colleague, John Salmon, for his help with the translation.

6. As Mary Morrison observed ('Catullus and the Poetry of the Renaissance in France', *BHR* 25 (1963) 28).
7. 'Feci autem, quod locupletes interdum oenopolae solent, qui multa hospitibus vini genera gustanda proponunt, electuris quod ad palatum maxime fecerit' (Muretus, *Iuvenilia*, in *Opera Omnia*, ed. C. H. Frotscher (Leipzig, 1834), ii. 243–4).
8. For the literary theory of the *Preface* see p. 153. For Muret and Du Bellay's *Deffense* see de Nolhac, *Ronsard et l'humanisme*, 17–18. Prefatory poems were contributed by Jean Dorat, George Buchanan, Baïf, Nicolas Denisot, and Etienne Jodelle as well as by Muret's favourite pupil, Memmius Fremiot. Muret wrote epistles to Baïf and Jodelle (c. 122, 123) and odes to Dorat (c. 124), Ronsard (c. 127), and Denisot (c. 128).
9. Laumonier, *Ronsard, poète lyrique*[2], 120–4; J. Hutton, *The Greek Anthology in France* (Ithaca, NY, 1946), 123, 357–8.
10. Laumonier, *Ronsard, poète lyrique*[2], 93–8. For the text of the *Folastries* see Pierre de Ronsard, *Œuvres complètes*, ed. P. Laumonier (Paris, 1928), v. 1–94.
11. A qui donnai-je ces sornettes, 1
Et ces mignardes chansonnettes?
A toy mon Janot, . . .
. . . . .
Pren le donc, Janot, tel qu'il est, 23
. . . . .
Afin que toy, moy, et mon livre, 29
Plus d'un siècle puissions revivre.

(Ronsard, *A Janot Parisien*, *Œuvres complètes* v. 3–5).

See Laumonier, *Ronsard, poète lyrique*[2], 96–7.

12. Laumonier, *Ronsard, poète lyrique*[2], 96.
13. The *Livret* also includes *Dithyrambes à la pompe du bouc de Jodelle*, a bacchic poem celebrating the success of Jodelle's tragedy, *Cléopâtre*. Ronsard places Muret next to himself in the

triumphal procession (*Dithyrambes*. 138, *Œuvres complètes*, v. 62).

14. Laumonier, *Ronsarde, poète lyrique*[2], 98.

15. 'Adopte moy aussi en la famille francoyse ces coulans et mignars hendecasyllabes, à l'exemple d'un Catulle, d'un Pontan et d'un Second . . .' (Joachim Du Bellay, *La Deffense et Illustration de la langue francoyse*, ed. H. Chamard (Paris, 1904) 228–9).

    For the vogue for Catullan poetry see Morrison, 'Ronsard and Catullus', 250; and 'Catullus and the Poetry of the Renaissance in France', 25–56.

16. See de Nolhac, *Ronsard et l'humanisme*, 92–101; Silver, 'Marc-Antoine de Muret et Ronsard', 36–48; E. S. Ginsberg, 'Change and Permanence in the French Renaissance: Muret and Ronsard', *Journal of Medieval and Renaissance Studies*, 16 (1986), 91–102. An important discussion, together with a facsimile of the 1623 edition of Book 1 of the *Amours* with Muret's commentary may be found in J. Chomarat, M. M. Fragonard, and G. Mathieu-Castellani (eds.), *Marc-Antoine de Muret, Commentaires au premier livre des* Amours *de Ronsard* (Geneva, 1985).

17. Là, venerable en une robe blanche, 193
Et couronne la teste d'une branche
Ou de Laurier, ou d'Olivier retors,
Guidant nos pas, . . .
. . . . .
Divin Muret, tu nous liras Catulle, 201

    (Ronsard, *Les Isles fortunées*,
    Œuvres complètes, v. 187–8).

18. *Les Isles fortunées*, 202–18.

19. 'Mais étant journellement solicité de me retirer de cette vile, par le commandement de ceus, ausquelz, apres Dieu, je doi le plus d'obeissance, & telement pressé qu'il me faloit presque à toute heure penser de mon depart, je ne pouvoi rien entreprendre, que d'un esprit troublé, & mal apte à produire fruits, qui fussent dignes de venir en lumière. Si est-ce qu'à la fin, je me suis hazardé, esperant que mon labeur trouvera quelque excuse envers ceus, qui sauront que j'en ai esté reduit à tel point qu'il me faloit autant composer par chacun jour, comme les imprimeurs en pouvoient metre en oeuvre' (Muret, *Preface . . . sur ses commentaires à Monseigneur Adam Fumee*, in Ronsard, *Œuvres complètes*, vol. v. p. xxv.

20. 'mihique divina quadam virgula contigisset, ut non pedem pene prius in hac civitate ponerem, quam in amicitiam ipsius familiarit-

atemque intimam admitterer . . .' (Muretus, *Catullus et in eum Commentarius* (Venice, 1554), p. iii).

21. See especially Grafton, *Joseph Scaliger*, 88–96.
22. 'Sed cum haud ita pridem venissem in Italiam, et ut eam regionem aspicerem, qua qui aequo animo carent, mihi quidem antiquitatis memoriam satis colere non videntur, et mehercule, verum ut dicam, cum alios eruditos homines, tum Paulum in primis Manutium ut cognoscerem; quod in eius scriptis mihi videbar animadvertisse expressas quasdam excellentis doctrinae, eximiaeque probitatis notas . . .' (Muretus, *Catullus*, p. iii).
23. 'non ille quidem ementitus Servius, cuius vulgo ineptiae quaedam in Terentium circunferuntur, sed vetus ille Servius . . .' (Muretus, *Catullus*, 72v). For Longinus see *Catullus*, 72 and pp. 163–4.
24. e.g. *ad* 3. 10; 14. 16; 53. 5; 67. 42.
25. Muret's copy of the *Variae lectiones* (now lost) was still in the Collegium Romanum in the eighteenth century. He bought it in Venice in June 1554, according to a note in his hand. See P. Lazeri, *Miscellaneorum ex Mss. Libris Bibliothecae Collegii Romani Societatis Iesu Tomus II* (Rome, 1757), 316; P. de Nolhac, 'La Bibliothèque d'un humaniste au xvie siècle: Les Livres annotés par Muret', *Mélanges d'archéologie et d'histoire*, 3 (1883), 232.
26. 'Hos quidem versus, nisi sibylla, ut ille ait apud Plautum Pseudolus, legerit, interpretari alium posse reor neminem' (Muretus, *Catullus,* 59 (*ad* 54)). Cf. Pier Vettori, *Variarum lectionum libri XXV* (Florence, 1553), v. 6, p. 61.
27. 'neque me id etiam cum bona ipsius Victorii gratia facturum esse diffido' (Muretus, *Catullus*, 47v (*ad* 39)). Cf. Vettori, *Variae lectiones*, vi. 12, pp. 83–4.
28. 'Quoniam autem Terentianus admonet, hortorum deo cecinisse Catullum huius generis versus, extantque inter Virgilianos lusus nonnulli, quod eruditi homines Catullo tribuunt, et nos quoque nunquam aliter credidimus, adscribemus eos, tum ut quasi postliminio ad auctorem redeant suum, tum ut cursim a nobis nonnulla in eis, quae ceteros fugere, annotentur' (Muretus, *Catullus*, 24v (*ad* 17)). Cf. Vettori, *Variae lectiones*, xii. 3, p. 173.
29. See Grafton, *Joseph Scaliger*, 89. For Vettori as an adherent of Poliziano's method, see Grafton, 44–70.
30. 17. 19 *suppernata*; 66. 94 *Oarion*; 98. 4 *crepidas . . . carbatinas*.
31. Baïf: on 4. 1 (*Faselus*) 'Campanum navigium est, ait Nonius. Plura nihil necesse: Baifii enim scrinia, ut ille ait, compilare hoc loco nolumus', (Muret, *Catullus*, 6. Muret may also be referring to

Lazare Baïf's work, *De re navali Commentarium* (Basle, 1537). *Galland's manuscript*: on 44. 5 (*Tiburs*), *Catullus*, 52. *Fremiot*: on 61. 54 (*te timens*), *Catullus*, 68v.

32. 'Praestantium poetarum . . . neque magna unquam copia, et semper magna laus fuit' (Muretus, *Catullus*, i).

33. 'ingenii bonitas, linguarum peritia et multarum magnarumque rerum comprehensa cognitio' (Muretus, *Iuvenilia*, in *Opera Omnia*, ii. 241).

34. 'nihil fere aliud comminisci possum, nisi esse quandam ut ceterarum rerum, ita studiorum quoque tempestivitatem: statisque quodammodo caeli conversionibus fieri, ut modo in hac, modo in illa facultate certi homines praestantes et egregii existant' (Muretus, *Iuvenilia*, 242).

35. 'In hac, nisi ab iis, quos ipsa quodam modo natura ad eam finxerit, labore, diligentia, vigiliis effici nihil potest. Ea ipsa res in hominum animis admirationem peperit poetarum: obstupefactis videlicet hominibus, cum viderent, alios sponte quadam et propensione naturae, sine ullo labore ea fundere, quae cum omnibus eloquentiae luminibus interlita, tum sparsa multifariam eruditionis variae notis, non tantum dulci sono tenerent aures, sed etiam omni genere affectuum, intimos audientium sensus, cogitationesque tentarent; alios contra ingenuarum artium scientia perpolitos, nulla tamen diligentia, aut diuturnitate studii consequi posse, ut aliquo inter poetas numero ac loco haberentur' (Muretus, *Catullus*, i). A few years later Muret was to set out the antithesis between *natura* and *ars* still more clearly in the *Variae Lectiones* (1559): 'Apes in struendis operibus suis naturam tantum magistram sequuntur: artem non adhibent. Sic et poetae natura tantum valent: arte si qui se poetarum nomen tueri posse confidunt, eos gravissimus auctor Plato pronunciat, nihi unquam egregium ac memorabile effecturos' (*Var. lect.* 8.1, in *Variarum lectionum libri xviiii* (Halle, 1891), i. 207).

36. See Morrison, 'Ronsard and Catullus', 250–1.

37. Par art, le Navigateur
Dans la Mer manie, & vire
La bride de son navire,
Par art, playde l'Orateur,
Par art, les Roys sont guerriers,
Par art, se font les ouvriers:
Mais si vaine experience
Vous n'aurez de tel erreur,
Sans plus ma saincte fureur
Polira vostre science.

(Ronsard, *Ode à Michel de l'Hospital*, 399–408,
Œuvres complètes iii. 141–2).

For discussions of the *Ode à Michel de l'Hospital* and the poetics of the Brigade see R. J. Clements, *Critical Theory and Practice of the Pléiade* Cambridge, Mass., 1942), 187–211; G. Castor, *Pléiade Poetics* (Cambridge, 1964), 24–50; D. Quint, *Origin and Originality in Renaissance Literature* (New Haven, Conn., 1983), 24–31.

38. Qu'encor les fredons de leur voix
Jusqu'aujourdhuy l'on entent bruire.
(Ronsard, *Ode à Michel de l'Hospital*, 601–2).

39. 'Ut autem omni elegantis doctrinae tractatione, ita huius quoque virtutis praestantia, longe supra ceteros / Graecorum hominum ingenia floruerunt. Romani et serius attigerunt poeticam, et coluerunt negligentius, et minime longo tempore in recte scribendorum poematum via perstiterunt. Siquidem cum a rudibus apud eos poetica profecta principiis, tandem per multos gradus ad Virgilium pervenisset, quo ego homine nihil statuo fieri potuisse divinius, ita postea coepere ingenia in deterius labi, ut mirum sit, quanta, quam brevi tempore, sit consecuta mutatio. Hispani poetae praecipue et Romani sermonis puritatem contaminarunt, et, cum inflatum quoddam, et tumidum, et gentis suae moribus congruens invexissent orationis genus, averterunt exemplo suo ceteros a recta illa et simplici, in qua praecipua poetarum sita laus est, et in quam superiores omni studio incubuerant, imitatione naturae' (Muretus, *Catullus*, ii–iiv).

40. 'inter Martialis autem et Catulli scripta tantum interesse arbitrer, quantum inter dicta scurrae alicuius de trivio, et inter liberales ingenui hominis iocos, multo urbanitatis aspersos sale. . . . Latinae quidem orationis nativa illa, minimeque quasi pigmentis infuscata germanitas in Martiale nulla est, in Catullo praecipua. Iis de causis cum ab illo altero, nescio quo modo, semper abhorruissem, Catullum contra nunquam non mirabiliter amavi' (Muretus, *Catullus*, iii).

41. See Hutton, *The Greek Anthology in France*, 51–3; K.-H. Mehnert, *Sal romanus und Esprit français. Studien zur Martialrezeption im Frankreich des sechzehnten und siebzehnten Jahrhunderts* (Bonn, 1970), 81–6.

42. For the commentaries of Partenio, Palladio, and Guarino see Chapter 2. For Valeriano see Chapter 3.

43. Commentaries on 61 were published by Francesco Robortello in 1548 (Adams R–621) and Costanzo Landi in 1550. In 1551 Bernardino Realino published a commentary on 64 (Adams R–237). See Gaisser, 'Catullus', 283–8.
44. See *Index Aureliensis. Catalogus librorum sedecimo saeculo impressorum*, Part I, (Aureliae Aquensis, 1982), vii. 206–8. But the important and rare Trincavelli edition is not listed in the *Index*.
45. See Morrison, 'Catullus and the Poetry of the Renaissance in France'; and 'Catullus in the Neo-Latin Poetry of France before 1550', *BHR* 17 (1955), 365–94.
46. Muret's text joins 2 and 2*b*, places 14*b* after 16. 13, adds three priapea after 17, divides 28 into two, places 58*b* after 55. 12, and joins 78 and 78*b* and 95 and 95*b*.
47. For the treatment of the Mentula poems (94, 105, 114, 115) and 35, 41, 42 in the first generation of commentators, see Chapter 3.
48. Thus on 2*b*. 1–2 (*Atalanta*): 'Fabula ex metamorphosi Ovidii, aut ex commentario in Comasten Theocriti nullo negocio peti potest' (Muretus, *Catullus*, 4). On 58*b*. 2 (*Pegasus*): 'Pegasi fabula notior est quam ut in hoc loco explicari debeat' (*Catullus* 60v). But he is not averse to an occasional learned digression, as at 68. 113. See p. 160 for his discussion of 68. 107–18.
49. 'Ne hic quidem me pudebit fateri, hos quattuor versus a me non intelligi. Possem, quae ab aliis adferuntur, refellere. Possem ipse quoque, si liberet, aliquid eorum exemplo confingere. Malo simpliciter id quod est, dicere: neque facere, quod isti, qui dum integra, corrupta, facilia, difficilia, nusquam haesitantes, sine ullo discrimine interpretantur, imperitis fortasse docti, doctis quidem et intelligentibus imperiti atque audaces videntur' (Muretus, *Catullus*, 133).
50. See Chapter 2, pp. 102–8.
51. The second Aldine was identified as the basis of Muret's text by the first Bipontine edition (*Catullus, Tibullus, Propertius* (Zweibrücken, 1783), p. xlv). But his text also has points in common with the first Aldine, on which the Gryphianae (1534, 1542, 1544, 1546, 1551) were based.

    Muret may have owned the second Aldine annotated by Antonio Petreio in 1528 with the corrections of Francesco Pucci (Berlin, Deutsche Staatsbibliothek, Bibl. Diez. oct. 2474). See L. Santen in *Sex. Aurelii Propertii Elegiarum Libri* IV, ed. P. Burmann (Utrecht, 1780), pp. v–vii.
52. For the procedure of the early editors see Chapter 1.
53. Goold credits Muret with nine emendations. 'A New Text', 99.

54. But between 1554 and 1558 he seems to have acquired a manuscript. He mentions it three times in the 1558 edition (at 38. 3; 44. 8; and 68. 52). Although the manuscript is apparently now lost, it was still in the possession of the Collegium Romanum in 1757: 'Hunc codicem nos unum ex Mureti libris qui fratris filio testamento ad nos redierint, habemus: continet vero Propertium, Tibullum, Catullum hoc ipso ordine, in fine haec nota adscripta est eadem manu: Catulli Veronensis liber feliciter explicit 5 Augusti 1460, et in fine Propertii, Propertii Aurelii Naute ad Cynthiam monobyblos explicit feliciter per me Ioannem Carpensem die 16 Februarii 1460' (P. Lazeri (ed.), *Miscellaneorum . . . Tomus II*, 414 n. 2).
55. e.g. at 12. 1 he correctly replaces Avanzi's *inter coenam Asini* with *Marrucine Asini*, which he attributes to *veteribus libris*. Avanzi had placed 37. 17–20 after 39. 9 (*Emendationes* 1495); Muret restores the verses to their correct position on the authority of *veteres libri*.
56. 'Has plagas sanare ipsi non possumus; non enim vates aut harioli sumus. Procul autem a nobis absit tantus furor, ut imitemur, quod, malo exemplo, alii quidam fecerunt, quibus religio non fuit, ubi quid deerat, hasce sacrosanctas venerandae antiquitatis reliquias, admistis ineptiis suis, intolerabili audacia, contaminare. Licuerit fortasse diis, (ut in fabulis est) cum humerum Pelopis Minerva depasta esset, veri loco eburneum apponere. Nobis certe non licet, ubi veros bonorum poetarum versus absumpsit vetustas, alios a nobis confictos eorum loco substituere. Docui supra, hoc a Parthenio in versibus Sapphicis [Cat. 51. 8] factum fuisse. Idem (ut incitata semel audacia non novit modum, multisque ut iterum peccare audeant, satis argumenti est semel peccasse) hoc etiam loco fecit, pentametrumque suum Catulli versibus immiscuit. Id ipse fassus ni [ne, *ed.*] esset, hodie fortasse versus / ille sine ulla dubitatione Catullo tribueretur' (Muretus, *Catullus*, 126r–v).
57. See Chapter 1, pp. 70–3.
58. See Chapter 2, p. 100.
59. '*Mane. Mane*. Prius adverbium est: posterius verbum. Est autem admodum iucunda παρήχησις.' (Muretus, *Catullus*, 15v).
60. The second Aldine prints 28 as a single poem (as does Guarino), but the Gryphianae divide it into two.
61. 'Nisi me valde animus fallit, poeta hic non ex sua persona loquitur, sed imitatur vocem alicuius, qui a Memmio praetore turpitudinem hanc passus fuerat. Nam neque credendum est generosae hominem indolis tantam suo corpore spurcitiem pertulisse; neque, si eo usque processisset impudentiae, tamen fuisse tam prodigiose

stultum, ut eam notam / sibi ipse versibus suis inurere voluerit' (Muretus, *Catullus*, 35v–36).

62. The most notorious example is Muret's Terence (1555), which Gabriele Faerno considered a threat to the reputation of Manuzio and his press. See Grafton, *Scaliger*, 92; P. Paschini, 'Gabriele Faerno, cremonese favolista e critico del '500', *Atti dell' Accademia degli Arcadi*, 13 (1929), 63–93; L. Ceretti, 'Critica testuale a Terenzio in una lettera del Faerno a Paolo Manuzio', *Aevum*, 28 (1954), 522–51.

63. For the enthusiasm of the Brigade and their friends for the Alexandrians, see de Nolhac, *Ronsard et l'humanisme*, 101–7.

64. 'Pulcherrima omnino haec elegia est, atque haud scio, an ulla pulchrior in omni Latina lingua reperiri queat. Nam et dictio purissima est, et mira quadam affectuum varietate permista oratio, et tot ubique aspersa verborum ac senten / tiarum lumina, ut ex hoc uno poemate perspicere liceat, quantum Catullus ceteris in hoc genere omnibus praestare potuerit, si vim ingenii sui ad illud excolendum contulisset' (Muretus, *Catullus*, 109v–110).

65. 'Quaerens autem occasionem admiscendi varias fabulas, iisque eruditionis quasi spargendis seminibus, exornandi opus suum, ait, amorem Laodamiae profundiorem fuisse palude quadam, quae erat in Thessalia, sed postea siccata est, Herculis opera, sumptaque occasione ad Herculis res gestas modice attingendas digreditur' (Muretus, *Catullus*, 111v).

Modern editors do not share Muret's enthusiasm. For Quinn the simile and its excursus on Hercules 'smell of the lamp' (*Catullus*, *ad* 68. 108–10). Fordyce calls the whole 'an extreme instance of the characteristically Alexandrian taste for the parade of mythological detail' and characterizes the excursus as 'whimsically precious' (*Catullus*, *ad* 108 ff.).

66. The marsh is near the town of Pheneus under Mt. Cyllene (*Pheneum prope Cyllenaeum*, 68. 109). The first Aldine had the right text, corrected by Avanzi (*Emendationes* 1500, o iii) from *Peneum prope Cyllenaeum* of the manuscripts. But Muret reproduced Partenio's innovation *Peneum propter amoenum*.

67. For discussions of the manuscript evidence see the commentaries of Ellis, Fordyce, and Quinn ad loc. See also Wiseman, *Cinna the Poet*, 77–90.

68. Thus Statius: 'Omnibus in manuscriptis. In deserto ali nomine, itaque legendum puto In deserto aliis nomine opus faciat' (Statius, *Catullus*, 341). Scaliger notes the same manuscript reading at 68. 50, and sees that *Alli*, not *aliis*, should be read at 150.

69. *Pun*: on *cita puppi* (64. 6) 'Videtur alludere ad id Argus etymon

[i.e., that *Argo* means "swift"] quod supra attulimus' (Muretus, *Catullus*, 90). Partenio and Palladio had noted the same connection, but did not treat it as a conscious trick of style. *Translation*: 64. 96 = Theocritus 15. 100. *Parallels*: 64. 14–15, Apollonius 1. 547–52.

70. 'Summa vis est in hac comparatione. Primum enim quod bacchanti Ariadnen comparat, significat eam et vultu et totius corporis gestu rabidum quendam concitatae mentis ardorem prae se tulisse. Quod autem addit saxeam effigiem, tantam vim doloris fuisse indicat, ut diu neque movere se potuerit, neque in ullam vocem erumpere. Omnis enim immodica affectio et eripere vocis usuram, et omnium corporis partium functiones impedire ad tempus solet. Atque hoc nimirum est, quod Nioben poetae, cum filios suos Apollinis et Dianae sagittis confossos videret, obriguisse in lapidem fabulantur' (Muretus, *Catullus*, 92).

71. Muretus, *Catullus*, 67v.

72. 'Videtur alludere ad eorum sententiam, qui aiunt, Bacchi numine effectum esse, ut Theseus oram solvens, Ariadnes penitus oblivisceretur. Itaque quod eam reliquerit, oblivione tantum, eaque divinitus immissa, non ingrato animo, effectum. Vide Theocritum Pharmaceutria, et in eum commentarios' (Muretus, *Catullus*, 92v).

And again, on Ariadne's prayer to the Eumenides (64. 200–1): 'Locus hic, si diligenter animadvertas, confirmat id, quod supra tetigimus . . . . Ipsa enim precatur deos, ut quali se mente reliquit Theseus, tali etiam funestet suos. Vota autem Iovi probata esse, infra dicitur. Cum ergo Theseus oblivione domum suam postea funestaverit, consequitur, ut oblivione quoque ante deseruisset Ariadnam' (*Catullus*, 94v).

73. C. Wendel (ed.), *Scholia in Theocritum vetera* (Stuttgart, 1967), 280.

74. e.g. Partenio and Palladio had discussed the name of the Argo (see n. 69); Bernardino Realino saw that 64. 96 was a translation of Theocr. 15. 100.

75. See T. B. L. Webster, 'The Myth of Ariadne from Homer to Catullus', *Greece and Rome*, 13 (1966), 22–31.

76. See Chapter 2, p. 73.

77. About 50 verses are preserved on a papyrus first published in 1929. See R. Pfeiffer, *Callimachus* (Oxford, 1949), vol. ii. p. ix. Pfeiffer prints 66 facing the *Lock of Berenice* (fr. 110); see *Callimachus* i. 112–23.

78. 'Iuvaret Graeca cum Latinis componere, inspicere non in singulis

modo vocibus, sed in figuris etiam luminibusque orationis, in ipsa ratione numerum, ac denique in tota structura poematis, quam apte et scienter Graeci poetae, in hoc genere, inter suos facile primi, vim ac leporem, Latinorum poetarum sine controversia politissimus assecutus fuisset' (Muretus, *Catullus*, 101).

79. For Call. fr. 110. 48–9 Poliziano had read: *Χαλύβων ὡς ἀπόλοιτο γένος / τηλόθεν* . . . . Muret corrects *τηλόθεν* to *γειόθεν* in 49 and suggests for 48 *Ζεῦ πάτερ, ὡς Χαλύβων πᾶν ἀπόλοιτο γένος* (cf. 66. 48: *Iuppiter, ut Chalybon omne genus pereat*).

80. For 66. 94 Muret prints *Proximus Arcturos fulgeat Erigonae*, with the comment: 'Postremus autem versus, ut a nobis scriptus est, ita legitur in veteribus libris' (Muretus, *Catullus*, 104v). He has no doubt derived the reading from Marullo's poem attacking Poliziano, which he prints *ad* 66. 94. Marullo's last couplet reads: 'Fecisti Oarionem ex Erigone, ex Arcturo / Hydrochoum. iam quod monstrum erit ipsa coma?' (Marullo, *Epigrammata varia* 1. 13–14).

81. For the manuscripts of Longinus see the editions of O. Jahn and J. Vahlen (Bonn, 1887); A. O. Prickard (Oxford, 1906); D. A. Russell (Oxford, 1964). For the early editions and commentaries see B. Weinberg, 'Translations and Commentaries of Longinus, *On the Sublime*, to 1600: A Bibliography', *Modern Philology*, 47 (1950) 145–51; Weinberg, 'Pseudo-Longinus', in *CTC* (Washington, 1971), ii. 193–8. The French printer, Henri Estienne, who was a friend of both Muret and Manuzio, included Sappho 31 in the second edition of his Anacreon (Paris, 1556); see M. Morrison, 'Henri Estienne and Sappho', *BHR* 24 (1962), 388–91. Porto brought out an edition of his own in 1569–70, and wrote a commentary on Longinus (first printed in 1733 in the edition of Longinus by Zacharias Pearce [Amsterdam, 1733]); see Weinberg, 'Pseudo-Longinus' and E. Legrand, *Bibliographie hellénique des XVe et XVIe siècles* (Paris, 1972), vol. ii. pp. vii–xx, 7–10.

82. 'Libet autem hoc potissimum loco singularem gratiam inire ab iis omnibus, qui antiquitatis studio et delicatorum versuum suavitate capiuntur. Etenim cum Dionysii Longini libellum *περὶ ὕψους* . . . Latine interpretari coepissem . . . cum alia in eo sane plurima deprehendi . . . tum oden suavissimam poetriae Sapphus, quam iis, qui proxime antecesserunt, versibus maxima ex parte Catullus expressit' (Muretus, *Catullus*, 57).

83. 'Quis autem est, duntaxat eorum, qui aliquem / literarum, atque humanitatis sensum habent, qui non summam voluptatem capiat, mulieris in hoc genere longe post homines natos praestantissimae,

et poetae Latinorum omnium mollissimi versibus invicem comparandis Muretus, *Catullus*, 57r–v).

84. 'Beatum esse ait, quicunque Lesbiae aspectu, et alloquio frui possit. Post castigat seipsum, affirmans, tales cogitationes non nisi ex ocio nasci, additque gravem sententiam, ocium multis regibus multisque urbibus exitii causam fuisse' (Muretus, *Catullus*, 57).

85. 'Neque vero diu fidem meam liberare distuli, ut qui inter varias occupationes, homo alioqui laboris non nimium tolerans, hoc tamen, quicquid est, trium mensium, aliquanto etiam minore spatio absolverim' (Muretus, *Catullus*, iii v).

86. Scaliger (1577) has a single note on 51 and no mention of Sappho. Statius (1566), however, claims to have identified 51. 9–10 as a translation of Sappho even before the publication of Longinus and makes some obvious comparisons, noting that Sappho treats the lover's symptoms in three stanzas, Catullus in only two, and that Catullus' final stanza on *otium* has no counterpart in Sappho. He argues that the stanza is a fragment that does not belong to the poem and amuses himself by composing a stanza describing Catullus' sufferings to correspond to Sappho's last stanza: 'Sudor it late gelidus trementi / Artubus totis, violamque vincit, / Insidens pallor moriens nec auras / Ducere possum' (Statius, *Catullus*, 141–2).

87. In his *Coniectanea et Notae* Dousa discusses Catullus' translations of individual words and phrases, finds parallels in Theocritus and Valerius Aedituus, and writes his own version of Sappho's last stanza ('Frigidus sudor fluit; horror artus / Pallidos herba magis it per omnes; / Et pati mortem videor morans in / Limine mortis.'). His work is most accessible in the Delphin edition of Catullus (London, 1822), ii. 682–702.

88. The poems are collected and discussed by D. A. Campbell, 'Galliambic Poems of the 15th and 16th Centuries', *BHR* 22 (1960), 490–510.

89. Morrison, 'Ronsard and Catullus', 257.

90. 'quorum unusquisque propius a summorum poetarum aberat, quam a mediocrium, laude, cum huiusmodi quaedam scribere aggressi essent, seseque totos ad imitationem Catulliani poematis contulissent, (neque enim aliud habebant, quod sibi proponerent ad imitandum) propter exemplaris ipsius corruptionem saepe peccarunt' (Muretus, *Catullus*, 75v–76).

91. 'Frequens autem est inter doctos viros opinio cui ego quoque Plinii auctoritate [Pliny, *NH* 28. 19] ductus assentior a Catullo alia quaedam poemata fuisse composita quae veterum negligentia iam diu perierunt' (Parthenius, 1491, f. 1v). See Introduction, n. 19.

92. ['Ut vero nomen quo carmen hoc Terentianus appellari tradit demum enuntiemus] sciendum est [ad Priapeium nuncupari a nonnullis Ithyphallicum, atque] alia huius numeri poemata composita a Catullo quae temporis iniuria periere' (Vat. lat. 5215, fol. 214).
93. 'Et plures similes sic conscripsisse Catullum scimus' (Terentianus Maurus, 2759–60, in Keil, *Grammatici latini*, vi. 407).
94. 'Elegans carmen, cuius falsus nunc est, aut incertus auctor, demonstratur Catulli esse' (Vettori, *Var. lect.* 12. 3).
95. Thus on Buecheler 85: 'Catulli esse hoc itemque sequens poematium et doctissimi iam viri admonuerunt et mihi non invito persuadent' (J. J. Scaliger, *Catalecta Virgilii et aliorum poetarum latinorum veterum poemata* (Leyden, 1617), 217). But on 17: 'Ex quo loco grammatici [Diomedes in Keil, *Grammatici latini* I. 512. 27–8] omnino convincitur eiusdem generis metrum, quod in custodem horti scriptum est inter Catalecta Virgiliana, recte Virgilio attribui: quanquam docti Catullo adscripserint' (*Castigationes in Valerii Catulli librum* (Paris, 1577), 16).
96. See Dejob, *Marc-Antoine Muret*, 70–83.
97. 'Kalendis Apr. omnino te, sin id minus, Catullum tuum expecto. Diem unum prorogari, e re mea non est' (Paulus Manutius, *Epistolarum libri quatuor* (Venice, 1560), 78). (Number 745 in E. Pastorello, *L'Epistolario Manuziano Inventario cronologico-analitico 1483–1597* (Florence, 1957).)
98. 'De Catullo, exiguam tu quidem mihi diem praesinis, sed tamen dabitur opera, ut satisfiat tibi' (Muretus, *Epistolae* (Leipzig, 1866) reprinted by Slatkine Reprints (Geneva, 1971), 10: Pastorello 746).
99. 'Sed quaeso te, quid tu facere cogitas? an forte eadem opera Catullum cum commentario meo, Tibullum autem et Propertium sine ullo commentario emittere, eosque tres unum in librum coniungere? Tale enim aliquid mihi venit in mentem suspicari. Hoc si est, non equidem reprehendo, neque improbo; etiam librum puto vendibiliorem fore: sed tamen novum, ut puto, multis videbitur' (Muretus, *Epistolae*, 11: Pastorello 751).
100. 'Rem tenes. Optime tres poetae coniungentur, ille, M. ANTONII MURETI COMMENTARIO ILLUSTRATUS; reliqui duo . . . AB EODEM EMENDATI' (Manutius, *Epistolarum libri quatuor* 79r–v: Pastorello 752).
101. Pastorello 754, 755.
102. Pastorello 778 (before 18 May 1558). See also Pastorello 797 (19 June 1558).
103. For Statius' life the best source is J. Gomes Branco, 'Un

umanista portoghese in Italia: Aquiles Estaço', *Relazioni storiche fra l'Italia ed il Portogallo*, Reale Accademia d'Italia (Rome, 1940), 135–48. See also P. de Nolhac, *La Bibliothèque de Fulvio Orsini* (Paris, 1887, repr. 1976), 263–5 and *passim*.

104. 'Nunc vos quid mi agitis? valetis ambo? / Ecquid luditis ambo, tenditisque / Vel Calvum superare, vel Catullum? / Cum magno magis an iuvat subire / Certamen Cicerone, iam iam et ipsum / Aequantes numerum, elegantiamque? / Quicquid nunc agitis vel edidistis, / Quicquid denique cogitatis ambo, / Vestris noscere litteris laboro: / Ac me nunquid ametis, anne vestro / Vester ex animo excidi sodalis?' (Lazeri *Miscellanea* ii. 436–7). Statius is borrowing from Andrea Navagero's *Lusus* 30, a verse letter to Pietro Bembo and Paolo Canalis. See Andrea Navagero, *Lusus*, ed. A. E. Wilson (Nieuwkoop, 1973), 58.

105. Statius is mentioned twice, rather coolly, in Manuzio's correspondence in the 1550s (Pastorello 554 and 809).

106. See A. Moreira de Sá, 'Manuscritos e obras impressas de Aquiles Estaço', *Arquivo per bibliografia portuguesa* (Coimbra), 3 (1957), 167–78.

107. See M. W. Croll, 'Muret and the History of "Attic Prose"', in *Style, Rhetoric, and Rhythm* (Princeton, NJ, 1966), 126–62.

108. Grafton, *Scaliger*, 89–100. Manuzio came to Rome in 1561 as official printer to Pope Pius IV. See P. Costil, 'Paul Manuce et l'humanisme à Padoue à l'époque du Concile de Trente', *Revue des questions historiques* 3: 21 [117] (1932), 342–7.

109. Only the commentaries on Catullus and Tibullus (1567) were published. Statius' Vergil is preserved in manuscript (Rome, Biblioteca Vallicelliana E.60.2), But his notes on Lucretius and Horace's *Odes* seem to have perished.

110. For Faerno see n. 62 above. For Orsini see de Nolhac, *La bibliothèque de Fulvio Orsini*.

111. 'Dionysius Lambinus, homo eruditissimus, mihique summus amicus, ait, se vidisse librum in quo esset, "Vorax venter". Ego, cum in meo manuscripto reperissem "meus vertet", suspicatus sum, legendum, "meus venter".' (Muretus, *Catullus* (1558) 58v).

112. 'Primus omnium, Gabriel Faernus ab hinc annos plus minus viiii fecit, 'Quam mihi meus venter'. quod suum ille inventum, ut erat homo aperto, liberalique ingenio, cum libentissime cum multis communicasset, non defuit, qui pro suo ederet. quod ut testarer suo nomine, multis ille me verbis, antequam diem obiret, est obtestatus' (Statius, *Catullus*, 125). Scaliger was to dismiss this dispute with characteristic acerbity: 'Iam ante quadraginta annos

plus minus, docti viri veram lectionem eruerunt, *quam mihi meus venter*' (Scaliger, *Castigationes* 38).

113. 'Itaque ad id opus antequam adgrederer, quo paratior hoc ipsum politis, ornatisque versibus praestarem, summos in suo quemque genere, Latinos poetas diligenter evolui. Inter legendum autem, quod adsolet, ita multa notaram, ut iustum prope volumen effectura viderentur. Ea mei studiosis hominibus cum placita essent, contenderunt a me scilicet etiam atque etiam, ne ceteros celarem, neve publico inviderem. Ergo, victus, a Catullo initium duxi, quem superior aetas omnis tanti fecit, ut elegantia illum poetis omnibus facile praestare censuerit. Certe Divus Hieronymus dignum putavit, cuius nomen Eusebii, quae convertebat in Latinum, Chronicis intexeret. Nam, quod idem lascivius, ac mollius scripsit, id vero temporum illorum sive mos, sive licentia potius, ac vitium fuit, quamquam de se ipse tamquam suppudens dicit, "Nam castum esse decet pium poetam / ipsum, versiculos nihil necesse est"' (Statius, *Catullus*, A 2v–A3).

114. On the period see Costil, 'Paul Manuce'; C. Dionisotti, 'La letteratura italiana nell' età del Concilio', in *Il Concilio di Trento e la riforma tridentina. Atti del Convegno storico internazionale. Trento. 2–6 settembre 1963* (Rome, 1965), i. 316–43; C. Dejob, *L'Influence du Concile de Trente sur la littérature et les beaux-arts chez les peuples catholiques* (Paris, 1884).

115. Pope Pius V was elected in January 1566, and Statius' commentary was published at the beginning of March. On Statius and the pope cf. Statius' comment, 'Cum autem operis huius editio in idem tempus incidisset, quo me Pius V. Pont. Max in suis esse voluisset . . .' (Statius, *Catullus*, A 3). The work is dedicated to the papal secretary Hieronymus Rusticuccius.

116. On Boccaccio see L. Pastor, *History of the Popes*, (London, 1928), xvi. 18 n. 4; Dejob, *L'Influence*, 152–82, 393–7.

117. Thus Rule VII of the Tridentine Index of 1564 bans all obscene books with this exception: 'Antiqui vero ab Ethnicis conscripti, propter sermonis elegantiam et proprietatem permittuntur; nulla tamen ratione pueris praelegendi erunt' (*Bibliothek des litterarischen Vereins in Stuttgart* 176 (Tübingen, 1886), 249).

118. Statius' poetry is preserved in a manuscript at the Biblioteca Vallicelliana in Rome; see M. La Tella Bartoli, 'A proposito di Aquiles Estaço e dei carmina del codice vallicelliano B 106', *Annali Istituto Univ. Orientale*, sez. Romanza 17 (1975), 293–362. See also Moreira de Sá, 'Manuscritos'.

119. Statius probably learned of some of these readings, as well as those he ascribes to Pontano and Valeriano, through Orsini, who had

annotated his own text of Catullus. Orsini's copy of the 1554 edition of Muret's commentary is preserved (Rome, Bibl. Angelica Aut. 1.18). Orsini may also be his source for Colocci's inscriptions, since Colocci, an early patron of Orsini's, died in 1549, a decade before Statius arrived in Rome.

120. 'De Catullo ipso, laudatissimo poeta, nihil amplius dicam, illius commendandi caussa' (Statius, *Catullus*, A 3v).

121. 'De lucubratione hac mea, vere videor posse dicere, eo consilio, et conatu institutam, quod me tamen adsecutum non profiteor, quem multa fugerint, plura fortasse fefellerint hominem vix mediocri praeditum ingenio, ut optimum poetam, neglegentia temporum valde corruptum, si non omnino resituerem, at paullo quidem certe meliorem redderem' (Statius, *Catullus*, A 3v).

122. 'Utinam quidem, quae deberet, ea in tractandis veterum monimentis, et servata esset a superioribus, et hodie servaretur religio. Simpliciora haud dubie omnia et integriora legerentur. Nunc, dum quisque, pro suo arbitratu, addit, delet, immutat, fiunt ex non integerrimis voluminibus manu scriptis impressa vitiosissima' (Muretus, *Catullus*, 1v).

123. '*Ora per virorum*, additum est a Ioviano Pontano . . . quod et Palladius indicat, et aperte, ex hoc ad ipsum Sannazarii epigrammate, cognoscitur: "Doctus ab Elysia redeat si valle Catullus, / . . . Ille tibi amplexus, atque oscula grata referret, / Mallet et hos numeros, quam meminisse suos." Amice Sannazarius, et venuste. Sed Catullus mallet profecto, ut opinor, suos. Ego, etsi non video, quid aptius appingi potuerit; satius tamen duco, esse lacunas in bonis libris, quam easdem ex cuiusquam ingenio expleri' (Muretus, *Catullus*, 2r–v).

124. For Pontano's version of 1. 9 and Muret's opinion of it see Chapter 3, n. 87. No one except Muret seems to have believed that there was a lacuna at 1. 9. In an early account Palladio reports: 'Caeterum Pontanus scriba regius vir impense doctus et qui Romae profitentur verba mutantes versum hunc ita scribunt *qualecunque per ora quod virorum*' (Palladius 1496, a iii).

125. '*Cui dono lepidum novum libellum*: in duobus manuscriptis, *cui*, ut est etiam impressum; in uno *quoi*; in Patavino altero *quin*, quae scriptura ad eam, quam veteres in scribenda voce hac tenebant, consuetudinem propius accedit, si tantum modo *N* litteram a fine sustuleris. Cuius rei auctor Donatus, illud in Andria Terentii interpretans . . .' (Statius, *Catullus*, 10).

126. 'cum est ipsum contra manuscriptorum fidem, tum veterum omnium auctoritatem' (Statius, *Catullus*, 11).

127. Statius' arguments have failed to convince. Modern editors

generally read *arida* with Servius (on *Aen.* 12. 587). Scaliger's comment is characteristically scathing: '*Arida modo*. Cur dubites de hac lectione, causa non est, si Servium locupletissimum auctorem habes. Quare enim illi minus, quam libris ab hinc centum annis scriptis tribuendum sit, non video' (Scaliger, *Castigationes*, 4).

128. 'in manuscriptis omnibus erat, *Qualecumque quod patrona virgo*' (Statius, *Catullus*, 15).

129. 'Ego vero, quid scriptum viderim, testari volui. legebam tamen, *Qualecumque quod est, patrona virgo*' (Statius, *Catullus*, 16).

130. B. L. Ullman, *The Identification of the Manuscripts of Catullus Cited in Statius' Edition of 1566* (Chicago, 1908). The four manuscripts identified by Ullman are Vatican Library, Vat. lat. 1608, Ottob. 1550, Ottob. 1829 (R); Padua, Biblioteca Capitolare C 77. The others have presumably perished. Statius calls them 'meus', 'Patavinus alter', and 'Zanchi liber'. Statius' readings are listed by Ullman, and, more fully, by G. B. Pighi, 'Achillis Statii lectiones atque emendationes Catullianae', *Humanitas* (Coimbra), 3 (1950), 37–160.

131. Goold, 'A New Text', 99.

132. 'In manuscriptis omnibus, *Detecta*, non, *Directa*. Legendum videtur, *Derecta*. Sic enim veteres, *Derigere* et *Derectus*, quod in meo vetustissimo Commentariorum Caesaris exemplo videre est, et in veteri inscriptione, quae est Romae in Basilica Sancti Petri, in qua nomen equi, Derector. Itaque ex *Derecta*, factum *Detecta*' (Statius, *Catullus*, 71).

133. 'In primo versu vitium inesse iampridem cum putassem, neque enim quid *unus* in eo loco significaret, aut quem salem ac leporem haberet, dispiciebam, et cum manuscriptos libros consulerem, et *Unus* et *Unius* scriptum reperiebam. Itaque *Intus* legendum putavi, idque magis etiam probavi post, cum in tertio manuscripto libro, *Imus*, scriptum animadverti' (Statius, *Catullus*, 192).

134. 'Hic versus in manuscriptis non erat, et in omnibus tantum spatii reliquum erat, quantum uni versui capiendo satis esset. Atque in uno annotatum in margine, Deficiebat hoc carmen in exemplo, itaque quicumque legitur versus hoc loco, nothus is est' (Statius, *Catullus*, 341). Statius makes similar comments on the supplements at 65. 9 and after 61. 108.

135. For the methods of Vettori and Faerno see Grafton, *Scaliger*, 52–70.

136. For the demonstration that Statius used R, see Ullman, *The Identification*, 10–17. After Statius, R, its value unrecognized,

slipped back into obscurity until its famous discovery by Hale in 1896. See Thomson, 'A New Look', 121–6.

137. Ullman, *The Identification*, 20–7.
138. Ibid. 62–4.
139. Thus, at 61. 176, where the base text correctly read *adeat*, he tries to justify *adeant* of the manuscripts. At 61. 79 and 61. 82–3 he reports the correct manuscript readings, *tardet* and *Arunculeia* or *Aurunculeia*, but rejects them for *tardat* and *Aruncleia* or *Hirculeia* of the base text. At 61. 140 he rejects *sola*, the reading of his manuscripts, as frigid, and emends to *soli*.
140. Since Statius always gives a full account of his evidence and line of reasoning, even his mistakes are instructive. For example, at 61. 46 he proposes an incorrect emendation, but only after reporting the readings of all the manuscripts and expelling a rewriting by Avanzi that had made its way into the Aldines and Muret. For more examples, see Pighi, 'Achillis Statii lectiones'.
141. The text printed with Statius' commentary has as its basis the second Aldine. See *Catullus, Tibullus, Propertius* (Zweibrücken, 1783), xlv.
142. For Valerianus' *Castigationes* see Grafton, *Scaliger*, 48–51.
143. For Giselinus and his edition see C. L. Heesakkers, *Praecidanea Dousana* (Amsterdam, 1976), 51–60.
144. See S. Timparano, *La genesi del metodo del Lachmann* (Florence, 1963), 8–10; Kenney, *The Classical Text*, 55–7; Grafton, *Joseph Scaliger*, 160–79; 'Joseph Scaliger's Edition of Catullus (1577) and the Traditions of Textual Criticism in the Renaissance', *JWI* 38 (1975), 155–81.
145. Although by this time they were probably calling themselves the Pléiade. See Chamard, *Histoire de la Pléiade*, 1–6. For Scaliger in Paris see J. Bernays, *Joseph Justus Scaliger* (Berlin, 1885; repr. New York 1965), 34–7, 119–31; de Nolhac, *Ronsard et l'humanisme*, 202–5; Grafton, *Scaliger*, 100–6.
146. Dejob, *Marc-Antoine Muret*, 153–60.
147. Dejob, *Marc-Antoine Muret*, 4–6. Several of the epigrams in Muret's *Iuvenilia* are dedicated to the elder Scaliger, including the first, which is entitled 'Divo Iulio Caesari Scaligero, Patri Meo'. (Muret, *Iuvenilia*, in *Opera Omnia*, ed. Frotscher, ii. 272.)
148. Grafton, *Joseph Scaliger*, 103–4. He also translated two elegies of Propertius (dedicated to Willem Canter in September 1561), and the *Moretum* of 'Vergil' (dedicated to Ronsard in 1563).
149. For the whole incident, see Bernays, *Scaliger*, 270–2 and Grafton, *Joseph Scaliger*, 161–2. Bernays prints the relevant texts from Scaliger and Muret.

150. 'Ne quis igitur amplius fallatur, et rem totam detegendam et carmina ipsa hic subiicienda duxi' (Muretus, *Orationes XXIII . . . eiusdem Interpretatio quincti libri Ethicorum Aristotelis ad Nicomachum. Eiusdem hymni sacri, et alia quaedam poematia* (Venice, 1575), 56). See also Bernays, *Scaliger*, 271.
151. Grafton, *Joseph Scaliger*, 161–3.
152. 'Praeterea ni grave est quaere diligenter ut possis requirere Catullum, Tibullum, Propertium cum commentario. Eo libro non amplius octo dies utar, ac bona fide remittam. Idque ut facias etiam atque etiam rogo' (R. L. Hawkins, 'The Relationship of Joseph Scaliger and François Vertunien', *Romantic Review*, 8 (1917), 128).
153. *Request for Statius' Catullus*: Scaliger to Dupuy, 13 Dec. 1575, in P. Tamizey de Larroque, (ed.), *Joseph Juste Scaliger: Lettres françaises inédites* (Agen, 1879; repr. Geneva, 1970), 36. *On the rumour of Muret's death*: 'je serois bien marri, qu'il s'en fust allé plustost, que je lui eusse rendu conte de ses vers d'Attius et Trabea.' Scaliger to Dupuy, 9 Feb. 1575, in Tamizey de Larroque, *Scaliger: Lettres françaises inédites*, 45. What seems to be another version of this comment is preserved in a *bon mot* in the *Prima Scaligerana*, collected in the 1560s and 1570s: 'Doleo obiisse Muretum, de cuius morte ad me scripsit Cujacius. Animus erat eum reprehendere in multis quae peroptabam ab eo videri' (*Prima Scaligerana nusquam antehac edita cum praefatione*, ed. T. Fabri (Utrecht, 1670), 76).
154. 'Qui rigidae flammas evaserat ante Tholosae, / Rumetus, fumos vendidit ille mihi.' The epigram is entitled 'In Rumetum, qui suos versus pro antiquis supposuerat' (Joseph Scaliger, *Poemata omnia*[2], ed. P. Scriverius (Berlin, 1864), 25).
155. 'Muretus fugit Tholosa, venit Venetias, sed quia primae nobilitatis filios volebat comprimere, ideo fugit Romam' (Joseph Scaliger, *Scaligerana, editio altera* (Cologne, 1667), 162).
156. 'c'étoit un homme docte; on ne l'a pas voulu endurer à Venise ob paederastiam' (Ibid.).
157. 'Muretus me vocabat fratrem, quia Pater illum vocabat filium. Tam bene scripsit quam ullus veterum. Voluit Italos imitari, ut multis verbis diceret pauca' (Ibid.).
158. 'Mureto nullus fuit post Ciceronem qui expeditius loqueretur et scriberet Romane. Lipsius nihil prae illo, et invidebat illi, furatus est emendationes. En ce mestier ego optime possum distinguere, quid hic vel ille possit. Fuerat pédant, et plerumque non emergunt nisi habeant animum non pedanticum, ut Muretus, qui vere regius erat' (Ibid. 163).

159. 'Scio magnae eruditionis viros non parum his auctoribus illustrandis contulisse. Equidem illis suam gloriam non invideo. Sed neque ipsi meam mihi praeripere si bene operam collocavi, neque si male conatum saltem vituperare possunt. Eum vero modum in istis brevibus ac pene nudis notis servavi, ut neminem vivum ne minima quidem animadversione perstrinxerim; mortuos autem, etiam quum ab eis dissentio, nunquam nisi honorificentissime appellarim. Illiberale enim facinus, propter nescio quas verborum quisquilias, aut propter errorem aliquem, qui humanitus contigerit, tantorum hominum eruditionem, atque adeo totum nomen et famam in periculum vocare' (Scaliger, *Castigationes*, a 5r–v).
160. See, for example, the similar sentiments expressed by Palladio Fosco: 'ut nemini unquam detraham et si quid ab aliis didicerim id acceptum referam' (Palladius 1496, f 6).
161. For Partenio and Guarino see Chapter 2, p. 82. For Muret and Vettori, see pp. 152–3.
162. In his discussion of 66. 94 Scaliger rejects the reading defended by Muret and viciously attacks its author, 'that Greekling, Marullo'. See Grafton, *Joseph Scaliger*, 169–72. He attacks Muret again through Marullo at 98. 3–4. See Grafton, 'Joseph Scaliger's Edition of Catullus', 180–1. Muret is also alluded to, but in a much more neutral way, in Scaliger's discussion of 17. See pp. 166–7 and n. 95 above.
163. 'stolidi isti' and 'vervecibus' *ad* 61. 115; 'sciolis' *ad* 61.170; 'minutilis magistris' *ad* 66.51; 'ineptis paedagogis' *ad* 66. 58; 'ineptis magistris' *ad* 61. 107; 'ineptorum magistellorum' *ad* 66. 63.
164. Scaliger to Dupuy 8 Feb. 1576; 8 Aug. 1576; 25 Sept. 1576 (Tamizey de Larroque, *Scaliger: Lettres françaises inédites*, 45, 54, 56).
165. 'Je trouve que nostre pouvre Statius est un grand fat, et ne me puis tenir de rire, quand je lis les commentaires *in Catullum et Tibullum*. Toustefois il ne dict pas tousjours mal et c'est *quando est dissimilis sui*' (Scaliger to Dupuy, 8 Feb. 1576: Ibid. 45–6).
166. 'et m'asseure que si nous n'avons faict nostre devoir, pour le moins, nous ne ferons tant le fat qu'a faict Messer Achille Statio, auquel Dieu doint bonne vie et longue, car s'il n'impètre cella par noz bonnes prières, à peine l'obtiendra il par son bon entendement' (Scaliger to Dupuy, 11 May 1576: Ibid. 48).
167. See R. Ellis, *A Commentary on Catullus* (Oxford, 1876), vi; and Grafton, 'Joseph Scaliger's Catullus', 179.
168. Scaliger's copy of the 1569 Plantin edition is now in Leiden University Library (shelf-mark 755 H 23). See Grafton, *Joseph Scaliger*, 165–7. He entered into it his collations from Jacques

Cujas' manuscript of Catullus (now British Library MS Egerton 3027). For the identification of the manuscript see R. Ellis and A. Palmer, 'Scaliger's Liber Cujacianus of Propertius, Catullus, etc.', *Hermathena*, 2 (1876), 124–58. For Scaliger's collations see Grafton, 'Joseph Scaliger's Edition of Catullus', 159–61; *Joseph Scaliger*, 165–7. As far as I know, no one has noticed the presence of Statius' readings in the Plantin edition or considered their importance for Scaliger's *Catullus*.

169. The table is based on the collation in Pighi, 'Achillis Statii lectiones'. I have added 68. 52 (*torruerit*), missed by Pighi.

170. For Cujas' manuscript see Chapter 1, n. 4.

171. 'Porro liber ille, quo usi sumus, cuiusque iam mentionem fecimus, longe alios huius poetae manuscriptos bonitate superare mihi videtur; quum tamen omnes ex uno exemplari descripti fuerint. Id exemplar ab homine Veronensi, quisquis ille fuit, in Galliis repertum, omnes illos codices eius poetae, qui in Italia extant, propagavit' (Scaliger, *Castigationes*, 3).

172. Quoted in Scaliger, *Castigationes*, 3.

173. 'Suspicor autem illud Gallicanum exemplar Langobardicis literis scriptum fuisse, quia errores, qui in postremis codicibus ab imperitis librariis disseminati sunt, non aliter videntur, quam a morosis illis characteribus nati, id quod suo loco diligenter admonebimus. Praeterea non character solum menda propagavit, sed et antiquaria lectio. Nam librarius semper scripserat QVOR, QVOM, LVDEI, LVCEI, ADEPTA'S, M'ALIVS, OCEANO'S, POPVL' ARBITRIO, DEVOLVIT ILL' ACVTO, ILI' ET. Item multa alia praeterea, quorum ignoratione quantum in hoc auctore edendo peccatum sit, postea docebo' (Scaliger, *Castigationes*, 4).

Grafton argues that Scaliger's model for the script of the lost exemplar was the ninth-century Visigothic manuscript that he used in preparing his text of Ausonius (Leiden MS Voss. Lat. fol. 111). See Grafton, *Joseph Scaliger*, 173–4 and 'Joseph Scaliger's Edition of Catullus', 171–2 and plate 24.

174. The correction *torruerit* was anticipated, but not explained, by Turnèbe and Statius.

175. Scaliger, *Castigationes* ad loc., p. 15.

176. 'Miraberis enim, studiose lector, tantam mendorum segetem hunc politissimum auctorem occupasse. Quam si non omnem extirpavero, tamen non magnum post me spicilegium relinquam' (Scaliger, *Castigationes*, 4).

177. 'Scaliger found *a–u* confusions in 6.12, 29.4, 66.43, 66.63, 67.32; *i–l* in 64.322, 80.8, 113.2; *c–t* in 25.7, 29.20, 34.22–3, 61.46, 64.308, 68.52, 95.7; *c–g* in 61.68' (Grafton, *Joseph Scaliger*, 313 n. 53).

178. At 6. 12, *ni stupra valet*, for *mi ista valet*. Thomson prints Haupt's *nil stupra valet*. Mynors obelizes the phrase.
179. 66. 43 *maximum* (Pucci); 67. 32 *supposita* (Pontano); 64.322 *perfidiae* (Statius attributes to *docti viri*); 80. 8 *ilia et emulso* (B. Guarino and Palladio); 68. 52 *torruerit* (Turnèbe).
180. 25. 7 *Tyrographos*; 29. 4 *unctum*; 29. 20 *inundat, extimae ecce Lusitaniae*; 34. 23 *Ancique*; 61. 46 *magis ah magis*; 61. 68 *iungier*; 64. 308 *excinxerat*; 66. 63 *vividulo a flatu*; 95. 7 *apuam porcentur*; 113. 2 *Moechi illi ah*.
181. Old corrections: 61. 134 *diceris* (1473); 61. 203 *ludi* (ed. Rom.). Wrong: 61. 46 *ah magis*; 61. 80 *quae*; 61. 102 *qui*; 61. 107 *quot o nimis*.
182. For Sophocles see Grafton, *Joseph Scaliger*, 114–16. For Festus ibid. 134–60.
183. 'Primum enim pro *paduam* non dubito *apuam* legere, deinde pro *portentur*, *porcentur*: C pro T, more aut potius errore usitato librariorum, quod supra toties memini me admonere. *Porcentur* eo tempore scribi solitum pro *porgentur*, quod etiamnum in meliore parte codicum scriptorum legitur. Et est usitatissima C, cum T commutatio. *Apua*, ἀφύη, ut etiam Glossarium notat, pisciculum esse omnes sciunt' (Scaliger, *Castigationes*, 98).
184. At 61. 68 he proposed *iungier* for the *vincier* in his manuscript and rejected Avanzi's correct *nitier*: 'At *nitier*, quod Avantius reposuerat, omnino cum ipsius Avantii fautoribus exibilandum est' (Scaliger, *Castigationes*, 47). At 61. 99 he rejected Calfurnio's *probra* as 'commentitium': 'Vetus enim lectio disertim habet, *Proca turpia*. Ego interpretor adulteram procam, virosam. Neque aliter scripsit Catullus.' *Castigationes*, 49).
185. 'Una litera minus veram lectionem eruere possumus, *Semihiante labello* . . .' (Scaliger, *Castigationes*, 55).
186. 'Quis de huius emendatione loci potius dubitabit, quam elegantiam mirabitur? (Ibid.).
187. For a modern analysis of the difficulties in 61. 189–228 and their causes and solution see M. L. West, *Textual Criticism and Editorial Technique* (Stuttgart, 1973), 132–41.
188. 'Locus inquinatissimus, quem ita, uti hodie legitur, reconcinnavit Parthenius. Mallem veterem lectionem depravatam reliquisset, quam suum somnium nobis interpretaretur' (Scaliger, *Castigationes*, 52).
189. 'Monstrum lectionis, ut vides, sed in quo solo istius loci depravandi et emendandi cardo versetur. Transposita enim haec Strophe locum cum superiore commutare debet, itaque sic omnia suo ordini reponimus, et tunc facile menda ipsa tollemus' (Ibid.).

190. 'Alii legunt *pulcher es*, alii *pulchra res*. Ego puto legendum *pulchra eris* . . .' (F. Robortello, *Explicationes*, 110).
191. For Muret, see n. 46 above. Statius improved on Muret by omitting 'Cat. 18, 19, 20', suggesting that 78*b* is a fragment, and separating 95 and 95*b*. Scaliger's sole improvement is the reuniting of 28. He joins 59–60, 77–78*b*, 93–94, 95–95*b*, and places 87 before 75 to form a single epigram.
192. 'Hic spurci homines verbum spurcum substituerunt, in quo non solum eos reprehendo, sed etiam quum eorum temeritate, qua hunc locum contaminarunt, ex uno Epigrammate duo non integra facta sunt. Atqui integrum totum hoc epigramma, si veterem lectionem in suas sedes restituas. Plane enim exaratum est: *Bononiensem Rufa Rufulum fallat*' (Scaliger, *Castigationes*, 44).
193. 'Fallare, est fallere, verbum antiquum eodem modo, quo et vanare. Attius Alcmena: *Tanta ut frustrando vanans, lactans protrahat*. Lactare, Vanare, Fallare, idem prope significare videntur' (Scaliger, *Castigationes*, 44).
194. 'Puto neminem huius poetae studiosum esse, qui huius aureoli epigrammatii vicem mihi gratias non agat' (Scaliger, *Castigationes*, 91).
195. 'Commendat poema Cinnae, quod ipse Smyrnam inscripserat; in eoque perpoliendo totos novem annos elaborarat' (Muretus, *Catullus*, 125 v).
196. 'Non enim magnum est, quod adfert Victorius, parva monimenta vocari vix posse, carmina tanto studio, per tantum tempus elaborata. Scimus libros bonitate, non mole, spectari, exiguasque gemmas ingentibus saepenumero colossis anteponi' (Muretus, *Catullus*, 127). For Vettori's argument, see *Variae Lectiones* xxii. 13, p. 345.
197. 'Ego vero, qui scirem istos tres poetas ab omnibus magnifieri, ut qui unum ex illis intelligere possit, non parum se in literis profecisse glorietur, quare pauculas horas male me collocasse putabo si effeci ut illos tres simul vel quivis mediocriter doctus nunc intelligat?' (Scaliger, *Castigationes*, a 5).
198. See, for example, his discussions of 74, 80, 112.
199. 'nunquam parcemus operae, quin quodcumque nobis a gravioribus studiis vacabit, totum id bonis auctoribus iuvandis impendamus, id quod in istis tribus luminibus poetices Romanae praestitimus, in quibus vix est, ut ullum animadversione dignum locum praetermiserimus, praeterquam si quae sunt, quae castae aures ferre non possunt. Ea enim attingere neque partes meae sunt, neque alius cuiuspiam, qui aliquem saltem pudorem habet. In istis commentatiunculis nostris ne verbulum quidem extat, quod me praeteriisse

melius fuerit, quam scripsisse. Vellem equidem ipsi veteres pudoris aliquam rationem habuissent, neque tot infamibus scriptis hominibus sese traduxissent. Sed quia aliter contigisse videmus, interea nos isto Catone contenti erimus; nam ex quibus Latinitatem, quam ex istis fontibus hauriemus? Et tamen isti tres poetae flagitiosius non loquuntur, quam vel una Aristophanis comoedia cuiusmodi tamen multas semper lectitasse Chrysostomum proditur. At quantum virum? Cui profecto eloquentia, probitate, pietate parem alium nulla post aetas tulit. Lectionem poetarum ego mari comparo: in eo sunt scopuli, ad quos tamen peritus nauta nunquam navem offendit. In poesi sunt quaedam non bona dicta, in quae nunquam pius animus offendit, sed ea strenuus secure praetervehitur. Quare ut quosdam rogatos volo, quos delectant poetica, ut ab illis praetextatis verbis aures, oculos, linguam, animam denique abstineant; ita alios castigandos censeo, qui propter unam, aut alteram, vel denique paucas aspersas labeculas totum opus maculosum putant' (Scaliger, *Castigationes*, a 4–5).

200. He has no discussion of 15, 47, 58, 106. For his lemmata, see, for example, at 6. 13, where he writes *e.* for *ecfututa* (Scaliger, *Castigationes*, 9).

201. Thus, on *irrumator* at 10. 12: 'Foedum verbum, quo praetorem hic appellat, non prima sua notione accipiendum est. Sed ita vocabant homines infestos, ut contra Spurci eadem tralatione dicebantur homines nulli rei. Quod dixi, ne quis aliquid foedi sub ea appellatione enunciari putet' (Scaliger, *Castigationes*, 12).

202. Emendations: 74. 3 *perdepsuit*; 78*b*. 2 *comminxit*. Explanations: e.g. at 21. 6; 88. 8; 112.

203. e.g. at 29. 13 he prints only the first three words in his lemma: *ut ista vostra*, omitting the essential *diffututa mentula*. He glosses: 'Id est, ut iste lastaurus vester Mamurra. . . . Quum libidinosum Mamurram vocat, quo nomine vocare soleat Catullus, clarius est, quam ut a me dici debeat' (Scaliger, *Castigationes*, 26). For Greek glosses on obscenities, see *inter alia ad* 21. 5; 33. 3–4.

204. Vettori: *ad* 55. 13; 64. 36; 64. 108; 66. 27. Turnèbe: *ad* 8. 19; 31. 13; 32. 1–2; 36. 12; 61. 189; 67. 42., etc. Genealogy of the Scaligers: *ad* 31. 1.

205. See Grafton, *Joseph Scaliger*, 184–5. Scaliger responded in an open letter to Joannes Stadius in July 1579. See Joseph Scaliger, *Epistolae Omnes quae reperiri potuerunt nunc primum collectae ac editae* (Frankfurt, 1628), 52–62, esp. 55–7.

206. See Gaisser, 'Catullus', 275–8.

207. See F.-R. Hausmann, 'Martialis', *CTC* (1980), iv. 256–8.

NOTES TO CHAPTER 5

1. For epithalamia see Morrison, 'Catullus in the Neo-Latin Poetry of France', 367–8; and 'Some Early Humanist Epithalamia', *Acta Conventus Neo-Latini Amstelodamensis* (Munich, 1979), 794–802. For galliambics see Campbell, 'Galliambic Poems of the 15th and 16th Centuries', 490–510. Poets also imitated parts of 68: see B. Coppel, 'Marginalien zu dichterischen Berührungspunkten zwischen Petrus Lotichius Secundus und C. Valerius Catullus', *Acta Conventus Neo-Latini Lovaniensis* (Louvain, 1973), 159–70.
2. On the proper length of poems in hendecasyllables see Pierio Valeriano's defence of Pontano, *Prolixitatem non incongruam hendecasyll.*: 'Pontani Hendecasyllabi notantur / Ut qui nil habeant Catullianum, / Ut qui luxurient nimis licenter / Centenis quoque versibus redundent' (*Prolixitatem*. 1–4, in P. Valerianus, *Praeludia* (Venice, 1509) E 1r–v). On iambic and trochaic openings see pp. 61–2 and 125–6.
3. The text is quoted from F. Arnaldi *et al.* (eds.), *Poeti latini del quattrocento*, 1152. Sannazaro is more explicit in verse 13: 'moechus ille sororis atque adulter'. For Clodius and Clodia see Cat. 79 and Cicero, *Pro Caelio* 36. See also Wiseman, *Catullan Questions*, 52–5.
4. For Statius see p. 169.
5. The text is quoted from Andrea Navagero *Lusus*, ed. Wilson, 58.
6. 'Non sunt Flaminio malo poeta / Digna carmina, sed tuo Catullo' (Marcantonio Flaminio, *Ad Blosium Palladium*, 7–8, quoted from *Carmina quinque illustrium poetarum* (Venice, 1558) 102v). For Colocci's epigrams on Adrian see V. Fanelli, 'Adriano VI e Angelo Colocci', 30–44.
7. For Muret see Chapter 4; for Dousa see Chapter 6.
8. *e.g.* in *1*. 1–2: *Cui dono lepidum | novum libellum / arida modo | pumice expolitum?* See Raven, *Latin Metre*, 139–40.
9. For the qualities of the hendecasyllable exploited by the Neo-Latin poets see Morrison, 'Catullus in the Neo-Latin Poetry of France', 376–9.
10. For vernacular poetry see pp. 149–50 above on Ronsard's *Folastries*. For cross-fertilization see the interesting discussion of E. Ginsberg of Muret and Du Bellay: 'Peregrinations of the Kiss: Thematic Relationships between Neo-Latin and French Poetry in the Sixteenth Century', *Acta Conventus Neo-Latini Sanctandreani* (Binghamton, NY, 1986), 331–42.
11. G. Pasquali, 'Arte allusiva', in *Stravaganze quarte e supreme*

(Venice, 1951) 11–20 (= *Pagine stravaganti* (Florence, 1968), ii. 275–83).

12. G. B. Conte, *The Rhetoric of Imitation: Genre and Poetic Memory in Virgil and other Latin Poets* (Ithaca, NY, and London, 1986), 28.
13. Ibid. 23–4.
14. Ibid. 32–4. Cf. *Aen*. 6. 692–3.
15. Conte, *Rhetoric*, 38. Cf. Pasquali: 'le allusioni non producono l'effetto voluto se non su un lettore che si ricordi chiaramente del testo cui si riferiscono' ('Arte allusiva', in *Pagine stravaganti* ii. 275).
16. 'La parola è come acqua di rivo che riunisce in sé i sapori della roccia dalla quale sgorga e dei terreni per i quali è passata' (Pasquali, 'Arte allusiva', 275).
17. See Conte, *Rhetoric*, 31, 37, and *passim*.
18. 'nam cum sequi, imitari, aemulari tria sint omnino specie diversa, genere tamen quodam sic sunt similia . . .' (Bartolomeo Ricci, *De imitatione libri tres* (Venice, 1545), 43v). For an excellent account of Ricci's categories, and of Renaissance imitation in general, see G. W. Pigman III, 'Versions of Imitation in the Renaissance', *Renaissance Quarterly*, 33 (1980), 1–32. The text of *De imitatione*, Book 1 is printed in B. Weinberg, ed., *Trattati di poetica e retorica del cinquecento* (Bari, 1970), i. 415–49, with bibliography on pp. 628–30.
19. Navagero, *Lusus* 43.
20. 'Rei materia simillima est, quod quidem imitationis proprium esse dicebamus, si quidem ille passerem mortuum, hic Catellum, ille heram, hic herum misere deflentem inducit, horum item lusus persimiles sunt, in saltu, morsu, pipatu, latratu, heri cognitione, sed cum omnia similia sunt, tum etiam commiseratio minime est dissimilis. postremo pro fletu assiduo, quo puellae suae turgidulos rubere oculos Catullus querebatur, longum Catelli desiderium hero suo relictum esse reposuit Navagerius . . .' (Ricci, *De imitatione*, 41v–42).
21. 'Sed eorum haec sunt, qui ad aliorum inventionem sibi quoque inveniendum esse, ac quasi alienis vestigiis eundum esse, probe censuerunt . . .' (Ricci, *De imitatione*, 43v).
22. 'Sane Catullum si solum legas, nihil melius desiderari posse videtur, verum si cum Marone conferas, vix iterum Catullum regustabis, ita hic illi quasi tenebras offudit, atque luminibus obstruxit omnibus' (Ricci, *De imitatione*, 44).
23. 'Quod lac lacti, quae aquae aqua similior, quam tota est ab usque initio ad ipsum finem Maronis imitatio? Quanto autem imitator

splendidius, quanto copiosius, quanto gravius agat, non arbitror te expectare, dum dicam. Ille enim narrat, hic vero canit, atque ea tuba canit qua nulla unquam gravior, atque nobilior inflabitur, ut isti tandem videant imitatorem non ita in ergastulis contineri, qui interdum tamen, quem sequatur, facile praecurrere non possit' (Ricci, *De imitatione*, 47v). With 'isti tandem videant' Ricci refers to those who believe that *imitatio* consists only in following and so exclude *aemulatio* (43v).

24. T. M. Greene, *The Light in Troy: Imitation and Discovery in Renaissance Poetry* (New Haven, Conn., 1980), 38.
25. Greene, *Light*, 46.
26. Thus Pasquali: 'Nelle arti figurative salta forse ancor meglio agli occhi quella che è caratteristica dell'allusione e la distingue da ogni riproduzione o imitazione povera di spiriti: la presenza del moderno in contrasto con l'antico o dentro l'antico, e quindi una certa tensione che dà movimento all' opera senza spezzarne l'unità. Ma insomma è tale e quale anche in letteratura' ('Arte allusiva', 276. See also James Hutton on the Latin translators of the *Greek Anthology*: 'At the point where the neo-Latin poet passed the boundary from *translatio* into *imitatio*, or even before, whatever his conscious intention may have been, his modern personality began to assert its rights. The tone of his work is a compromise between on the one hand a medium (Latin) and a theme shaped in an alien world, and on the other the mental directions given him by his own time and place' (*The Greek Anthology in France*, 36).
27. Greene, *Light*, 20.
28. cf. Greene, *Light*, 11: 'The signifier is rooted in the activity of a society which alters, but the word in its apparent stability fails to respond sensitively to that alteration. Beneath the apparent constancy of the *verbum*, the *res* of experience is sliding into new conformations with the immense complexity of history.'
29. For Martial manuscripts see F.-R. Hausmann, 'Martial', in *CTC*, iv. 250–9.
30. His first collection, the *Liber Spectaculorum* (AD 80), is not numbered. Some editors treat his *Xenia* and *Apophoreta* (AD 84/5) as Books 13 and 14. For the chronology of the *Epigrams* see L. Friedlaender (ed.), *M. Valerii Martialis Epigrammaton Libri*, 50–67; M. Citroni (ed.), *M. Valerii Martialis Epigrammaton Liber I* (Florence, 1975), pp. ix–xxi.
31. Quoted from P. Howell, *A Commentary on Book One of the Epigrams of Martial* (London, 1980), 104.
32. P. White, 'The Presentation and Dedication of the *Silvae* and the *Epigrams*', *Journal of Roman Studies*, 64 (1974), 56.

33. On Martial and Catullus see R. Paukstadt's dissertation, *De Martiale Catulli imitatore* (Halle, 1876); J. Ferguson, 'Catullus and Martial', *Proceedings of the African Classical Society*, 6 (1963), 3–15; and, especially, H. Offermann, 'Uno tibi sim minor Catullo', *Quaderni Urbinati de Cultura classica*, 34 (1980), 107–39.
34. Muretus, *Catullus*, p. iii. For the Latin text see Chapter 4, n. 40.
35. Life in Rome is vividly characterized by Wiseman in *Catullus and his World*, 4: 'Studying ancient Rome should be like visiting some teeming capital in a dangerous and ill-governed foreign country; nothing can be relied on, most of what you see is squalid, sinister or unintelligible . . .'. And in n. 8: 'It was, after all, a city where a dog might pick up a human hand in the street (Suet. *Vesp.* 5. 4).'
36. For Martial and his times see S. d'Elia, 'Appunti su Marziale e la civiltà letteraria dell'età flavia', in *Letterature comparate: problemi e metodo. Studi in onore di Ettore Paratore* (Bologna, 1981), ii. 647–66; P. White, 'Presentation'; 'The Friends of Martial, Statius, and Pliny, and the Dispersal of Patronage', *Harvard Studies in Classical Philology*, 79 (1975), 265–300.
37. Tacitus, *Agricola*, 2–3, quoted from *Tacitus on Britain and Germany*, trans. H. Mattingly (Harmondsworth, 1948), 52–3.
38. Book 11 appeared in December 96, three months after Domitian's death.
39. See Mart. 7. 12 and 7. 72. In both epigrams Martial pleads with patrons to confirm that slanderous verses circulated in his name are counterfeits.
40. Catullus addresses his own verses in 35 and 42, and the *annales* of Volusius in 36. For lists of Martial's personifications see P. Howell, *A Commentary*, 110; Citroni, *M. Valerii Martialis Epigrammaton Liber I*, 23. Martial's models for the personified book are Horace and Ovid. See Citroni, 'Le raccomandazioni del poeta: apostrofe al libro e contatto col destinatario', *Maia*, 36 (1986), 111–46.
41. 'Aetherias, lascive, cupis volitare per auras: / I, fuge, sed poteras tutior esse domi' (Mart. 1. 3. 11–12). For Horace *Ep.* 1. 20 see Fraenkel, *Horace*, 356–9.
42. cf. Conte's remarks on the reader's role in interpreting allusive poetry: 'The reader's collaboration is indispensable to the poet if the active phase of allusion is to take effect. Thus allusion will occur as a literary act if a sympathetic vibration can be set up between the poet's and the reader's memories when these are directed to a source already stored in both' (*Rhetoric*, 35). See also n. 15 above.

43. The translation is by Howell, *A Commentary*, 55.
44. The commentators note that Martial's metaphorical use of the word is the source for its modern meaning, 'literary thief': *plagium* (stealing another man's slave or forcing a free man into slavery) and its derivatives refer to literary theft nowhere else in classical Latin. See Howell, *A Commentary*, 230.
45. See 35 (*Poetae tenero meo sodali, / velim Caecilio, papyre, dicas*).
46. But contrast the more optimistic pose in two later poems, Mart. 8. 3 and 10. 2.
47. For the conventions of dedication poems see Citroni, 'Le raccomandazioni del poeta'.
48. *Pace* Offermann, '*Uno tibi sim minor Catullo*', 108.
49. cf. Martial's ambiguous phrase *frontis gemino decens honore* (Mart. 3. 2. 8).
50. See especially Prop. 4. 5 and Ovid *Amores* 1. 8.
51. For the patron's role in promoting the poet's work see the important studies of P. White, '*Amicitia* and the Profession of Poetry', *JRS* 68 (1978), 74–92; and R. Saller, 'Martial on Patronage and Literature', *CQ* 33 (1983), 246–57.
52. Elsewhere, however, Martial explicitly rejects the artistic criteria of 95, treating its hero Cinna as the very type of the obscure, unreadable poet (cf. Mart. 10. 21), and cheerfully describing his own work as prolific and uneven (cf. Mart. 1. 16, 7. 81, and 7. 90). Much of his poetry was written 'to order', and perhaps extemporaneously (see White, 'Presentation', 42–3).
53. See D. F. S. Thomson, 'Catullus 95. 8: "Et laxas scombris saepe dabunt tunicas"', *Phoenix*, 18 (1964), 30–6.
54. *Pace* Friedlaender, *M. Valerii Martialis Epigrammaton Libri*, ad loc.
55. Tacitus *Annales* 15. 44, in *The Works of Tacitus: The Oxford Translation, Revised* (London, 1854), i. 423. For the *tunica molesta* see also Mart. 10. 25; Juv. 1. 155; Seneca, *Ep.* 14. 5.
56. See also Mart. 3. 69.
57. See J. N. Adams, *The Latin Sexual Vocabulary* (London, 1982) *sub vocibus*.
58. 'lasciva est nobis pagina, vita proba' (Mart. 1. 4. 8). He uses the idea again to conclude 11. 15: 'mores non habet hic meos libellus' (Mart. 11. 15. 13).
59. 'vita verecunda est, Musa iocosa mea' (*Tristia* 2. 354).
60. On the *topos* see G. R. Throop, 'The Lives and Verse of Roman Erotic Writers', *Washington University Studies*, 1 (1914), 160–83; and G. Williams, 'Poetry in the Moral Climate of Augustan Rome', *JRS* 52 (1962), 39–41.

61. For the meanings of *pius* and *castus* see T. P. Wiseman, 'Catullus 16', *Liverpool Classical Monthly*, 1 (1976), 15.
62. *Emperors*: Both Augustus and Domitian took a hard line on immorality. For the zeal with which Domitian exercised his censorship (referred to at Mart. 1. 4. 7) see Suetonius, *Domitian* 8. *Pliny*: *Ep*. 4. 14. 4: 'Scimus alioqui huius opusculi illam esse verissimam legem, quam Catullus expressit [Cat. 16. 5–8].'
63. The poem was first noted by L. Bertalot in 1931 in 'Forschungen über Leonardo Bruni Aretino', *Archivum Romanicum*, 15 (1931), 284–323 (reprinted in his *Studien zum italienischen und deutschen Humanismus*, ed. P. O. Kristeller (Rome, 1975) ii. 375–420 (394)). It appears in Naples, Biblioteca Nazionale V E 18 and VIII G 45, as well as in Seville, Biblioteca Capitular y Columbina 7.1.36.

    For a discussion of Bruni and his poem see J. Hankins, 'The Latin Poetry of Leonardo Bruni', *Humanistica lovaniensia*, 39 (1990), 1–39. I am extremely grateful to Professor Hankins for allowing me to study his article before publication and for valuable information on the manuscripts.
64. For Bruni's life see G. Griffiths, J. Hankins, and D. Thompson, trans., *The Humanism of Leonardo Bruni: Selected Texts*, Medieval and Renaissance Texts and Studies, 46 (= Renaissance Society of America Text Series, 10 (Binghampton, NY, 1987), 3–50).
65. See Hankins, 'Latin Poetry', 23–4. The *Oratio Heliogabali* was written in 1407.
66. For Salutati and his manuscript see p. 20. For Poggio see A. C. de la Mare and D. F. S. Thomson, 'Poggio's Earliest Manuscript?' 16 (1973), 179–95; and Thomson, *Catullus*, 29–33; Table of Manuscripts, p. 60 no. 115. Thomson now suggests that the date may even be as early as 1397–8. According to L. Gualdo Rosa (cited by Hankins, n. 44) R contains some notes that may be in the hand of the young Bruni.
67. Hankins, 'Latin Poetry', 24. The manuscript (Naples, BN VIII G 45) also contains Bruni's translations of the *Economics* of pseudo Aristotle and Plutarch's *Life of Marc Antony* in addition to the *Oratio Heliogabali*. For a description of the manuscript see 'Latin poetry', n. 32.
68. S. Mariotti, 'Cornelii Galli Hendecasyllabi', in *Tra latino e volgare: Per Carlo Dionisotti*, ed. G. Bernardoni Trezzini *et al.* (Padua, 1974), ii. 547–68. For the differences between Bruni and pseudo Gallus, see Hankins, 'Latin Poetry', 21–3.
69. The meaning of *percitemur* is uncertain. Pseudo Gallus reads

percitentur, which is equally problematic. See Mariotti, 'Cornelii Galli endecasyllabi', 557–8.

70. For Bruni's borrowings see Mariotti, 'Cornelii Galli endecasyllabi', 554–6. For the transmission of 40–48 see Appendix 1. Mariotti (555 n. 1) says that 40–42 were separated from the rest of the block only around the time of the first edition (1472).

71. For the interpretations of Partenio, Palladio, and Guarino, see p. 90. Avanzi separated 41 and 42 in his *Emendationes* (1495), but printed them together in the first and second Aldines (1502 and 1515). See p. 308 n. 152.

72. See Mariotti, 'Cornelii Galli endecasyllabi', 551–2.

73. For a survey of early Catullan imitation see W. Ludwig, 'Catullus renatus: Anfänge und frühe Entwicklung des catullischen Stils in der neulateinischen Dichtung', in *Litterae Neolatinae* (Munich, 1989), 162–94. A shorter version of this article appears as 'The Catullan Style in Neo-Latin Poetry', in *Latin Poetry and the Classical Tradition: Essays in Medieval and Renaissance Literature*, ed. P. Godman and O. Murray (Oxford, 1990), 183–97.

74. For the chronology see A. Perosa (ed.), *Christophori Landini Carmina Omnia* (Florence, 1939), p. xxxvii. The text of Landino is quoted from Perosa's edition. For Landino and his poetry see G. Bottiglioni, *La lirica latina in Firenze nella secunda metà del secolo XV* (Pisa, 1913); and R. Cardini, *La critica del Landino* (Florence, 1973).

75. Ludwig, 'Catullus renatus', 172.

76. For Martial's dedications see pp. 202–8.

77. For books in a hurry see Mart. 1. 3. 11; 3. 5. 1; 8. 72. 3. Landino's book is characterized as limping (*claudus*) in other personifications as well; see *X*. 38. 3 (= A 1. 32. 3) and *X*. 53. 2 (= A 1. 33. 2), both in elegiacs. The pun on 'bad feet' occurs at Cat. 14. 22; in 36. 7 bad verses are to be sacrificed to *tardipedi deo* (cf. Landino A 1. 33. 11–12: 'claudo Veneris sua sacra marito / confice: . . .').

78. See C. Grayson, 'Alberti', *DBI* (1960), i. 706; and A. Perosa, 'Miscellanea umanistica', *Annali di scuola normale superiore de Pisa*, 2: 7 (1938), 73–80.

79. See p. 7.

80. *X*. 50 (= A. 1. 30) imitates 11, and *X*. 6 (= A 1. 6), *X*. 34 (= A 1. 16), and *X*. 35 (= A 1. 17) imitate 8. See Ludwig, 'Catullus renatus', 171–2. (Ludwig does not mention *X*. 34.)

81. Landino uses hendecasyllables twice, but not in direct imitation of Catullus: in *X*. 1 his hendecasyllables and imitation of Martial present him as a Catullan poet, but he evokes no particular

Catullan poem; *X*. 46 (= A 1. 26) is a *paraclausithyron* loosely modelled on Horace, *Odes* 1. 25.

82. The first couplet of *X*. 6, though imitated from 87, corresponds to 8. 5 (*amata nobis quantum amabitur nulla*): 'Xandra mihi tantum quondam crudelis amata / quantum dilecta est femina nulla viro' (*X*. 6. 1–2). Landino's refrain, *iamque puella vale*! (*X*. 6. 8, 12, 16, 20), is a formal echo of Catullus' repetitions (*fulsere . . . candidi tibe soles*, 8. 3, 8; and *obdura*, 8. 11, 19).
83. 'Quid facis infelix? (*X*. 35 (= A. 17) 1) . . . Desine iam vanos tibimet nutrire dolores. (35. 5) . . . Pone modum lacrimis et quae deperdita cernis / perdita iam ducas, paeniteatque tui' (35. 7–8).
84. The title of *X*. 34 in the 1443–4 collection was *Ad Musas*. (See Perosa, *Christophori Landini Carmina Omnia*, ad loc.) For the titles in the archetype, McKie, *The Manuscripts of Catullus*, 95*a–c*.
85. cf. the final verses in the 1443–4 collection: 'Nam mea quae dici cupiat reperire puellam / non dubito, cuius solus amator ero' (*X*. 6. 23–4).
86. Compare, Ovid, *Amores* 1. 4, for example, and *X*. 18 (= A I. 20), *De Gnognia*: 'Cum matutinus peterem pia sacra beatae / Luciae venit Gnognia nostra simul, / . . . / Inde abitum simulans, ut se coniungat amanti / me petit atque premit muta puella pede / et lateri nostro turba suadente coherens, / murmure submisso dixit: Amice, vale!' (*X*. 18. 1–2, 9–12).
87. See Cardini, *La critica del Landino*, 356–82.
88. See Ludwig, 'Catullus renatus', 172–80. For a succinct account of Pontano's life and works see L. Monti Sabia, 'Giovanni Gioviano Pontano', in *Poeti latini del quattrocento*, ed. F. Arnaldi, L. Gualdo Rosa, and L. Monti Sabia, 307–14.
89. For Panormita, see pp. 20–2 above.
90. See Ludwig, 'Petrus Lotichius Secundus and the Roman Elegists: Prolegomena to a Study of Neo-Latin Elegy', in *Litterae Neolatinae*, 202–17, reprinted from *Classical Influences on European Culture A.D. 1500–1700* (Cambridge, 1976), 171–90.
91. For the chronology see Ludwig, 'Catullus renatus', especially pp. 172–80. For Ludwig's reconstruction of the contents of the *Pruritus* see p. 173 n. 47. For the text and composition of the *Hendecasyllabi* see L. Monti Sabia (ed.), *Ioannis Ioviani Pontani, Hendecasyllaborum Libri* (Naples, 1978), 1–19.
92. It is only in the *Amores* that fewer than half of the poems are in hendecasyllables.
93. For the hendecasyllabic style see p. 195. Ludwig lists some of the

Catullan features of the hendecasyllables in the *Pruritus* ('Catullus renatus', 175). In the absence of a detailed stylometric study comparing Pontanus' hendecasyllables with those of earlier poets and tracing his own metrical development from the *Pruritus* to the *Hendecasyllabi*, one is reduced to suggestions and impressions. It seems likely, however, that Pontano's hendecasyllables were influenced not only by Catullus, Martial, and the *Priapea*, but also by mediaeval and Italian lyric and Italian popular song, and that they became more fluid and lyrical in the course of their development.

94. See pp. 208–11.
95. B. Soldati (ed.), *Ioannis Ioviani Pontani Carmina* (Florence, 1902), ii. 406.
96. See Soldati, *Ioannis Ioviani Pontani Carmina* i. 48–50 and ii. *App*. 8.
97. See Pontano, *Am*. 2. 8. 12; and L. Monte Sabia, 'Giovanni Gioviano Pontano', 427.
98. The point emerges more sharply in a later version (*App*. 8, Soldati), which Ludwig dates after 1451 ('Catullus renatus', 173), dedicated to Tito Strozzi (1424–1505), Pontano's contemporary and fellow poet. There verse 1 reads: 'Facunde Tite, corculum Guarini,'; and 'Samarrae' in verse 5 is replaced by 'Aurispae', i.e. the humanist and manuscript hunter, Giovanni Aurispa (1369–1459), a man in his eighties at the time of the *Pruritus*.
99. 'I munus lepido meo sodali / Non dura nimium, libelle, fronte' (Pontano, *Am*. 1. 1. 1–2) The text of the *Parthenopeus sive Amores* is quoted from Soldati, *Ioannis Ioviani Pontani Carmina* ii. For Landino's influence on Pontano see Ludwig, 'Catullus renatus', 178.
100. i.e. Bonincontri, who came from San Miniato.
101. As Ludwig observed; see 'Catullus renatus', n. 70.
102. On this point see the interesting discussion of E. Paratore, *La poesia di Giovanni Pontano* (Rome, 1967), 75–93.
103. On Catullus see Ross, *Style and Tradition*, 80–95. For elegy see E. Burck, 'Römische Wesenzüge der augusteischen Liebeselegie', *Hermes*, 80 (1952) 163–200.
104. For *Am*. 1. 28 as the final poem of the first version of the *Parthenopeus* see Ludwig, 'Catullus renatus', 173 n. 47.
105. See Pliny, *Epist*. 4. 27. 4. For the text of Augurinus see p. 280 n. 37.
106. For Mart. 3. 2 see p. 204. For the allusion to Prop. 3. 3, see Ludwig, 'Catullus renatus', 178 n. 71.
107. The seductions of Baiae were notorious in Antiquity, e.g. Martial's

comment on the chaste woman who went to Baiae: 'Penelope venit, abit Helene' (Mart. 1. 62. 6).

108. The text of the *Hendecasyllabi* is quoted from Monti Sabia, *Ioannis Ioviani Pontani, Hendecasyllaborum Libri*.

109. 'quot, quot oscula morsiunculasque, / quot, quot enumerabitis duella! / Quot suspiria, murmura et cachinnos . . .' (Pontano, *Hend.* 1. 1. 25–7).

110. 'senex salaxque', *Hend.* 1. 1. 35; 'nimio supinus usu' (1. 1. 37).

111. 'Haec [vis] est [tabulae] vigorque fontis' (Pontano, *Hend.* 1. 7. 19).

112. 'thermae nam iuvenes decent, tabernae / Lenaeae invalidos senes. . . .' (Pontano, *Hend.* 2. 1. 27–8).

113. 'est certus quoque terminus cachinnis' (Pontano, *Hend.* 2. 38. 6).

114. For Panormita and Guarino see pp. 21–2.

115. For the *Folastries* see pp. 149–50.

116. *Salmonii Macrini Iuliodunensis Carminum libellus* (Paris, 1528) a i v. On Macrin see M. Morrison, 'Catullus in the Neo-Latin Poetry of France', *passim*; and I. D. MacFarlane, 'Jean Salmon Macrin', *BHR* 21 (1959), 55–82, 311–47, and 22 (1960) 73–87.

117. For Macrin's early poetry see MacFarlane, 'Jean Salmon Macrin', 55–71. The epithalamial nature of the collection is announced in the programme poem, side by side with the 'Catullan law': 'Dum carmen tibi nuptiale, proles / O regum inclyta, Caesarumque sanguis / Honorate dico, levesque nugas / Volui abs te nimis impudenter insto: / Frontem exporrige blandus ad iocosas / Festi delicias Thalassionis. . . .' (*Carminum libellus* 1528, 1. 1–6).

118. For Mantuan and Marullo see the short bio-bibliographies in Arnaldi, *Poeti latini del quattrocento*, 885–7 and 939–41. Ludwig ('Catullus renatus', 181–2) notes the criticism of Pontano by Mantuan and Marullus, but implies the opposite chronology.

The publication of the first two books of Marullo's *Epigrammata* is dated between June 1488 amd July 1489 by Alessandro Perosa, 'Studi sulla formazione delle raccolte di poesie del Marullo', *Rinascimento*, 1. 2 (1950–51), 128–34. Recently Kidwell has argued that the collection was not published until 1490. See C. Kidwell, *Marullus. Soldier Poet of the Renaissance* (London, 1989), 156–7. Mantuan's poem was published in a volume dated 1 April 1489 (*BMC* vi. 823), but the poem itself bears the date: Rome, 20 October 1487. Marullo was in Rome from 1485 to July or August 1489 (see Perosa, 'Studi' *loc. cit.*, especially 130 n. 3).

119. Mantuan's text is quoted from Baptista Mantuanus, *Contra poetas impudice scribentes Carmen* (Paris, *c.*1490); Goff B–83.

120. 'Casta dei genetrix, castus regnator olympi. / Mens capit ambrosias non nisi casta dapes' (Mantuan, *Contra poetas* 35–6).
121. 'Pierides castae, castae libethrides undae. / Tota pudicitiam vera poesis amat. / Est helicon virgo, virgo peneia Daphne. / Castalidasque aiunt virgine matre satas. / Ite procul veneris vates heliconis ab amne. / Virgineus vestro leditur ore liquor' (Mantuan, *Contra poetas*, 39–44).
122. 'Castalium veri potant non vina poetae' (Mantuan, *Contra poetas*, 83).
123. cf. the gloss of Mantuan's contemporary commentator, Jodocus Badius Ascensius: '*in pectore vapido*: i. vini pleno unde vapores eriguntur' (Mantuan, *Contra poetas* (Paris, *c.*1490), C. c. i).
124. e.g., in *Amores* I. 28. 15–24.
125. For Mart. I. 35 see pp. 208–11.
126. The text of Marullo is quoted from the edition of A. Perosa, *Michaelis Marulli Carmina* (Zurich, 1951).
127. 'Marsumque feras doctumque Catullum / Et quoscunque alios Martia Roma legit / Non tamen efficies, ut Phrynae scribere malim, / Quam tibi vel turbae, Laodamia, tuae' (Marullo, *Ep.* I. 62. 9–12). cf. 'sic scribit Catullus, sic Marsus, sic Pedo, sic Gaetulicus, sic quicumque perlegitur' (Martial, *Praef.* I). Since Phryne was a famous prostitute, *Ep.* I. 62. 11–12 answers Martial's assertion that he writes for the audience of the Floralia (where prostitutes performed naked on the stage).
128. Ludwig, 'Catullus renatus', 181.
129. 'Sit procul a nobis obscoena licentia scripti: / Ludimus innocuae carmina mentis opus' (Marullo, *Ep.* I. 62. 15–16). For the text of Mantuan *Contra poetas*, 39–42 see n. 121.
130. 'Haec ego: Phoebus / Annuit et sanctis ora rigavit aquis' (Marullo, *Ep.* I. 62. 27–8.
131. *Sparrows*: See G. Herrlinger, *Totenklage um Tiere in der antiken Dichtung, mit einem Anhang, byzantinischer, mitellateinischer und neuhochdeutscher Tierepikedien* (Stuttgart 1930); T. Sorbelli, 'Della fortuna del Carme terzo di Catullo presso gli Umanisti', *Classici e neo-latini* (1912), 170–81.

    Kisses: In addition to many separate poems by individual poets there are 11 kiss poems in Book I of Pontano's *Amores* alone (see Ludwig, 'Catullus renatus', 179 n. 74). Johannes Secundus' masterpiece, the *Basia* (a cycle of 19 poems), had many imitators, including Joachim Du Bellay (*Basia Faustinae*), Janus Dousa the Elder (*Basia*), Janus Lernutius (*Ocelli*), and Janus Dousa the younger (*Eratopaignion*). See A. Ramminger, *Motivgeschichtliche Studien zu Catulls Basiagedichten mit einem Anhang: Aus dem*

Nachleben der catullischen Basiagedichte (Würzburg, 1937); G. Braden, '*Vivamus mea Lesbia* in the English Renaissance', *English Literary Renaissance*, 9 (1979), 199–224; N. J. Perella, *The Kiss, Sacred and Profane* (Berkeley, 1969).

132. 'Tantum dat tibi Roma basiorum / post annos modo quindecim reverso / quantum Lesbia non dedit Catullo' (Mart. 12. 59. 1–3). Martial's language is ambiguous. The Loeb translates, 'Rome gives you as many kisses . . . as Lesbia never gave Catullus.' W. C. A. Ker, *Martial: Epigrams* (London, 1927), ii. 361.

133. In Greene's classification Martial's technique in the presentation poems would be described as 'heuristic', while that in the kiss poems would be 'dialectical'. 'Heuristic imitations come to us advertising their derivation from the subtexts they carry with them, but having done that, they proceed to distance themselves from the subtexts and force us to recognize the poetic distance traversed.' Greene, *Light*, 40. In dialectical imitation the imitator enters into a dialogue or a contest (*aemulatio*) with the subtext: 'And just as heuristic imitation involves a passage from one semiotic universe to another, so dialectical imitation, when it truly engages two eras or two civilizations at a profound level, involves a conflict between two *mundi significantes*' (Greene, 46).

134. For Mart. 12. 59 see n. 132 above. In Mart. 6. 34. 7–8 Lesbia is *exorata* ('pleaded with'), and the jest is sharper if her kisses were few or none.

135. cf. Mart. 3. 35 and 3. 40. For more examples see White, 'Presentation', 43 n. 12.

136. See Offermann, '*Uni tibi sim minor Catullo*', 128–9.

137. 'ars et gratia, lusus et voluptas, / Romani decus et dolor theatri / atque omnes Veneres Cupidinesque / hoc sunt condita, quo Paris sepulchro' (Mart. 11. 13. 4–7). See N. M. Kay, *Martial Book XI: A Commentary* (Oxford, 1985), 94–7.

138. See pp. 11–12.

139. Mart. 1. 7. 1–3.

140. See Howell, *A Commentary*, 121–4; R. W. Hooper, 'In Defence of Catullus' Dirty Sparrow', 162–78.

141. Rome is 'dressed in the freedom cap' (*pilleata*) as a sign of licence. The cap (*pilleus*) was awarded to manumitted slaves, appears on coins with the goddess Libertas, and was a special token of the Saturnalia, when normal conventions of good behaviour were suspended. See Kay, *Martial Book XI*, 71–2.

142. See the discussions in Kay, *Martial Book XI*, 71–6, and Hooper, 'In Defence of Catullus' Dirty Sparrow', 168–70.

143. The story is told in Tacitus, *Annales* 15. 37. Strictly speaking, the

analogy is imperfect, since Nero took the role of bride in this wedding (although Pythagoras seems to have been a eunuch); but the context of the wedding (which was the climax of the most notorious banquet of Nero's reign) provides a nice parallel with Martial's Saturnalia symposium.

144. 'Pollicetur . . . se tale carmen in eius gratiam scripturum, quale Catullus de passere Lesbiae . . .' (Guarinus, *Expositiones*, B 2v. Domizio Calderini had proposed the same interpretation fifty years earlier in his commentary on Martial (1474), i.e. *before* Poliziano's discussion (see Jocelyn, 'On Some Unnecessarily Indecent Interpretations', 424).

145. For a defence of the *passer* as poem see Jocelyn, 'On Some Unnecessarily Indecent Interpretations', 423–4.

146. 'tanto Stella meus tuo Catullo / quanto passere maior est columba' (Mart. 1. 7. 4–5). The translation is from Howells, *A Commentary*, 33.

147. See Hooper, 'In Defence of Catullus' Dirty Sparrow', 171–2.

148. *Impotence*: e.g. Tibullus 1. 5. 39–40; Ovid, *Amores* 3. 7. *Salacious sparrows*: Hooper, 'In Defence of Catullus' Dirty Sparrow', 163–4. *Doves*: The kissing of doves was especially erotic—e.g Pliny, *NH* 10. 58: 'Columbae proprio ritu osculantur ante coitum.' For the modern debate compare Jocelyn, 'On Some Unnecessarily Indecent Interpretations' with Hooper, 'In Defence' and G. Giangrande, 'Catullus' Lyrics on the *Passer*', *Museum Philologum Londiniense*, 1 (1976), 137–46.

149. Stella's is the only imitation of 3 we can point to with any confidence, although some might want to include Ovid's *epicedion* on Corinna's parrot in *Amores* 2. 6.

150. Pliny, *Ep*. 9. 25. 3. See Introduction, pp. 11–12.

151. For the composition of the *Pruritus* see Ludwig, 'Catullus renatus', 173 n. 47. For the *columba* in *Am*. 1. 5, see Ludwig, 175 n. 58.

152. For 1 and Mart. 3. 2, see pp. 204–6.

153. 'Non vobis dabimus, mali cinaedi; / Non vos munere tam elegante digni. / Quin ite, illepidi atque inelegantes / Ales nam Veneris nitore gaudet, / Odit sorditiem inficetiasque, / Insulsos fugit et parum venustos, / Sed cuinam cupis, o columba, munus / Deferri? Scio; nam meam puellam / Amas plus oculis tuis, nec ulla / Vivit mundior elegantiorve' (Pontano, *Am*. 1. 5. 4–13). Verses 6–9 replace three verses perhaps from the *Pruritus* in which the attack on the catamites is more explicit: 'Quin ite in miseram crucem, diuque / Concisis maceremini mariscis, / Insulsi, illepidi et parum venusti.' See Soldati, *Pontani Carmina*, ii. 63.

154. Pontano continued to exploit Martial's interpretation. In *Appendix* 18 (Soldati) he urges his young pupil, Alfonso, Duke of Calabria (1448–95), not to wear himself out studying the Latin poets, but to enjoy the pleasures of love: 'Nunc te dum cupide illa et illa et illa / Optat et tenero fovere sinu, / Surrige et basiolis catullianis. / Hispanos fuge quae secuta amores, / Et novam tibi compara puellam; / Laeva sit liceat et superba, fiet / Attutu facilis tuisque amatrix, / Dones dummodo passerem Catulli' (Pont. *Ap.* 18. 27–34). The poem was probably written before 1465 or so, since Alfonso is described as 'tenelle lector' (*Ap.* 18. 17)—an unlikely appellation after his marriage to Ippolita Sforza in 1465 and his military successes in the late 1460s. For Alfonso see R. Moscati, 'Alfonso II d'Aragona', *DBI* (1960), ii. 331–2.

155. For Pontano's anticipation of Poliziano see Ludwig, 'Catullus renatus', 176 n. 59. For Poliziano's discussion in the *Miscellanea* see pp. 75–6.

156. For an account of Sannazaro's life and poetry see A. Altamura, *Jacopo Sannazaro* (Naples, 1951).

157. *Iacobi Sannazarii Opera Omnia Latine Scripta* (Venice, 1535) 44r–v.

158. See, for example, Poliziano, *Lamia*, ed. Wesseling, 16–18.

159. For the text of *Misc.* 6 see p. 314, n. 35.

160. See Altamura, *Jacopo Sannazaro*, 47.

161. On *Misc.* 2: Marullo, *Ep.* 3. 27; on *Misc.* 69: Marullo, *Ep.* 3. 11 and *Ep. Var.* 1; on *Misc.* 73: Marullo, *Ep.* 3. 39.

162. For Marullo see Perosa, 'Studi sulla formazione', 136–7. For Pontano see *Pontani Hendecasyllaborum Libri*, ed. L. Monti Sabia, 7–8. Sannazaro, *Ep.* 1. 6 is undated: see Altamura, *Jacopo Sannazaro*, 172.

163. *Counting*: 'Non tot Oceano moventur undae, / Non tantus numerus Lybissae arenae: / Quot suspiria, quot, Neaera, pro te / Vesanos patior die dolores' (Marullo, *Ep.* 1. 49. 9–12). *Snatching kisses*: 'Suaviolum invitae rapio dum casta Neaera, / Imprudens vestris liqui animam in labiis' (*Ep.* 2. 4. 1–2).

164. 'At vos interea, labella cara, / An est cur ego pressa non resuggo / Et centum fero basiationes? / . . . / 'Saevo pectoris halitu perussi' (Marullo *Ep.* 3. 31. 19–21, 29).

165. 'Sexcentas, Nina, da, precor, roganti' (Sannazaro, *Ep.* 1. 6. 1. The text is quoted from Arnaldi *et al.* (eds.), *Poeti latini del quattrocento*, 1150–2.

166. 'sed totam cupio tenere linguam / insertam humidulis meis labellis, / hanc et sugere morsiunculasque / molles adiicere et, columbulorum / in morem, teneros inire lusus / ac blandum simul excitare murmur.

/ Haec sunt suavia dulciora melle / Hyblaeo et Siculae liquore cannae. / Haec sola ambrosiaeque nectarisque / succos fundere, sola habere possunt' (Sannazaro, *Ep.* 1. 6. 11–20). Cf. Pont. *Am.* 1. 5. 26–31, quoted on p. 243.

167. 'quales Menaliae canunt puellae' (Pont. *Hend.* 1. 29. 3).
168. On Flaminio see C. Maddison, *Marcantonio Flaminio: Poet, Humanist, and Reformer* (London, 1965). The trip is mentioned on p. 14. See also E. Cuccoli, *M. Antonio Flaminio* (Bologna, 1897) 32–3.
169. The text is quoted from *Michaelis Tarchaniotae Marulli Neniae . . . M. Antonii Flaminii Adulescentis Amoenissimi Carminum Libellus* (Fano, 1515) e i v–e ii r. See also Maddison, *Marcantonio Flaminio*, 22–3. According to Cuccoli, (*M. Antonio Flaminio*, 35), Flaminio omitted *Ad Septimillam* from later editions of his poetry.
170. *Pace* Ludwig, 'Catullus renatus', 191–2.
171. 'Appellabo ego te meam columbam, / Tu me, blandula, passerem vocabis' (Muret, *Ep.* 23. 6–7). The text is quoted from Frotscher, ed., *M. Antonii Mureti Opera Omnia*, ii. 274–5.
172. The text is quoted from *The Attic Nights of Aulus Gellius* ed. Rolfe, iii. 392.
173. For the text see n. 163 above.
174. For the importance of Pontano, especially *Hend.* 1. 16, see Ludwig, 'Catullus Renatus', 183–94. Important general studies include Ramminger, *Motivgeschichtliche Studien zu Catulls Basiagedichten*, 76–119, and especially Perella, *The Kiss*.
175. Secundus' text is quoted from F. J. Nichols, *An Anthology of Neo-Latin poetry* (New Haven, Conn., 1979) 508–10. Nichols also gives a short biobibliography (*An Anthology*, 701–2). For the *Basia* see Ludwig, 'Catullus renatus', 188–92 and the important studies of P. Godman: 'Johannes Secundus and Renaissance Latin Poetry', *Review of English Studies*, 39 (1988), 258–72; and especially, 'Literary Classicism and Latin Erotic Poetry of the Twelfth Century and the Renaissance', in *Latin Poetry and the Classical Tradition* ed. Godman and Murray, 149–82. In 'Literary Classicism' Godman suggests an interpretation of *Basia* 16 complementary to my own (see 175–6).
176. *Latonae . . . sidere* is the moon, hence Diana (daughter of Latona).
177. See Nichols, *An Anthology*, 703. On the power of a single word to establish an allusion see Conte, *Rhetoric*, 35.
178. Thus of Venus in 68. 17–18: 'non est dea nescia nostri, / quae dulcem curis miscet amaritiem.' And of Cupid in 64. 95: 'sancte

puer, curis hominum qui gaudia misces'. Cf. Sappho 130 LP: Ἔρος . . . / γλυκύπικρον ἀμάχανον ὄρπετον.

179. For the sense of *publica verba* see Godman, 'Johannes Secundus', 262. I read *quales* at v. 21 instead of Nichols' *qualeis*.

180. See, for example, Horace *C*. 1. 4; 1. 9; 4. 7; and the discussion of S. Commager, *The Odes of Horace* (New Haven, Conn., 1962), 265–306.

181. 'nec dulcis amores / sperne puer neque tu choreas, / donec virenti canities abest / morosa' Horace *C*. 1. 9. 15–18. The text is quoted from *Q. Horatii Flacci, Opera*, ed. D. R. Shackleton Bailey (Stuttgart, 1985).

NOTES TO CHAPTER 6

1. For the style and metre of 4 see Fordyce, *Catullus*, *ad loc*.
2. See Fordyce, *Catullus*, 99. On *Catal*. 10 see especially R. E. H. Westendorp Boerma (ed.), *P. Vergili Maronis Catalepton* (Assen, 1963), ii. 28–48; G. I. Carlson and E. A. Schmidt, 'Form and Transformation in Vergil's *Catalepton*', *AJP* 92 (1971), 252–65; N. Zorzetti, 'L'ironia della differenza (a proposito di Catull. 4 e *Catal*. 10)', in *Interpretazioni latine* (Padua, 1978), 43–77.
3. The text is that of Westendorp Boerma, *P. Vergili Maronis Catalepton*.
4. For the interpretation of *iugum tulisse* (18) and *proximum* (22) see Carlson and Schmidt, 'Form and Transformation', 263–4.
5. See Zorzetti, 'L'ironia della differenza', 67–8.
6. Greene, *Light*, 46.
7. *Phaselus Catulli, et ad eam, quotquot extant, Parodiae. Cum annotationibus doctissimorum virorum. Accesserunt alia quaedam eiusdem generis, Edita a Sixto Octaviano. Eboraci, Apud Ioannem Marcantium. MDLXXIX*. See H. van Crombruggen, *Lernutiana*, Mededelingen van de koninklijke vlaamse Academie voor Wetenschappen, Letteren en schone Kunsten van Belgie, 21 (1959); Gaisser, 'Catullus', 280–3.
8. For a detailed description of the volume see van Crombruggen, *Lernutiana*, 4–7. For the parodies of Cat. 4 see n. 36 below.
9. 'Ad Clarissimum et Eruditissimum Virum N. Ascanium: Catulle optime, et optimi Catulli / Vos vestigia proxime insecuti / Vates, quos parili Thalia cursu / In certamine dispari, phaselum / Illam maximi et optimi poetae / Vidit non parili arte consecutos: / Vos o vos lepidissimi poetae / Ite, et Ascanium tenete vestrum. / Vestris

deliciis leporibusque; / Quem nunc Curia seriis severis / In rebus tenet occupatque totum. . . ' (*Phaselus*, 67–8).

10. Van Crombruggen, *Lernutiana*, 3–11.
11. See Heesakkers, *Praecidanea Dousana*, 14–21.
12. For Giselinus' plans see his correspondence with Dousa in Heesakkers, *Praecidanea Dousana*, 51–60. Heesakkers (p. 136) suggests that part of Giselinus' dedication may be preserved in a fragment in pure iambics in Dousa's *Nova poemata* ((Antwerp, 1576), 2G1r–2G2r) that urges Dousa to repair the text of Catullus. For Statius' readings see p. 178.
13. Heesakkers, *Praecidanea Dousana*, 21–4.
14. Thus, in an affectionate invitation to Giselinus: 'Sunt ioca, sunt seria, quae in sinum tuum cupio effundere, sinum, et amore et fide mihi perspectum. Cum te Castore, Pollucem exspectabo Lernutium. Mihi crede, non illae ipsae stellae tam gratae nautis turbante mari adfulgent, quam mihi vos . . .' (Justus Lipsius, *Epistolicae Quaestiones* 2. 6, in *Epistolicarum Quaestionum Libri V* (Antwerp, 1577), 51).
15. See H. van Crombruggen, *Janus Lernutius (1545–1619): Een biografische studie*, Verhandelingen van de koninklijke vlaamse Academie voor Wetenschappen, Letteren en schone Kunsten van Belgie, Klasse der Letteren, 23 (1955), 33–197. Lernutius' correspondence with Dousa appears on 101–12.
16. See J. H. Waszink, 'La filologia nei paesi bassi', *Annali della Scuola Normale Superiore di Pisa*, 8 (1978), 124–5.
17. See Heesakkers, *Praecidanea Dousana*, 14–15, 128–9.
18. Ibid. 129–30. Heesakkers notes that Dousa had also promised the poems to Georgius Ratallerus, and in nearly the same words that he used to Lernutius.
19. 'Ac ne in opera te gratuita esse pigeat diutius, nosque ex eorum hominum ingeniis aestimare pergas porro, qui (ne non apud te quoque solenne illud meum, ut Plautissem, obtineam solens), "Lingua tantummodo largiuntur, opera vero ac factis fallunt", en tibi pro geminis germanis illis, lepidissimis libellis inquam tuis, *Praecidanea* haec nostra, "Plena ruris, et inficetiarum [36. 19]."' (Janus Dousa, *Praecidanea Pro Q. Valerio Catullo*, in *Catullus, Tibullus, et Propertius*, ed. J. G. Graevius (Utrecht, 1680), ii. 379).
20. 'priscae illius ac Catullianae festivitatis imaginem maxime in scriptis tuis recognosere videor mihi, praesertim quoties OCELLOS istos contemplor . . .' (Dousa, *Praecidanea* 1680, 382).
21. 'Sed quoniam Phaseli incidit mentio, haud alienum a more et instituto meo videor facturus, si, explendae Parodiarum tuarum

Decuriae, Iambos etiam nostros, huic libello per causam subtexuero' (Dousa, *Praecidanea* 1680, 382). The parody, 'In effigiem Rosillae defunctae', begins: 'Et os, et ista, quae vides, labellula / ferunt fuisse pyxidem Dioneam / Ubi reposta margarita conderet / . . .' (*Praecidanea* 1680, 405).

22. For an excellent account of the rôles of Scaliger and Estienne in the development of sixteenth-century parody see E. Schäfer, *Deutscher Horaz* (Baden, 1976), 92–101.

23. 'Est igitur Parodia Rhapsodia inversa mutatis vocibus ad ridicula sensum retrahens' (Scaliger, *Poetices Libri Septem*, facsimile of the edition of Lyon, 1561 (Stuttgart-Bad Cannstatt, 1964), 46).

24. 'Personae in Parodiis amantes foeminae aut temulentae. Item Ganeones, qui bona sua abligurierunt. Patres eorundem Nepotum et Gurgitum Alcumistarum imposturae' (Scaliger, *Poetices Libri Septem*, 46).

25. 'Lusus in malos poetas ex persona cauponis aut pistoris. Irrisio mali medici ex recitatione podagrici' (Scaliger, *Poetices Libri Septem*, 46).

26. Scaliger prints *Boletus* in verses 1 and 15, *Doletus* in 10. In other printings of the poem the name appears as *Doletus* throughout.

27. As Schäfer observes: 'Das antike Vorbild ist für Scaliger das Vergil zugeschriebene Gedicht Catalepton 10, in dem Vers für Vers Catulls c.4 abgewandelt wird. Parodia war damit auf die Veränderung bestimmter Verse oder zusammenhängender Texte, nicht allgemeiner Stilzüge und Darstellungsformen festgelegt. Scaliger übernahm dieses Kontrafakturprinzip und schuf mit einer eigenen Parodia zu Catulls c.4 das neuzeitliche Muster dieses Typs' (*Deutscher Horaz*, 93).

28. 'tanto difficilius quod neque Catulli ἐκμαγεῖον neque Virgilii deprompta mihi ponere licuit: sed alia longe diversa, quae tamen ad rem facerent, quaerenda' (Scaliger, *Poetices Libri Septem*, 46).

29. 'at παρῳδοῖς in eo tantum adhibenda cautio est, ut quae furati verba fuerint, in alium usum convertant, qui tam remotus sit ab eo quem apud suum auctorem habebant . . . ut nihil tale illi dum iis uteretur, in mentem venisse dici possit' (Henri Estienne, *Homeri et Hesiodi certamen . . . Matronis et aliorum Parodiae*, in *Phaselus*, 5). His example is Matro's notorious parody of the opening of the *Odyssey*:

Δεῖπνά μοι ἔννεπε Μοῦσα πολυτρόφα καὶ μάλα πολλά.

'Cum enim caneret Homerus, ἄνδρά μοι ἔννεπε Μοῦσα πολύτροπον, ὃς μάλα πολλά [*Od.* 1. 1], quid minus in mentem ei venisse putandum est, quam rogare suam Calliopen ut ipsi Δεῖπνα πολυτρόφα καὶ μάλα πολλά memoraret?' (*Phaselus*, 5).

30. 'ita ut, velut Proteum quendam vultus alios atque alios sumere coegerim' (Estienne, *Parodiae morales*, p. iv).
31. 'donec paucas veterum poetarum gnomas, id est sententias, in adeo multas propagavi aut (si mihi ita loqui potius concedis) in unumquenque ex illis quos delegi veterum poetarum versibus, velut surculos in veteres arbores insevi' (Estienne, *Parodiae morales*, p. iv).
32. 'in parodiis contra non probatur solum, sed valde etiam amatur, si modo quis ea qua decet immutatione adhibita, efficiat ut qui ex uno eodemque loco et servata eadem serie adduntur versus, non trahi sed sponte sequi videantur' (Estienne, *Parodiae morales*, 130).
33. 'Existimo enim aliquem maiore non solum cum delectatione, sed etiam fructu, musam suam in hoc poeseωs genere posse exercere: quod hic spatiis iniquis exclusa, viam vi facere, vel potius viam per avia invenire interdum cogatur' (Estienne, *Parodiae morales*, 168).
34. His Catullan examples are 4 with five parodies—by Vergil, J. C. Scaliger (*Doletus ille* and *Maranus ille*), J. J. Scaliger (*Magirus ille*), and Paul Melissus (*Colonus ille*); 57 with J. C. Scaliger's parody (*Pulchre convenit hispidis molossis*); and 3 with Estienne's parody (*Lugete o calices capidinesque*).
35. Quoted from *Parodiae morales*, 179. For the text of 3 see pp. 236–7.
36. The *Phaselus* includes the following parodies of 4 (an * marks those appearing also in *Parodiae morales*). My description is much indebted to van Crombruggen, *Lernutiana*, 5–6.

*Parody 1, p. 15. Vergil, *Sabinus ille*, (*Catalepton* 10).

Parody 2, p. 22. Giorgio Anselmi, *Libellus ille* (*In P. Virgilii opera*), *Ep.* 1.5 in *Epigrammaton libri septem* (Parma, 1526).

*Parody 3, p. 23. J. C. Scaliger, *Doletus ille*, in *Poetices libri septem*, 46.

*Parody 4, p. 24. J. C. Scaliger, *Maranus ille*, (*In Vidorem, qui ex pharmacario factus erat clinicus*), in *Poemata* ([Heidelberg?] 1574), 352.

*Parody 5, p. 25. J. J. Scaliger, *Magirus ille*, in *Parodiae morales*, 173.

Parody 6, p. 26. Janus Lernutius, *Ocellus ille*, in *Carmina* (Antwerp, 1579) 20–1.

*Parody 7, p. 28. Paulus Melissus Schedius, *Colonus ille*, in *Schediasmata poetica* (Frankfurt, 1574), 39–40.

Parody 8, p. 29. Joannes Matthaeus Toscanus, *Atimus ille*, in *Carmina illustrium poetarum italorum* (Paris, 1576), f. 64.

Parody 9, p. 30. 'Sixtus Octavianus' (= Giselinus), *Tricongio ille*. (Later printed under Giselinus' name with the title *In Ludo(vicum) C(arrionem) Pontanum* in R. Gherus, *Delitiae C. Poetarum Belgicorum*, (Frankfurt, 1614) ii. 468–9.)

Parody 10, p. 31. 'Sixtus Octavianus' (= Giselinus), *Lavernio ille*. (Later printed under Giselinus' name with the same title as Parody 9 in *Delitiae* ii., 469–70.)

Parody 11, p. 33. 'Sixtus Octavianus' (= Giselinus), *Melissa, Lipsii illa* (*In Caniculam Iusti Lipsii, de qua Epistolicarum quaestionum lib. III. epist. v.*). (Later reprinted under Giselinus' name in *Delitiae* ii., 470–1.)

37. Thus in the preface to their notes: 'Fecit admiratio Catulli, poetae non tam communi nomine quam re vera doctissimi, quicquid sentiant alii qui contra sentiunt, ut propter voluptatem, quam ex hoc etiam poematio singularem capiebamus, in mentem nobis venerit, alios omnes, qui et olim et hodie idipsum imitari summa ingenii contentione sunt conati, in unum quasi fascem colligere, eosdem inter se mutuo componere. Quae voluptas cum liberalibus ingeniis maxime sit digna, neque inutilis iis qui ad veram ac rectam imitandi rationem adspirant, libuit nonnulla, quae praeter aliorum inventa eodem annotavimus in commune conferre' (*Phaselus*, 34).

38. Parodies 3, 4, 5, 8, 9, 10.

39. For Dolet see R. C. Christie, *Étienne Dolet, the Martyr of the Renaissance 1508–1546* (London, 1899). For the enmity of Scaliger see Christie, 195–228 and V. Hall, 'Life of J. C. Scaliger', *Transactions of the American Philosophical Society* 40. 2 (1950), 106–14, 153–4.

40. See van Crombruggen, *Janus Lernutius*, 26–8, 40–7.

41. For Muret's trick see p. 179. For an amusing account of Chrestien's parody (which Muret attributed to Scaliger himself) see B. Jacobsen, *Florent Chrestien: Ein Protestant und Humanist in Frankreich zur Zeit der Religionskriege* (Munich, 1973), 124–5.

42. Paris, *BN*, MS Dupuy 837, fol. 174. The parody is printed in *Mémoires-Journaux de Pierre de L'Estoile* (Paris, 1889), xi. 308–9.

43. It is mentioned by Giovanni Vincenzo Pinelli in a letter to Claude Dupuy of 3 September 1578. Paris, *BN*, MS Dupuy, 704, fol. 63.

44. 'Ridebis? an indignaberis? sed indignare potius aut mehercules ego indignabor. Melissa mea, delicium illud caniculae, pessimo furto mihi periit. Prae cuius ingenio et fide ille Ulyssis, Lysimachi, aut Sabini canis, merae nugae. Amabo te, dic Lernutio, dic Modio, Hendecasyllabos parent' (Lipsius, *Epistolicae Quaestiones* 3. 5, in *Quaestiones*, 95).

45. *'Parody of a parody'*: 'Cum enim Doletum suum ex Valerii phaselo ante edolasset, hic in Marano suo depingendo maluit expressam aliunde delineationem sibi proponere, ipsamque parodiam παρῳδεῖν' (*Phaselus*, 39). *Giselinus' pair*: Parodies 9 and 10.
46. 'Hic a Catullo longissime omnium abscessit, eundem enim facit proxenetam, latronem, harpagatorem, disertum, ludimagistrum, et libidinosum' (*Phaselus*, 39).
47. For Anselmi see M. Quattrucci, 'Anselmi, Giorgio,' *DBI* (Rome, 1961) iii. 378–9; F. Römer, 'Martial in drei Monodistichen des Giorgio Anselmi', *Wiener Studien*, 102 (1989), 339–50.
48. Quoted from *Phaselus*, 22–23.
49. It was published in 1526. See n. 36 above. But Anselmi may not have been the first to imitate 4. Valeriano wrote an imitation in the form of an epode (iambic trimeter alternating with iambic dimeter): 'Venator ille, quem videtis, Naides; / Cui nomen a re ipsa inditum' (*Pierii Valeriani Hexametri Odae et Epigrammata* (Venice, 1550) 65v–66v). Although published much later, the poem commemorates a hunting party given by Cardinal Alessandro Farnese for Pope Leo X in January 1514. From the more famous poem on this hunt (*Palietum*, by Molosso Tranquillo) it is clear that Anselmi was among those present. For the hunting party see D. Gnoli, 'Le Cacce di Leon X', *Nuova Antologia*, 43 (1893), 433–58 and 617–48, but especially 617–21.
50. 'Desideramus hic certis de caussis Parodiam Georgii Anselmi Nepotis, quae primo libro epigrammaton eius exstat, de operibus Virgilianis, cuius initium Libellus ille. Eam tu nobis indaga et investiga, quoquo modo poteris' (Giselinus to Franciscus Nansius, 9 March 1579, quoted by van Crombruggen, *Lernutiana*, 4 n. 9).
51. *Style*: 'exsiccatum dicendi genus' (Lilii Gregorii Gyraldi, *De Poetis nostrorum temporum*, (repr. Berlin, 1894) 33). *Erudition*: '. . . Georgius Anselmus, poeta vulgo hodie rarus, et rarae item eruditionis' (*Phaselus*, 38).
52. Anselmi's contemporary Valeriano identified and discussed Catullus' pure iambics in his lectures; see p. 123. The first published commentary to identify the metre was that of Muret (1554). Anselmi seems to have had a penchant for very close imitation. The *Phaselus* also includes his version of 3 (pp. 43–4), and he wrote an imitation of Catullus' galliambics, on *Stupor*, 'intoxication'. See Campbell, 'Galliambic Poems of the 15th and 16th Centuries', 496–500.
53. See p. 262.
54. Parthenius, Palladius, and the first Aldine (1502) read *Phasellus*. The second Aldine and Guarinus print *Phaselus*.

55. 'Qui tamen ingenio efficere non potuit, quin relinqueret nonnulla digna animadversione' (*Phaselus*, 38).
56. 'Quod bona venia boni poetae dictum sit; non ut comata silva in buxiferi Cytori stetit iugo, sic amica Deorum seu divina Delfici specus vox in Lycaei piniferi cacumine potuit stetisse' (*Phaselus*, 38).
57. *Chronology*: Lernutius' parody is from his *Ocelli*, published in January 1579. (See van Crombruggen, *Janus Lernutius*, 29–30.) He could not have had a text of Anselmi by that time (see p. 267), but perhaps, like Giselinus, knew Anselmi's first verse. Giselinus' parody, inspired by a letter in Lipsius' *Quaestiones epistolicae*, could have been written any time after its publication (1577). *Seventeenth-century omnium-gatherum*: Andreas Seuftleben and Nicolaus Henelius, *Phaselus Catulli, et ad eundem Parodiarum a diversis auctoribus scriptarum, Decades quinque* (Leipzig, 1642).
58. *Carolus Rocasius*: *Phaselus* 1642, 37–8, first published in Ianus Dousa, *Epodon ex puris Iambis libri II* (Antwerp, 1584), 8v. *Daniel Heinsius*: *Phaselus 1642*, 32–3, first published in *Laus Asini* (Leiden, 1623). See C. C. Coulter, 'A Seventeenth-Century Parody of Catullus 4', *CP* 12 (1917), 198–200; R. E. H. Westendorp Boerma, 'Navolgingen van Catullus 4', *Hermeneus*, 33 (1961), 59–61. *Caspar Barthius*: *Phaselus 1642*, 42–3.
59. *Puellus iste quem videtis Aemuli*, Joannes Niess, SJ, *Phaselus 1642*, 58–9; *Puellus ille, qui prehendit Aspidem*, Conradus Bachmannus, Prof. Giessenus, pp. 60–1; *Puellus iste, quem virago parturit*, Johan. Blausus, pp. 63–4. See also *Redemptor ille, quem videtis Angeli*, Christophorus Ansorge, pp. 79–80. For seventeenth-century *parodia sacra* see Schäfer, *Deutscher Horaz*, 93–101.
60. 'Filiolo auctum me scito, salva puerpera. Et viden', Carmen te Genethliacum debere?' (Dousa, *Praecidanea* 1680, 384).

APPENDIX 1

Unseparated Poems and their Titles

R^2 Coluccio Salutati (following McKie)	Venice 1472
2–3 Fletus passeris lesbie	2–3 Fletus passeris Lesbię
9–10 Ad Verannium	9–10 Ad [V]erannium
14–14*b* ad calvum. poetam	14–14*b* Ad Calvum Poetam
15–16 Ad Aurelium	
23–24 Ad Furium	
32–33 Ad Ipsicillam	32–33 Ad Ipsithillam
37.17–39 Ad Egnatium	37.17–39 Ad Egnatium
40–48 Ad Ravidum	40–42 Ad Ravidum
	44.21–48 De Septimio
52–53.4 In Novium	52–53.4 In Novium
53.5–54.5 De Ottonis capite	53.5–54.5 De Othonis Capite
54.6–55 In Camerium	54.6–55 In Camerium
56–58*b* Ad Catonem	56–57 Ad Catonem
	58–58*b* Ad Caelium
59–60 In Rufum	59–60 In Rufum
65–66 Ad Ortalem	65–67 Ad Ortalem
69–71 In Rufum	69–71 In Rufum
72–76 Ad Lesbiam	72–76 Ad Lesbiam
77–79 Ad Rufum	77–79 Ad Rufum
80–88 Ad Gellium	
	83–84 Ad Mullum
	85–88 De Quintia
89–91 In Gellium	89–91 Ad Gellium
92–99 In Cesarem	
	93–95*b* In Cesarem
	96–98 De Aemylio
103–104 no title	
105–116 no title	
	111–112 Ad Aufilenam
	114–115 De Salio Firmano

APPENDIX 2

A Survey of Unseparated Blocks in the Fifteenth Century

Venice 1472	Parma 1473 Puteolanus	Vicenza 1481 Calphurnius	Brescia 1485/6 Parthenius	Poliziano	Avanzi 1495
2–3	2–3	2–3	2–3	2–3	
9–10					
14–14*b*	14–14*b*	14–14*b*	14–14*b*		
32–33					
37.17–39	37.17–39	37.17–39	37.17–39		37.1–16, 39.9–37.17–20 39.10–21
40–42	40–42	40–42	41–42		
44.21–48	45–47				
52–53.4	52–54.1–50.16–17–54.2–5	53–54.1	53.–54.1–50.16–17–54.2–3	53–54.1–50.16–7	53–54.1
53.5–54.1–50.16–17–54.2–5		50.16–17–54.2–5	54.4–7	54.2–7	54.2–5[a]
54.6–55	54.6–55	54.6–55			54.6–55
56–57	56–57	56–57			
58–58*b*					
59–60	59–60	59–60			
65–67	65–66	65–66	65–66	65–66	65–66
69–71	70–71				
72–76	72–76	72–76	72–73	72–73 75–76	
77–79	78–78*b*	78–78*b*	78–78*b*	78–78*b*	78–78*b*
83–84	83–84				
85–88	85–87	85–86.4 86.5–87	86–87		
89–91	89–91	89–91	89–90	89–90	89–90
93–95*b*	93–94	93–94	93–94		93–94
	95–95*b*	95–95*b*	95–95*b*		95–95*b*
96–98					
111–112	111–112	111–112			
114–115	114–115	114–115	114–115	114–115	114–115

[a] Avanzi does not mention 50. 16–17.

APPENDIX 3

Poliziano's Corrections to Venice 1472

Note: In order to establish the most likely source for Poliziano, manuscripts are credited only with corrections not found in editions before 1494. For items 8–13 in Section B an * marks corrections found first in that source and a † marks corrections not printed in later editions. The attributions are taken from Thomson's *apparatus*. Exceptions are noted.

A. Corrections Made in the *Miscellanea*.

66.48 Chalybum (*Misc.*: Chalybon)
84.2 hinsidias[a]

B. Corrections to the 1472 Edition Available in Sources before 1494.

1. T (Paris, BN Lat. 8071)
   62.7 oeteos
2. *α*
   63.4 animis
   63.10 quatiensque
3. *β*
   64.21 tum[b]
4. Cod. Leidensis anni mccccliii [= (*γ*)]
   61.179 viris
5. (*δ*)
   98.1 inquenquam[c]
6. *ζ* / *η*
   66.63 deum me
7. *θ*
   17.10 putideque
   61.196 iuverit
8. Parma 1473 (Puteolanus)
   4.4 nequisse
   10.24 decuit
   11.2 penetrabit
   *22.6 novi
   †*[22.5 palinxesto][d]
   22.14 infacetior
   25.12 minuta
   27.5 quo lubet
   29.3 Mamurram

29.13 vestra
29.13 diffututa
36.1,20 annales Volusi
36.14 colis quaeque
45.1 septimius
48.1 iuventi
53.5 disertum
55.12 hic
61.187 velut
61.198 abscondis
61.226 bene vivite et
64.11 prima
64.298 natisque
64.341 praevertet
64.368 madefient
66.12 vastatum
66.24 sollicitae
66.70 autem
66.80 unanimis
68.40 defferrem
68.49*a* *deletes*
68.64 lenius
88.2 prurit
90.6 omentum
†*[92.3 cui ego quasi eadem totidem][e]
95.5 cavas

9. [Rome 1475]
†*44.19 Sexti recepso
†[*66.58 Canopieis][f]

10. Vicenza 1481 (Calphurnius)
*4.2 ait
†*4.3 ullius
*4.3 trabis
12.13 *μνημόσυνον*
34.12 amniumque
*38.1 *deletes* si
61.180 bene
*61.194 remoratus
*63.9 tua
*63.23 hederigerae
*63.66 corollis
63.68 ferar
*63.70 nive

63.71 columinibus
63.79 ictu
*63.81 verbera
64.36 ac moenia Larissea
*64.77 *deletes* quom
*64.138 miserescere
66.5 sub Latmia
*66.27 adepta es
66.35 tetulisset
*66.79 quas
*67.7 dum
*67.22 ad
[68.41 Mallius][g]
*68.61 levamen
68.141 componier
*69.3 illam rarae
76.12 dis (*Calph.* diis)
*77.3 surrepsti
*78*b*.4 fama loquetur anus
*84.1 chommoda
84.11 arrius (*Calph.* arius)
84.12 Hionios
100.6 perspecta

11 Brescia 1485 (Parthenius)
45.1 Acmen
45.21 Acmen
*63.46 sine quis
[*64.3 aeetheios][h]
*64.307 vestis
*64.386*a* *perhaps deletes*[i]
*66.66 Lycaoniae
*84.4 hinsidias

12. B Guarinus (*c*.1485?)[j]
*34.17 menstruo
41.1 defututa
*63.14 *deletes* celeri[k]
*64.308 talos

13. Beroaldus (1488)
93.2 albus an ater homo[l]

C. Corrections to the 1472 Edition Attributed to Sources after 1494.

1. Avantius (1495)
9.2 antistans
17.14 cui cum[m]

36.5 desissemque[n]
38.1 cornifici
46.5 uber

2. Venice 1496 (Palladius)
36.19 ruris[o]
50.18 cave sis

3. Avantius (1500)
64.96 golgos[p]
93.2 scire

4. Venice 1502 (Aldine, ed. Avantius)
95*b*.1 sodalis

5. F. Puccius (1502)
64.344 *adds* campi[q]

6. Venice 1521 (A. Guarinus)
107.7–8 hac quid / optandum[r]

7. Venice 1535 (Trincavellium, ed. Avantius)
42.4 nostra

8. Venice 1566 (Statius)
95*b* *separated from* 95

9. Berlin 1829 (Lachmann)
66.70 restituit

[a] It is difficult to understand why Poliziano has been credited with this emendation, for the text in the *Miscellanea* is essentially the same as in Calfurnio and Partenio: *Dicere, et hinsidias Arrius insidias*. Modern editions aspirate the second *insidias*, not the first. In the marginalia, however, Poliziano aspirates the second *insidias*. See Chapter 2, p. 70 and Plate 4.

[b] Thomson: β; Mynors: *Aldina*.

[c] Thomson: (δ); Avantius. Mynors: *Aldina*. The correction does not appear in the 1495 edition of Avanzi.

[d] Mynors and Thomson read *palimpseston*, Parma 1473 *palimpsesto*.

[e] Not printed in modern editions. Venice 1472 omitted 92. 3–4; Poliziano's reproduction of this idiosyncratic version of 92. 3 proves that he consulted Parma 1473. See p. 33.

[f] Not printed in Mynors or Thomson. Mynors: *Canopitis*; Thomson: *Canopeis*.

[g] Not printed in modern editions. The 'corrected' verse reads . . . *qua Mallius in re*.

[h] Not printed in Mynors or Thomson. Mynors: *Aeeteos*; Thomson: *Aeetaeos*. Poliziano has added the gloss *Aeetheus* in the margin, which suggests that perhaps he meant his correction to read *Aeetheos*. Venice 1472 reads *oetheios*, which Poliziano corrected by striking out the *oe* and writing *aee* above. He has not stricken the *i*.

[i] Venice 1472 prints a spurious verse (= 67. 21) after 64. 386, which Partenio deletes. In Poliziano's marginalia there is no line striking out the verse, but there is a *very* faint two-word note in the margin, which may read *delendum puto*. *Puto* is clear.

[j] For the date of Battista Guarino's emendations see pp. 84–5.

[k] Venice 1472 reads: *Alienaque petentes velut exules loca celeri*. In the margin Poliziano has *velut exules loca*.

[l] Beroaldo had suggested the correction, claiming it had its source *ex probatissimis codicibus*. Thomson attributes it to *Edin.*, *Urb.* 812, *Diez.* 56[2], and Beroaldus.

[m] Thomson: *Avantius* (recte); Mynors: *Palladius*. But A. Guarinus also claims *cui cum* for B. Guarinus.

[n] The ink is brighter and the script more angular than in most notes.

[o] The ink is brighter and the script more angular than in most notes.

[p] Thomson: *Ald.*; Mynors: *Hermolaus Barbarus teste Mureto*. The reading was assigned by Muret to H. Barbarus and by Statius to P. Bembus.

[q] Thomson: *Puccius* (et β^2); Mynors: *Statius*. This is one of several cases in which Poliziano has made more than one correction. The last word in the 1472 edn. is *teucri*. Poliziano has written *campi* above it, but in the margin he has written *rivi* (Calfurnio's correction). It is impossible to say whether he regarded either correction as final. Similarly, at 63. 47 (*extuante rursum, extuanter usus*); 63. 71 (*columinibus* Calph., *culminibus*); 66. 63 (*decumme* V, *deum me*); 66. 79 (*que*, *quas* Calph.); 68. 64 (*leviter, lenius*); 69. 3 (*labefacta est, labefactas*).

[r] Thomson prints *hac quid / optandum* and credits A. Guarinus. Mynors prints (and obelizes) *hac est / optandus* and does not mention this reading.

APPENDIX 4

Summary of Sabellico's *Ex Catullo*

Note: An * marks readings found in modern editions. A † indicates the reading for which Sabellico is credited.

1.9	Discussion: read *patroa virgo* (i.e., Diana) or *patrona virgo* (i.e., Minerva).
*3.1	Discussion: 3.1 begins a new epigram.
4.24	Read *novissime* (not *novissem*)[a]
10.16	Read *hominum* (not *hominis*).
*10.30	Read *Caius* (not *gravis*).
11.6	Red *seu sacas partosque feros sagittis* (not *seu saccas sagittiferosque parthos*).
11.15	Read *nunc aite* (not *nunciate*).
*14.5	Read *male* (not *malis*).
25.5	Read *mater ales* (not *mulier aves*).
27.2	Read *meratiores* (not *amariores*).
29.11	Discussion: 29.11 begins a new epigram.
29.13	Read *vesca* (not *vestra*).
31.6	Read *in tutu* (not *in tuo*).
34.8	Discussion: *Deliam olivam* is a spring on Mt. Delos.[b]
50.2	Read *in vicem* (not *in meis*).
64.16	Read *haudque alia* (not *atque alia*).
*64.25	Read *taedis* (not *thetidis*).
*64.106	Read *conigeram* (not *cornigeram*).
64.159	Discussion: *prisci parentis* refers not to Aegeus but to Cecrops.
†*64.243	Read *infecti* (not *inflati*).[c]

[a] Thomson prints *novissime*, Mynors *novissimo*.

[b] Sabellico may have stolen this idea from Aulo Giano Parrasio. Both use a passage in Plutarch's *Pelopidas* to explain *Deliam olivam* as a fountain named Oliva on Mt. Delos in Laconia, but Parrasio, writing in 1501, claims priority (without naming Sabellico): 'Olivam fontem Catullus intelligit in sacro Dianae carmine . . . quem locum decimo ab hinc anno primi omnium declaravimus . . . Neque mentiri me sinet Tideus Actianus . . . non Aelius Gorgonius aut Putius florentinus . . . Possem praeterea sexcentos adiicire qui rem ita (ut diximus esse) probe tenent, ni vererer Sanctissimis viris iniuriam facere, si suam fidem quasi minus per se firmam novi testimonii autoritate fulcirem. Quid tamen refert quom nonnulli inventi sint qui nostrum qualecunque hoc inventum pro suo recitent ae ostentent?' ad ii. 135–6, *De raptu Proserpinae* (Milan, 1501). See also Richardson. 'Pucci, Parrasio and Catullus', 281–2.

[c] Mynors prints *infecti*, Thomson *inflati*. See Goold, 'A New Text', 99.

APPENDIX 5

Avanzi and the Printed Tradition

Note: The table shows readings found *only* in Avanzi and the edition or editions cited. It includes readings about which Avanzi's judgement agrees with that of modern editors, but is not based on a complete collation of the *Emendationes* with earlier editions. No reading in the table is attributed by Avanzi to a manuscript.

Parthenius (Brescia 1485): Readings rejected by Avanzi

63.82	loca *omitted*	64.249	accedentem . . . carina
64.41	frondatoris	64.274	magis *omitted*
64.44	splendet	64.286	impedientes
64.48	aedibus	64.372	animis
64.78	decus *omitted*	64.377	coluum
64.80	augusta	68.126	compar seu quicquid
64.87	costus	95.3	vilia

Calphurnius (Vicenza 1481) and Parthenius: Readings rejected

8.3	tibi candidi	63.69	vis
10.15	aere	66.80	vincula
15.11	moneto	66.84	in puro
29.22	cuncta	86.2	sic *omitted*
30.3	fallere *omitted*		

Calphurnius: Readings rejected

67.45	ardebat

[*Rome 1475*]*: Readings adopted*

44.19	Sexti recepso	61.176	adeat
60.5	ah nimis	63.28	thiasus

[*Rome 1475*)*, Venice 1472,* [*Milan*] *1475: Readings adopted*

8.6	cum	29.7	perambulabit
10.19	quod	29.16	helluatus est
13.9	meros	63.25	divae

Venice 1472 and [*Milan*] *1475: Readings rejected*

66.35	audisset

Parma 1473 and Reggio 1481: Readings adopted

39.1	Egnatius quod	64.96	quaeque . . . quaeque
59.2	sepulchretis	64.165	externata
63.42	somnus	65.4	animi

APPENDIX 6

The Muses in Ficino and Valeriano

FICINO	VALERIANO
Calliope Musa vox est, ex omnibus saltans sphaerarum vocibus.	. . . omnium suprema Calliope est, quippe vox ea, quae ex omnibus spherarum vocibus resultat . . .
Urania, coeli stelliferi, per dignitatem sic dicta.	. . . Uranie a stelliferi coeli dignitate sic cognominata . . .
Polymnia Saturni, propter memoriam rerum antiquarum quam Saturnia exhibet et siccam frigidamque complexionem.	. . . Polyhymnia, quae propter memoriam rerum antiquarum, et altiorem naturae cognitionem in Saturni regia sedem habere fertur . . .
Terpsichore, Iovis, salutifer enim choro hominum.	Therpsichore . . . quam hominum choro salutiferam interpretantur, eam in orbe Iovis residere ferunt . . .
Clio Martis, propter gloriae cupiditatem.	. . . Clio, quae Gloriae cupiditatem ac ingentem aeternitatis amorem afflat . . . Hanc apud Martem hospitari tradunt . . .
Melpomene solis, quia totius mundi temperatio est.	. . . Melpomene, quae totius mundi temperatio est. Ea Soli addicitur . . .
Erato Veneris, propter amorem.	. . . Erato, ab amore nimirum, quem spirat appellata. In orbe autem tertio Venus collocata est . . .
Euterpe Mercurii, propter honestam in gravibus rebus delectationem.	. . . Euterpe a fandi delectatione ita nuncupata . . . Mercurium autem cui omnes fandi veneres sunt attributae huius spherae, quae supra Lunam est dominum praedicant . . .

Thalia lunae, propter viriditatem eius humore rebus exhibitam.	. . . in lunari globo Thalia sedem habere fertur, quam *παρὰ τὸ θάλλω* dictam volunt, hinc viriditatem et exundantem copiam emanare . . .

APPENDIX 7

Valeriano and the Division of the Catullan Hendecasyllable

1. Modern analysis: glyconic + bacchiac
   × × – ∪ ∪ – ∪ – | ∪ – –

2. Valeriano's 'elementary' account: spondee + dactyl + 3 trochees
   – – | – ∪ ∪ | – ∪ | – ∪ | – –

3. Dactylic *Tome* + Iambic or Trochaic *Tome*

   – – – ∪ ∪ – | ∪ – ∪ – –
   Cui dono lepidum | novum libellum

   – – – ∪ ∪ – ∪ | – ∪ – –
   Corneli tibi namque | tu solebas

   Hexameter: cui dono lepidum | Corneli docte | libellum
   Corneli tibi namque | meas tu saepe | solebas

   Iambics: novum libellum | quum videtis hospites
   putare nugas | esse cognitissimas

   **Archilochean* (= Alcaic): novum libellum | nunc dabimus tibi
   cf. vides ut alta stet nive candidum (Horace *Odes* 1. 9. 1)

4. *Whole Choriamb (= Glyconic) + Bacchiac

   – – – ∪ ∪ – ∪ – | ∪ – –
   Cui dono lepidum novum | libellum

   †*Priapean*: cui dono lepidum novum | nuncupoque | libellum
   Asclepiadean (by insertion of a second choriamb – ∪ ∪ –):
   cui dono lepidum | cui dabimus | novum
   cf. Maecenas atavis edite regibus (Horace *Odes* 1. 1. 1)

5. Molossus + (Anaclastic) Ionic Dimeter

   – – – | ∪ ∪ – ∪ – ∪ – –
   Cui dono | lepidum novum libellum

   Galliambic: lepidum novum libellum | tibi pumice poliam
   cf. Super alta vectus *atys celeri rate maria (63. 1)

* Valeriano's term or reading.

† After this example Valeriano says (fol. 29v): cuius modi genus carminis Catullus in priapum cecinit, ex quo pauca recitasse sufficiat: Nam te praecipue in suis urbibus colit ora / Hellespontia caeteris ostreosior oris. [Cat. frag. 1, 3–4] (The verses are quoted from Terentianus 2756–7.)

APPENDIX 8

Statius and the Vulgate in 61

The table lists Statius' correct readings in 61 against the readings of the base text, which is defined here as the texts of the Aldines, Guarino, and Muret. When the tradition is not unanimous the readings are designated as follows: A1 = the first Aldine (1502), A2 = the second Aldine (1515), A = both Aldines, G = Guarino (1521), M = Muret (1554).[a] Readings printed by Robortello (*Explicationes in Catulli Epithalamium*, Florence, 1548) are printed in brackets. Readings of the base text that entered the printed tradition in the fifteenth century are accompanied by the date and edition of their first appearance. Statius' emendation is marked with an *.

	STATIUS	BASE TEXT (Aldines, Guarinus, Muret)
61.16	Iunia	Iulia (Venice 1472)
[61.20	nubet]	nubit
61.34	huc et huc	hac et hac (Venice 1472)
61.36	vosque	vos (Parma 1473)
61.81	est	sit
61.107–8	quod omnibus candido pede lecti	quot omine/candido lacteo pede (A1) quot omine/candido pede lectuli (A2) quod homine/candido pede lectulis (G) quot omina/candido pede lectulis (M)
61.112	gaudeat	gaudeas (Parthenius, 1485)
61.115	video venire	video venite (A1) videor videre (A2, G, M)
61.121	nec	neu
*61.164	intus	unus
61.179	vos bonae senibus viris	vos unis senibus bonae (A, M) binae in aedibus unius (G)
[61.199	pulveris]	pulvis
61.202	volt	vult

[a] The notations are those of Pighi ('Achillis Statii lectiones'), who compares Statius' readings with those of the Aldines, Guarino, and Muret.

APPENDIX 9

Readings shared by Statius and Scaliger

The table lists readings not found in the Aldines, Guarino, or Muret. Section (A) lists readings printed in Mynors' edition and not discussed by Scaliger. Section (B) lists readings printed in Mynors that Scaliger discusses. Section (C) lists readings not printed in Mynors.

An * marks readings appearing in the text (as opposed to the margins) of the Plantin edition. A ‡ marks readings not found in the Plantin edition. A § marks readings Scaliger attributes to his manuscript. Emendations are accompanied by the names of their authors (the attributions are taken from Mynors).

A. Readings Printed in Mynors (Not Discussed by Scaliger)

* 2.4	acris	64.207	mentem
2.10	tristis	64.257	divolso
24.6	illo	65.14	absumpti
59.3	rapere de rogo	66.12	finis
61.202	volt	68.72	constituit solea
*64.52	litore	68.76	caelestis
64.170	auris	68.102	penetralis
‡64.171	ne	68.133	hinc illinc

B. Readings Printed in Mynors (Discussed by Scaliger)

‡10.15	dicitur esse	64.237	aetas
17.19	suppernata[a] (*Sc.* subpernata)	§65.9	spurious verse omitted
§28.11	fuistis	§66.11	novo auctus hymenaeo
§28.13	farti estis	66.85	a mala dona levis bibat inrita
29.8	columbus aut Adoneus [Statius][b]	67.27	et quaerendum unde ⟨unde⟩ [Statius]
29.15	quid est alid [Statius][c]	§68.47	spurious verse omitted
39.19	russam[d]	‡68.51	Amathusia
42.8	mimice [Turnebus]	68.52	torruerit [Turnebus]
‡56.7	protelo	§68.147	is
‡§61.108	lecti	74.3	perdepsuit [vir eruditus apud Statium][f]
§61.112	gaudeat		
§61.115	video venire		
§61.179	vos bonae senibus viris[e]		

§92.2	Lesbia me dispeream nisi
108.1	populi arbitrio [Statius]

C. Readings Not Printed in Mynors († marks readings not discussed by Scaliger)

†10.9	mihi nec ipsi (*Sc.* neque)
§24.4	divitias mihi
§45.14	uno
§61.176	adeant
*†64.42	robigo
*†64.327	subtemina
§64.353	cultor
67.30	imminxerit[g]
§68.112	audet
§68.128	quamquam (*sc.* quanquam)
68.148	quem lapide illa diem candidiore notat[h]
†101.8	tristis
§114.2	quot res in se
§114.6	dum modo (*Mynors obelizes* modo)

[a] The reading goes back to Poliziano (see p. 75), but was ridiculed by his detractors. It is printed for the first time in Scaliger's edition.

[b] Scaliger liked this emendation well enough to try to steal it. Thus: 'Ego, quum Valentiae Cavarum hunc locum scriptae lectionis perpenderem, succurrit posse legi, *Aut albulus columbus, aut Adoneus*, quia Adoneus pro Adonis Plauto, et Ausonio antiquario dictum memineram. Itaque nondum me eius coniecturae poenitet' (Scaliger, *Castigationes*, 26). Statius had already cited Plautus and Ausonius.

[c] Misprinted in the Plantin edition: 'Stat. quid est abit'.

[d] Both Scaliger and Statius make the correction from Apuleius, *Ap*. 6. Giselinus' note ('Scalig. et Stat. *russam*') vindicates Scaliger's claim to have made the correction as a young man (*Castigationes*, 35).

[e] Scaliger reports *vos bone senibus unis* from his manuscript.

[f] Statius attributes *perdepsuit* to a *vir eruditus*, Giselinus to 'Cauchus et alii'. Scaliger claims it for himself: 'Primi omnium olim adolescentes docuimus *perdepsuit* legendum esse. Quam emendationem nemo postulet se mihi praeripere, quod tamen quidam conati sunt. Non quod ego tanti mea faciam, neque quod hac existimationem meam stare aut cadere censeam, sed quia perfrictas frontes ferre non possum' (*Castigationes*, 90–1).

[g] Statius found *imminxerit* in one manuscript (identified by Ullman as Padua, Biblioteca capitolare C77, *The Identification*, 54). cf. Scaliger: 'Placet, quod adolescentes olim reposuimus, *imminxerit*' (*Castigationes*, 83).

[h] Thomson reads *diem*.

BIBLIOGRAPHY

ADAMS, J. N., *The Latin Sexual Vocabulary* (London, 1982).

AFFÒ I., *Memorie degli scrittori e letterati parmigiani* ii (Parma, 1789).

ALBERTINI, A., 'Calfurnio Bresciano: La sua edizione di Catullo,' *Commentari dell' Ateneo di Brescia* (1953), 29–79.

ALLEN, M. J. B., *The Platonism of Marsilio Ficino* (Berkeley, Calif., 1984).

ALLENSPACH, J., and FRASSO, G., 'Vicende, cultura e scritti di Gerolamo Squarzafico, Alessandrino', *IMU* 23 (1980), 233–92.

ALPAGO-NOVELLO, L., 'Spigolature vaticane di argomento bellunese. I. Un' opera inedita ed ignorata di Pierio Valeriano', *Archivio Veneto Tridentino*, 9 (1926), 69–96.

—— 'Nuove notizie intorna a Pierio Valeriano con documenti inediti', *Archivio storico di Belluno, Feltre, et Cadore*, 6 (1934), 477–84.

ALTAMURA, A., *Jacopo Sannazaro* (Naples, 1951).

ANDERSON, R. D., PARSONS, P. J., and NISBET, R. G. M., 'Elegiacs by Gallus from Qaṣr Ibrîm', *JRS* 69 (1979), 125–55.

APULEIUS, *Apulei Apologia*, ed. H. E. Butler and A. S. Owen (Oxford, 1914).

ARNALDI, F., GUALDO ROSA, L., MONTI SABIA, L. (eds.), *Poeti latini del quattrocento* (Milan/Naples, 1964).

Atti del Convegno internazionale di studi su Albio Tibullo (Rome, 1986).

AVANTIUS, HIERONYMUS, *Emendationes Catullianae* (Venice, 1495) (= *Emendationes*, 1495).

—— *Emendationes Catullianae* (Venice, 1500) (= *Emendationes*, 1500).

AVESANI, R., 'Doctos viros tu aliis gentibus dedisti', in *Verona e il suo territorio* (Verona, 1984), IV. ii. 193–263.

—— and PEEBLES, B., 'Studies in Pietro Donato Avogaro of Verona', *IMU* 5 (1962), 1–84.

BAÏF, ANTOINE DE, *Les Amours* (Paris, 1552).

BARBARUS, HERMOLAUS, *Castigationes Plinianae* (Rome, 1492).

—— ed. G. Pozzi, *Hermolai Barbari Castigationes Plinianae et in Pomponium Melam*, 4 vols. (Padua, 1973).

BARTOLI, M. LA TELLA, 'A proposito di Aquiles Estaço e dei carmina del codice vallicelliano B 106', *Annali Istituto Univ. Orientale*, sez. Romanza 17 (1975), 293–362.

BECCADELLI, A., *Antonii Bononiae Beccatelli Cognomento Panhormitae Epistolarum Libri V* (Venice, 1553).

—— *Beccadelli, L'Ermafrodito, e Pacifico Massimo, L'Ecatelegio*, ed. A. Ottolini (Milan, 1922).

BERG, W., *Early Virgil* (London, 1974).

BERNAYS, J., *Joseph Justus Scaliger* (Berlin, 1885; repr. New York, 1965).

BERTALOT, L., 'Forschungen über Leonardo Bruni Aretino', *Archivum Romanicum*, 15 (1931), 284–323 (repr. in *Studien zum italienischen und deutschen Humanismus*, ed. P. O. Kristeller (Rome, 1975), ii. 375–94).

BIETENHOLZ, P. G., and DEUTSCHER, T. B., *Contemporaries of Erasmus*, 3 vols. (Toronto, 1986).

BILLANOVICH, GIUSEPPE, 'Dal Livio di Raterio al Livio del Petrarca', *IMU* 2 (1959), 103–78.

—— 'Terenzio, Ildemaro, Petrarca', *IMU* 17 (1974) 1–60.

—— 'Livio e Catullo nella Cattedrale di Verona', in *La tradizione del testo di Livio e le origini dell' umanesimo*, (Padua, 1981), i. 241–81.

—— 'Il Catullo della Cattedrale di Verona, in *Scire Litteras* = Bayerische Akad. der Wissenschaften, Philosophisch-Historische Klasse Abhandlungen 99 (Munich, 1988), 37–52.

BILLANOVICH, GUIDO, '*Veterum vestigia vatum* nei carmi dei preumanisti Padovani', *IMU* 1 (1958), 155–243.

BIRT, T., *Das antike Buchwesen* (Berlin, 1882).

BOBER, P. P., 'The "Coryciana" and the Nymph Corycia', *JWCI* 40 (1977), 223–39.

BONITO, V., *The Saint Anne Altar in Sant' Agostino, Rome*, Ph.D. diss. (New York Univ., 1983).

BOSCO, U., 'Il Petrarca e l'umanesimo filologico', *GSLI* 120 (1942), 108–16.

BOTTIGLIONI, *La lirica latina in Firenze nella secunda metà del secolo XV* (Pisa, 1913).

BRADEN, G., '*Vivamus mea Lesbia* in the English Renaissance', *English Literary Renaissance*, 9 (1979), 199–224.

BRANCO, JOSE GOMES, 'Un umanista portoghese in Italia: Aquiles Estaço', *Relazioni storiche fra l'Italia et il Portogallo*, Reale Accademia d'Italia (Rome, 1940).

BREWER, J. S., GAIRDNER, J., and BRODIE, R. (eds.), *Letters and Papers of Henry VIII* (London, 1920).

BUCHHEIT, V., 'Catull an Cato von Utica (c. 56)', *Hermes*, 89 (1961), 345–56.

—— *Studien zur Corpus Priapeorum*, Zetemata 28 (Munich, 1962).

BÜHLER, C. F., *The University and the Press in Fifteenth Century Bologna* (Notre Dame, Ind., 1958).

BURCK, E., 'Römische Wesenzüge der augusteischen Liebeselegie', *Hermes*, 80 (1952), 163–200.

Burgess, D., 'Catullus c. 50: The Exchange of Poetry', *AJP* 107 (1987), 576–86.

Bustico, G., 'Pierio Valeriano, poeta bellunese del sec. XVI', *Atti della R. Accademia roveretana degli Agiati*, 11 (1905), 155–76.

Butrica, J., 'Pontanus, Puccius, Pocchus, Petreius, and Propertius', *Res Publica Litterarum*, 3 (1980), 5–9.

—— *The Manuscript Tradition of Propertius* (Toronto, 1984).

Cairns, F., *Tibullus: A Hellenistic Poet at Rome* (Cambridge, 1979).

Callimachus, *Callimachus*, 2 vols., ed. R. Pfeiffer (Oxford, 1949–53).

Calonghi, F., 'Marginalia', in *Miscellanea Pandiani* (Genoa, 1921), 97–114.

Campbell, D., 'Galliambic Poems of the 15th and 16th Centuries: Sources of the Bacchic Odes of the Pléiade School', *BHR* 22 (1960), 490–510.

Cardini, R., *La critica del Landino* (Florence, 1973).

Carlson, G. I., and Schmidt, E. A., 'Form and Transformation in Vergil's *Catalepton*', *AJP* 92 (1971), 252–65.

Carmina quinque illustrium poetarum (Venice, 1558).

Castor, G., *Pléiade Poetics* (Cambridge, 1964).

Catullus: *C. Valerii Catulli Opera Omnia ex Editione F. G. Doeringii cum Notis et Interpretatione in Usum Delphini*, 2 vols. (London, 1822).

—— *Catulli Veronensis Liber*, ed. R. Ellis (Oxford, 1878).

—— *Catullus: A Commentary*, ed. J. Fordyce (Oxford, 1961).

—— *C. Valerii Catulli Carmina*, ed. R. A. B. Mynors (Oxford, 1958).

—— *Catullus. The Poems*², ed. K. Quinn (London, 1973).

—— *Catulli Veronensis Liber*², ed. L. Schwabe (Berlin, 1886).

—— *Catullus: A Critical Edition*, ed. D. F. S. Thomson (Chapel Hill, NC, 1978).

Cavazzocca-Mazzanti, 'Due illustri lazisiensi', *Pro Verona*, nos. 8–10 (1911), 13–27.

Ceretti, L., 'Critica testuale a Terenzio in una lettera del Faerno a Paolo Manuzio', *Aevum*, 28 (1954), 522–51.

Chastel, A., *Marsile Ficino et l'art* (Geneva and Lille, 1954).

Chomarat, J., Fragonard, M. M., and Mathieu-Castellani, G. (eds.), *Marc-Antoine de Muret, Commentaires au premier livre des Amours de Ronsard* (Geneva, 1985).

Christie, R. C., *Étienne Dolet, the Martyr of the Renaissance 1508–1546* (London, 1899).

Cian, V., 'Un umanista bergamasco del Rinascimento. Giovanni Calfurnio', *Archivio storico lombardo*, 4: 14 (1910), 221–35.

Ciapponi, L. A., 'Bartolomeo Fonzio e la prima centuria dei "*Miscellanea*" del Poliziano', *IMU* 23 (1980), 165–77.

Citroni, M., 'Le racommandazioni del poeta: apostrofe al libro e contatto col destinatario', *Maia*, 36 (1986), 111–46.

Cittadella, L., *I Guarini: famiglia nobile ferrarese oriunda da Verona* (Bologna, 1870).

Clausen, W., 'Callimachus and Latin Poetry', *GRBS* 5 (1964), 181–96.

—— 'Catulli Veronensis Liber', *CP* 71 (1976), 37–43.

Clements, R. J., *Critical Theory and Practice of the Pléiade* (Cambridge, Mass., 1942).

Commager, S., *The Odes of Horace* (New Haven, Conn., 1962).

Conte, G. B., *The Rhetoric of Imitation: Genre and Poetic Memory in Virgil and other Latin Poets* (Ithaca, NY, and London, 1986).

Coppel, B., 'Marginalien zu dichterischen Berührungspunkten zwischen Petrus Lotichius Secundus und C. Valerius Catullus', *Acta Conventus Neo-Latini Lovaniensis* (Louvain, 1973). 159–70.

Coryciana, ed. Blosio Palladio (Rome, 1524).

Cosenza, E. M., *Biographical and Bibliographical Dictionary of the Italian Humanists and of the World of Classical Scholarship in Italy. 1300–1800* (Boston, 1962).

Costil, P., 'Paul Manuce et l'humanisme à Padoue à l'époque du Concile de Trente', *Revue des questions historiques*, 3: 21 [117] (1932), 321–62.

Coulter, C. C., 'A Seventeenth-Century Parody of Catullus 4', *CP* 12 (1917), 198–200.

Croll, M., 'Muret and the History of "Attic Prose"', in *Style, Rhetoric, and Rhythm* (Princeton, NJ, 1966), 126–62.

Crombruggen, H. van, *Janus Lernutius (1545–1619): Een biografische studie*, Verhandelingen van de koninklijke vlaamse Academie voor Wetenschappen, Letteren en schone Kunsten van Belgie, Klasse der Letteren, 23 (Brussels, 1955).

—— *Lernutiana*, Mededelingen van de koninklijke vlaamse Academie voor Wetenschappen, Letteren en schone Kunsten van Belgie, 21 (Brussels, 1959).

Crowther, N. B., '*ΟΙ ΝΕΩΤΕΡΟΙ*, Poetae Novi, et Cantores Euphorionis', *CQ* 20 (1970), 322–7.

—— 'Parthenius and Roman Poetry', *Mnemosyne*, 29 (1976), 65–71.

Cuccoli, E., *M. Antonio Flaminio* (Bologna, 1897).

Cuppini, M. T., 'L'arte a Verona tra i secoli xv e xvi', in *Verona e il suo territorio*, iv. 1 (Verona, 1981), 261–75.

D'Amico, J., *Renaissance Humanism in Papal Rome* (Baltimore, 1983).

De Caprio, V., 'L'area umanistica romana (1513–1527)', *Studi romani*, 29 (1981), 321–35.

Dejob, C., *Marc-Antoine de Muret: Un professeur français en Italie dans la seconde moitié du XVIe siècle* (Paris, 1881).

DEJOB, C., *L'Influence du Concile de Trente sur la littérature et les beaux-arts chez les peuples catholiques* (Paris, 1884).

DE LA MARE, A. C., 'The Return of Petronius to Italy', in *Medieval Learning and Literature: Essays Presented to Richard W. Hunt*, ed. J. J. G. Alexander and M. T. Gibson (Oxford, 1976), 220–54.

—— and D. F. S. THOMSON, 'Poggio's Earliest Manuscript?' *IMU* 16 (1973), 179–95.

D'ELIA, S., 'Appunti su Marziale e la civiltà letteraria dell'età flavia', in *Letterature comparate: problemi e metodo. Studi in onore di Ettore Paratore* (Bologna, 1981), ii. 647–66.

DELLA CORTE, F., 'L'altro Catullo', in *Due studi catulliani* (Genoa, 1951).

DIONISOTTI, C., 'La letteratura italiana nell' età del Concilio', in *Il Concilio di Trento e la riforma tridentina. Atti del Convegno storico internazionale. Trento. 2–6 settembre 1963* i (Rome, 1965), 317–43.

—— 'Calderini, Poliziano e altri', *IMU* 11 (1968), 151–79.

—— *Aldo Manuzio Editore* i (Milan, 1975).

DOUSA, J., *Praecidanea Pro Q. Valerio Catullo*, in *Catullus, Tibullus, et Propertius* ed, J. G. Graevius, ii (Utrecht. 1680).

DU BELLAY, JOACHIM, *La Deffense et Illustration de la langue francoyse*, ed. H. Chamard (Paris, 1904).

ELLIS, R., *A Commentary on Catullus*^{2} (Oxford, 1889).

—— *Catullus in the XIVth Century* (Oxford, 1905).

—— and PALMER, A., 'Scaliger's *Liber Cujacianus* of Propertius, Catullus, etc.', *Hermathena*, 2 (1876), 124–58.

ESTIENNE, H., *Parodiae morales* (s.l., 1575).

FABBRI, R., 'Approcci umanistici a Catullo', *Materiali e Discussioni per l'analise dei testi classici*, 19 (1987), 171–83.

FANELLI, V., 'Adriano VI e Angelo Colocci' in *Ricerche su Angelo Colocci e sulla Roma cinquecentesca*, Studi e testi 283 (Vatican City, 1979), 30–44.

FERGUSON, J., 'Catullus and Martial', *Proceedings of the African Classical Society*, 6 (1963), 3–15.

FESTUS, *De verborum significatione*, ed. C. O. Mueller (Leipzig, 1839).

—— *De verborum significatione*, ed. W. M. Lindsay (Leipzig, 1913).

FICINO, MARSILIO, *De poetico furore*, in *Opera Omnia*, ii (Torino, 1959).

FLETCHER, H. G., III, *New Aldine Studies* (San Francisco, 1988).

FRAENKEL, E., *Horace* (Oxford, 1957).

FRANK, T., 'Can Grande and Catullus', *AJP* 48 (1927), 273–5.

FUSCUS, PALLADIUS, *In Catullum Commentarii* (Venice, 1496).

GAISSER, J. H., 'Catullus and his First Interpreters: Antonius Parthenius and Angelo Poliziano', *TAPA* 112 (1982), 83–106.

—— 'The Catullan Lectures of Pierius Valerianus', in *Acta Conventus Neo-Latini Guelpherbytani* (Binghamton, NY, 1988), 45–53.

—— 'Catullus', *CTC* (1992) vii, 197–292.

Gamberini, F., *Stylistic Theory and Practice in the Younger Pliny* (Hildesheim, 1983).

Geiger, L., 'Der älteste römische Musenalmanach', *Vierteljahrsschrift für Kultur und Literatur der Renaissance* 1 (1886), 145–61.

Gellius, Aulus, *The Attic Nights of Aulus Gellius*, ed. J. C. Rolfe (London, 1927; repr. 1967).

Gherus, R., ed., *Delitiae C. Poetarum Belgicorum* (Frankfurt, 1614).

Giangrande, G., 'Catullus' Lyrics on the *Passer*', *Museum Philologum Londiniense*, 1 (1976), 137–46.

Giehlow, K., 'Hieroglyphenkunde des Humanismus in der Renaissance', *Jahrbuch der kunsthistorischen sammlungen des aller höchsten Kaiserhauses*, 32 (1915), 113–29.

Ginsberg, E. S., 'Change and Permanence in the French Renaissance: Muret and Ronsard', *Journal of Medieval and Renaissance Studies*, 16 (1986), 91–102.

—— 'Peregrinations of the Kiss: Thematic Relationships between Neo-Latin and French Poetry in the Sixteenth Century', *Acta Conventus Neo-Latini Sanctandreani* (Binghamton, NY, 1986), 331–42.

Giovio, P., 'Vita Hadriani Sexti Pont. Max.', in *Elogia virorum bellica virtute illustrium*, ii (Florence, 1551).

Giuliari, G. C., *Della letteratura veronese al cadere del secolo XV* (Bologna, 1876).

Gnoli, D., 'Un giudizio di lesa romanità sotto Leone X', *Nuova Antologia*, 115 (1891), 251–75, 691–716, ibid. 116 (1891), 34–63.

—— 'Le Cacce di Leon X', *Nuova Antologia*, 43 (1893), 433–58, 617–48.

—— *La Roma di Leon X* (Milan, 1938).

Godman, P., 'Johannes Secundus and Renaissance Latin Poetry', *Review of English Studies*, 39 (1988), 258–72.

—— 'Literary Classicism and Latin Erotic Poetry of the Twelfth Century and the Renaissance', in *Latin Poetry and the Classical Tradition*, ed. P. Godman and O. Murray, (Oxford, 1990), 149–82.

Goold, G. P., 'A New Text of Catullus', *Phoenix*, 12 (1958), 93–116.

—— 'Catullus 3. 16', *Phoenix*, 23 (1969), 186–203.

Grafton, A., 'Joseph Scaliger's Edition of Catullus (1577) and the Traditions of Textual Criticism in the Renaissance,' *JWCI* 38 (1975), 161–79.

—— 'On the Scholarship of Politian and its Context', *JWCI* 40 (1977), 150–88.

—— *Joseph Scaliger: A Study in the History of Classical Scholarship*, i (Oxford, 1983).

—— and Jardine, L., *From Humanism to the Humanities* (London, 1986).

Granarolo, J., 'L'Époque néotérique ou la poésie romaine d'avant garde au dernier siècle de la République (Catulle excepté)', *Aufstieg und Niedergang der römischen Welt*, i. 3 (Berlin, 1973), 278–360.

Greene, T. M., *The Light in Troy: Imitation and Discovery in Renaissance Poetry* (New Haven, Conn., 1980).

Griffiths, G., Hankins, J., and Thomson, D. (trans.), *The Humanism of Leonardo Bruni: Selected Texts*, Medieval and Renaissance Texts and Studies, 46 (= Renaissance Society of America Text Series, 10 (Binghampton, NY, 1987)).

Guarinus, Alexander, *Alexandri Guarini Ferrariensis in C. V. Catullum Veronensem per Baptistam Patrem Emendatum Expositiones cum Indice* (Venice, 1521).

Hale, W. G., 'Benzo of Alexandria and Catullus', *CP* 5 (1910), 56–65.

Hall, V., 'Life of J. C. Scaliger', *Transactions of the American Philosophical Society* 40. 2 (1950).

Hankins, J. 'The Latin Poetry of Leonardo Bruni', *Humanistica lovaniensia*, 39 (1990), 1–39.

Hausmann, F.-R., 'Enea Silvio Piccolomini "Poeta" und die Rezeption der heidnischen Antike', *BHR* 35 (1972), 454–61.

—— 'Untersuchungen zum neulateinische Epigramm italiens im Quattrocento', *Humanistica lovaniensia*, 21 (1972), 1–35.

—— 'Martial in Italien', *Studi medievali*, 17. 1 (1976), 173–218.

—— 'Martialis', *CTC* iv (1980), 249–96.

Hawkins, R. L., 'The Relationship of Joseph Scaliger and François Vertunien', *Romantic Review*, 8 (1917), 117–44 and 307–27.

Heesakkers, C. L., *Praecidanea Dousana* (Amsterdam, 1976).

Herrlinger, *Totenklage um Tiere in der antiken Dichtung, mit einem Anhang, byzantinischer, mitellateinischer und neuhochdeutscher Tierepikedien* (Stuttgart, 1930).

Hooper, R. W., 'In Defence of Catullus' Dirty Sparrow', *Greece and Rome*, 32 (1985), 162–78.

Horace: *Q. Horatii Flacci, Opera*, ed. D. R. Shackleton Bailey (Stuttgart, 1985).

Howell, P., *A Commentary on Book One of the Epigrams of Martial* (London, 1980).

Hutton, J., *The Greek Anthology in France* (Ithaca, NY, 1946).

Ijsewijn, J., 'Poetry in a Roman Garden: The *Coryciana*', in *Latin Poetry and the Classical Tradition: Essays in Medieval and Renaissance Literature*, ed. P. Godman and O. Murray (Oxford, 1990), 211–31.

JACOBSEN, B., *Florent Chrestien: Ein Protestant und Humanist in Frankreich zur Zeit der Religionskriege* (Munich, 1973).

JOCELYN, H. J., 'On Some Unnecessarily Indecent Interpretations of Catullus 2 and 3', *AJP* 101 (1980), 421–41.

KAY, N. M., *Martial Book XI: A Commentary* (Oxford, 1985).

KEIL., H., *Scholia in Nicandri Theriaca*, in O. Schneider, *Nicandrea Theriaca et Alexipharmaca* (Leipzig, 1856).

—— *Grammatici latini*, vi (Leipzig, 1874).

KENNEY, E. J., 'The Character of Humanist Philology', in *Classical Influences on European Culture A.D. 500–1500*, ed. R. R. Bolgar (Cambridge, 1971), 119–28.

—— *The Classical Text: Aspects of Editing in the Age of the Printed Book* (Berkeley, Calif., 1974).

—— 'Books and Readers in the Ancient World', *Cambridge History of Classical Literature* (Cambridge, 1982), ii. 23–37.

KENYON, F. G., *Books and Readers in Ancient Greece and Rome*[2] (Oxford, 1951).

KIDWELL, C., *Marullus: Soldier Poet of the Renaissance* (London, 1989).

LANDINUS, C., *Christophori Landini Carmina Omnia*, ed. A. Perosa (Florence, 1939).

LAUMONIER, P., *Ronsard, poète lyrique*[2] (Paris, 1923).

LAZERI, P., *Miscellaneorum ex Mss. Libris Bibliothecae Collegii Romani societatis Iesu Tomus II* (Rome, 1757).

LEGRAND, E., *Bibliographie hellénique des XVe et XVIe siècles* (Paris, 1972).

L'ESTOILE, PIERRE DE, *Mémoires-Journaux de Pierre de L'Estoile* (Paris, 1889).

LEVY, H., 'Catullus and Cangrande della Scala', *TAPA* 99 (1968), 249–53.

LIPSIUS, J., *Epistolicarum Quaestionum Libri V* (Antwerp, 1577).

LOWRY, M., *The World of Aldus Manutius* (Cambridge, 1979).

LUCCHETTA, G., 'Contributi per una biografia di Pierio Valeriano', *IMU* 9 (1966), 461–76.

LUDWIG, W., 'Petrus Lotichius Secundus and the Roman Elegists: Prolegomena to a Study of Neo-Latin Elegy', in *Litterae Neolatinae*, 202–17, repr. from *Classical Influences on European Culture A.D. 1500–1700* (Cambridge, 1974), 171–90.

—— 'Kannte Lovato Catull?', *RhM* 129 (1986), 329–57.

—— 'Catullus renatus: Anfänge und frühe Entwicklung des catullischen Stils in der neulateinischen Dichtung', in *Litterae neolatinae* (Munich, 1989), 162–94.

—— 'The Catullan Style in Neo-Latin Poetry', in *Latin Poetry and the*

Classical Tradition: Essays in Medieval and Renaissance Literature, ed. P. Godman and O. Murray (Oxford, 1990), 183–97.

LUZIO, A., and RENIER, R., 'La coltura e le relazioni letterarie di Isabella d'Este Gonzaga', *GSLI* 35 (1900), 212–20.

LYNE, R. O. A. M. (ed.), *Ciris* (Cambridge, 1978).

——'The Neoteric Poets', *CQ* 28 (1978), 167–87.

MACFARLANE, I. D., 'Jean Salmon Macrin', *BHR* 21 (1959), 55–82, 311–47; 22 (1960), 73–87.

MCKIE, D. S., *The Manuscripts of Catullus: Recension in a Closed Tradition*, diss. (Cambridge Univ., 1977).

MCNALLY, R. E., SJ, 'Pope Adrian VI and Church Reform', *Archivum Historiae Pontificiae*, 7 (1969), 253–86.

MACRIN, SALMON, *Salmonii Macrini Iuliodunensis Carminum libellus* (Paris, 1528).

MADDISON, C., *Marcantonio Flaminio: Poet, Humanist, and Reformer* (London, 1965).

MAFFEI, S., *Verona illustrata*, iii. (Milan, 1825).

MAÏER, I., *Les Manuscrits d'Ange Politien* (Geneva, 1965).

——*Ange Politien: la formation d'un poète humaniste* (Geneva, 1966).

MANTUANUS, B., *Contra poetas impudice scribentes Carmen* (Paris, *c*.1490) (Goff B–83).

MANUTIUS, P., *Epistolarum libri quatuor* (Venice, 1560).

MANZO, A., 'Testimonianze e tradizione del "Liber" Catulliano nella letteratura esegetico-scolastica antica', *Rivista di Studi classici*, 15 (1967), 137–62.

MARIOTTI, S., 'Cornelii Galli endecasyllabi', in *Tra latino e volgare: Per Carlo Dionisotti*, ed. G. Bernardoni Trezzini *et al*. (Padua, 1974), ii. 547–68.

MARTIAL, *M. Valerii Martialis Epigrammaton Libri*, ed. L. Friedlaender (Leipzig, 1886).

——*Martial: Epigrams* ii, ed. W. C. A. Ker (London, 1927).

——*M. Val. Martialis, Epigrammata*, ed. W. M. Lindsay (Oxford, 1929; repr. 1981).

——*M. Valerii Martialis Epigrammaton Liber I*, ed. M. Citroni (Florence, 1975).

MARUCCI, V., MARZO, A., and ROMANO, A., *Pasquinate Romane del Cinquecento* (Rome, 1986).

MARULLUS, M., *Michaelis Tarchaniotae Marulli Neniae . . . M. Antonii Flaminii Adulescentis Amoenissimi Carminum Libellus* (Fano, 1515).

——*Michaelis Marulli Carmina*, ed. A. Perosa (Zurich, 1951).

MEHNERT, K.-H., *Sal romanus und Esprit français. Studien zur Martial-rezeption im Frankreich des sechzehnten und siebzehnten Jahrhunderts* (Bonn, 1970).

MONFASANI, J., 'Calfurnio's Identification of Pseudepigrapha of Ognibene, Fenestella, and Trebizond, and His Attack on Renaissance Commentaries', *RQ* 41 (1988), 32–43.

MOREIRA DE SÁ, A., 'Manuscritos e obras impressas de Aquiles Estaço', *Arquivo per bibliografia portuguesa* (Coimbra), 3 (1957), 167–78.

MOREL, W. (ed.), *Fragmenta poetarum latinorum*[2] (Stuttgart, 1975).

MORETTI, G., 'Il cardinale Ippolito de' Medici dal trattato di Barcellona alla morte (1529–1535)', *Archivio storico italiano*, 98 (1940), 137–78.

MORRISON, M., 'Catullus in the Neo-Latin Poetry of France before 1550', *BHR* 17 (1955), 365–94.

—— 'Ronsard and Catullus: The Influence of the Teaching of Marc-Antoine de Muret', *BHR* 18 (1956), 240–74.

—— 'Henri Estienne and Sappho', *BHR* 24 (1962), 388–91.

—— 'Catullus and the Poetry of the Renaissance in France', *BHR* 25 (1963), 25–56.

—— 'Some Early Humanist Epithalamia', *Acta Conventus Neo-Latini Amstelodamensis* (Munich, 1979), 794–802.

MÜLLNER, K., *Reden und Briefe italienischer Humanisten* (Vienna, 1899). Reprint with introduction, summaries, bibliography, and indexes by B. Gerl (Munich, 1970).

MURET, Marc-Antoine, *Catullus et in eum Commentarius* (Venice, 1554). Second edition Venice, 1558.

—— *Orationes XXIII . . . eiusdem Interpretatio quincti libri Ethicorum Aristotelis ad Nicomachum. Eiusdem hymni sacri, et alia quaedam poematia* (Venice, 1575).

—— *Scripta Selecta* (Heidelberg, 1809).

—— *Iuvenilia*, in *Opera Omnia*, ii, ed. C. H. Frotscher (Leipzig, 1834).

—— *Epistolae* (Leipzig, 1866), repr. Slatkine Reprints (Geneva, 1971).

—— *Variarum lectionum libri xviii* (Halle, 1891).

NARDI, B., Saggi sull'aristotelismo padovano dal secolo XIV al XVI (Florence, 1958).

NAUERT, C., 'Plinius', *CTC* iv (Washington, DC, 1980), 297–422.

NAVAGERO, ANDREA, *Andrea Navagero. Lusus*, ed. A. E. Wilson (Nieuwkoop, 1973).

NEGRI, G., *Lettere di Principi*, i (Venice, 1581).

NETTLESHIP, H., *Lectures and Essays* (Oxford, 1885).

NEUDLING, C., *A Prosopography to Catullus*, Iowa Studies in Classical Philology, 12 (1955).

NICHOLS, F., *An Anthology of Neo-Latin Poetry* (New Haven, Conn., 1979).

NOLHAC, P. DE, 'La Bibliothèque d'un humaniste au xvie siècle: Les livres annotés par Muret', *Mélanges d'archéologie et d'histoire*, 3 (1883), 202–38.

——'Le *Festus* d' Ange Politien', *Revue de Philologie*, 10 (1886), 145–8.

——*La Bibliothèque de Fulvio Orsini* (Paris, 1887, repr. 1976).

——*Ronsard et l'humanisme* (Paris, 1921).

OCTAVIANUS, S., (= Lernutius, J. and Giselinus, V.) *Phaselus Catulli, et ad eam, quotquot extant, Parodiae. Cum annotationibus doctissimorum virorum. Accesserunt alia quaedam eiusdem generis, Edita a Sixto Octaviano* ('York', 1579).

OFFERMANN, 'Uno tibi sim minor Catullo', *Quaderni urbinati di Cultura classica*, 34 (1980), 107–39.

OKSALA, P., 'Das Geschlecht des Attis bei Catull', *Arctos*, 6 (1969), 91–6.

PACE, RICHARD, *De Fructu qui ex doctrina percipitur*, ed. and trans. F. Manley and R. Sylvester (New York, 1967).

PAGE, D., *Sappho and Alcaeus* (Oxford, 1955).

——*Poetae Melici Graeci* (Oxford, 1967).

PALERMINO, R. J., 'The Roman Academy, the Catacombs, and the Conspiracy of 1468', *Archivum Historiae Pontificiae*, 18 (1980), 117–55.

PALMER, A., and ELLIS, R., 'Scaliger's Liber Cuiacianus of Propertius, Catullus, etc.', *Hermathena*, 2 (1876), 124–58.

PARATORE, E., *La poesia di Giovanni Pontano* (Rome, 1967).

PARTHENIUS, ANTONIUS, *Antonii Parthenii Lacisii Veronensis in Catullum Commentationes* (Brescia, 1485; Venice, 1491; etc.).

PASCHINI, P., 'Gabriele Faerno, cremonese favolista e critico del '500', *Atti dell' Accademia degli Arcadi*, 13 (1929), 63–93.

PASQUALI, G., 'Arte allusiva', in *Stravaganze quarte e supreme* (Venice, 1951), 11–20 (= *Pagine stravaganti* (Florence, 1968), ii. 275–83).

PASTOR, L., The *History of the Popes*[2] (London, 1923).

PASTORELLO, E., *L'Epistolario Manuziano Inventario cronologico-analitico 1483–1597* (Florence, 1957).

PAUKSTADT, R., *De Martiale Catulli imitatore*, diss. (Halle, 1876).

PÈRCOPO, E., (ed.), *Le rime del Chariteo* (Naples, 1897).

——*Vita di Giovanni Pontano* (Naples, 1938).

PERELLA, N. J., *The Kiss, Sacred and Profane* (Berkeley, Calif., 1969).

PEROSA, A., 'Miscellanea umanistica', *Annali di scuola normale superiore di Pisa*, 2: 7 (1938), 73–80.

——'Studi sulla formazione delle raccolte di poesie del Marullo', *Rinascimento*, 1. 2 (1950–1), 125–56.

——*Mostra del Poliziano nella Biblioteca Medicea–Laurenziana:*

manoscritti, libri rari, autografi e documenti. Firenze, 23 settembre—30 novembre 1954 (Florence, 1954).

PERPOLLI, C., 'L'*Actio Panthea* e l'umanesimo veronese', *Atti e memorie, Accademia di agricoltura scienze e lettere, Verona* s. iv. 16 (1915), 1–162.

PICTORIUS, LUDOVICUS BIGUS, *Tumultuariorum carminum libri* (Mutina, 1492).

PIGHI, G. B., 'Achillis Statii lectiones atque emendationes Catullianae', *Humanitas* (Coimbra), 3 (1950), 37–160.

PIGMAN, G. W., III, 'Versions of Imitation in the Renaissance', *RQ* 33 (1980), 1–32.

PLATO, *Ion*, trans. Lane Cooper, in *The Collected Dialogues of Plato*, ed. E. Hamilton and H. Cairns (Princeton, NJ, 1978), 215–28.

POLIZIANO, ANGELO, *Epistole inedite di Angelo Poliziano (Lettere latine estratte dal codice Vaticano-Capponiano 235)*, ed. L. D'Amore (Naples, 1909; repr. *Opera Omnia*, ed. Maïer).

—— *Miscellanea* i, in *Opera Omnia*, i.

—— *Opera Omnia*, ed. I. Maïer (Turin, 1971).

—— *Lamia*, ed. and comm. A. Wesseling (Leiden, 1986).

PONTANO, GIOVANNI GIOVIANO, *Liber de Aspiratione* (Naples, 1481).

—— *De immanitate*, ed. Pietro Summonte (Naples, 1512).

—— *Ioannis Ioviani Pontani Carmina*, ed. B. Soldati: 2 vols (Florence, 1902).

—— *Ioannis Ioviani Pontani Hendecasyllaborum Libri*, ed. L. Monti Sabia (Naples, 1978).

QUINN, K., *Catullus: An Interpretation* (London, 1972).

QUINT, D., *Origin and Originality in Renaissance Literature* (New Haven, Conn., 1983).

RAMBAUD, M., 'César et Catulle', in *Actes du Colloque L'Élégie romaine: Enracinement, Thèmes, Diffusion (16–18 mars 1979)*, Bulletin de la Faculté des Lettres de Mulhouse, fasc. 10. (Paris, 1980), 37–50.

RAMMINGER, A., *Motivgeschichtliche Studien zu Catulls Basiagedichten mit einem Anhang: Aus dem Nachleben der catullischen Basiagedichte* (Würzburg, 1937).

RATHERIUS, *Sermones Ratherii Episcopi Veronensis*, ed. B. Reece (Worcester, Mass., 1969).

RAVEN, D. S., *Latin Metre: An Introduction* (London, 1965).

REYNOLDS, L. D., and WILSON, N. G., *Scribes and Scholars: A Guide to the Transmission of Greek and Latin Literature* (Oxford, 1974).

RICCI, BARTOLOMEO, *De imitatione libri tres* (Venice, 1545).

—— *De imitatione*, Book 1. Repr. in *Trattati di poetica e retorica del cinquecento*, ed. B. Weinberg, i (Bari, 1970), 415–49, with bibliography on 628–30.

RICHARDSON, B., 'Pucci, Parrasio, and Catullus', *IMU* 19 (1976), 277–89.

RIZZO, S., *Il lessico filologico degli umanisti* (Rome, 1973).

ROBORTELLO, F., *Explicationes in Catulli Epithalamium* (Florence, 1548).

RÖMER, F., 'Martial in drei Monodistichen des Giorgio Anselmi', *Wiener Studien*, 102 (1989), 339–50.

RONSARD, PIERRE DE, *Œuvres complètes*, ed., P. Laumonier (Paris, 1928).

ROSIVACH, V., 'Sources of Some Errors in Catullan Commentaries', *TAPA* 108 (1978), 203–16.

ROSS, D. O., Jun., *Style and Tradition in Catullus* (Cambridge, Mass., 1969).

RUYSSCHAERT, J., 'Les Péripéties inconnues de l'édition des "Coryciana" de 1524', in *Atti del Convegno di Studi sul Angelo Colucci: Jesi: 13–14 settembre 1969* (Jesi, 1972), 45–56.

SABBADINI, R., *Le scoperte dei codici latini e greci ne' secoli xiv e xv* (Florence, 1914).

——*Epistolario di Guarino Veronese*, 3 vols. (Venice, 1915).

——*Il metodo degli umanisti* (Florence, 1920).

SABELLICUS, MARCUS ANTONIUS, *Annotationes in Plinium et alios auctores* [Venice?, 1497].

——*Epistolae familiares*, in *Opera* (Venice, 1502).

SADOLETO, JACOPO, *Opera Omnia* (Verona, 1737).

SALLER, R., 'Martial on Patronage and Literature', *CQ* 33 (1983), 246–57.

SANNAZARO, J., *Jacobi Sannazarii Opera Omnia Latine Scripta* (Venice, 1535).

SANUTO, MARINO, *I Diarii* (Venice, 1892).

SCAGLIONE, A., 'The Humanist as Scholar and Politian's Conception of the Grammaticus', *Studies in the Renaissance*, 8 (1961), 49–70.

SCALIGER, JOSEPH JUSTUS, *Castigationes in Valerii Catulli librum* (Paris, 1577).

SCALIGER, JULIUS CAESAR, *Poetices Libri Septem*, facsimile of the edition of Lyon, 1561 (Stuttgart-Bad Cannstatt, 1964).

——*Catalecta Virgilii et aliorum poetarum latinorum veterum poemata* (Leiden, 1617).

——*Epistolae Omnes quae reperiri potuerunt nunc primum collectae ac editae*, (Frankfurt, 1628).

——*Scaligerana, editio altera* (Cologne, 1667).

——*Prima Scaligerana nusquam antehac edita cum praefatione*, ed. T. Fabri (Utrecht, 1670).

——*Poemata omnia*[2], ed. P. Scriverius (Berlin, 1864).

SCHÄFER, E., *Deutscher Horaz* (Baden, 1976).

SCHOLDERER, V., 'Printing at Venice to the End of 1481', in *Fifty Essays* (Amsterdam, 1966), 74–89.

SCOTT, W., *Fragmenta Herculanensia* (Oxford, 1885).

SCOTT, W. C., 'Catullus and Cato (c. 56)', *CP* 64 (1969), 24–9.

SENFTLEBEN, A., and HENELIUS, N., *Phaselus Catulli, et ad eundem, Parodiarum a diversis auctoribus scriptarum, Decades quinque* (Leipzig, 1642).

SEVERYNS, A., *Texte et Apparat: Histoire critique d'une tradition imprimée*, *Mémoires* Acad. Royale de Belgique 66. 2 (1962).

SEZNEC, J., *The Survival of the Pagan Gods: The Mythological Tradition and its Place in Renaissance Humanism and Art*, trans. B. F. Sessions. (Princeton, NJ, 1972).

SHERWIN-WHITE, A. N., *The Letters of Pliny: A Historical and Social Commentary* (Oxford, 1966).

SICCO POLENTON, *Sicconis Polentoni Scriptorum Illustrium Latinae Linguae*, ed. B. L. Ullman. Papers and Monographs of the American Academy in Rome 6 (Rome, 1928).

SIGHINOLFI, L., 'Francesco Puteolano e le origini della stampa in Bologna e in Parma', *Bibliofilia*, 15 (1913), 263–467.

SILENZI, R. and F., *Pasquino: Cinquecento Pasquinate* (Milan, 1932).

SILVER, I., 'Marc-Antoine de Muret et Ronsard', in R. Antonioli, R. Aulotte, *et al.*, (eds.), *Lumières de la Pléiade* (Paris, 1966).

SKINNER, M., *Catullus' Passer: The Arrangement of the Book of Polymetric Poems* (New York, 1981).

SKUTSCH, O., 'Metrical Variations and Some Textual Problems in Catullus', *Bulletin of the Institute of Classical Studies of the University of London*, 16 (1969), 37–9.

—— 'The Book under the Bushel', *Bulletin of the Institute of Classical Studies of the University of London*, 17 (1970), 148.

SOLDATI, B., 'Un emistichio di Manilio e quattro lacune di Tibullo', *Rivista di filologia e d'istruzione classica*, 28 (1900), 287–90.

SORBELLI, T., 'Della fortuna del Carme terzo di Catullo presso gli Umanisti', *Classici e neo-latini* (1912), 170–81.

STATIUS, ACHILLES, *Catullus cum commentario* (Venice, 1566).

STEINER, G., 'Source Editions of Ovid's *Metamorphoses*', *TAPA* 82 (1951), 219–31.

—— 'The Textual Tradition of the Ovidian Incunabula', *TAPA* 83 (1952), 312–18.

STEPHANUS BYZANTINUS, *Ethnikon*, ed. A. Westermann (Leipzig, 1839).

STINGER, C. L., *The Renaissance in Rome* (Bloomington, Ind., 1985).

SYMONDS, J. A., *The Renaissance in Italy*, ii. (New York, 1881).

TACITUS, *Tacitus on Britain and Germany*, trans. H. Mattingly (Harmondsworth, 1948).

TAMIZEY DE LARROQUE, P. (ed.), *Joseph Juste Scaliger: Lettres françaises inédites* (Agen, 1879; repr. Geneva, 1970).

THEWREWK, A. (ed.), *Codex Festi Farnesianus* (Budapest, 1893).

THOMSON, D. F. S., 'Catullus 95. 8: "Et laxas scombris saepe dabunt tunicas"', *Phoenix*, 18 (1964), 30–6.

—— 'The Codex Romanus of Catullus: A Collation of the Text', *RhM* 113 (1970), 97–110.

—— 'A New Look at the Manuscript Tradition of Catullus', *Yale Classical Studies*, 23 (1973), 113–29.

THROOP, G. R., 'The Lives and Verse of Roman Erotic Writers', *Washington University Studies*, 1 (1914), 160–83.

TICOZZI, S., *Storia dei letterati e degli artisti del dipartimento del Piave* (Belluno, 1813), i. 85–150.

TIMPARANO, S., *La genesi del metodo del Lachmann* (Florence, 1963).

TIRABOSCHI, G., *Storia della letteratura italiana* (Florence, 1805).

TOMASINI, J. P., *Bibliothecae patavinae manuscriptae* (Udine, 1639).

TRAGLIA, A., *Poetae novi*[2] (Rome, 1974).

TRISTANO, C., 'Le postille del Petrarca nel Vat. lat. 2193', *IMU* 17 (1974), 365–468.

UBALDINI, F., *Vita di Mons. Angelo Colocci*, ed. V. Fanelli (Città del Vaticano, 1969).

ULLMAN, B. L., *The Identification of the Manuscripts of Catullus Cited in Statius' Edition of 1566* (Chicago, 1908).

—— 'Hieremias da Montagnone and his Citations from Catullus', in *Studies in the Italian Renaissance* (Rome, 1955), 81–116.

—— 'Petrarch's Acquaintance with Catullus, Tibullus, Propertius', in *Studies in the Italian Renaissance* (Rome, 1955), 181–200.

—— *The Humanism of Coluccio Salutati* (Rome, 1958).

—— 'The Transmission of the Text of Catullus', in *Studi in onore di Luigi Castiglioni* 2, 1027–57 (Florence, 1960).

VALERIANUS, PIERIUS, *Praeludia Quaedam* (Venice, 1509).

—— *Amorum Libri V* (Venice, 1549).

—— *Hexametri, odae, et epigrammata* (Venice, 1550).

—— *Hieroglyphica* (Basle, 1552; repr. 1602).

—— *De litteratorum infelicitate* (Venice, 1620; repr. Geneva, 1821).

VASARI, G., *Le opere di Giorgio Vasari*, ed. G. Milanesi (Florence, 1973).

VETTORI, PIER, *Variarum lectionum libri XXV* (Florence, 1553).

WAGENWOORT, H., '*Ludus Poeticus*', in *Studies in Roman Literature, Culture, and Religion* (Leiden, 1954), 30–42.

WALTERS, K. R., 'Catullan Echoes in the Second Century A.D.', *Classical World*, 69 (1976), 353–60.

WASZINK, J. H., 'La filologia nei paesi bassi', *Annali della Scuola Normale Superiore di Pisa*, 8 (1978), 97–133.

WEBSTER, T. B. L., 'The Myth of Ariadne from Homer to Catullus', *Greece and Rome*, 13 (1966), 22–31.

WEGG, J., *Richard Pace: A Tudor Diplomat* (London, 1932).

WEINBERG, B., 'Translations and Commentaries of Longinus, *On the Sublime*, to 1600: A Bibliography', *Modern Philology*, 47 (1950), 145–51.

—— 'Pseudo-Longinus', in *CTC* ii (1971), 193–8.

—— (ed.), *Trattati di poetica e retorica del cinquecento* (Bari, 1970).

WEISS, R., 'Geremia da Montagnone', in *Il primo secolo dell' umanesimo* (Rome, 1949).

—— 'Benvenuto Campesani (1250/5?–1323)', *Bollettino del Museo Civico di Padova*, 44 (1955), 129–44.

—— 'In memoriam Domitii Calderini', *IMU* 3 (1960), 309–21.

WENDEL, C. (ed.), *Scholia in Apollonium Rhodium Vetera* (Berlin, 1935).

—— (ed.), *Scholia in Theocritum Vetera* (Stuttgart, 1967).

WEST, M. L., *Textual Criticism and Editorial Technique* (Stuttgart, 1973).

—— *Greek Metre* (Oxford, 1982).

WESTENDORP BOERMA, R. E. H. (ed.), 'Navolgingen van Catullus 4', *Hermeneus*, 33 (1961), 59–61.

—— *P. Vergili Maronis Catalepton*, ii (Assen, 1963).

WHEELER, A. L., *Catullus and the Traditions of Ancient Poetry* (Berkeley, Calif., 1934).

WHITE, P., 'The Presentation and Dedication of the *Silvae* and the *Epigrams*', *JRS* 64 (1974), 40–61.

—— 'The Friends of Martial, Statius, and Pliny, and the Dispersal of Patronage', *Harvard Studies in Classical Philology*, 79 (1975), 265–300.

—— '*Amicitia* and the Profession of Poetry', *JRS* 68 (1978), 74–92.

WILAMOWITZ-MOELLENDORF, U. VON, *Griechische Verskunst* (Berlin, 1921).

WILLIAMS, G., 'Poetry in the Moral Climate of Augustan Rome', *JRS* 52 (1962), 26–46.

WIND, E., *Pagan Mysteries in the Renaissance* (New York, 1968).

WISEMAN, T. P., *Catullan Questions* (Leicester, 1969).

—— *Cinna the Poet* (Leicester, 1974).

—— 'Catullus 16', *Liverpool Classical Monthly*, 1 (1976), 14–16.

—— *Catullus and his World* (Cambridge, 1985).

ZABUGHIN, V., *Vergilio nel Rinascimento italiano* (Bologna, 1923).

ZAFFAGNO, E., 'L'epigramma di Benvenuto di Campesani: *de resurectione Catulli poetae Vernonensis*', *I classici nel medioevo e nell' umanesimo*, Università di Genova Pubblicazioni dell' Istituto di filologia classica e medievale, 42 (Genoa, 1975), 289–98.

ZETZEL, J. E. G., *Latin Textual Criticism in Antiquity* (Salem, NH, 1981).

ZICÀRI, M., 'A proposito di un "altro Catullo"', *Rendiconti dell' Istituto Lombardo*, 85 (1951), 246–58 (= *Scritti Catulliani*, 29–42).

—— 'Calfurnio, editore di Catullo', *Atene e Roma*, 2 (1957), 157–9 (= *Scritti Catulliani*, 105–8).

—— 'Ricerche sulla tradizione manoscritta di Catullo', *Bollettino del comitato per la preparazione dell' edizione nazionale dei classici greci e latini*, 6 (1958), 79–99 (= *Scritti Catulliani*, 79–104).

—— 'Sul primo carme di Catullo', *Maia* 17 (1965), 232–40 (= *Scritti Catulliani*, 143–52).

—— *Scritti Catulliani* (Urbino, 1976).

ZORZETTI, N., 'L'Ironia della Differenza (a proposito di Catull. 4 e *Catal.* 10)', in *Interpretazioni latine* (Padua, 1978), 43–77.

ZWIERLEIN, O., *Prolegomena zu einer kritischen Ausgabe der Tragödien Senecas*, Abhandlungen der Geistes- und Sozialwissenschaftlichen Klasse der Akademie der Wissenschaften und der Literatur (Mainz, 1983), Nr. 3.

INDEX LOCORUM

GENERAL INDEX